The Soccer Coach's Toolkit

The content of this book was carefully researched. All information is supplied without liability. Neither the author nor the publisher will be liable for possible disadvantages, injuries, or damages.

# Rob Ellis

# THE
# SOCCER COACH'S
# TOOLKIT

**More Than
250 Activities
to Inspire and
Challenge Players**

Meyer & Meyer Sport

British Library of Cataloguing in Publication Data
A catalogue record for this book is available from the British Library

**The Soccer Coach's Toolkit**
Maidenhead: Meyer & Meyer Sport (UK) Ltd., 2022
ISBN: 978-1-78255-217-8

All rights reserved, especially the right to copy and distribute, including the translation rights. No part of this work may be reproduced—including by photocopy, microfilm or any other means—processed, stored electronically, copied or distributed in any form whatsoever without the written permission of the publisher.

© 2022 by Meyer & Meyer Sport (UK) Ltd.
Aachen, Auckland, Beirut, Dubai, Hägendorf, Hong Kong, Indianapolis, Cairo, Cape Town, Manila, Maidenhead, New Delhi, Singapore, Sydney, Tehran, Vienna
Member of the World Sport Publishers' Association (WSPA), www.w-s-p-a.org

Printed by Print Consult GmbH, Munich, Germany
Printed in Slovenia

ISBN: 978-1-78255-217-8
E-Mail: info@m-m-sports.com
www.thesportspublisher.com

# Contents

Introduction ............................................................................................................. 14
How to Use This Book ........................................................................................... 16
Key to Diagrams ..................................................................................................... 19
Technical Guidance ................................................................................................ 20
    Warm-Up Activities ....................................................................................... 20
    Physical/Movement Development ................................................................ 21
    Ball Manipulation .......................................................................................... 23
    Short Passing ................................................................................................. 23
    Long Passing ................................................................................................. 24
    Receiving ....................................................................................................... 24
    Support Play .................................................................................................. 25
    Dribbling ........................................................................................................ 26
    Running With the Ball .................................................................................. 27
    Turning and Shielding .................................................................................. 27
    Crossing ......................................................................................................... 28
    Shooting ........................................................................................................ 29
    Finishing ........................................................................................................ 30
    Volleys ........................................................................................................... 30
    Heading ......................................................................................................... 31
    Goalkeeping .................................................................................................. 32
    Attacking and Defending ............................................................................. 34
    Tactical/Team Shape ..................................................................................... 36
Tactical Guidance ................................................................................................... 38
    Decision-Making ........................................................................................... 38
    Creativity ....................................................................................................... 39
    Pressing ......................................................................................................... 40
    Counterattacking .......................................................................................... 40
    Defending Against an Overload .................................................................. 41
    Defensive Support ........................................................................................ 41
    Defending in Wide Areas ............................................................................. 41
    Attacking With an Overload ........................................................................ 42

# 6　THE SOCCER COACH'S TOOLKIT

   Attacking in Wide Areas .................................................................. 42
   Attacking in Central Areas ............................................................... 43

Type of Activity .......................................................................................... 44
   Unopposed Technical Practice ......................................................... 45
   Opposed Technical Practice ............................................................. 45
   Implementation Practice ................................................................. 46
   Small-Sided Game .......................................................................... 47
   Simulated Match Activity ................................................................ 48

Session Planning ...................................................................................... 50

Warm-Up Activities .................................................................................. 54
   Activity 1: Cats and Dogs ................................................................ 54
   Activity 2: Paint Pots ....................................................................... 56
   Activity 3: Forward March ............................................................... 58
   Activity 4: Magpies ......................................................................... 60
   Activity 5: Box-to-Box ..................................................................... 62
   Activity 6: Ready for Action ............................................................. 64
   Activity 7: Under Orders .................................................................. 66
   Activity 8: Battle Stations ................................................................ 68
   Activity 9: King of the Ring ............................................................. 70
   Activity 10: Square Affair ................................................................ 72

Physical/Movement Development ............................................................. 74
   Activity 11: Grand Prix .................................................................... 74
   Activity 12: Team Warm-Up ............................................................ 76
   Activity 13: 3v2 in the Ring ............................................................. 78
   Activity 14: Possession Switchover .................................................. 80
   Activity 15: Combinations ............................................................... 82
   Activity 16: Four Linked Activities .................................................. 84
   Activity 17: Reactions ..................................................................... 86
   Activity 18: SAQ Circuit .................................................................. 88
   Activity 19: Rapid-Fire Soccer ......................................................... 90
   Activity 20: Blast ............................................................................ 92

Short Passing ............................................................................................ 94
   Activity 21: Touch the Line ............................................................. 94
   Activity 22: Passing Croquet ........................................................... 96
   Activity 23: Crown Green Balls ....................................................... 98
   Activity 24: End-to-End Passing .................................................... 100

Activity 25: Across the Square ........................................................................ 102
Activity 26: Passing by Numbers .................................................................... 104
Activity 27: Crash, Bang, Wallop .................................................................... 106
Activity 28: Ball Switch .................................................................................. 108
Activity 29: Soccer Ice Hockey ....................................................................... 110
Activity 30: Passing Breakaway ...................................................................... 112
Activity 31: Six and Out ................................................................................. 114
Activity 32: Rewards ...................................................................................... 116
Activity 33: Give-and-Go Glory ...................................................................... 118
Activity 34: Escape to Victory ........................................................................ 120
Activity 35: Play Out, Go Out ........................................................................ 122
Activity 36: Four-Goal Takeaway .................................................................... 124
Activity 37: Hole or Nothing .......................................................................... 126
Activity 38: Attacking Overloads .................................................................... 128
Activity 39: Pass at Pace ................................................................................ 130

Long Passing ............................................................................................................. 132
Activity 40: Knock on Wood .......................................................................... 132
Activity 41: Ping King .................................................................................... 134
Activity 42: High-Flying Balls ........................................................................ 136
Activity 43: Long Distance ............................................................................. 138
Activity 44: Double Cross Passing .................................................................. 141
Activity 45: Ready, Aim, Fire ......................................................................... 143
Activity 46: Perilous Passing .......................................................................... 145
Activity 47: Find a Keeper ............................................................................. 147
Activity 48: Seek and Score ........................................................................... 149
Activity 49: Range Finders ............................................................................. 151

Receiving ................................................................................................................... 153
Activity 50: Changing Angles ......................................................................... 153
Activity 51: Red or Blue ................................................................................ 156
Activity 52: Pele 7 ......................................................................................... 158
Activity 53: Passing Traffic ............................................................................ 160
Activity 54: Shift It ....................................................................................... 162
Activity 55: 4v1 Possession ............................................................................ 164
Activity 56: Tennis Ball Keep-Ups .................................................................. 166
Activity 57: Aerial Control ............................................................................. 168
Activity 58: Three Teas ................................................................................. 170
Activity 59: Middleman ................................................................................. 172

Activity 60: Gate Instinct...... 174
Activity 61: Friends and Enemies...... 176
Activity 62: Tricolour...... 178
Activity 63: Triple Chance Passing...... 180
Activity 64: Possession v Penetration...... 182

Dribbling...... 184
Activity 65: Superstar Dribbling...... 184
Activity 66: Traffic Lights...... 186
Activity 67: American Penalty...... 188
Activity 68: Four-Corner Dribbling...... 190
Activity 69: Dribble Slalom...... 192
Activity 70: Volcano...... 194
Activity 71: Copycat...... 196
Activity 72: Moving Targets...... 198
Activity 73: Show Your Skills...... 200
Activity 74: Dribble From Danger...... 202
Activity 75: Through the Gate...... 204
Activity 76: Dribbling Fakes...... 206
Activity 77: Through the Forest...... 208
Activity 78: Eyes Open...... 210
Activity 79 1v1 Dribbling to Score...... 212
Activity 80: Mini-Goal Face-Off...... 214
Activity 81: Gate Patrol...... 216
Activity 82: Prison Break...... 218
Activity 83: Messi v Ronaldo...... 220
Activity 84: Hunter Gates...... 222

Running With the Ball...... 224
Activity 85: End-to-End Stuff...... 224
Activity 86: Catch Up...... 226
Activity 87: Circle Running With the Ball...... 228
Activity 88: Robin Hood...... 230
Activity 89: What's the Time, Coach?...... 232
Activity 90: Ball Relay...... 234
Activity 91: Premier League...... 236
Activity 92: Road Runner...... 238
Activity 93: Running Partners...... 240
Activity 94: Running With the Ball (Circuit)...... 242
Activity 95: All in the Timing...... 244

|     |     |
| --- | --- |
| Activity 96: Break Out | 246 |
| Activity 97: Across the Sea | 248 |
| Activity 98: Roadblock | 250 |
| Activity 99: On Your Marks | 252 |

## Turning .................................................................................................. 254

|     |     |
| --- | --- |
| Activity 100: Skill of the Day | 254 |
| Activity 101: Turning and Receiving | 256 |
| Activity 102: Turning and Shooting | 258 |
| Activity 103: Dodgems | 260 |
| Activity 104: Turn, Turn, Turn | 262 |
| Activity 105: Turning Development | 264 |
| Activity 106: Find a Corner | 266 |
| Activity 107: Tennis Ball Turning | 268 |

## Shielding ............................................................................................. 270

|     |     |
| --- | --- |
| Activity 108: Shielding Strength | 270 |
| Activity 109: Show of Strength | 272 |
| Activity 110: Lose Your Shadow | 274 |
| Activity 111: Shielding and Scoring | 276 |
| Activity 112: Aerial Shielding | 278 |
| Activity 113: 2v2 Shielding | 280 |
| Activity 114: Stuck Like Glue | 282 |

## Crossing ............................................................................................... 284

|     |     |
| --- | --- |
| Activity 115: Crossing Basics | 284 |
| Activity 116: Cross on the Run | 286 |
| Activity 117: Crossing, Headers and Volleys | 288 |
| Activity 118: In to Out Crossing | 290 |
| Activity 119: Crossing and Movement | 292 |
| Activity 120: Out on the Wing | 294 |
| Activity 121: Crossing Under Pressure | 296 |
| Activity 122: Crossing Passage of Play | 298 |
| Activity 123: Crossing Gates | 300 |
| Activity 124: Crossing Overloads | 302 |

## Shooting .............................................................................................. 304

|     |     |
| --- | --- |
| Activity 125: Continuous Shooting | 304 |
| Activity 126: Ready to Fire | 306 |
| Activity 127: Shooting Relay | 308 |

Activity 128: Shooting Fundamentals .......................................................... 310
Activity 129: Hit the Target ........................................................................ 312
Activity 130: Receive and Shoot ................................................................. 314
Activity 131: Shooting Fiesta ...................................................................... 316
Activity 132: Shooting Fiesta 2 ................................................................... 318
Activity 133: Open Corner ......................................................................... 321
Activity 134: Four-Way Shooting ................................................................ 323
Activity 135: Stylish Shooting .................................................................... 325
Activity 136: Shots on the Run ................................................................... 327
Activity 137: Raining Shots ........................................................................ 329
Activity 138: Shooting in the Arc ............................................................... 331
Activity 139: Shooting Options .................................................................. 333
Activity 140: Striking Instinct ..................................................................... 335

Finishing ........................................................................................................... 337
Activity 141: Attacking Waves .................................................................... 337
Activity 142: Angled Finishing ................................................................... 339
Activity 143: Strike Force ........................................................................... 341
Activity 144: Coconut Shy .......................................................................... 343
Activity 145: 4v1 Finishing ......................................................................... 345
Activity 146: Three-Second Finish ............................................................. 347
Activity 147: Set to Score ........................................................................... 349
Activity 148: Thinking Finishing ................................................................ 351
Activity 149: Dream Goals ......................................................................... 353
Activity 150: High-Pressure Finishing ........................................................ 355
Activity 151: Find a Finish ......................................................................... 357

Volleys .............................................................................................................. 359
Activity 152: Volley Basics .......................................................................... 359
Activity 153: Volley and Move .................................................................... 361
Activity 154: Wall Volleys ........................................................................... 363
Activity 155 Soccer Tennis ......................................................................... 365
Activity 156: Pressure Volleys .................................................................... 367
Activity 157: Volleys Keep Ball ................................................................... 369
Activity 158: Soccer Volleyball ................................................................... 371
Activity 159: Volley to Score ...................................................................... 373
Activity 160: Open Play Volleys ................................................................. 375
Activity 161: Volley Rules ........................................................................... 377

Heading ........................................................................................................... 379
    Activity 162: Heading Basics ............................................................. 379
    Activity 163: Piggy in the Middle ...................................................... 381
    Activity 164: Heading Workout ......................................................... 383
    Activity 165: Pairs Heading ............................................................... 385
    Activity 166: Bullet Headers .............................................................. 387
    Activity 167: Speed Heading ............................................................. 389
    Activity 168: Heading Medley ........................................................... 391
    Activity 169: 4v1 Heading ................................................................. 393
    Activity 170: Heading Finesse ............................................................ 395
    Activity 171: In the Onion Bag .......................................................... 397
    Activity 172: Throw, Head and Catch ................................................ 399
    Activity 173: Head Scramble ............................................................. 401
    Activity 174: King of Headers ............................................................ 403
    Activity 175: Take Your Chances ........................................................ 406

Goalkeeping .................................................................................................. 408
    Activity 176: Goalkeeping Basics ...................................................... 408
    Activity 177: Goalkeeper Ball Skills ................................................... 410
    Activity 178: Goalkeeper Duos ......................................................... 412
    Activity 179: Long Kick Outs ............................................................. 414
    Activity 180: Diamond Roll ............................................................... 416
    Activity 181: Five in a Throw ............................................................. 418
    Activity 182: Get Down ..................................................................... 420
    Activity 183: Goalkeeper 1v1s .......................................................... 422
    Activity 184: Claim and Distribute .................................................... 424
    Activity 185: On Your Toes ................................................................ 426
    Activity 186: Stop All Six .................................................................... 428
    Activity 187: Close-Range Saves ....................................................... 430
    Activity 188: Leaping Keepers .......................................................... 432
    Activity 189: 50 Saves ....................................................................... 434
    Activity 190: Play It Safe .................................................................... 436
    Activity 191: 1, 2, Throw .................................................................... 438
    Activity 192: One for the Cameras ................................................... 440
    Activity 193: Keeper Is the Key .......................................................... 442
    Activity 194: Keeper Re-starts ........................................................... 444

Attacking and Defending: ............................................................................. 446
    Activity 195: Stick or Twist ................................................................ 446

Activity 196: Numbers ..... 448
Activity 197: Cross the Line ..... 450
Activity 198: 1v1 Continuous Drill ..... 452
Activity 199: Both Sides of the Fence ..... 454
Activity 200: Hold Firm ..... 456
Activity 201: 1v1 Finishing ..... 458
Activity 202: 1v1 Speed Play ..... 460
Activity 203: Pick Your Path ..... 462
Activity 204: Attacking Angles ..... 464
Activity 205: 3v3 Attacking and Defending ..... 466
Activity 206: 21 ..... 468
Activity 207: Close to Home ..... 470
Activity 208: Four Goals Close to Home ..... 472
Activity 209: No Easy Option ..... 474
Activity 210: Leading From the Front ..... 476
Activity 211: Build Up to Score ..... 478
Activity 212: Powerball ..... 480
Activity 213: Cover All Bases ..... 482
Activity 214: Break Through or Break Free ..... 484
Activity 215: Five Goals Five Ways ..... 486
Activity 216: Narrow Pitch SSG ..... 488
Activity 217: Wide Pitch SSG ..... 490
Activity 218: Volleys SSG ..... 492
Activity 219: One Big, Two Small ..... 494
Activity 220: Mystery Box ..... 496
Activity 221: Triple Target ..... 498
Activity 222: Player Power ..... 500
Activity 223: Double Trouble ..... 502
Activity 224: Empty the Net ..... 504

Tactical Development/Team Shape ..... 506
Activity 225: Crossing and Finishing ..... 506
Activity 226: Bull's-eye ..... 509
Activity 227: Defending Deep ..... 511
Activity 228: Go Create ..... 513
Activity 229: Attacking Overloads ..... 515
Activity 230: Attacking Team Play ..... 517
Activity 231: Hog the Ball ..... 519

## Contents

Activity 232: Pressing Matters ............................................................................ 521
Activity 233: Counterattacks ............................................................................... 523
Activity 234: 4v4 Playing Out of Defence ........................................................ 525
Activity 235: Scenarios ......................................................................................... 527
Activity 236: Checkpoint Soccer ......................................................................... 529
Activity 237: Defending in Wide Areas .............................................................. 531
Activity 238: Attacking in Wide Areas ............................................................... 533
Activity 239: Attacking in Central Areas ........................................................... 535
Activity 240: Creating Space ............................................................................... 537
Activity 241: Principles of Defending ................................................................ 539
Activity 242: Defending Against Overloads ..................................................... 541
Activity 243: Principles of Attack ....................................................................... 544
Activity 244: Movement and Finishing in Central Areas ............................... 546
Activity 245: Goal Scoring on the Turn and Running Onto Passes ............ 548
Activity 246: Pressing as a Team ........................................................................ 550
Activity 247  Improve Goalkeeping ................................................................... 552
Activity 248: Movement to Create Space ......................................................... 554
Activity 249: Create Space to Make Goal-Scoring Opportunities ............... 556
Activity 250: Combination Plays Between Team Units ................................. 558
Activity 251: Support Play ................................................................................... 560
Activity 252: Creative and Penetrative Attacking ........................................... 562

# INTRODUCTION

I have written this book as an educational guide for soccer coaches. The activities and the technical and tactical guidance offered in this book will help coaches to deliver challenging, stimulating and enjoyable soccer coaching sessions. The content of this book is based on my 22 years of soccer coaching experience and 12 years of physical education teaching.

My experiences over those 22 years are wide and varied. I have been a Football Association (FA) county coach, a grassroots coach for a Championship club and the head coach at a player development centre for a Premier League soccer club for 6 years. I have worked in semi-professional soccer as a 1st team coach and as an overseas developmental coach in America and Turkey for a Premier League club.

During these 22 years, I have seen and delivered many coaching activities that work well and many that do not. I know from my own experience that one of the most important things for a coach to know before the session is that their session plan and coaching activities work as well in practice as they do in theory.

As a PE teacher, I have overseen many junior school teams and hundreds of school fixtures, as well as creating a player development centre for talented school players.

# Introduction

Thanks to tens of thousands of hours of teaching and coaching, I have developed a strong understanding of how to make coaching activities and sessions work effectively for the players and the coach.

I am confident that the activities in this book work well in practice and are also easy to understand, require only basic coaching equipment and can be adapted to challenge players of vastly different ability levels. Each of the activities has a primary, secondary and additional technical or tactical focus to help the coach plan and deliver well-balanced and adaptable activities and sessions.

There are 252 coaching activities in this book, which will give coaches a lifetime of activities and the right ingredients for all types of training sessions. The activities are suitable for coaches working with elite youth and adult players, coaches or PE teachers delivering a soccer scheme of work/coaching curriculum, and coaches working at grassroots soccer camps. The activities range in difficulty level from basic to intermediate and advanced to help the coach select suitable activities for each group of players.

The activities in this book will help players to improve their performance across a wide range of techniques and tactics. For each key soccer technique, there is a selection of activities to improve that specific technique. There is a tactical and team play section in the book, to improve player performance across a wide range of tactical and team-play aspects.

For each of the activities, there is a diagram and a written description of how to organise and deliver the activity; an activity classification (e.g., an opposed or unopposed technical practice); the technical and tactical areas of key focus and coaching points; the number of players (ideally) required for the activity; the equipment required to coach the activity; and finally, how to progress or adapt the activity depending on the performance and ability of the players.

I hope that the coaches that use this book find it useful, and that it helps to make planning coaching activities and sessions as easy as possible. The activities are designed to be enjoyable and stimulating for the players and the coach and can also stimulate ideas for coaches to develop their own activities. Good luck and happy coaching!

# HOW TO USE THIS BOOK

Each coaching activity has a name to help the coach remember and distinguish the activities from each other. During coaching sessions, the organisation and function of activities can be forgotten or confused with other activities particularly when activities are similar. By giving each activity a catchy name, it can help the coach to memorise and visualise the key features of the activity and maintain focus during coaching sessions.

Each activity is classified in terms of the nature of the activity (see the "type of activity" section for guidance on these classifications) as each activity differs in organisation in order to maximise player technical and tactical development. If, for example, the coach wants to improve short passing technique then it is necessary to consider what type of activity is best suited for improving that technique in terms of organisation. The warm-up activities do not have any additional classification as their only purpose is to warm up the players.

There are many ways to organise coaching activities, for example, unopposed or opposed technical practices; area-specific activities (e.g., in the penalty area); and activities that are performed individually or in small/large groups. Any coaches that are unfamiliar or new to activity classifications should pay particular attention to the "type of activity" section of this book.

Each activity has a diagram. The diagram includes approximate pitch dimensions in yards. Please remember that the dimensions are approximate and should be altered depending on the number of players involved in the activity; their age, ability and physical condition; and the amount of space available. The diagrams show typical starting positions for all players and the movement of the players and ball. The diagrams also show specific areas of play, e.g., offside lines or parts of the playing area that need to be coned off for specific purposes. Specialist equipment, e.g., coaching mannequins or agility poles are also shown in the diagrams.

Each activity has a written description of how it is organised and how it starts. In this section, the purpose of the activity and specific guidelines or rules that must be followed are also explained in order to deliver the activity effectively. The description of the activity works in conjunction with the diagram to illustrate how the activity should look and how it works.

Each activity includes progressions (ways of making the activity more challenging) and/or adaptations (ways of tweaking the activity to increase/decrease the challenge, the level of performance-related pressure and to add more technique-specific focus). The progressions and adaptations don't have to be used in each activity; however, they can be used to support player progress and development as the activity progresses.

Each activity is rated as **basic, intermediate or advanced.** This serves as a guide to how difficult the activity is in terms of technical demands/tactical understanding. The activity ratings can help the coach select appropriate activities for the ability of the players; however, they can and should be used flexibly. There is nothing wrong with using and adapting a basic activity for higher ability players or using and adapting an advanced activity for intermediate players.

As an example, unopposed short passing in small groups is a basic activity as well as a necessary and relevant technique for advanced players to practice. In such a case, the coach should insist on a consistently high level of technical performance and focus in more detail on the specifics of the technique in order to challenge the players.

Each activity in the "Tactical and team shape" section is rated **basic, intermediate or advanced**. However, I would suggest that even basic activities in this section should be used sparingly and introduced gradually with lower ability and beginner players. The activities in this section provide a high level of challenge for more experienced/advanced players. The organisation, number of players involved and the tactical focus in these activities will prove particularly challenging for players that are still developing basic techniques. Even an activity that is rated as basic in this section requires a certain level of exposure to match play and game understanding.

# 18  THE SOCCER COACH'S TOOLKIT

Each activity has a primary, secondary and additional focus. The primary focus indicates the main area of development within the activity (e.g., short passing) and the secondary and additional focuses suggest the next most relevant areas of development. The secondary and additional areas of focus provide flexibility and variety, as they allow the coach to develop multiple techniques in one coaching activity.

There is a suggested number of players to be used in each activity. The numbers stated should be used as a guide and represent an ideal number of players for the activity. If, for example, the activity suggests that 12 players are required, the activity can still function well with a smaller or larger number of players, but the coach will need to adapt aspects of the activity, e.g., by changing the size of the playing area or removing/adding playing positions to accommodate the players in the group.

For each activity, there is a list of recommended equipment to be used. Most of the activities require only basic coaching equipment, e.g., a bag of soccer balls, a stack of cones and 2 sets of bibs. The use of simple equipment enables the coach to deliver the activities in basic coaching environments. More specialist equipment, e.g., agility poles are suggested very rarely and the activity will still function by using alternative equipment. For example, coaches working outside of a club or school environment may not have access to goals with nets or even free-standing goals. If this is the case, there is nothing wrong with using cones/domes/agility poles to mark out goals.

The use of bibs is not necessary for every activity; however, in most cases they are listed as equipment. For example, during individual (1 ball per player) or non-competitive activities it is not essential to wear bibs. They may still be used to help players identify their partner. Players do need to wear bibs during competitive partner, group or team activities and target players/floating players (players that play for both teams) should wear a bib of a different colour to all other players so that they are distinguishable from the rest of the group.

The "playing area" refers to the space in which the activity takes place. The playing area is a generic term that replaces all others such as "pitch", "square" or "grid". The term "playing area" is used for each activity regardless of size, shape and sub-divisions of the area. "Zones" refer to parts of the playing area that perform specific functions within each activity. Zones can be anywhere inside or outside of the playing area depending on what purpose they serve in the activity and should be clearly marked out.

# Key to Diagrams

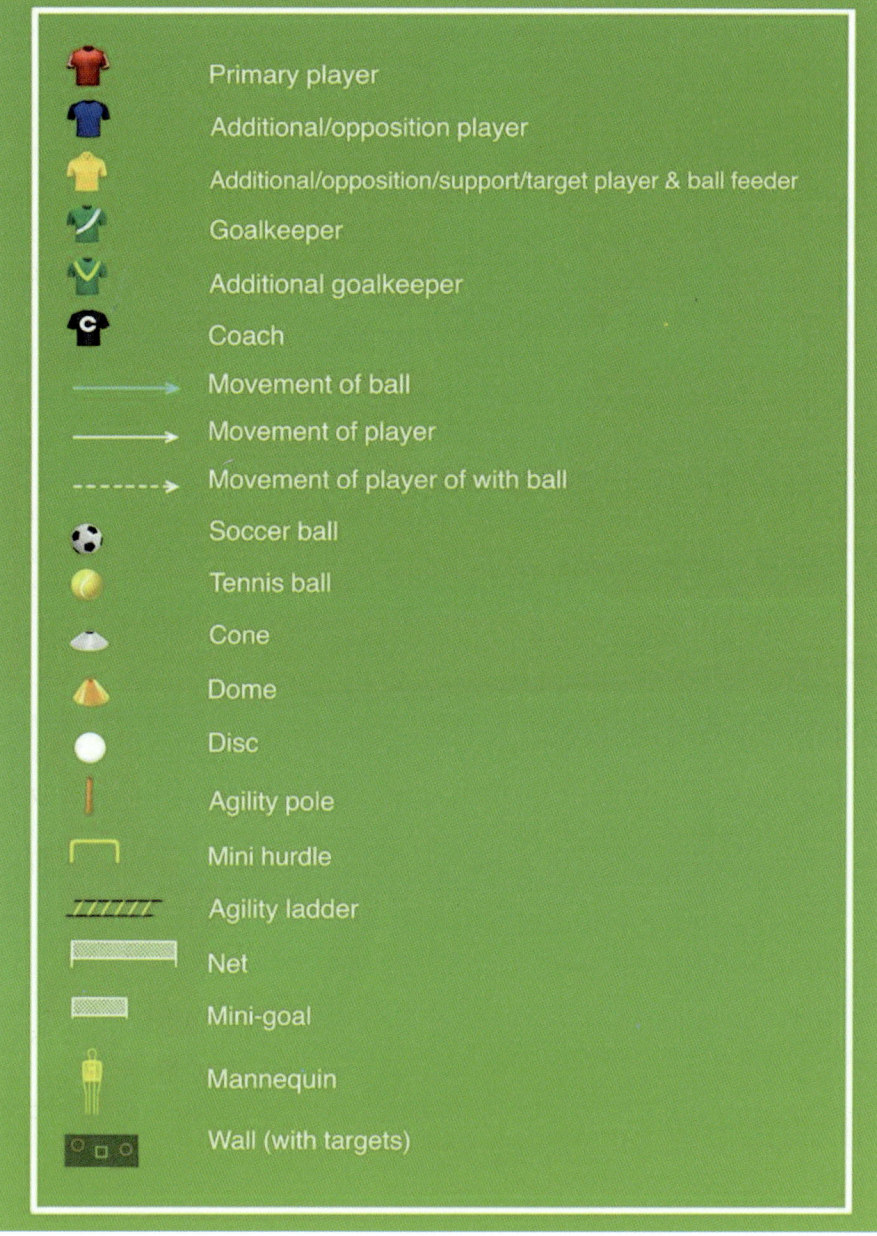

# TECHNICAL GUIDANCE

## Warm-Up Activities

Warm-up activities are an important part of every coaching session. There are hundreds of different games and activities that can be used to get your players warmed up and ready for the rest of the session. There are a many reasons why players need to perform a warm-up:

- To reduce the risk of muscular injuries, pulls, strains and tears.

- To increase blood flow to working muscles, making them more able to meet the physical demands of running, jumping and kicking.

- To gradually increase heart rate. This reduces the physical shock of going from a resting heart rate to a high working heart rate, which can be dangerous, particularly in cold conditions.

- To allow players to psychologically prepare to play. Warm-up activities help players to focus their minds and increase levels of mental and physical arousal.

During a warm-up activity, it is important that the players increase their heart rate, stretch muscles and mobilise joints. The warm-up activities in this book will help to increase players' heart rates; however, they do not prescribe specific stretches or joint mobilisation exercises. Coaches should learn about basic muscle stretching and joint mobilising as part of the preparation for each session. During the warm-up, players should start at a low intensity, gradually rising to a high intensity towards the end of the activity. Muscle stretching and joint mobilisation should be introduced after heart rate and body temperature have increased.

## Physical/Movement Development

Through the development and increasing use of sports science, soccer players are increasingly required to be fitter and physically more developed. It is important that players at all levels try to develop all aspects of physical fitness and development in order to meet the physical and competitive demands of the sport.

At every level of soccer, a high level of physical and movement development is beneficial to the player. When players and teams of similar technical ability compete against each other, the players/teams that have reached a higher level of fitness often prevail and so it is particularly important that coaches try to develop specific areas of physical fitness with their players.

Soccer players need to develop key aspects of physical fitness; aerobic endurance, speed, agility, balance, muscular strength and muscular endurance. Good all-round physical and movement development means that players are well equipped to perform basic soccer movements, e.g., running, jumping, kicking, tackling and contesting the ball against an opponent.

The physical/movement development activities in this book involve high intensity running/sprints. Some of the activities focus more on agility and coordination. In both cases, I have tried to use a soccer ball as much as possible to keep the activities soccer-specific and technically challenging. The key thing to remember with these activities is that the players must work hard and push themselves physically in order to maximise physical and movement development.

To improve physical conditioning, the coach must focus on soccer-specific areas of fitness as well as general physical and movement development. The activities in this section work on the key components of soccer specific fitness. Below is a guide to what these components mean in practical terms.

**Speed:** Essentially, speed is about the player moving from point A to point B as quickly as possible – whether in or out of possession. Speed usually refers to movement in a straight line, but also involves changes of direction when necessary. Speed is developed by high-intensity running over short distances.

**Quickness:** Being able to move feet and legs at high speed when running or moving at high speed on the spot. An example of quickness on the spot is when a striker quickly moves the ball out from under their feet and quickly fires a shot at goal. This example involves the striker having to quickly move specific body parts without moving from where they are standing. Quickness also refers to speed of thought. A quick and alert mind helps to produce quick actions. Quickness can be developed by performing movements and techniques that make players move their feet as fast as they can.

**Agility:** The ability to move quickly in different directions for example, side-to-side and up-and-down. A goalkeeper diving to save a deflected shot or an acrobatic goal line clearance are examples of soccer-specific agility and can be improved by making players practice jumping, skipping, hurdling and movement in different directions.

**Reaction time:** The ability to react as quickly as possible to a stimulus. In soccer, the stimulus could be the ball, teammates or opposition players. Reaction time can involve moving the whole body or specific body parts quickly in response to the stimulus. Reaction time can be developed by coaching players to react quickly to verbal and visual cues, including the movement of the ball and other players.

**Strength:** Strength means exerting a physical force against another object. Physical strength is important in soccer, as it is a contact sport that requires the application of force against opponents, e.g., when tackling or shielding the ball. Strength is also required to kick the ball with power to make it travel at high speed and over long distances. The development of physical strength can help players to win physical contests, which can be the difference between retaining or losing possession of the ball. Activities that involve safe and sensible physical contact against opponents will help players to develop physical strength and develop confidence in contact situations.

**Coordination:** Moving multiple body parts effectively and gracefully at the same time. Soccer players move all limbs during play to perform a wide array of techniques, which makes coordination a vital physical attribute. Good coordination allows players to efficiently prepare and get into good positions to perform techniques, which increases the likelihood of successfully performing the technique. Good coordination allows players to learn techniques quickly and effectively. Activities that allow players to perform multiple movements at the same time (e.g., hurdling and jumping) can help improve coordination.

**Endurance:** The ability to withstand fatigue and maintain physical work for prolonged periods of time. Soccer is a sport that places a high level of stress on cardiovascular endurance, as players must cover a lot of ground with little rest. Players that develop high levels of endurance will find it easier to cope with the demands of soccer and maintain good performance levels even when tired. Activities that emphasise running for an extended period will help players improve their endurance.

# Ball Manipulation

Ball manipulation is the ability to master and develop control over the soccer ball. Every soccer technique requires the player to manipulate the ball in order to keep the ball under control. Ball manipulation in its simplest form can be conceptualised as keeping the ball under control and moving it successfully into a desired space. Good ball manipulation helps players to create space in possession and provides a foundation to perform the next technique successfully.

Ball manipulation involves using different body surfaces (mainly feet) to move the ball, keeping possession and avoiding opponents. Good ball manipulators are incredibly good at working in tight areas and can create enough space and time to make the next move, e.g., a pass, dribble or shot. Good ball manipulation allows the player to remain calm and composed when under pressure. With practice, players can learn to treat the ball as an extension of their body rather than as a foreign object.

Ball manipulation can be greatly improved by individual practices, i.e., 1 ball per player. Good examples of ball manipulation activities include dribbling around obstacles in a tight space and performing keep-ups with different body surfaces. These kinds of activities help the player learn how to creatively move the ball and move with the ball. Lionel Messi is perhaps the most obvious contemporary example of a player that manipulates the ball expertly well – using subtle body movements, excellent control over the ball and by finding space in crowded areas.

# Short Passing

It important to impress upon young players that a firmly struck pass is the quickest way of moving the ball from point A to point B and retaining team possession. Unless a pass is badly hit or played with little power, it will always travel faster than any player can dribble or run with the ball. Short passing is a quick and effective way of building attacks without attempting higher risk techniques, e.g., long passing or running with the ball.

Short passing is one of the most frequently used techniques in any training or match situation, so it is vital that players practice it regularly to master the technique. Players should be encouraged to use different foot services, e.g., inside, outside, back-heel and even toes to pass the ball over short distances.

Short passing activities create opportunities to coach player movement and show how teammates can make each pass as easy as possible for the player in possession. Coaching short passing should challenge the players to think about when and where to pass. The player in possession needs to develop an understanding of when to pass to the feet and when to pass into space. The activities must challenge the players to use the type of pass most likely to reach their teammate, e.g., ground or aerial passes. The players need to practice the finer technical details of short passing such as passing at different angles and using different types of spin.

# Long Passing

A long pass is a direct way of transferring the ball to a teammate over 25 yards away. All players need to perform long passes during competitive play. It is important to perform the long passing technique accurately as poorly executed long passes can easily be misdirected and intercepted by opponents.

Long passing is an advanced technique due to the distance of the pass, the high level of accuracy required and the potential for interceptions. The activities in this book allow players to practice different types of long passes and find ways to use them in competitive play.

There are many different types of long pass including: flat drive, lofted drive, chip, and curved passes with the inside and outside of the foot. Players that improve and can perform these types of long pass provide valuable attacking options to the team in possession. Allow players to initially practice long passes over shorter distances (25 yards) and with minimal pressure before increasing the distance and amount of pressure.

# Receiving

Good ball receiving allows players to keep the ball close, under control and in the best possible position to perform the next technique. For example, when a player receives the ball in the opponent's penalty area, it may be to create a shooting opportunity whereas a player receiving the ball in a wide attacking area may do so to create an opportunity to cross. Receiving the ball well and with confidence is a critical technique to develop and essential for player development.

How the player receives the ball depends on many factors. Some of these factors include how much space is available, how much time the player has, what part of the playing area they are in (e.g., wide, central, defensive or attacking) and where the ball is (e.g., on the floor, bouncing or in the air). When receiving the ball on the bounce or in the air, players need to be comfortable using different body surfaces to receive the ball including feet, thighs, chest and head.

Ball receiving forces players to use their brains and quickly assess the picture in front of them. Players need to quickly decide how to receive the ball and when it is necessary to play the ball first-time. The activities in this book will allow beginner players to learn ball receiving techniques with minimal pressure and more advanced players to receive the ball under pressure and in complex situations.

When receiving the ball, try to encourage players to change the angle of the pass they have received. Receiving the ball into a new space outside the line of where the pass has travelled from creates new passing angles and makes it difficult for opponents to block the next pass. Changing the angle of a pass allows the player in possession to move away from congested areas of play and keeps defenders guessing about where to move to next.

How players receive the ball depends on the amount of space available to them and the positioning of teammates and opponents. This makes it important to coach the movement of teammates as well as the player receiving the pass. Creating space and passing options makes it easier to receive passes, as the ball receiver faces less time- and space-related pressure. During ball receiving activities, try to encourage players to look for gaps between defenders and open spaces before attempting to receive passes.

## Support Play

Support play is about players moving into space to keep/receive possession when attacking or to stop attacks and regain possession when defending. Support play is of fundamental importance to the development of successful soccer players. Support play requires players to continuously find positions to help teammates and team functions in and out of possession. The basics of support play can be developed with low numbers, e.g., 2v2 and developed in more detail with greater numbers.

During support play activities, players need to learn about different types of movement to receive possession/attack (e.g., diagonal or overlap runs) and prevent/stop attacks when defending (e.g., side-to-side or recovery runs). Coaching support play requires players to consider their own position in relation to the ball, teammates and opponents, how to maintain a balance of players in different areas of the pitch and ways to create/minimise space through movement. Teams and individual players perform to a higher level when they can support each other effectively and so it should be coached as regularly as possible.

# Dribbling

Dribbling is an individual technique used to travel while in possession of the ball. Players often use the dribble to retain possession when there is no clear passing, crossing or shooting option available to them. While dribbling, players should use small and frequent foot touches on the ball to keep it close to their feet, under good control and move away from/past defenders.

Dribbling is hard to perform well in competitive play, as it is performed while switching focus between the ball, the playing area and the other players. To dribble effectively in competitive play requires a high level of technical competence and lots of practice. In the early stages of coaching dribbling, allow the players the chance to master the technique without too much external stimuli, i.e., teammates and opponents.

Players should practice using different parts of their foot to dribble (front, outside, and inside), as this helps to control and manipulate the ball as well as change direction. When coaching dribbling, give players the opportunity to learn tricks and skills to use, as this will give them more confidence to use the dribble in competitive play. Tricks and skills should initially be practiced unopposed before using them in 1v1 and small group activities.

Try to encourage players to be creative when dribbling and give them the freedom to dribble in the right areas of play without too much fear of losing the ball. Developing dribbling technique and confidence takes time and can be quickly damaged by negative coach responses when players lose the ball. Learn to expect mistakes and be patient with players as they practice dribbling.

Like any technique, it is important to discuss with players the right time and the right areas of play in which to use it. Good, accurate passes are more than often not an easier way to retain possession than dribbling, and so it is important to help players identify and understand their passing options before using the dribble in competitive play.

## Running With the Ball

Running with the ball is a similar technique to dribbling in that it involves the player using their feet to travel into space while retaining individual ball possession. It is different from dribbling in that bigger touches are used to move the ball and it is usually performed over longer distances than dribbling. Running with the ball requires sufficient space between the ball and the nearest defender so that the player in possession is not under immediate threat of being tackled.

Running with the ball is a quicker way of moving with the ball than dribbling, as essentially it is a touch of the ball followed by a sprint rather than dribbling, which involves more ball contacts and as a result, a slower running speed. The distance between the player running with the ball and the nearest defender determines the ideal distance between the foot and the ball while travelling and the strength of each ball contact. If, for example, a player has a clear path to goal from the halfway line, the distance between the player running with the ball and ball could be up to 20 yards.

In competitive play, the player running with the ball will rarely get the opportunity to run with the ball over more than 30-40 yards. It is difficult to find large areas of open space and defenders will attempt to close the space. When coaching running with the ball, keep the distances covered realistic for competitive play and develop speed while keeping the ball under control. As the technique develops, introduce defenders to add pressure. The presence of defenders increases the difficulty of performing the technique and exposes the player to decisions about when and where to release the ball.

## Turning and Shielding

Turning and shielding the ball are quite different techniques; however, they are linked in competitive play. When a player in possession is unable to shoot at goal or pass to a teammate in a better attacking position, they will need to travel into a space where this is possible, either by dribbling or running with the ball. If the space to travel into is blocked by opponents, then the player may need to use a turn to move away from the opponent(s) into an open space. If the turn is not possible, or turning would risk losing possession, the player will need to shield the ball until an opportunity to turn, dribble or pass becomes available.

Turns can be performed while dribbling with a moving ball or on the spot with a still ball. Turns are used when the player in possession needs to move into open space if facing a congested area of play and/or they are under close pressure from opponent(s). Players should be encouraged to turn when and where necessary, i.e., to move out of danger. If a player has space and time available to them, there is no need to turn.

Shielding is a technique to protect the ball from opponents by positioning the body between the ball and the player challenging for the ball. When a player is shielding the ball, they must move their body and use their physical strength to resist the challenge and protect the ball. Shielding the ball is used in competitive play when the player in possession has no available space to move into or teammates to pass to, e.g., when facing the touchline with an opponent blocking off space and in-field passing options.

The activities in this book are designed to help players explore the relationship between shielding and turning and which technique is most appropriate to use in different situations. Shielding the ball is necessary until an opportunity to either turn and dribble into space or pass to a teammate becomes available. Knowing when to shield and when to turn is an important skill and should be worked on when coaching shielding technique.

The turning and shielding activities in this book will give players opportunities to practice turning and shielding under varying degrees of pressure. Beginner players should be taught how to turn without defensive pressure in the early stages and then be exposed to passive and active pressure as the technical competence progresses. Similarly, shielding should be developed gradually with increasing physical pressure from defenders.

# Crossing

The activities in this section will allow players to learn the fundamental techniques of crossing the ball. Crossing is the technique of transferring the ball from a wide area of the pitch to a central and potentially goal-scoring area of the pitch. Crosses can be from deep positions, e.g., near the halfway line or from advanced positions, e.g., near to the goal line. Crossing is a type of pass but is classified as a cross because of the area of the playing area it comes from and travels to.

Crossing is a challenging technique for players to develop. Firstly, it is a long pass often performed while moving at high speed and secondly, it is often performed side-on to the area/players being aimed at. It is important to make sure that players develop sufficient power to cross the ball from wide to central areas of play and can successfully pass the ball when side-on to play before adding defensive pressure. If defensive pressure is added too early, the technique may fail, causing players to avoid opportunities to cross during competitive play.

The ability to create goal-scoring opportunities from crosses requires a lot of practice. Good crossing requires a combination of good technique and quick decision making. The decision-making aspect of crossing involves varying the type and direction of the cross, as the position of other attacking and defending players is different for each cross.

The crossing position and positions of other players means that the crosser must develop the ability to deliver different types of crosses such as flat, lofted, pull-backs, in-swingers and out-swingers. When appropriate, encourage players to cross early because the longer it takes to deliver a cross, the more time defenders have to take up good defensive positions.

# Shooting

Goals win games of soccer and so shooting is a vital technique for all players to practice. To varying degrees, all players from defenders to strikers need to learn to shoot because when the opportunity to shoot comes along it is often at the critical point of an attack and whoever the ball falls to needs to be able to finish the attack with a good shot. It stands to reason that the more players that can shoot well within a team, the more likely they are to score more goals and win more games.

Shooting is a difficult technique to perform successfully and score goals regularly from in competitive play. Shooting is never unopposed in match situations, as the goalkeeper and defenders provide obstacles to scoring, adding difficulty to the execution of the technique. Once players have developed a good shooting technique with minimal external pressure, they should practice with increasingly match realistic pressure. Pressure can be increased by raising the intensity of the activity (e.g., set a shooting time limit), adding defenders to block shots and force early attempts at goal, and reducing the size of the target.

It is rare that shots are scored from distances greater than 30 yards, so players should focus on shooting from realistic distances (between 18 and 30 yards). In this book, shots from closer than 18 yards are classified as finishes, which involve different techniques and skill sets. Shots should be attempted from central and wide areas and players should be encouraged to use the instep, inside and outside of the foot to beat the goalkeeper. The better the player is at using different types of shots, the more ways they have of beating the goalkeeper.

If possible, try to use ball retrievers (a safe distance behind the goal) to collect balls and maintain a good supply of balls for the shooters. It helps to keep the flow and intensity of shooting activities.

# Finishing

In the same way that turning and shielding techniques can overlap and be coached simultaneously, the same can be said of finishing and shooting. Finishing is a type of shot from closer range (approximately 18 yards and under) and is a clear goal-scoring chance. Finishing is sometimes a direct contest between the attacker and the goalkeeper; however, finishes are often in crowded penalty areas with defenders blocking the path to goal.

Finishing is a varied technique as there are many different types of finish, e.g., 1v1 with the goalkeeper, close and long range, on the turn, half-volleys, volleys, headers and finishes that depend more on power or accuracy. The activities in this book allow players to practice finishes from different distances, angles, with varying degrees of defensive pressure and moving/bouncing balls to develop different aspects of finishing. When coaching finishing, try to develop good decision making in order to select the appropriate technique in each situation.

An important aspect of finishing is player movement to create goal-scoring opportunities. The finishing activities in this book (particularly those with defensive pressure) give the coach opportunities to show players how to find space to finish and anticipate where chances to score will arise before the defenders. There are many types of movement to coach such as diagonal runs, straight runs, in-to-out and out-to-in movements, overlaps and curved runs.

Successful finishing requires a clear head and the ability to cope with the pressure of completing attacking moves. Finishers may not have touched the ball in the attacking movement until the very last moment – and the success of the move depends on this final touch. Even the best finishers miss chances, so remember to be positive with players during finishing activities and remind them that the next chance to score is always the most important one.

# Volleys

Volleys are a way of moving an aerial ball onwards before it touches the floor. Volleys are usually performed with the feet; however other body parts can also be used to volley the ball. When coaching volleys, allow players the chance to practice using all legal body parts to volley the ball, including different foot surfaces, thighs, chest, head and even shoulders.

There are 3 main types of volleys: volleys to keep possession (i.e., passes), volleys to make attempts at goal (i.e., shots) and volleys to clear danger when defending. The activities in this book allow players to practice all these different types of volleys and improve volleying technique. Encourage players to be on their toes during volleying activities as the flight of the ball can be unpredictable. Being alert and ready to adjust body position will help players to execute the technique well.

Volleys are a difficult technique to master, and it is generally harder to volley the ball accurately than receive and pass the ball along the floor. Improving volleys can take a long time and a lot of practice. One of the reasons that volleying the ball is difficult is due to environmental factors such as wind. Wind can make the flight, speed and spin on the ball variable. In the early stages of coaching volleys, be mindful of the weather before attempting volleying activities. Volleys are an important technique in competitive play and occur naturally in different situations. Tackles, for example, can cause the ball to leave the floor, and passes, crosses and shots through the air can lead to a volley.

**Half-volleys** are either shots or passes performed immediately after a ball has bounced. Players may choose to hit a half-volley or can be forced to hit a half-volley if they cannot reach the ball in time to hit a volley. When coaching half-volleys, it is important to get players to strike the ball as soon as possible after the bounce. A bouncing ball travels upwards above shin height very quickly. Any half-volley above shin height is extremely hard to control and it is difficult to prevent the ball from ballooning up in the air. Remind players that half-volleys are best executed "as" the ball bounces rather than "after" the ball bounces.

# Heading

*As of February 2020, all coaches in England must follow the Football Association's guidelines about how to safely coach (or in the case of some age groups, not coach) heading in training sessions. At the start of the heading section in this book, there is a brief summary of the FA's heading safety advice for coaches to follow. Safety guidelines may vary from country to country, so coaches should research the safety advice from their own country's governing body before coaching headers in sessions.*

When coaching age groups that are allowed to practice headers there are ways to minimise heavy impact between the head and soccer ball. If a coach has concerns about the safety implications of coaching heading (even with age groups that are allowed to practice heading), try using balls that are slightly deflated or use a softer type of ball altogether. The main technical aspects of heading can be effectively coached to players using adapted balls. Balls suitable for practicing heading that reduce impact on the head include volleyballs and sponge balls.

The activities in this section allow the players to practice the main uses of headers:

- **Attacking heading**
- **Defensive heading**
- **Possession heading**

All players need to improve their heading technique, particularly heading techniques that are most common to their preferred playing position. Before working on position specific headers, players need to develop basic heading technique and practice making good ball contact with power and accuracy. In terms of position-specific headers, strikers should focus on headers to score (often under pressure from defenders). Defenders should focus on headers to clear danger from their goal whilst contesting an aerial dual. Midfielders need to practice headers to retain possession as well as attacking and defensive headers.

Once basic and position-specific heading techniques have been improved, it is important to introduce players to aerial duals and performing headers under pressure. The ability to win aerial duals and head the ball well under pressure is an asset in different areas of play and creates the possibility of a positive team outcome. For attackers, it creates the opportunity to score; for defenders it allows them to clear danger from their goal; and for midfielders it allows them to transfer possession to a teammate with a headed pass.

Heading is an essential technique in competitive play and one that occurs in many different situations. Headers often occur as a result of a re-start in play such as a goal kick, a corner, a free kick or a throw-in, where the ball is usually transferred through the air. During open play, players may perform headers as the ball travels through the air after a long pass, a cross or a block tackle. In all these situations, players must be able to challenge for the ball and in the process execute headers effectively.

# Goalkeeping

A soccer coach does not need to have played as a goalkeeper or have specialist goalkeeping qualifications to be a competent goalkeeping coach. Basic goalkeeping techniques can be coached effectively by non-specialist coaches if they have a good understanding of fundamental techniques and a willingness to learn.

Goalkeepers performing for elite-level teams will receive advanced coaching from goalkeeping experts; but at lower levels of soccer, techniques can be coached by non-specialist coaches. Advanced/elite-level goalkeepers need expert technical and tactical coaching in order to develop advanced techniques. The activities in the goalkeeping section of this book are designed for, and can be delivered by, non-specialist coaches.

A better understanding of what fundamental goalkeeping techniques are will help to make it a less daunting topic to coach. Below is a brief explanation of what these techniques mean in relation to goalkeeping.

## Movement

Goalkeepers need to be able to move quickly forwards, backwards and sideways around their goal area in order to position and re-position themselves. Any running activities that allow goalkeepers to cover short distances in different directions and at high speeds are suitable for improving goalkeeping movement.

## Agility

Good agility requires quick movement in different directions. For goalkeepers this means high speed up and down and side-to-side movement in order to react to the ball and make saves. Jumping, lunging, squatting and hurdling, as well as speed, agility, and quickness (SAQ) activities performed at high speed, are all useful for improving agility.

## Shot Preparation and Positioning

The ability to make saves is linked to how well prepared and positioned the goalkeeper is before an attempt at goal. Being ready and in the best possible position before an attempt at goal increases the chances of making a save. Activities that involve quick movement, ball anticipation and reacting quickly to the ball will help to improve shot preparation and positioning.

## Catching and Deflecting

Both are ball handling techniques and are vital techniques to practice regularly. The ability to catch crosses and shots is important, as is the ability to deflect, push and parry attempts at goal. Simple throwing, catching and parrying activities with the ball travelling at different heights, speeds, trajectories and spins will help to improve catching and deflecting.

## Shot Stopping

Shot stopping is the technique of making saves and stopping goal attempts. Shot stopping encompasses diving saves, tipping the ball over the crossbar or wide of the goalposts and standing blocks/deflections to prevent goals. Shots at the goalkeeper with power from close-/mid-/long-range and from varying angles will improve shot-stopping technique. It is important to spend time coaching safe and correct diving and landing technique before shot-stopping activities.

## Distribution

Short and long passes when the ball is on the ground, long kicks from hands and short and long throws and rolls are all types of goalkeeper distribution. Short and long passes for goalkeepers are the same techniques used by outfield players; however, as the last line of defence, the decision-making process is different. Kicking from hands is a similar technique to volleys performed by outfield players, although the context is different. Goalkeepers should regularly practice passing, kicking, rolling and throwing to teammates over different distances to improve their all-round distribution.

# Attacking and Defending

Any invasion game (e.g., soccer, hockey, rugby, basketball) is a competition between attack and defence. Soccer players are constantly involved in a contest between attack and defence, depending on who is in possession of the ball. The team in possession is the attacking team, and the team out of possession is the defending team. The only time when neither team is attacking, or defending is when the ball is loose, and players are contesting possession.

The activities in this book help players to understand and improve the technical and tactical aspects related to attacking and defending. It is an extremely broad theme, which depending on how the activity is organised and conditioned, creates opportunities to develop other relevant areas of technical and tactical play. For example, conditioning a 5v5 match attack v defence activity so that the attacking team must complete 5 passes to score, emphasises the importance of passing and receiving and creates opportunities to link this to the main topic.

There are five key attacking principles and five key defending principles that are part of all attack v defence activities:

**Attacking:**

- Movement
- Dispersal
- Support
- Creativity
- Penetration

**Defending:**

- Delay
- Depth
- Cover and balance
- Concentration and compactness
- Control and restraint

Try to coach one topic, i.e., attacking or defending and focus on one team during these activities. It is possible (but not recommended) to coach the principles of attacking and defending to one team, depending on if they are in or out of possession. It is also possible, but again not recommended, to coach the principles of attacking and defending to both teams depending on which team is in and out of possession.

Bear in mind that the non-recommended approaches make it difficult to provide a detailed technical and tactical focus and require a lot of expertise to do well. If using one of the non-recommended approaches, try to use half of the activity to coach each team. This allows the coach to focus on one group of players at a time and coach the topic in more detail.

Each activity in this section is organised and conditioned so that there is an emphasis on either attacking or defending. The secondary and additional focus varies for each activity and either emphasises attacking or defensive techniques and tactics. If, for example, the secondary focus is short passing and the additional focus is dribbling, then this suggests that the activity is better suited to focusing on attacking rather than defending. In each activity, there is room for coach interpretation and adaptation. Even when there is a suggested attacking or defending emphasis, the activity can still be used to coach either attacking or defending.

Try to refer to the 5 defensive principles and the 5 attacking principles when coaching these activities. Look out for opportunities to develop individual players, small units, team units and whole-team play.

# Tactical/Team Shape

Tactics are strategies employed by the coach to maximise team efficiency and success. Team shape is how a team organises itself inside the playing area when in and out of possession. The activities in this section are designed to help the coach improve specific areas of tactical play and improve team shape in different situations. They will help any coach that needs to improve and organise teams that are involved in competitive matches or to provide advanced players with a high level of challenge. The activities will help to condition the team as a whole and improve specific features of attacking and defending.

The tactical activities in this section cover a wide range of topics. They will develop player understanding of how to perform effectively in relation to the topic as an individual and within the team. To improve as a player and to win games of soccer, players must understand how to play as part of a team and how to react to specific events during competitive play as well as develop technical skills.

All coaches have different ideas about how they want their team to play. Some coaches prefer a defensive/counter-attacking style of play (particularly if they are playing against technically stronger opposition), whereas other coaches prefer a more attacking approach regardless of the opposition. Some coaches like to build attacks in as few passes as possible, while other coaches regard prolonged periods of possession as the key ingredient to success. Some coaches like to use a high defensive line and try to catch attackers offside, whereas others prefer to drop deep towards their own goal and block the centre of the pitch. The activities in this section allow the coach to practice and experiment with different tactical approaches.

Coaching from a tactical/team-shape perspective requires attention to detail from the coach and the players. Players that are not in correct positions will have a negative impact on the whole team and cause it to function inefficiently. The activities in this section of the book require players to concentrate and understand their role and how to play within their team. Younger players may find it hard to concentrate on tactical and team-shape activities for prolonged periods of time. Build these activities into sessions gradually with younger players to develop their mental application.

For every coach, it is important to find the most suitable way of coaching tactical/team-shape activities for each group of players. Some players may enjoy tactical activities, whereas others may struggle to apply themselves to the task. It is hard to coach tactical/team-shape activities well without regularly spending time on them. There is lots for the coach to organise and improve within these activities; however, this must be balanced out against the concentration span of the players and their willingness to absorb ideas. Over time and with consistency, players will start to see the benefits of tactical coaching and team-shape activities.

# TACTICAL GUIDANCE

The information in this section will help the coach to understand the activities in the tactical/team-shape section of the book. This section explains what each tactic means and how it is relevant to competitive play. Coaches need to be aware of the purpose of tactical/team-shape activities and how they will improve player performance before coaching them. Tactical and team-shape activities help condition players and the team to play in a certain style, so it is essential that coaches think about what they want to achieve from coaching each activity. Below is a guide to different aspects of tactical and team-shape play.

## Decision-Making

Decision-making activities should give players the opportunity to think carefully about what they are doing during play. Decision making, e.g., where to run to, which player to pass to or when to attempt a tackle is a continuous process when playing soccer, so it is important for players to learn and practice making good technical and tactical decisions.

Decision-making activities take players beyond technical decision making (e.g., how to pass, dribble or shoot) and gets them to think about when to use techniques to maximum effect and about the fine details of each technique. Using shooting as an example, a player may have good shooting technique, but they must also learn to make decisions about what type of shot to use (e.g., low, high, near post or far post) and understand why they are choosing to use that specific type of shot within the context of play. Decision making in soccer is based on many external stimuli, e.g., player distance from the goal, the position of the goalkeeper, teammates and opponents.

The fine detail of techniques are specific technical requirements that improve the quality and chances of technical success. Examples of fine technical details are applying spin to a pass or a shot to eliminate defenders, subtle adjustments to body position in relation to the ball and using decoys/fakes to disguise techniques. Players start to think about and use fine details once they have developed good technique and are confident in using the technique. Advanced players employ fine technical details much more regularly than lower-ability players, as their basic techniques are well established and reliable.

Decision-making activities should be performed at high speed. This forces players to think quickly, process information under pressure and make pressurised decisions. Activities that focus on decision making are organised in such a way that the players are frequently placed under pressure from opponents. This forces players to think creatively and find ways to outwit the opponents. The coach should encourage players to think about the best technical and tactical approach to succeed in each aspect of the activity.

# Creativity

Creativity is one of the five key principles of attack and is a key ingredient in successful attacking play. Creativity is about developing ways and moments to use attacking techniques to expose defences and create goal-scoring opportunities. Creativity sometimes involves using less commonly used and higher risk techniques such as a back-heeled pass, a trick to beat a defender or an unexpected chip over the goalkeeper.

Players should be encouraged to use attacking techniques creatively and express themselves without fear of failure. Activities that focus on creativity should be coached in a way that gives responsibility to the players to think for themselves, as this is the essence of creative play. The activities are organised in such a way that players are faced with a situation that requires some risk taking in possession and instinctive decision making.

# Pressing

Pressing refers to the organised and efficient application of pressure to the player and team in possession of the ball. Effective pressing happens when individual players, team units and the whole team understand how to close the player and team in possession and minimise space for the opposition. In order to press successfully, players need to be well organised and understand where and when to press the opposition. Pressing is an individual and team movement that involves hard physical work and carefully choreographed movements to pressurise the opposition.

Activities that have a focus on pressing allow players to learn about how to press within a team unit and the most appropriate situations in which to press. Pressing cannot be a constant defensive tactic, as there are times when dropping off and allowing time to recover to a balanced formation is equally necessary. Understanding the balance between when to press and when to drop off and recover shape is a key principle of successful pressing.

# Counterattacking

When the defending team wins back possession of the ball, they can counterattack. A quick counterattack creates opportunities to penetrate the opposition before they have transitioned from an attacking to a defensive shape. To launch a successful counterattack, the balance of the team needs to be organised so that after winning possession, players are in good positions to receive the ball and penetrate the opposition. Organising players to win the ball back and then transition quickly into a good attacking shape is a key coaching aspect of counterattacks. The longer the delay between winning possession and starting a counterattack, the more time there is for the opposition to filter back into a well-organised defensive shape.

Activities that focus on counterattacking relate specifically to the quick, organised and appropriate transition from defence to attack. They are organised in such a way that when the defending team wins possession of the ball, they must quickly transition from a defensive to an attacking team shape and start a counterattack as quickly as possible. Counter attacking activities should provide a high level of difficulty for the team in possession. This creates a high potential for turnovers in possession and regular counterattacks.

## Defending Against an Overload

This is a defensive situation in which there are fewer defenders (not including the goalkeeper) closer to their own goal than there are attackers (including the player in possession of the ball). Defending against an overload is difficult to do successfully and teams should try to avoid these situations as much as possible. Defending against an overload often occurs when the defending team faces a counterattack.

## Defensive Support

Defensive support is about individual players and the defensive unit working together to cover space, slow down and ultimately break up attacks. The coach should show defenders where the greatest attacking threat is in each attack and where defenders should position themselves to minimise the threat. It is important for defenders to always keep a balanced defensive formation to minimise areas of defensive risk.

The coach should focus on showing defenders where and when to move as a defender in relation to the ball, attacking players and rest of the defensive unit. The overall stability and balance of the defensive unit is the most important aspect of defensive support. Defensive support must be practiced regularly so that players develop an understanding of how to maintain it during competitive play.

## Defending in Wide Areas

Defending in wide areas requires individual players and the defensive unit to minimise space for attackers in wide positions. Well-organised wide defending can force the attackers to lose possession or push them into less dangerous attacking areas. Defending in wide areas requires vigilance and good positioning to minimise the risk of the attack moving into central and potentially goal-scoring areas of play. Defenders must also be aware of the threat of danger on the opposite side of the pitch and be ready to re-position if the attack switches to the opposite side of play.

Defending players need to support each other to prevent attacking players from penetrating the defensive line in wide positions or breaking into central positions. The defenders need to organise themselves to defend the wide area without flooding the area and losing a balanced defensive shape. Key skills to coach when defending in wide areas are: 1v1 defending, preventing crosses and forcing attackers into congested areas of play/away from goal.

## Attacking With an Overload

This is an attacking situation where there are more attackers (including the player in possession of the ball) closer to the goal than there are defenders (not including the goalkeeper). Creating attacking overloads creates vulnerability in the defensive unit and makes it impossible for each attacking player to be marked. Attacking overloads performed efficiently and at high speed can lead to the creation of goal-scoring opportunities. The longer the attack takes, the more time there is for the defending team to restore defensive balance, solidity and redress their numerical disadvantage.

Attacking overloads often occur after dispossessing the opposition and transitioning quickly from defence to attack. Quick penetration of the defensive unit is a key principle for the coach to develop when attacking with an overload. The coach should work on the effective movement of all players involved in the attack to penetrate the defensive unit. The attackers need to know where and when to move in order to exploit defensive vulnerability and how to best support the player in possession to penetrate the defence as quickly as possible.

## Attacking in Wide Areas

When attacks develop in wide areas, all attacking players need to understand how to best support the attack – whether they are directly involved in the wide attack, slightly more distant (in the centre of the playing area) or more distant (the opposite side of the playing area). The movement and position of every attacking player in wide attacks play a part in its success or failure. The defenders position themselves in relation to where the attackers position themselves and so good attacking positioning can cause weaknesses in the defensive unit.

Wide attacks need to be well supported to create attacking opportunities; however, if the wide area becomes saturated with attacking players, there is less space to penetrate the defence. The more attacking players there are in a wide area, the more defending players will be drawn into this area, causing congestion. It is important for the attacking team to focus on the principles of support and creating space as well as maintaining a balanced attacking shape.

Creating space behind the full-backs during wide attacks is an effective way to penetrate the defensive unit. Once the attacking team is beyond the full-backs, there is space to dribble into or to cross from. Effective ways of finding this space are quick interplay and movement of the ball and dribbles past the full-backs. The coach should try to develop player understanding of how and when to use the dribble and how and when to combine quickly with teammates. As with any attack, the more space that is created by movement and support, the more opportunities there are to penetrate the opposition.

## Attacking in Central Areas

Successful attacks in central areas offer a quick and direct path to goal. The ability to penetrate the defence in central areas of play is a vital attacking weapon for individual players and attacking units to develop. Attacking in central areas is a difficult task as the defending team often has most of their defensive players in the central area of play. This is to prevent shots on goal or passes in between or behind the central defenders. The amount of congestion in the central attacking area of play creates difficulties for the attacking team to overcome.

Attacking players involved a central attack need to work on finding space in tight areas, moving into areas that create gaps in the defence and attacking with a creative mentality. The closer the attack gets to the goal, the more the attacking players should be encouraged to take appropriate risks in possession if it means that the chance of breaking through the central area is increased. Playing quick 1- and 2-touch passes, and using the dribble to go past defenders, can help to de-stabilise the defensive unit. When coaching these activities, the coach should try to improve quick and creative passing combinations and 1v1 dribbles.

# TYPE OF ACTIVITY

The only activities that do not have a category type are warm-up activities and some of the physical/movement development activities. Warm-up activities can be used as an introduction to coach certain techniques, but they are organised differently to other types of coaching activities and generally should be used as stand-alone warm-up activities.

Physical/movement development activities are varied in the way that they are organised and performed. Some of the activities have a technical aspect to them; however, some are purely physical or movement-based and therefore do not fit into the other types of activity category.

Every other activity in this book has been categorised into a type of activity, depending on how it is organised and how it approaches coaching player technique and/or tactical play/team shape. Each activity type has been organised so that the structure is most conducive to player development for the selected topic. Familiarisation with the types and methodology of each activity structure will help coaches to understand how the different types of activity help players to learn and develop. It is important for the coach to understand how the structure of each activity fits into a whole session so that sessions are balanced and progressive. Following is an explanation of what the different activity types are.

# Unopposed Technical Practice

Activities in this category are performed with minimal external pressures, e.g., opponents, time and space pressures that occur when playing against other players. Unopposed technical practices are activities designed to help players learn the correct body shape, movements and sequential stages of performance, which with repetition will facilitate good technique.

This type of activity can be performed individually, in partners or in small groups. Generally, the more players that are involved in an activity the greater the level of technical pressure, as greater numbers add complexity to decision making, which in turn adds difficulty to the technique. When coaching unopposed technical practices, players should be given adequate time and space to perform the technique without the pressure of relating it to competitive situations.

The success of techniques in unopposed activities can be judged visually by the coach and kinesthetically by the player, for example: How accurate was the pass? How many mistakes were made (for example, shots off target)? Did the body shape look correct? How did the technique feel when it was executed? Coaches should give clear technical instructions during unopposed technical practice, starting with advice on basic body movements and key coaching points.

# Opposed Technical Practice

An opposed technical practice is an activity that requires players to perform techniques under pressure from opponents during a form of competitive play. The more opponents that are added to pressurise the player in possession, the greater the level of technical difficulty. With beginner players, try to start with only 1 or 2 opponents before taking the technique into more competitive arenas such as a 5v5 match.

Try not to expose players to heavy external technical pressure too quickly, as it can have negative outcomes for players. If players experience too much pressure, too early, they are likely to make regular technical errors. Players become demotivated by frequent errors, which can lead to the development of bad technical habits, to generate short-term success but ultimately cause long-term technical failings. Typically, no more than 12-14 players should take part in opposed technical practices. If the number of players rises above 12-14, the focus on the technique can become lost due to lack of space and time in possession and the high number of alternative technical options when in possession.

Players should be set realistic targets during opposed technical practices. For example, when coaching players how to dribble, make sure that they can beat 1 defender before adding a second defender. If the coach wants to continue to raise the level of technical challenge, they could add a teammate(s) as well as other defenders to offer support as well as opposition. This will also encourage players to make technical decisions about how and when to use or not use the technique during competitive play.

The nature of opposed technical practices forces players to consider why, when and how techniques can be successfully performed in competitive play. For example, an attacking player may want to dribble, but if there is minimal space to dribble into and opponents in proximity, they need to consider their chances of success in relation to an alternative technique, e.g., a short pass. Opponents force the player in possession to make technical why, when and how decisions. This pressure facilitates a greater understanding of how the technique is relevant to competitive play.

## Implementation Practice

Implementation practices allow players to perform activities under pressure in a similar way to opposed technical practices. The key difference is that during implementation practices, players perform techniques under pressure from opponents in the areas most specific and relevant to the technique. For example, during an implementation practice, crosses would be performed under pressure in wide areas, as this is the area where crosses are delivered from. Implementation practices simulate key aspects of realistic and competitive match play and therefore place realistic pressure on the technique.

During implementation practices, players develop an understanding of how their technical performance impacts team performance and effectiveness in specific situations. These activities allow players to experience realistic pressure, technical success and failure. For example, if a coach wants to improve short passing from defence into midfield, then it is important to practice the technique starting in the defensive third of the playing area. The specific area of play adds pressure through realism and consequences, i.e., if a defender plays an inaccurate short pass in their defensive third, the opposition may gain possession in a dangerous and potentially goal-scoring area of play.

Implementation practices are competitive, and players should experience realistic pressure from the opposition. As with all types of activity, give the players some time to understand the activity and experience some success before increasing pressure and difficulty too much. If the level of difficulty is too high, then consider adding teammates and removing opposition players so that players can practice and develop techniques with success. Typically, the number of players involved in implementation practices ranges between 12-16.

Try to encourage players to play with discipline and play to the requirements of their position to give the activity realism. To maintain realism and technical specificity, only use players that are directly relevant to the technique being coached. If, for example, a winger is not directly relevant to the technique being coached, then do not use one just for the sake of it. Employ the players in positions and areas of the pitch that will directly influence, and are most relevant to, the activity.

# Small-Sided Game

Small-sided games are competitive soccer matches using teams of less than 11 players (typically teams of 7-8) including goalkeepers. For each small-sided game there is a technical/tactical focus to impress upon the players, e.g., counterattacks. During small-sided games, teams attack opposite ends of the playing area, in contrast to opposed technical practices where the method and direction in which players score varies.

Small-sided games replicate and allow players to experience realistic match play. The coach may need to alter certain rules or conditions of play to meet the needs of the technical/tactical focus. For example, an offside line may be used so that players can only be offside within a specific area of play. Similarly, the coach may condition play so that only a certain number of players are allowed in each half at any time to maintain a specific formation or team shape.

There are enough players involved in small-sided games to divide them into small team units, i.e., defence, midfield and attack. This allows the players to experience playing within a team unit and to see how their performance affects the whole team. During small-sided games, the coach can help players to develop tactical awareness and see how their performance and decisions affect the whole team's function. Small-sided games are a good way of coaching the key principles of defensive and attacking play as they expose players to realistic match play.

During small-sided games, it is recommended to coach only 1 team at a time. There are too many players involved to thoroughly coach both teams at the same time. It is good practice to focus on coaching 1 team and conditioning the other team in such a way that they offer a specific and relevant challenge to the team being coached. Examples of conditioning play are selecting a playing formation, limiting the number of passes they can make in an attack or giving them a scenario to play to, e.g., 2-0 down with 20 minutes to play.

# Simulated Match Activity

A simulated match activity has many similarities to 11v11 match play but incorporates slightly fewer players. The 2 teams can be even in terms of numbers; however, the team being coached usually has a numerical advantage of 1-2 players. Only the team being coached requires a goalkeeper. A typical simulated match activity involves a team of 10 against a team of 8-9.

Both teams require 2 complete team units (these units vary depending on the coaching topic) and the most relevant player(s) from the remaining team unit. For example, if the team being coached consists of 10 players, they could be organised as: 1 goalkeeper, 3 defenders, 4 midfielders and 2 attackers. This formation replicates a 4-4-2, however, 1 defender has been removed from the defensive unit. The organisation of simulated match activities allows the coach and players to focus on the team units most relevant to the topic and minimises the influence of peripheral players.

Simulated match activities are usually played on a full-width but reduced-length (commonly 2/3 of a full pitch), playing area. The team being coached defends a goal at 1 end of the playing area (with goalkeeper) and the opposition team defends the opposite end (with no goalkeeper). Depending on the coaching topic, the opposition team's end may vary in layout; however, it is usually a line, which the team being coached trying to penetrate this line with a dribble or a pass to a target player or players.

The team being coached attacks an end line rather than a goal to help create disciplined play. Players can sometimes play unrealistically, selfishly or not in an appropriate style when there is a goal to be scored in. Instinctively, players are excited by the goal and their thinking and playing intent can be influenced by shooting at goal as much as possible. Of course, shooting and scoring are important, but using a different method of scoring helps to focus on the coaching topic.

The organisation of simulated match activities enhances player performance and their understanding of the coaching topic. The removal of players that are not critical to the coaching topic means that the coach can focus in greater detail on the players that are involved. This also helps the coach to focus on the development of player techniques and team tactics that are most critical to the activity.

The reduction in the size of the playing area maximises the amount of time that players spend in the areas that are most relevant to the activity. It also minimises the space to play in areas that are less relevant to the topic focus. Simulated match activities give the players the opportunity to experience small group, team unit and whole-team competitive play.

## Type of Activity

The coach should focus on coaching 1 team and conditioning the opposition to play in a style that best suits the focus of the topic. It is helpful to give the opposition players targets or challenges to help motivate them to play in the style that is required. The use of targets/challenges helps to keep the opposition team conditioned to play in the way that the coach requires and lets the coach focus on coaching the team they want to coach. For example, if the coach requires the opposition team to play with a direct attacking style, they could be conditioned to use a maximum of 3-4 passes before they break into the penalty area.

# SESSION PLANNING

When planning a coaching session, it is important to consider the objectives and structure of the session before selecting the activities. The technical/tactical objectives and structure vary from session to session, but in each session the coach should try to make the activities enjoyable, developmental and motivational for the players. It is important that players progress and develop in each session, so try to plan activities that increase in difficulty as the session progresses and finish with an activity that assesses the level of player progress. Competitive activities such as a small-sided game allow the coach and player to see how much they have progressed during the session.

There are many factors to consider before planning a session. Some of the most important factors for consideration are:

- **Length of session**
- **Number of players**
- **Ability of players**
- **Session context:** Are the players part of a team? Is it primarily a recreational session? Is it a one-off session or part of a large block of sessions?

- **Coaching environment:** How much space is available? What equipment is available? Is it an open or closed environment and therefore will there be possible distractions and disturbances?

- **Concentration level of players:** How long will players be able to focus on the activity? How many activities will I need to include depending on the concentration span of the players?

- **Physical considerations:** Are there any disabled players in the group? Are there any players with existing injuries or illness that will affect their participation in certain activities?

Session planning and structure are also dependent on the length of the session. A typical coaching session will last somewhere between 1-2 hours, with 90 minutes considered a good amount of time. A session of 90 minutes allows the coach to deliver a productive and well-balanced session without over-tiring the players. Using 90 minutes as a guide, the session templates below suggest how the coach can structure sessions using a mixture of activity types for different ability levels. The session templates can be adapted and modified as required to consider the requirements of the players and the objectives of the coach.

*Mixed ability group* session template:

- Warm-up activity (10 minutes)
- Unopposed technical practice (15 minutes)
- Opposed technical practice (15 minutes)
- Implementation practice (25 minutes)
- Small-sided game or simulated match activity (25 minutes)

For lower ability/recreational groups, it is advisable to spend less time on pressurised activities, e.g., opposed technical practices and tactical/team-shape activities. As the players progress technically and are ready for a higher degree of pressure and challenge, then the emphasis of the session can be modified to reflect this. Initially, the coach should plan more activities that allow players to learn new techniques with minimal pressure, e.g., unopposed technical practices and experience competition through small-sided games.

*Lower ability group* session template:

- Warm-up activity (15 minutes)

- Unopposed technical practice (15 minutes)
- Unopposed technical practice – more advanced than previous activity (15 minutes)
- Opposed technical practice (20 minutes)
- Small-sided game (30 minutes)

With higher ability groups, the session structure should emphasise high pressure and competitive play activities, e.g., opposed technical practices and implementation practices. Higher ability players generally enjoy activities that are pressurised, as it encourages them to raise their performance levels to meet technical and tactical challenges. Activities that create technical pressure and challenge players tactically, e.g., simulated match activities also help to keep higher ability players stimulated and focused.

*Higher ability group* session template:

- Warm-up activity (10 minutes)
- Opposed technical practice – incorporating 1-2 progressions (25 minutes)
- Implementation practice (30 minutes)
- Small-sided game or simulated match activity (25 minutes)

For all ability groups, the context of the session is a key factor in planning a good session. If, for example, a group of players is taking part in a one-off session and want to play for enjoyment rather than development, it is unlikely that they will enjoy multiple activities working on a specific technique. In such a case, it is a good idea to plan activities that focus on a range of techniques, e.g., a dribbling activity, followed by a physical/movement development activity, followed by a shooting activity. This is an example of context-based planning, which will help the players enjoy the session and stay engaged.

For higher ability players or team training, the session structure and plan should focus on technical/tactical improvement and development. In order to facilitate this, try to coach only 1-2 techniques/tactics in a session so that coaching can be detailed. If focusing on 1 technique/tactic in a session, each activity type should focus on the chosen technique/tactic. For example, to focus on shooting, each activity should have a primary focus on shooting. If the coach wants to work on multiple techniques or tactics, it is helpful if they are linked, e.g., turning and shielding.

When coaching higher ability players or teams, the activities should increase in difficulty throughout the session and culminate in a competitive activity designed to challenge technical/tactical development. When appropriate, the coach can broaden the technical/

tactical focus by using the secondary and additional activity focus to increase the level of difficulty. If, for example, the secondary focus for a shooting activity is short passing, the coach can refer to and coach aspects of short passing in relation to shooting, e.g., accurate short passing in attacking areas can create good shooting opportunities.

Following is an example of how to select activities from this book and use a range of activity types to plan a session with 1 technical focus.

*Shooting session template:*

- **Warm-up activity** – *Under orders* (activity number 7) 10 minutes.

- **Unopposed technical practice** – *Shooting fundamentals* (activity number 128) 15 minutes (include progressions).

- **Unopposed technical practice** – *Hit the target* (activity number 129) 15 minutes.

- **Opposed technical practice** – *Raining shots* (activity number 137) 25 minutes.

- **Small-sided game** – *Empty the net* (activity number 224) 25 minutes.

# WARM-UP ACTIVITIES

## ACTIVITY 1   CATS AND DOGS

**Level:** Basic

**Number of participants:** 2-16

**Equipment required:** Soccer balls, cones, discs and 2 sets of bibs

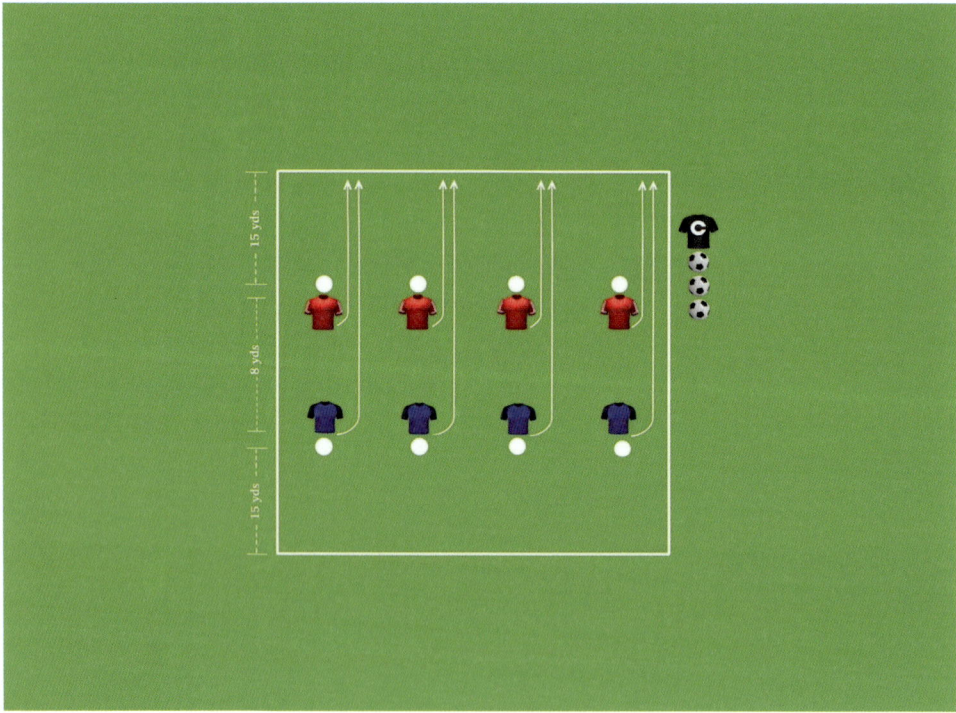

## Description

Divide players into pairs. Mark out a playing area. Position the pairs facing each other on two lines in the middle of the playing area, 8-10 yards apart. The distance from each line to the nearest end of the playing area should be 12-15 yards. Nominate 1 player in each pair as a "cat" and their partner as a "dog".

The activity starts when the coach calls either "cat" or "dog". If the coach calls "cat", the cat chases the dog, in which case the dog must turn and try to sprint to their nearest end of the playing area before the cat taps them on the back. If the coach calls "dog" then the dog chases the cat who turns and sprints to their nearest end of the playing area. If either player makes it back to their end of the playing area before they are tapped on the back, they win 1 point. If the chasing player taps their partner on the back, they win 1 point.

## Key focus/Coaching points

**Primary focus:** Reaction time

**Secondary focus:** Agility

**Additional focus:** Speed

## Progressions/Adaptations

- Give a ball to each player. The player that is chased must dribble their ball to their nearest end line. The player that is chasing must leave their ball and chase without it.

- The chasing player also must dribble their ball.

- Nominate one player in each pair to be the chasing player and the player being chased. The player being chased requires a ball. On the command "Go", the player with the ball is chased to their nearest end line by their partner. Rather than trying to tap their partner on the back, the chasing player now tries to tackle their partner before they reach their nearest end line. If the chasing player wins possession of the ball, they try to dribble the ball to their end line.

# 56 THE SOCCER COACH'S TOOLKIT

## ACTIVITY 2  PAINT POTS

**Level:** Basic

**Number of participants:** 4-16

**Equipment required:** 4 sets of different coloured cones

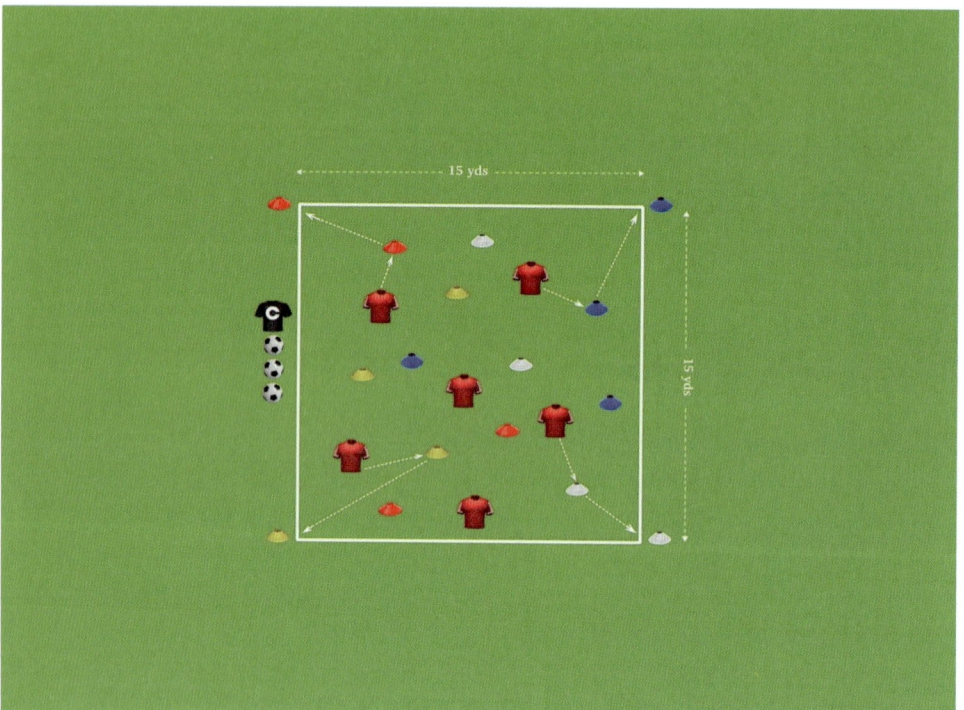

## Description

Place a different coloured cone at each corner of the playing area, e.g., red, blue, yellow and white. Scatter an equal amount of the corresponding coloured cones inside the playing area. Players must pick up the cones one at a time and place them on the corresponding cone in each corner. Encourage the players to work as fast as they can. Complete the activity two or three times and time each one to see how fast the players managed to collect all the cones. See if the players can get a faster time with each attempt.

# Warm-Up Activities

## Key focus/Coaching points

Primary focus: Speed

Secondary focus: Agility

Additional focus: Dribbling

## Progressions/Adaptations

- Divide players into four teams, each corresponding to a set of differently coloured set of cones, e.g., red, blue, yellow and white teams. The teams race to clear the playing area of their coloured cones and put them in their corner. The first team to collect all their cones is the winner.

- Players have a ball each and must complete the same activity while dribbling their ball.

# 58  THE SOCCER COACH'S TOOLKIT

## ACTIVITY 3   FORWARD MARCH

**Level:** Basic

**Number of participants:** 8-20

**Equipment required:** Soccer balls, cones and 1 set of bibs per group

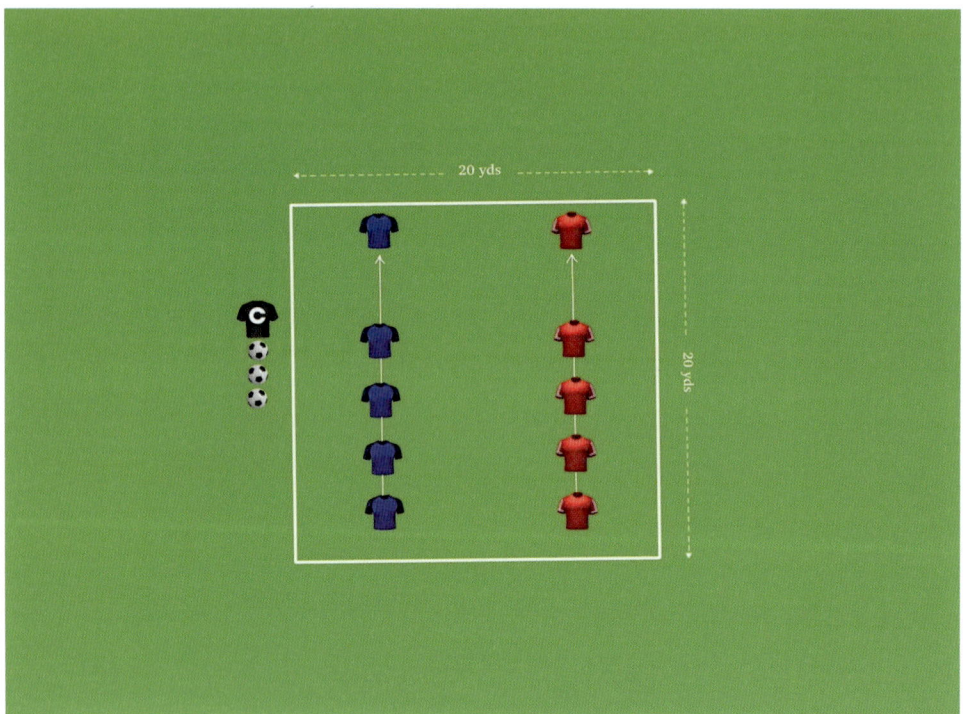

## Description

Divide players into groups of four to five. Position the players in single-file lines inside the playing area and number them 1-5. Player number 1 should be at the front of the line. The groups jog around the playing area trying to maintain a straight line. Instruct the player at the front of each line to change direction. Every 10-15 seconds, the coach calls out a number and the corresponding player must run to the front of their line as quickly as possible. Repeat until all players have been at the front of the line at least once.

## Key focus/Coaching points

Primary focus: Agility

Secondary focus: Coordination

Additional focus: Dribbling

## Progressions/Adaptations

- All players must dribble a ball.
- Add rewards, forfeits for the fastest/slowest team to get their player to the front of their line.
- Call 2 numbers and the corresponding players must swap places in the line.
- On command, all players dribble one lap of the playing area as fast as they can and re-form the line.

## ACTIVITY 4    MAGPIES

**Level:** Basic

**Number of participants:** 8-16

**Equipment required:** Soccer balls, cones and 2 sets of bibs

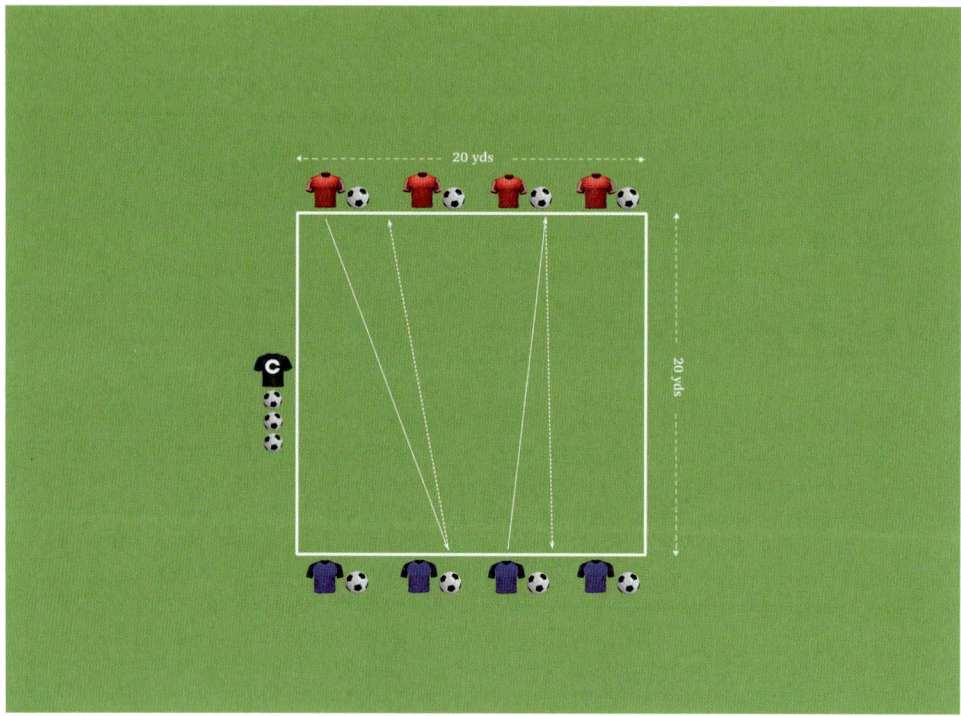

## Description

Divide players into two teams of four to eight. Position the teams at opposite ends of the playing area. Instruct the players to spread out along their line. Each player has a ball next to their feet. On the command of the coach, the players leave the ball next to their feet and run to the opposite end to steal a ball from the other team. The players steal balls by dribbling a ball back to their end of the playing area. Once a player has stolen a ball they run back to the opposite end and repeat.

This is a competition for 1-2 minutes and the team with most balls on their end line at the end of the competition is the winning team. It is important that teams start with the same number of soccer balls. Players can steal any of the balls from opposite end. Only one ball can be stolen at a time by each player and players are not allowed to remain on their own line and guard soccer balls.

## Key focus/Coaching points

Primary focus: Running with the ball.

Secondary focus: Speed

Additional focus: Endurance

## Progressions/Adaptations

- Each team places a defender in the middle of the playing area. This player tries to prevent opponents from dribbling balls back to their end line by tackling or intercepting. If the defender makes a tackle or interception, they dribble the ball back to their end line. The player that was tackled must run to their own end line before attempting to steal another ball.

## ACTIVITY 5  BOX-TO-BOX

**Level:** Intermediate

**Number of participants:** 4-16

**Equipment required:** Soccer balls and cones

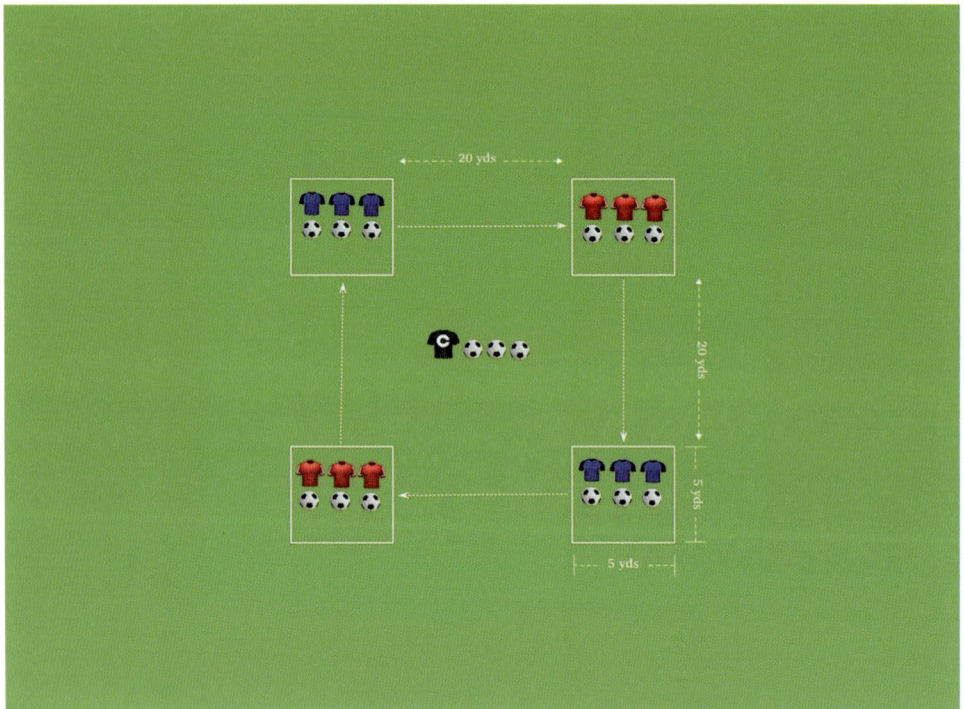

## Description

Divide players into four teams of one to four. Mark out a playing area with a small square in each corner. Position one team inside each of the squares. On the command of the coach, all teams race clockwise around and through each square until they are back at their starting square. At each square, all players must complete a physical or technical challenge before they can move onto the next square. This activity can have a more physical or technical focus depending on the type of challenges.

# Warm-Up Activities

## Key focus/Coaching points

Primary focus: Speed

Secondary focus: Running with the ball.

Additional focus: Physical/movement development

## Progressions/Adaptations

- All players within each team complete the challenge individually. Once all players are back to their starting square, their team has finished the race.

- Teams must wait at each square until all the players in their team have completed the challenge. Once all players from their team have completed the challenge, they can move on to the next square.

- Example of activities to emphasise physical development: **square 1** – 10 star jumps; **square 2** – 10 squat thrusts; **square 3** – 10 knee-to-chest jumps; **square 4** – 10 burpees.

- Example of activities to emphasise technique: **square 1** – 10 keep-ups; **square 2** – 10 Cruyff turns; **square 3** – 10 ball taps; **square 4** – 10 step-overs.

# 64   THE SOCCER COACH'S TOOLKIT

## ACTIVITY 6   READY FOR ACTION

**Level:** Intermediate

**Number of participants:** 8-16

**Equipment required:** Soccer balls and cones

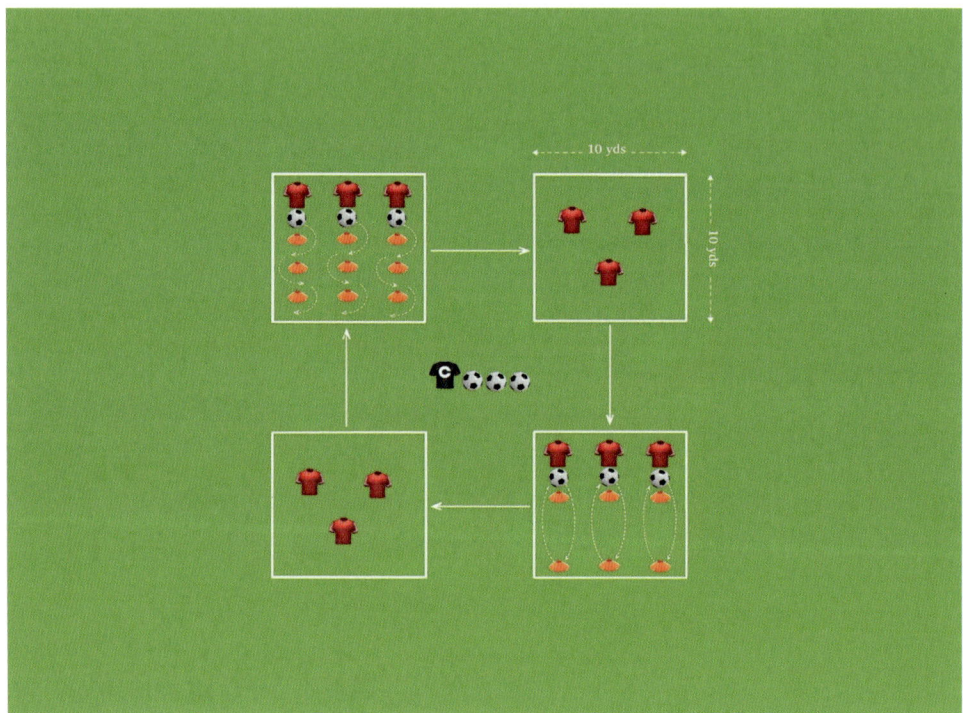

## Description

Divide players into four groups of three. Mark out four activity stations (shown next). Each group spends 1-2 minutes at each activity station. After each activity move, all groups move one station clockwise until all activities are completed. Players should complete two full circuits of activities twice.

- **Activity 1:** High intensity dribbling in and out of cones.
- **Activity 2:** Static stretching.

# Warm-Up Activities

- **Activity 3**: Dribble between 2 cones and perform a turn at both ends. Dribbling and turns should be completed at high speed.
- **Activity 4**: Dynamic stretching.

## Key focus/Coaching points

Primary focus: Dribbling

Secondary focus: Speed

Additional focus: Agility

## Progressions/Adaptations

- Condition the activities so that players must use both feet when performing ball activities.
- Under coach supervision, encourage the players to do their own stretches.

# 66  THE SOCCER COACH'S TOOLKIT

## ACTIVITY 7   UNDER ORDERS

**Level:** Intermediate

**Number of participants:** 2-16

**Equipment required:** Soccer balls and cones

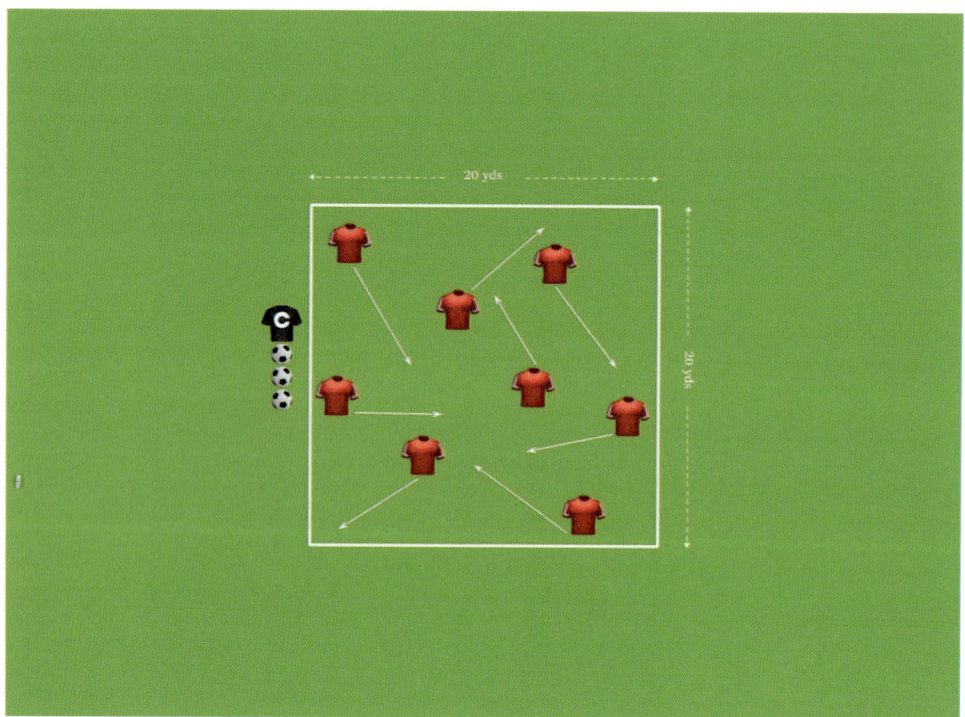

## Description

Position all players inside the playing area. The players jog around inside the playing area and the coach gives players a series of commands to follow. Encourage players to jog with their heads up and to maintain space for themselves as much as possible. Examples of suitable commands:

High 5s, players tap feet against each other, jump up and touch chests, jump up and touch backs, assemble in groups of 2-4.

## Key focus/Coaching points

**Primary focus:** Coordination

**Secondary focus:** Reaction time

**Additional focus:** Agility

## Progressions/Adaptations

- As the players warm up, gradually increase the tempo of the movements.
- Any other activities can be added that encourage movement and player interaction.
- Players perform activities whilst dribbling a ball around the playing area.

# 68  THE SOCCER COACH'S TOOLKIT

## ACTIVITY 8   BATTLE STATIONS

**Level:** Advanced

**Number of participants:** 2-16

**Equipment required:** Cones and 2 sets of bibs

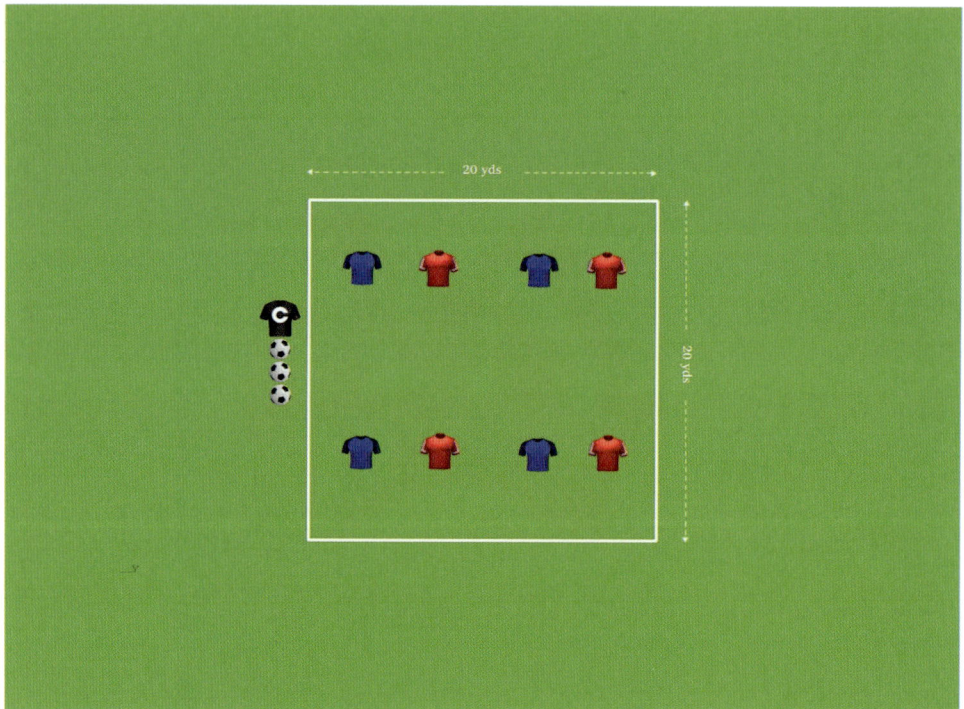

## Description

Divide players into pairs. Position each pair in a good amount of space inside the playing area. The pairs engage in a series of 1v1 contests. Each contest is completed three to four times. These contests develop a determined mentality and encourage players to use their strength, agility and coordination to beat their partner.

**Activity 1** – Face-to-face, arms on partner's shoulders. Players try to push themselves through the gate by pushing their partner backwards (progress to standing on 1 leg).

**Activity 2** – Grip partner's forearms. Forearms facing upwards. Players try to pull their partners through the gate.

# Warm-Up Activities

**Activity 3** – Stand back-to-back, legs bent 45-90 degrees (depending on strength and balance of players). Players try to push themselves through the gate by pushing their partner backwards.

**Activity 4** – Players face-to-face on floor in spider position (palms on floor, torso raised off floor and standing on balls of feet). Players try to grab either of their partner's wrists and hold on without losing balance.

**Activity 5** – Players stand back-to-back on either side of gate. Players take turns spinning around and scrambling through the gate as their partner tries to prevent them from getting through.

**Activity 6** – Unopposed activity. Players lie flat on their back and try to get up without arms or hands touching the floor.

**Activity 7** – Partners stand face-to-face, balancing on one leg, and grip one of their partner's forearms. Players try to pull their partner through the gate.

**Activity 8** – 1 player lies flat on their back and makes their body rigid. Their partner tries to roll them over onto their front.

*These activities are meant to enable players to gain confidence in physical contests. Encourage players to use their strength and be determined to win but exercise caution. None of these activities should involve excessive force, nor should players deliberately try to hurt or humiliate an opponent. If it is obvious that players are physically mismatched, intervene and suggest working with a partner of similar height, weight and strength.

## Key focus/Coaching points

**Primary focus:** Strength

**Secondary focus:** Agility

**Additional focus:** Coordination

## Progressions/Adaptations

- Introduce a 60-second time limit for each activity. Players perform the activity as many times as they can in 60 seconds and the player that wins most contests wins 1 point. After all exercises are completed, see how many players each player has won.

# 70  THE SOCCER COACH'S TOOLKIT

## ACTIVITY 9   KING OF THE RING

**Level:** Advanced

**Number of participants:** 6-16

**Equipment required:** Soccer balls and cones

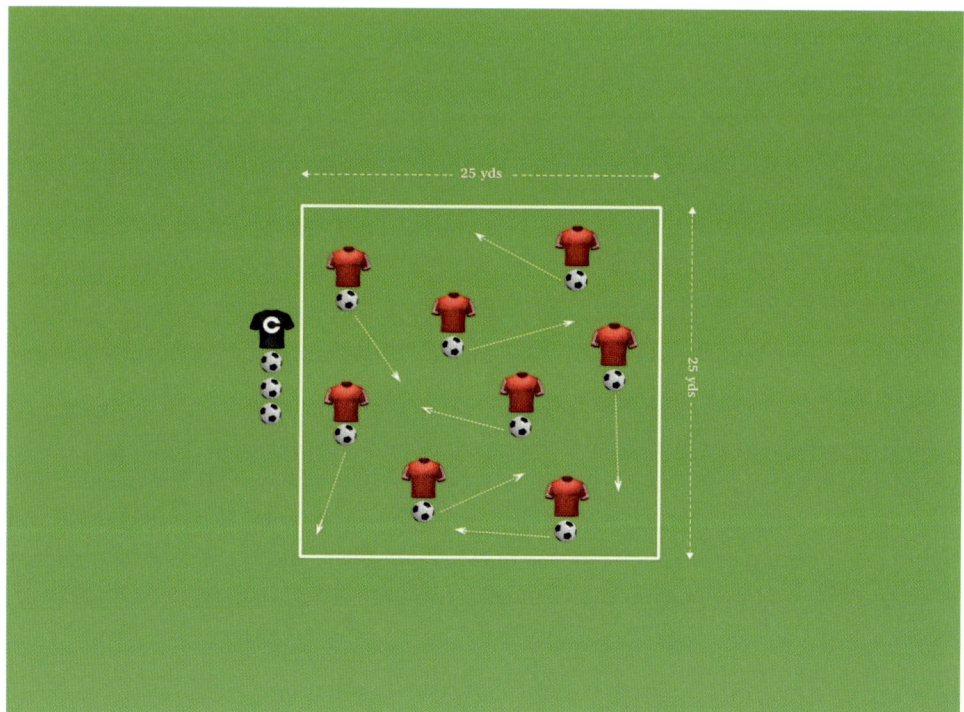

## Description

Position all players inside the playing area with a ball each. The players dribble their soccer balls around inside the playing area. At the same time as dribbling the ball, players try to kick other players' balls out of the playing area. Players will develop dribbling and shielding technique while also trying to challenge for other balls. If a player has their ball kicked out, they are eliminated from game. To prevent eliminated players from waiting for long periods of time, allow them to practice a skill challenge to return to game, e.g., 10 keep-ups.

## Key focus/Coaching points

**Primary focus:** Agility

**Secondary focus:** Movement

**Additional focus:** Dribbling

## Progressions/Adaptations

- To make the elimination of players more difficult, balls can only be kicked out across 1 line of the playing area.

## ACTIVITY 10 SQUARE AFFAIR

**Level:** Advanced

**Number of participants:** 12

**Equipment required:** Soccer balls, cones and 3 sets of bibs

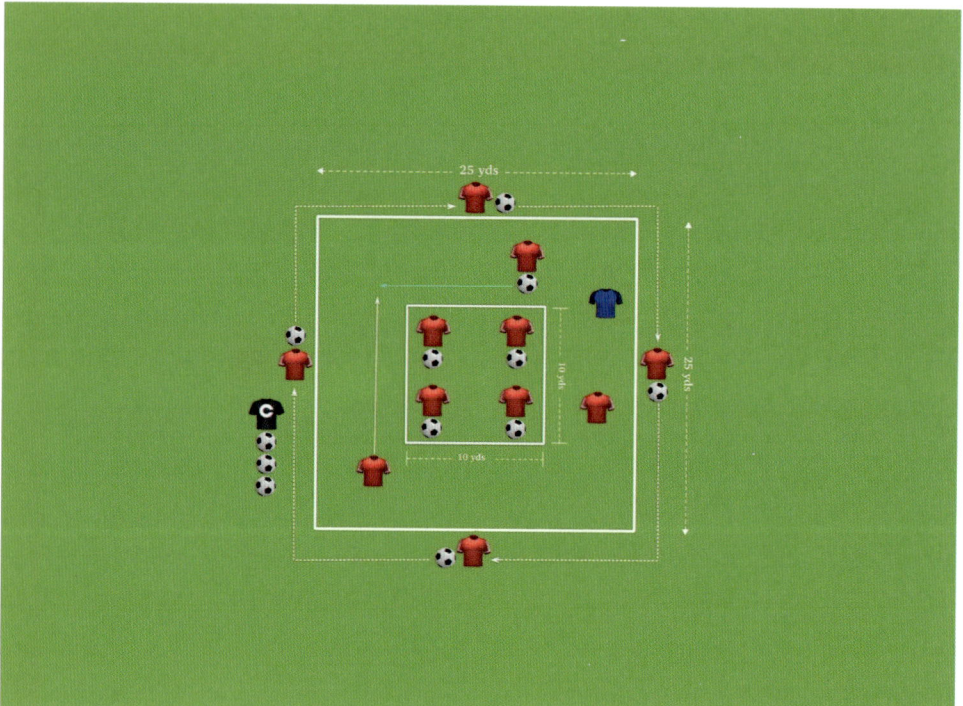

## Description

Divide players into three groups of four. Mark out a playing area with a square in the middle. Position one group inside the middle square, a second group inside the playing area and third group outside the main playing area. Each player has a ball. The groups perform three warm-up activities (see below) for 2-3 minutes each. After each activity, the groups move onto another activity:

- **Activity 1 (inside small square):** Players perform keep-ups.
- **Activity 2 (inside main playing area):** 3v1 possession.
- **Activity 3 (outside main playing area):** Players dribble laps of the playing area.

# Warm-Up Activities

## Key focus/Coaching points

Primary focus: Ball manipulation

Secondary focus: Receiving

Additional focus: Dribbling

## Progressions/Adaptations

- Activity 1 – Nominate specific body parts for keep-ups, e.g., head only.
- Activity 2 – Players have 2 touches maximum on the ball during 3v1 possession.
- Activity 3 – Use weaker foot, use alternate feet, use small touches or big touches.

74 THE SOCCER COACH'S TOOLKIT

# PHYSICAL/MOVEMENT DEVELOPMENT

## ACTIVITY 11  GRAND PRIX

**Level:** Basic

**Type of activity:** Unopposed technical practice

**Number of participants:** 12

**Equipment required:** Soccer balls, cones and 4 sets of bibs

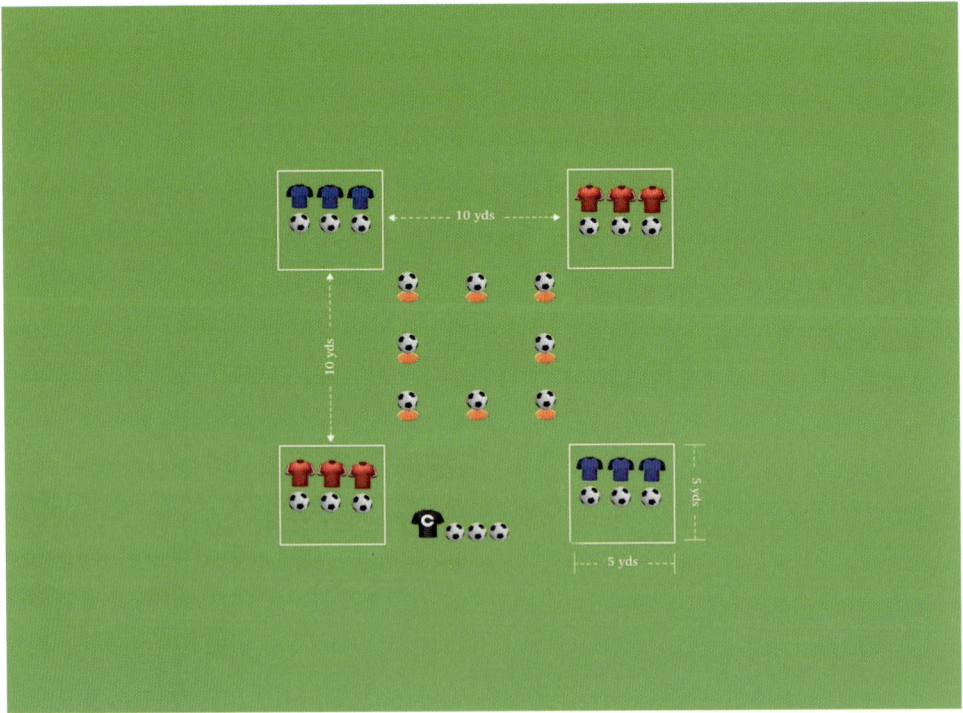

## Description

Divide players into four teams of three. Mark out a playing area with a square in each corner. Position 8-10 balls, balanced on cones in a square shape in the centre of the playing area. Position one team inside each square. Each player requires one ball.

The activity starts when the first player from each team runs around the perimeter of the playing area and back to their square. From their squares, each player retrieves their ball and passes it into the centre of the playing area to try to knock a ball off a cone. After the pass, the next player in the team repeats until all balls are knocked off the cones. The team that knocks the most balls off the cones is the winning team.

## Key focus/Coaching points

Primary focus: Physical/movement development

Secondary focus: Speed

Additional focus: Short passing

## Progressions/Adaptations

- Dribble the ball around the perimeter of the playing area and then pass.

# ACTIVITY 12  TEAM WARM-UP

**Level:** Basic

**Number of participants:** 2-16

**Equipment required:** Soccer balls and cones

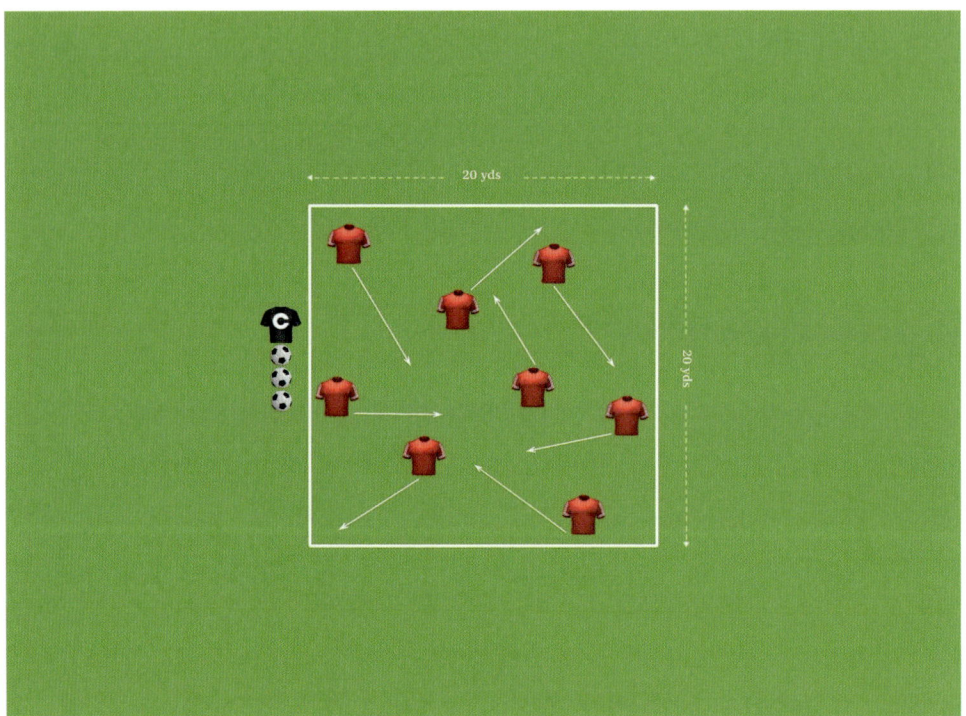

## Description

Position all players inside the playing area. The players jog around inside the playing area and the coach calls out the names of an international soccer player every 10 seconds. For each of the international soccer players, the players mimic one of their typical playing actions (the coach should nominate the actions before the activity). Each player represents one of the four main playing positions (goalkeepers, defenders, midfielders and attackers). Use the players and actions below as examples:

# Physical/Movement Development

England:

**Jordan Pickford (goalkeeper)**: players perform dive to the floor and then stand up.

**Harry Maguire (defender)**: players jump up and head an imaginary soccer ball.

**Raheem Sterling (midfielder)**: players perform step-overs with imaginary soccer ball.

**Marcus Rashford (striker)**: players shoot an imaginary soccer ball and celebrate a goal.

This activity can be adapted to any international or club team. Let the players pick the team, players and actions.

## Key focus/Coaching points

**Primary focus:** Physical/movement development

**Secondary focus:** Coordination

**Additional focus:** Speed

## Progressions/Adaptations

- Each player moves around the playing area dribbling a soccer ball and uses the ball to perform actions, e.g., dive and grab the ball or throw the ball up, jump and header.

# 78    THE SOCCER COACH'S TOOLKIT

## ACTIVITY 13  3V2 IN THE RING

**Level:** Basic

**Type of activity:** Opposed technical practice

**Number of participants:** 11

**Equipment required:** Soccer balls, cones and 3 sets of bibs

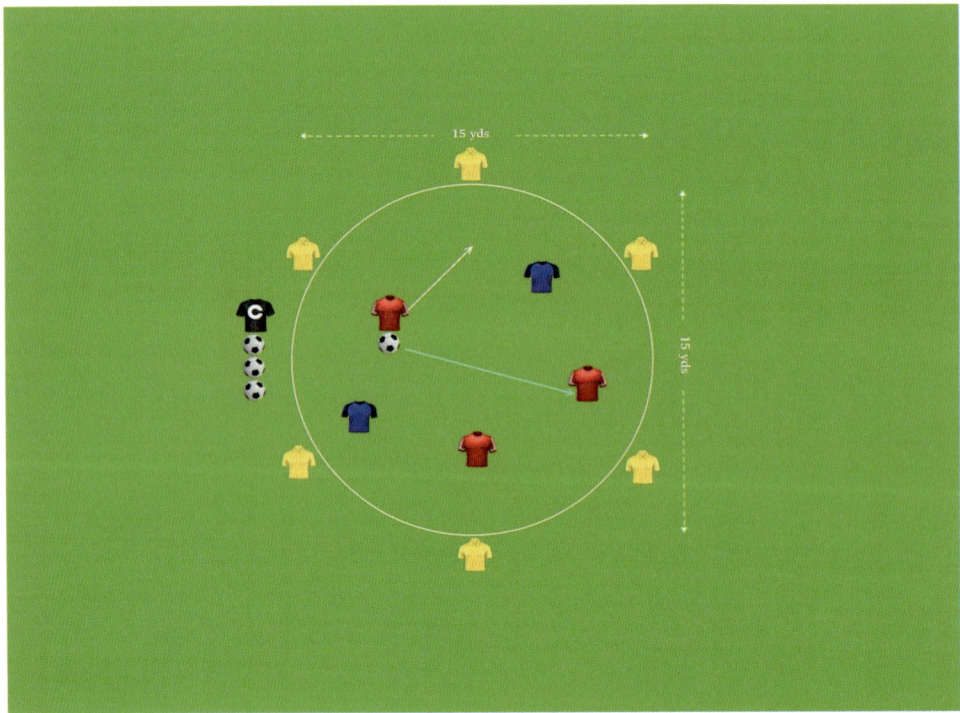

## Description

Divide players into a group of six and a group of five. Mark out a circular playing area. Position the group of six players around the outside of the playing area. Organise the group of five into a team of three and a team of two players. Position the two teams inside the playing area.

The activity starts when the coach feeds a ball into the playing area. The two teams compete to retain possession of the ball. The team of three players can only use each other to retain possession, whereas the team of two players can pass to and receive back from the players around the playing area. The players around the playing area can exchange passes but should try to pass back to the team of two players as soon as possible.

## Key focus/Coaching points

Primary focus: Physical/movement development

Secondary focus: Short passing

Additional focus: Receiving

## Progressions/Adaptations

- The team of 2 players rotate with the player they pass to, each time they pass the ball to a player outside the playing area.
- Limit the number of touches for each player in the team of 3.
- Limit the number of touches for each of the players outside the playing area.

## ACTIVITY 14 POSSESSION SWITCHOVER

**Level:** Intermediate

**Type of activity:** Opposed technical practice

**Number of participants:** 12

**Equipment required:** Soccer balls, cones and 2 sets of bibs

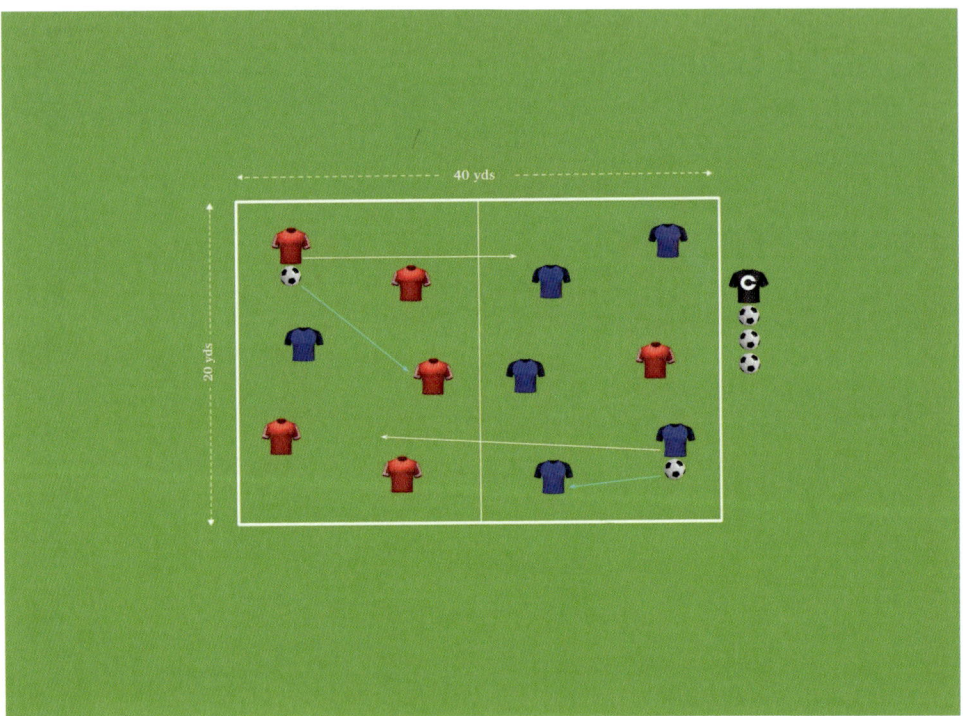

## Description

Divide players into two groups of six. Organise both groups into five attackers and one defender. Divide the playing area into two zones with one ball in each zone. Position one group inside each zone. In both zones, the five attackers try to keep possession and avoid interceptions from the defender. Both zones play at the same time. After each successful pass, the player immediately runs into the opposite zone. The aim is to maintain a 5v1 attack v defence in both zones with the attackers moving between zones.

There will be lots of player movement and rotation between zones as each successful pass requires the passer to move to a new zone. Rotate the defenders every 60 seconds as they will become fatigued. Encourage attackers to count their passes before interception and see how many they can complete.

## Key focus/Coaching points

Primary focus: Physical/movement development

Secondary focus: Speed

Additional focus: Receiving

## Progressions/Adaptations

- Change from 5v1 to 4v2 in both zones.

# 82    THE SOCCER COACH'S TOOLKIT

## ACTIVITY 15  COMBINATIONS

**Level:** Intermediate

**Type of activity:** Unopposed technical practice

**Number of participants:** 5 + 1 goalkeeper

**Equipment required:** Soccer balls, cones, discs, 2 sets of bibs and 1 goal

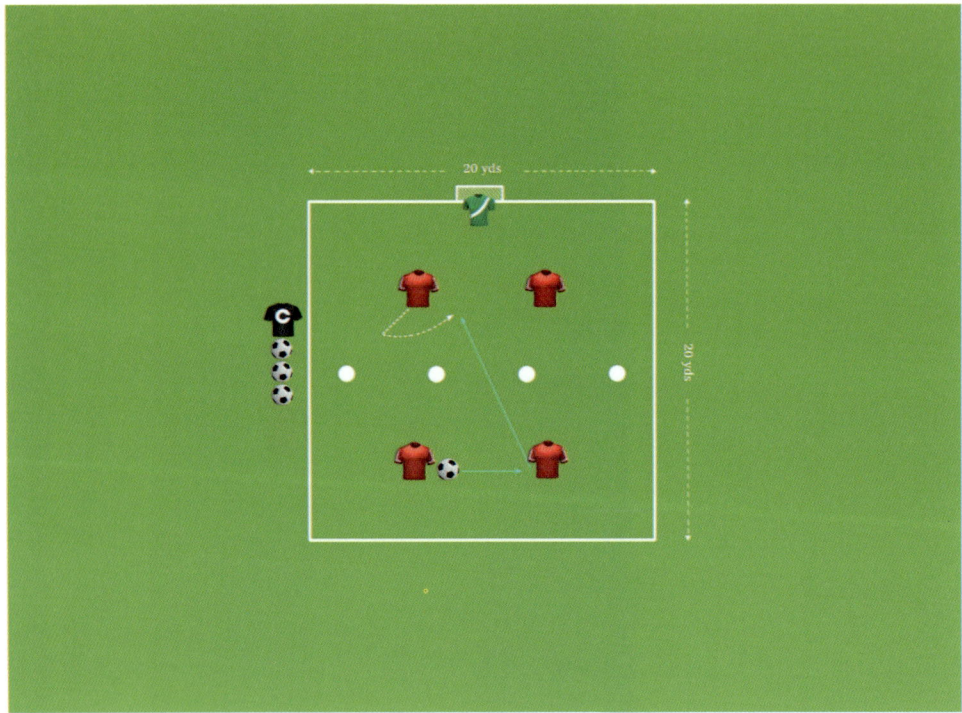

## Description

Divide players into groups of five (including goalkeeper). Divide the playing area into two small zones. In zone 1, position two players standing side-by-side (10 yards apart) with one soccer ball. In zone 2, position two attacking players without a ball. Position a goal and goalkeeper on the end line of zone 2.

The activity starts with the players in zone 1 exchanging passes while the players in zone 2 make attacking runs to receive a pass and support the movement of the ball (examples of attacking runs include lateral, diagonal and cross-over.) At any stage, a player in zone 1 can pass the ball to an attacker in zone 2. As soon as an attacker is in possession they must combine with their partner and attempt a shot at goal.

Encourage players in both zones to play quickly. When players in zone 1 have the ball try to encourage them to move the ball quickly between themselves and make a forward pass after no more than four to five passes. When the attacking players have possession ask them to combine quickly and try to score as soon as possible.

## Key focus/Coaching points

**Primary focus:** Physical/movement development

**Secondary focus:** Support play

**Additional focus:** Finishing

## Progressions/Adaptations

- Add a defender in zone 2 to apply passive and then active pressure to the attackers.

# 84   THE SOCCER COACH'S TOOLKIT

## ACTIVITY 16  FOUR LINKED ACTIVITIES

**Level:** Intermediate

**Type of activity:** Unopposed leading to opposed technical practices

**Number of participants:** 12

**Equipment required:** Soccer balls, cones and 2 sets of bibs

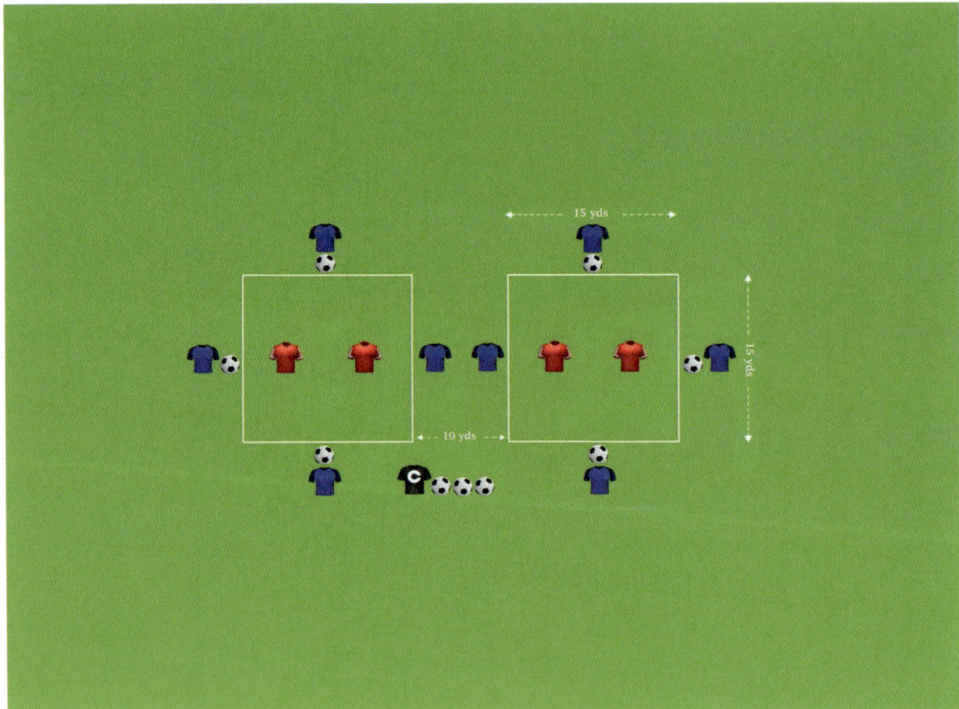

## Description

These activities are linked and progress from activity 1 to 4. The transition from activity to activity is simple and requires little moving of equipment. All the activities develop fitness, movement, receiving and short passing.

Divide players into a group of 12. Mark out two playing areas next to each other with a 10-yard channel in between. For the first activity, position two players inside each playing area and one player outside each line of both playing areas. Give a ball to three of the players outside the lines of both playing areas. This is the initial organisation for activity 1:

**Activity 1:** Players inside the playing area move and create space to receive a pass from one of the players outside the playing area. The players inside the playing area call for a pass from outside, receive the pass, dribble off into a new space and then pass to a player outside the playing area without a ball. After this, the players inside the playing area move and look to receive a pass from another player. The activity is continuous for 60 seconds. After 60 seconds, rotate the players.

**Activity 2:** Remove two balls from the outside of both playing areas so that only one outside player has a ball. The four players outside the playing area try to keep possession among themselves by passing through the playing area to each other. The two players inside the playing area act as defenders and try to intercept the passes. Rotate the players every 60 seconds.

**Activity 3:** Position all the outside players inside the playing area to create a 4v2 inside each playing area. The teams of four try to keep possession from the teams of two. Rotate players every 2-3 minutes.

**Activity 4:** Remove the channel between the playing areas so that it is a now one large playing area. Organise players into an 8v4 possession game. The team of eight tries to keep possession from the team of four. Rotate players every 2-3 minutes.

## Key focus/Coaching points

Primary focus: Physical/movement development

Secondary focus: Receiving

Additional focus: Short passing

## Progressions/Adaptations

- Change the 8v4 to a 6v6. The first team to complete 10 passes is the winner.
- Organise the players into a 6v4 with 2 floating players that play for the team in possession.

# 86   THE SOCCER COACH'S TOOLKIT

## ACTIVITY 17  REACTIONS

**Level:** Advanced

**Type of activity:** Opposed technical practice

**Number of participants:** 12 + 4 goalkeepers

**Equipment required:** Soccer balls, cones, 2 sets of bibs and 4 goals

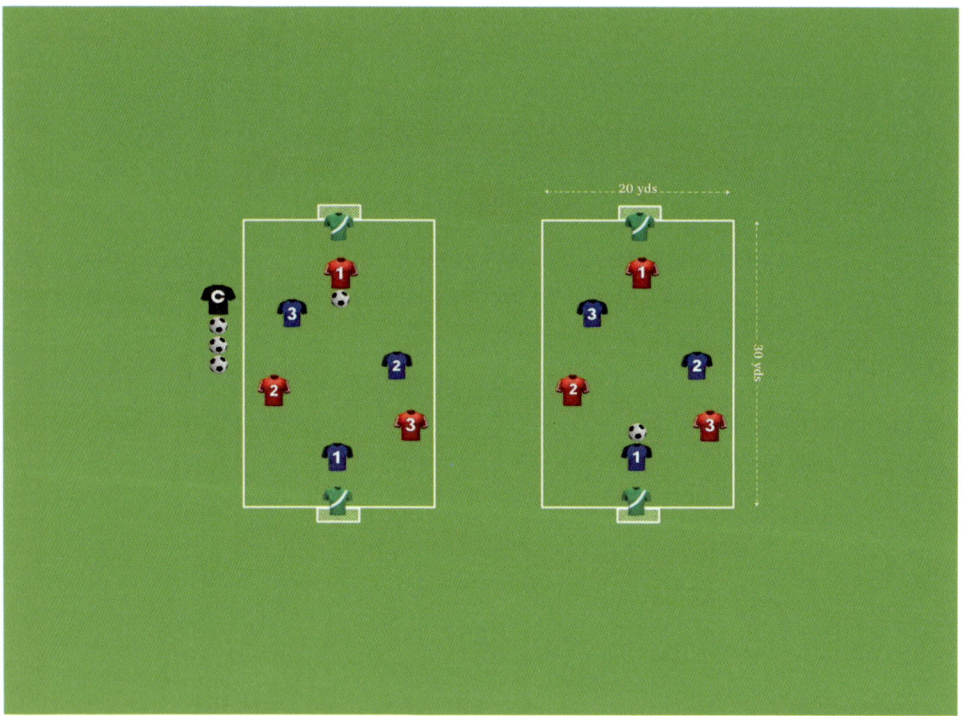

## Description

Divide players into two 4v4 mini matches (including goalkeepers). Mark out two small playing areas (side-by-side) with goals at both ends of the playing areas. Number each outfield player in all teams from 1-3. Organise players so that each team is wearing the same-coloured bib as one other team on the opposite playing area (e.g., red v blue and red v blue) on both playing areas.

# Physical/Movement Development

During the matches, the coach can call out any number between 1 and 3. When the coach calls out a number, the players of the corresponding numbers in each team switch playing areas and join the team wearing the same-coloured bibs on the other playing area. The matches are continuous and should not pause during player transitions. Encourage players to switch playing areas as quickly as possible to maintain 3v3 play.

## Key focus/Coaching points

Primary focus: Physical/movement development

Secondary focus: Reaction time

Additional focus: Attacking and defending

## Progressions/Adaptations

- The coach can call more than one number at a time.

# 88 THE SOCCER COACH'S TOOLKIT

## ACTIVITY 18 SAQ CIRCUIT

**Level:** Advanced

**Number of participants:** 12-20

**Equipment required*:**

Station 1: 4 mini hurdles and 2 agility poles

Station 2: 1 set of agility ladders and 2 agility poles

Station 3: 6 agility poles

Station 4: 7 agility poles

*Mini hurdles are small arch-shaped hurdles used for jumping exercises. Agility poles are plastic poles with a sharp point at one end that stick into grass. Agility ladders are plastic squares joined together by a cord to make a ladder shape that can be placed flat on the floor. If agility poles are not available, use domes or cones.

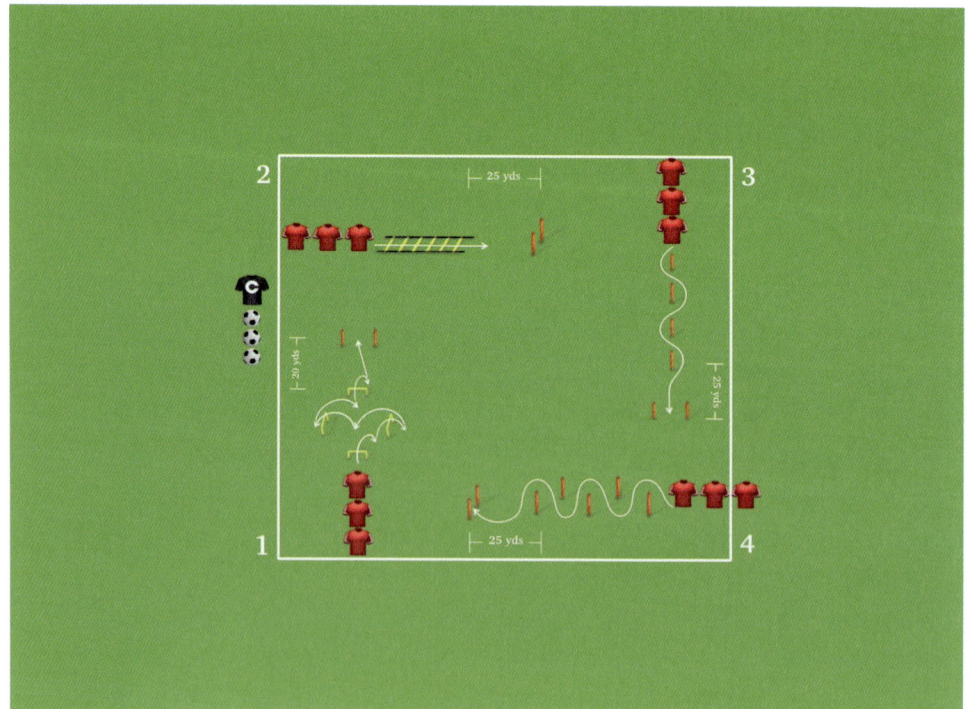

## Description

Divide players into groups of three to five. Mark out four activity stations (see below). All groups complete a four-station SAQ (speed, agility, quickness) circuit. Players should spend 1-2 minutes at each activity station. Coaches can vary the amount of time spent at each station depending on the fitness of the players and the intensity of work. After each completed circuit allow 60 seconds recovery time. During work periods encourage players to work at high intensity.

**Station 1:** Two-footed jumps over mini hurdles (jump forward over mini hurdle; jump right over mini hurdle; jump left to the middle; jump left over mini hurdle; jump right to the middle; jump forward over mini hurdle; followed by 20-yard sprint.)

**Station 2:** Sprint activities through agility ladders (**exercise 1** – slalom sprint in and out of ladders followed by 25-yard sprint; **exercise 2** – sprint 1 foot in each square followed by 25-yard sprint; **exercise 3** – sprint 2 feet in each square followed by 25-yard sprint.)

**Station 3:** Slalom sprint through agility poles followed by 25-yard sprint.

**Station 4:** Wide slalom sprint around agility poles followed by 25-yard sprint.

## Key focus/Coaching points

Primary focus: Speed

Secondary focus: Agility

Additional focus: Quickness

## Progressions/Adaptations

- Alter the **intensity** of work periods, **time spent** at each station and the **number of circuits completed** to suit the physical needs and capabilities of the players. Try to set realistic, challenging and safe expectations for players to work toward. Get player feedback about the physical demands of the circuit to help plan future circuits.

# 90  THE SOCCER COACH'S TOOLKIT

## ACTIVITY 19  RAPID-FIRE SOCCER

**Level:** Advanced

**Type of activity:** Opposed technical practice

**Number of participants:** 12 + 1 goalkeeper

**Equipment required:** Soccer balls, cones, 3 sets of bibs and 1 goal

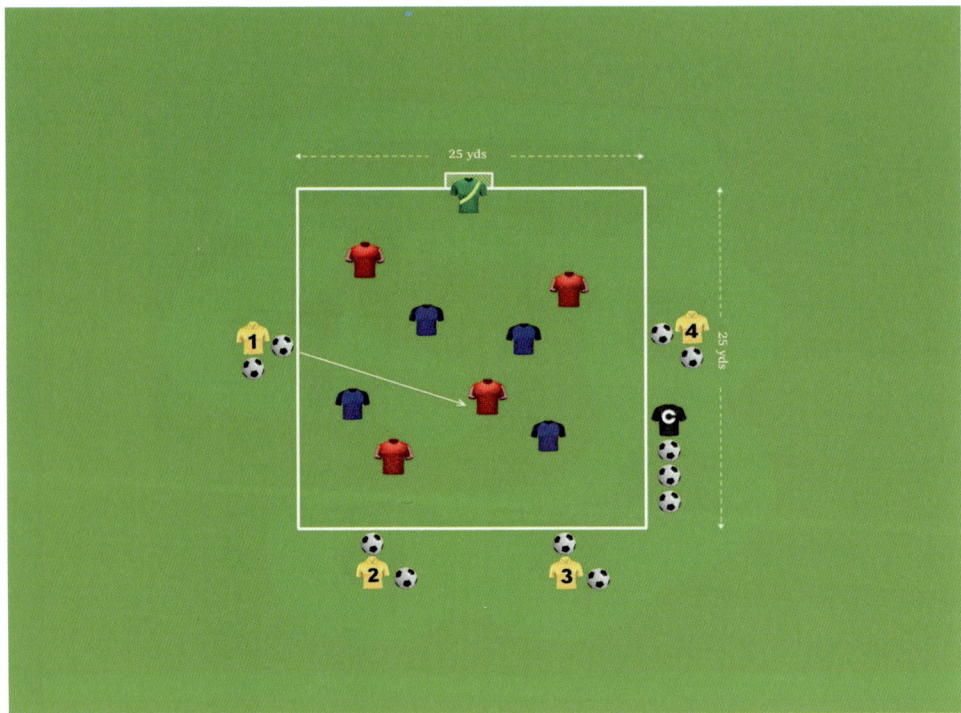

## Description

Divide players into three teams of four. Position two teams inside the playing area to compete in a 4v4 match. Position the third team around the outside of the playing area and number them 1-4 with two balls per player. Position a goal and goalkeeper at one end of the playing area.

The activity starts when player number 1 passes a ball to either of the teams inside the playing area. The two teams inside the playing area compete to score past the goalkeeper. When a goal is scored or the ball goes out of play, the next ball is immediately passed in from player 2 and continues in this way up to player 4. Player numbers 2-4 should pass to the team that has just scored, got a shot on target or had a shot blocked. After the first set of balls have been used up, player number 1 continues the activity and passes their ball into the playing area. Play until all balls are used up and then rotate one team on and off.

## Key focus/Coaching points

Primary focus: Physical/movement development

Secondary focus: Finishing

Additional focus: Receiving

## Progressions/Adaptations

- Players outside the playing area can be used as bounce players for team in possession. Condition players outside the playing area to use no more than 1-2 touches to keep the activity high intensity.
- Give the team in possession a set number of passes, e.g., no more than 6 in each attack.

# 92   THE SOCCER COACH'S TOOLKIT

## ACTIVITY 20  BLAST

**Level:** Advanced

**Number of participants:** 2-20

**Equipment required:** Cones and stopwatch

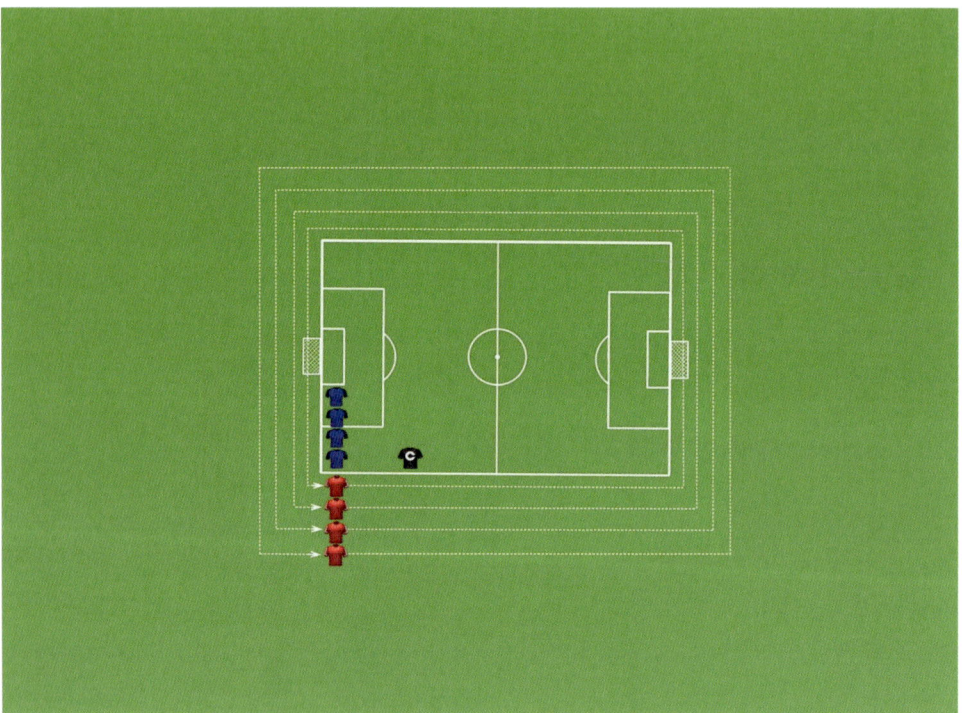

## Description

The "blast test" is a high intensity speed/endurance running activity. It is designed to challenge players physically and improve cardiovascular/speed endurance running. The test is completed around the perimeter of a full-sized soccer pitch; however, if this amount of space is not available, use an area as close as possible in size.

The blast test is hard work and is ideally used in sessions to improve fitness. It should not be delivered before or along with activities that require high levels of technical performance. The level of fatigue caused by the blast test may significantly reduce technical performance. If the test is used a technical/tactical session, it is best to do it at the end of the session when players can rest immediately afterwards.

Divide players into two groups. The groups complete four sections of running with the aim of running the distances within the specified time limits (see below). Group one performs section one of the test first, while group two rests. As soon as group one has completed section one, group two performs section one of the test and group one rests. The groups alternate between running and rest periods until all sections of the test have been completed.

**The following times are a guide**. If the players are not used to high-intensity running and/or have low/moderate cardiovascular fitness levels, the time limits should be made easier. If the test is too demanding for the players, the coach can also reduce the sections of work from 4 to 3.

- **Section 1:** Complete 4 laps of a soccer pitch in **3 minutes 40 seconds**.
- **Section 2:** Complete 3 laps of a soccer pitch in **2 minutes 45 seconds**.
- **Section 3:** Complete 2 laps of a soccer pitch in **1 minute 50 seconds**.
- **Section 4:** Complete 1 lap of a soccer pitch in **55 seconds**.

## Key focus/Coaching points

Primary focus: Physical/movement development

Secondary focus: Endurance

Additional focus: Speed

## Progressions/Adaptations

There are 3 variables that coaches can alter/adapt in this test:

- **Time limit, sections of work and distance covered.**
- The running area should not be bigger than a full-sized soccer pitch. The suggested sections of work offer a high level of physical challenge. The coach can increase or decrease the above variables as they see fit.

# 94 THE SOCCER COACH'S TOOLKIT

# SHORT PASSING

## ACTIVITY 21  TOUCH THE LINE

**Level:** Basic

**Type of activity:** Opposed technical practice

**Number of participants:** 12

**Equipment required:** Soccer balls, cones and 2 sets of bibs

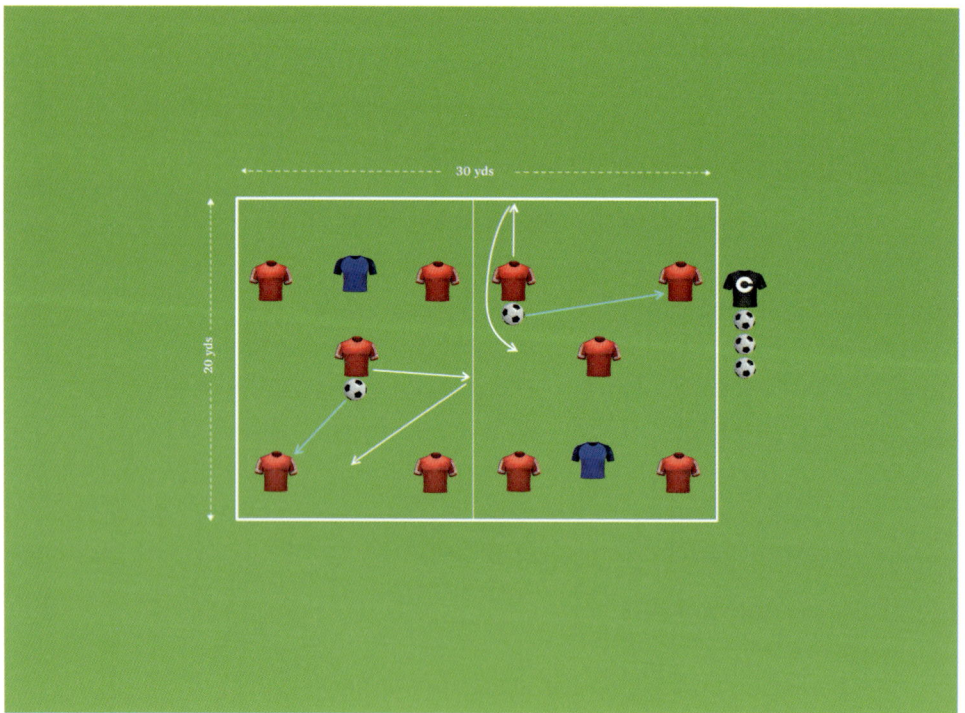

## Description

Divide players into two groups of six. Mark out a playing area with two equal-sized zones. Organise the groups into five attackers v one defender and position one group in both

# Short Passing 95

zones with one ball in each zone. Both groups perform the activity at the same time. The five attackers in both zones try to keep possession from the defender who tries to make a tackle or interception. After each pass, the player that passed the ball must run to the nearest playing area line and touches it before re-entering play. Each player takes a turn as a defender (swap every 60 seconds.)

## Key focus/Coaching points

Primary focus: Short passing

Secondary focus: Movement

Additional focus: Receiving

## Progressions/Adaptations

- Progress to a passing contest between the groups. The group that completes the most consecutive passes in 60 seconds scores 1 point. Play until all players within the teams have taken a turn as the defender. The team with the most points after each 6 rounds of possession is the winner.

- To make the activity easier, remove the defenders and play unopposed possession.

# 96  THE SOCCER COACH'S TOOLKIT

## ACTIVITY 22  PASSING CROQUET

**Level:** Basic

**Type of activity:** Unopposed technical practice

**Number of participants:** 2-20

**Equipment required*:** Soccer balls, cones/domes and 2 sets of bibs

*A dome is a large cone, which in this case makes it harder to avoid when receiving the pass and shooting, thus increasing the difficulty of the technique.

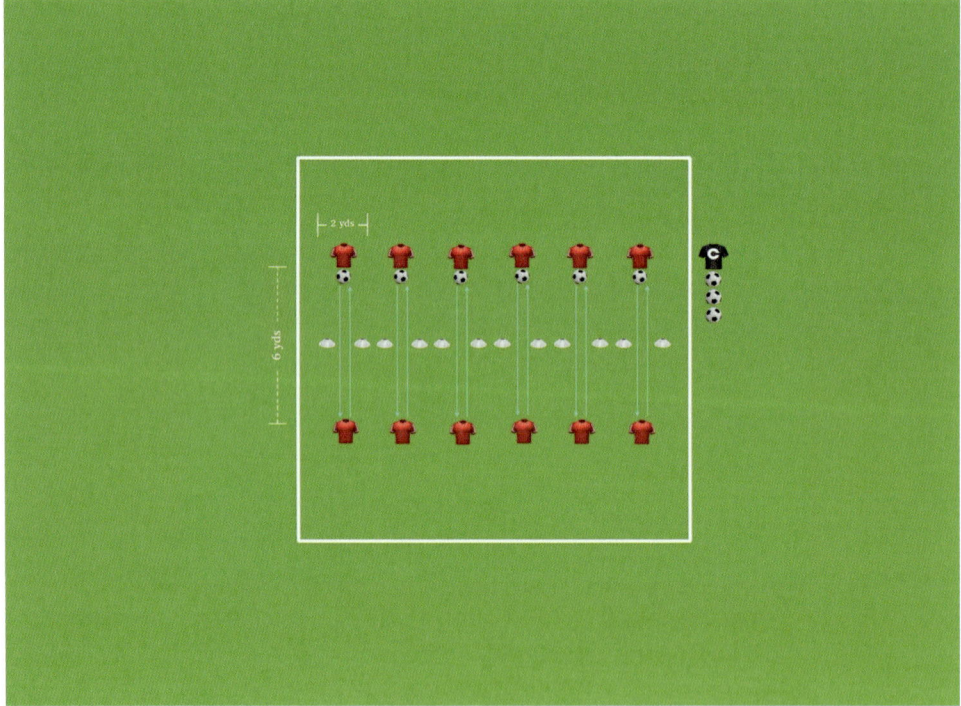

## Description

Divide players into groups of two with one ball per group. Position the pairs of players 6 yards apart from their partner between two cones positioned side-by-side on the floor. The gap between each set of cones should be approximately two yards. The players exchange passes through the gap between the cones.

# Short Passing

## Key focus/Coaching points

**Primary focus:** Short passing

**Secondary focus:** Receiving

**Additional focus:** Ball manipulation

## Progressions/Adaptations

- After each successful pass through the gap each player takes 1 step backwards. The player that gets farthest from the gap is the winner.

- Players work as a pair to complete as many passes as they can through the gap in 60 seconds. Compete against other pairs.

- Compete against partner. The player with most passes through the gap in 60 seconds is the winner.

- Can be turned into a ladder competition. The player that gets the most successful passes in 60 seconds moves up 1 place to the right to play a new opponent. Losing player moves down 1 place to the left to play a new opponent. The idea is to get to the contest at the far-right end of the ladder.

# 98 THE SOCCER COACH'S TOOLKIT

## ACTIVITY 23 CROWN GREEN BALLS

**Level:** Basic

**Type of activity:** Unopposed technical practice

**Number of participants:** 1+

**Equipment required:** Soccer balls (if balls with different markings or colours are available, they will help with ball identification) and cones

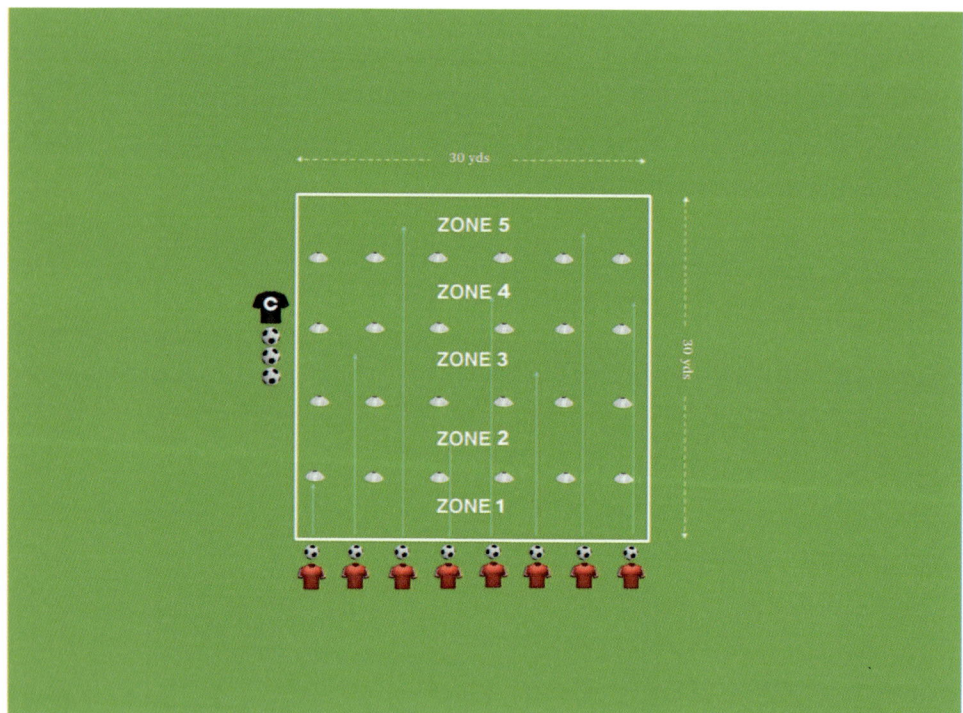

## Description

Position all players side-by-side at one end of the playing area. Divide the playing area into equal-sized zones. The zone farthest from the players has the highest value and the nearest zone has the lowest value.

For each zone, there is a point value. The players take turns passing their balls forwards. The zone in which the ball stops determines the player's score. The more balls each player has the better so that they can perform multiple passes. If possible, use different coloured cones to mark out the different zones as a visual aid. Below is an example of how to create a scoring system:

- **Zone 1** = 1 point.
- **Zone 2** = 3 points.
- **Zone 3** = 5 points.
- **Zone 4** = 7 points.
- **Zone 5** = 10 points.
- **Beyond zone 5** = 0 points.

## Key focus/Coaching points

Primary focus: Short passing

Secondary focus: Long passing

Additional focus: Ball manipulation

## Progressions/Adaptations

- Create a team competition by forming teams and adding points together to make team scores. Players are permitted to try to knock other teams' balls out of zones.
- The teams have 2 minutes to score as many points as they can. Each team has 1 ball. The players take turns passing their ball and scoring points. After each pass, the player retrieves the ball and dribbles it back to next player in team.

## ACTIVITY 24  END-TO-END PASSING

**Level:** Basic

**Type of activity:** Opposed technical practice

**Number of participants:** 8

**Equipment required:** Soccer balls, cones and 2 set of bibs

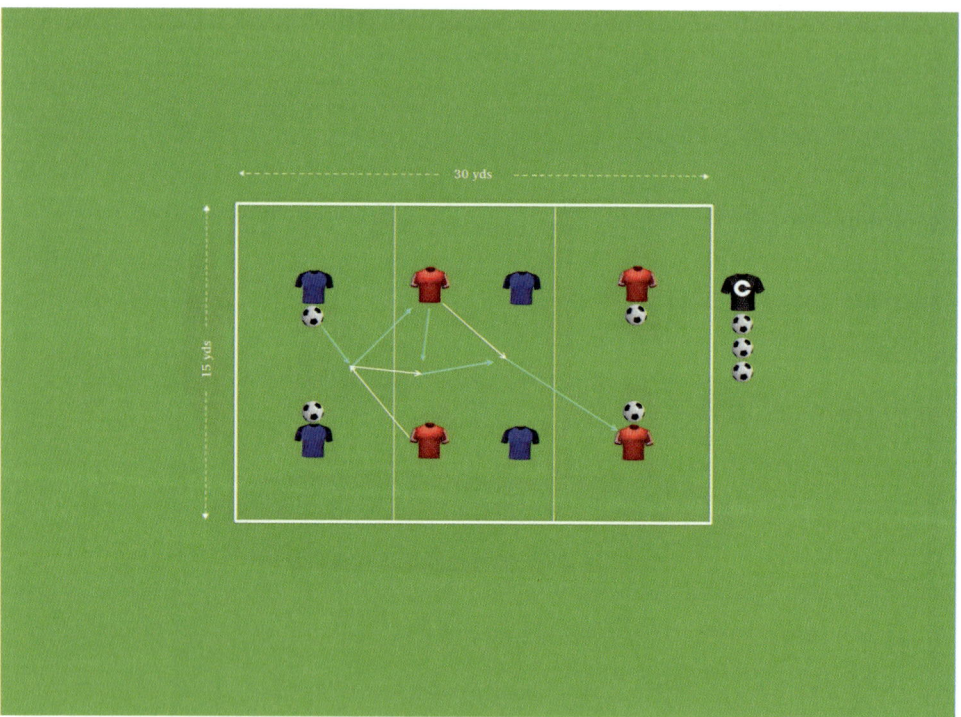

## Description

Divide players into four groups of two. Divide the playing area into three zones. Position two of the groups inside the middle zone and the remaining two groups in opposite end zones. Each player in the end zones requires a ball.

The activity starts when one player from both groups in the middle zone moves into an end zone and receives a pass. The players in the middle must coordinate their movements so that they receive the passes in opposite end zones.

The player that received a pass then either dribbles into or passes to their partner inside the middle zone. The partners then play two to three combination passes and pass the ball to the free player in the opposite end zone. After the ball has been transferred from one end zone to the other, all middle players take up new positions in the middle zone.

The two players that did not receive the previous pass move into the end zone that their group just passed to and receive a pass from either end zone player. The groups in the middle of the playing area repeat the activity and pass to the free player in the opposite end zone. Repeat for 2-3 minutes and then rotate players.

## Key focus/Coaching points

**Primary focus:** Short passing

**Secondary focus:** Receiving

**Additional focus:** Movement

## Progressions/Adaptations

- Add a defender in middle zone to try to intercept interplay between pairs.
- Turn the activity into a timed competition. Challenge the pairs to complete as many end-to-end transfers as possible in 2-3 minutes.

# 102 THE SOCCER COACH'S TOOLKIT

## ACTIVITY 25 ACROSS THE SQUARE

**Level:** Basic

**Type of activity:** Unopposed technical practice

**Number of participants:** 8

**Equipment required:** Soccer balls and cones

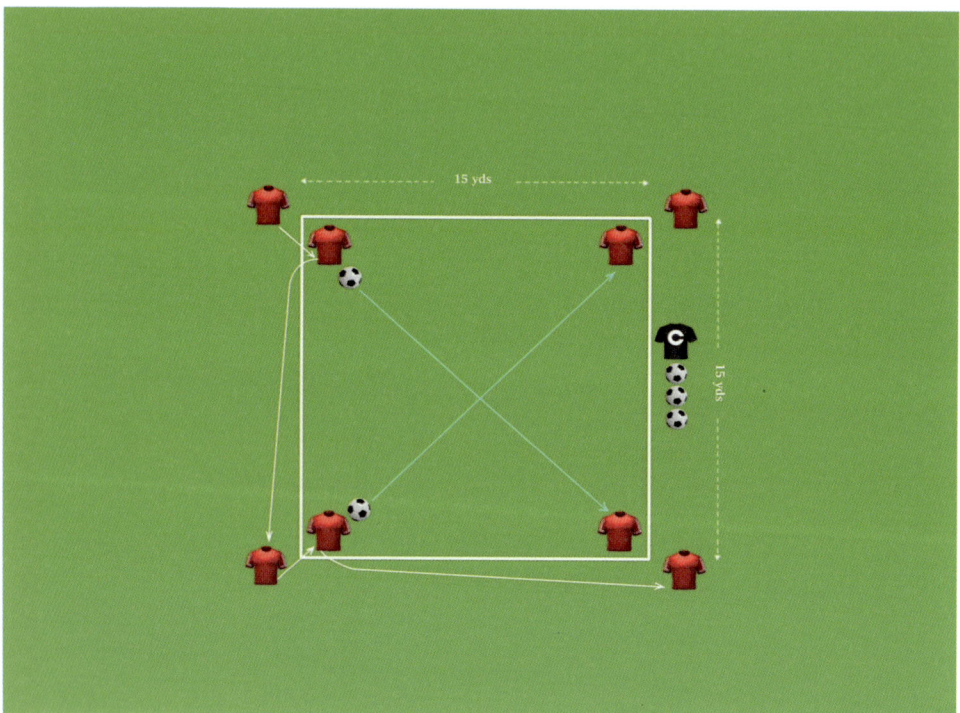

## Description

Divide players into groups of eight and position two players in each corner of the playing area. Position balls at two of these corners (make sure they are not in diagonally opposite corners). The players in possession of the ball pass diagonally across the playing area and move one corner to the right. Play is continuous and should be at high tempo.

## Key focus/Coaching points

**Primary focus:** Short passing

**Secondary focus:** Receiving

**Additional focus:** Movement

## Progressions/Adaptations

- Vary the type of pass, e.g., inside, outside of foot and driven pass.
- Add a defender in the centre of the playing area as a passive defender. Encourage players to take a touch out of their feet to widen the passing angle.

## ACTIVITY 26  PASSING BY NUMBERS

**Level:** Basic

**Type of activity:** Unopposed technical practice

**Number of participants:** 6

**Equipment required:** Soccer balls and cones

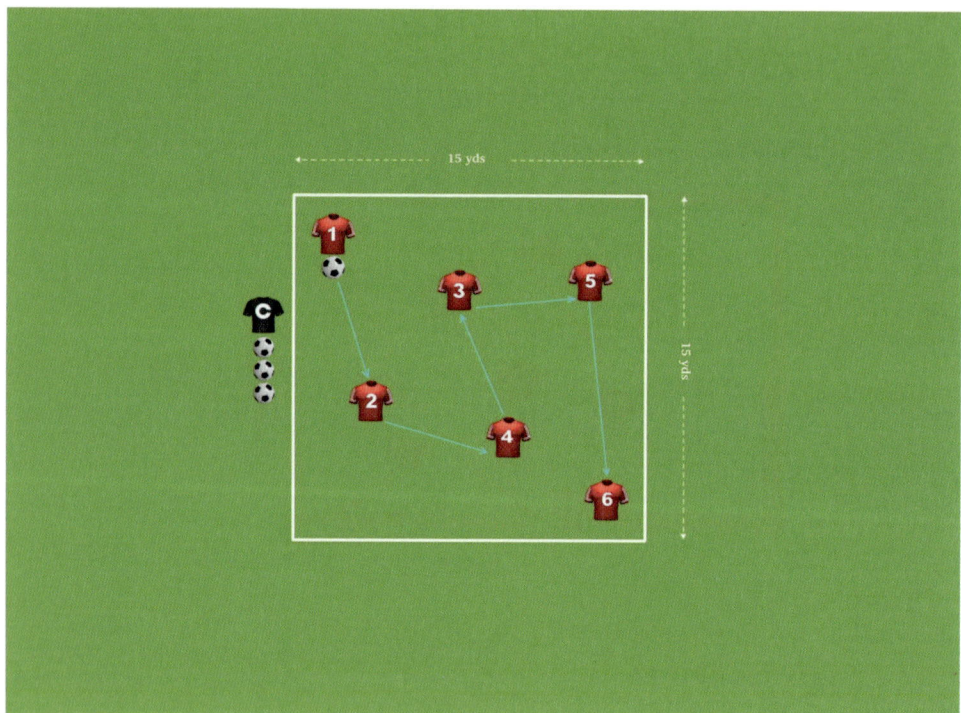

## Description

Divide players into groups of six and number them 1-6. Position all players inside the playing area with one ball. The players pass the ball to each other in ascending numerical order and then when number 6 is reached, they perform passes in descending numerical order down to number 1. Repeat for 5 minutes.

## Key focus/Coaching points

**Primary focus:** Short passing

**Secondary focus:** Receiving

**Additional focus:** Movement

## Progressions/Adaptations

- Players can only have 2 touches in possession.
- Players can only play a first-time pass.
- Introduce movements after each pass, e.g., overlap or underlap run.

# 106  THE SOCCER COACH'S TOOLKIT

## ACTIVITY 27  CRASH, BANG, WALLOP

Level: Basic

Type of activity: Unopposed technical practice

Number of participants: 2-20

Equipment required: Soccer balls, cones and 2 sets of bibs

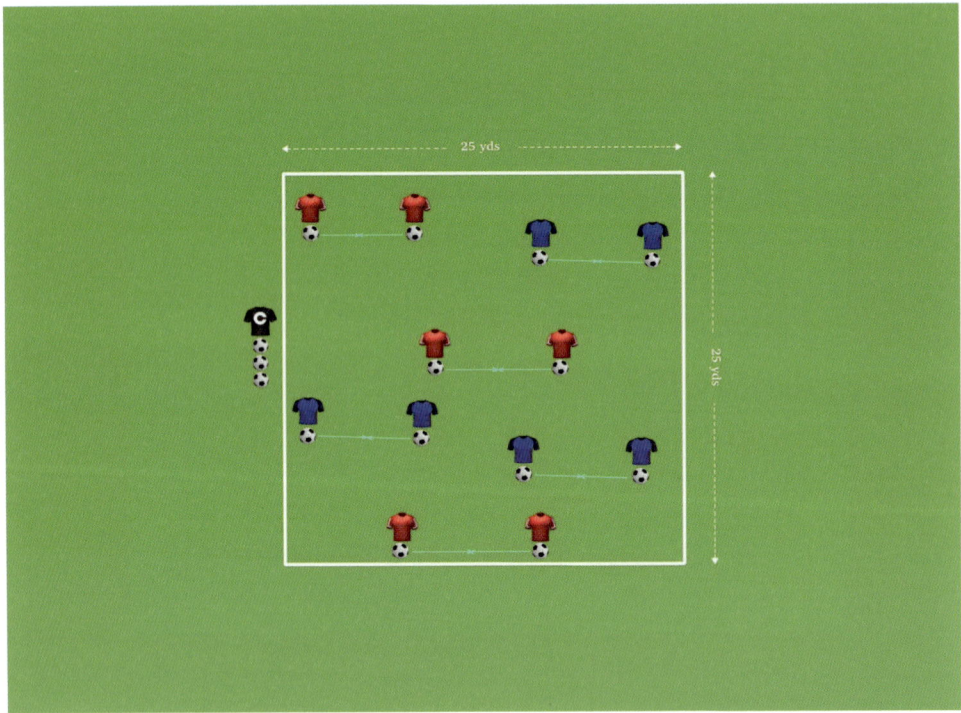

## Description

Divide players into pairs with one ball per player. Position the pairs opposite each other and approximately 8 yards apart. The players pass their balls at the same time as their partner and try to make the balls collide.

## Key focus/Coaching points

Primary focus: Short passing

Secondary focus: Ball manipulation

Additional focus: Decision making

## Progressions/Adaptations

- Players use different types of short pass, e.g., outside of foot/toe-poke.
- Gradually increase the distance as players become more successful.
- Players dribble around area and try to collide soccer balls with other players. Turn the activity into a timed competition. The players count many ball collisions they complete 60 seconds.

# 108 THE SOCCER COACH'S TOOLKIT

## ACTIVITY 28 BALL SWITCH

**Level:** Basic

**Type of activity:** Unopposed technical practice

**Number of participants:** 8-12

**Equipment required:** Soccer balls, cones and 2 sets of bibs

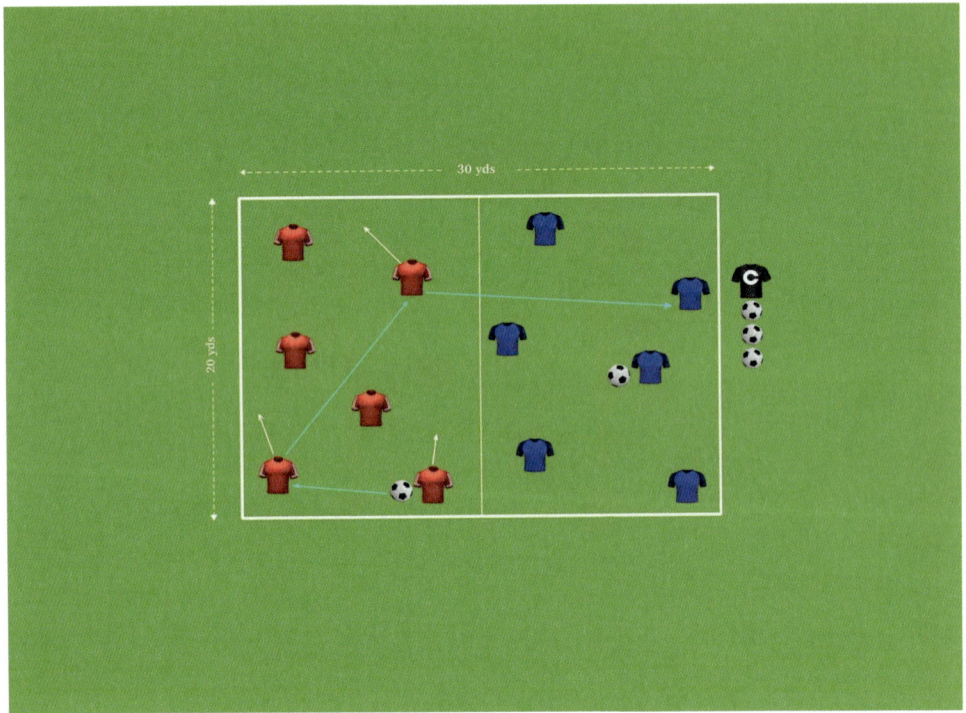

### Description

Divide players into two groups of six. Divide the playing area into two zones. Position one group in each zone with one ball per group. Players pass among themselves at high intensity and move into a new space after each pass. On the command of "Switch", the players in possession in both zones transfer the ball to the other group with a long pass. As soon as the long pass is received, the activity continues.

## Key focus/Coaching points

**Primary focus:** Short passing

**Secondary focus:** Long passing

**Additional focus:** Receiving

## Progressions/Adaptations

- Condition the type of long pass to, e.g., chip, low drive, high drive or curled.
- Organise both groups into 5 attackers v 1 defender in each zone. The defender tries to intercept passes.
- Position 2 balls in each zone.

## ACTIVITY 29  SOCCER ICE HOCKEY

**Level:** Intermediate

**Type of activity:** Opposed technical practice

**Number of participants:** 8

**Equipment required:** Soccer balls, cones, agility poles and 2 sets of bibs

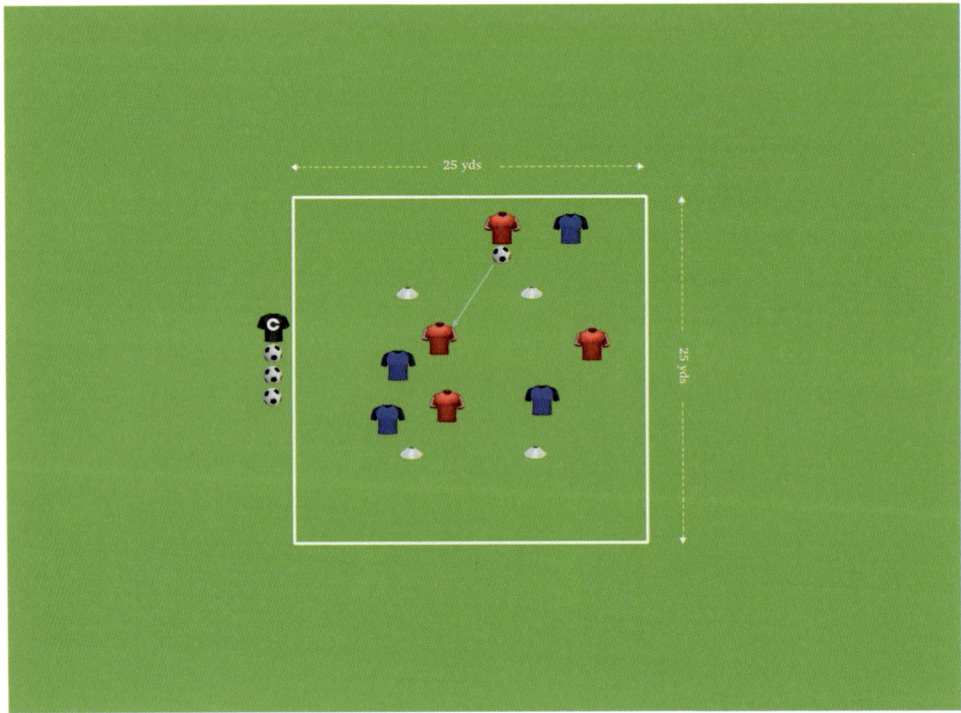

### Description

Divide players into two teams of four. Position two mini-goals 10 yards in from either end of the playing area. Make the goals using cones or poles (**the activity will not work if goals with nets are used**). The teams compete against each other and try to score by passing through either side of goal to a teammate.

# Short Passing

Goals can be scored sequentially through the front and back end of the same goal. Both teams can attack and score in either goal. Encourage the players to think about using the whole of the playing area to create opportunities to score through the front and back of the goals.

## Key focus/Coaching points

Primary focus: Short passing

Secondary focus: Receiving

Additional focus: Movement

## Progressions/Adaptations

- To make scoring more difficult, add goalkeepers (using feet only) to defend the goals.

## 112 THE SOCCER COACH'S TOOLKIT

### ACTIVITY 30 PASSING BREAKAWAY

**Level:** Intermediate

**Type of activity:** Opposed technical practice

**Number of participants:** 12 + 2 goalkeepers

**Equipment required:** Soccer balls, cones, 2 sets of bibs and 2 goals

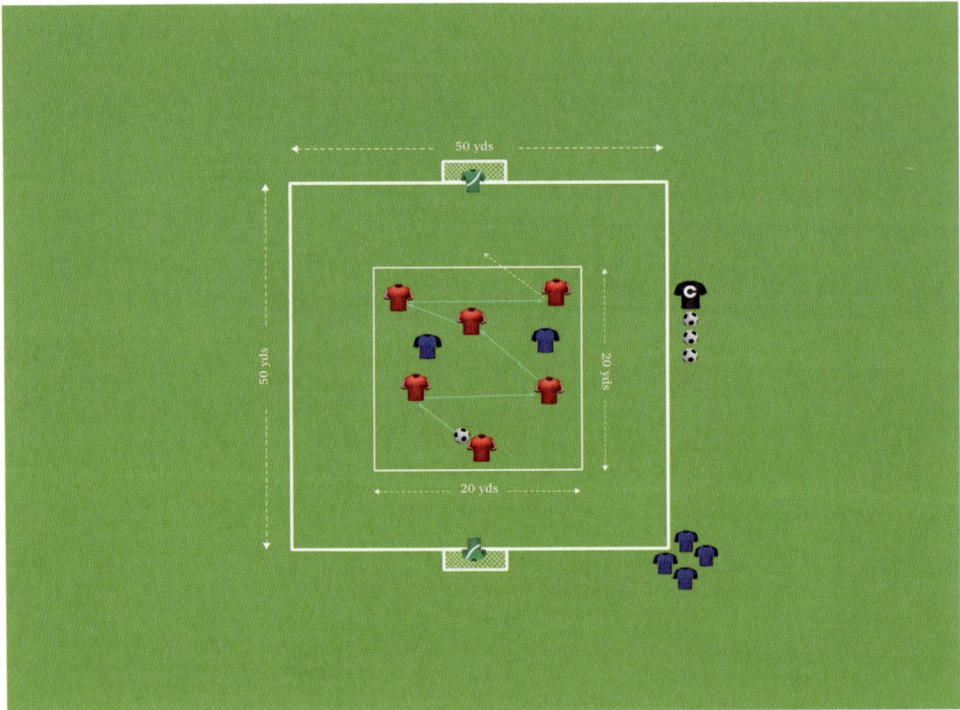

### Description

Divide players into one team of six attackers and one team of six defenders. Organise the defenders into groups of two. Mark out a playing area with a main playing area in the middle. Position the attackers and two defenders inside the main playing area. Position the remaining defenders in a corner of the playing area. Position a goal and a goalkeeper at opposite ends of the playing area.

The activity starts when the coach feeds a ball into the main playing area. The six attackers try to complete five passes without interception. After five successful passes, the attacker that receives the fifth pass tries to dribble out of the main playing area and score at either end of the playing area. The defenders try to prevent five passes from being completed.

If either of the defenders wins possession of the ball inside the main playing area, the defender in possession can dribble out to score in either goal. If the attackers win possession back from the defenders, they try again to complete five passes and score. If the ball is kicked out of the main playing area, the coach feeds a new ball in to re-start the activity. When an attacker successfully dribbles out of the main playing area, they have two touches to score.

Once every episode of play has finished, the defenders run out of the main playing area and tag two new defenders who replace them to defend the next episode of play. Rotate the attackers and defenders after 5 minutes.

**Scoring system:**

- If the attackers complete 5 passes, they receive 1 point.
- If the attackers then go on to score a goal after the 5 passes, they score a second point.
- If the defenders intercept a pass or knock ball out of the main playing area, they score 1 point.
- If a defender intercepts a pass and breaks out of the main playing area and then scores, they score 2 extra points.

## Key focus/Coaching points

Primary focus: Short passing

Secondary focus: Receiving

Additional focus: Finishing

## Progressions/Adaptations

- A second attacker can break out of the main playing area with the attacker in possession. The defenders can also break out of the playing area.

# 114 THE SOCCER COACH'S TOOLKIT

## ACTIVITY 31 SIX AND OUT

Level: Intermediate

Type of activity: Opposed technical practice

Number of participants: 12

Equipment required: Soccer balls, cones and 2 sets of bibs

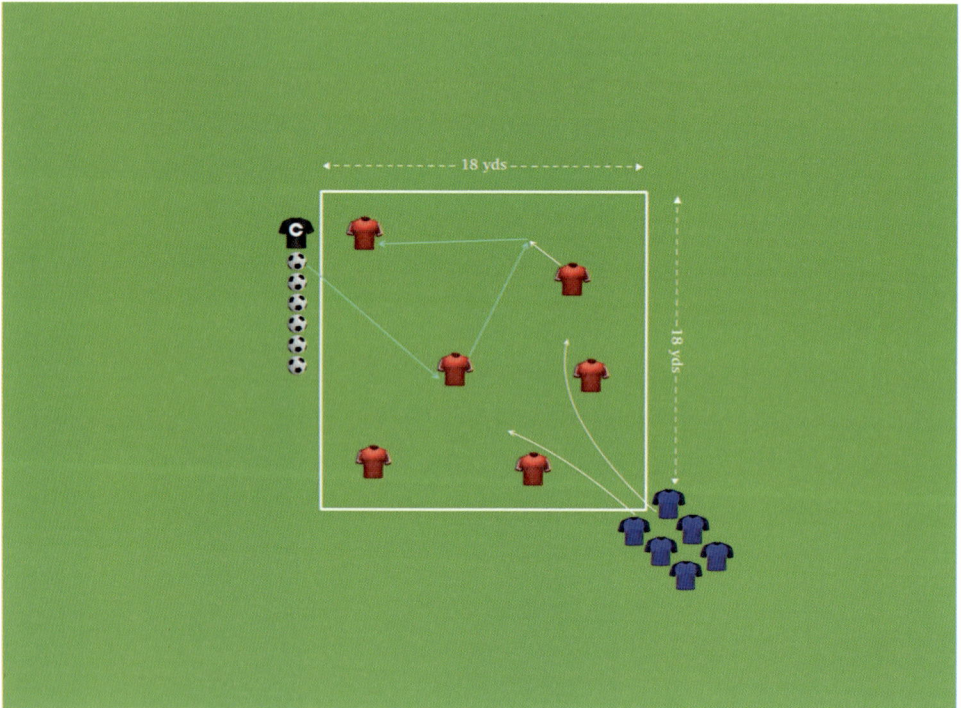

## Description

Divide players into two groups of six. Position one group of players inside the playing area. Divide the other group of six players into pairs. Position the pairs side-by-side in a line in a corner of the playing area. The coach should be positioned outside the playing area with six balls.

The activity starts when the coach feeds the first ball into the playing area. As soon as the first ball has been fed in, the coach starts timing with a stopwatch. The first two

# Short Passing

defenders sprint into the playing area and try to intercept or knock the first ball out while the six players try to keep possession for as long as possible.

When the first ball has been won by the defenders, they sprint out of the playing area and tag two new defenders who replace them inside the playing area. The coach feeds in the next ball and play continues until all 6 balls have been won by the defenders. As soon as the final ball has been won by the defenders, the coach stops timing and the groups swap roles. The activity is repeated, and the team that keeps possession for the longest period is the winning team.

## Key focus/Coaching points

Primary focus: Short passing

Secondary focus: Receiving

Additional focus: Long passing

## Progressions/Adaptations

- Players can only use 2-3 touches in possession.
- Increase the number of defenders to 3.

# 116 THE SOCCER COACH'S TOOLKIT

## ACTIVITY 32 REWARDS

**Level:** Intermediate

**Type of activity:** Opposed technical practice

**Number or participants:** 8 + 1 goalkeeper

**Equipment required:** Soccer balls, cones and 2 sets of bibs

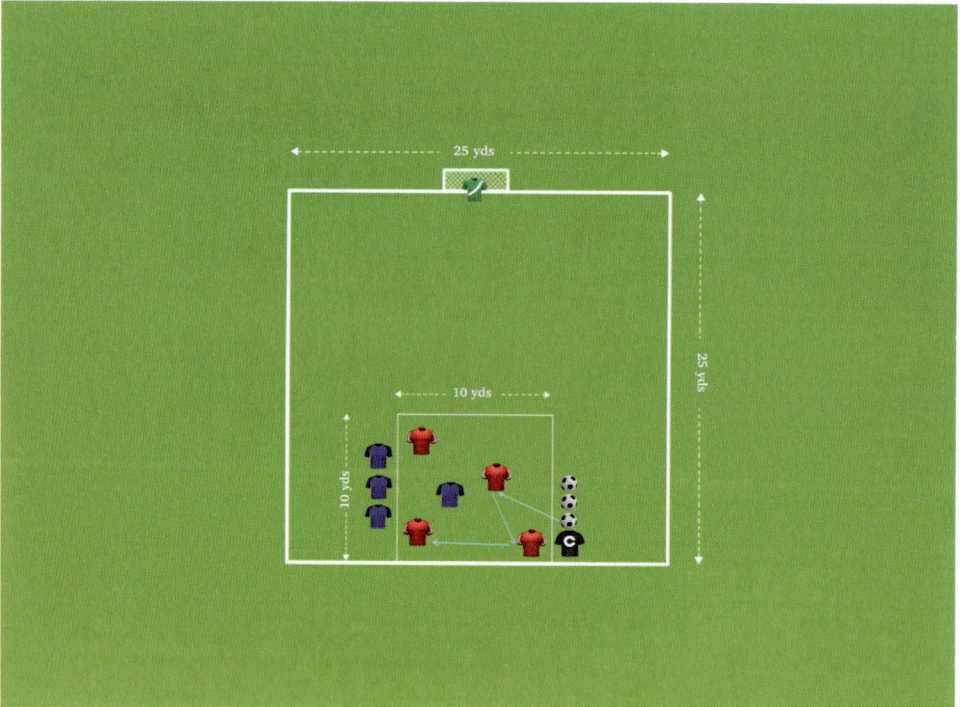

## Description

Divide players into a group of four possession players and a group of four defenders. Mark out a playing area with a small square positioned in the middle of an end line. Position the four possession players and one defender inside the small square. Position the remaining three defenders to the side (10 yards away) of the small square. Position a goal and a goalkeeper at the opposite end of the playing area.

The activity starts when the coach feeds a ball into the small square. The possession team tries to complete 10 passes without interception to score 1 point. If the defender wins possession before 10 passes are completed, they can try to dribble out of the small square and score in the goal. If the defender scores, they receive 1 point for the defending team.

Each defender has two episodes of play inside the possession square and then is replaced by another defender. Once each defender has had two episodes of play inside the possession square, the teams switch roles. Once both teams have been the possession team and the defending team, add up the points scored to find out the winning team.

## Key focus/Coaching points

**Primary focus:** Short passing

**Secondary focus:** Receiving

**Additional focus:** Movement

## Progressions/Adaptations

- Players can only use 2-3 touches in possession.
- Add a second defender inside the possession square.
- If 10 passes are too difficult for the possession team, reduce the number to 6-7.

## ACTIVITY 33 GIVE-AND-GO GLORY

**Level:** Intermediate

**Type of activity:** Opposed technical practice

**Number of participants:** 6

**Equipment required:** Soccer balls, cones and 3 sets of bibs

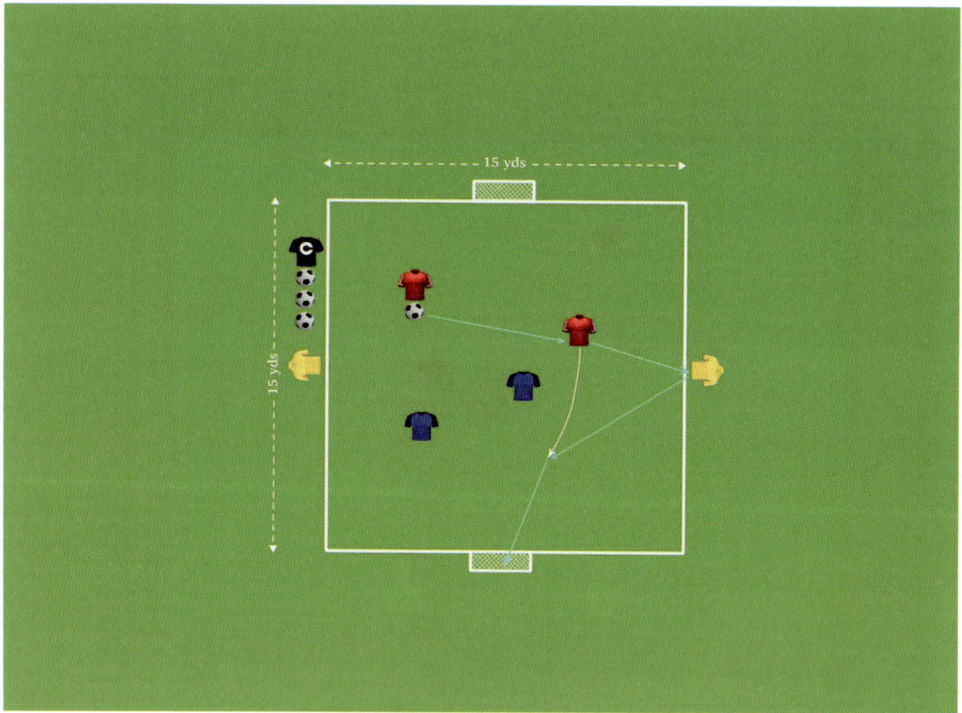

## Description

Divide players into a group of six. Organise the players into two teams of two inside the playing area and one support player outside each of the sidelines. Position mini goals at both ends of the playing area. The teams compete in a 2v2 mini-match and attack opposite ends of the playing area. Both teams can pass to and receive passes back from the support players. Encourage the players to play quickly and look for opportunities to play a give and go pass to penetrate the opposition's defence. Encourage the support players to move up and down the sidelines to support the team in possession.

## Key focus/Coaching points

Primary focus: Short passing

Secondary focus: Movement

Additional focus: Creativity

## Progressions/Adaptations

- 3 passes must be completed before an attempt to score. This encourages the player to keep possession and build attacks patiently.
- Change the method of scoring from a pass to a dribble into the mini goal.
- The players can only score with a first-time pass into a mini goal.
- Mark out a scoring zone at both ends of the playing area. Players can only score from inside the zone at their attacking end of the playing area.

# 120 THE SOCCER COACH'S TOOLKIT

## ACTIVITY 34 ESCAPE TO VICTORY

**Level:** Advanced

**Type of activity:** Opposed technical practice

**Number of participants:** 10 + 4 goalkeepers

**Equipment required:** Soccer balls, cones, 2 sets of bibs and 4 goals

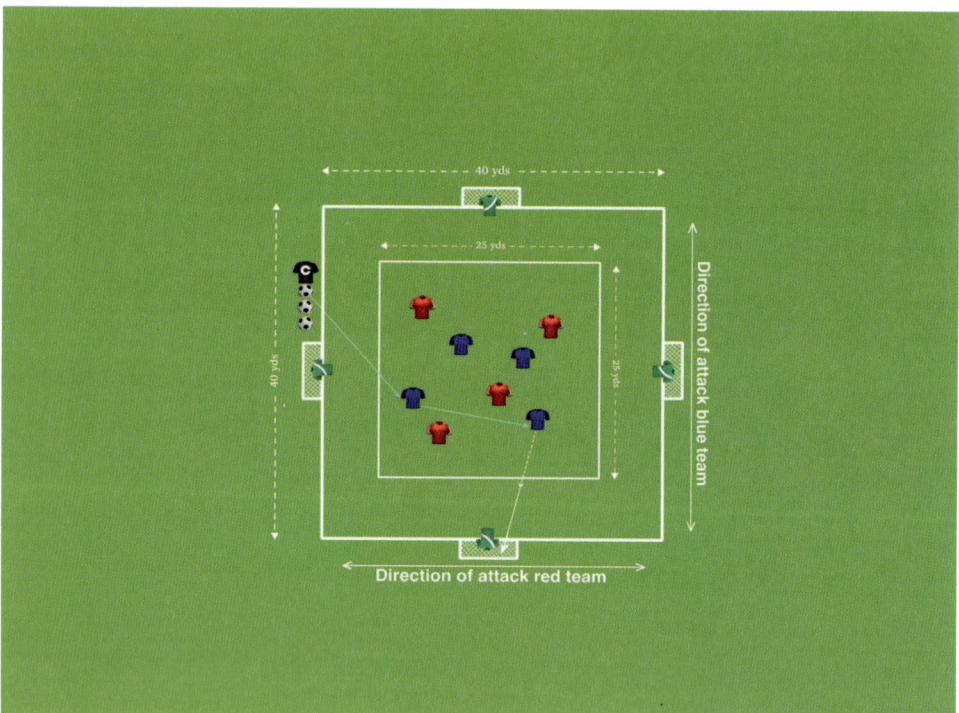

## Description

Divide players into two teams of seven (including two goalkeepers per team). Mark out a playing area with a main playing area in the middle. Position the two teams of outfield players inside the main playing area. Position a goal in the centre of each end line. Position the goalkeepers of both teams in the goals at opposite ends of the playing area. Both teams can only score in two of the goals. Nominate goals at opposite ends of the playing area for both teams to score in, i.e., one team plays up and down and the other plays across.

The activity starts when the coach feeds the ball into the main playing area. The teams try to keep possession of the ball until one of their players can dribble out of the main playing area and try to score. When a player dribbles out of the main playing area, they have a maximum of three touches to score. Once the attack is over, the coach re-starts the activity with a pass into the main playing area.

## Key focus/Coaching points

**Primary focus:** Short passing

**Secondary focus:** Receiving

**Additional focus:** Finishing

## Progressions/Adaptations

- 1 defending player can break out of the main playing area to defend the attack.
- Teams must complete 4-5 passes before one of their players can dribble out of the main playing area.

## ACTIVITY 35 PLAY OUT, GO OUT

**Level:** Advanced

**Type of activity:** Opposed technical practice

**Number of participants:** 12

**Equipment required:** Soccer balls, cones, discs and 3 sets of bibs

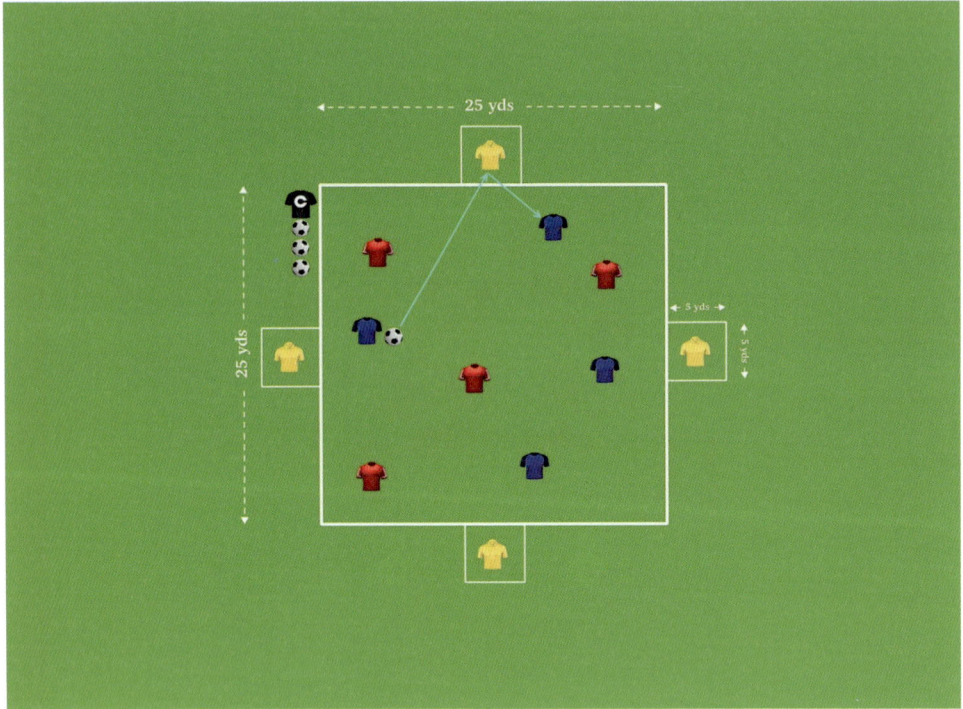

### Description

Divide players into three teams of four. Mark out a playing area with a small square in the centre of each playing area line. Position two teams inside the playing area and one player from the remaining team in each of the squares.

The teams inside the playing area compete to keep possession and try to score with a pass to a player in one of the squares. Each successful pass to a player inside a square is worth 1 point. After a pass to a player inside a scoring square, the player that received the pass has a maximum of two touches to pass back to any player in the team that scored. The teams are not allowed to score consecutively in the same square.

## Key focus/Coaching points

Primary focus: Short passing

Secondary focus: Receiving

Additional focus: Movement

## Progressions/Adaptations

- Teams must complete 3 passes inside the playing area before passing to a player in a square.
- Both teams are only allowed to score in 2 of the squares.
- Players swap positions after each successful pass into a scoring square, i.e., the player that passes into the square follows their pass and the player receiving the pass then follows their pass out into the playing area.

# 124 THE SOCCER COACH'S TOOLKIT

## ACTIVITY 36  FOUR-GOAL TAKEAWAY

**Level:** Advanced

**Type of activity:** Opposed technical practice

**Number of participants:** 7

**Equipment required:** Soccer balls, cones, domes and 2 sets of bibs

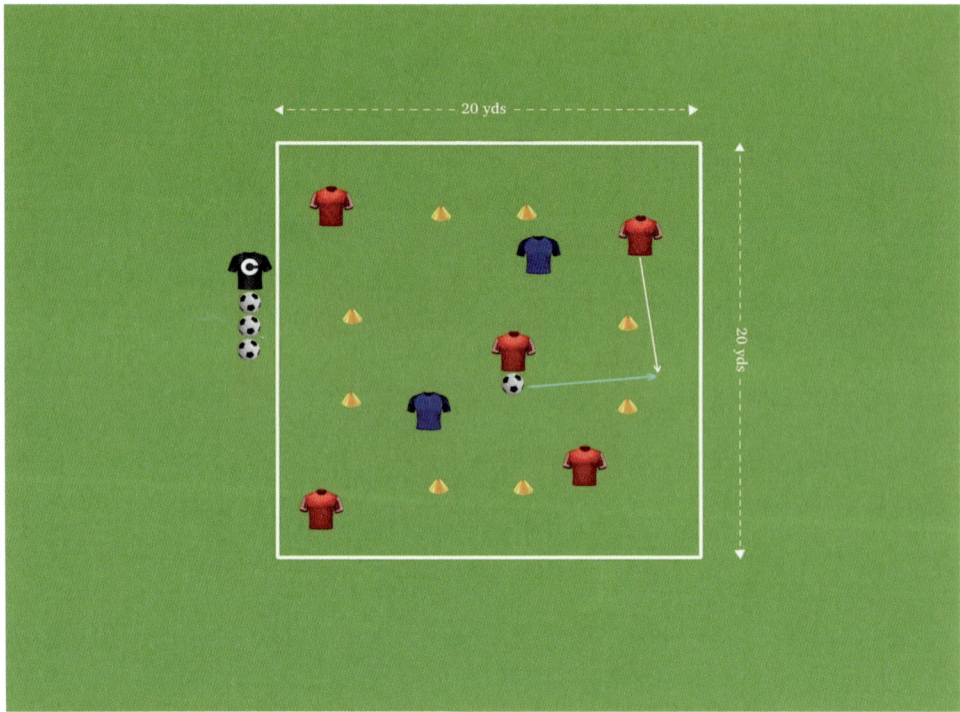

## Description

Divide players into a team of five attackers and a team of two defenders. Mark out a playing area and position four mini goals inside the playing area (**make sure the mini goals do not have nets, or the activity will not work**). The team of attackers tries to score by completing passes to a teammate through any of the mini goals. Each completed pass through a mini goal is worth 1 point.

# Short Passing

The attacking team has 3 minutes to score as many points as possible. If either of the defenders wins possession of the ball, they try to pass it out of the playing area to score 1 point. The attackers can try to win possession back from the defenders if they lose possession. Rotate the players after 3 minutes.

## Key focus/Coaching points

Primary focus: Short passing

Secondary focus: Receiving

Additional focus: Movement

## Progressions/Adaptations

- Each time the attacking team scores, the coach removes the mini goal that was scored in from the playing area. The attacking team has 3 minutes to score in every goal.
- If the defending team wins possession, they can win the competition by scoring in any of the goals.

## ACTIVITY 37  HOLE OR NOTHING

**Level:** Advanced

**Type of activity:** Opposed technical practice

**Number of participants:** 8

**Equipment required:** Soccer balls, cones and 2 sets of bibs

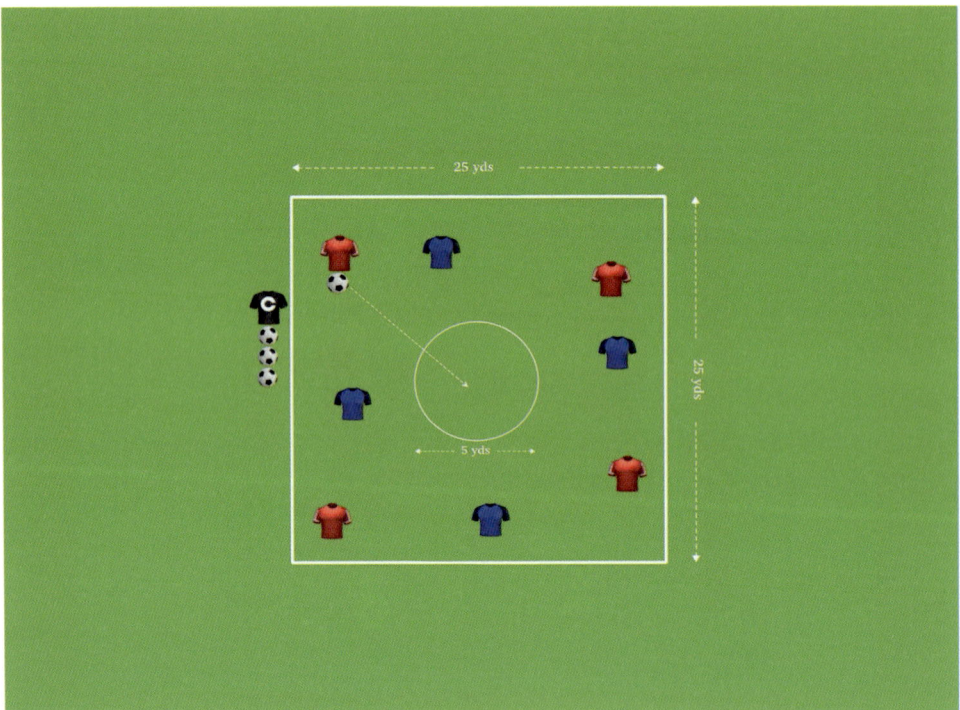

### Description

Divide players into two teams of four. Mark out a playing area with a circle in the centre. The teams compete for possession and try to score by dribbling the ball into the circle. If a player successfully dribbles into the circle, they re-start the activity with a pass out to the opposition. The opposition players must disperse around the outside of the playing area and only re-enter play once the ball has been received by one of their players.

## Key focus/Coaching points

**Primary focus:** Short passing

**Secondary focus:** Dribbling

**Additional focus:** Movement

## Progressions/Adaptations

- Teams must complete 3 passes before scoring.
- Change the method of scoring from a dribble to a received pass into the circle.
- To make the activity easier, increase the number of scoring circles to 2-3.

# 128  THE SOCCER COACH'S TOOLKIT

## ACTIVITY 38  ATTACKING OVERLOADS

**Level:** Advanced

**Type of activity:** Opposed technical practice

**Number of participants:** 11 + 1 goalkeeper

**Equipment required:** Soccer balls, cones, discs, 2 sets of bibs and 1 goal

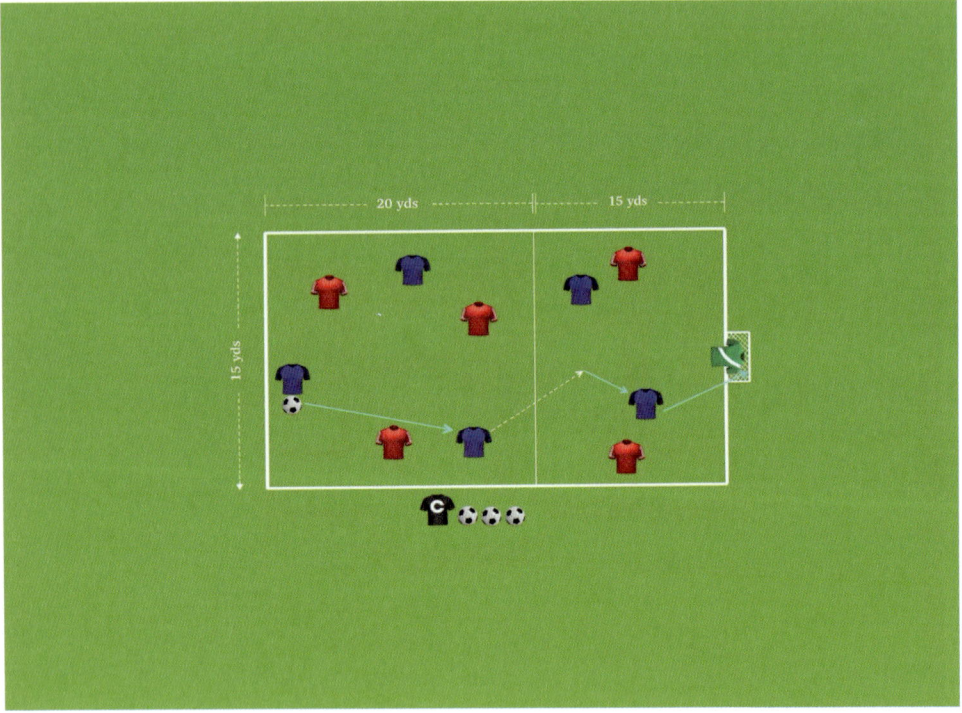

## Description

Divide players into two teams of five. Organise both teams into three midfielders and two attackers. Mark out a playing area with a midfield and an attacking zone. Position a goal and goalkeeper at one end of the playing area. Position both sets of midfielders in the midfield zone and both sets of attackers in the attacking zone.

The activity starts when the coach passes to any of the midfielders. The two sets of midfielders compete for possession and try to pass to a teammate in, or dribble into, the attacking zone. Any midfielder that passes or dribbles into the attacking zone joins in the attack to create a 3v2 attacking overload. When a player has possession in the attacking zone, they can combine with their teammates and try to score. Both teams attack the same goal. If the defending team wins possession in the attacking zone, they become the attacking team and try to score.

Play until a goal is scored or the ball goes out of play. After each attack, the midfielder returns to the midfield zone. The coach re-starts play with a pass to any midfielder.

## Key focus/Coaching points

Primary focus: Short passing

Secondary focus: Finishing

Additional focus: Receiving

## Progressions/Adaptations

- Once an attacker has possession in the attacking zone, they can pass back into the midfield zone to retain possession. If this happens, the midfielder that has moved into the attacking zone must retreat to the midfield zone.

- If it is too difficult to get players into the attacking zone, add a floating player in the midfield zone to support the team in possession. Initially, the floating player cannot pass or dribble into the attacking zone but can be allowed to do so as the activity progresses.

# 130 THE SOCCER COACH'S TOOLKIT

## ACTIVITY 39 PASS AT PACE

**Level:** Advanced

**Type of activity:** Opposed technical practice

**Number of participants:** 12

**Equipment required:** Soccer balls, cones, discs and 3 sets of bibs

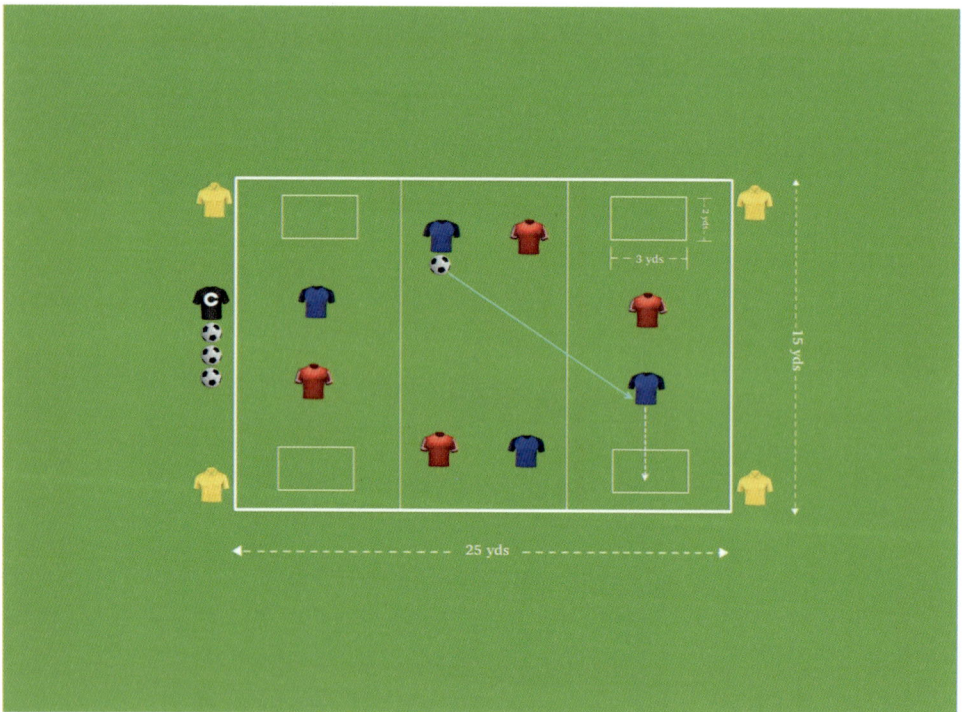

## Description

Divide players into two teams of four and one group of four target players. Mark out a playing area with three zones. Position a small square on the left and right sides of both end zones. Organise both teams into a 1-2-1 formation with one player in each end zone and two players in the middle zone. Position two support players at both ends of the playing area.

The teams compete in a 4v4 and can score at both end zones by either dribbling into or receiving a pass inside one of the squares. Initially, only the players in the end zones can score and players cannot move between zones. The support players at both ends can be used at any time during the activity to pass to and receive passes back from. Encourage the support players to move along the end lines to support the player in possession.

When a team scores, they immediately attack the opposite end zone. When a player has scored, they are allowed 3 seconds alone inside the square to pass to a teammate to re-start the attack.

## Key focus/Coaching points

**Primary focus:** Short passing

**Secondary focus:** Receiving

**Additional focus:** Speed

## Progressions/Adaptations

- Players in the middle zone can enter an end zone by passing to their teammate or dribbling into the end zone. Once possession is lost, they must immediately retreat to the middle zone.
- 1 support player must be used in every attack before a goal can be scored.
- Players can only use 3 touches in possession.
- Teams must complete 2 passes in the middle zone before they can score.
- Players can only score after a pass has been played directly from end zone to end zone. The middle zone is allowed to be used during build-up play but not directly leading to scoring.

# 132 THE SOCCER COACH'S TOOLKIT

# LONG PASSING

## ACTIVITY 40 KNOCK ON WOOD

**Level:** Basic

**Type of activity:** Unopposed technical practice

**Number of participants:** 16

**Equipment required:** Soccer balls, cones and 4 goals

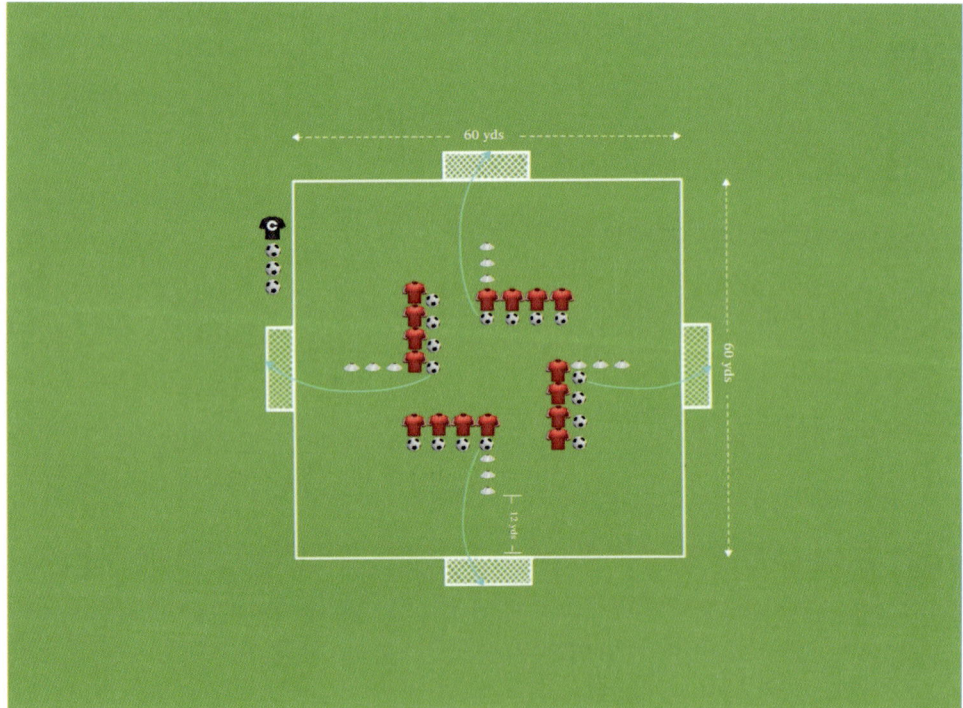

## Description

Divide players into groups of four with one ball per player. Position one goal in the middle of each line of the playing area. Position each group in front of and facing a goal. Players take turns trying to hit the crossbar with a long pass from three different distances. The players can decide which distance they want to pass from and after 10 minutes, the players with the most points in their group are the winners.

- 12 yards from goal = 3 points
- 18 yards from goal = 5 points
- 20-25 yards from goal = 10 points

If necessary, two groups can share one goal. In this case, position the groups 10-15 yards apart and make sure that all players are behind the ball before each attempt. The goals do not have to be full size. The use of 8-a-side or 5-a-side goals is suitable for this activity.

## Key focus/Coaching points

**Primary focus:** Long passing

**Secondary focus:** Ball manipulation

**Additional focus:** Decision making

## Progressions/Adaptations

- Condition the type of pass, e.g., chip or drive.
- Turn the activity into a team competition. The teams compete for 5 minutes. The players in each team take turns to try to hit the crossbar from any of the 3 positions. All points scored go to the team total. Encourage players to move quickly to attempt their pass and to retrieve their ball. Make sure that no players are in front of the ball before each attempt.

# 134 THE SOCCER COACH'S TOOLKIT

## ACTIVITY 41  PING KING

**Level:** Basic

**Type of activity:** Unopposed technical practice

**Number of participants:** 2-16

**Equipment required:** Soccer balls, cones and 2 sets of bibs

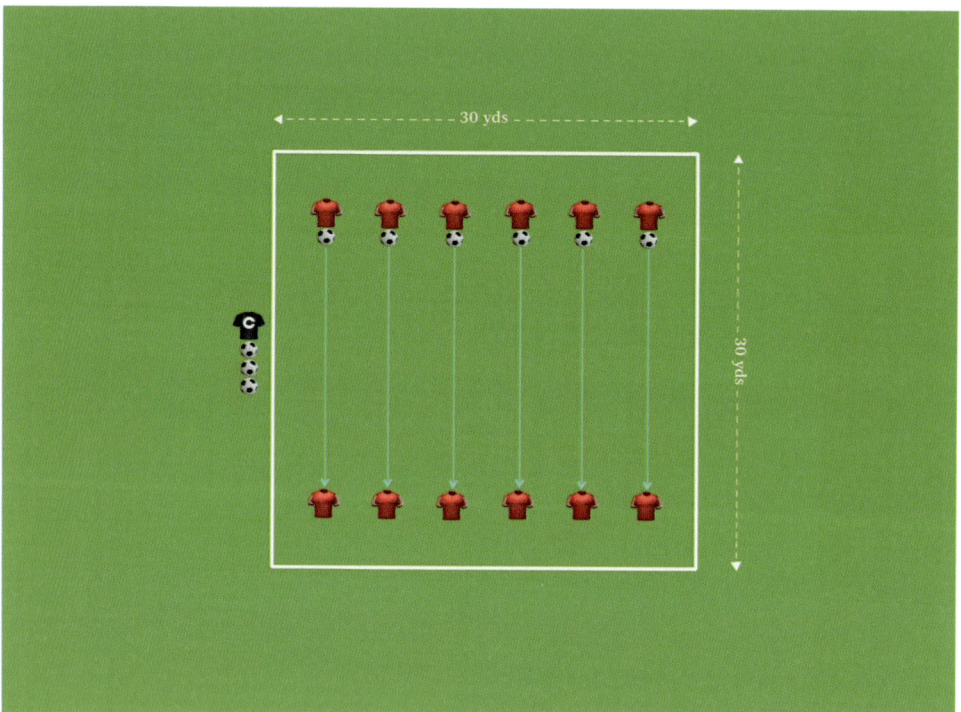

## Description

Divide players into pairs with one ball per pair. Position each pair facing each other at opposite ends of the playing area. The distance between the pairs should be 30 yards. The players perform different types of long pass (see below) to their partner across the playing area:

- Drive
- Chip

- Inside foot curl
- Outside foot curl
- Drive with 1 bounce

Note: The title of this activity is called "Ping king" as a long pass is commonly referred to by soccer players as a "ping".

## Key focus/Coaching points

Primary focus: Long passing

Secondary focus: Ball manipulation

Additional focus: Receiving

## Progressions/Adaptations

- Add a target (use agility poles, domes or cones) in between each pair for the ball to travel through.
- Encourage players to add more power to each pass.
- Advanced players can perform the passes with a rolling ball.

# 136 THE SOCCER COACH'S TOOLKIT

## ACTIVITY 42 HIGH-FLYING BALLS

**Level:** Basic

**Type of activity:** Unopposed technical practice

**Number of participants:** 12

**Equipment required:** Soccer balls, cones and 3 sets of bibs

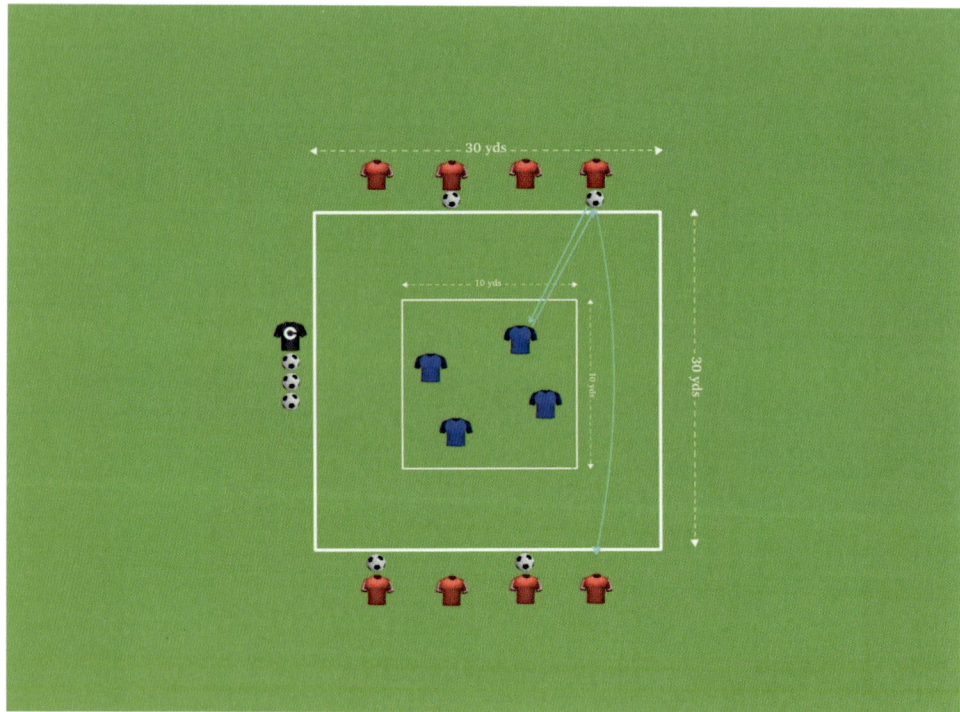

## Description

Divide players into one group of eight and one group of four. Organise the group of eight players into pairs with one ball per pair. Mark out a playing area with a square in the middle. Position the group of 4 players inside the square. Position the pairs facing each other at opposite ends of the playing area. Organise the balls so that there are two in the possession of players at opposite ends of the playing area.

The activity starts when the four players in possession of a ball pass to an available player inside the square. The players inside the square pass back to the players that passed to them. Once the players have received the pass back, they have 1 touch to receive and then play a long pass across and over the square to their partner.

When the ball travels across and over the square, the partners on the other side receive the ball and pass to an available player inside the playing area. The players inside the playing area pass the balls back to the players that passed to them. Once the players have received the pass back, they have one touch to receive the pass and then play a long pass across and over the square to their partner. The activity continues from end to end.

Encourage the players inside the square to move, make angles and check both ends for passes to receive. Rotate players after 5 minutes.

## Key focus/Coaching points

**Primary focus:** Long passing

**Secondary focus:** Receiving

**Additional focus:** Ball manipulation

## Progressions/Adaptations

- Players are allowed only 1 touch to receive a long pass before passing the ball into the square.
- Players can only pass with their weaker foot.
- Change the positions of the players at one end of the playing area so that partners are not directly opposite each other.

# 138 THE SOCCER COACH'S TOOLKIT

## ACTIVITY 43 LONG DISTANCE

**Level:** Intermediate

**Type of activity:** Unopposed technical practice

**Number of participants:** 1-21

**Equipment required: Station 1** – Cones and 1 goal or 2 agility poles to mark out goalposts

**Station 2** – Cones and domes to mark out a square

**Station 3** – Cones and 1 mini-goal

**Station 4** – Cones and 1 goal

**Station 5** – Cones and a wall. If a wall is not available, use another kind of upright and stable target, e.g., a net or fence

**Station 6** – Cones to mark out a square

**Station 7** – Cones and 1 goal or mini-goal

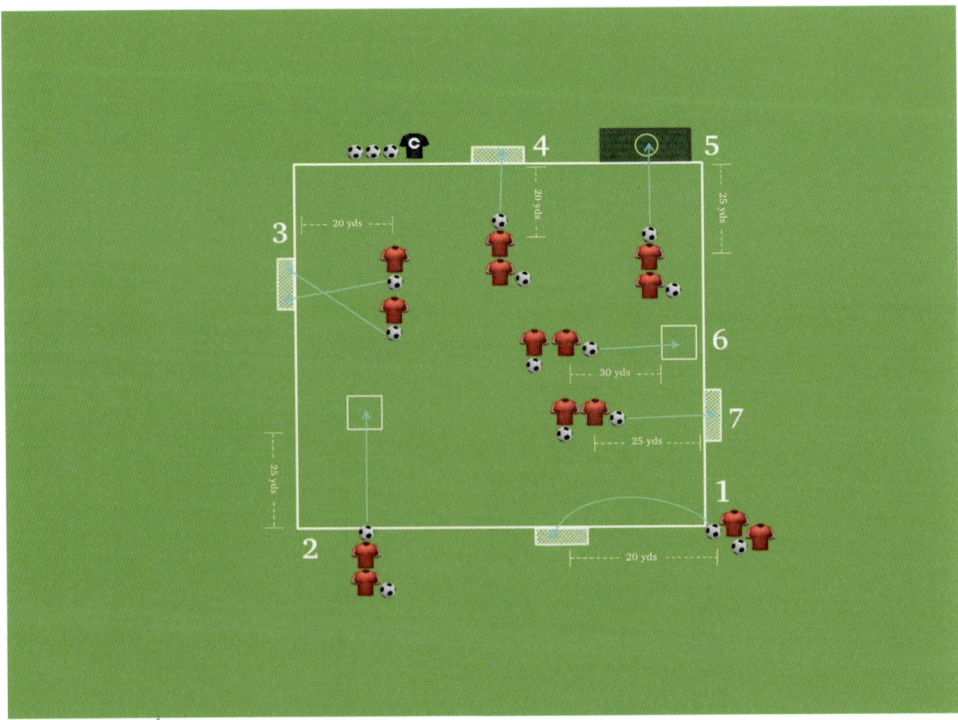

## Description

Mark out seven activity stations (see below). Position two to three players at each activity station with a ball each. The players attempt the task at their activity station and can move on to another activity station after successful completion of the task. Set a time limit of 20-25 minutes, in which the players try to complete all the activity stations.

The players work through the activity stations as individuals. They do not need to wait for the other players at their activity station to complete the task before they can move on. The activity stations can be completed in any order. Encourage players to move to activity stations with the fewest number of players. This maintains a good flow of activities and creates space for all the players.

At each activity station, make sure that players take alternate attempts and do not kick the ball when there are other players in front of them. Encourage the players to use as much space as is available to them. When setting up the activity stations, try to keep them as far apart as possible and set up to avoid players kicking in the direction of other activity stations.

**Station 1** – Player is positioned parallel to a goalpost, curl the ball into an empty goal (20 yards).

**Station 2** – Straight lofted drive pass into a square from 20-25 yards. The ball should only bounce inside the square.

**Station 3** – Player positioned on the right side of the goal, pass the ball diagonally with the inside of the right foot into the goal's left side netting. Player positioned on the left side of the goal, pass the ball diagonally with the inside of the left foot into the goal's right-side netting (20 yards).

**Station 4** – Player positioned side-on to and in front of a goal, hold the ball, let it bounce once and volley it into the goal. The ball must not bounce before it travels into the goal (20 yards).

**Station 5** – Player positioned facing a wall. Mark a target on the wall. Perform a lofted drive pass to hit the target (25 yards).

**Station 6** – Drive pass along the floor into a square from a straight position. The ball must stop inside the square (30 yards).

**Station 7** – Player positioned in front of a goal. Perform a lofted drive pass into the goal. The ball must not bounce before it travels into the goal (25 yards).

## Key focus/Coaching points

**Primary focus:** Long passing

**Secondary focus:** Short passing

**Additional focus:** Shooting

## Progressions/Adaptations

- Players complete all activity stations using their weaker foot.
- Encourage the players to add spin, vary the trajectory and experiment with different foot surfaces for each pass.

# Long Passing

## ACTIVITY 44 DOUBLE CROSS PASSING

**Level:** Intermediate

**Type of activity:** Unopposed technical practice

**Number or participants:** 12

**Equipment required:** Soccer balls and cones

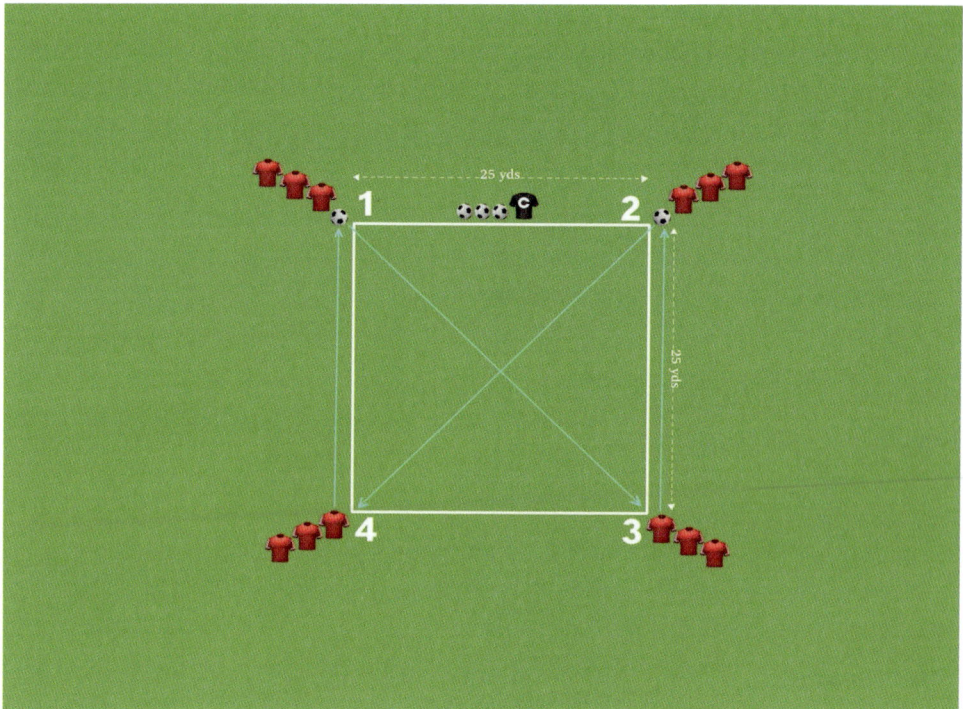

## Description

Divide players into groups of three. Mark out a playing area and position one group in each corner of the playing area. Organise the groups to face the diagonally opposite corner and make sure they are in straight lines. The distance between each group should be 25-30 yards.

Give each corner a number to help with the organisation and explanation of the activity. Starting in any corner, number the first group as 1 and continue clockwise around the playing area up to group 4. Position a ball with two of the groups, but make sure that the groups are not diagonally opposite each other. For example, if group 1 has a ball, group 2 should also have a ball; or if group 3 has a ball, then group 4 should also have a ball. **For the purpose of this description, groups 1 and 2 start with a ball.**

The activity starts when the first players in groups 1 and 2 perform a lofted drive pass diagonally across the playing area. The group 1 players pass to the first player in group 3 and the group 2 player passes to the first player in group 4. After the passes, the players in groups 1 and 2 jog to the back of their line.

The players in possession in groups 3 and 4 now perform a low drive pass along the side of the playing area. The group 3 player passes to the first player in group 2 and the group 4 player passes to the first player in group 1. After the passes, the players in groups 3 and 4 jog to the back of their line.

The balls are now back in their starting positions and the next players in line repeat the activity. The activity continues with this order and direction of passes for 5 minutes. After 5 minutes, rotate the players so that those who were passing diagonally across the area are now passing along the side of the playing area and vice versa.

## Key focus/Coaching points

**Primary focus:** Long passing

**Secondary focus:** Receiving

**Additional focus:** Short passing

## Progressions/Adaptations

- Players must use their weaker foot to pass.
- Vary the type of long pass, e.g., inside-foot curl, outside-foot curl and chip.

# Long Passing 143

## ACTIVITY 45 READY, AIM, FIRE

**Level:** Intermediate

**Type of activity:** Unopposed technical practice

**Number of participants:** 4 per wall/goal

**Equipment required:** Soccer balls, walls or goals (1 per group) and equipment suitable for making targets, e.g., chalk, sticky shapes that attach to the wall, hula hoops and string

## Description

Divide players into groups of four. Position each group in front of and 30 yards away from a wall or a goal. The aim of the activity is to practice long passes and hit targets on the wall/goal. Targets can be drawn on walls with chalk or stuck to the wall, e.g., square or circle shapes. They can also be placed in or hung from the crossbar/post of goals, e.g., hula hoops.

Give each group 10-15 minutes to try to hit each target. Introduce a point system for each target depending on the level of difficulty. Players in each group should spread out and use the space available to them. Multiple players can perform passes at the same time, but make sure the target area is free of players before each pass.

## Key focus/Coaching points

**Primary focus:** Long passing

**Secondary focus:** Ball manipulation

**Additional focus:** Decision making

## Progressions/Adaptations

- Players must hit all targets with both feet.
- Increase the distance from the targets.
- Condition the type of passes, e.g., chip, drive or inside/outside foot curl.

# ACTIVITY 46 PERILOUS PASSING

**Level:** Intermediate

**Type of activity:** Opposed technical practice

**Number of participants:** 15

**Equipment required:** Soccer balls, cones, discs (ideal for this activity, as they ensure that the passes between zones travel without disturbance) and 3 sets of bibs

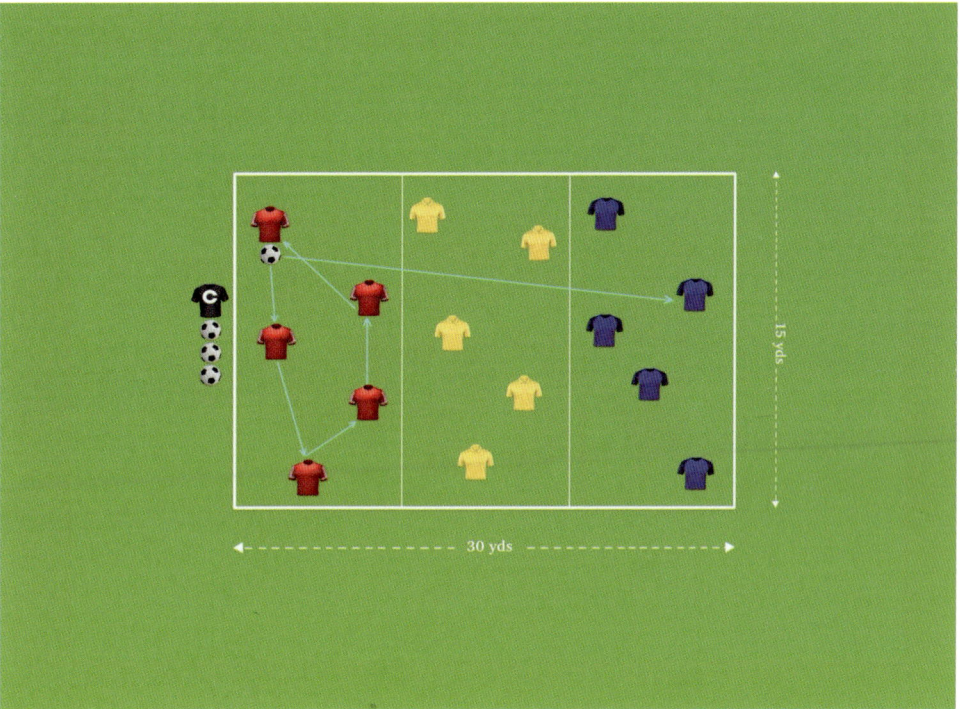

## Description

Divide players into three teams of five. Mark out a playing area with three playing zones of equal size. Position one team in each of the zones. The team in the middle zone starts the activity as the defending team. The teams in the end zones work together to try to keep possession and avoid interceptions from the team in the middle zone.

The activity starts when the coach passes to either of the teams in the end zones. The team in possession completes five passes among themselves. After the fifth pass, the player in possession tries to pass the ball through the middle zone to the opposite end zone. The players in the middle zone try to intercept the pass.

If the pass through the middle zone is successful, the activity continues immediately at the opposite end zone with five passes followed by a pass through the middle zone. If the defending team manages to intercept a pass, they swap zones with the team that lost possession for the next period of play. Players in both end zones should move and create angles to support the player in possession. Encourage the team in possession to play quickly.

## Key focus/Coaching points

**Primary focus:** Long passing

**Secondary focus:** Receiving

**Additional focus:** Short passing

## Progressions/Adaptations

- Allow 1-2 defenders to enter the end zones to try to win possession. If 5 successful passes and a pass to the opposite end zone have been completed, the defenders retreat to the middle zone and 1-2 new defenders enter the opposite end zone to try to win possession.

## ACTIVITY 47  FIND A KEEPER

**Level:** Advanced

**Type of activity:** Unopposed technical practice

**Number of participants:** 8 + 2 goalkeepers

**Equipment required:** Soccer balls, cones and 2 sets of bibs

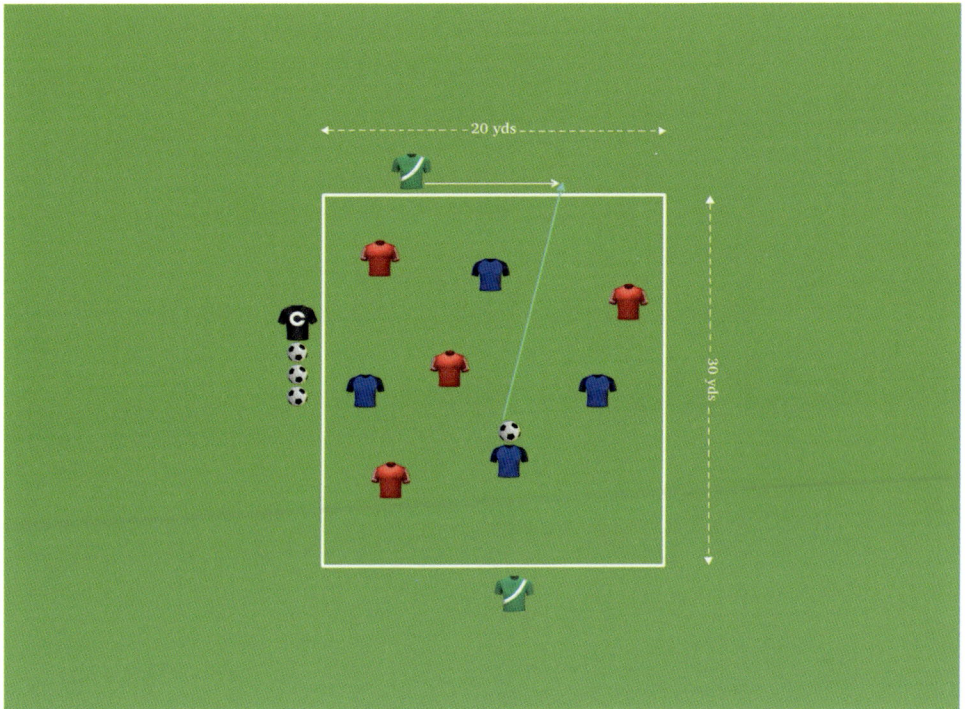

## Description

Divide players into two teams of four (including goalkeepers). Mark out a playing area and position the goalkeepers at opposite ends of the playing area. The two teams of outfield players compete to keep possession and try to score with an aerial pass into the hands of their goalkeeper. Encourage the goalkeepers to move along the line to support teammates.

## Key focus/Coaching points

**Primary focus:** Long passing

**Secondary focus:** Catching

**Additional focus:** Movement

## Progressions/Adaptations

- Alter the type of pass to the goalkeeper, e.g., low drive, lofted drive, inside/outside of foot and chip.

- The teams can score at both ends of the playing area and can try to score consecutively at opposite ends of the playing area. The goalkeepers re-start the activity with a roll out to the team that scored.

- Condition the number of passes completed inside the playing area before a pass to the goalkeeper.

- Add 1 outfield player to both teams.

# Long Passing

## ACTIVITY 48 SEEK AND SCORE

**Level:** Advanced

**Type of activity:** Opposed technical practice

**Number of participants:** 10

**Equipment required:** Soccer balls, cones, discs and 2 sets of bibs

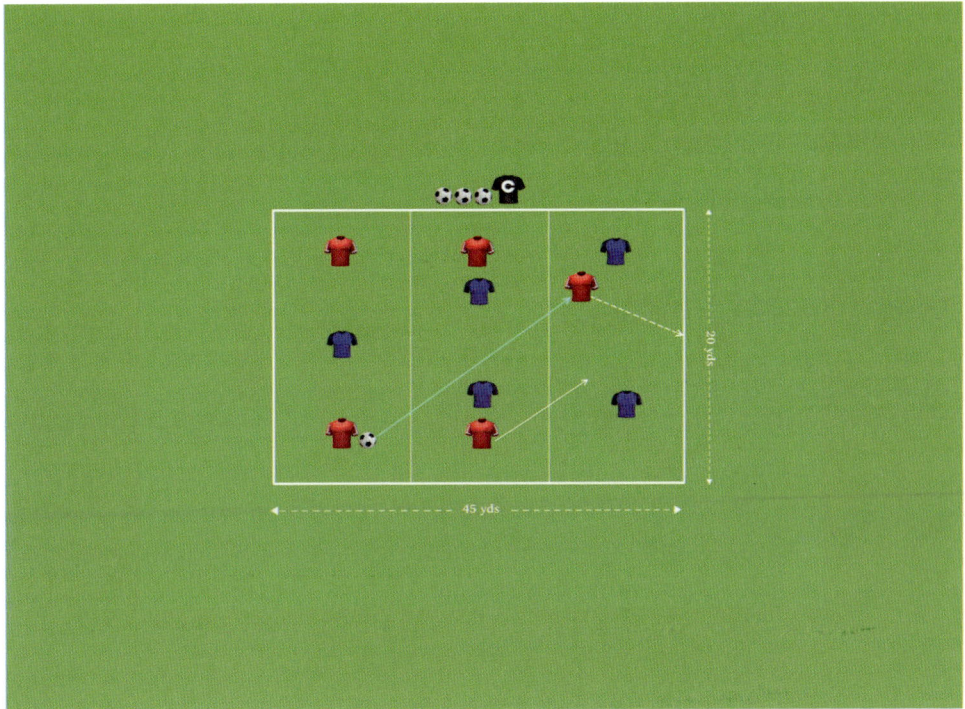

## Description

Divide players into two teams of five. Organise both teams into a 2-2-1 formation. Divide the playing area into three zones. The teams compete in a 5v5 match and attack opposite ends of the playing area. Goals are scored by dribbling over the end line. Organise both teams with two defenders in their defensive zone, two midfielders in the middle zone and one attacker in their attacking zone.

Goals can only be scored after a long pass from the defensive zone to the attacking zone. The middle zone can be used at any time during the build-up but cannot be used immediately before an attempt to score. Once a pass has been played into the attacking zone from the defensive zone, one player from the middle zone can enter the attacking zone to create a 2v2. Once a goal has been scored or their team has lost possession, the midfield player must retreat to the middle zone.

### Key focus/Coaching points

Primary focus: Long passing

Secondary focus: Dribbling

Additional focus: Receiving

### Progressions/Adaptations

- Once a pass has travelled directly from the defensive zone to the attacking zone, the ball must stay in the attacking zone and cannot be passed back into another zone.

- After a pass from the defensive zone to the attacking zone, the player that played the pass and a midfielder can travel into attacking zone to make a 3v2 attacking overload. Once a goal has been scored or their team has lost possession, the defender and the midfielder must retreat to their zones.

# Long Passing

## ACTIVITY 49 RANGE FINDERS

**Level:** Advanced

**Type of activity:** Opposed technical practice

**Number of participants:** 12

**Equipment required:** Soccer balls, cones, discs and 3 sets of bibs

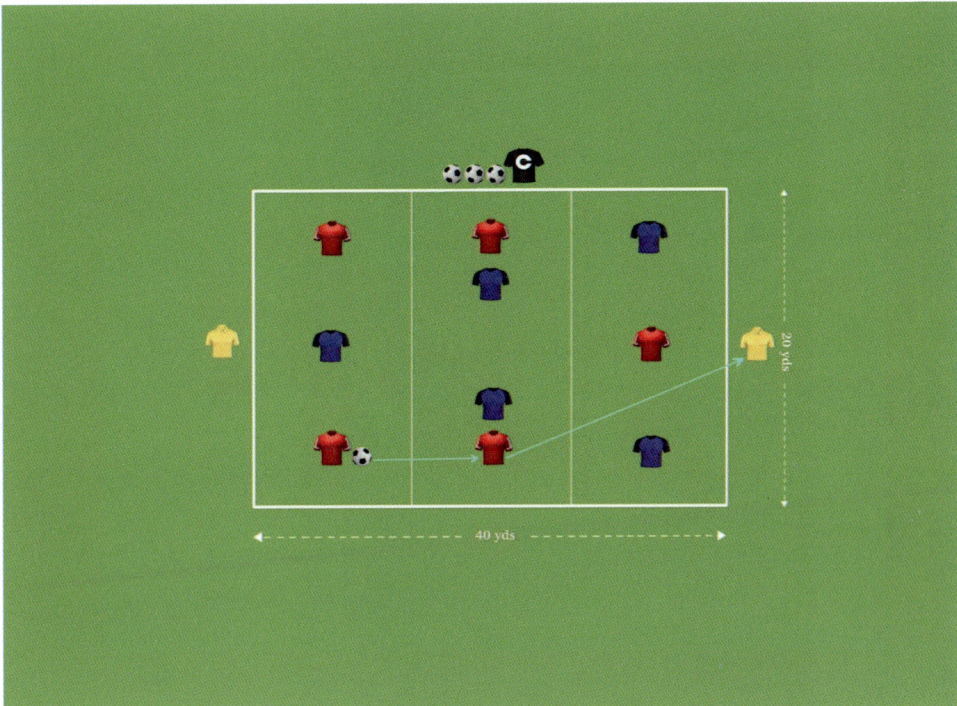

## Description

Divide players into two teams of six. Organise both teams into a 2-2-1 formation plus one target player. Divide the playing area into three zones. Organise both teams with two defenders in their defensive zone, two midfielders in the middle zone, one attacker in their attacking zone and the target player beyond the attacking zone. The teams inside the playing area compete in a 5v5 match and attack opposite ends of the playing area. All players are initially restricted to play within their zones.

Goals are scored by a pass to the target player. Condition the activity so that scoring passes can only be played directly from the defensive or middle zone to the target player. Attackers can receive passes and take part in attacks but cannot pass to the target player.

## Key focus/Coaching points

**Primary focus:** Long passing

**Secondary focus:** Attacking and defending

**Additional focus:** Speed

## Progressions/Adaptations

- Player can move forward 1 zone after passing or dribbling into the next zone. When this happens, there must be a rotation of players to maintain the team formation. For example, if a defender breaks into the middle zone, 1 midfielder must drop into the defending zone.

- Condition the type of scoring pass, e.g., low drive pass, inside/outside of foot or chip.

Receiving **153**

# RECEIVING

## ACTIVITY 50  CHANGING ANGLES

**Level:** Basic

**Type of activity:** Unopposed technical practice

**Number of participants:** 2-20

**Equipment required*:** Soccer balls, cones (mannequins can also be used as obstacles), domes and 2 sets of bibs

*A mannequin is a metal or plastic figure in the shape of a player's torso. The lower half is either a plastic base that stands on the floor or is spike to stick into the ground. They are used as static opponents. They are used to add pressure to the player in possession and provide an obstacle to avoid during technical practices.

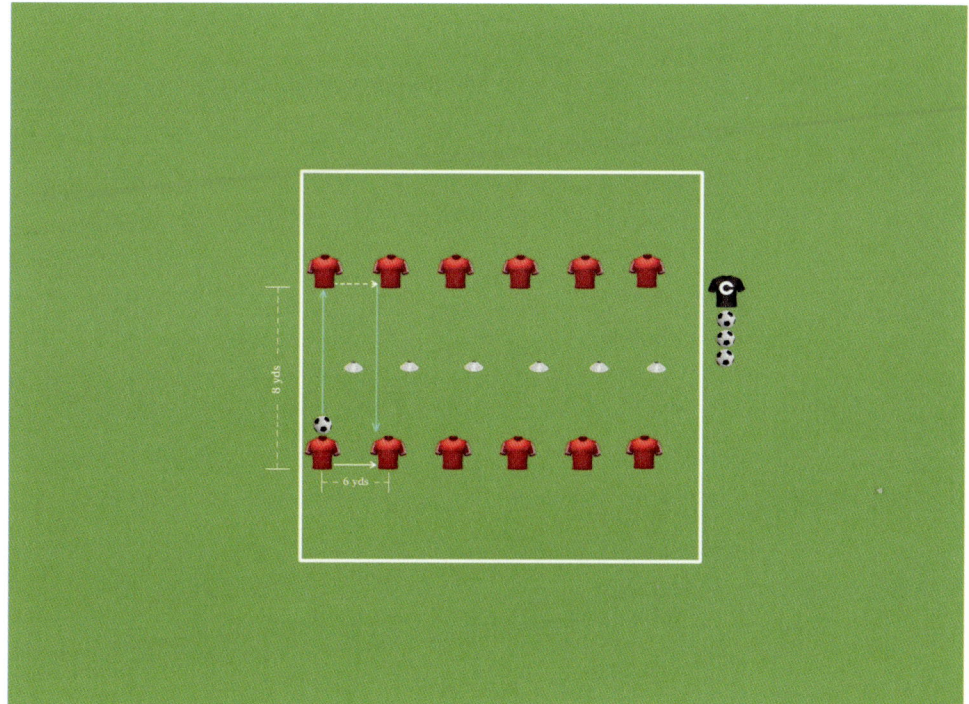

## Description

Divide players into pairs with one ball per pair. Position the players in each pair 8 yards apart and facing each other. Position a cone in between the players in each pair as an obstacle to avoid when passing and receiving the ball. The players pass to each other and receive the ball, while trying to avoid touching the cone. Allow 6 yards of space to the side between the pairs of players.

Before the players start passing, the coach should explain the type of pass, the method of receiving each pass and the direction in which to receive the pass. Both players must follow these instructions - otherwise the activity will break down. Before the first pass, both players should stand to the side of the cone to avoid the cone with the pass so that the receiver is in position to receive the pass.

In the early stages of this activity, some players may need one touch to receive the ball and a second touch to move the ball to the side of the cone. Use the following types of passes, methods of receiving the ball and directions in which to receive each pass. The tasks below are for both players to follow. The players perform each task for 60 seconds:

- Pass with the inside of the left foot past the left side of the cone. Partner receives the pass with the outside of the left foot to the left side of the cone. Repeat.

- Pass with the inside of the left foot past the left side of the cone. Partner receives the pass with the inside of the right foot to the left side of the cone. Repeat.

- Pass with the outside of the left foot past the right side of the cone. Partner receives the pass with the outside of the right foot to the right side of the cone. Repeat.

- Pass with the outside of the left foot past the right side of the cone. Partner receives the pass with the inside of the left foot to the right side of the cone. Repeat.

- Pass with the inside of the right foot past the right side of the cone. Partner receives the pass with the outside of the right foot to the right side of the cone. Repeat.

- Pass with the inside of the right foot past the right side of the cone. Partner receives the pass with the inside of the left foot to the right side of the cone. Repeat.

- Pass with the outside of the right foot past the left side of the cone. Partner receives the pass with the outside of the left foot to the left side of the cone. Repeat.

- Pass with the outside of the right foot past the left side of the cone. Receive the pass with the inside of the right foot to the left side of the cone. Repeat.

## Key focus/Coaching points

**Primary focus:** Receiving

**Secondary focus:** Short passing

**Additional focus:** Ball manipulation

## Progressions/Adaptations

- Use a dome, 2-3 cones side-by-side or 2 cones placed 1-2 steps apart to make the obstacle wider.

- Players are free to choose how to receive and pass the ball. Before they start, the players must decide on the direction of play, e.g., clockwise or anti-clockwise.

# 156 THE SOCCER COACH'S TOOLKIT

## ACTIVITY 51 RED OR BLUE

Level: Basic

Type of activity: Unopposed technical practice

Number of participants: 2-20

Equipment required: Soccer balls, cones (need 2 different colours, e.g., red and blue) and bibs

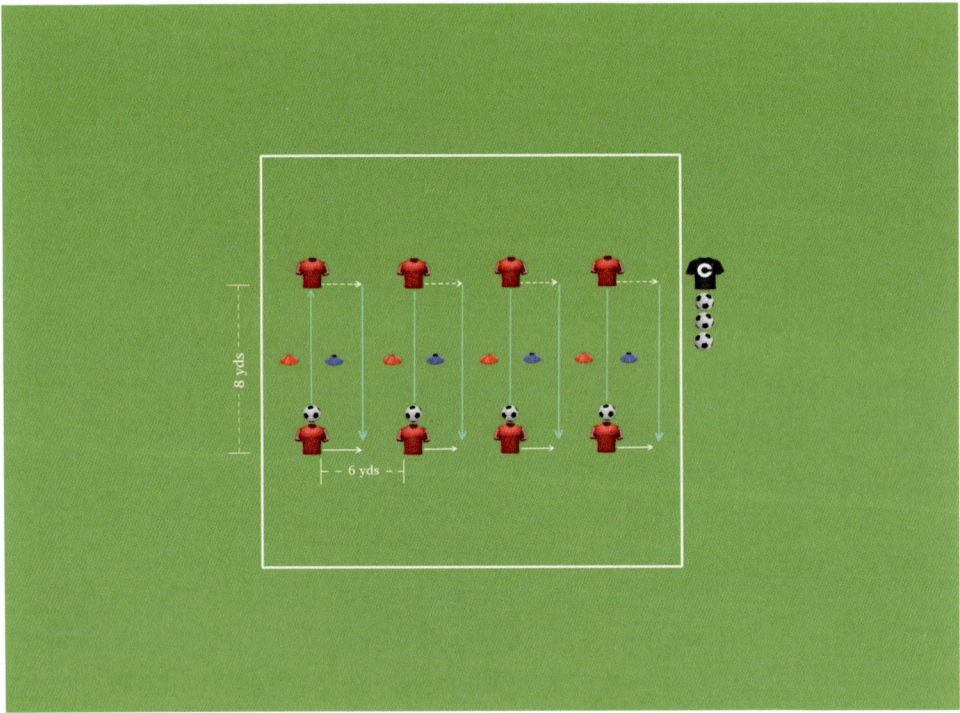

## Description

**This activity can be used as a progression from activity 50 ("Changing angles").**

Divide players into pairs with one soccer ball per pair. Position each pair of players 8 yards apart and facing each other. Position two cones side-by-side as a mini gate in between each pair of players as an obstacle to avoid when passing and receiving the ball.

The cones should be of any two different colours, but for the purpose of this description they will be red and blue.

The activity starts when the player with the ball performs a side-foot pass to their partner through the gate. As the player passes the ball, they must call aloud "Red" or "Blue". After they have passed the ball, they must move 1-2 steps to the outside of the cone they have nominated. The player that receives the pass must receive it in the direction of and to the outside of the cone with the corresponding colour. After receiving the pass, the player must then perform a side-foot pass to their partner past the outside of the cone.

After receiving the pass past the outside of the cone, the player receives the ball towards the middle of the mini gate. The player again passes to their partner through the gate and calls out a colour. The activity continues in this manner for 1-2 minutes. Rotate roles.

**Encourage the players to use different methods of receiving the ball, e.g., inside or outside of the foot. Let the players also develop their own techniques and use different foot surfaces to receive the ball in new ways.**

## Key focus/Coaching points

**Primary focus:** Receiving

**Secondary focus:** Short passing

**Additional focus:** Agility

## Progressions/Adaptations

- With each pass, the players must call out a colour. The receiving player must receive the ball and move it to the outside of the cone with the corresponding colour. As soon as they have done this, they must pass to their partner and call out a colour. Players must move quickly and be in position to receive each pass. If a player makes a mistake and either hits a cone with a pass or is unable to receive and move it to the outside of the correct cone, 1 point is awarded to their partner. The first player to 10 points wins.

- Allow lower ability players 1 touch to receive the ball and a second touch to move the ball to the outside of the nominated cone.

## ACTIVITY 52 PELE 7

**Level:** Basic

**Type of activity:** Unopposed technical practice

**Number of participants:** 1+

**Equipment required:** Soccer balls and cones

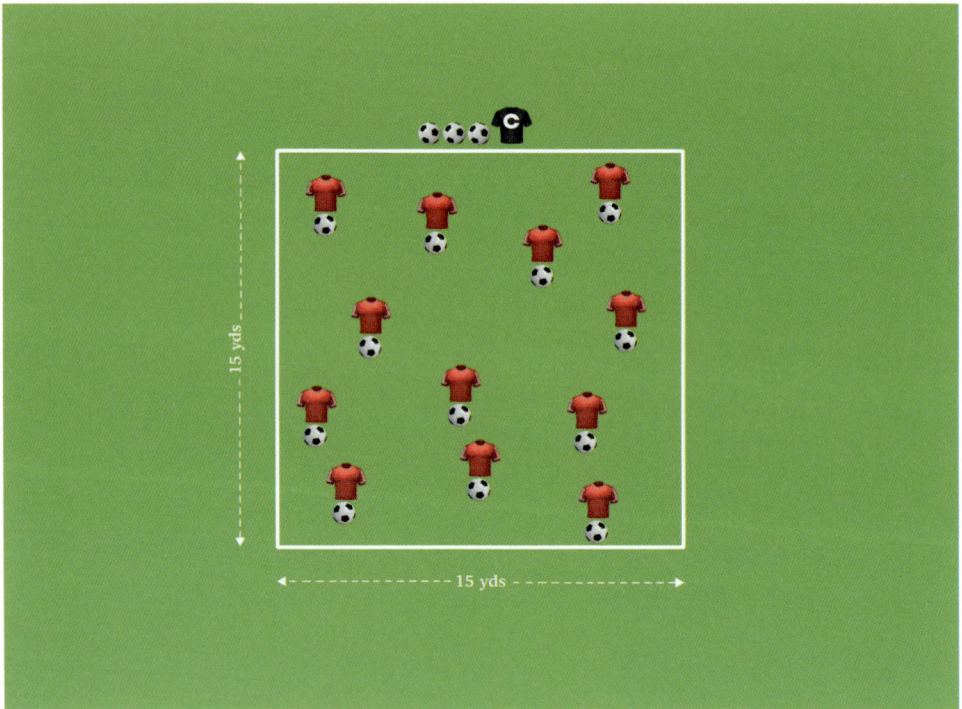

### Description

Players work individually with one ball each. Position all players inside the playing area. The players try to complete a "Pele 7". A "Pele 7" is a sequence of keep-ups using different parts of the body. The sequence is as follows:

Left foot, right foot, left thigh, right thigh, left shoulder, right shoulder and head.

## Key focus/Coaching points

**Primary focus:** Receiving

**Secondary focus:** Ball manipulation

**Additional focus:** Coordination

## Progressions/Adaptations

- Beginner players can catch the ball after every ball contact, e.g., left foot, catch, right foot, catch.

- Intermediate players: allow 1 touch to "steady" the ball before moving on to the next body part, e.g., left foot, left foot, right foot, right foot.

- Advanced players: any player that completes a "Pele 7" must then try to complete a "Pele 14": **Left foot, right foot, left thigh, right thigh, left shoulder, right shoulder, head, head, right shoulder, left shoulder, right thigh, left thigh, right foot and left foot.**

## ACTIVITY 53 PASSING TRAFFIC

**Level:** Basic

**Type of activity:** Unopposed technical practice

**Number of participants:** 12

**Equipment required:** Soccer balls, cones and 2 sets of bibs

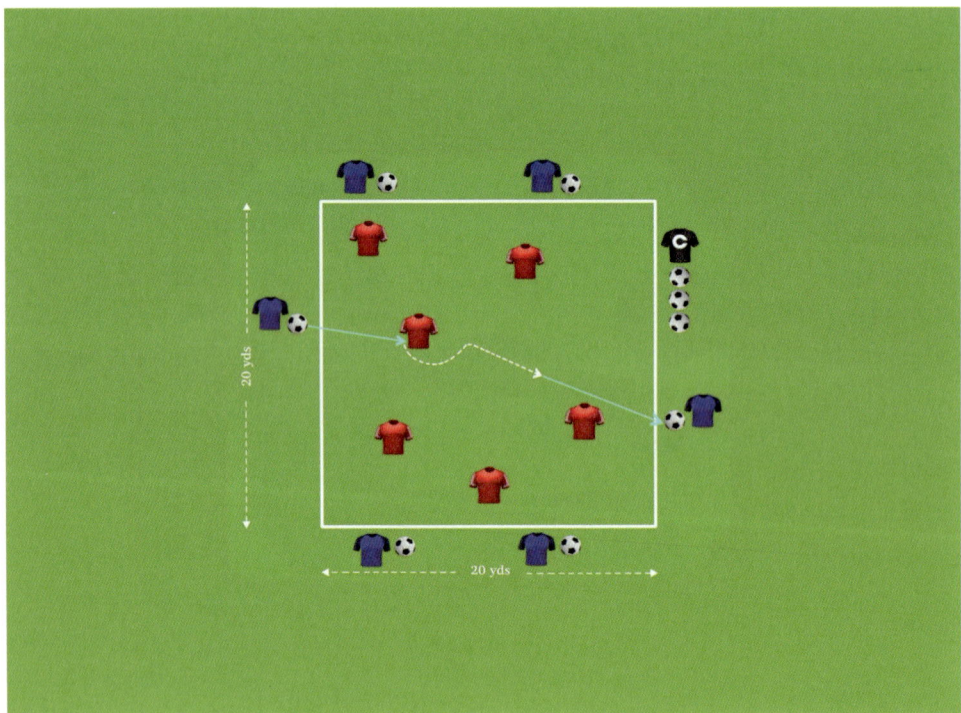

### Description

Divide players into two groups of six. Position one group of players inside the playing area and the other group of players around the outside of the playing area with one ball each. The activity starts when the players outside the playing area pass to an available player inside the playing area. There are six players in both groups, so there will always be at least one player available for each pass.

When the players inside the playing area receive a pass, they then turn and dribble into a new space and pass out to a different player. The players inside the playing area may be able to find an available player to pass to immediately, or they may have to hold on to possession until a free player becomes available to receive a pass.

After passing out, the players inside the playing area make a small movement away from the player they passed to and then move back towards them to receive another pass. The activity continues following this sequence for 1-2 minutes. Rotate the players after 1-2 minutes.

## Key focus/Coaching points

Primary focus: Receiving

Secondary focus: Movement

Additional focus: Short passing

## Progressions/Adaptations

- After the players inside the playing area have passed out to an available player, they must move to a different player and receive a pass.

- Position one of the outside players as a defender inside the playing area. The defender tries to intercept passes and can tackle any of the players inside the playing area. There should now only be 5 players on the outside of the playing area. The players inside the playing area may have to shield the ball or turn away from the defender until a player on the outside is ready to receive a pass. They will also have to be aware of and move quickly to receive passes from outside the playing area, as there are fewer players available to receive passes from.

- Position two of the outside players as defenders inside the playing area. The defenders try to intercept passes and can tackle any of the players inside the playing area. There should now only be 4 players on the outside of the playing area. The players inside the playing area may have to shield the ball or turn away from the defenders until a player on the outside is ready to receive a pass. They will also have to be aware of and move quickly to receive passes from outside the playing area, as there are fewer players available to receive passes from.

# 162 THE SOCCER COACH'S TOOLKIT

## ACTIVITY 54 SHIFT IT

**Level:** Basic

**Type of activity:** Unopposed technical practice

**Number of participants:** 9

**Equipment required:** Soccer balls, mannequins (domes or cones positioned side-by-side can be used as an alternative), 2 sets of bibs and 2 mini-goals

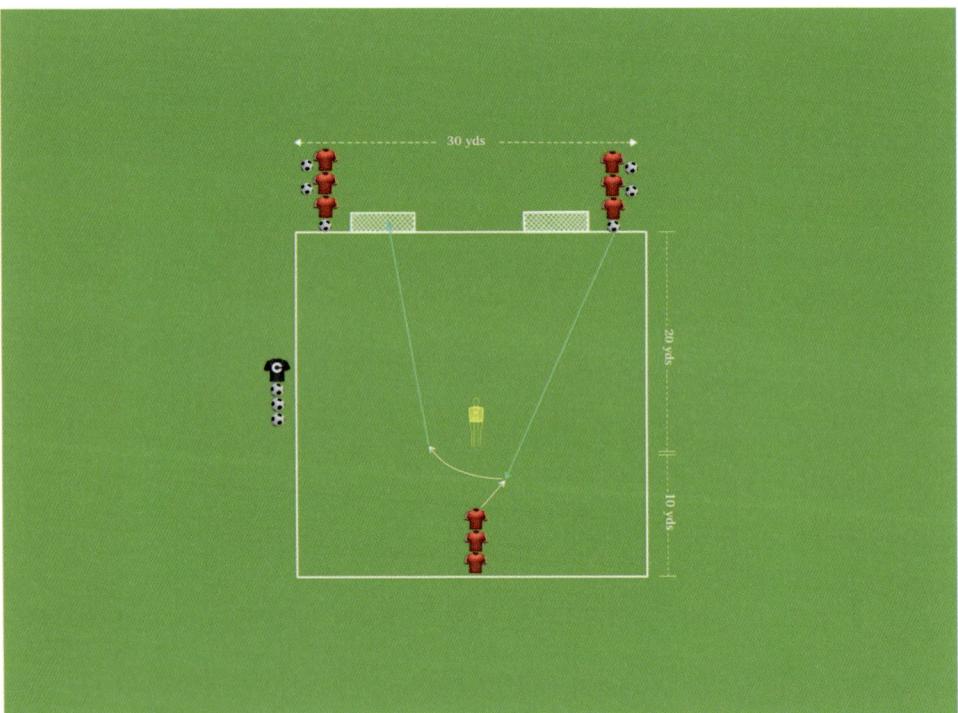

## Description

Divide players into a group of nine. Mark out a playing area and position one mini goal in each corner at one end of the playing area. Organise the group into two sets of three ball feeders and one group of three attackers. Position one set of ball feeders a safe distance to the right side of the mini goal in the right corner of the playing area. Position one set of ball feeders a safe distance to the left side of the mini goal in the left corner of the playing area. Both sets of ball feeders require a supply of soccer balls. Position a mannequin 20 yards from and in the middle of the mini goals. Position the attackers in a straight line behind the mannequins.

The activity starts when the first ball feeder from either group passes to the first attacker in line. The attacker must move to the side of the mannequin and be in line with the ball to receive the pass. The attacker receives the pass across and to the other side of the mannequin. The attacker then finishes into the mini goal that they received the pass from. The attackers must finish using the correct foot, i.e., if after receiving the pass, the ball is to the left of the mannequin, they should finish with their left foot. After the attacker has performed the finish, the attacker and the ball feeder run to the back of each other's lines.

The activity continues immediately from the other group of ball feeders. Emphasise fitness development with the players by encouraging them to run at high intensity between positions. Following are some methods to use for receiving the passes:

- Outside of the foot across the body for a finish with the same foot.

- Inside of the foot receive across the body for a finish with the other foot.

- Two-touch (inside/outside of the foot) receive across the body for a finish with the same foot.

## Key focus/Coaching points

**Primary focus:** Receiving

**Secondary focus:** Movement

**Additional focus:** Finishing

## Progressions/Adaptations

- The ball feeder follows their pass and tries to pressure the finish.

- Encourage the ball feeders to make the passes more difficult to receive by varying the flight, trajectory, power and spin applied to each pass.

# 164 THE SOCCER COACH'S TOOLKIT

## ACTIVITY 55  4V1 POSSESSION

**Level:** Intermediate

**Type of activity:** Opposed technical practice

**Number of participants:** 8

**Equipment required:** Soccer balls, cones and 2 sets of bibs

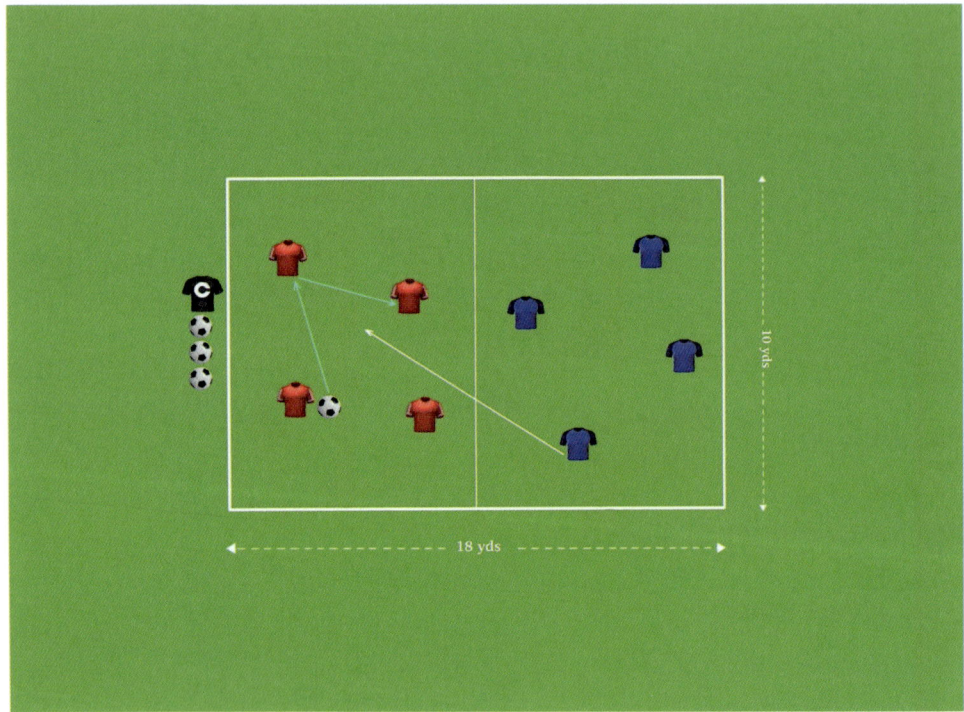

## Description

Divide players into two teams of four. Mark out a playing area and divide it into two zones. Position one team in each zone. Before the activity starts, position one ball in either of the zones. The activity starts with the team in possession passing the ball among themselves. One player from the other team runs into the possession team's zone and tries to win possession of the ball. If the player manages to win possession, they can either try to pass or dribble the ball into their own zone. The team of four players can try to win possession back before the ball leaves their zone.

Once the ball and the player that won possession have transferred to the other zone, the team now in possession tries to keep the ball among themselves. One player from the team that has just lost possession runs into the possession team's zone and tries to win back possession of the ball. The activity is continuous between zones with a 4v1 possession organisation constantly in place.

If at any stage of the activity, the ball travels out of the playing area, the coach feeds new a ball into the team that most recently has possession.

## Key focus/Coaching points

Primary focus: Receiving

Secondary focus: Short passing

Additional focus: Movement

## Progressions/Adaptations

- 2 defenders try to win the ball back.
- Players can only use 2 touches in possession of the ball.

## ACTIVITY 56  TENNIS BALL KEEP-UPS

**Level:** Intermediate

**Type of activity:** Unopposed technical practice

**Number of participants:** 1-20

**Equipment required:** Tennis balls and cones

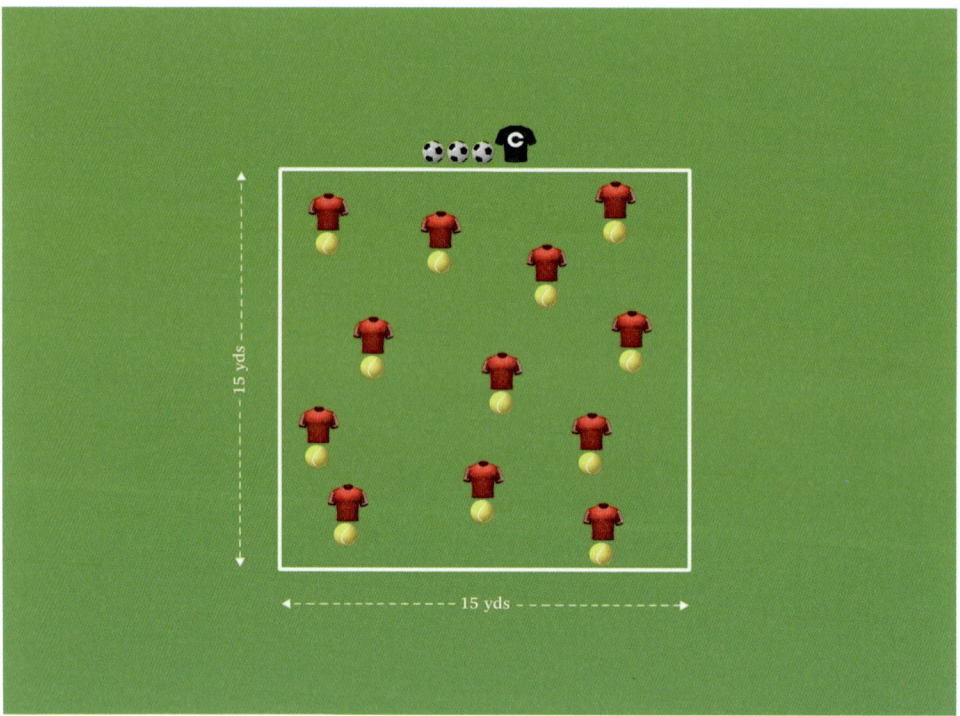

## Description

Players perform individually. Position all players inside the playing area with a tennis ball. The players perform keep-ups with their tennis ball. Allow the players 5 minutes of free practice to get used to using a tennis ball. After 5 minutes, instruct the players to perform the tasks listed below in the **progressions and adaptations** section.

## Key focus/Coaching points

Primary focus: Receiving

Secondary focus: Ball manipulation

Additional focus: Coordination

## Progressions/Adaptations

The players will find performing keep-ups with a tennis ball challenging, particularly if they have never used a tennis ball before. Encourage the players to develop sequences gradually to build confidence. For beginner players, allow them to catch the ball after each ball contact, i.e., one touch and catch until the technique feels more comfortable.

Tasks:

- Feet only.
- Thighs only.
- Weaker foot only.
- Small and big touches.
- Combinations using all body parts.

# 168  THE SOCCER COACH'S TOOLKIT

## ACTIVITY 57  AERIAL CONTROL

**Level:** Intermediate

**Type of activity:** Opposed technical practice

**Number of participants:** 10 + 2 goalkeepers

**Equipment required:** Soccer balls, cones, 2 sets of bibs and 2 goals

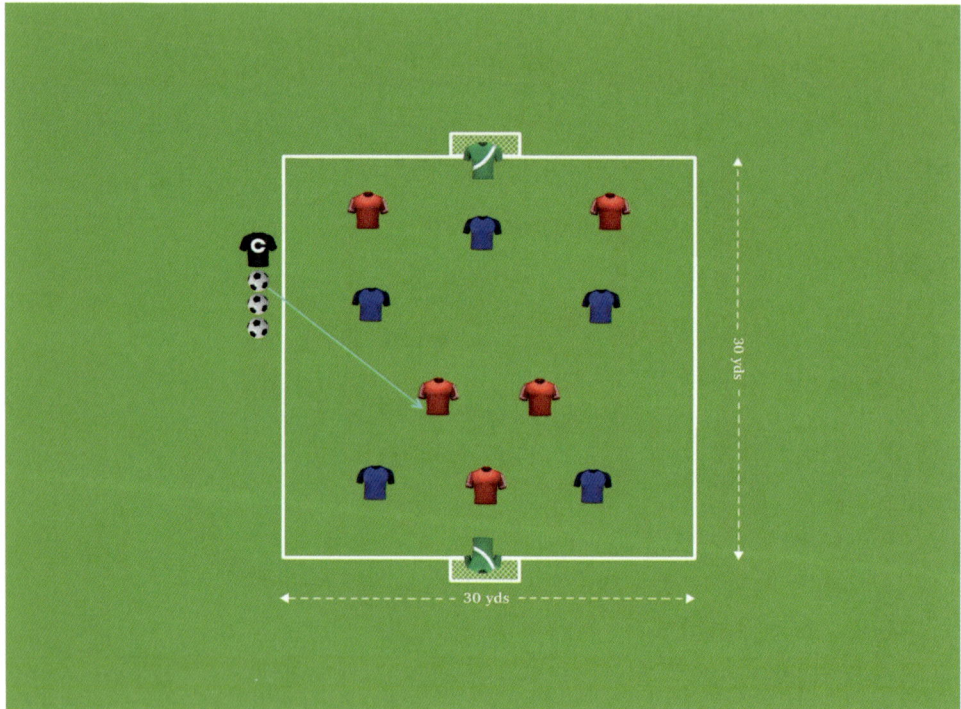

## Description

Divide players into two teams of 6 (including goalkeepers). Position one goal at both ends of the playing area. The teams compete in a 6v6 match following normal game rules apart from the following adaptations to re-starts in play:

- When the ball goes out of play for a throw-in, the coach serves a high aerial ball into the team whose throw-in it is to re-start play. A player from this team must receive the ball before it bounces. If they fail to receive the ball before it bounces, feed a high aerial ball into the opposition.

- When the ball goes out of play for a corner, the corner must be played through the air and received by a teammate before the ball bounces. If they fail to receive the ball before it bounces, award a goal kick to the opposition.

- When the ball goes out of play for a goal kick, it must be kicked through the air and received by a teammate before it bounces. If they fail to receive the ball before it bounces, award a goal kick to the opposition.

- Re-starts should initially be unopposed to allow players to receive the ball without pressure.

## Key focus/Coaching points

Primary focus: Receiving

Secondary focus: Volleys

Additional focus: Attacking and defending

## Progressions/Adaptations

- Increase the difficulty of re-starts by varying the speed, height and spin on ball.

- To make re-starts easier, encourage teams to decrease the distance between the player performing the re-start and the intended receiver.

- Both teams contest re-starts.

# 170 THE SOCCER COACH'S TOOLKIT

## ACTIVITY 58 THREE TEAS

**Level:** Intermediate

**Type of activity:** Opposed technical practice

**Number of participants:** 14

**Equipment required:** Soccer balls, cones, discs and 3 sets of bibs

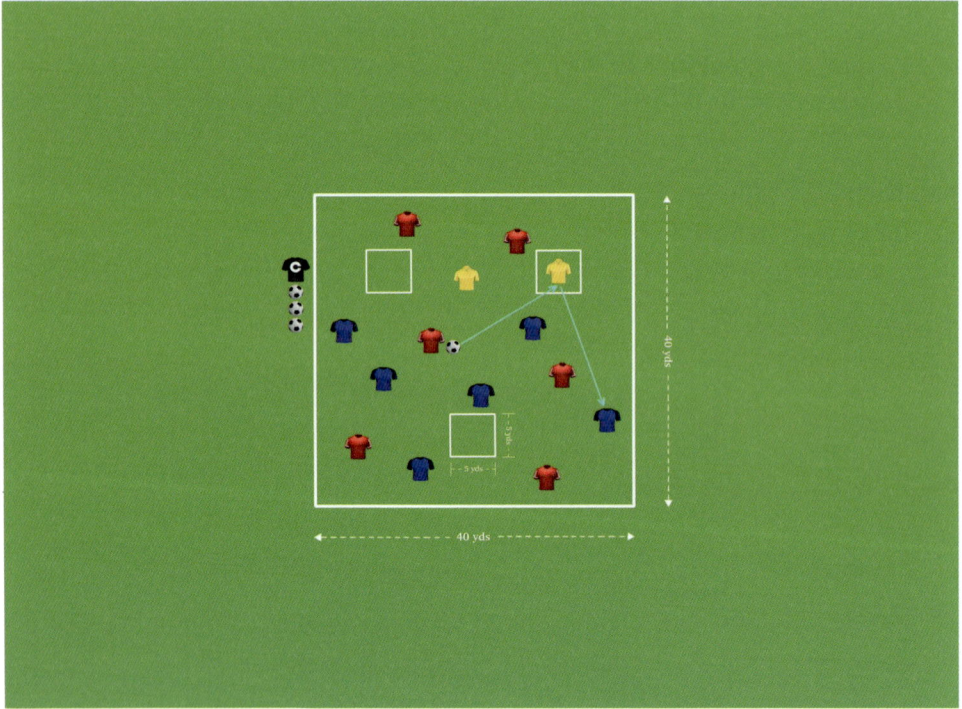

## Description

Divide players into two teams of six and two floating target players. Mark out a playing area with three squares positioned around the inside of the area. The teams compete for possession and try to score a goal by either dribbling the ball into or passing to either of the floating target players inside one of the squares.

Encourage the floating target players to move and support the team in possession and make runs into the squares. If a floating target player receives a pass inside one of the squares, they re-start the activity with a pass out to the other team. If a player successfully dribbles into one of the squares, a goal is awarded, and play continues. The teams cannot score successive goals in the same square, so after each goal, they must attack a new square.

## Key focus/Coaching points

**Primary focus:** Receiving

**Secondary focus:** Movement

**Additional focus:** Decision making

## Progressions/Adaptations

- Nominate 1 floating target player to play for 1 team only.
- When either team tries to score with a pass, only award a goal if the target player arrives inside the square at the same time as the pass.

# ACTIVITY 59 MIDDLEMAN

**Level:** Advanced

**Type of activity:** Opposed technical practice

**Number of participants:** 12

**Equipment required:** Soccer balls, cones, discs and 2 sets of bibs

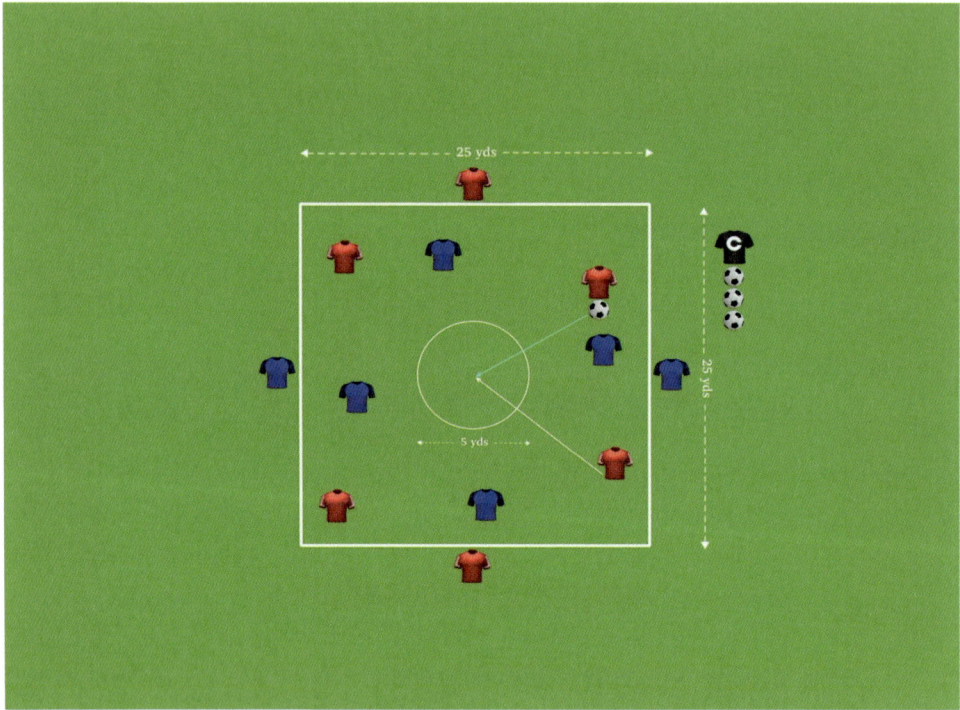

## Description

Divide players into two teams of six. Mark out a playing area with a circle in the middle. Position four players from each team inside the playing area and one player from each team at opposite ends of the playing area. The teams compete for possession and try to score by passing into the circle to a teammate. Teams can pass to their teammates at the ends of the playing area at any time to help keep possession. Encourage players to keep out of the circle unless they are making a run into it to receive a pass.

## Key focus/Coaching points

**Primary focus:** Receiving

**Secondary focus:** Short passing

**Additional focus:** Movement

## Progressions/Adaptations

- One of or both teammates at the ends of the playing area must be passed to in each attack before a team can attempt to score.
- Allow players to score with a dribble into the circle.
- Condition the number of passes that must be played before attempting to score.

# 174 THE SOCCER COACH'S TOOLKIT

## ACTIVITY 60 GATE INSTINCT

**Level:** Advanced

**Type of activity:** Opposed technical practice

**Number of participants:** 8-10

**Equipment required:** Soccer balls, cones, domes 2 sets of bibs

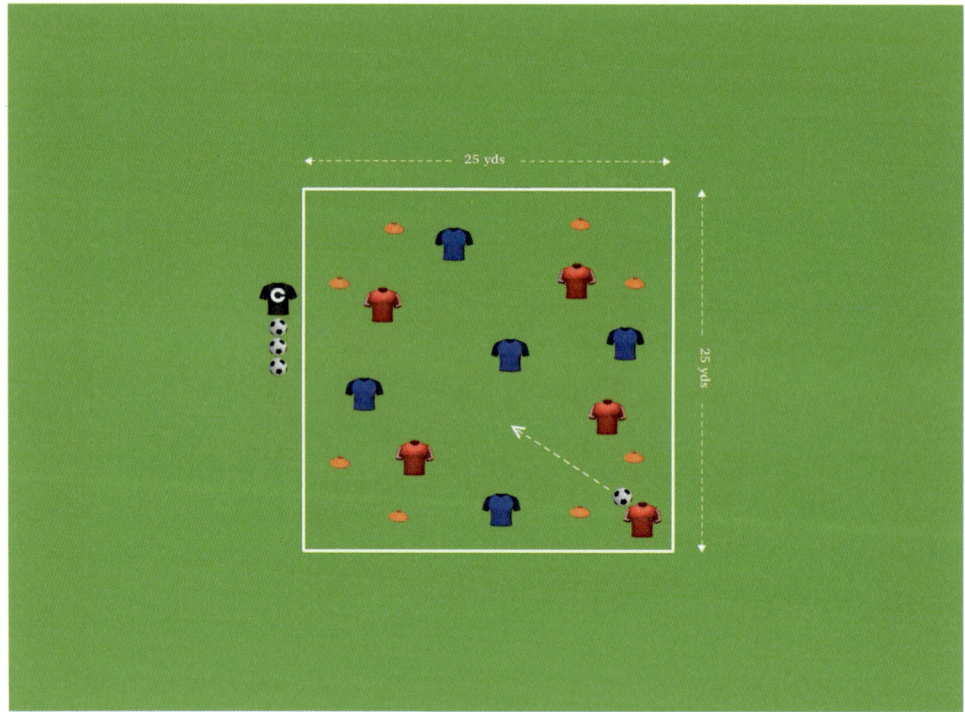

## Description

Divide players into two teams of four to five. Mark out a playing area and position four sets of gates inside the playing area. The teams compete for possession and try to score by either dribbling through or completing a pass to a teammate through one of the gates.

## Key focus/Coaching points

Primary focus: Receiving

Secondary focus: Short passing

Additional focus: Dribbling

## Progressions/Adaptations

- Players can only use 2-3 touches in possession.
- Condition the number of passes that must be completed before a goal can be goal.

# 176 THE SOCCER COACH'S TOOLKIT

## ACTIVITY 61  FRIENDS AND ENEMIES

**Level:** Advanced

**Type of activity:** Opposed technical practice

**Number of participants:** 8-10

**Equipment required:** Soccer balls, cones and 2 sets of bibs

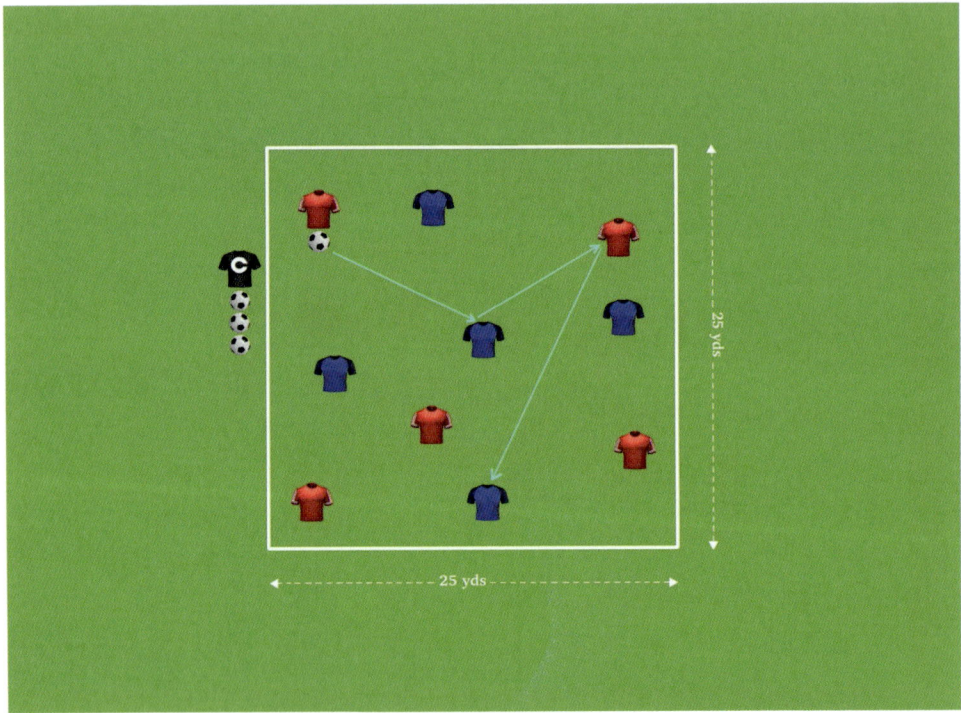

## Description

Divide players into two groups of three to four. Position both groups inside the playing area. Both groups work together to keep possession of one ball. The players can only receive the ball from and pass the ball to players in the other group. Passing to and receiving passes from players in the same group is not permitted. The activity requires concentration, as the players will take time to get used to receiving the ball from players that are not in their group. Encourage the players to play with their heads up and to be mentally alert to minimise mistakes.

It is important to make sure that the groups are wearing different coloured bibs. This will help players to identify the players they can and cannot pass to and receive passes from.

## Key focus/Coaching points

**Primary focus:** Receiving

**Secondary focus:** Decision making

**Additional focus:** Movement

## Progressions/Adaptations

- Players can only use 2 touches in possession.
- Add 1-2 defenders to try to intercept passes and tackle players.
- Players try to keep possession of 2 balls at the same time.

## ACTIVITY 62 TRICOLOUR

Level: Advanced

Type of activity: Opposed technical practice

Number of participants: 9-15

Equipment required: Soccer balls, cones and 3 sets of bibs

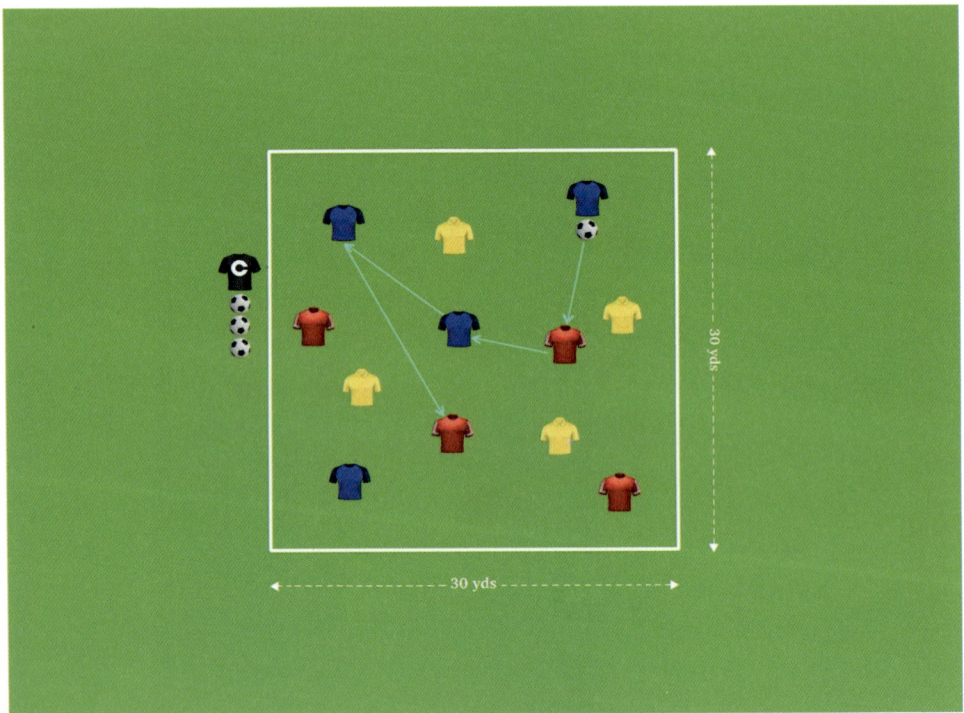

## Description

Divide players into three groups of three to five. Position all the groups inside the playing area. Make sure that the groups are wearing different coloured bibs. Nominate two groups to start as the possession groups and the remaining group to start as the defending group. The two possession groups work together to keep possession from the defending group. The coach requires a supply of balls and should feed a new ball into the playing area each time a ball goes out of the playing area.

When a group loses possession (e.g., by losing control of the ball, having a pass intercepted, a player being tackled or passing the ball out of the playing area) they immediately become the defending group. The group that was the defending group then becomes one of the possession groups. There must always be two groups working together in possession against one defending group. The defending group can intercept, tackle or knock the ball out of play. Encourage quick transitions between the defending and possession groups to help the activity flow.

## Key focus/Coaching points

**Primary focus:** Receiving

**Secondary focus:** Short passing

**Additional focus:** Movement

## Progressions/Adaptations

- Players can only use 2 touches in possession.
- When a player receives possession of the ball they must pass to a teammate in their group and then to a teammate in the other possession group. The players must maintain this sequence of possession.

# 180 THE SOCCER COACH'S TOOLKIT

## ACTIVITY 63 TRIPLE CHANCE PASSING

Level: Advanced

Type of activity: Opposed technical practice

Number of participants: 10

Equipment required: Soccer ball, cones, domes and 3 sets of bibs

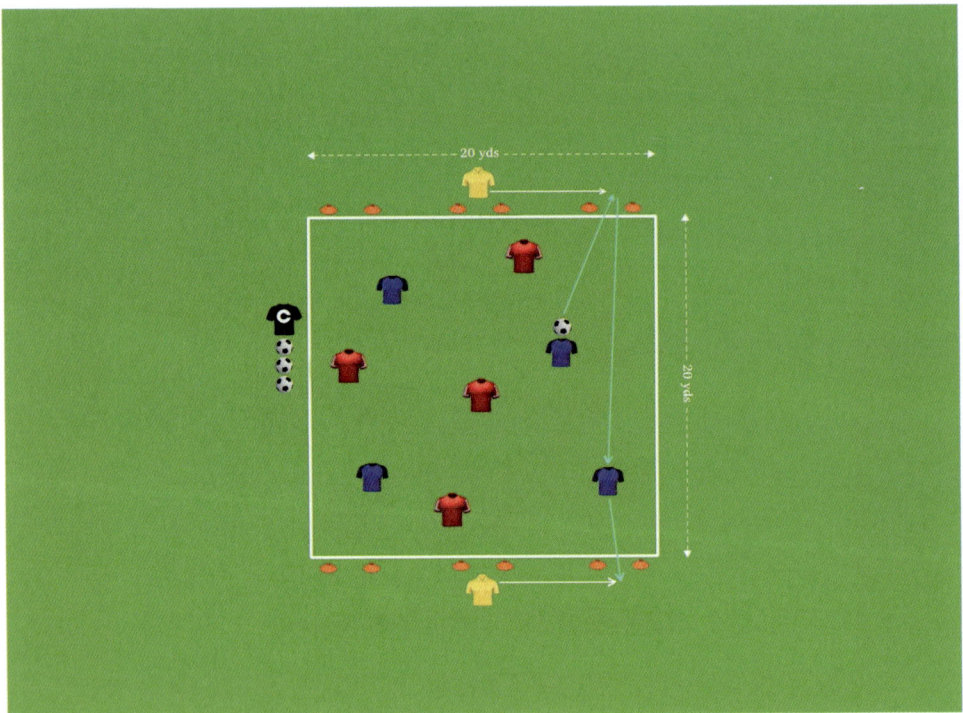

## Description

Divide players into two teams of four and two target players. Mark out a playing area with three gates spread out along both end lines. Position one target player at both ends of the playing area. The teams compete for possession and try to score by passing to a target player through any of the gates.

The teams can score at both ends of the playing area but cannot score consecutive goals at the same end. The target players should move along the end line and make positions to receive passes through the gates. When a goal has been scored, the target player immediately passes back to the scoring team, who then attacks the other end of the playing area.

## Key focus/Coaching points

Primary focus: Receiving

Secondary focus: Short passing

Additional focus: Movement

## Progressions/Adaptation

- The teams attack opposite ends of the playing area. After each goal, the target player immediately passes to the team that has just conceded the goal.

- After a goal is scored remove the gate that was scored through. The first team to score through all the gates at the end that they are attacking are the winning team.

- The teams must complete 4 passes before scoring.

# 182 THE SOCCER COACH'S TOOLKIT

## ACTIVITY 64 POSSESSION V PENETRATION

**Level:** Advanced

**Type of activity:** Opposed technical practice

**Number of participants:** 10 + 1 goalkeeper

**Equipment required:** Soccer ball, cones, 2 sets of bibs and 1 goal

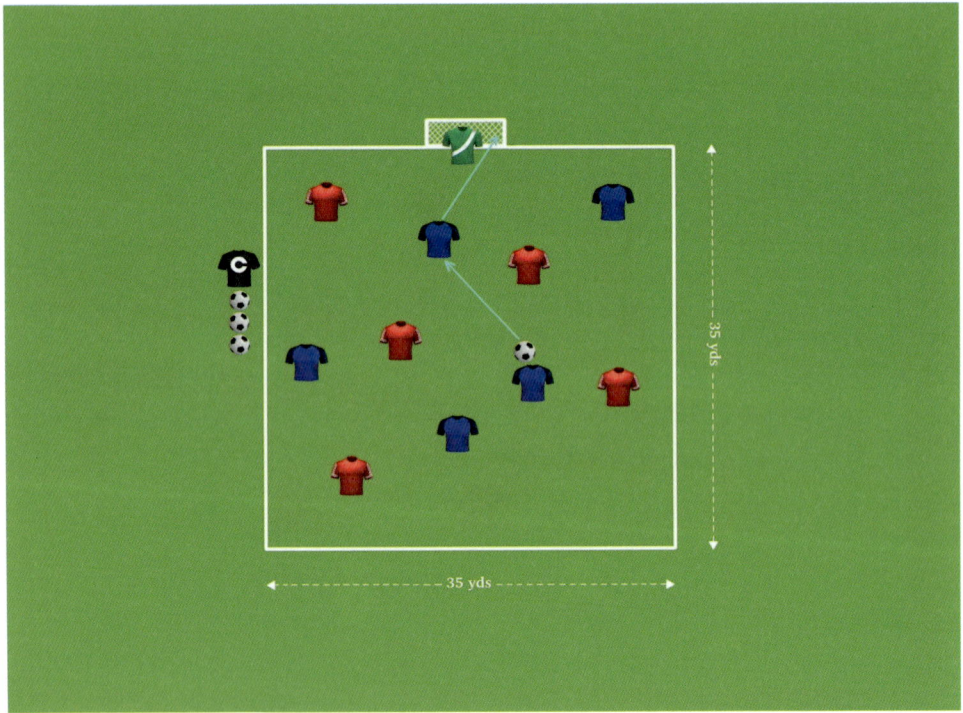

## Description

Divide players into two teams of five. Position one goal and a goalkeeper at one end of the playing area. The teams compete against each other inside the playing area. At the start of the activity nominate a possession team and an attacking-with-penetration team. The possession team scores 1 point each time that they complete seven passes without interception. The attacking-with-penetration team scores 1 point each time they score past the goalkeeper. Rotate the teams after 10-15 minutes.

## Key focus/Coaching points

Primary focus: Receiving

Secondary focus: Movement

Additional focus: Decision making

## Progressions/Adaptations

- Increase/decrease the number of passes required to score a goal so that the level of challenge is equal to that of scoring a goal.
- Condition the methods of scoring in the goal, e.g., first-time finish.
- Condition the type of the possession team must use in their possession sequence, e.g., 3 lofted passes, 3 passes with the outside of the foot and 1 pass over 20 yards in distance.

# 184 THE SOCCER COACH'S TOOLKIT

# DRIBBLING

## ACTIVITY 65  SUPERSTAR DRIBBLING

**Level:** Basic

**Type of activity:** Unopposed technical practice

**Number of participants:** 1-16

**Equipment required:** Soccer balls and cones

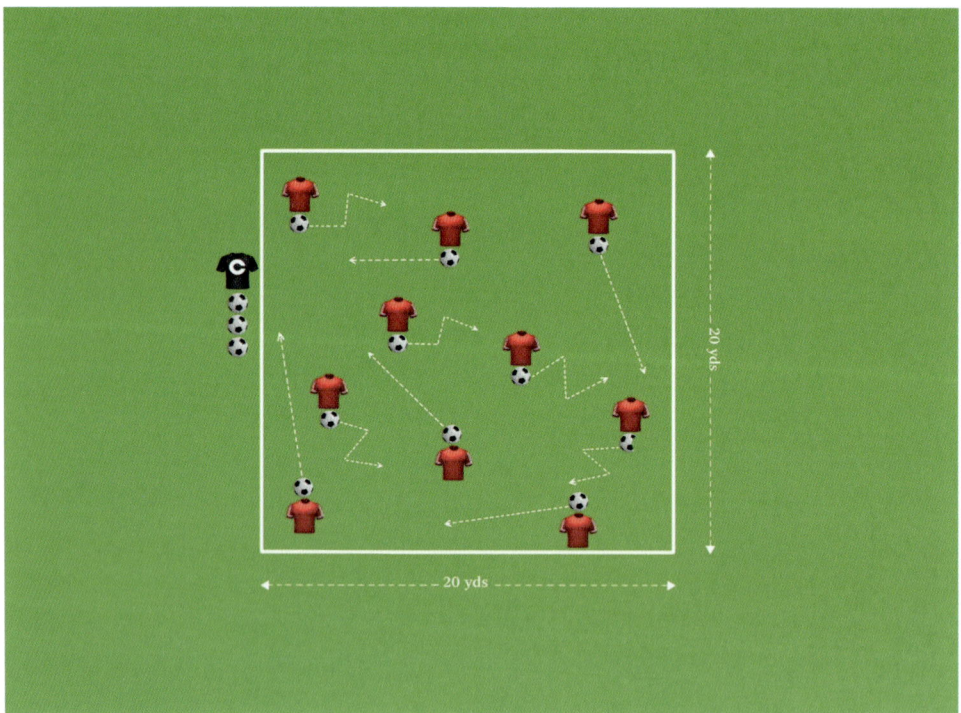

## Description

Players perform individually inside the playing area with a ball each. The players dribble around the playing area in the style of Lionel Messi and Cristiano Ronaldo. Before the activity, the coach should give technical advice on the dribbling styles of Messi and

Ronaldo (see below). Using these two soccer greats as examples can help players to understand and experiment with different approaches to dribbling.

- **Messi:** dribble with small touches and lots of quick touches of the ball. Change direction regularly and use different foot surfaces to move the ball.
- **Ronaldo:** dribble using bigger touches followed by a high-speed chase after the ball. Encourage explosive changes of speed and direction with fewer touches of the ball.

## Key focus/Coaching points

Primary focus: Dribbling

Secondary focus: Running with the ball

Additional focus: Turning

## Progressions/Adaptations

- Other famous players can be introduced to further explore different dribbling styles:
    - **Bale** – dribble with the outside of the foot. Keep the ball on the foot farthest from the sidelines.
    - **Gnabry** – dribble with the front of the foot. Keep the ball on the foot nearest to the sidelines.
    - **Neymar** – dribble with the inside, outside, sole and back of the foot. Use tricks and turns while dribbling.

# 186   THE SOCCER COACH'S TOOLKIT

## ACTIVITY 66  TRAFFIC LIGHTS

**Level:** Basic

**Type of activity:** Unopposed technical practice

**Number of participants:** 1-16

**Equipment required:** Soccer balls and cones

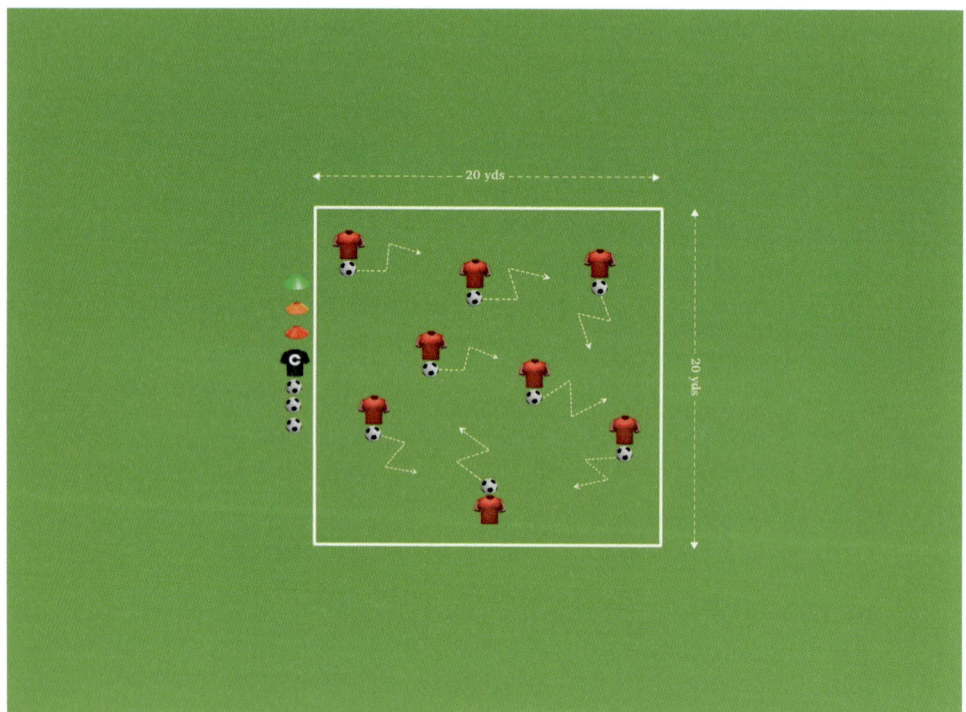

## Description

Players perform individually inside the playing area with a ball each. Allow players to dribble freely around the playing area for 2-3 minutes. Introduce the following commands and related tasks for the players to perform:

- **Red light** – the players stop dribbling and place the sole of their foot on top of the ball.

- **Orange light** – the players perform ball taps side-to-side with the insides of both feet.
- **Green light** – the players dribble in different directions around the playing area, dodging each other while they dribble.
- **Roundabout** – the players turn with the ball in a 360-degree circle and continue dribbling.
- **Pit stop** – the players dribble out of the playing area and then back inside.
- **Pick-up truck** – the coach enters the playing area and tries to steal balls from the players. The players dribble and dodge the coach with their soccer balls. The coach should play sensibly and avoid physical contact with the players. If a player clearly loses control of their ball, the coach can gently kick it out of the playing area. The players can return to the playing area once they have retrieved their ball.

## Key focus/Coaching points

Primary focus: Dribbling

Secondary focus: Ball manipulation

Additional focus: Turning

## Progressions/Adaptations

- Replace verbal commands with visual commands. The coach should hold up red, orange and green cones for the players to respond to. If these colours are not available, use any 3 colours but make sure that the players understand what each colour represents.
- Encourage the players to use different dribbling speeds (gears) while dribbling.

# 188 THE SOCCER COACH'S TOOLKIT

## ACTIVITY 67 AMERICAN PENALTY

**Level:** Basic

**Type of activity:** Opposed technical practice

**Number of participants:** 6

**Equipment required:** Soccer balls, cones and 1 goal

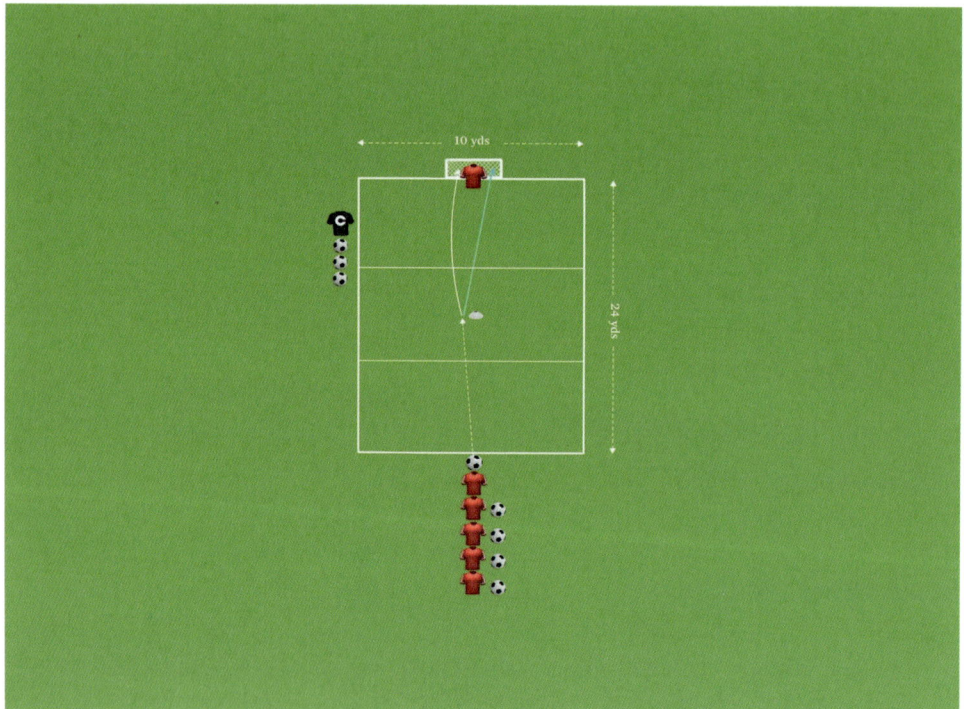

## Description

Divide players into a group of six. Mark out a playing area with three zones. Position a cone in the centre of the middle zone and a goal beyond one end zone. Position one player in goal. Position the remaining five players in a straight line with a ball each beyond the opposite end zone.

The activity starts when the player at the front of the line dribbles to the cone. When they reach the cone, they stop the ball and try to score with a shot past the goalkeeper. As soon as the player has taken their shot, the player in goal runs to the back of the line and the player that shot runs to the goal to act as the goalkeeper for the next shot.

The next player in line dribbles to the cone, stops the ball and tries to score with a shot past the goalkeeper. The activity is continuous for 5 minutes. Encourage the players to perform the activity at high intensity.

## Key focus/Coaching points

Primary focus: Dribbling

Secondary focus: Shooting

Additional focus: Goalkeeping

## Progressions/Adaptations

- Progress to an elimination game. If a player fails to score, they must save the next shot to stay in the game. If they fail to score and to save the next shot, they are eliminated. If a player scores with their shot they must still try to save the next shot, even though they cannot be eliminated in that round.

## ACTIVITY 68 FOUR-CORNER DRIBBLING

Level: Basic

Type of activity: Unopposed technical practice

Number of participants: 4-16

Equipment required: Soccer balls, cones, domes and 1 set of bibs

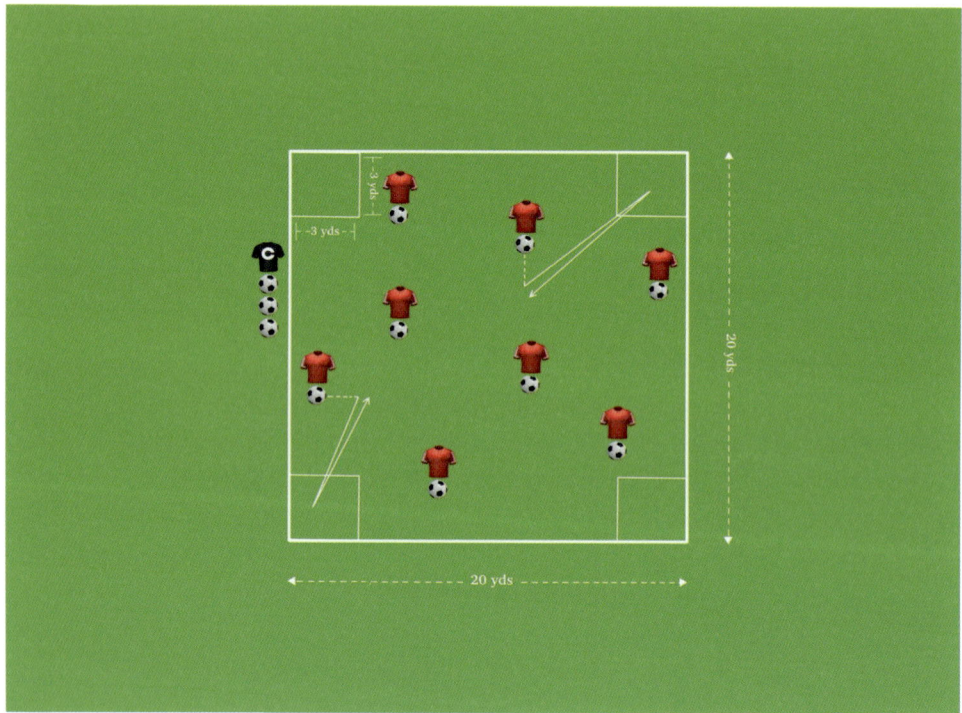

## Description

Players perform individually with a ball each. Mark out a playing area with a square in each corner. Position all players inside the playing area. Allow the players to dribble freely around the playing area for 1-2 minutes. On the coach's command, the players must leave their ball inside the playing area, sprint to any of four squares and then back to their ball. Once all the players are back with their ball, they carry on dribbling until the next command from the coach.

## Key focus/Coaching points

**Primary focus:** Dribbling

**Secondary focus:** Running with the ball

**Additional focus:** Speed

## Progressions/Adaptations

- The players must dribble their soccer balls to a square and then back into the playing area.

- The players stop, switch balls with another player, dribble to a square and then back into the playing area.

- Add 2-3 defenders inside the playing area. The defenders try to kick the balls out of the playing area. When a player loses possession of their ball, they become a defender. The last player in possession of their ball is the winner.

# 192 THE SOCCER COACH'S TOOLKIT

## ACTIVITY 69 DRIBBLE SLALOM

Level: Basic

Type of activity: Unopposed technical practice

Number of participants: 2-16

Equipment required: Soccer balls and cones

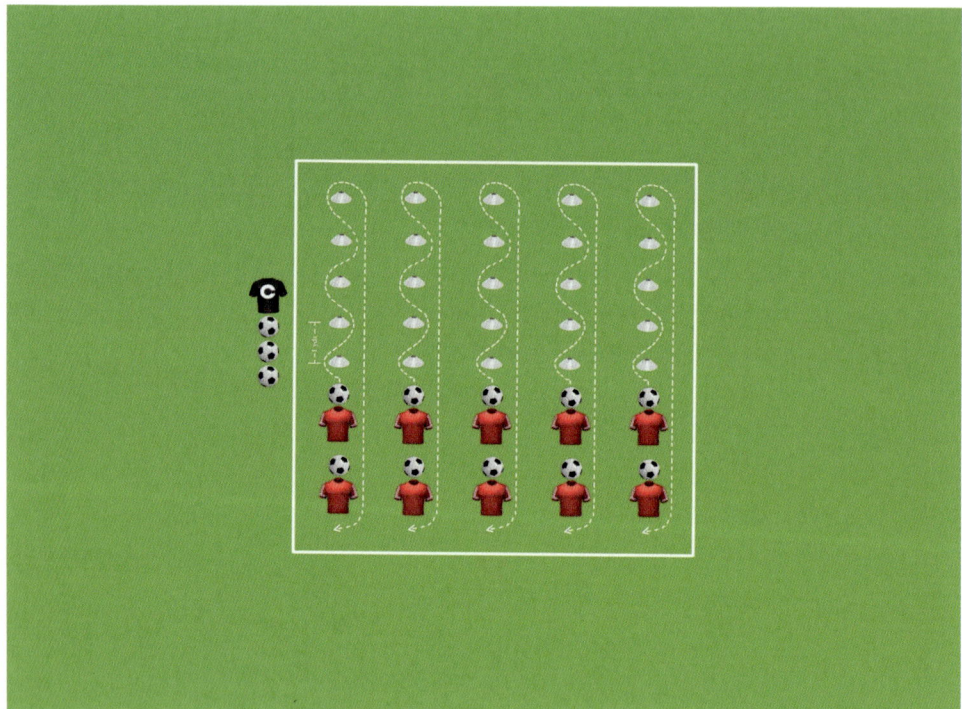

## Description

Divide players into pairs. Each player requires a ball. Position a line of five cones in front of each pair. The players take turns dribbling in and out of the cones. On the way back, the players dribble straight to, rather than in and out of, the cones.

Instruct the players to perform the dribbling styles and techniques for 1-2 minutes each:

- Left foot only.
- Right foot only.
- Outside then the inside of the right foot followed by the outside then the inside of the left foot.
- 2 touches with the outside of the right foot then 2 touches with the outside of the left foot.
- Alternate right and left foot step-overs at each cone.
- Double step-over at each cone.

## Key focus/Coaching points

**Primary focus:** Dribbling

**Secondary focus:** Ball manipulation

**Additional focus:** Coordination

## Progressions/Adaptations

- Players perform a skill challenge after each dribble, e.g., 5 keep-ups.
- Decrease the space between each cone.
- Encourage the players to gradually increase their dribbling speed and then make all pairs race against each other.

## ACTIVITY 70 VOLCANO

Level: Basic

Type of activity: Unopposed technical practice

Number of participants: 2-16

Equipment required: Soccer balls, cones and 2 sets of bibs

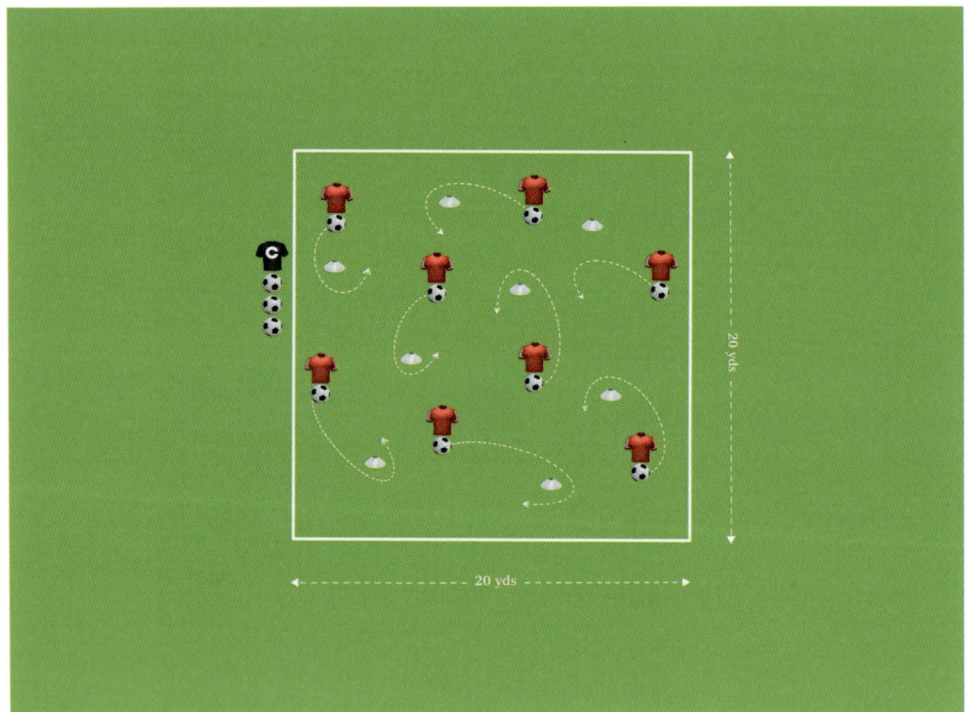

### Description

Players perform individually with a ball each. Position all players inside the playing area. Scatter cones inside the playing area (1 per player inside the playing area is a good amount). The players dribble around the playing area and avoid touching the cones with their soccer balls.

## Key focus/Coaching points

**Primary focus:** Dribbling

**Secondary focus:** Turning

**Additional focus:** Ball manipulation

## Progressions/Adaptations

- Players must perform a trick (e.g., step-over) or a turn (e.g., inside hook) every time they dribble past a cone.

- Add 2-3 defenders to pressurise the dribbling players. The defenders can kick any stray balls out of the playing area.

# 196 THE SOCCER COACH'S TOOLKIT

## ACTIVITY 71 COPYCAT

**Level:** Basic

**Type of activity:** Unopposed technical practice

**Number of participants:** 2-16

**Equipment required:** Soccer balls, cones and 2 sets of bibs

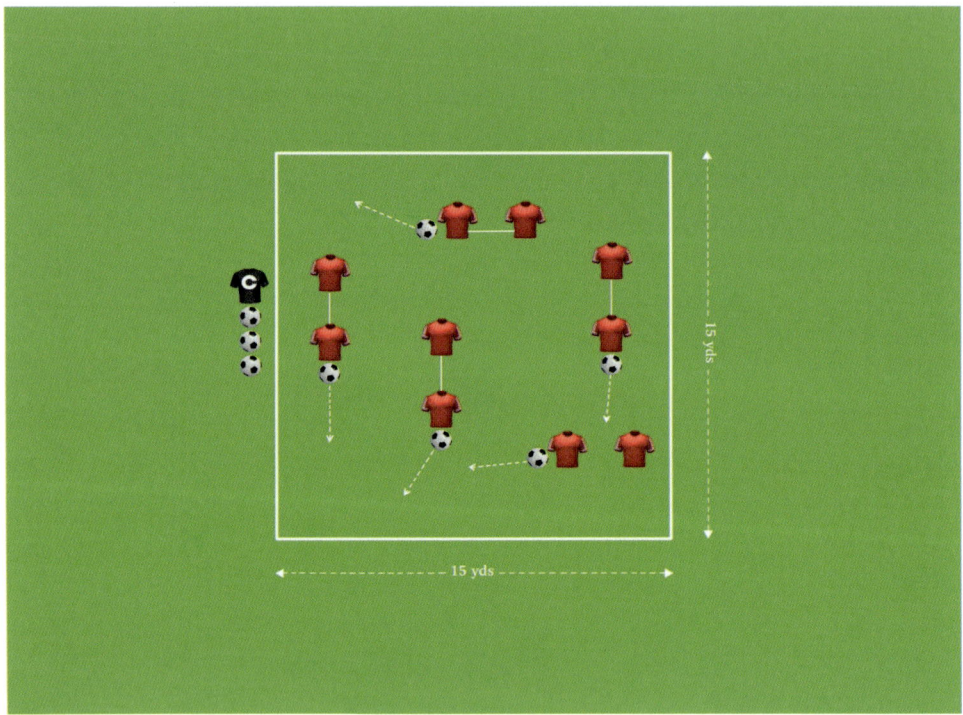

## Description

Divide players into pairs with 1 ball per pair. Position all players inside the playing area. In each group, nominate a lead player and a shadow player. The lead player starts the activity with the ball and dribbles around the playing area. The shadow player follows wherever the leader dribbles to. Encourage the lead player to change direction, vary the speed of dribbling and use different turns to change direction. Encourage the shadow player to keep as close as possible to the lead player. Switch roles every 30 seconds.

## Key focus/Coaching points

**Primary focus:** Dribbling

**Secondary focus:** Running with the ball

**Additional focus:** Turning

## Progressions/Adaptations

- Both players dribble a soccer ball.
- Make the activity more competitive. Ask the leader to get as far away from the shadow player as possible and the shadow player to stay as close to the leader as possible.

# 198 THE SOCCER COACH'S TOOLKIT

## ACTIVITY 72 MOVING TARGETS

**Level:** Intermediate

**Type of activity:** Opposed technical practice

**Number of participants:** 12

**Equipment required:** Soccer balls, cones and 2 sets of bibs

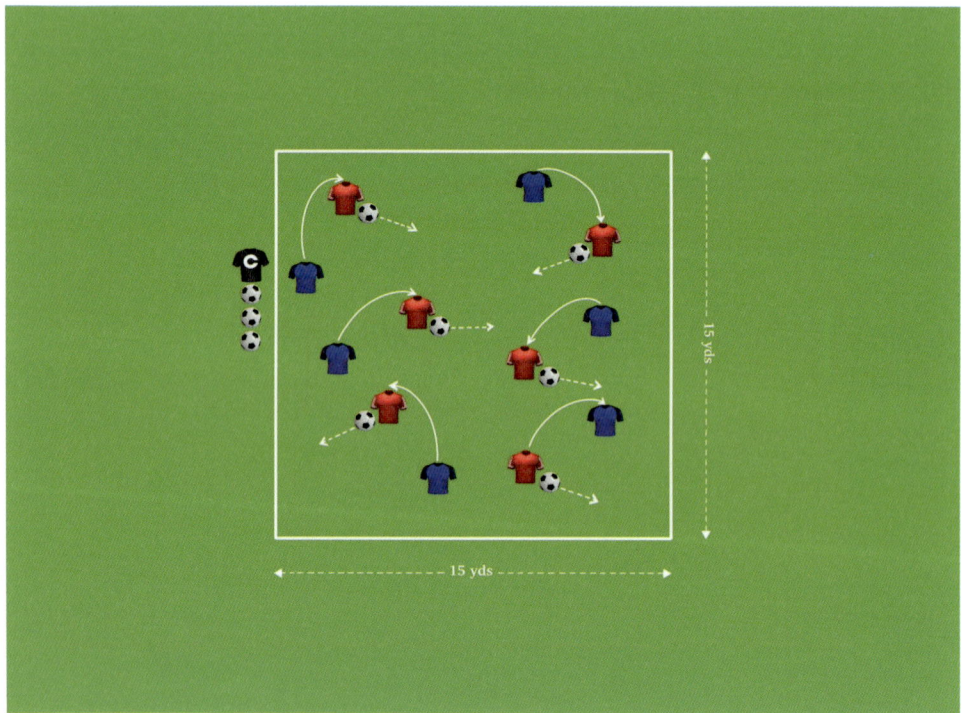

## Description

Divide players into two teams of six. Position all players inside a small playing area. Organise one team with one ball per player and the other team without soccer balls. The team without soccer balls jogs around the playing area and tries to tag the players with soccer balls. The players with soccer balls try to dribble away from the players without soccer balls. When a player is tagged (1-2 hands placed on the upper body), they must stand still. When all players are tagged, the players swap roles.

## Key focus/Coaching points

**Primary focus:** Dribbling

**Secondary focus:** Running with the ball

**Additional focus:** Turning

## Progressions/Adaptations

- Condition the dribbling players to use different types of dribbling, e.g., weaker foot only.

- When a player has been tagged, they can be released by a teammate passing the ball through their legs.

# 200 THE SOCCER COACH'S TOOLKIT

## ACTIVITY 73 SHOW YOUR SKILLS

**Level:** Intermediate

**Type of activity:** Unopposed technical practice

**Number of participants:** 6

**Equipment required:** Soccer balls, cones and mannequins (if not available use domes)

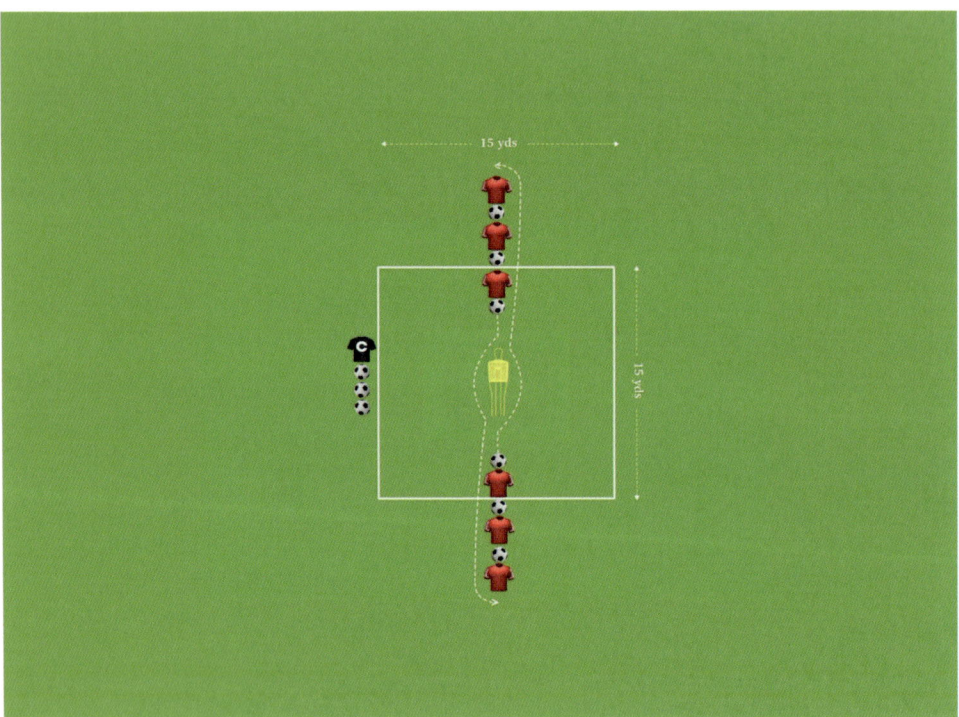

## Description

Divide players into two groups of three. Mark out a playing area with a mannequin in the middle. Position the groups in straight lines at opposite ends of the playing area. Both groups should be facing the mannequin. Each player requires a ball.

The first players in each line dribble up to and past the mannequin. Nominate which side the players dribble to before the activity starts, i.e., left or right. Once the players have dribbled past the mannequin, they continue their dribble to the back of the opposite line. It is important that the players dribble to the nominated side of the mannequin to prevent collisions.

## Key focus/Coaching points

**Primary focus:** Dribbling

**Secondary focus:** Running with the ball

**Additional focus:** Ball manipulation

## Progressions/Adaptations

- Players must dribble past the mannequin with a trick or 1v1 move: **step-over, 2-touch (inside/outside of foot), sidestep or the players can use their own trick or 1v1 move.**

# 202 THE SOCCER COACH'S TOOLKIT

## ACTIVITY 74 DRIBBLE FROM DANGER

**Level:** Intermediate

**Type of activity:** Opposed technical practice

**Number of participants:** 10

**Equipment required:** Soccer balls, cones and 2 sets of bibs

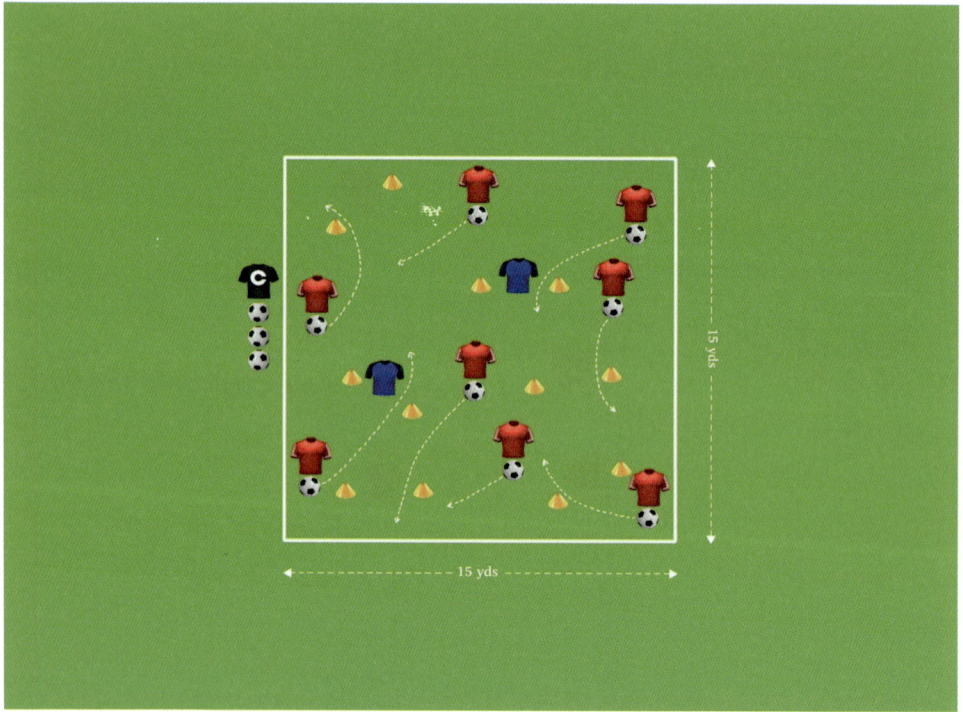

## Description

Divide players into a group of eight and a group of two defenders. The group of eight players requires a ball each. Mark out a playing area with six gates scattered around the inside. Position all players inside the playing area. The players with soccer balls dribble inside the playing area and try to score points by dribbling through the gates.

Each time that a player dribbles through a gate, they score 1 point. Set a time limit of 60 seconds for the players to score as many points as they can. The defenders move around the playing area and try to tag the dribbling players (by placing 1-2 hands on their upper body). If a defender tags a player with a ball, the player loses all their points. Rotate the defenders every 60 seconds.

## Key focus/Coaching points

Primary focus: Dribbling

Secondary focus: Turning

Additional focus: Shielding

## Progressions/Adaptations

- Decrease the number of gates.
- Increase the number of defenders.

## ACTIVITY 75 THROUGH THE GATE

**Level:** Intermediate

**Type of activity:** Unopposed technical practice

**Number of participants:** 12

**Equipment required:** Soccer balls, cones and 2 sets of bibs

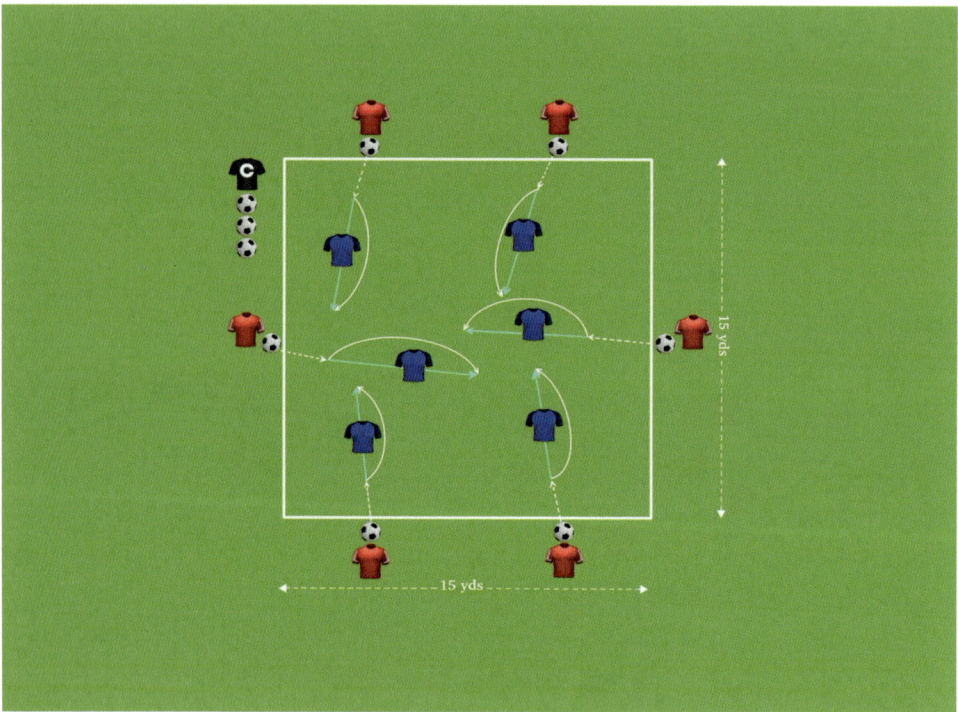

### Description

Divide the players into two groups of six. Position one group around the outside of the playing area. Each player in this group requires a ball. Position the other group inside the playing area. The players in this group do not require a ball and should stand with their legs shoulder-width apart. During the activity, they should stand still.

The activity starts when the players outside the playing area dribble into the playing area. Once inside the playing area, they try to score points by passing their ball through the legs of the players in the other group. The passes should be gentle enough to receive the ball on the other side of the player. Each pass scores 1 point. After each pass, the player with the ball must dribble to and pass through the legs of a new player. Set a time limit of 60 seconds for the players to score as many points as they can.

## Key focus/Coaching points

Primary focus: Dribbling

Secondary focus: Turning

Additional focus: Speed

## Progressions/Adaptations

- After each pass, the player standing still must pick up the ball and gently feed it into the air. The other player must receive the ball before it bounces and then continue dribbling.
- Give the balls to the players inside the playing area. The players in possession of the ball should stand still with the ball at their feet. The other group moves around the playing area and tries to play as many 1-2 passes with available players. Each 1-2 pass is worth 1 point for the player without the ball. After each pass, the players without soccer balls move to a new player.

# 206  THE SOCCER COACH'S TOOLKIT

## ACTIVITY 76  DRIBBLING FAKES

**Level:** Intermediate

**Type of activity:** Unopposed technical practice

**Number of participants:** 12

**Equipment required:** Soccer balls, cones and 1 mannequin (domes or cones can be used instead of a mannequin)

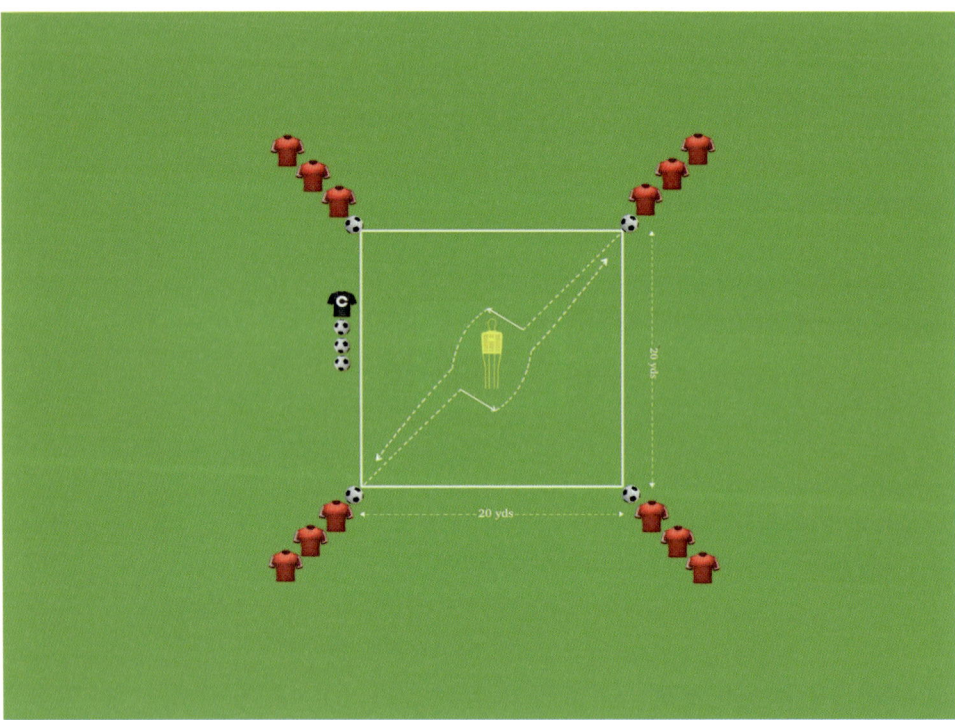

## Description

Divide players into four groups of three. Mark out a playing area with a mannequin in the middle. Position one group in each corner of the playing area. Position each group in a straight line and facing the middle of the playing area. The first player in each line should have a ball.

Nominate the first players in line from two opposite diagonal corners to start the activity. Both players dribble to the mannequin and perform a sidestep past it. Before the activity starts, inform the players which foot they should dribble with and which side they should perform the sidestep to, e.g., right foot dribble, feint to the left and sidestep to the right. This will prevent players from colliding as they pass the mannequin.

After the sidestep, the players continue their dribble to the opposite diagonal corner. When the players reach the corner, they stop the ball for the next player in line and run to the back of the line. The activity continues with the first players in line from the other two opposite diagonal corners. After 5 minutes, the players should switch feet and perform the dribbling and the trick with their other foot.

## Key focus/Coaching points

Primary focus: Dribbling

Secondary focus: Ball manipulation

Additional focus: Running with the ball

## Progressions/Adaptations

Work through the following progressions:

- Feint to the left, sidestep to the right with right foot after a right foot dribble.
- Feint to the right, sidestep to the left with left foot after a left foot dribble.
- 2-touch to the right after a right foot dribble (touch with the inside then the outside of the foot).
- 2-touch to the left after a left foot dribble (touch with the inside then the outside of the foot).
- Step-over to the right after a right foot dribble.
- Step-over to the left after a left foot dribble.

# 208 THE SOCCER COACH'S TOOLKIT

## ACTIVITY 77 THROUGH THE FOREST

**Level:** Intermediate

**Type of activity:** Unopposed technical practice

**Number of participants:** 6-12

**Equipment required:** Soccer balls, cones and 1 set of bibs

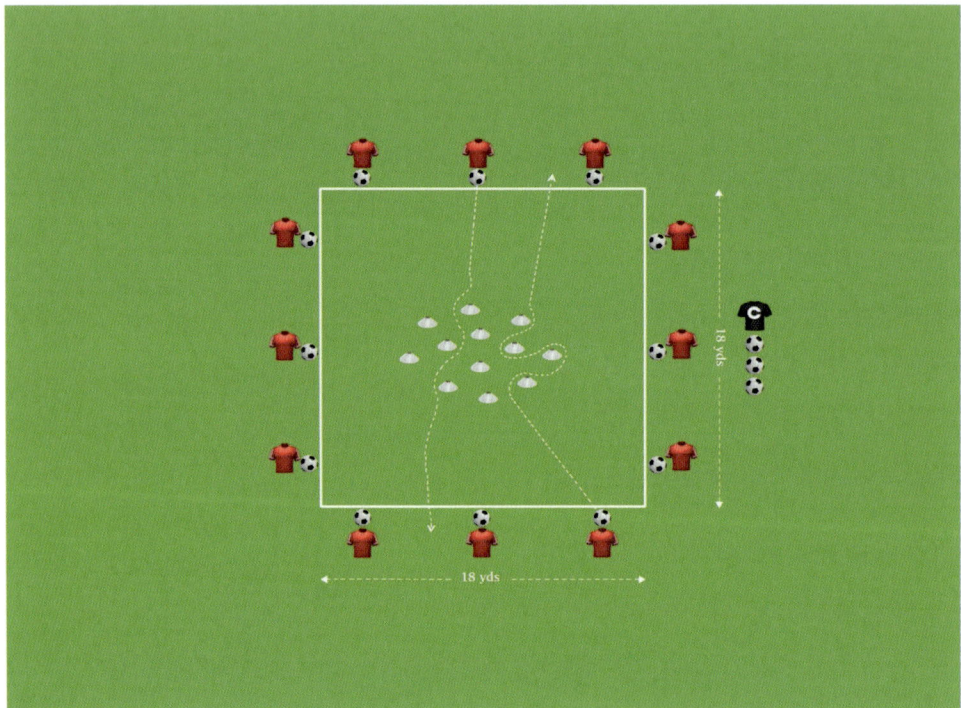

## Description

Players perform individually with a ball each. Mark out a playing area with 12-15 cones scattered around the centre of the playing area. Position the players around the outside of the playing area. The players have 60 seconds to dribble across the playing area as many times as they can.

The players must dribble through and around the cones and avoid touching them with their soccer balls. Each successful journey across the playing area scores 1 point. If a player loses control of their ball and it touches a cone, they lose all their points.

## Key focus/Coaching points

**Primary focus:** Dribbling

**Secondary focus:** Running with the ball

**Additional focus:** Turning

## Progressions/Adaptations

- Decrease the distance between the cones.
- Position 1-2 defenders inside the playing area to pressurise and tackle the dribbling players. If a player is tackled by a defender, they lose all their points.
- Increase the number of cones and the area they cover.

# 210 THE SOCCER COACH'S TOOLKIT

## ACTIVITY 78 EYES OPEN

**Level:** Intermediate

**Type of activity:** Unopposed technical practice

**Number of participants:** 12

**Equipment required:** Soccer balls and cones

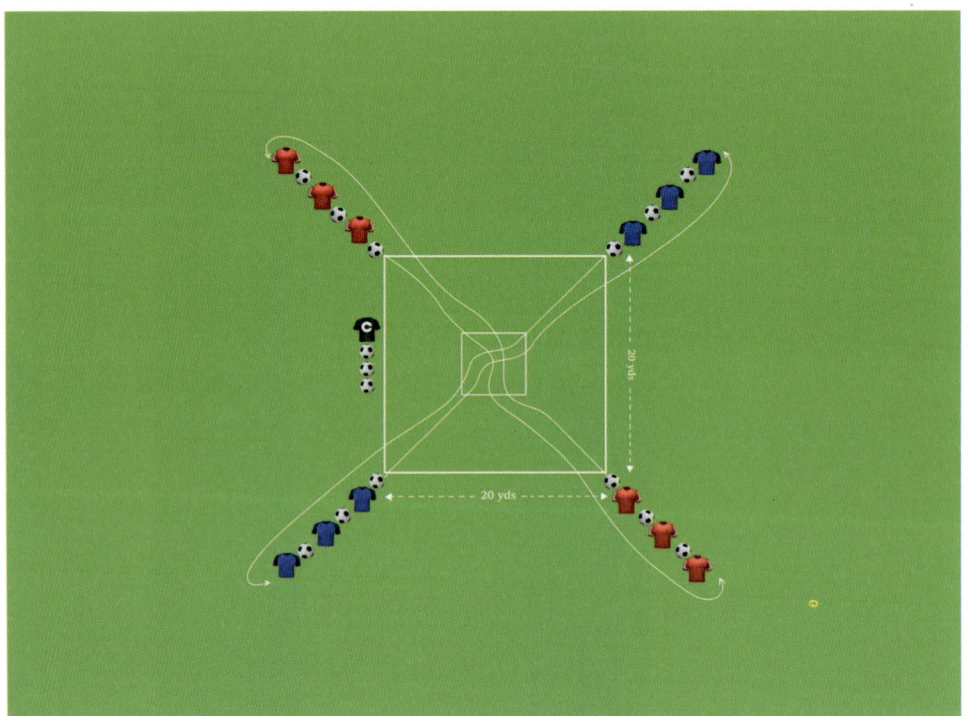

## Description

Divide players into four groups of three. Mark out a playing area with a square in the middle. Position one group of players in each corner of the playing area with a ball each. Organise the groups into straight lines and facing the square.

The activity starts when first player in each group dribbles into square. The players must keep their soccer balls under control and avoid each other while dribbling through the square. Once the players have dribbled through the square, they dribble to the back of the opposite diagonal line.

The next group of players continues the activity as soon as the previous group has reached the back of the opposite diagonal line. Encourage the players to keep the activity fast paced and work at a high intensity.

## Key focus/Coaching points

**Primary focus:** Dribbling

**Secondary focus:** Decision making

**Additional focus:** Turning

## Progressions/Adaptations

- Before dribbling out of the square, the players must perform 1-2 turns.
- After dribbling through the square, the players dribble can to any corner.

## ACTIVITY 79 1V1 DRIBBLING TO SCORE

**Level:** Advanced

**Type of activity:** Opposed technical practice

**Number of participants:** 8

**Equipment required:** Soccer balls, cones, domes and 2 sets of bibs

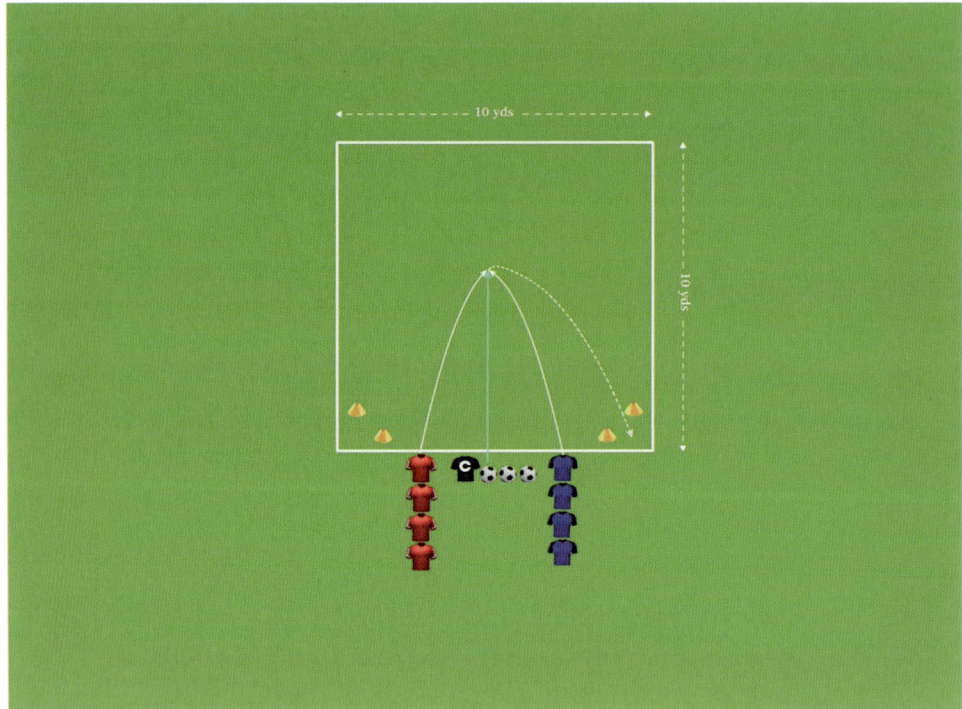

### Description

Divide players into two teams of four. Mark out a playing square with a gate in two of the corners. The gates should be positioned on the same line, i.e., not in diagonal corners. The coach should be positioned in between the gates with a supply of balls. Position the teams in straight lines and facing the playing area on either side of the coach.

The activity starts when the coach feeds a ball into the middle of the playing area. The first players in line from each team run into the playing area. The players compete for possession and try to score by dribbling the ball through either of the gates. Play continues until a goal is scored or the ball goes out of the playing area. When the 1v1 is over, both players join the back of their line. The activity continues with a feed into the playing area for the next player in line from both teams.

## Key focus/Coaching points

**Primary focus:** Dribbling

**Secondary focus:** Turning

**Additional focus:** Shielding

## Progressions/Adaptations

- Progress to a 2v2 inside the playing area.
- Change the position of the gates, e.g., opposite ends of the playing area.
- Increase/decrease the size of the gates.

# 214  THE SOCCER COACH'S TOOLKIT

## ACTIVITY 80 MINI-GOAL FACE-OFF

Level: Advanced

Type of activity: Opposed technical practice

Number of participants: 8

Equipment required: Soccer balls, cones, domes and 2 sets of bibs

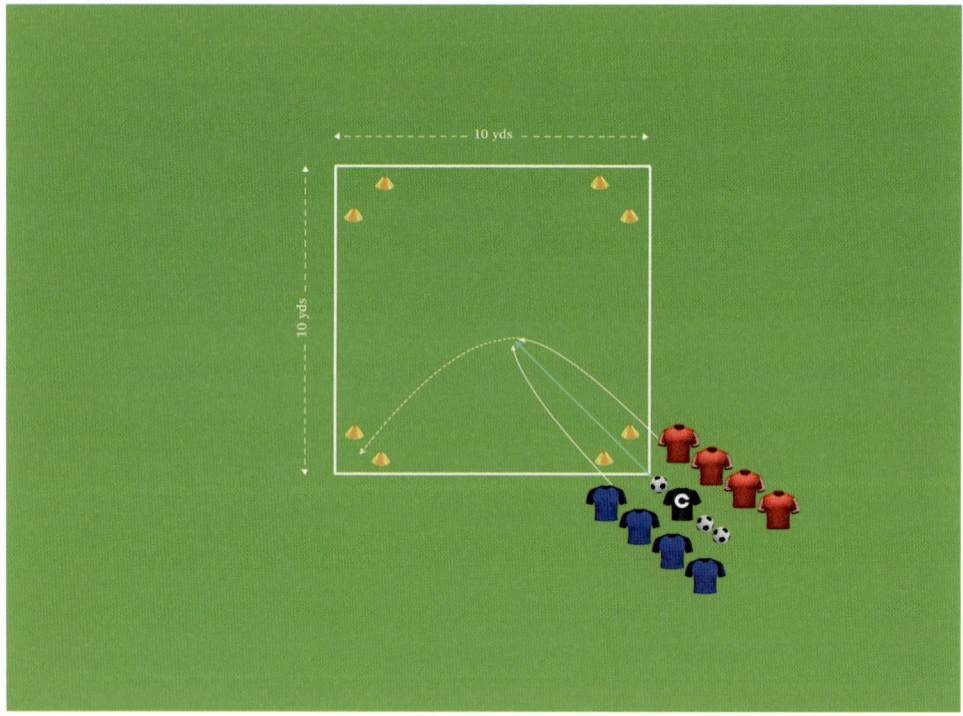

## Description

Divide the players into two groups of four. Mark out a playing area with four gates inside the playing area. The coach should be positioned in any corner of the playing area with a supply of balls. Position the teams in straight lines and facing the middle of the square on either side of the coach.

The activity starts when the coach feeds a ball into the playing area. The first player in line from both teams run into the playing area. The players compete for possession and try to dribble through any of the gates. The first player to score through one gate is the winner. Each 1v1 continues until a goal is scored or the ball goes out of the playing area. When the 1v1 is over, both players join the back of their line. The activity continues with a feed into the playing area for the next player in line from both teams.

## Key focus/Coaching points

Primary focus: Dribbling

Secondary focus: Turning

Additional focus: Attacking and defending

## Progressions/Adaptations

- Players must score through 2 gates.
- Progress to a 2v2 inside the playing area.

## ACTIVITY 81  GATE PATROL

**Level:** Advanced

**Type of activity:** Opposed technical practice

**Number of participants:** 14

**Equipment required:** Soccer balls, cones, domes and 2 sets of bibs

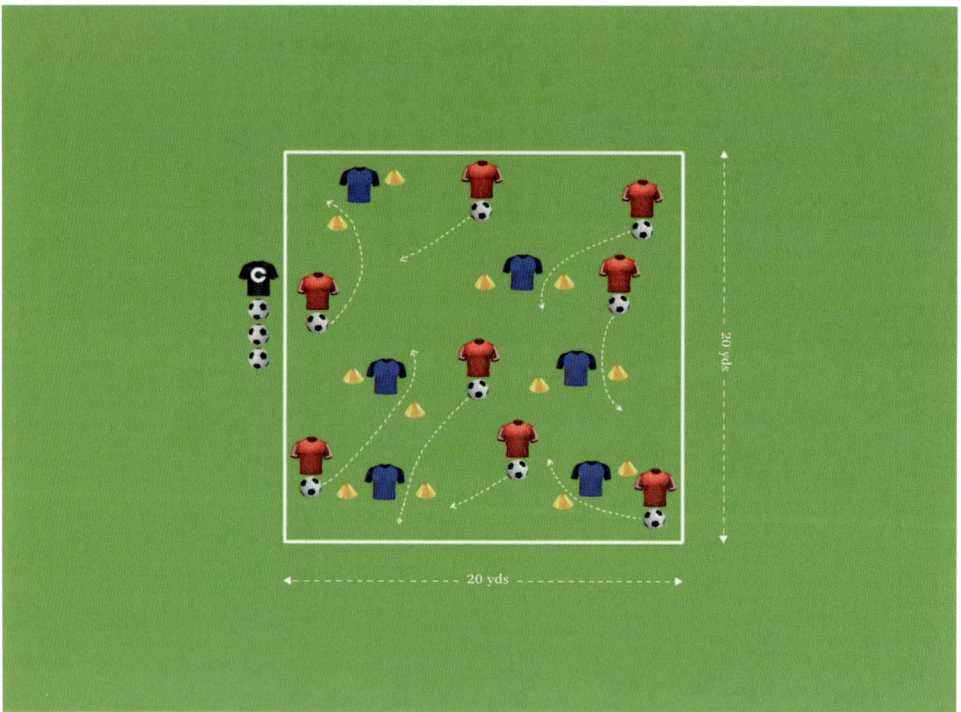

## Description

Divide players into a group of eight and a group of six defenders. Mark out a playing area with six large gates positioned inside. The group of eight players requires one ball each. Position 1 defender between each of the gates. The players with soccer balls have 60 seconds to dribble through as many gates as they can. After each successful dribble, they must try to dribble through a new gate.

The defenders try to tackle players as they approach/pass through the gates. Each time that a player dribbles through a gate, they score 1 point. If they are tackled by a defender, they lose all their points.

## Key focus/Coaching points

Primary focus: Dribbling

Secondary focus: Decision making

Additional focus: Turning

## Progressions/Adaptations

- The players with soccer balls must dribble through both sides of each gate to score 1 point.
- Allow the defenders to move away from their gates to tackle players. The defenders can move between gates and defend any gate they want to.

# 218 THE SOCCER COACH'S TOOLKIT

## ACTIVITY 82 PRISON BREAK

**Level:** Advanced

**Type of activity:** Opposed technical practice

**Number of participants:** 12

**Equipment required:** Soccer balls, cones, domes and 2 sets of bibs

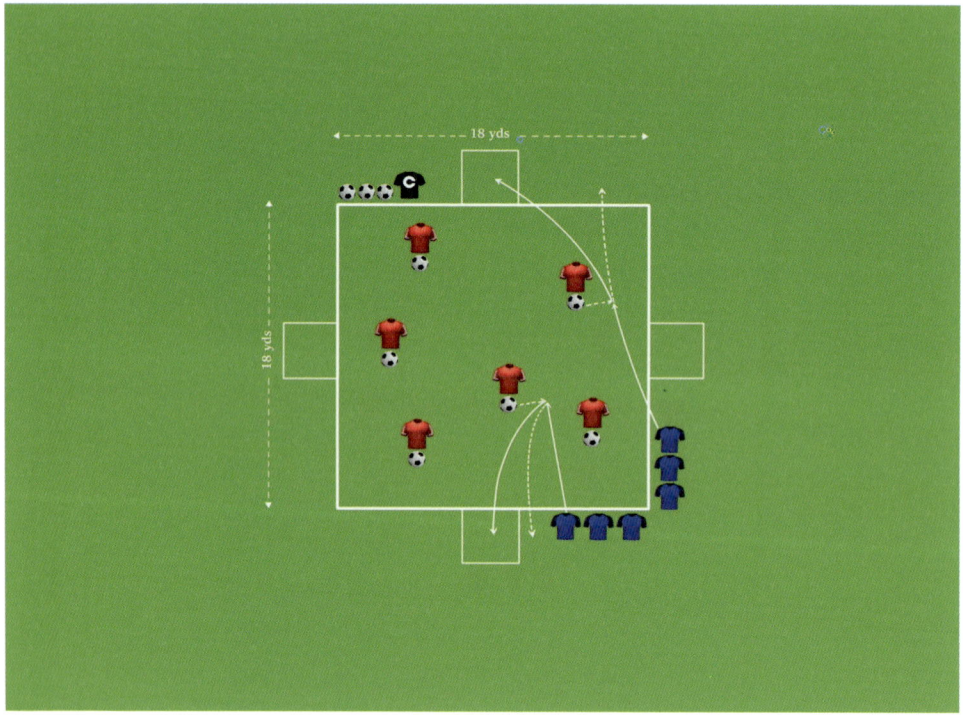

## Description

Divide players into one team of six and one team of six defenders. Mark out a small square in the centre of each of the playing area lines. Position the team of defenders outside the playing area. Position the other team inside the playing area with a ball per player. The players with soccer balls dribbles around the playing area. After 10-20 seconds of unopposed dribbling, the defending team enters the playing area and tries to win possession/tackle the dribbling players.

If any of the defenders manage to win possession of a ball, they must try to dribble it out of the playing area. If they manage to achieve this, the dribbling player must retrieve their ball and take it into the nearest square. When the players are inside the squares, they are frozen out of the activity. The players can be released from the squares if another player in their team can dribble into their square and tag them. The defending team attempt to get all the balls out of the playing area in the shortest time possible and get all the dribbling players inside the squares.

**Note:** Try to make sure that no more than two defenders attempt to tackle a player at the same time. If there are too many players competing for the same ball, the chances of collisions increase. Encourage sensible and safe play from the defending team.

## Key focus/Coaching points

Primary focus: Dribbling

Secondary focus: Turning

Additional focus: Shielding

## Progressions/Adaptations

- When a player loses their ball, they remain inside the playing area as a support player for their teammates. They must move around the playing area to create space for 1-2 passes to support teammates under pressure from the defenders.

# 220 THE SOCCER COACH'S TOOLKIT

## ACTIVITY 83 MESSI V RONALDO

Level: Advanced

Type of activity: Opposed technical practice

Number of participants: 2-16

Equipment required: Soccer balls, cones, domes and 2 sets of bibs

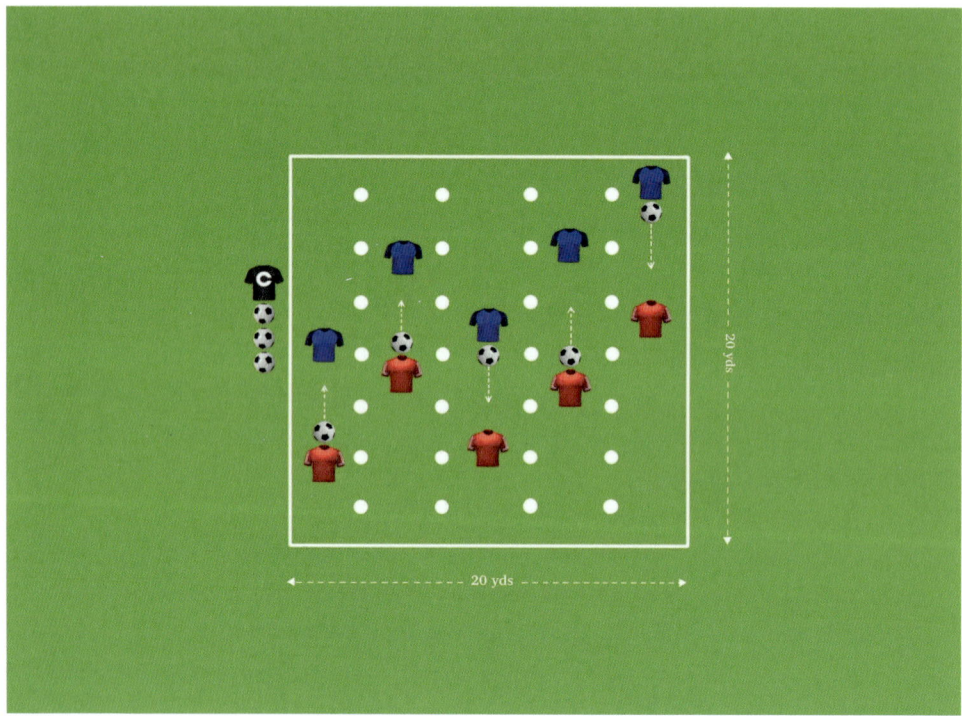

## Description

Divide players into pairs with one ball per group. Mark out a playing area divided into lanes. The lanes should be a suitable width for 1v1 contests. The pairs compete in 1v1 matches and try to score a goal by dribbling to and stopping the ball on their opponent's end line.

Condition the match so that one player has the task of dribbling in the style of **Lionel Messi (small touches, ball close to their feet and lots of changes of direction)** and the other player has the task of dribbling in the style of **Cristiano Ronaldo (bigger touches, greater distance between the ball and the feet and explosive changes of speed)**. After 2-3 minutes the players switch roles.

## Key focus/Coaching points

Primary focus: Dribbling

Secondary focus: Running with the ball

Additional focus: Attacking and defending

## Progressions/Adaptations

- Make the lanes bigger and divide players into 2v2 matches. Give each player a dribbling style, e.g., Messi and Messi v Ronaldo and Ronaldo, or Messi and Ronaldo v Messi and Ronaldo.

- Award a bonus point to any player or team that does the best job of impersonating Messi or Ronaldo.

# 222 THE SOCCER COACH'S TOOLKIT

## ACTIVITY 84 HUNTER GATES

**Level:** Advanced

**Type of activity:** Opposed technical practice

**Number of participants:** 12

**Equipment required:** Soccer balls, cones and 2 sets of bibs

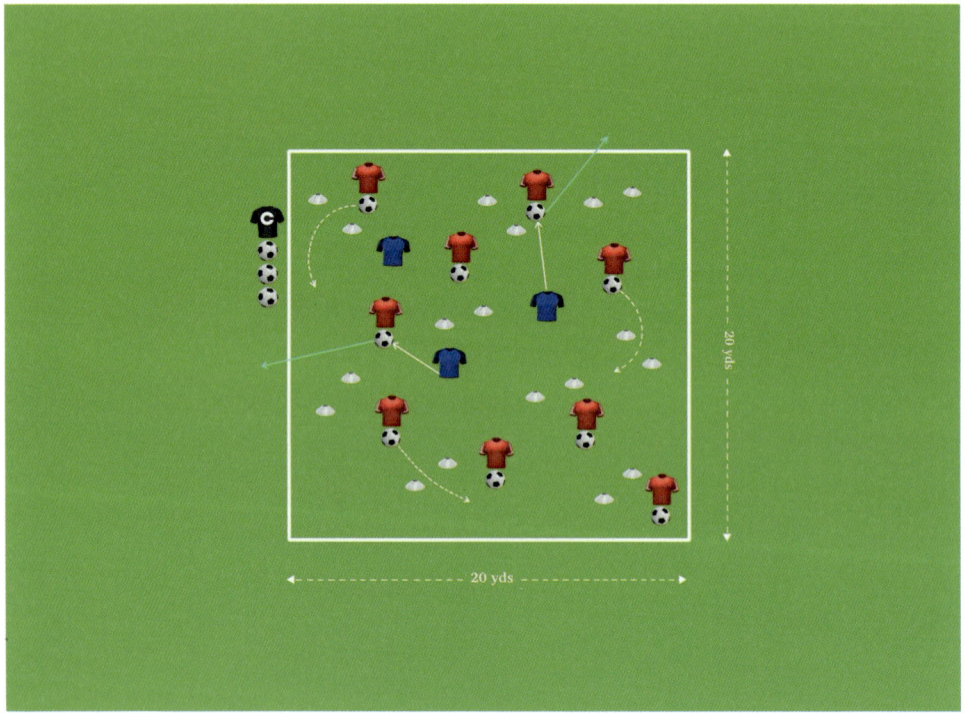

## Description

Divide players into a group of nine and a group of three defenders. Mark out a playing area with nine gates inside. The group of nine players requires one ball each. The players with soccer balls dribble around the playing area and try to score points by dribbling through the gates. The players score 1 point for each gate that they dribble through.

The defenders move around the playing area and try to stop the players from dribbling through the gates by tackling and kicking the balls out of the playing area. If a player with a ball has their ball kicked out of playing area, they must retrieve it and complete a challenge, e.g., 5 keep-ups. Set a time limit of 60 seconds for the players to score as many points as they can.

## Key focus/Coaching points

Primary focus: Dribbling

Secondary focus: Turning

Additional focus: Shielding

## Progressions/Adaptations

- Reduce the number of dribbling players and increase the number of defenders.
- Make the dribbling players perform a turn to travel through both sides of each gate.

## 224 THE SOCCER COACH'S TOOLKIT

# RUNNING WITH THE BALL

### ACTIVITY 85 END-TO-END STUFF

**Level:** Basic

**Type of activity:** Unopposed technical practice

**Number of participants:** 8

**Equipment required:** Soccer balls, cones and 2 sets of bibs

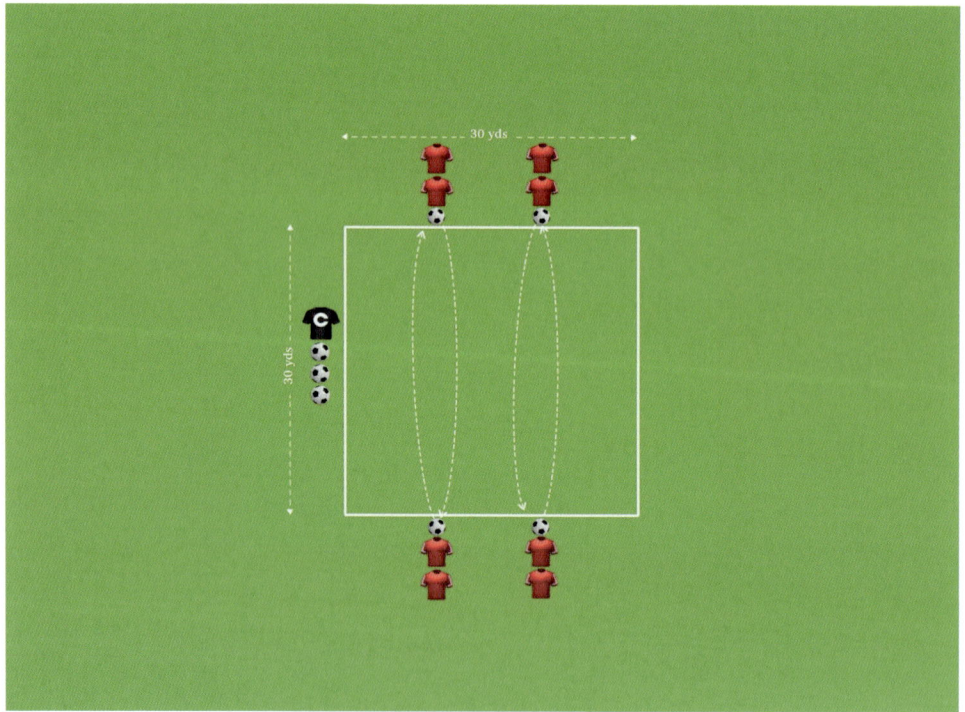

## Description

Divide players into two groups of four. Position the groups in straight lines and facing each other, 30 yards apart. Position a ball with a player at the front of either group. The player with the ball runs with it to the opposite end and stops it at the feet of the player

# Running With the Ball

at the front of the line. After stopping the ball, the player joins the back of the line. The activity continues with each player in turn running with the ball to the opposite end. The activity is continuous for 5 minutes and should be performed at high speed.

## Key focus/Coaching points

**Primary focus:** Running with the ball

**Secondary focus:** Speed

**Additional focus:** Ball manipulation

## Progressions/Adaptations

- The second player in line chases the player with the ball to the opposite end. The player with the ball should have a 5- to 10-yard head start.
- Players can only touch the ball 4 times before they reach the opposite end.

# 226 THE SOCCER COACH'S TOOLKIT

## ACTIVITY 86 CATCH UP

**Level:** Basic

**Type of activity:** Unopposed technical practice

**Number of participants:** 8

**Equipment required:** Soccer balls and cones

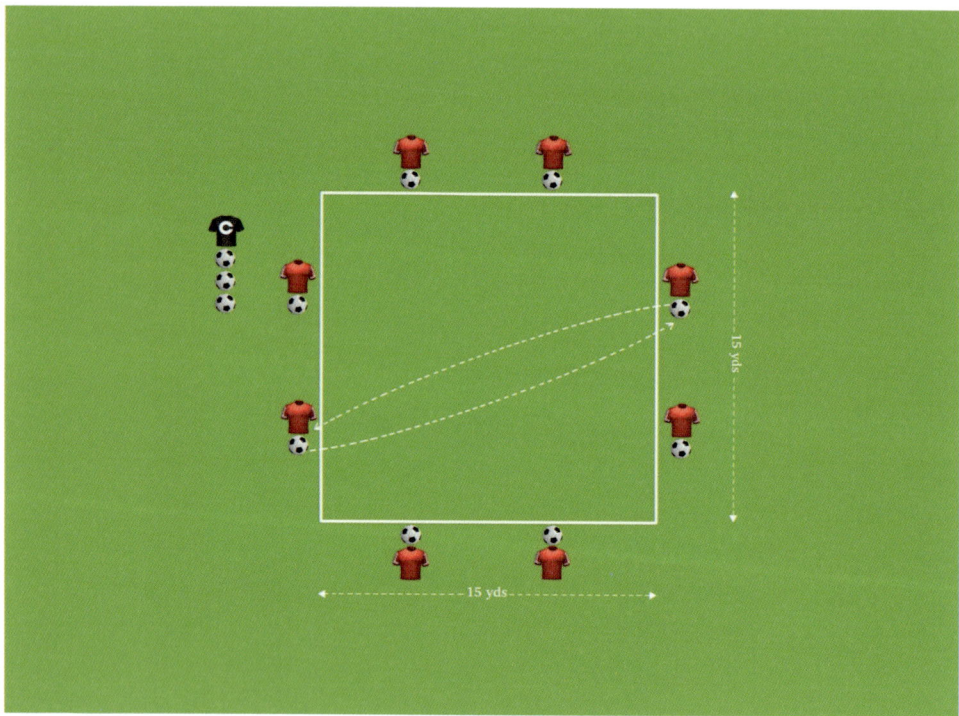

## Description

Divide players into a group of eight with one ball per player. Number the players 1-8 and position around them around the outside of the playing area. The activity starts when the coach calls out two numbers between 1-8. The players with the corresponding numbers run with their soccer balls across the playing area. It is a race to see which player can fill the position vacated by the other player first. As soon both players have reached their new position, the coach calls out another two numbers.

## Key focus/Coaching points

**Primary focus:** Running with the ball

**Secondary focus:** Speed

**Additional focus:** Turning

## Progressions/Adaptations

- Add obstacles in the centre of the playing area for players to dribble through/around.
- Players must race around the outside of the playing area and stop at the position vacated by the other player.

# 228 THE SOCCER COACH'S TOOLKIT

## ACTIVITY 87 CIRCLE RUNNING WITH THE BALL

**Level:** Basic

**Type of activity:** Unopposed technical practice

**Number of participants:** 8

**Equipment required:** Soccer balls and cones

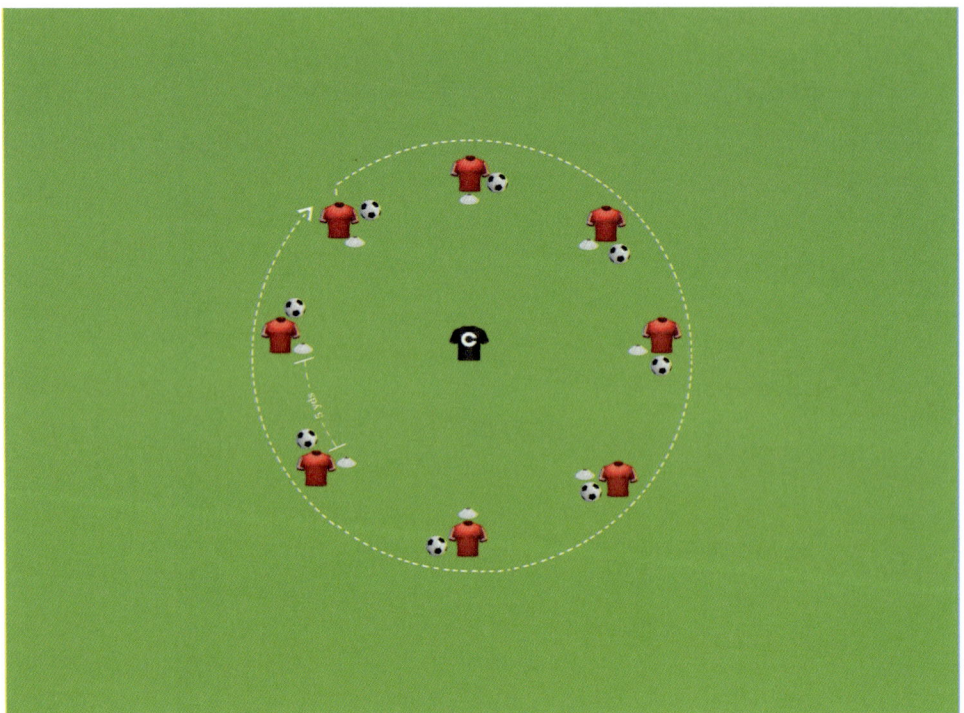

## Description

Divide players into a group of eight with one ball per player. Mark out a circular playing area using eight cones. Position one player on each cone. On the coach's command, the players run with their ball as fast as they can, clockwise around the playing area. Award 1 point to the first player to arrive back at their starting cone. After each lap of the playing area, allow 10 seconds recovery time before starting the next race.

## Key focus/Coaching points

**Primary focus:** Running with the ball

**Secondary focus:** Ball manipulation

**Additional focus:** Speed

## Progressions/Adaptations

- Add a skill challenge at each cone, e.g., 2 keep-ups.
- On the coach's command, the players must change direction and race clockwise around the playing area back to their starting position.

# 230 THE SOCCER COACH'S TOOLKIT

## ACTIVITY 88  ROBIN HOOD

**Level:** Basic

**Type of activity:** Unopposed technical practice

**Number of participants:** 12

**Equipment required:** Soccer balls, cones and 4 sets of bibs

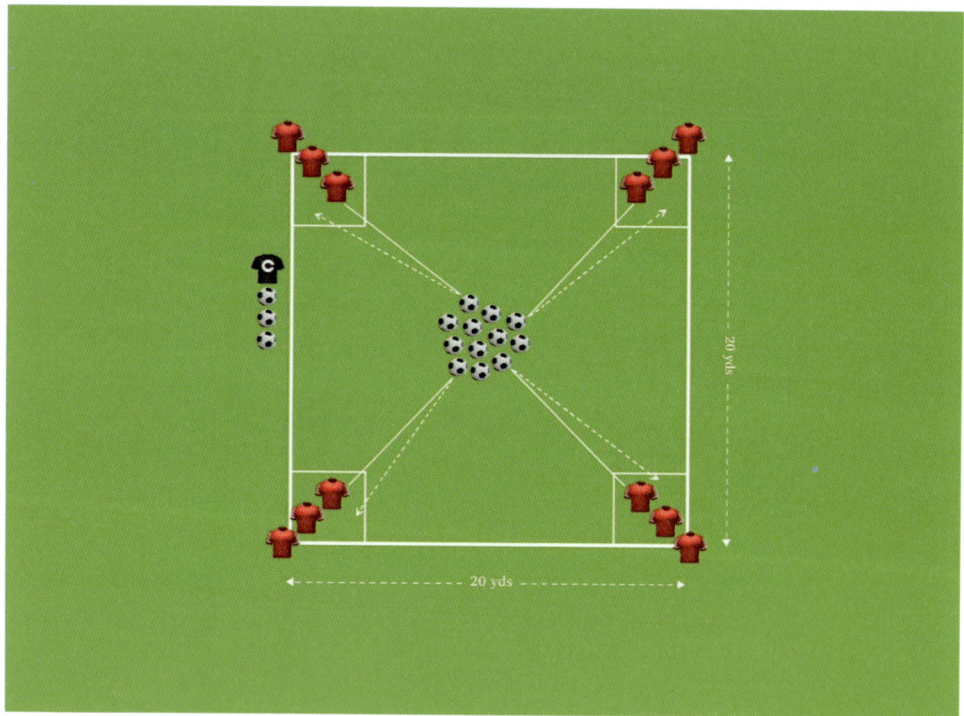

## Description

Divide players into four groups of three. Mark out a playing area with a square in each corner. Position all the balls in the middle of the playing area. Position one group of players in each square. Organise the players into straight lines and facing the balls.

The activity starts when the first player from each group runs into the middle of the playing area, collects one ball and runs with it back to their square. Once the ball is inside the square, the player runs to the back of their line and the player at the front of the line repeats the task. When all the balls are out of the middle of the playing area, the team with the most soccer balls inside their square is the winning team.

If any ball goes out of the playing area, it cannot be retrieved and must remain outside the playing area for the remainder of the activity. Encourage the players to run fast but to maintain good control over the ball.

## Key focus/Coaching points

Primary focus: Running with the ball

Secondary focus: Speed

Additional focus: Movement

## Progressions/Adaptations

- Players must complete 3 keep-ups before running with the ball back to their square.
- Once all the balls are out of the middle of the playing area, the groups can take balls from each other. All players can move at the same time but can only take 1 ball at a time from another team. Players are not allowed to stay in their home square and protect their team's supply of balls. Set a time limit of 60 seconds.

## ACTIVITY 89  WHAT'S THE TIME, COACH?

**Level:** Basic

**Type of activity:** Unopposed technical practice

**Number of participants:** 2-16

**Equipment required:** Soccer balls, cones and 1 set of bibs

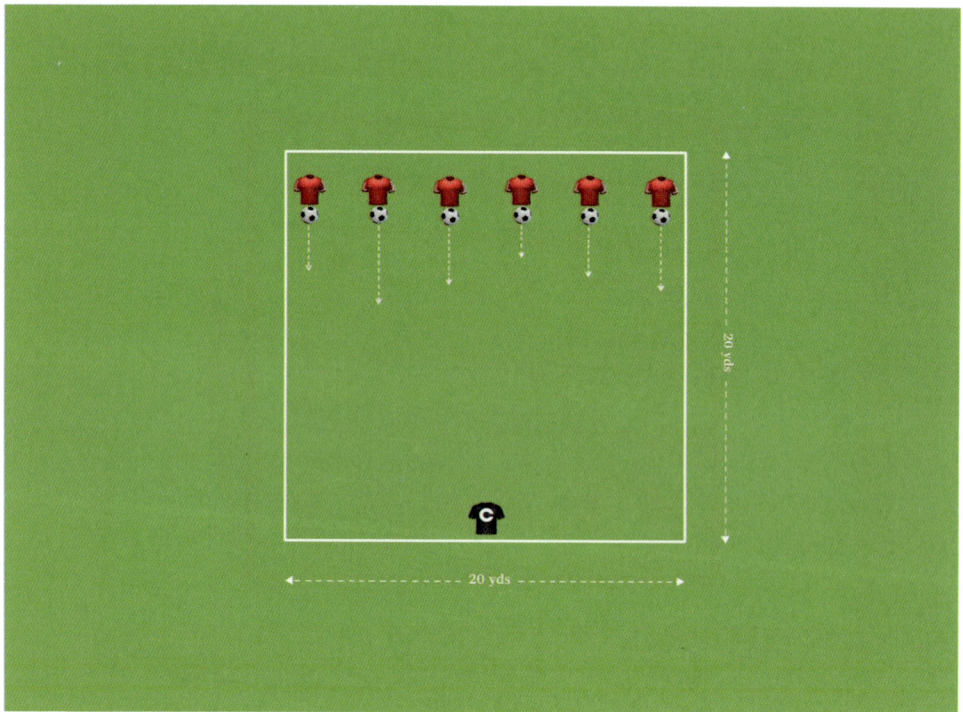

## Description

Position all players at one end of the playing area with a ball each. The coach should position themself at the opposite end of the playing area with their backs to the players. The activity starts when the players shout the question "What's the time, Coach?" The coach replies with the time, e.g., "4 o'clock" and proceeds to count aloud from 1 to 4.

The players take the corresponding number of touches forwards (e.g., 4) and then stop the ball with the sole of their foot. After calling out the final number, the coach quickly turns around to face the group. Any player whose ball is moving when the coach turns around is sent back to the players' end of the playing area. The first player to dribble their ball to and stop it on the coach's end line is the winner.

## Key focus/Coaching points

**Primary focus:** Running with the ball

**Secondary focus:** Dribbling

**Additional focus:** Ball manipulation

## Progressions/Adaptations

- Add a defender in the middle of the playing area to tackle players and knock balls back to their end of the playing area.

- Encourage the players to run with the ball using different foot surfaces, e.g., inside/outside of the foot.

# 234 THE SOCCER COACH'S TOOLKIT

## ACTIVITY 90 BALL RELAY

**Level:** Intermediate

**Type of activity:** Unopposed technical practice

**Number of participants:** 6-10

**Equipment required:** Soccer balls, cones and 2 sets of bibs

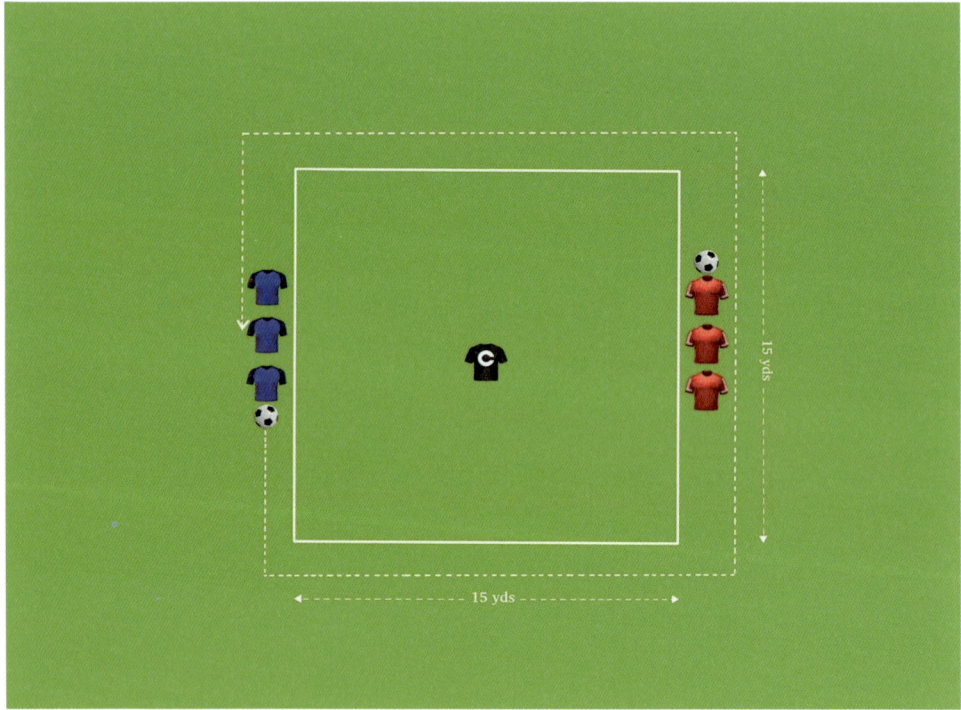

## Description

Divide players into two teams of three to five. Position the teams in straight lines opposite each other on the outside middle of the playing area. Each team requires one ball. Nominate one of the teams to race clockwise and the other to race anti-clockwise around the playing area.

# Running With the Ball

The first player in both teams runs with the ball once around the outside of the playing area as fast as they can. After completing one lap, the player stops the ball for the next player in their team to continue the race. The first team of players to complete one lap each is the winning team.

## Key focus/Coaching points

**Primary focus:** Running with the ball

**Secondary focus:** Speed

**Additional focus:** Ball manipulation

## Progressions/Adaptations

- This activity can be performed as a team relay or a series of individual races. If it is performed as individual races, number the players in both teams 1-3/5. The coach calls out a number and the corresponding player from each team races 1 lap with the ball. The winning player from each race scores 1 point for their team.

- Players complete a skill challenge at each corner of the playing area, e.g., 5 keep-ups.

- If group numbers are large, divide the players into 4 teams and position 1 team in each of the corner of the playing area.

# 236 THE SOCCER COACH'S TOOLKIT

## ACTIVITY 91 PREMIER LEAGUE

**Level:** Intermediate

**Type of activity:** Unopposed technical practice

**Number of participants:** 4-16

**Equipment required:** Soccer balls and cones

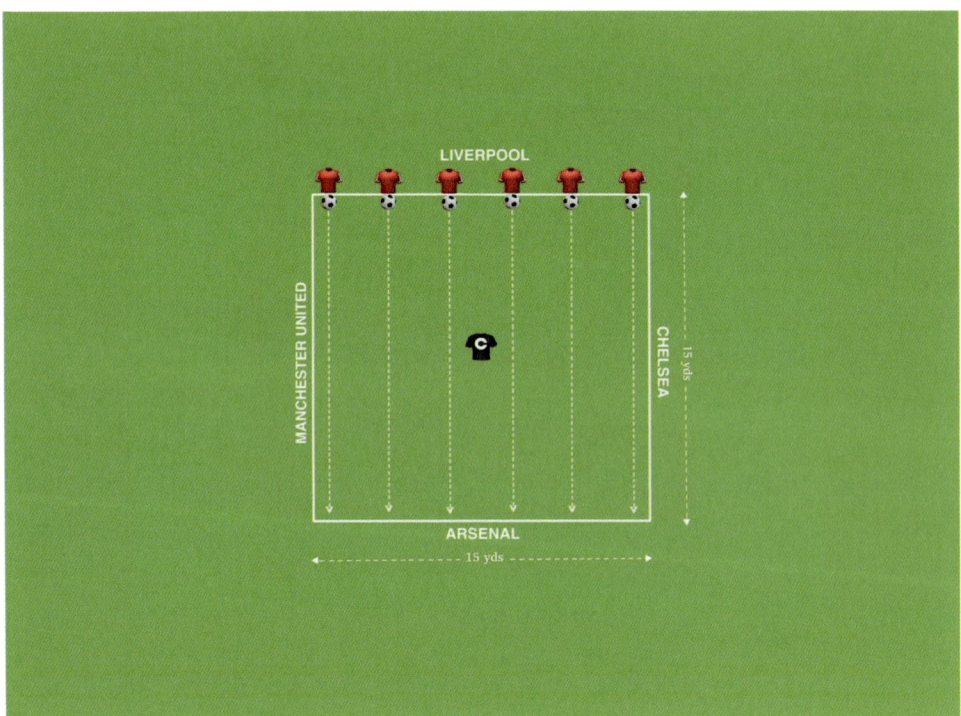

## Description

Players perform individually with a ball each. Position all players side-by-side at one end of the playing area. Before the activity starts, give each of the four playing area lines the name of a Premier League team, e.g., Arsenal, Chelsea, Liverpool and Manchester United.

The coach calls out the name of one of the teams. The players run with their soccer balls and stop on the corresponding line. The coach should call out each of the team names until the players have visited and memorised each line. After visiting each line, encourage the players to increase their speed on subsequent visits. After 5 minutes of practice, add the following features to the activity:

- Call out the name of the team that is currently at the bottom of the Premier League. The players must stop the ball with the sole of their foot wherever they are and sit down on their ball.
- Call out the name of a stylish and attacking Premier League team (a good current example is Manchester City). The players must stop the ball wherever they are and complete a challenge as quickly as they can, e.g., 3 step-overs.

## Key focus/Coaching points

**Primary focus:** Running with the ball

**Secondary focus:** Dribbling

**Additional focus:** Turning

## Progressions/Adaptations

- Call out the names of multiple teams so that the players must change direction as they run with the ball. Try to call out each team name when the players are at least halfway across the playing area.
- Progress to an elimination activity. The last 2 players to arrive at each line are eliminated from the activity. The eliminated players leave the playing area and must complete a skills challenge in order to re-enter the competition, e.g., 10 keep-ups. The last player to be eliminated from the activity is the winner.

## ACTIVITY 92 ROAD RUNNER

**Level:** Intermediate

**Type of activity:** Unopposed technical practice

**Number of participants:** 16

**Equipment required:** Soccer balls, cones and 2 sets of bibs

### Description

Divide players into 2 groups of 8. Position 1 group of players inside the playing area with a ball each. Position the other group of players around the outside of the playing area.

The activity starts when the players with soccer balls run with the ball to an available player on the outside of the playing area. When the players are 10 yards apart, the player with the ball passes to the available player. There will always be at least 1 player available for each player in possession.

The player that passed the ball follows their pass, runs around the back of the player they passed to and back onto the playing area. As they re-enter the playing area, the player with the ball returns the pass to them. After receiving the return pass, the players with the ball then run with the ball to a new available player and repeat the task. Rotate the players after 60 seconds.

## Key focus/Coaching points

**Primary focus:** Running with the ball

**Secondary focus:** Short passing

**Additional focus:** Turning

## Progressions/Adaptations

Condition how the players must run with the ball:
- Weaker foot only.
- Alternate foot touches.
- Big/small touches.

# 240 THE SOCCER COACH'S TOOLKIT

## ACTIVITY 93 RUNNING PARTNERS

**Level:** Intermediate

**Type of activity:** Unopposed technical practice

**Number of participants:** 16

**Equipment required:** Soccer balls and cones

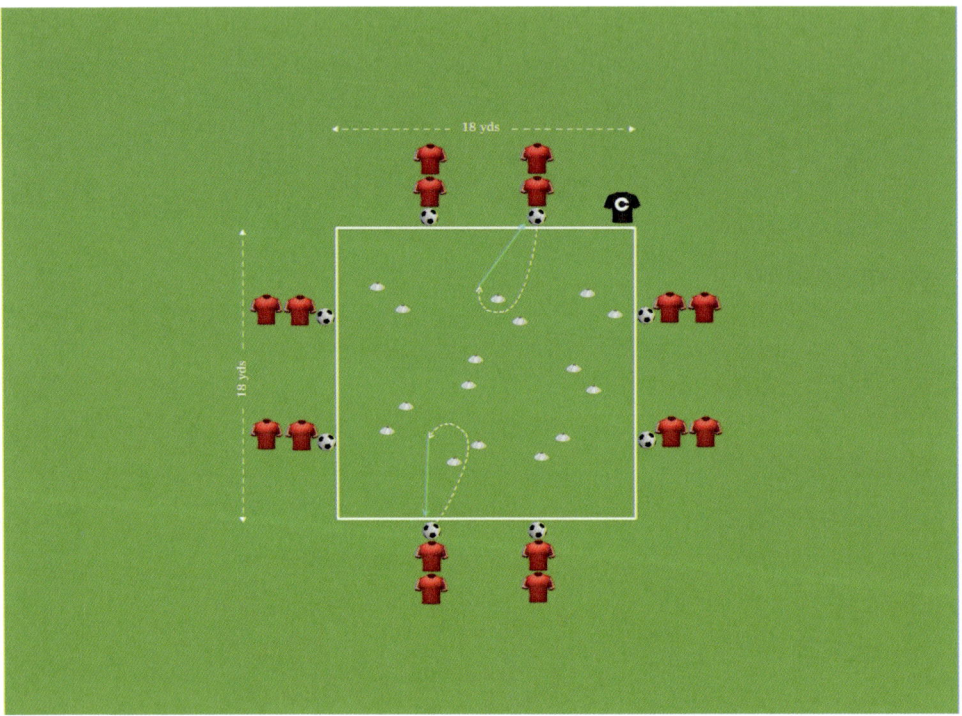

## Description

Divide players into eight pairs with one ball per pair. Position eight gates inside the playing area. The activity starts when one player from each pair runs with their ball into the playing area and through an available gate. After travelling through the gate, the player with the ball must turn and pass through the gate to their partner. After the pass, the players should follow their pass out of the playing area.

The players in each pair perform the task alternately and must travel through a new gate each time that they enter the playing area. Each time a player completes a travel through a gate and a pass to their partner, they score 1 point. Perform the activity for 60 seconds and see which pair scores the most points.

## Key focus/Coaching points

**Primary focus:** Running with the ball

**Secondary focus:** Turning

**Additional focus:** Short passing

## Progressions/Adaptations

Condition how the players must run with the ball:

- Weaker foot only.
- Alternate foot touches.
- Big/small touches.

# 242 THE SOCCER COACH'S TOOLKIT

## ACTIVITY 94 RUNNING WITH THE BALL (CIRCUIT)

Level: Intermediate

Type of activity: Opposed technical practice

Number of participants: 10-15

Equipment required: Soccer balls and equipment for each station:

Activity station 1: 4 agility poles or domes

Activity station 2: 5 agility poles or domes

Activity station 3: 4 cones

Activity station 4: 4-6 agility poles or domes

Activity station 5: 4 agility poles or domes

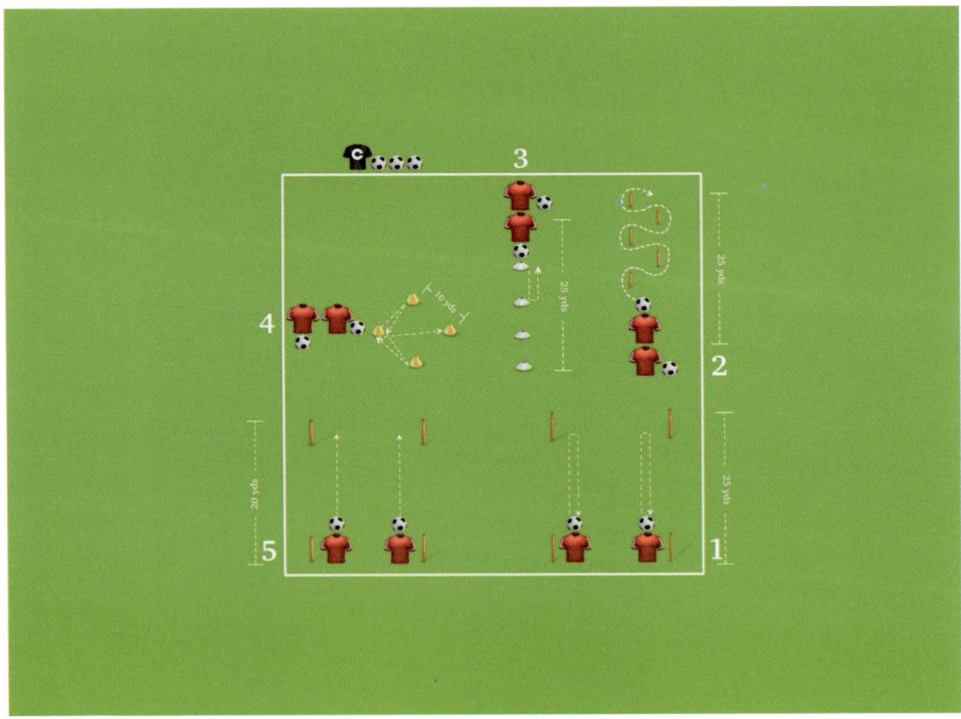

## Description

Divide players into groups of two to three. Mark out five activity stations (see below) and position one group per activity station. All players require a ball. The groups perform the task at each activity station for 1-2 minutes. After completing each station, the players should have 20-30 seconds of recovery time before moving onto the next activity station. When each group has completed all five activity stations, the circuit is complete.

- **Station 1** – 25-yard high-intensity straight line run with the ball followed by low-intensity run back to the start position.
- **Station 2** – 25-yard zigzag slalom run with the ball.
- **Station 3** – Shuttle runs with the ball (cone 1 to 2 and back, cone 1 to 3 and back, cone 1 to 4 and back).
- **Station 4** – Multi-directional run with the ball (forwards, backwards and sideways). The coach can position the cones in a variety of shapes to challenge the players.
- **Station 5** – The players race against each other, running with the ball over 20 yards. The first player to the finish is the winner. Players take turns giving the starting command for each race.

## Key focus/Coaching points

**Primary focus:** Running with the ball

**Secondary focus:** Ball manipulation

**Additional focus:** Agility

## Progressions/Adaptations

- Encourage different styles and techniques when running with the ball, e.g., bigger touches, alternate foot touches or weaker foot only.
- Vary the duration and intensity of each activity station depending on the fitness and physical conditioning of the players.

# 244 THE SOCCER COACH'S TOOLKIT

## ACTIVITY 95 ALL IN THE TIMING

**Level:** Advanced

**Type of activity:** Opposed technical practice

**Number of participants:** 10

**Equipment required:** Soccer balls, cones and 2 sets of bibs

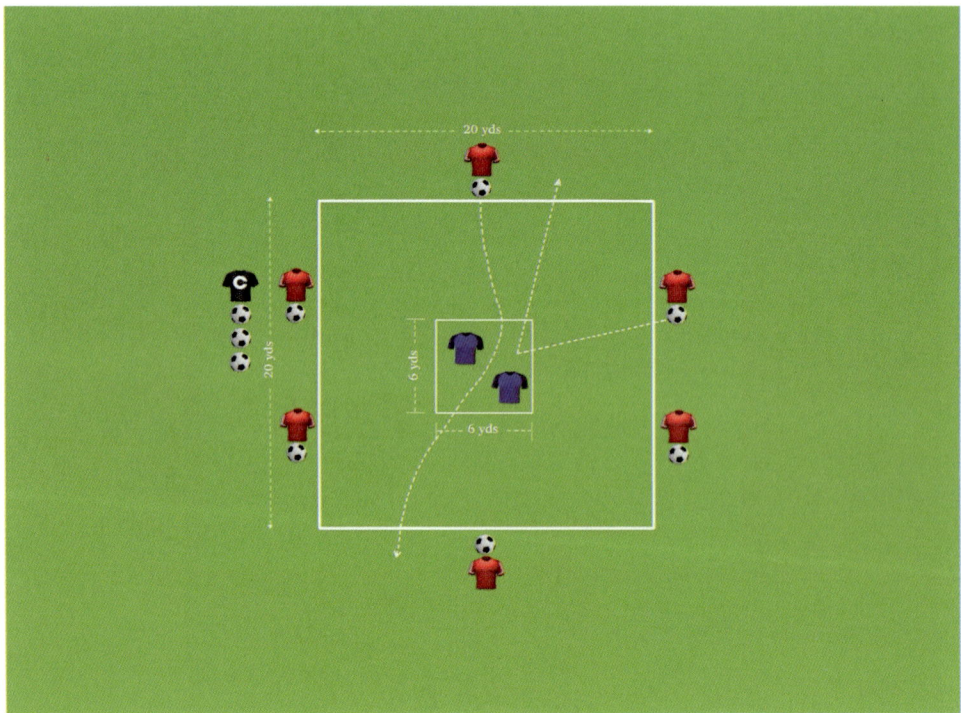

## Description

Divide players into one group of six and one group of two defenders. The players in the group of six require a ball each. Mark out a playing area with a small square in the middle. Position the two defenders inside the square and the group of six around the outside of the playing area.

The players on the outside of the playing area try to run with their ball through the square and out to any side of the playing area without being tackled by a defender. The players score 1 point if they manage to travel into the square and out through either side of the square and 3 points if they manage to travel through and to the opposite side of the playing area.

Set a time limit of 60 seconds for the players to score as many points as they can. If a player is tackled their score returns to zero.

## Key focus/Coaching points

**Primary focus:** Running with the ball

**Secondary focus:** Speed

**Additional focus:** Decision making

## Progressions/Adaptations

- Add a third defender into the square.
- Add a support player into the square. The players with soccer balls can play a 1-2 with the support player as they travel through the square.

# 246 THE SOCCER COACH'S TOOLKIT

## ACTIVITY 96 BREAK OUT

**Level:** Advanced

**Type of activity:** Opposed technical practice

**Number of participants:** 9

**Equipment required:** Soccer balls, cones and 2 sets of bibs

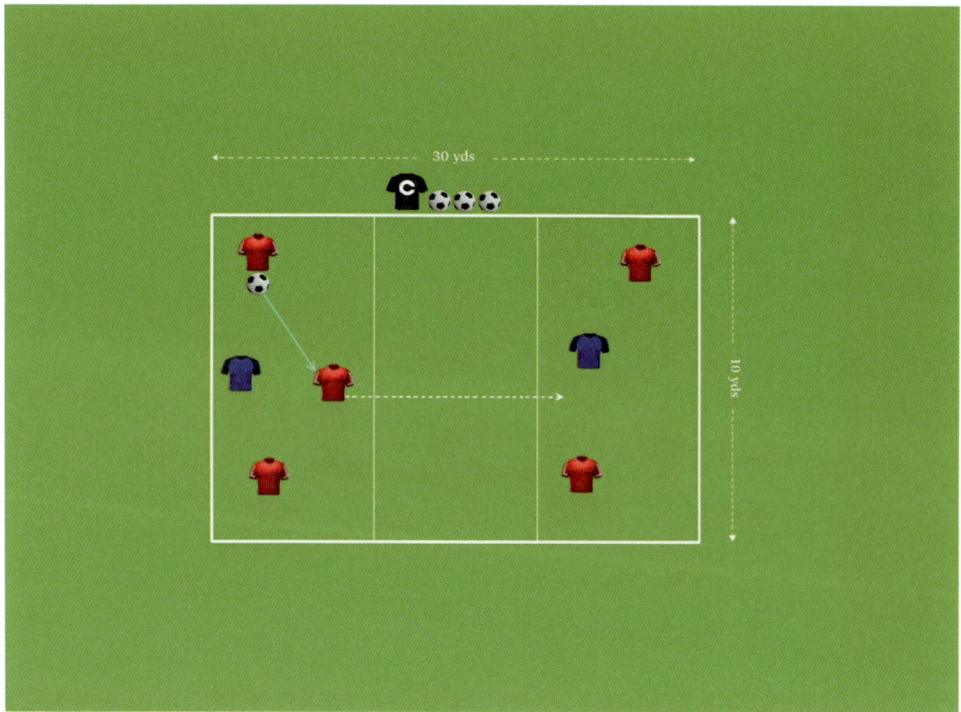

## Description

Divide players into a group of five attackers and a group of two defenders. Mark out a playing area divided into three zones. Position three attackers and one defender in one of the end zones and two attackers and one defender in the other end zone. The middle zone should be unoccupied. The group of three attackers should have one ball.

The activity starts with the three attackers trying to keep possession from the defender inside their zone. When an opportunity arises, an attacking player must run with the ball out of their zone, through the middle zone and into the opposite end zone to create three attackers v one defender. When this happens, the three attackers now in possession try to repeat the task and transfer the ball to the opposite end of the playing area. The activity continues from end to end.

## Key focus/Coaching points

Primary focus: Running with the ball

Secondary focus: Short passing

Additional focus: Speed

## Progressions/Adaptations

- Add 1 defender into the middle zone to challenge the player with the ball as they travel to the opposite end of the playing area.

- Add a second defender into the end zone where there are 2 attackers. The activity should start in the opposite end zone. When an opportunity arises, 2 attackers can travel out of the opposite end zone and through the middle to create a 4v2. When an opportunity arises, allow 2 attackers to travel out of this zone, through the middle zone and back to the original zone to create a 3v1. The activity continues from end to end.

# 248  THE SOCCER COACH'S TOOLKIT

## ACTIVITY 97  ACROSS THE SEA

**Level:** Advanced

**Type of activity:** Opposed technical practice

**Number of participants:** 13

**Equipment required:** Soccer balls, cones and 2 sets of bibs

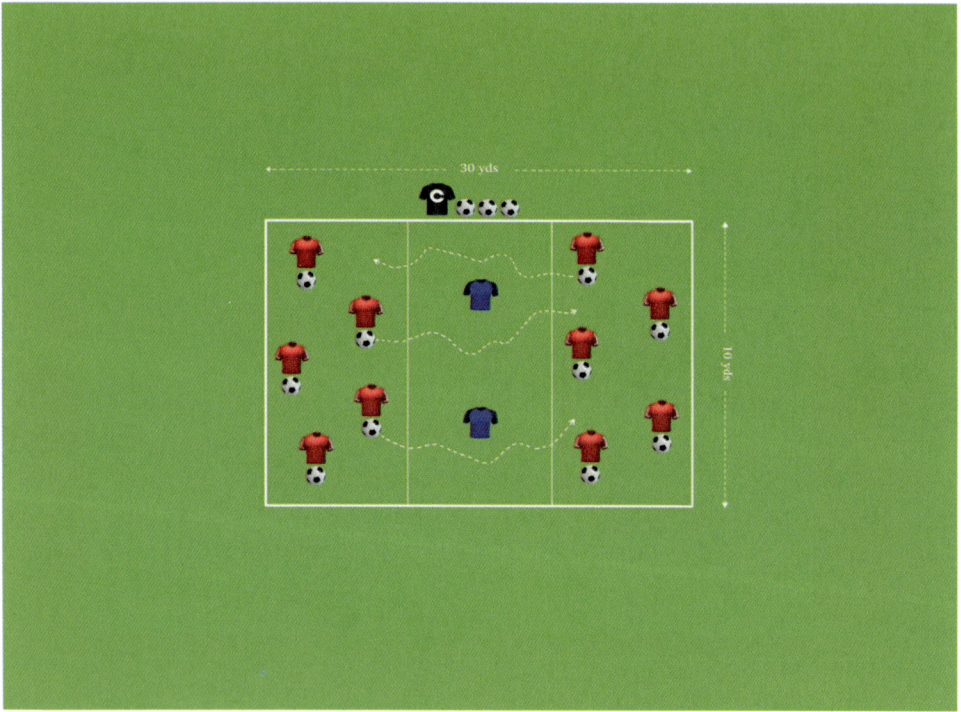

## Description

Divide players into two groups of five and a group of two defenders. The groups of five players require a ball each. Mark out a playing area and divide it into three zones. Position two defenders inside the middle zone and the groups of five players at opposite ends of the playing area.

The two groups simultaneously try to run with the ball through the middle zone to the opposite end of the playing area. The defenders try to tackle the players or force them out of the playing area. If a player loses possession of their ball, they swap roles with the player that lost their ball. The defenders can try to tackle any of the players as they pass through the middle zone.

## Key focus/Coaching points

**Primary focus:** Running with the ball

**Secondary focus:** Dribbling

**Additional focus:** Ball manipulation

## Progressions/Adaptations

- Decrease/increase the size of the middle zone.
- Add a third defender into the middle zone.

# 250 THE SOCCER COACH'S TOOLKIT

## ACTIVITY 98 ROADBLOCK

Level: Advanced

Type of activity: Opposed technical practice

Number of participants: 12

Equipment required: Soccer balls, cones and 2 set of bibs

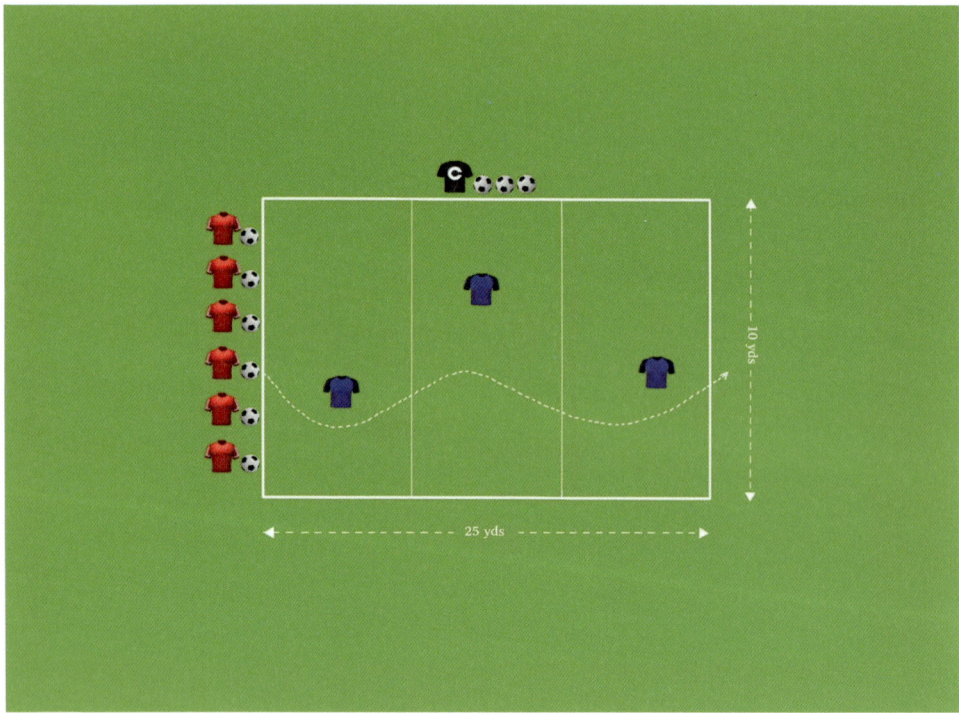

## Description

Divide players into one group of six and one group of three defenders. The group of six players require a ball each. Mark out a playing area divided into three zones. Position one defender in each zone. Position the players with soccer balls at one end of the playing area.

The players with soccer balls try to run with their ball through each zone to the opposite end of the playing area. In each zone, the defender tries to tackle the players with soccer balls or force them out of the playing area. When a player loses possession of their ball, they become a defender in the zone where they lost possession of their ball. The last player to lose possession of their ball is the winner.

## Key focus/Coaching points

**Primary focus:** Running with the ball

**Secondary focus:** Dribbling

**Additional focus:** Ball manipulation

## Progressions/Adaptations

- Position 2 defenders in each zone.
- Players work in pairs with 1 ball. As they travel through each zone, they must complete 2 passes before they can travel into the next zone.

# 252 THE SOCCER COACH'S TOOLKIT

## ACTIVITY 99 ON YOUR MARKS

**Level:** Advanced

**Type of activity:** Opposed technical practice

**Number of participants:** 8-10 + 1 goalkeeper

**Equipment required:** Soccer balls, cones, 2 sets of bibs and 1 goal

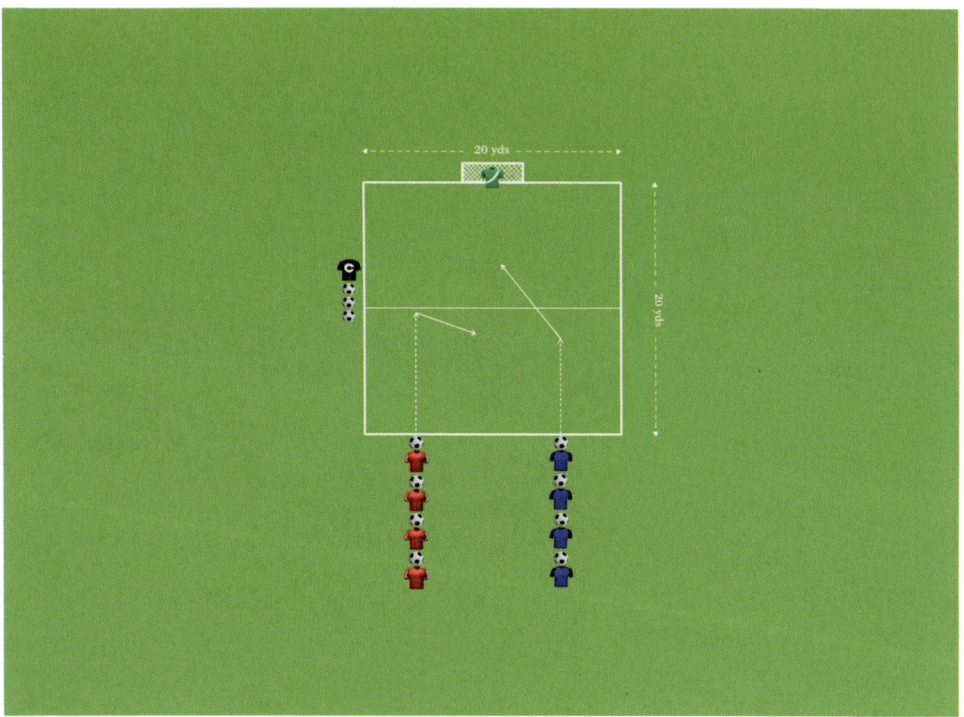

### Description

Divide players into two teams of four to five. Each player requires a ball. Divide the playing area into two zones. Position a goal and a goalkeeper at one end of the playing area. Position the teams side-by-side and in straight lines at the end of the playing area opposite the goal.

On the coach's command, the first player from both lines runs with their ball to the middle line of the playing area. The first player to reach the middle line becomes the attacker and keeps possession of their ball. The second player to the middle line becomes the defender and knocks their ball to the side of the playing area.

The defender backs off 10 yards towards the goal and faces the attacker. The attacker tries to dribble past the defender and score past the goalkeeper. The activity continues until a goal is scored, the defender wins the ball or the ball travels out of the playing area. When 1v1 is over, the two players run to the back of their lines and the next two players repeat the activity.

## Key focus/Coaching points

Primary focus: Running with the ball

Secondary focus: Dribbling

Additional focus: Attacking and defending

## Progressions/Adaptations

- Add a scoring system:
    - The first player to the middle line wins 1 point for their team.
    - If the attackers score a goal, they earn an additional 3 points for their team.
- If the defender wins the ball, they can then attack the goal and try to score. If the defender scores, they earn 2 points for their team.

# 254 THE SOCCER COACH'S TOOLKIT

# TURNING

## ACTIVITY 100  SKILL OF THE DAY

**Level:** Basic

**Type of activity:** Unopposed technical practice

**Number of participants:** 1-12

**Equipment required:** Soccer balls and cones

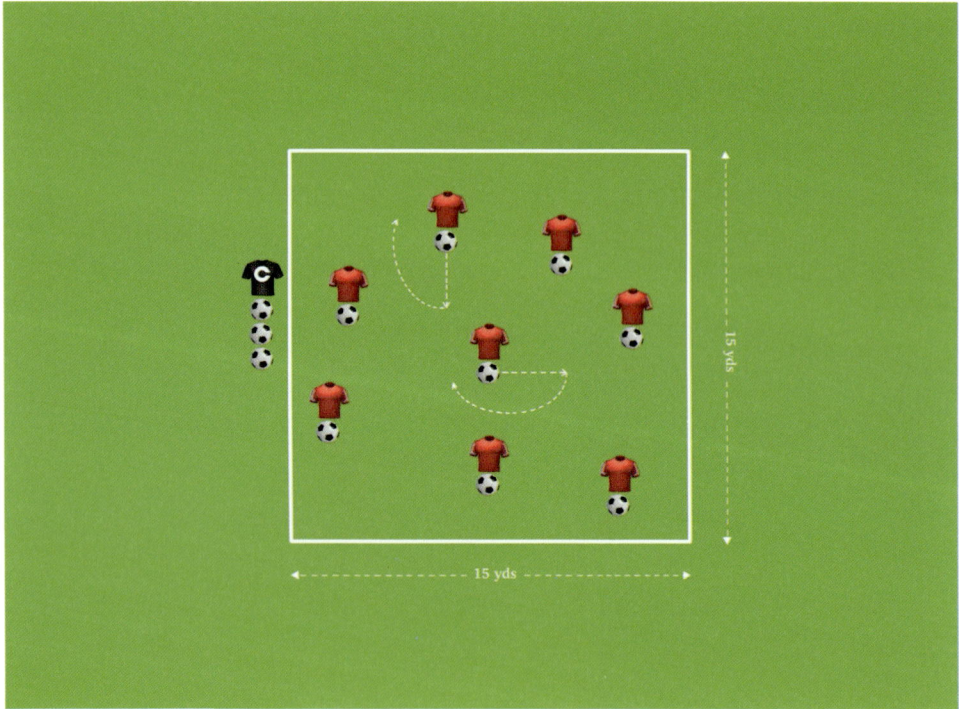

## Description

Players perform individually with a ball each. Position all players inside the playing area. The players dribble around inside the playing area, performing the following turns.

The coach should introduce the turns 1 at a time and allow the players 2-3 minutes to practice each turn:

- Inside and outside hook.
- Stop turn.
- Dragback.
- Cruyff turn.
- Ronaldo chop.
- Double dragback.
- Step-over.

## Key focus/Coaching points

**Primary focus:** Turning

**Secondary focus:** Ball manipulation

**Additional focus:** Dribbling

## Progressions/Adaptations

- Players create their own sequence of 2-4 turns.
- Freestyle – players have time to develop their own turns.
- Players use their weaker foot only.
- If the players are struggling to perform the turns with good technique, allow them to perform the turns standing still.

## ACTIVITY 101  TURNING AND RECEIVING

**Level:** Basic

**Type of activity:** Unopposed technical practice

**Number of participants:** 18

**Equipment required:** Soccer balls, cones and 2 sets of bibs

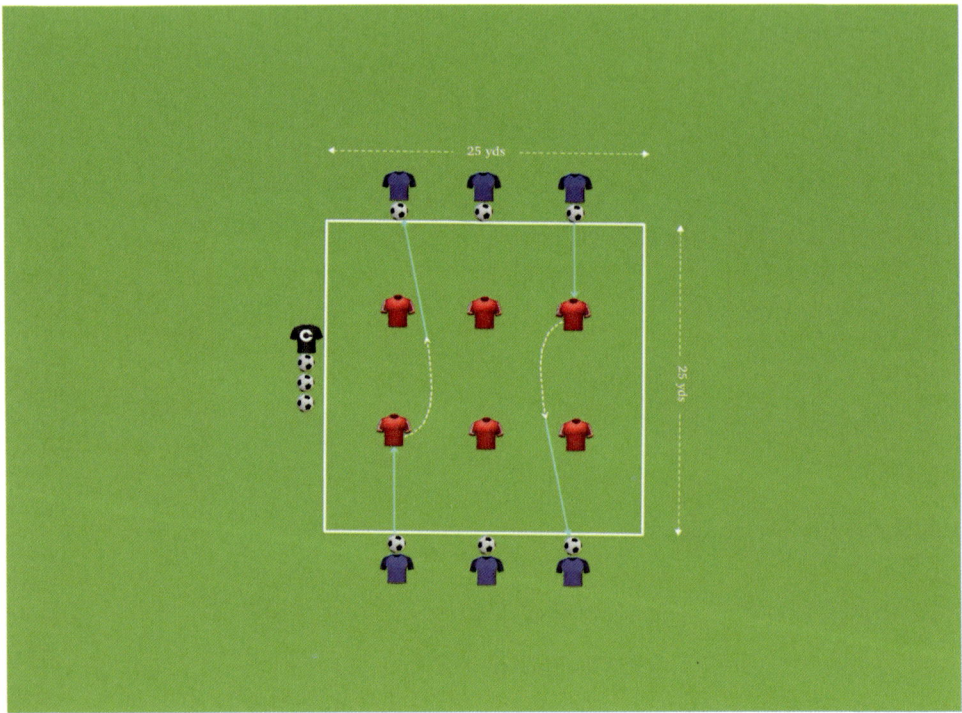

### Description

Divide players into two groups of six. Organise one group into two sets of three ball feeders. Position one set of ball feeders at opposite ends of the playing area with a ball each. Position the ball feeders 6-8 yards apart. Position the other group inside the playing area with each player opposite a ball feeder, i.e., three players opposite the ball feeders at both ends of the playing area. The distance between the players inside the playing area and the ball feeders should be 10-15 yards.

# Turning

The players inside the playing area receive a pass from the ball feeder opposite them. When they have received the pass, the players turn and dribble towards the ball feeder at the opposite end of the playing area. From 10-15 yards, the player passes the ball to the ball feeder. The players inside the playing area re-position themselves opposite the ball feeders and repeat the task to the opposite end of the playing area. Rotate the players after 2 minutes.

## Key focus/Coaching points

**Primary focus:** Turning

**Secondary focus:** Receiving

**Additional focus:** Short passing

## Progressions/Adaptations

- Add passive defenders to shadow the movements of the players inside the playing area.
- Condition the type of turn after each pass, e.g., inside-of-the-foot turn, outside-of-the-foot turn and 2-touch turn (inside and outside of the foot).

# 258 THE SOCCER COACH'S TOOLKIT

## ACTIVITY 102  TURNING AND SHOOTING

**Level:** Basic

**Type of activity:** Unopposed technical practice

**Number of participants:** 6 + 1 goalkeeper

**Equipment required:** Soccer balls, cones, 1 mannequin (agility pole can be used instead) and 1 goal per group

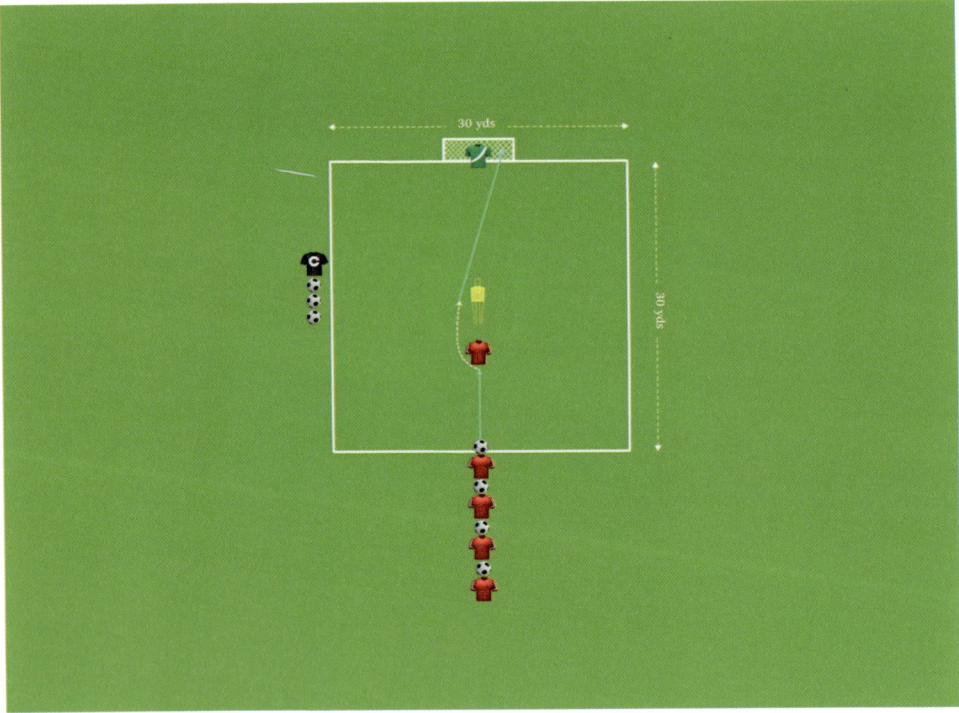

## Description

Divide players into a group of six (including a goalkeeper). Position a goal and the goalkeeper at one end of the playing area. Position a mannequin 20-25 yards from the goal. Position one player in front of the mannequin with their back to goal. Position the remaining four players in a straight line facing and 10 yards away from the mannequin. The group requires five balls, one with each player in the line and one spare ball.

# Turning

The first player in the line passes to the player in front of the mannequin. The receiving player turns past the mannequin towards the goal and shoots at goal. After the shot, the player that took the shot joins the back of the line and the player that passed the ball moves in front of the mannequin to receive the next pass. The activity is continuous for 10 minutes.

The coach should focus on two types of turn and encourage the players to practice turns with both feet. Use the following turns:

- Inside-of-the-foot turn and shoot with the same foot.
- Outside-of-the-foot turn and shoot with the opposite foot.

## Key focus/Coaching points

**Primary focus:** Turning

**Secondary focus:** Receiving

**Additional focus:** Shooting

## Progressions/Adaptations

- Use 1 player as a passive defender instead of the mannequin to add gentle pressure to each turn.
- Encourage the defender to defend competitively and try to prevent each turn.

# 260 THE SOCCER COACH'S TOOLKIT

## ACTIVITY 103  DODGEMS

**Level:** Intermediate

**Type of activity:** Unopposed technical practice

**Number of participants:** 12

**Equipment required:** Soccer balls, cones and 1 set of bibs

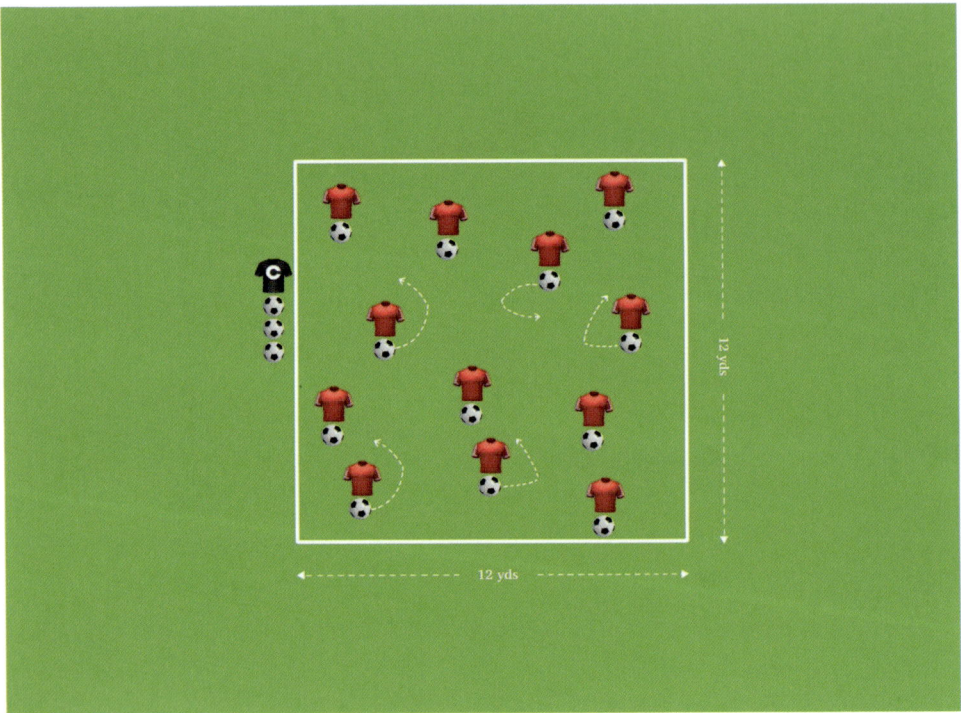

## Description

Mark out a small playing area and position all players inside with a ball each. The players dribble around the playing area and try to maintain good control of their soccer balls. Encourage the players to perform turns and changes of direction to find space and to avoid each other. Many of the turns will happen naturally due to the size of the playing area.

# Turning

Encourage the players to work at high intensity to challenge their turning and dribbling techniques. Make sure that the playing area is big enough to ensure that players have enough room to avoid colliding with each other, but small enough to ensure that turning and maintaining good control of the ball is difficult.

## Key focus/Coaching points

Primary focus: Turning

Secondary focus: Dribbling

Additional focus: Decision making

## Progressions/Adaptations

- Award each player 5 points. The players lose 1 point each time that their ball goes out of the playing area, or it collides with another player's ball.
- Add a defender to try to tackle players (slightly increase the size of the playing area).

# 262 THE SOCCER COACH'S TOOLKIT

## ACTIVITY 104  TURN, TURN, TURN

**Level:** Intermediate

**Type of activity:** Unopposed technical practice

**Number of participants:** 1-12

**Equipment required:** Soccer balls, cones (4 colours) and 1 set of bibs

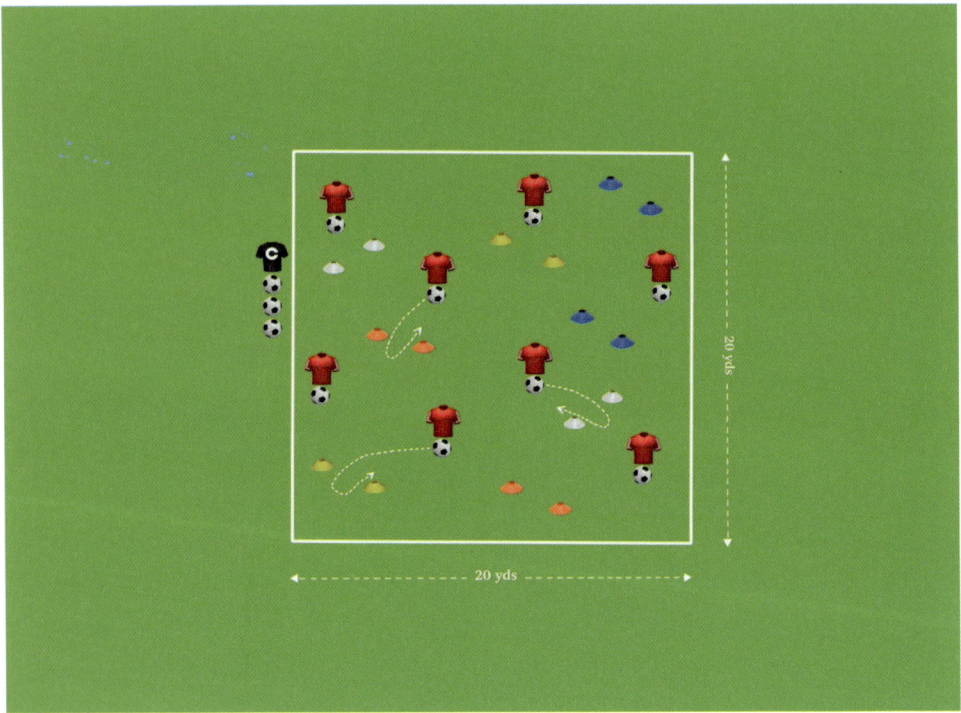

## Description

Players perform individually inside the playing area with a ball each. Mark out a playing area and position the same number of mini gates as there are players, i.e., 12 players = 12 mini gates inside the playing area. Use four different coloured sets of cones to mark out the gates. Each colour represents a different turn, for example:

- **Orange cones** – Inside hook.
- **Blue cones** – Cruyff turn.

- **White cones** – Stop turn.
- **Yellow cones** – Outside hook.

If possible, mark out the same number of mini gates for each colour, e.g., 3 orange, 3 blue, 3 white and 3 yellow. The players dribble around the playing area. Each time that a player dribbles through a gate, they perform the turn that corresponds to that colour back out through the gate.

## Key focus/Coaching points

Primary focus: Turning

Secondary focus: Ball manipulation

Additional focus: Dribbling

## Progressions/Adaptations

- The players try to complete as many turns as they can in 60 seconds.
- Add 1-2 floating defenders. If a dribbler is tackled or has their ball kicked out of the playing area, they lose all their points.

# 264  THE SOCCER COACH'S TOOLKIT

## ACTIVITY 105   TURNING DEVELOPMENT

**Level:** Intermediate

**Type of activity:** Unopposed technical practice

**Number of participants:** 1-14

**Equipment required:** Soccer balls and cones (4 colours)

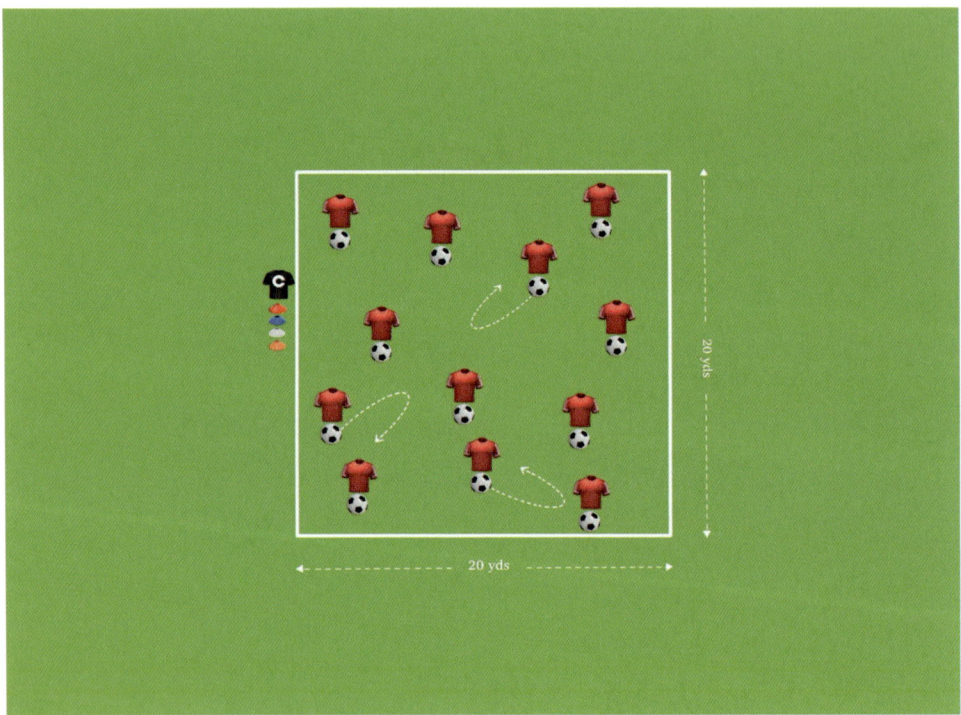

## Description

Players perform individually inside the playing area with a ball each. The coach should hold four cones in their hands (each one should be a different colour). Before the activity starts, the coach explains that each colour represents a different turn, for example:

- **Red** – Cruyff turn.
- **Blue** – Ronaldo chop.

- **White** – Step-over.
- **Orange** – Dragback.

The players dribble around the playing area and respond to the visual command of the coach holding one of the cones up. Every 5-10 seconds, the coach holds a different cone up. Each time that the coach holds a cone aloft, the players perform 2-3 repetitions of the turn that corresponds to that colour. Encourage the players to dribble with their heads up as much as possible in order to see the cones.

## Key focus/Coaching points

Primary focus: Turning

Secondary focus: Dribbling

Additional focus: Ball manipulation

## Progressions/Adaptations

- Decrease the size of playing area to increase the difficulty of the turns.
- Add 1-2 defenders to try to win possession from the players as they perform the turns.

# 266   THE SOCCER COACH'S TOOLKIT

## ACTIVITY 106   FIND A CORNER

**Level:** Advanced

**Type of activity:** Opposed technical practice

**Number of participants:** 8-16

**Equipment required:** Soccer balls, cones and 2 sets of bibs

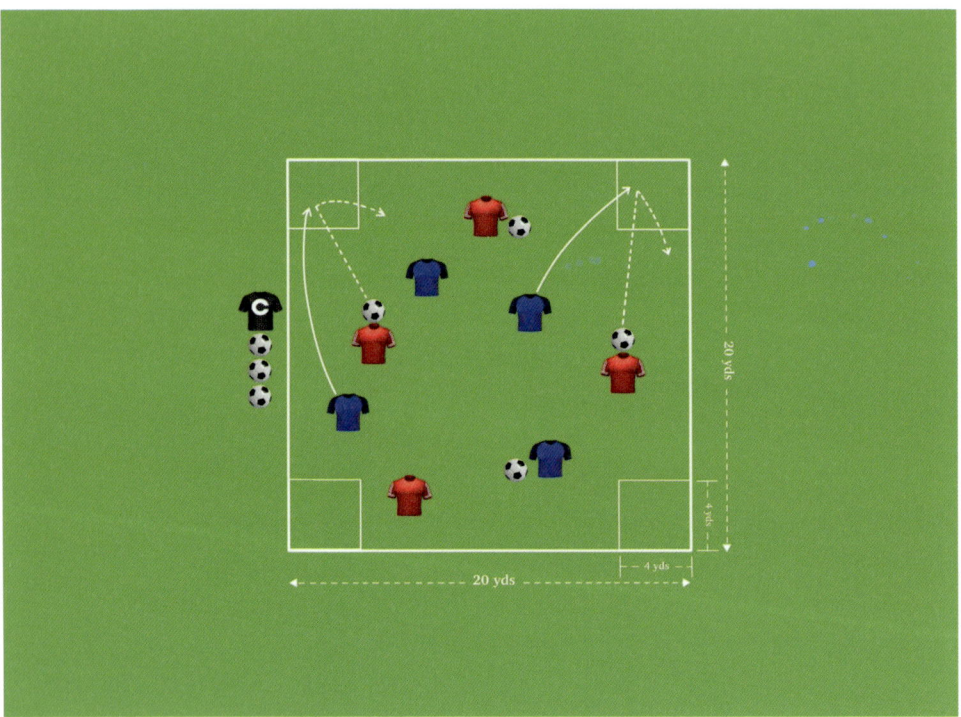

## Description

Divide players into pairs with one ball per pair. Mark out a playing area with a square in each corner. Position all players inside the playing area. The players in each pair compete against each other for possession and try score points by dribbling into and turning out of any of the squares.

As the players turn out of the square, they must retain possession of the ball for the point to be awarded. The players cannot score consecutive points in the same square. All pairs compete at the same time, so encourage the players to keep their heads up as much as possible and to be aware of other players.

## Key focus/Coaching points

Primary focus: Turning

Secondary focus: Dribbling

Additional focus: Shielding

## Progressions/Adaptations

- Add a passive defender inside each square box to pressurise the turn.
- Progress to 2v2 contests.

# 268  THE SOCCER COACH'S TOOLKIT

## ACTIVITY 107  TENNIS BALL TURNING

**Level:** Advanced

**Type of activity:** Unopposed technical practice

**Number of participants:** 1-16

**Equipment required:** Tennis balls and cones

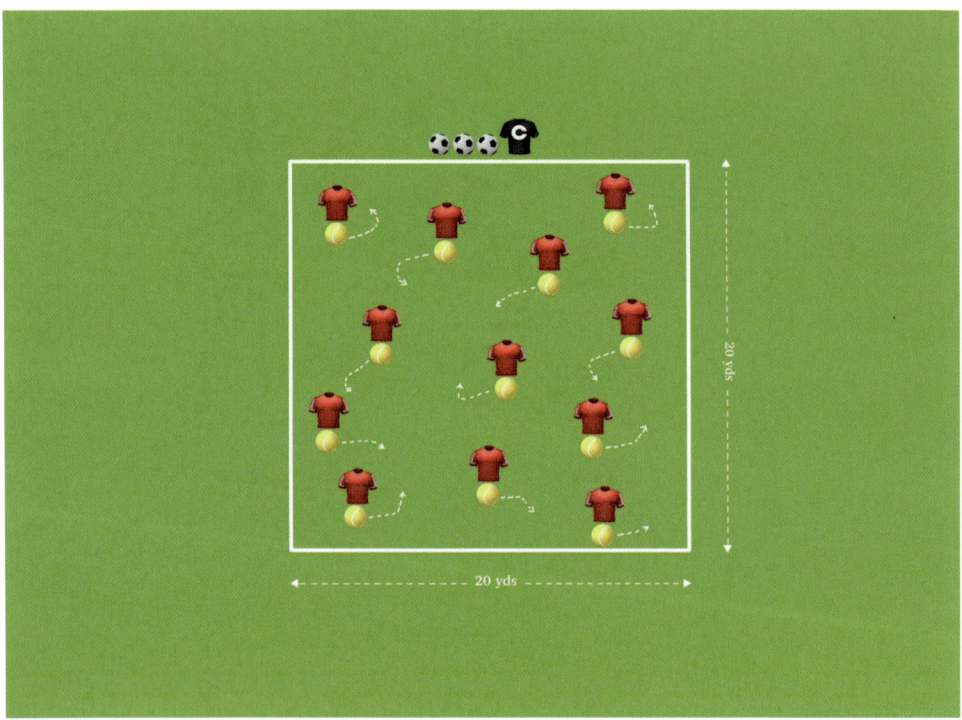

## Description

Position all players inside the playing area with one tennis ball each. The players dribble inside the playing area and practice changing direction and turning with the tennis ball. The players will find this activity difficult, particularly the players that have never practiced with a tennis ball before. There will be lots of opportunities to coach and improve technical weaknesses. Allow players time at the start of the activity to get used to dribbling the tennis ball before getting them to practice turns. Initially, keep the turns simple (e.g., stop turn) and as players develop confidence, make the turns more advanced, e.g., Cruyff turn.

## Key focus/Coaching points

Primary focus: Turning

Secondary focus: Ball manipulation

Additional focus: Dribbling

## Progressions/Adaptations

- Decrease the size of the playing area.
- Encourage players to dribble and perform turns with their weaker foot/both feet.

# SHIELDING

## ACTIVITY 108  SHIELDING STRENGTH

**Level:** Basic

**Type of activity:** Opposed technical practice

**Number of participants:** 8

**Equipment required:** Soccer balls, cones and 2 sets of bibs

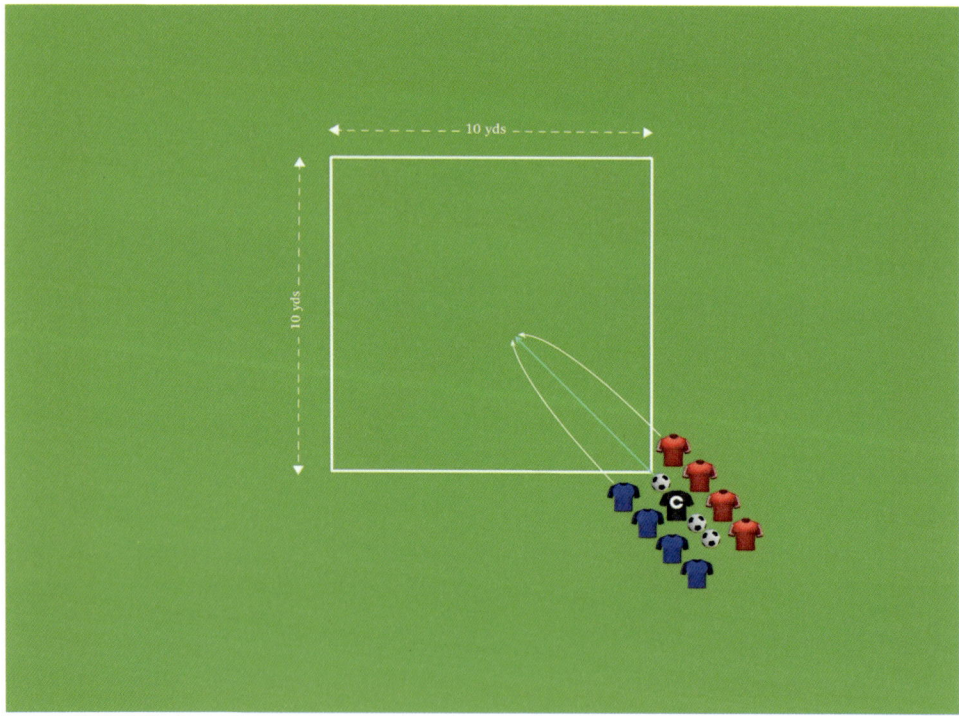

### Description

Divide players into two teams of four. The coach should be positioned in any corner of the playing area with a supply of balls. Position the teams in straight lines on either side of the coach and facing the playing area.

The activity starts when the coach feeds a ball into the playing area. The first player in line from each group runs into the playing area. The players compete for possession of the ball for 20 seconds. The player in possession of the ball after 20 seconds wins 1 point for their team.

After the first contest, the two players run to the back of their lines, and the coach feeds a ball into the playing are for the next two players. Encourage determined and competitive play in order to develop opportunities to shield the ball and hold off the opponent.

## Key focus/Coaching points

**Primary focus:** Shielding

**Secondary focus:** Turning

**Additional focus:** Dribbling

## Progressions/Adaptations

- 2 players from each team enter the playing area at the same time and compete for possession in a 2v2.
- Feed the ball into the playing area aerially. Encourage players to use safe shoulder contact and shielding to contest possession as it drops to the floor.

## ACTIVITY 109　SHOW OF STRENGTH

**Level:** Basic

**Type of activity:** Opposed technical practice

**Number of participants:** 4

**Equipment required:** Soccer balls, cones and 2 set of bibs

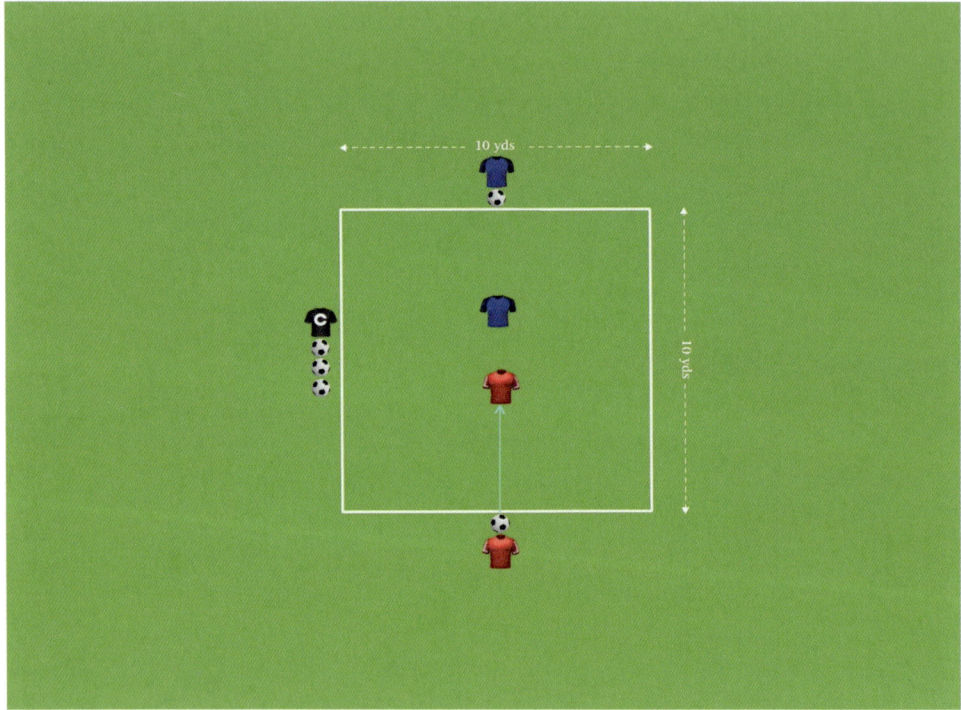

## Description

Divide players into a group of four. Organise the group into one shielding player, one defender and two ball feeders. Position the shielding player and the defender inside the playing area and the ball feeders at opposite ends of the playing area. The ball feeders require a soccer ball each.

The activity starts when the shielding player runs towards a ball feeder. From 5 yards, the ball feeder passes to the shielding player. The shielding player attempts to shield the ball and retain possession from the defender for 5 seconds before passing the ball back to the ball feeder. The shielding player should try to shield the ball without dribbling or turning away from the defender.

After each shielding contest, the shielding player and the defender switch roles. The passes to the shielding player should be played from alternate ends of the playing area. The players inside the playing area perform six to eight shielding contests and then swap roles with the ball feeders.

## Key focus/Coaching points

Primary focus: Shielding

Secondary focus: Receiving

Additional focus: Physical/movement development

## Progressions/Adaptations

- After a ball feeder passes into the playing area; both ball feeders enter the playing area and compete in a 2v2 against the players originally inside the playing area. The teams compete for possession for 30 seconds. The players can shield the ball, turn into space and pass to their teammate when necessary to retain possession.

# 274 THE SOCCER COACH'S TOOLKIT

## ACTIVITY 110   LOSE YOUR SHADOW

**Level:** Intermediate

**Type of activity:** Opposed technical practice

**Number of participants:** 12

**Equipment required:** Soccer balls, cones and 3 sets of bibs

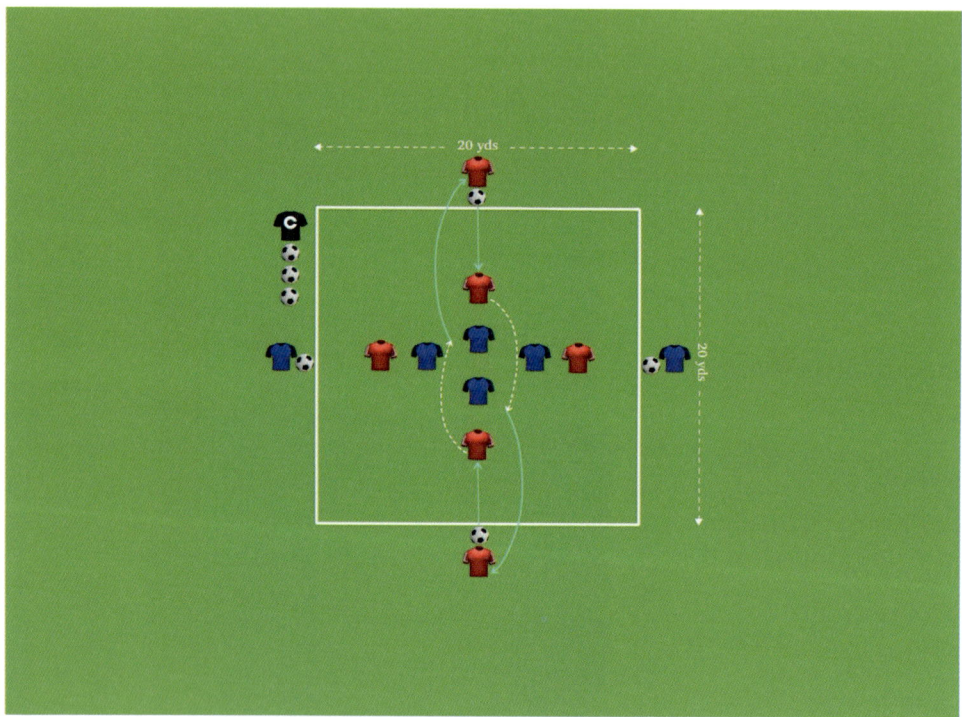

## Description

Divide players into four sets of pairs and one group of four ball feeders. Position one player from the group of ball feeders outside each playing area line. Each ball feeder requires a ball. Position each pair of players inside the playing area. Nominate one player in each pair to start the activity as the receiving player and the other player as a passive defender.

# Shielding

The activity starts when each of the receiving players moves into space to receive a pass from a ball feeder. The passes from the ball feeders to the receiving players should be from 6-8 yards. After receiving the pass, the receiving players turn past their defending partners and pass to another available ball feeder from 6-8 yards.

The receiving players then move into a new space inside the playing area and receive a pass from a different ball feeder. The passive defenders follow their partners throughout the activity and pressurise each turn but should not attempt to win possession of the ball. After 2 minutes rotate the roles of all players.

## Key focus/Coaching points

**Primary focus:** Shielding

**Secondary focus:** Turning

**Additional focus:** Dribbling

## Progressions/Adaptations

- Allow active pressure from the defenders, i.e., they try to win possession of the ball.
- If the defenders win possession of the ball, they try to pass the ball outside the playing area to a ball feeder. The player that passes the ball out to a ball feeder should receive the next pass from a new ball feeder.

# 276 THE SOCCER COACH'S TOOLKIT

## ACTIVITY 111  SHIELDING AND SCORING

**Level:** Intermediate

**Type of activity:** Implementation practice

**Number of participants:** 10 + 1 goalkeeper

**Equipment required:** Soccer balls, cones, discs, 2 sets of bibs and 1 goal

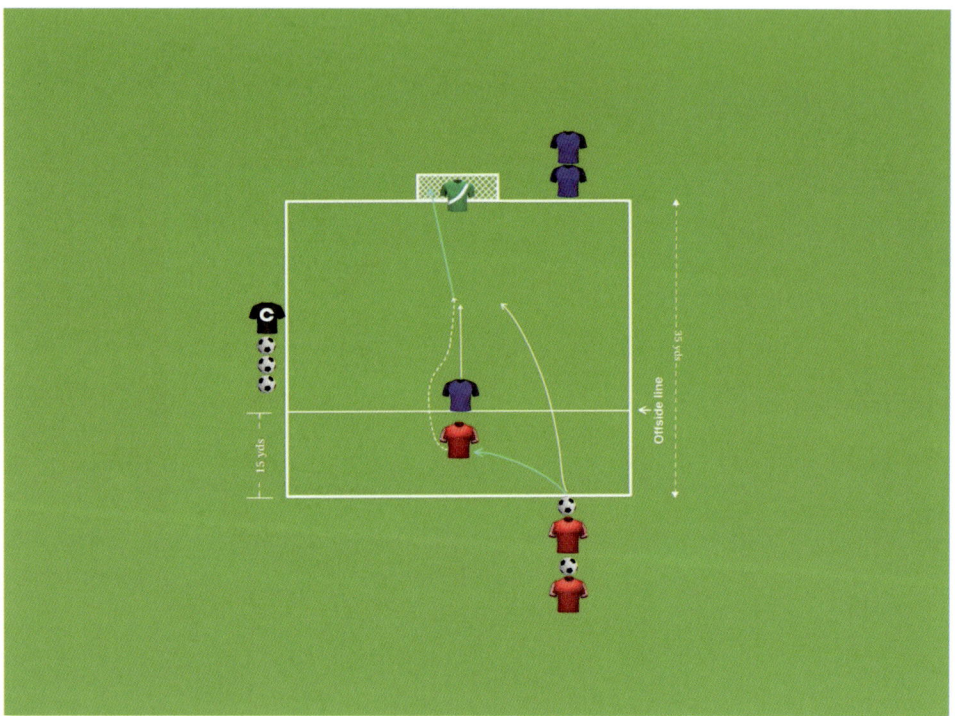

## Description

Divide players into one group of three attackers and one group of three defenders. Position a goal and goalkeeper at one end of the playing area. Mark out an offside area 20 yards from goal. Position two of the attackers in a straight line 35 yards from goal and 10 yards to the side of either goalpost. The two attackers require a supply of balls. Position the remaining attacker 25 yards out from and with their back to the centre of the goal. Position one defender behind central the attacker in a marking position. Position the other two defenders a safe distance to the side of the goal.

The activity starts when the first attacker in line passes to the central attacker. The attacker that passed the ball makes a supporting run to create a 2v1 attacking overload. The central attacker has the choice to either try to turn past the defender and score or shield the ball and play a pass to the supporting attacker.

If the central attacker chooses to pass, the two attackers combine to build an attack. If the attackers combine to score, they score 1 point for the attackers. If the central attacker turns and scores without using the supporting attacker, they score 3 points for the attackers.

The defender tries to stop the attacker(s) from scoring by tackling, intercepting passes or forcing the ball out of play. The defender and the goalkeeper work together to try to prevent goals. The attackers can be caught offside beyond the offside line. If the attackers fail to score, the defenders score 1 point.

After each attack, rotate the attackers for the next attack. The central attacker drops out of the next attack and the supporting attacker becomes the central attacker. The attacker that was not involved in the previous attack becomes the supporting attacker. The defender runs to their line and is replaced by a new defender for the next attack. After 10-12 attacks, rotate the players. Keep a score of the points and see which team wins the most points overall.

## Key focus/Coaching points

**Primary focus:** Shielding

**Secondary focus:** Turning

**Additional focus:** Finishing

## Progressions/Adaptations

- If the supporting attacker is used in the attack, then a second defender runs onto the playing area to create a 2v2.
- Add a second central attacker and a supporting midfielder. Position the midfielder 10 yards opposite the central attackers. Add a second defender to mark the central attackers and a third defender to mark the supporting midfielder. Position the third defender next to the supporting midfielder at the start of each attack.

# 278  THE SOCCER COACH'S TOOLKIT

## ACTIVITY 112  AERIAL SHIELDING

Level: Intermediate

Type of activity: Opposed technical practice

Number of participants: 12

Equipment required: Soccer balls, cones and 3 sets of bibs

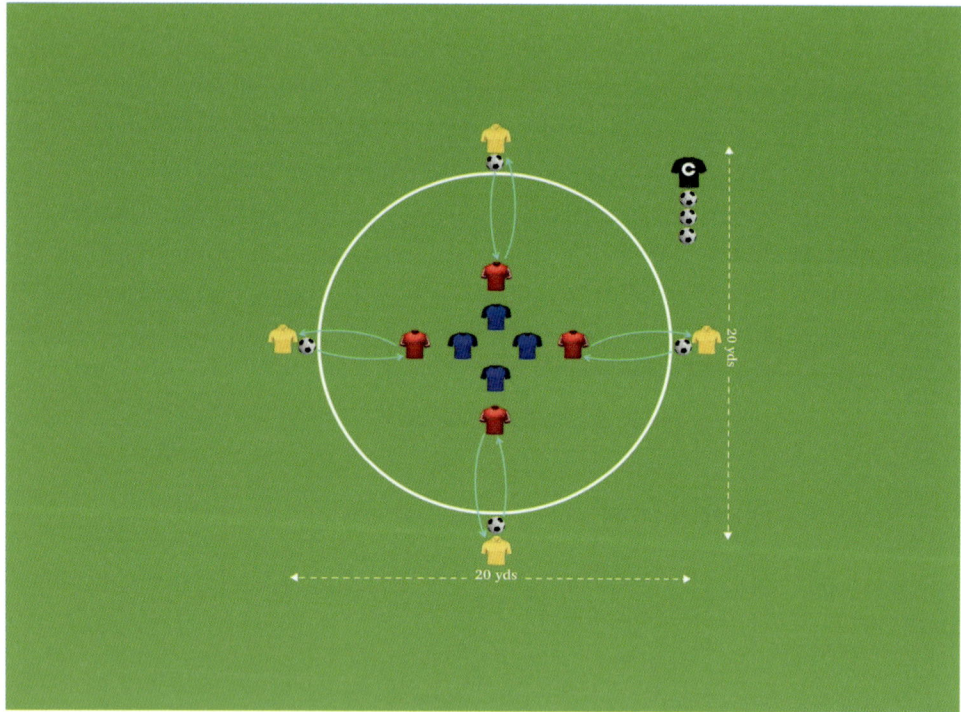

## Description

Divide players into one group of four shielding players, one group of four defenders and one group of four ball feeders. Mark out a circular playing area. Position the ball feeders around the outside of the playing area with a ball each. Position the shielding players inside the playing area. Position the defenders inside the playing area with each one marking a shielding player. The defenders should only apply passive pressure to the ball shielders.

The shielding players move around the circle and try to create space away from the defenders. When the shielding players manage to create some space, they run to and call for an aerial feed from an available ball feeder. The ball feeders underarm throw the ball to the shielding players.

The shielding players must receive the ball with the most appropriate body surface and shield it from the defender for 2-3 seconds. After shielding the ball, the shielding player must pass the ball back to the ball feeder. The shielding players repeat the activity of creating space and then receiving an aerial feed from a new ball feeder. Rotate the players after 1-2 minutes.

## Key focus/Coaching points

Primary focus: Shielding

Secondary focus: Receiving

Additional focus: Turning

## Progressions/adaptations:

- After receiving and shielding the ball, the shielding player tries to turn past the defender, dribble towards and pass to another available ball feeder.
- The defenders apply full pressure to the ball shielders and try to win possession of the ball.

## ACTIVITY 113  2V2 SHIELDING

**Level:** Advanced

**Type of activity:** Opposed technical practice

**Number of participants:** 8

**Equipment required:** Soccer balls, cones and 3 sets of bibs

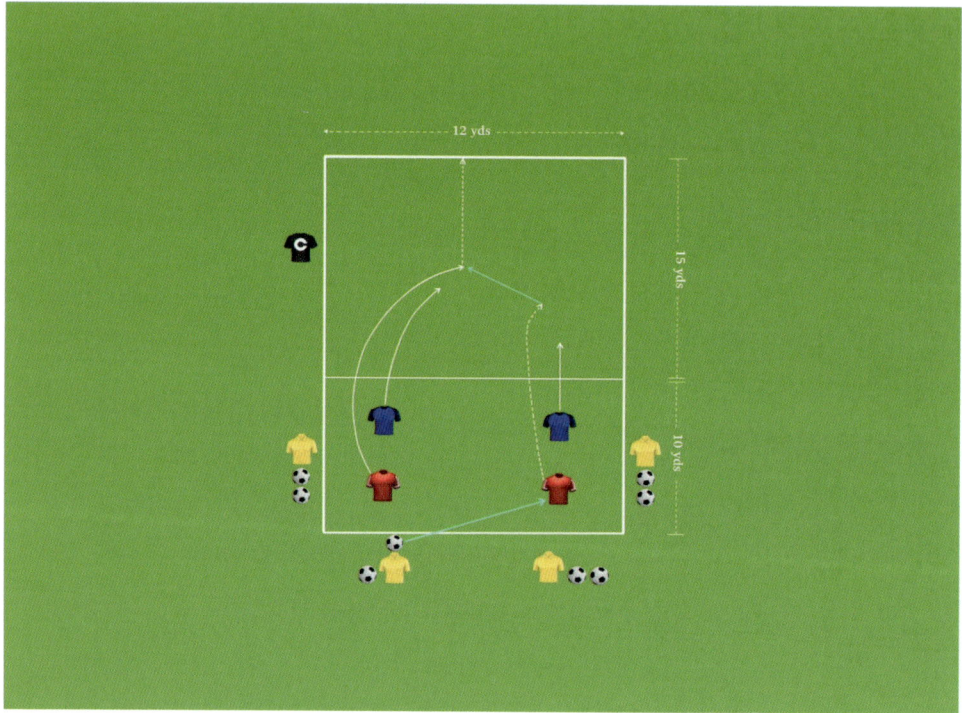

## Description

Divide players into one team of two attackers, one team of two defenders and one group of four support players. Mark out a main playing area with a scoring zone positioned at one end of the playing area. Position the support players around the outside of the main playing area with a supply of balls each. Position the group of attackers and the group of defenders inside the main playing area.

The activity starts when one of the support players passes to the attacking team. The attackers try to keep possession of the ball until there is an opportunity to dribble or play a through pass into the scoring zone. The attackers can pass to and receive passes back from the support players at any time when they have possession inside the main playing area.

When one of the attackers either dribbles into or receives a through pass into the scoring zone, the second attacker and both defenders run into the scoring zone to create a 2v2 in the scoring zone. Once the attackers are in the scoring zone, they try to score by dribbling the ball and stopping it on the line at the end of the scoring zone.

The attackers are allowed a maximum of three passes in the scoring zone. After each attack, the attackers and defenders retreat to the main playing area for the next attack. Rotate the players after 5 minutes.

## Key focus/Coaching points

**Primary focus:** Shielding

**Secondary focus:** Turning

**Additional focus:** Running with the ball

## Progressions/Adaptations

- The attackers are allowed a maximum of 5 passes inside the main playing area.
- Add 1 support player to the attacking team and 1 to the defending team to create a 3v3 with 2 support players.

# 282 THE SOCCER COACH'S TOOLKIT

## ACTIVITY 114　STUCK LIKE GLUE

**Level:** Advanced

**Type of activity:** Opposed technical practice

**Number of participants:** 10 + 2 goalkeepers

**Equipment required:** Soccer balls, cones, discs, 2 sets of bibs and 2 goals

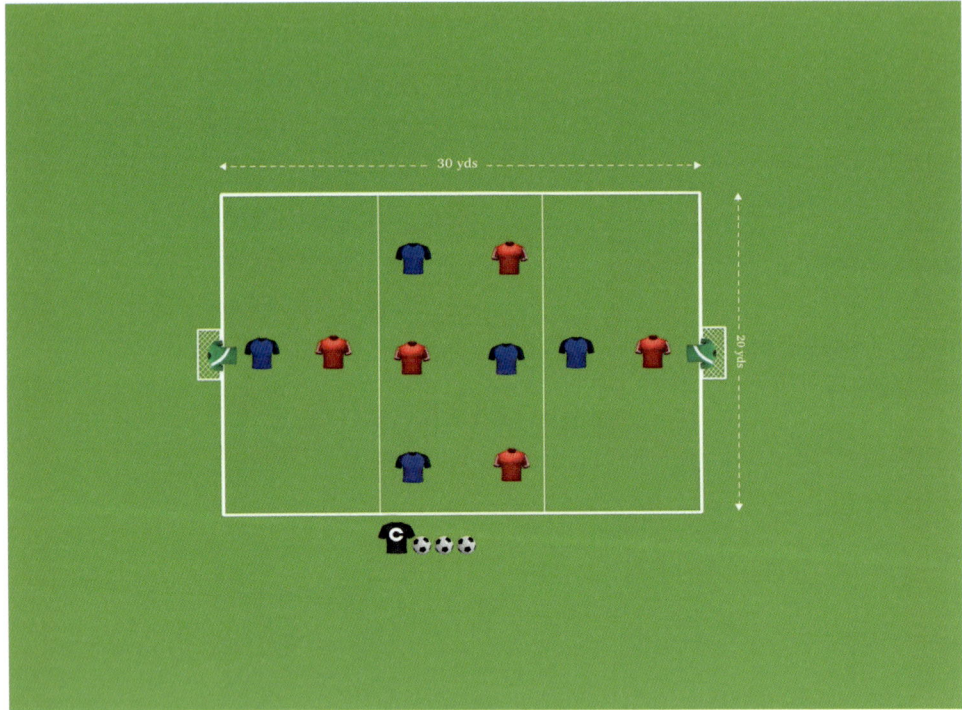

## Description

Divide players into two teams of six (including goalkeepers). Divide the playing area into three zones with a goal and goalkeeper at both ends of the playing area. Organise both teams of outfield players into a 1-3-1 formation. The teams compete in a 6v6 match and attack opposite ends of the playing area. Position one defender in the defensive zone, three midfielders in the middle zone and one attacker in the attacking zone for both teams. Initially, all players must play within their zones.

Before the activity starts, the coach nominates an opposition player to compete against for all players. The players are not allowed to mark or challenge any opposition player, other than the one they have been assigned to. In the defensive and attacking zones, it is a 1v1 contest so the opposition players in these zones compete against each other. In the midfield zone, the coach must organise opponents into three sets of opponents.

## Key focus/Coaching points

**Primary focus:** Shielding

**Secondary focus:** Turning

**Additional focus:** Physical/movement development

## Progressions/Adaptations

- The players must take more than 1 touch in possession to create opportunities for their opponent to challenge them.
- Allow the players to move between zones when they pass or dribble into a new zone. When this happens, their opponent follows them. When the attacking player's team loses possession, both players return to their original zone.

# CROSSING

## ACTIVITY 115  CROSSING BASICS

**Level:** Basic

**Type of activity:** Unopposed technical practice

**Number of participants:** 12 +1 goalkeeper

**Equipment required:** Soccer balls, cones and 1 goal

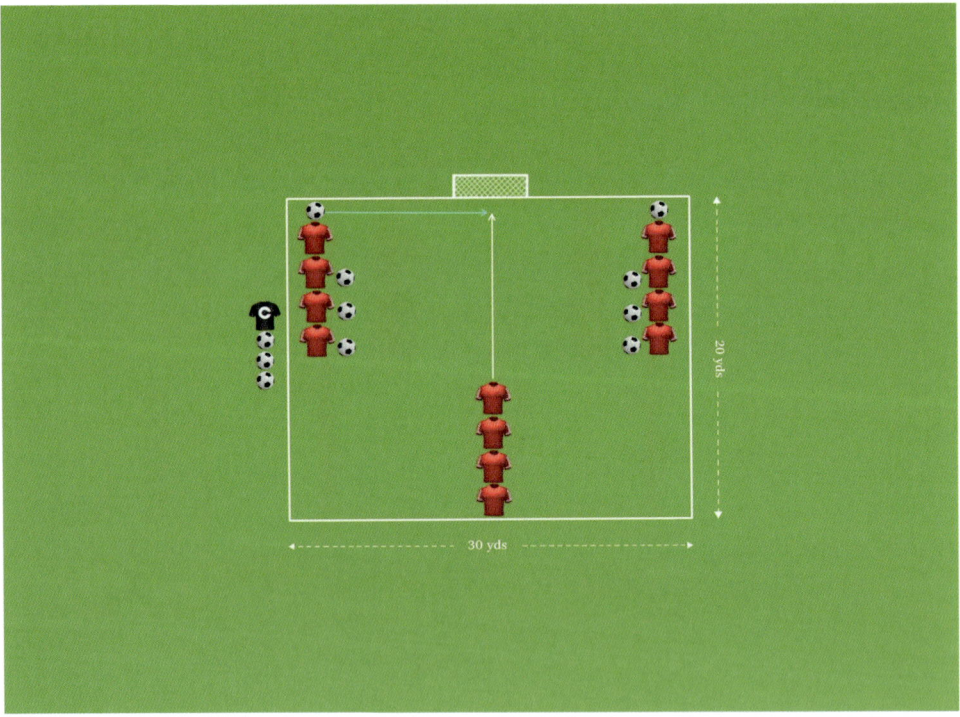

### Description

Divide players into three groups of four. Position a goal at one end of the playing area. Position one group on the left and one group on the right side of the playing area, and the third group in the centre of the playing area. Position the groups on the left and right approximately 6 yards from the goal end of the playing area and the central group 20 yards back from the goal end of the playing area. The players on the left and right require a soccer ball each.

The activity starts when the first player from the central group makes a forwards run until they are in line with the front of the group on the left. The first player in line from the group on the left crosses their ball, aiming at the central player's hands, which should be held high above their head. The central player tries to catch the cross. After the cross, the player that crossed the ball runs to the back of the central line group and the player from the central group runs to the back of the line on the left.

The activity continues with a forwards run from the next central player in line until they are level with the front of the group on the right. The first player in line from the group on the right crosses their ball, aiming at the central player's hands, which should be held high above their head. The central player tries to catch the cross. After the cross, the player on the right runs to the back of the central group line and the player from the central group runs to the back of the line on the right.

## Key focus/Coaching points

Primary focus: Crossing

Secondary focus: Long passing

Additional focus: Ball manipulation

## Progressions/Adaptations

- The wide players aim their crosses at head height and the central players aim their headers into the goal.
- Add goalkeepers to save the headers.
- Progress onto low crosses and crosses along the floor so that the central players must try to score with shots or volleys.

# 286 THE SOCCER COACH'S TOOLKIT

## ACTIVITY 116   CROSS ON THE RUN

**Level:** Basic

**Type of activity:** Unopposed technical practice

**Number of participants:** 13

**Equipment required:** Soccer balls, cones, 1 set of bibs and 1 goal

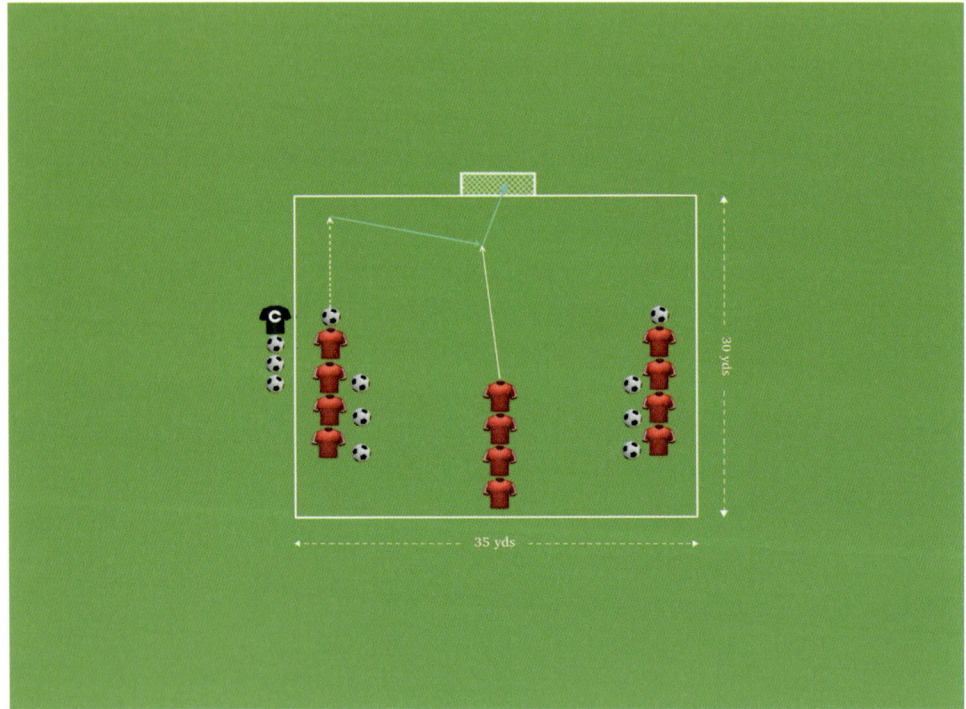

## Description

Divide players into three groups of four. Position a goal at one end of the playing area. Position one group in a straight line on the left side of the playing area with a ball each, a second group in a straight line on the right side of the playing area with a ball each (approximately 18 yards out from the end of the playing area) and the third group in line with the middle of the playing area approximately 20 yards out from the end of the playing area.

# Crossing

The activity starts when one player from the central group makes a run towards the goal and stops approximately 6 yards from the goal. At the same time, the first player in line on the left performs a dribble towards the end of the playing area. When the dribbling player is approximately 6 yards out from the end of the playing area, they cross the ball for the central player to finish in the goal. The player on the left then runs to the back of the central line and the central player runs to the back of the line on the left.

The activity continues with a dribble and cross from the player at the front of the line on the right of the playing area and a run towards goal from the next player in the central line. After the cross and finish, the player on the right runs to the back of the line in the central group and the central player runs to the back of the line on the right.

## Key focus/Coaching points

Primary focus: Crossing

Secondary focus: Dribbling

Additional focus: Long passing

## Progressions/Adaptations

- The wide players must perform a dribble in and out of 4 cones before crossing.
- Introduce a passive defender to pressurise the dribble and cross.

# 288 THE SOCCER COACH'S TOOLKIT

## ACTIVITY 117 CROSSING, HEADERS AND VOLLEYS

**Level:** Basic

**Type of activity:** Unopposed technical practice

**Number of participants:** 6 + 1 goalkeeper

**Equipment required:** Soccer balls, cones, 2 sets of bibs and 1 goal

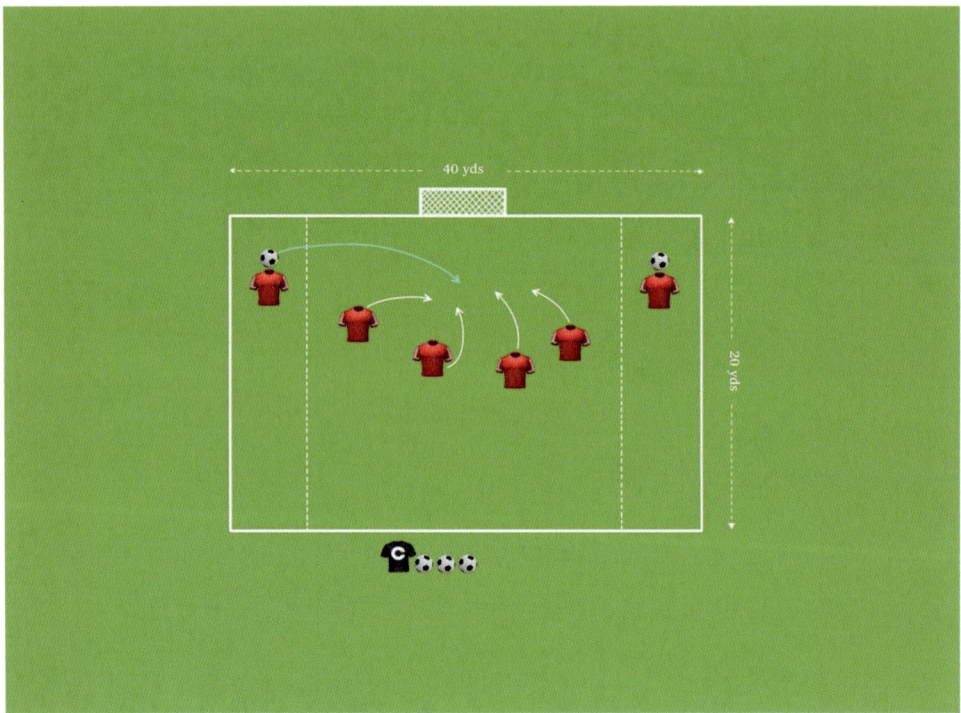

## Description

Divide players into one group of six. Mark out a main playing area (similar in size to a penalty area) with a channel running the length of the playing area on both sides. Position a goal and goalkeeper at the end of the playing area. Position four players inside the main playing area and one player in each channel. Position a ball with either of the players in the channels.

The activity starts when the channel player in possession of the ball crosses the ball into the main playing area for the attackers to either volley or header at goal. As soon as the first cross has been delivered, the goalkeeper counts aloud from 1-60 seconds. The attackers try to score one goal in 60 seconds with either a header or a volley from a cross.

If the attackers score the required number of goals in 60 seconds, the clock is re-set, and they try to score an additional goal in the next 60 seconds. The attackers try to score an additional goal in each 60-second period until they fail to score the required number of goals.

If during play an attempt at goal is off target, saved by the goalkeeper or a cross is misdirected or bounces before it reaches an attacker, the activity continues with a pass to the player in the opposite channel. The player in possession in the channel delivers another cross for the attackers to try to score from. The crosses are delivered alternately from opposite channels for each 60-second period. If the goalkeeper catches the ball from a cross/attempt at goal at any time, the activity stops, and the last player to have touched the ball switches positions with the goalkeeper for the next round of 60 seconds.

## Key focus/Coaching points

**Primary focus:** Crossing

**Secondary focus:** Headers

**Additional focus:** Volleys

## Progressions/Adaptations

- If the activity is too difficult, allow the players to score with half-volleys.
- Divide the attackers into 2 teams of 2. The teams contest each cross. The first team to score the required number of goals wins the round.

# 290 THE SOCCER COACH'S TOOLKIT

## ACTIVITY 118  IN TO OUT CROSSING

**Level:** Intermediate

**Type of activity:** Unopposed technical practice

**Number of participants:** 8-12 + 1 goalkeeper

**Equipment required:** Soccer balls, cones and 1 goal

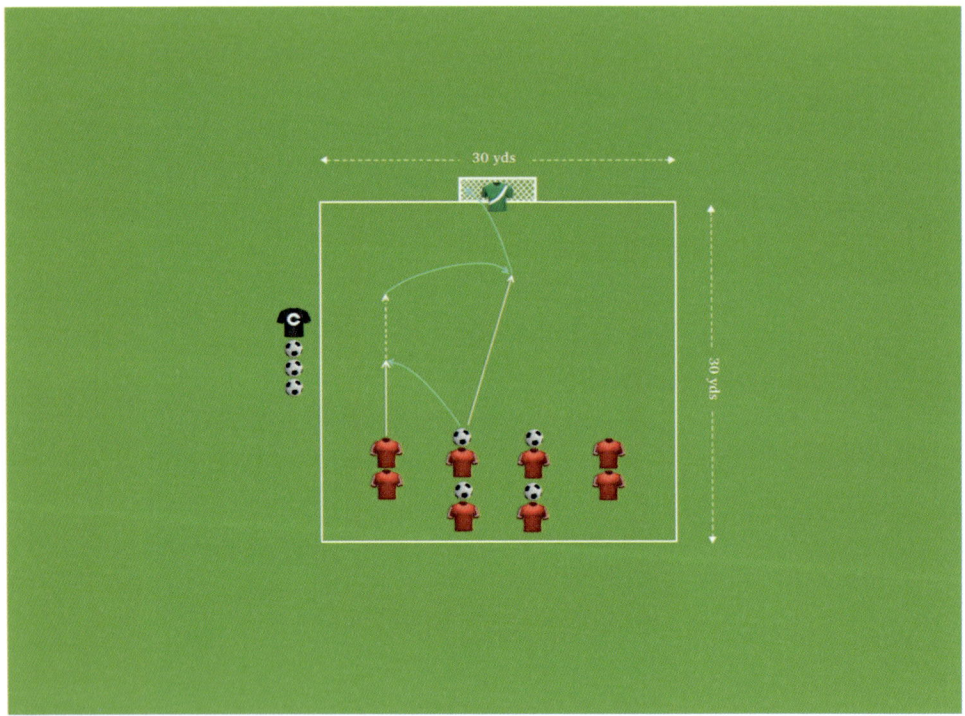

## Description

Divide players into four groups of two to three. Position two of the groups in the centre the playing area side-by-side and facing one end of the playing area. Position a goal (approximately 30 yards away) and goalkeeper at the end of the playing area that the groups are facing. Each player in these two groups requires a ball. Position the other two groups on the left and right side of the playing area, level with the central groups.

The activity starts when the first player from the central group nearest to the left passes to the first player in the line on the left. The pass should be forwards and into the path of the player on the left. The player that passed the ball makes a run towards the goal and the player on the left crosses the ball for the central player to finish into the goal.

After the attack, the players that were involved in the attack run to the back of each other's starting line and the activity continues immediately with the central group nearest to the right and the group on the right.

## Key focus/Coaching points

Primary focus: Crossing

Secondary focus: Finishing

Additional focus: Speed

## Progressions/Adaptations

- Encourage the players to vary the type of cross, e.g., flat, high, cut-back depending on the position and movement of the central player.
- The second player in line in each group acts as a recovering defender and chases the player crossing the ball.

# 292 THE SOCCER COACH'S TOOLKIT

## ACTIVITY 119   CROSSING AND MOVEMENT

**Level:** Intermediate

**Type of activity:** Implementation practice

**Number of participants:** 10-12 + 1 goalkeeper

**Equipment required:** Soccer balls, cones, 3 sets of bibs and 1 goal

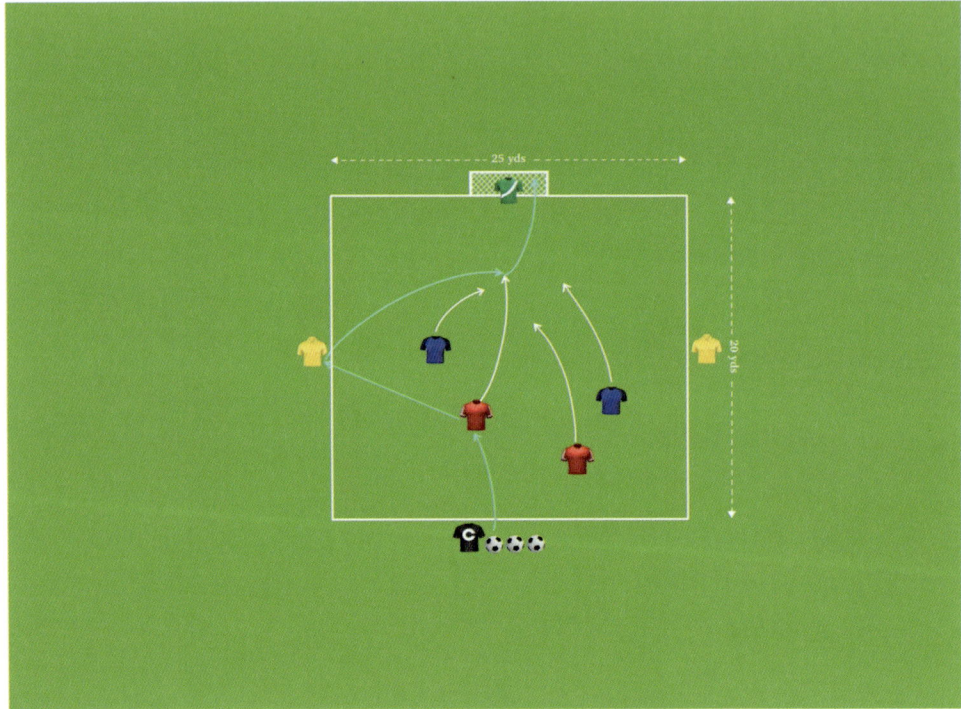

## Description

Divide players into two teams of two to three and one group of two support players. Position one goal and a goalkeeper at one end of the playing area. Position the two teams of two to three players inside the playing area. Position one support player on each side of the playing area.

The activity starts when the coach passes a ball into the playing area and both teams compete for possession. The first team to pass out to a support player becomes the nominated attacking team. The players in the nominated attacking team and the players in the other team make attacking runs towards the goal. The support player tries to cross the ball to a player in the nominated attacking team to finish however, both teams contest the cross and try to score.

If the cross is not converted into a goal but stays within the playing area, both teams have 10 seconds to try to score from open play. If neither team has scored after 10 seconds, the team in possession of the ball passes it out to either support player. The support player tries to cross the ball to a player in the nominated attacking team. Again, both teams can attack and try to score from the cross. After 8-10 crosses, rotate the positions of all players.

## Key focus/Coaching points

**Primary focus:** Crossing

**Secondary focus:** Movement

**Additional focus:** Finishing

## Progressions/Adaptations

- Add a passive defender on each side of the playing area to make the crosses more difficult.

- Add a second support player on each side of the playing area. The support players can combine to create a crossing opportunity. The defender should now apply full pressure and try to block the crosses or win possession of the ball.

# 294 THE SOCCER COACH'S TOOLKIT

## ACTIVITY 120   OUT ON THE WING

**Level:** Intermediate

**Type of activity:** Opposed technical practice

**Number of participants:** 10 + 2 goalkeepers

**Equipment required:** Soccer balls, cones, 3 sets of bibs and 2 goals

## Description

Divide players into two teams of five (including goalkeepers) and two support players. Mark out a wide playing area. Position a goal and goalkeeper at both ends of the playing area. Position both teams inside the playing area and one support player on the outside of both sidelines. The teams inside the area compete in a 4v4 match.

The support players support the team in possession. They should move up and down the outside of the playing area to support attacks. Both teams must play a pass to either support player and receive a pass or cross back from them before they can attack the goal. Encourage the wide players to deliver crosses as often as possible and when appropriate.

If a team scores after converting a cross, it is worth two goals. If a cross is delivered but the attacking team fail to convert it, they have a maximum of three passes to score if they have retained possession of the ball. In this case, if the attacking team score, the goal value is 1. If, after three passes, the attacking team has failed to score, award possession to the other team to re-start the activity. If the defending team wins possession from a cross, play continues as normal.

## Key focus/Coaching points

**Primary focus:** Crossing

**Secondary focus:** Movement

**Additional focus:** Attacking and defending

## Progressions/Adaptations

- The support players can only have 1 touch before crossing or passing the ball.
- The support players must cross first time.
- If players are taking too long to pass the ball to the support players, limit the number of passes allowed inside the playing area.

## ACTIVITY 121   CROSSING UNDER PRESSURE

**Level:** Advanced

**Type of activity:** Opposed technical practice

**Number of participants:** 15 + 1 goalkeeper

**Equipment required:** Soccer balls, cones, 2 sets of bibs and 1 goal

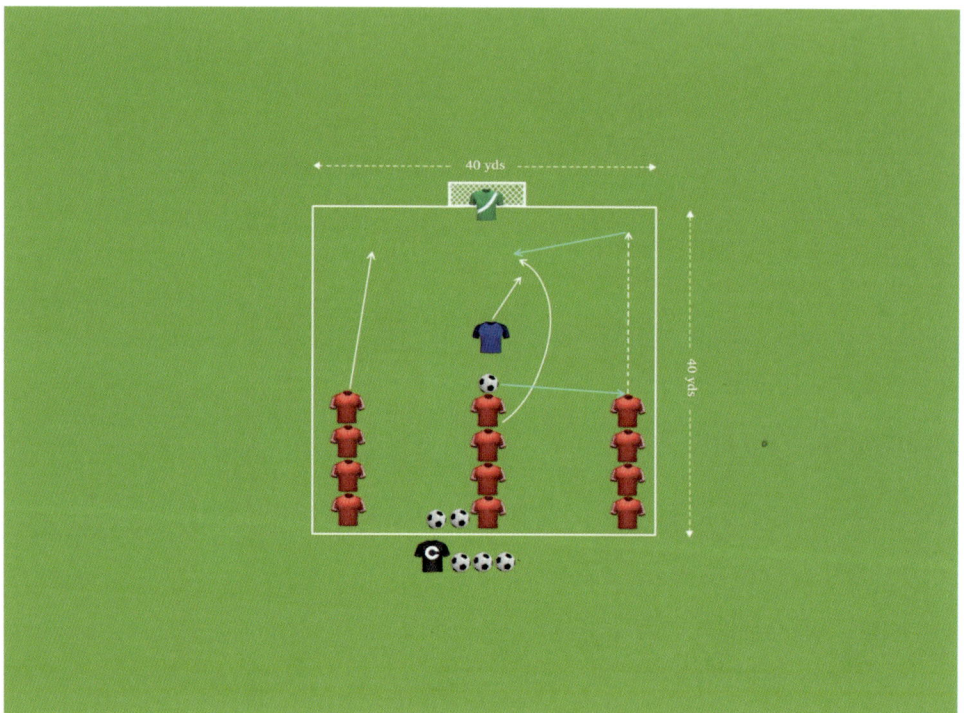

## Description

Divide players into one group of four central attackers, one group of four left wingers, one group of four right wingers and one defender. Position a goal at one end of the playing area. Position the groups in straight lines facing the goal. Position the left wingers on the left side, the right wingers on the right side, and the central attackers in the centre of the playing area. All the groups should be 35-40 yards away from the goal. Position the defender 10 yards from the line of central attackers. Position a supply of balls with the central attackers.

The activity starts when the first player in the line of central attackers passes to the first player in the line of left or right wingers. The central attacker makes an attacking run towards the goal. The defender follows and marks the central attacker. The winger in possession of the ball dribbles towards the end of the playing area.

The first player in the other line of wingers supports the attack and makes a run towards the far post. The winger in possession of the ball crosses to either the central attacker or the other winger. The attackers try to score from the cross and the defender tries to clear the ball to end the attack.

Once the attack is over, the wingers run to the back of their line, the central attacker becomes the defender for the next attack and the defender joins the back of the central attackers' line. The next attack starts with a pass to the first player in line in the other group of wingers. After 5-10 minutes rotate the wingers and central attackers.

### Key focus/Coaching points

**Primary focus:** Crossing

**Secondary focus:** Movement

**Additional focus:** Ball manipulation

### Progressions/Adaptations

- Position a line of 3 defenders at a safe distance to the side of the goal. As soon as each attack starts, 1 defender from the line runs towards the goal and supports the other defender to create a 2v2 attack v defence.
- Add a goalkeeper.

## ACTIVITY 122  CROSSING PASSAGE OF PLAY

**Level:** Advanced

**Type of activity:** Implementation practice

**Number of participants:** 17 + 1 goalkeeper

**Equipment required:** Soccer balls, cones, 2 sets of bibs and 1 goal

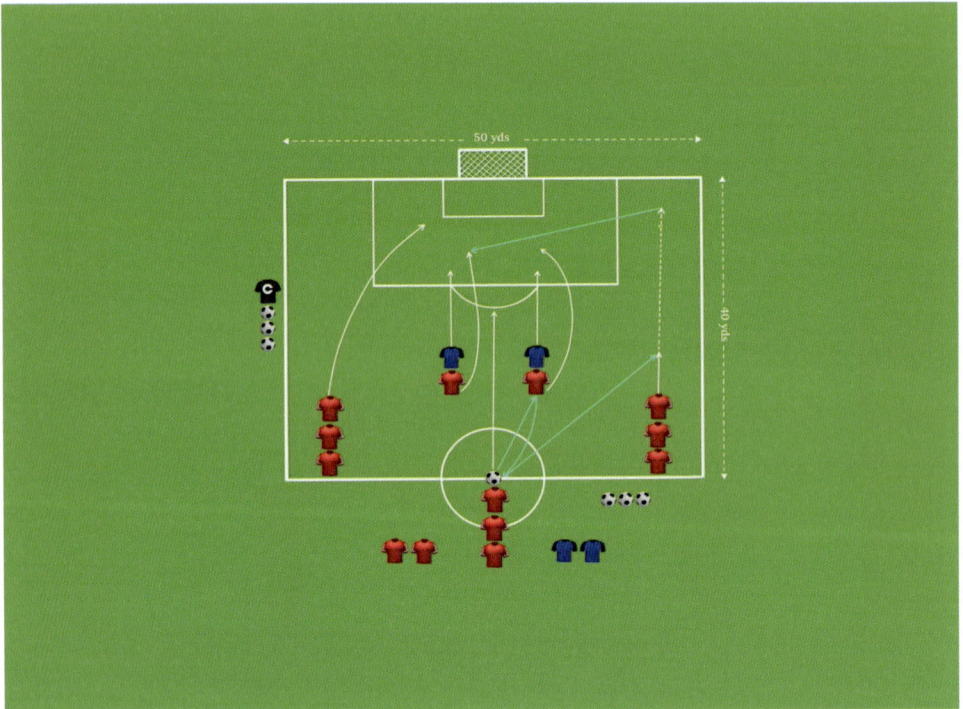

### Description

Divide players into one group of three central midfielders, one group of three right wingers, one group of three left wingers, one group of four central attackers and one group of four central defenders. Position a goal at one end of the playing area. Position both groups of wingers and the central midfielders facing the goal. Position the left wingers on the left side, the right wingers on the right side and the central midfielders in the centre of the playing area. All the lines should be 40-50 yards away from the goal. Position a supply of balls with the central midfielders.

Position two of the central attackers 10 yards opposite the line of central midfielders with their backs to goal. Position two of the defenders behind the central attackers in marking positions. Position the remaining two central attackers and two defenders behind the line of central midfielders.

The activity starts when the first central midfielder in line passes to either of the central attackers. The attacker that receives the ball then passes the ball back to the central midfielder. The central midfielder then passes to the first player in line in either group of wingers.

The two central attackers make runs towards goal. The defenders follow and mark the central attackers. The winger in possession of the ball dribbles towards the end of the playing area. The first player in the line of other wingers makes an attacking run towards the far post and the central midfield player makes a supporting run towards the goal.

The winger in possession of the ball crosses to either of the central attackers or the other winger. If the cross is misplaced or the defenders clear the ball to the central midfielder, they must pass the ball back to the winger that crossed the ball for a second attempt.

Once the attack is over, the wingers and the central midfielder run to the back of their lines. The central attackers and defenders rotate with the other two central attackers and defenders. The next attack starts when the next central midfielder in line passes to the central attackers. After 5-10 minutes rotate the attackers and defenders and rotate the wingers and central midfielders.

## Key focus/Coaching points

Primary focus: Crossing

Secondary focus: Movement

Additional focus: Long passing

## Progressions/Adaptations

- Add a goalkeeper. Encourage the goalkeeper to try to catch or punch the crosses when appropriate.
- Add a third defender and another central midfielder to each attack. The central midfielder should make an attacking run towards the goal.

# 300 THE SOCCER COACH'S TOOLKIT

## ACTIVITY 123   CROSSING GATES

**Level:** Advanced

**Type of activity:** Opposed technical practice

**Number of participants:** 10 + 2 goalkeepers

**Equipment required:** Soccer balls, cones, discs, 2 sets of bibs and 2 goals

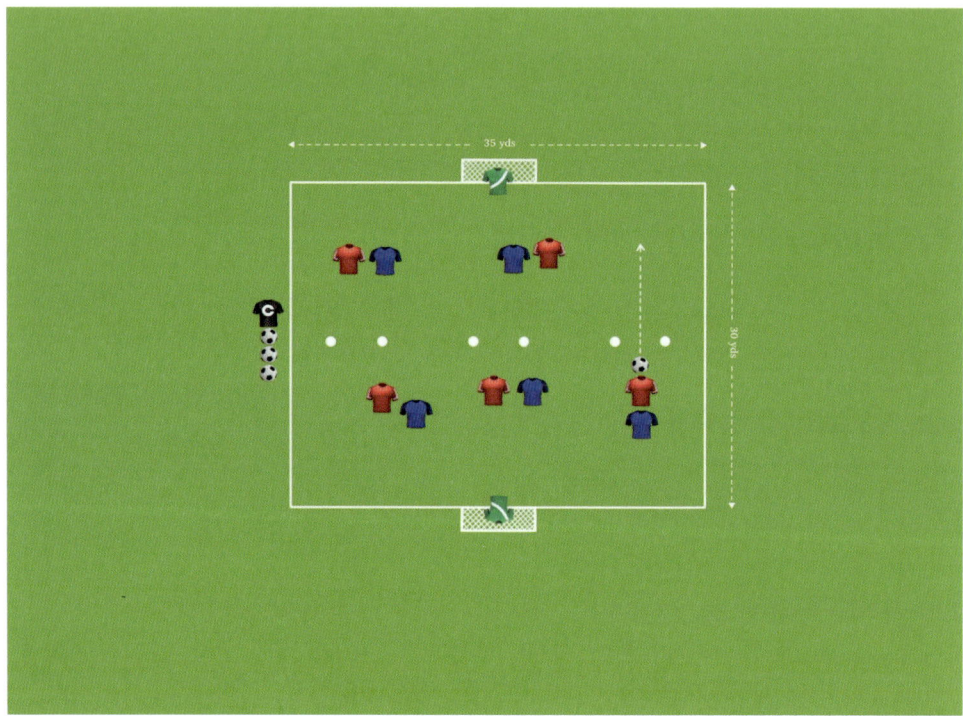

## Description

Divide players into two teams of six (including goalkeepers). Mark out a wide playing area and position a goal and goalkeeper at both ends of the playing area. Position both teams inside the playing area. Position one gate on both sides of the playing area and one in the centre of the playing area.

# Crossing

The teams play a 6v6 match. Condition play so that a team can only try to score once of their players has either dribbled or passed through one of the gates to a teammate. When an attacking player is in possession after they have travelled through one of the wide gates, they should be encouraged to deliver a cross rather than pass to retain possession.

## Key focus/Coaching points

Primary focus: Crossing

Secondary focus: Short passing

Additional focus: Movement

## Progressions/Adaptations

- Position the gates closer to the goals.
- Allow goals to be scored without travelling through a gate; however, if a team scores after travelling through a gate award 3 goals.

# 302 THE SOCCER COACH'S TOOLKIT

## ACTIVITY 124   CROSSING OVERLOADS

**Level:** Advanced

**Type of activity:** Opposed technical practice

**Number of participants:** 10 + 2 goalkeepers

**Equipment required:** Soccer balls, cones, discs, 2 sets of bibs and 2 goals

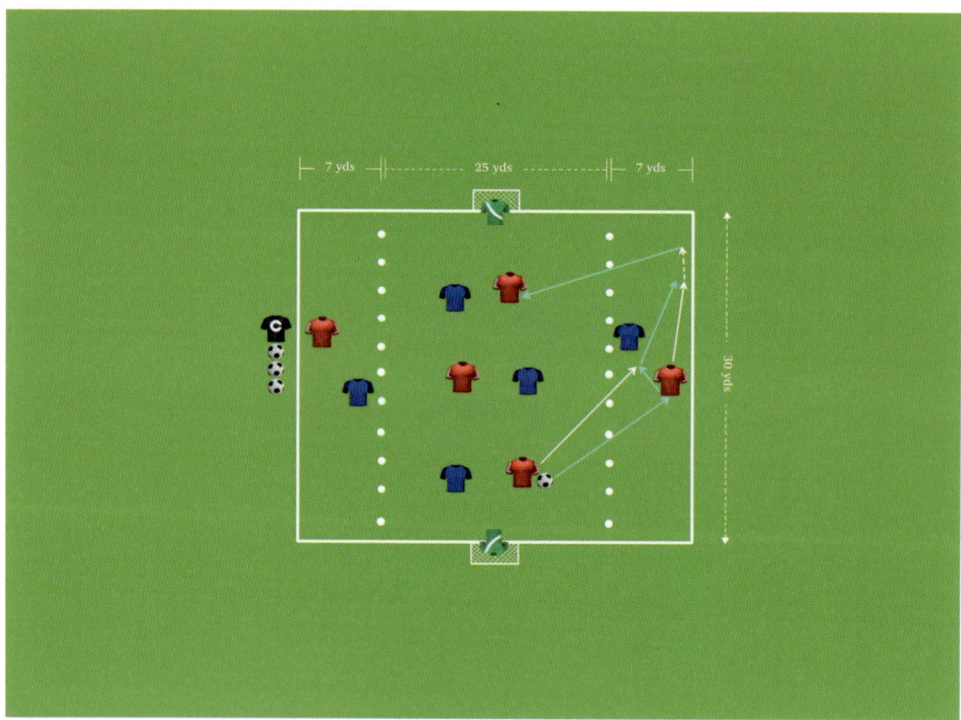

## Description

Divide players into two teams of six (including goalkeepers). Mark out a main playing area with a channel on either side. The channels should cover the full length of the playing area. Position a goal and goalkeeper at both ends of the playing area. Position three players from both teams inside the main playing area. Position one player from each team in both channels.

The teams play a 5v5 match with the condition that before either team can try to score, they must pass to a teammate in either channel. After a pass into the channel, the player that passed the ball runs into the channel to create a 2v1 attacking overload.

Once the ball and the player that passed the ball are inside the channel, the two attacking players try to create an opportunity to cross the ball back into the main playing area. Once the ball has been crossed or possession is lost, the player that was originally inside the channel runs into the main playing area and the player that passed the ball remains in the channel. If the opposition player in the channel wins possession, they then pass to a teammate inside the main playing area and play continues.

## Key focus/Coaching points

Primary focus: Crossing

Secondary focus: Dribbling

Additional focus: Support play

## Progressions/Adaptations

- 1 defender from inside the main playing area must follow each pass into the channel to create a 2v2. If the defenders win possession in the channel, they can either pass into the main playing area or stay inside the channel and attack the other end. Once the ball is back inside the main playing area, the defender that followed the pass out stays inside the channel and the other defender runs into the main playing area.

- The attacking players inside the channel can only use 2 passes before they must deliver a cross.

# 304 THE SOCCER COACH'S TOOLKIT

# SHOOTING

## ACTIVITY 125  CONTINUOUS SHOOTING

**Level:** Basic

**Type of activity:** Unopposed technical practice

**Number of participants:** 12 + 1 goalkeeper

**Equipment required:** Soccer balls, cones, 2 sets of bibs and 2 goals

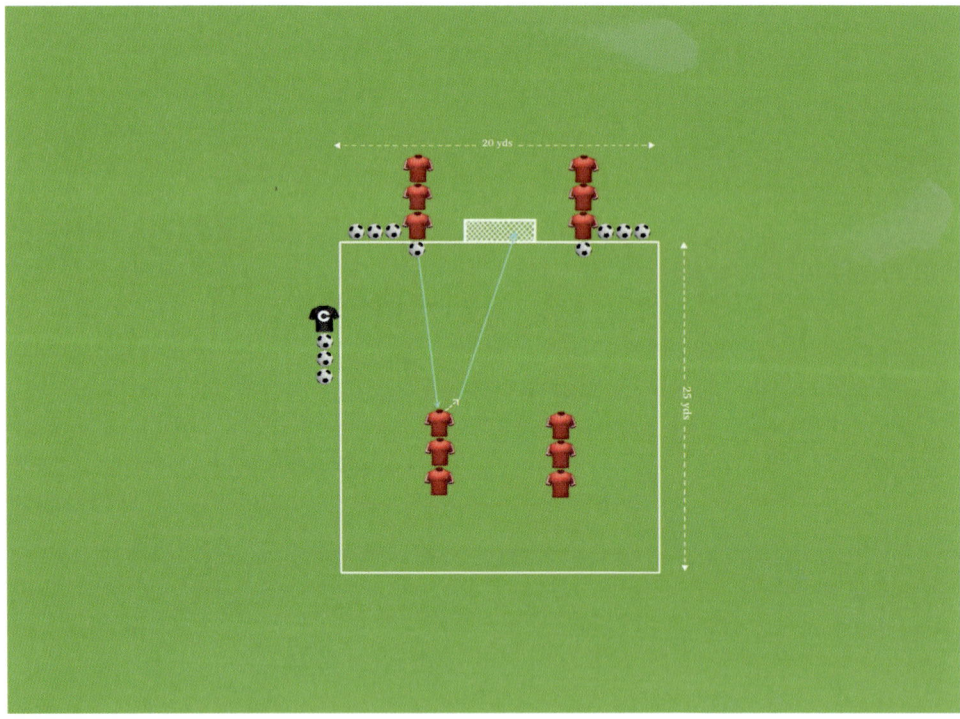

## Description

Divide players into two groups of three attackers and two groups of three ball feeders. Mark out a playing area with a goal at one end. Position one line of attacking players 20 yards from and in line with either goalpost. Position one line of ball feeders opposite each group of attackers and a safe distance to the side of the goal. Position a supply of balls with both groups of ball feeders.

The activity starts when the first player in either group of ball feeders passes to the first attacker in the opposite line. The attacking player receives the pass and shoots at goal. The attacker follows their shot to the back of the opposite line of ball feeders. The ball feeder follows their pass to the back of the opposite line of attackers. The activity continues immediately from the other group of ball feeders.

## Key focus/Coaching points

Primary focus: Shooting

Secondary focus: Receiving

Additional focus: Finishing

## Progressions/Adaptations

Work through the following variations:
- 1 touch and shoot.
- First time shot.
- Left-foot/right-foot shots.
- Receive the pass to the left/right before shooting.
- Vary the type of feed, e.g., flat, bobbly or aerial.
- The feeder follows their pass and tries to block the shot.
- The receiving player passes to the first player in the other line of attackers to shoot.
- Play for 3 minutes and see which line scores most goals.
- Add a goalkeeper.

## ACTIVITY 126   READY TO FIRE

**Level:** Basic

**Type of activity:** Unopposed technical practice

**Number of participants:** 4 + 1 goalkeeper

**Equipment required:** Soccer balls, cones, 2 sets of bibs and 1 goal

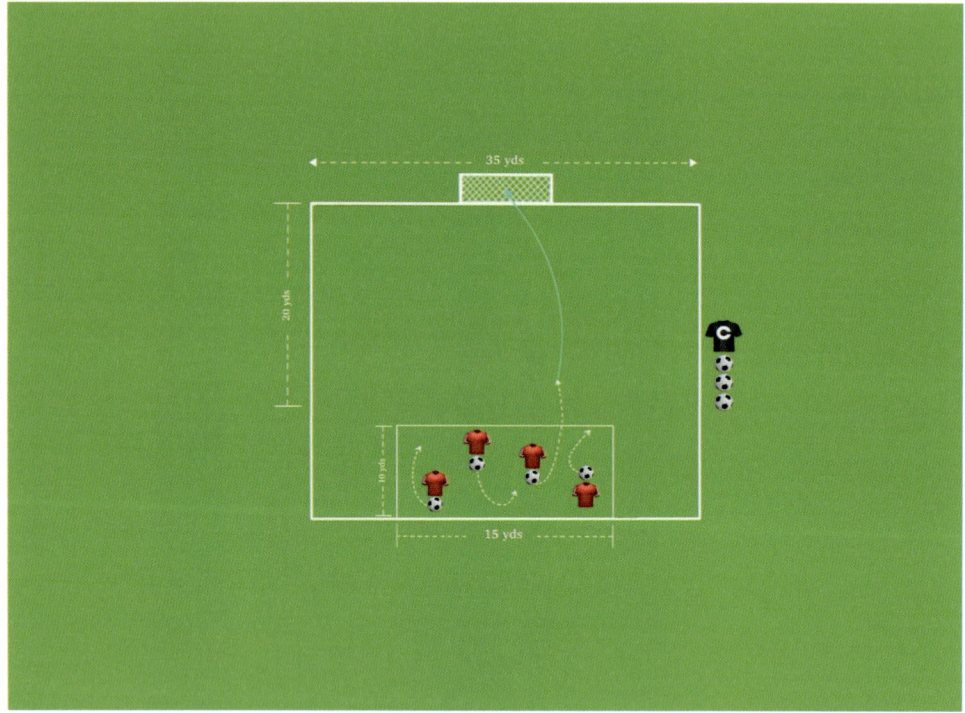

## Description

Divide players into one group of four. Number the players 1-4. Mark out a playing area and a shooting zone beyond the playing area. Position a goal at the end of the playing area beyond the shooting zone. Each player requires one ball.

The activity starts with all the players dribbling and turning inside the playing area. The coach calls out a number from 1-4 and the corresponding player dribbles into the shooting zone and shoots at goal. After the shot, the player quickly retrieves their ball and re-enters the playing area. The coach should call out a number every 5 seconds to maintain a regular flow of shots and give all players lots of opportunities to shoot.

## Key focus/Coaching points

**Primary focus:** Shooting

**Secondary focus:** Finishing

**Additional focus:** Dribbling

## Progressions/Adaptations

- The players must shoot from inside the main playing area rather than inside the shooting zone. Make sure that all other players quickly move clear of the goal before the shot.

- Use only 2 balls inside the main playing area. The players pass and move to each other using the 2 balls. The players in possession of the balls when the coach calls "Shoot" dribble into the shooting zone to shoot.

- Divide players into a team of 3 attackers and 1 defender. Use 1 ball. The attackers try to keep possession from the defender. When the coach calls "Shoot", the attackers have 5 seconds to create an opportunity for an attacker to dribble into the shooting zone. If an attacker manages to dribble into the shooting zone, the defender follows the attacker and tries to stop them scoring.

- Add a goalkeeper.

# 308 THE SOCCER COACH'S TOOLKIT

## ACTIVITY 127 SHOOTING RELAY

**Level:** Basic

**Type of activity:** Unopposed technical practice

**Number of participants:** 8 + 2 goalkeepers

**Equipment required:** Soccer balls, cones, 2 sets of bibs and 2 goals

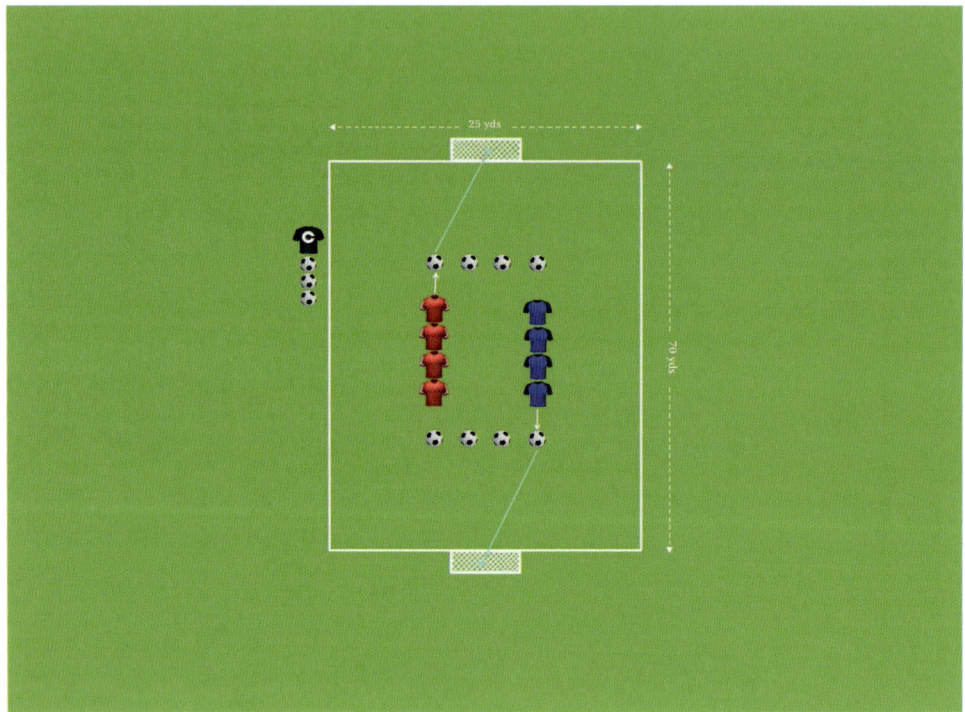

## Description

Divide players into two teams of four. Mark out a playing area with a goal positioned at both ends of the playing area. Position the teams side-by-side in straight lines and in the middle of the playing area. Position the teams so that they are facing opposite goals. Both teams of players should be approximately 35 yards from the goal they are facing. Position a line of four balls 10 yards in front of both teams.

The activity starts when the players at the front of both lines sprint to their supply of balls and try to score with a shot into their goal. After the shot, the player sprints back to their line and tags the next player.

Every player in the team repeats the run and shot until each ball has been shot. The teams race to shoot all their balls as quickly as possible. The first team to shoot all their soccer balls and get into line wins 2 points. Encourage the players to shoot accurately and award 3 points for every goal scored. The team with the most points overall wins the race.

## Key focus/Coaching points

**Primary focus:** Shooting

**Secondary focus:** Finishing

**Additional focus:** Speed

## Progressions/Adaptations

- Add goalkeepers.
- Switch from a team race to individual player races. The player that completes the shot and runs to the back of their line first scores 1 point for their team. Add an extra point for each shot on target and 3 points for each goal.
- Add 1 ball feeder to each team. Position the ball feeders 10 yards in front of and to the side of their team. Position 4 balls with each ball feeder. As the players in each team run towards the goal, the ball feeders pass to the player in their team. The shooting player is allowed 1 touch to receive the pass and then shoot.

# 310  THE SOCCER COACH'S TOOLKIT

## ACTIVITY 128  SHOOTING FUNDAMENTALS

**Level:** Basic

**Type of activity:** Unopposed technical practice

**Number of participants:** 2-20

**Equipment required:** Soccer balls, cones and 2 sets of bibs

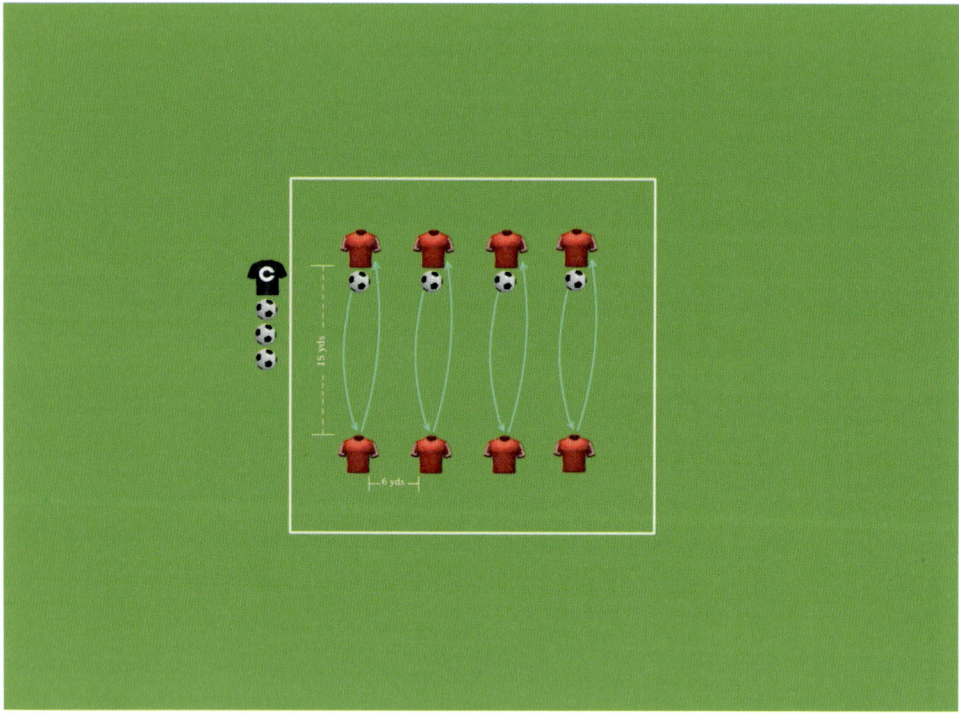

## Description

Divide players into pairs with one ball between them. Position all pairs inside the playing area. Position the players in each pair 15-20 yards apart and opposite each other. Nominate one player to perform a shot towards the chest area of their partner. The shot should be moderately powerful so that the player catching the ball can do so comfortably. Each player performs 10 shots and then the players rotate roles. The players should rotate roles two to three times. Emphasise good shooting technique and work on accurate shooting into the chest area.

Make sure that each pair are positioned at least 5-6 yards apart. Ensure that the players catching the shots are directly opposite their partner. This will help to minimise the risk of players getting hit by balls.

## Key focus/Coaching points

Primary focus: Shooting

Secondary focus: Goalkeeping

Additional focus: Physical/movement development

## Progressions/Adaptations

- Divide players into groups of 4. Position 3 of the players facing and at different angles to the shooter. The shooters perform shots towards the chest area of each player in their group.
- Change the target area for the shots, e.g., shin height and the trajectory of each shot, e.g., 1 bounce.
- Increase the distance between the shooters and their partner(s) to 20-25 yards.

## ACTIVITY 129   HIT THE TARGET

**Level:** Basic

**Type of activity:** Unopposed technical practice

**Number of participants:** 9 + 1 goalkeeper

**Equipment required:** Soccer balls, cones, 2 sets of bibs and 1 goal

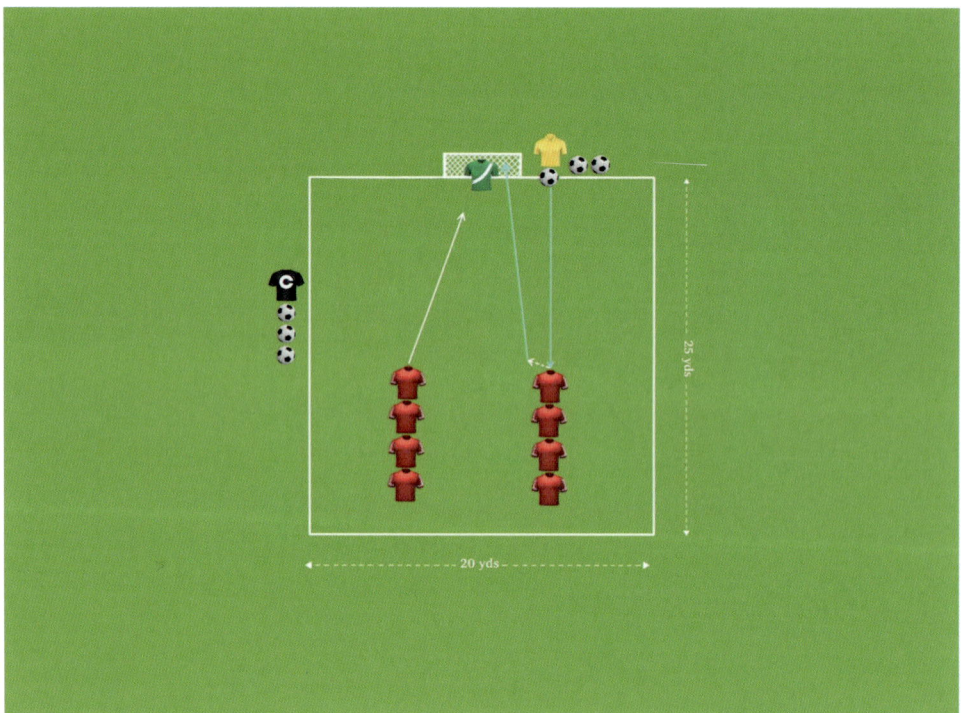

## Description

Divide players into two groups of four attackers and 1 ball feeder. Position a goal and a goalkeeper at one end of the playing area. Position each group of players 20 yards from the goal. Position one group opposite each goalpost. Position the ball feeder a safe distance to the side of either goalpost with a supply of balls.

The activity starts when the ball feeder passes to the first attacker in line from either group. The attacker that receives the pass has one touch to receive the ball and then shoot at goal. The first attacker in line from the other group runs towards the goal and tries to convert any rebounds from the goalkeeper.

Any rebound finishes must be first-time. If the attacker scores, award 3 points to their group. If the shot rebounds and the other attacker converts the rebound, award 1 point to their group. After each shot, the attackers run to the back of their lines.

The ball feeder passes to each attacker in line from the same group until all the balls have been shot. When all the balls have been shot, re-load the balls. The activity re-starts when the ball feeder passes to the first attacker in line from the other group. After one round of shooting each, the team with the most points are the winning team.

## Key focus/Coaching points

Primary focus: Shooting

Secondary focus: Finishing

Additional focus: Volleys

## Progressions/Adaptations

- Vary the type of pass to the attackers, e.g., flat, lofted or 1-2 bounces.
- The attackers must shoot first time.

# 314 THE SOCCER COACH'S TOOLKIT

## ACTIVITY 130   RECEIVE AND SHOOT

**Level:** Basic

**Type of activity:** Unopposed technical practice

**Number of participants:** 13 + 1 goalkeeper

**Equipment required:** Soccer balls, cones, 1 set of bibs and 1 goal

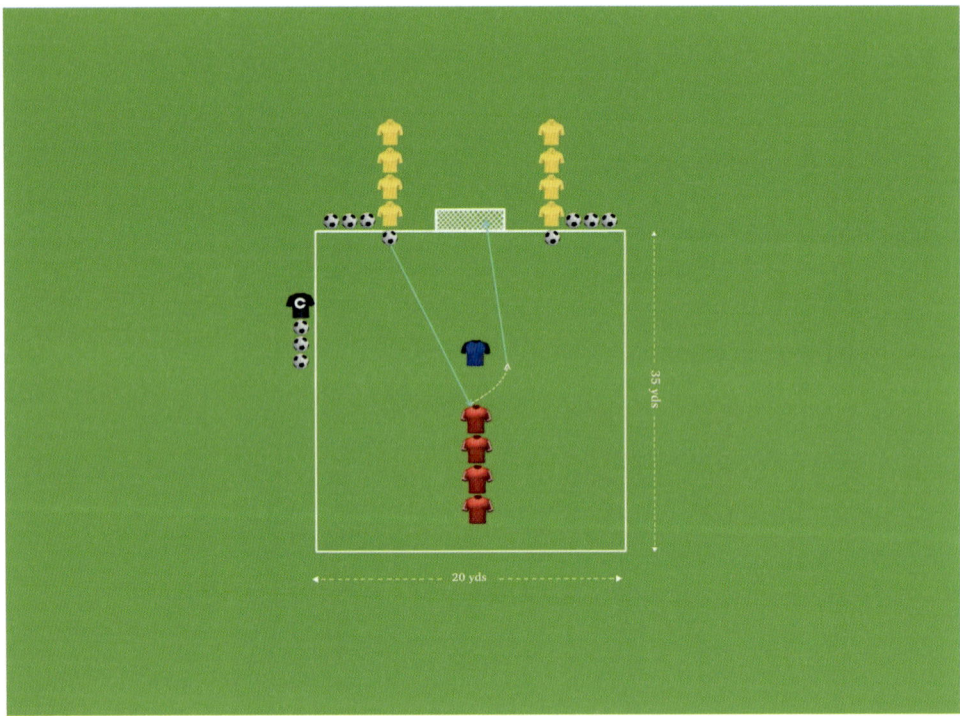

## Description

Divide players into one group of four attackers, two groups of four ball feeders and one defender. Mark out a playing area with a goal at one end of the playing area. Position the group of attackers 20-25 yards from the centre of the goal. Position one group of ball feeders on the left and one group of ball feeders on the right, diagonally in front of the attackers. Each group of ball feeders requires a supply of balls. Position one defender 10 yards in front of and facing the line of attackers.

The activity starts when the first player in line from either ball-feeding group passes to the first attacker in line. The attacker receives the pass to the side of the defender to shoot at goal with their next touch. The defender should apply passive pressure to the attacker. After the shot, the ball feeder and the attacker run to the back of each other's lines. The activity continues with a pass to the next attacker in line from the first player in line from the other group of ball feeders.

## Key focus/Coaching points

Primary focus: Shooting

Secondary focus: Finishing

Additional focus: Receiving

## Progressions/Adaptations

- Players must shoot first time.
- Vary the type of pass to the attackers, e.g., flat, aerial or 1-2 bounces.
- Add a goalkeeper.

# 316 THE SOCCER COACH'S TOOLKIT

## ACTIVITY 131   SHOOTING FIESTA

**Level:** Intermediate

**Type of activity:** Unopposed technical practice

**Number of participants:** 11 + 1 goalkeeper

**Equipment required:** Soccer balls, cones, 2 mannequins or domes and 1 goal

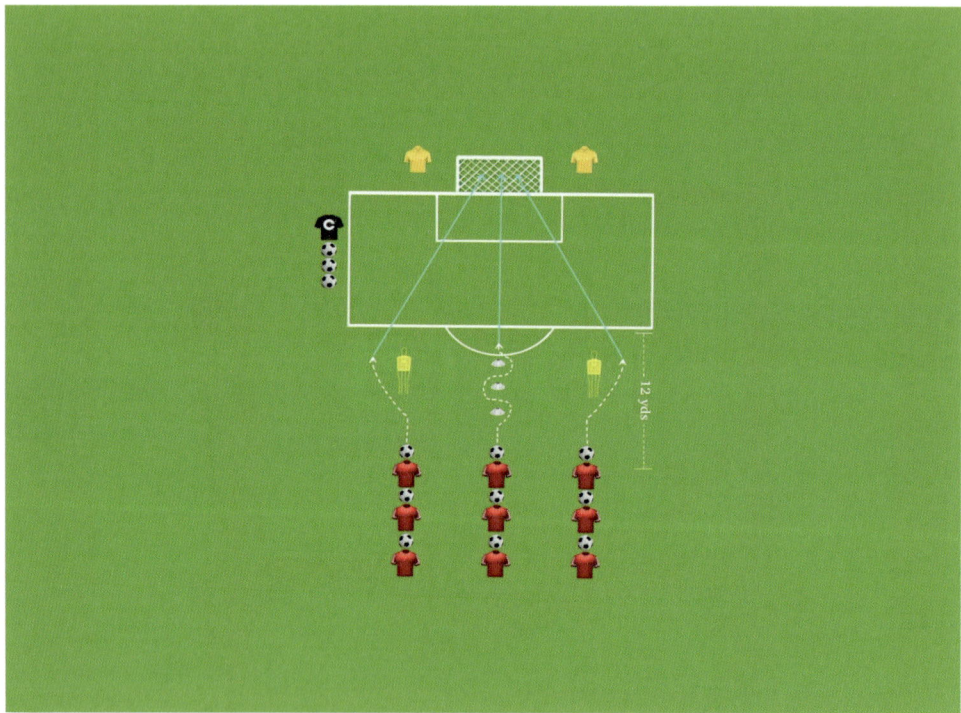

## Description

Divide players into three groups of three and two ball retrievers. Mark out a playing area with a goal at one end of the playing area. Position one group of players 10 yards to left of the left goalpost, one group of players in line with the centre of the goal and one group 10 yards to the right of the right goalpost. Position each group in straight lines and 30 yards from goal. Each player requires a ball. Position the ball retrievers a safe distance behind the goal to collect stray shots.

The activity starts when the first player in line from the group on the left shoots at goal, immediately followed by the first player in line from the central group and then the first player in line from the group on the right.

After each player has performed their shot, the players run to collect their soccer balls and then to the back of their line. As soon as the players are at the back of their lines, the next players in line from each group follow the same sequence. Once the players are comfortable with the organisation of the activity, add in the following requirements before shooting:

- **Group on the left** – dribble past and to the left of a mannequin 10 yards ahead and shoot with the left foot.
- **Group in the centre** – slalom dribble through 3 cones and shoot with either foot.
- **Group on the right** – dribble past and to the right of a mannequin 10 yards ahead before shooting with the right foot.

Rotate the ball retrievers every 3-4 minutes.

## Key focus/Coaching points

Primary focus: Shooting

Secondary focus: Finishing

Additional focus: Dribbling

## Progressions/Adaptations

- Add a goalkeeper. Allow a short pause in between each shot so the goalkeeper can prepare for the next shot.
- The next player in line chases the shooter and applies passive pressure.

## ACTIVITY 132  SHOOTING FIESTA 2

**Level:** Intermediate

**Type of activity:** Opposed technical practice

**Number of participants:** 11 + 1 goalkeeper

**Equipment required:** Soccer balls, cones, 1 mannequin or domes and 1 goal

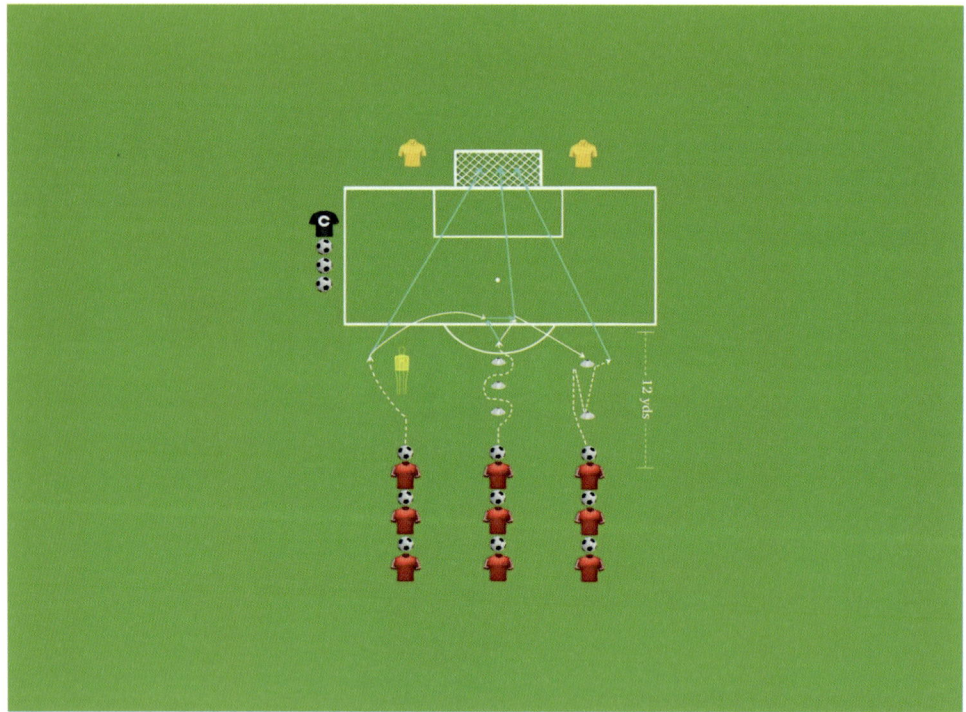

## Description

Divide players into three groups of three and two ball retrievers. Mark out a playing area with a goal at one end of the playing area. Position one group of players 10 yards to left of the left goalpost, one group of players in line with the centre of the goal and one group 10 yards to the right of the right goalpost. Position each group in straight lines and 30 yards from goal. Each player requires a ball. Position the ball retrievers a safe distance behind the goal to collect stray shots.

The activity starts when the first player in line from the group on the left shoots at goal, immediately followed by the first player in line from the central group and then the first player in line from the group on the right.

After the player from the group on the left has performed their shot, they run to face the first player in line from the central group. As soon as the player from the group on the left is in position, the first player in the central group completes the task (see below) and performs their shot. After the shot, the player from the group on the left runs to the back of the central group line and the player from the central group runs to stand opposite the first player in line from the group on the right.

As soon as the player from the central group is in position, the player from the group on the right completes the dribbling task (see below) and then performs their shot. Each time the player dribbles to cone 2, the player opposite them should apply passive pressure. After performing the shot, the player from the central group runs to the back of the group on the right and the player from the group on the right runs to the back of the line on the left.

To maintain a continuous flow of this activity, encourage players to work quickly and move as fast as they can to their new line after each shot. This will encourage players in each group to start their dribbling task immediately and ensure the activity moves quickly. Re-load the ball and rotate the ball retrievers every 3-4 minutes.

- **Group 1** – Dribble to mannequin 10 yards ahead, sidestep left or right and shoot.
- **Group 2** – Dribble in and out of 4 cones, perform a 1-2 pass and shoot.
- **Group 3** – Start on cone 1, dribble to and around cone 2, dribble back to and around cone 1, dribble to cone 2, sidestep left or right and shoot.

## Key focus/Coaching points

**Primary focus:** Shooting

**Secondary focus:** Finishing

**Additional focus:** Dribbling

## Progressions/Adaptations

- Add a goalkeeper. Allow a short pause in between each shot so the goalkeeper can prepare for the next shot.
- Players must shoot with their weaker foot.
- The next player in line chases the shooter and applies passive pressure.

# ACTIVITY 133  OPEN CORNER

**Level:** Intermediate

**Type of activity:** Unopposed technical practice

**Number of participants:** 16 + 4 goalkeepers

**Equipment required:** Soccer balls, cones and 4 goals

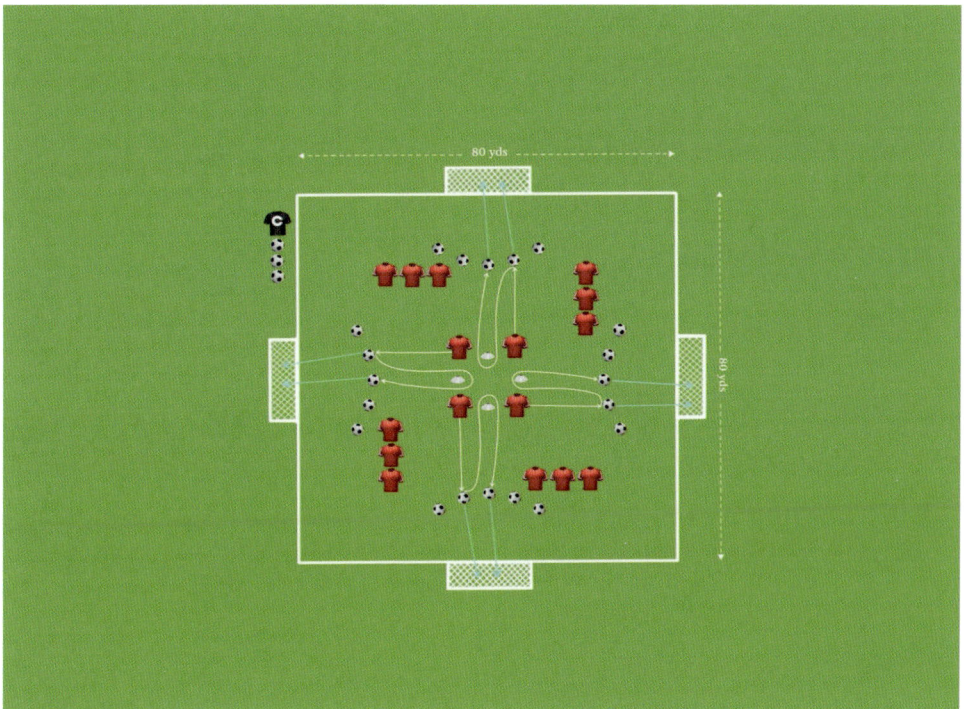

## Description

Divide players into four groups of four. Position a goal at each end of the playing area. Position five balls in an arc shape 25 yards from each goal. The inside of the arc should be facing the goal. Position a cone 10 yards opposite the ball in the centre of each arc. The players in each group take turns to perform the following shooting activity:

Run to any of the balls and shoot. After the shot, run back to and around the cone. Repeat for the task for all 5 balls. Encourage the players to run as fast as possible and shoot with as much power as possible.

Make sure that the goals are clear of other players before each shot.

## Key focus/Coaching points

Primary focus: Shooting

Secondary focus: Finishing

Additional focus: Goalkeeping

## Progressions/Adaptations

- Position a goalkeeper in 1 corner of each goal. The goalkeeper is not allowed to move across the goal line, but they can dive if the shot comes near enough to save and divert it away from the goal.
- Allow the goalkeepers to move and make saves as they would in competitive play.

Shooting **323**

## ACTIVITY 134 FOUR-WAY SHOOTING

**Level:** Intermediate

**Type of activity:** Unopposed technical practice

**Number of participants:** 16 + 4 goalkeepers

**Equipment required:** Soccer balls, cones and 4 goals

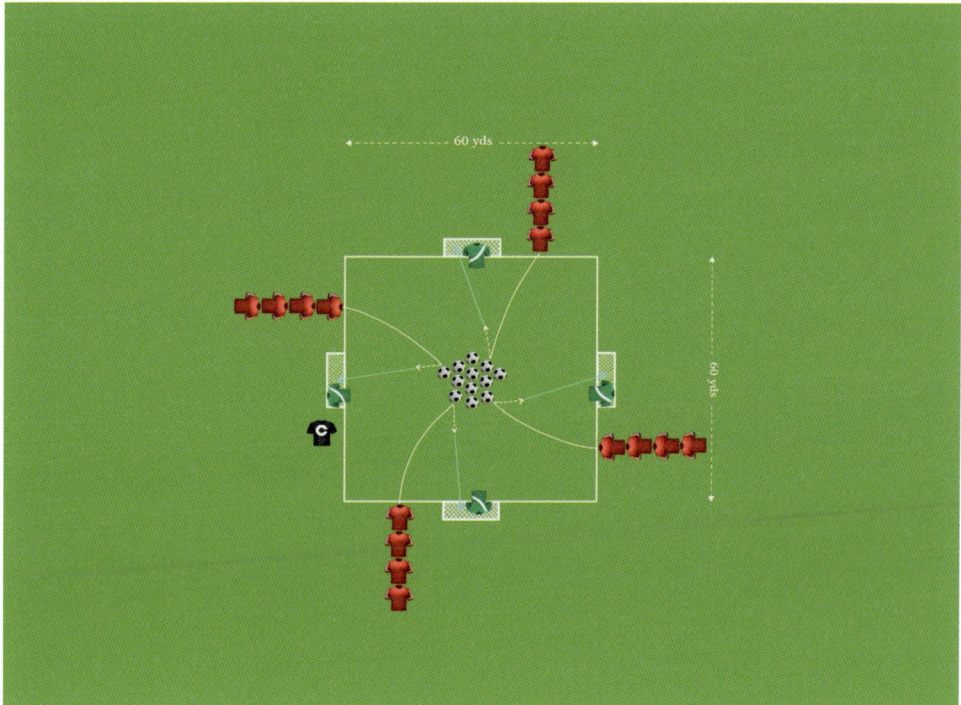

## Description

Divide players into four groups of four. Position one goal and goalkeeper on all sides of the playing area. Position each group in a straight line 10 yards to the side of their goal. Ensure that the players are a safe distance away from the goal and are alert to stray shots. Position all balls in a tight circle in the centre of the playing area. The balls should be approximately 30 yards from each goal.

The activity starts when first player in line from each group runs into the middle of the playing area, collects a ball, dribbles it towards and shoots at their goal from 20-25 yards. After each player has performed their shot, they must run to retrieve their ball and return it to the centre of the playing as quickly as possible.

After returning the balls to the centre of the playing area, the players that performed a shot run to the back of their line. As soon as the players are at the back of their lines, the next player in line repeats the task. The players should perform the activity continuously for 5 minutes. Award 5 points each time a player scores. The activity should continue for 5 minutes. The player with the most points in each group is the winner.

## Key focus/Coaching points

**Primary focus:** Shooting

**Secondary focus:** Finishing

**Additional focus:** Speed

## Progressions/Adaptations

- Players must shoot using their weaker foot.
- Encourage the goalkeepers to start 2-3 steps forwards from their goal line to narrow the shooting angle.
- Condition the style of shot, e.g., low, high, near post and far post.

# ACTIVITY 135  STYLISH SHOOTING

**Level:** Intermediate

**Type of activity:** Unopposed technical practice

**Number of participants:** 16 + 4 goalkeepers

**Equipment required:** Soccer balls, cones and 4 goals

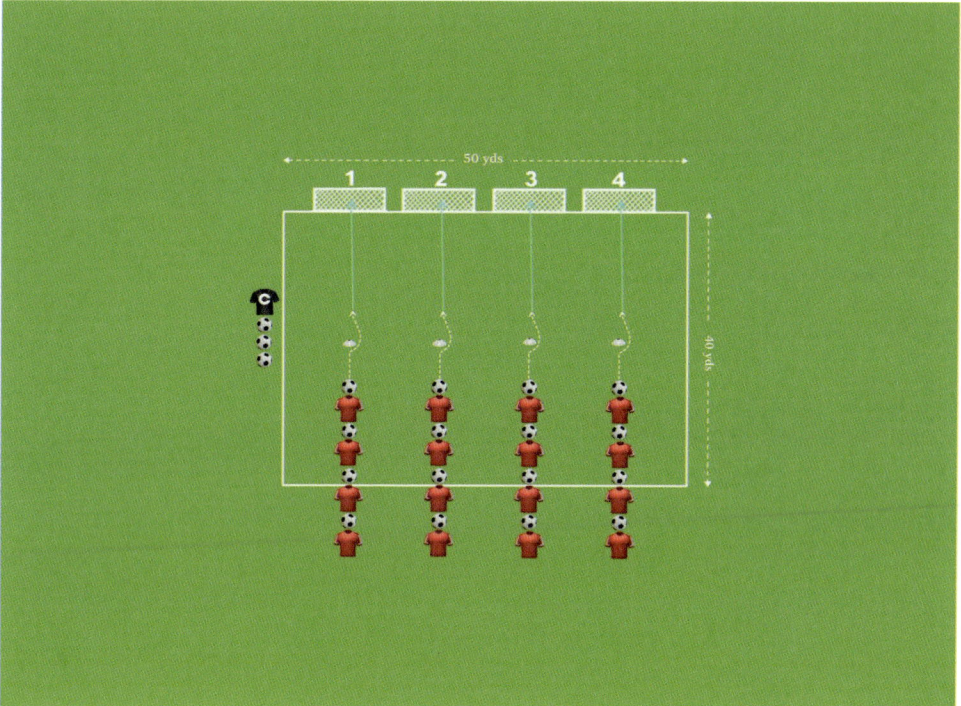

## Description

Divide players into four groups of four. Position four goals at one end of the playing area 12 yards apart. Position each group of players in a straight line opposite one of the goals. Position each group approximately 30 yards away from their goal. Each player requires a ball. Position a cone 5 yards ahead of each line of players.

The activity starts when the first player from each group dribbles their ball around the cone and shoots at goal. As the players dribble past the cones, they must perform a different trick (see below). After the players have shot, they should move up one group to the right and join the back of that line. This rotation does not apply to the players in the group on the far right who should move to the back of the line in the group on the far left. Number the goal on the far left of the playing area number 1.

- **Goal 1** – 2-touch.
- **Goal 2** – Step-over.
- **Goal 3** – Double step-over.
- **Goal 4** – Sidestep.

## Key focus/Coaching points

**Primary focus:** Shooting

**Secondary focus:** Volleys

**Additional focus:** Ball manipulation

## Progressions/Adaptations

- After each dribble and trick, the players must pick up their ball and feed themselves a half-volley or volley.
- Add a goalkeeper in each goal.

# Shooting 327

## ACTIVITY 136   SHOTS ON THE RUN

**Level:** Intermediate

**Type of activity:** Unopposed technical practice

**Number of participants:** 9 + 2 goalkeepers

**Equipment required:** Soccer balls, cones, 1 mannequin or dome, 1 set of bibs and 2 goals

## Description

Divide players into two groups of four. Position a goal at opposite ends of the playing area (approximately 40 yards apart). Position the groups in straight lines and a safe distance to the side of opposite goals. Position the groups so that they are facing each other diagonally. Position a mannequin in the centre of the playing area. Each player requires a soccer ball.

The activity can start from either end when the first player in line runs with their ball towards the mannequin. As they approach the mannequin, the player side steps it to either side and shoots at goal. As soon as the player has performed their shot, the first player in the opposite line repeats the task in the opposite direction. The activity continues end to end and should be performed at high speed to keep all players involved. After 5 minutes, position both groups on the other side of their goalpost.

Make sure that the player collecting their ball from the goal is out of the goal before another shot is attempted at this goal.

## Key focus/Coaching points

Primary focus: Shooting

Secondary focus: Running with the ball

Additional focus: Goalkeeping

## Progressions/Adaptations

- Players must use a different trick or skill to go past the mannequin, e.g., step-over.
- Replace the mannequin with a passive defender to pressurise the shooters.
- The next player in line chases the shooter to add pressure from behind.
- Add a goalkeeper.

# ACTIVITY 137  RAINING SHOTS

**Level:** Advanced

**Type of activity:** Opposed technical practice

**Number of participants:** 12 + 3 goalkeepers

**Equipment required:** Soccer balls, cones, 3 sets of bibs and 2 goals

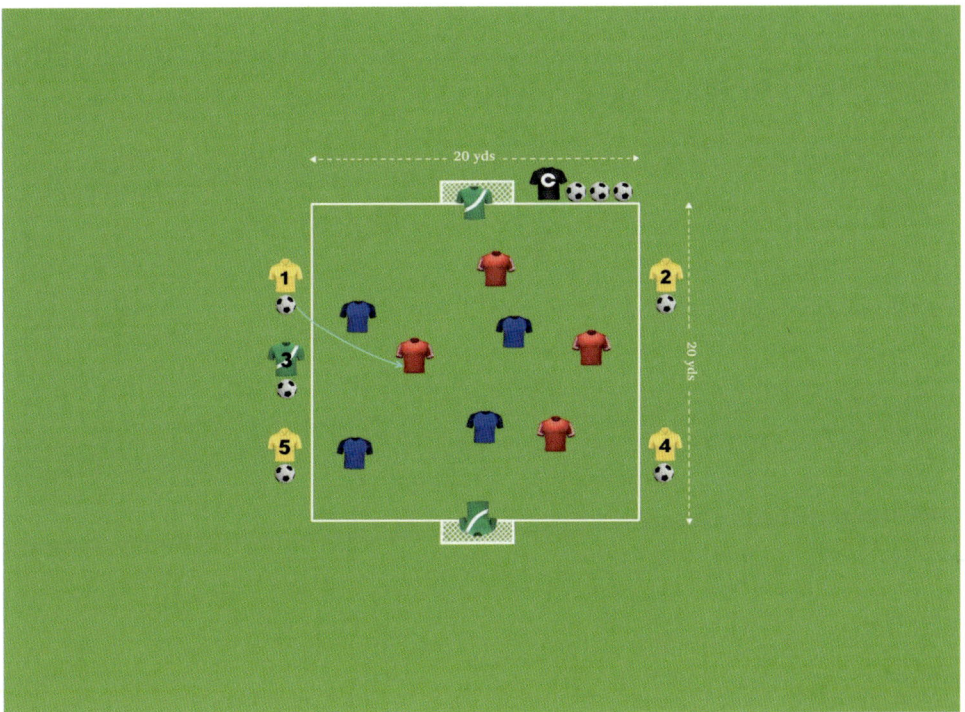

## Description

Divide players into three teams of five (including goalkeepers). Mark out a short and narrow playing area. Position a goal and goalkeeper at both ends of the playing area. Position two of the teams inside and the remaining team outside the playing area. Number the players outside the playing area 1-5. Try to position two to three players in this group on each side of the playing area. The teams inside the playing area attack opposite goals.

The activity starts when player number 1 passes their ball into the playing area to either team. The two teams inside the playing area compete against each other until a goal is scored or the ball goes out of play. As soon as either of these things happens, player number 2 passes their ball into the team that had the last touch in the previous episode of play. The activity continues until all the balls have been used. Rotate one team from inside the playing area with the team outside the playing area.

## Key focus/Coaching points

**Primary focus:** Shooting

**Secondary focus:** Creativity

**Additional focus:** Finishing

## Progressions/Adaptations

- The teams can use a maximum of 5 passes in each attack.
- Players can only score with a first-time finish/shot.

# Shooting 331

## ACTIVITY 138  SHOOTING IN THE ARC

**Level:** Advanced

**Type of activity:** Opposed technical practice

**Number of participants:** 9 + 1 goalkeeper

**Equipment required:** Soccer balls, cones, 3 sets of bibs and 1 goal

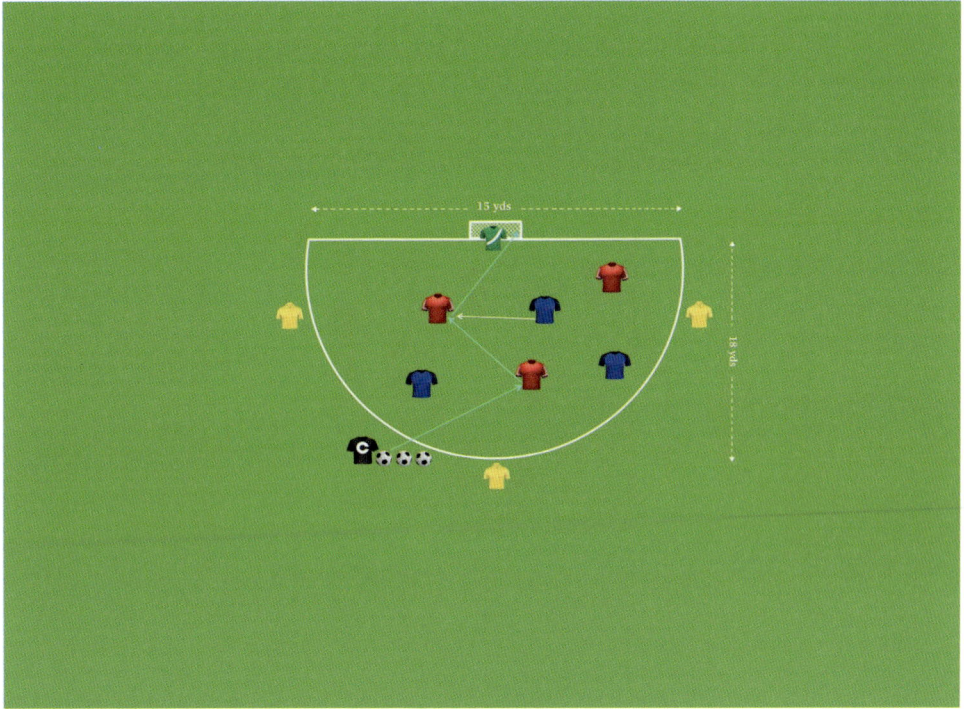

## Description

Divide players into two teams of three and one team of three support players. Mark out an arc-shaped playing area. Position a goal and goalkeeper at the straight end of the playing area. Position two teams inside the playing area and the support players around the outside of the playing area. The coach should be positioned outside the playing area with a supply of balls.

The activity starts when the coach feeds a ball into the playing area. The two teams inside the playing area compete for possession and try to score. The teams are allowed a maximum of three passes inside the playing area before they must try to score.

The teams can earn three extra passes if they need them by passing to and receiving a pass back from a support player. The support players can be used if the team in possession is unable to create an attempt at goal with three passes. The support players can only be used twice during each attack. Encourage the teams to try to create chances to score using as few passes as possible and to use the support players only when necessary.

The two teams play until a goal is scored. After each failed attack, the coach feeds another pass into the playing area. When a goal is scored, the team that scored stays inside the playing area for the next game. The losing team swaps roles with the support players.

## Key focus/Coaching points

Primary focus: Shooting

Secondary focus: Finishing

Additional focus: Attacking and defending

## Progressions/Adaptations

- The support players can only be used once in each attack.
- The teams must complete 3 passes and then pass to one of the support players. The support player has 1 touch to receive the pass and a second touch to shoot. If the support player scores, the goal counts for the team that passed the ball to them. If the shot stays inside the playing area, the activity continues.

# ACTIVITY 139  SHOOTING OPTIONS

**Level:** Advanced

**Type of activity:** Opposed technical practice

**Number of participants:** 13 + 2 goalkeepers

**Equipment required:** Soccer balls, cones, 3 sets of bibs and 2 goals

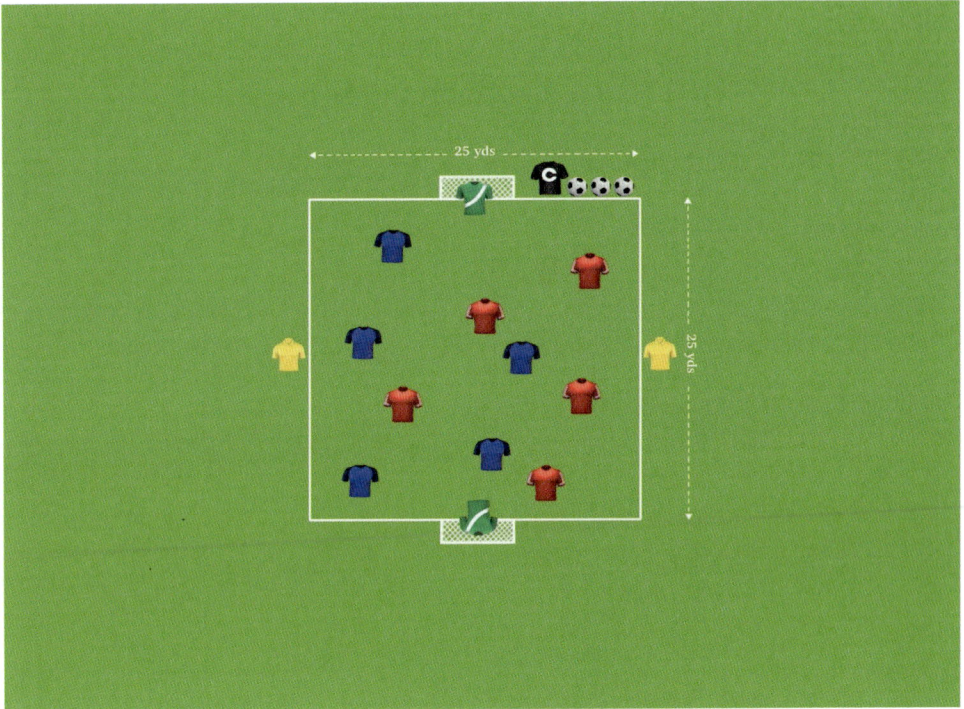

## Description

Divide players into two teams of six (including goalkeepers) and two support players. Position a goal and goalkeeper at both ends of the playing area. Position the two teams inside the playing area and one support player on both sides of the playing area.

The teams compete for possession and try to score at opposite ends of the playing area. The teams are allowed a maximum of three passes before attempting to score. If after the third pass an attempt at goal is not realistically possible, the team in possession can pass to and receive a pass back from a support player to allow three extra passes.

The support players cannot be used more than three times in each attack. Encourage the teams to shoot as early as possible and only use the support players when necessary. The support players should move up and down the length of the playing area to support attacks.

## Key focus/Coaching points

**Primary focus:** Shooting

**Secondary focus:** Finishing

**Additional focus:** Speed

## Progressions/Adaptations

- Position 1 extra support player inside the playing area. The extra support player can be passed to at any time in each attack but must not score for either team.

- Add 1 support player from outside the playing area into each team to create a 7v7 (+ 1 support player). The teams are allowed a maximum of 5 passes before each attempt at goal.

# Shooting

## ACTIVITY 140  STRIKING INSTINCT

**Level:** Advanced

**Type of activity:** Opposed technical practice

**Number of participants:** 12 + 2 goalkeepers

**Equipment required:** Soccer balls, cones, discs, 2 sets of bibs and 2 goals

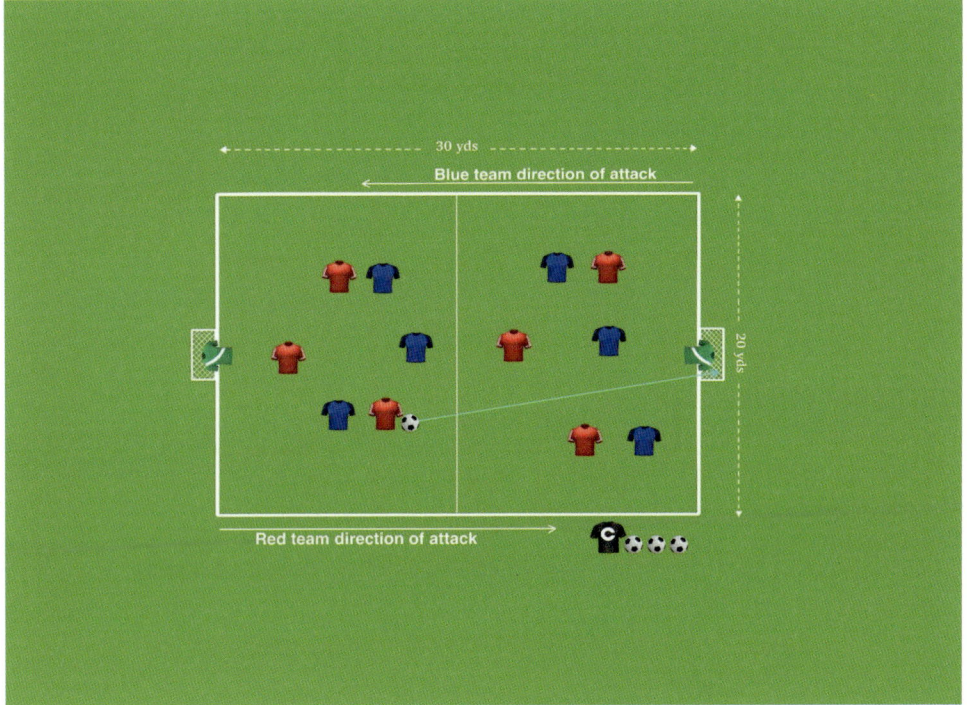

## Description

Divide players into two teams of seven (including goalkeepers). Mark out a playing area with a halfway line. Position a goal and goalkeeper at both ends of the playing area. Position three outfield players from each team in both halves of the playing area. The teams compete for possession and try to score at opposite ends of the playing area.

The teams can only score with a shot from their defensive half. The exception to this condition is if the attacking team has a shot blocked or saved in their attacking half of the playing area. In this instance, the attacking team has a maximum of three passes to try to score. If after three passes, an attempt at goal is not possible, they must pass back into their defensive half to start a new attack. If the defending team wins possession in their defensive half after the blocked shot or save, they then attack the other goal.

If the attacking team loses possession in their defensive half while building an attack, the team that won possession have a maximum of three passes to try to score. If after three passes, an attempt at goal is not possible, the team in possession must pass back into their defensive half.

## Key focus/Coaching points

**Primary focus:** Shooting

**Secondary focus:** Receiving

**Additional focus:** Finishing

## Progressions/Adaptations

- Change both teams' formations so that they have 2 players in their defensive half and 4 players in their attacking half.
- The teams are allowed a maximum of 4 passes in their defensive half of the playing area before they must shoot.

# FINISHING

## ACTIVITY 141   ATTACKING WAVES

**Level:** Basic

**Type of activity:** Unopposed technical practice

**Number of participants:** 18 +2 goalkeepers

**Equipment required:** Soccer balls, cones, discs, 1 set of bibs and 2 goals

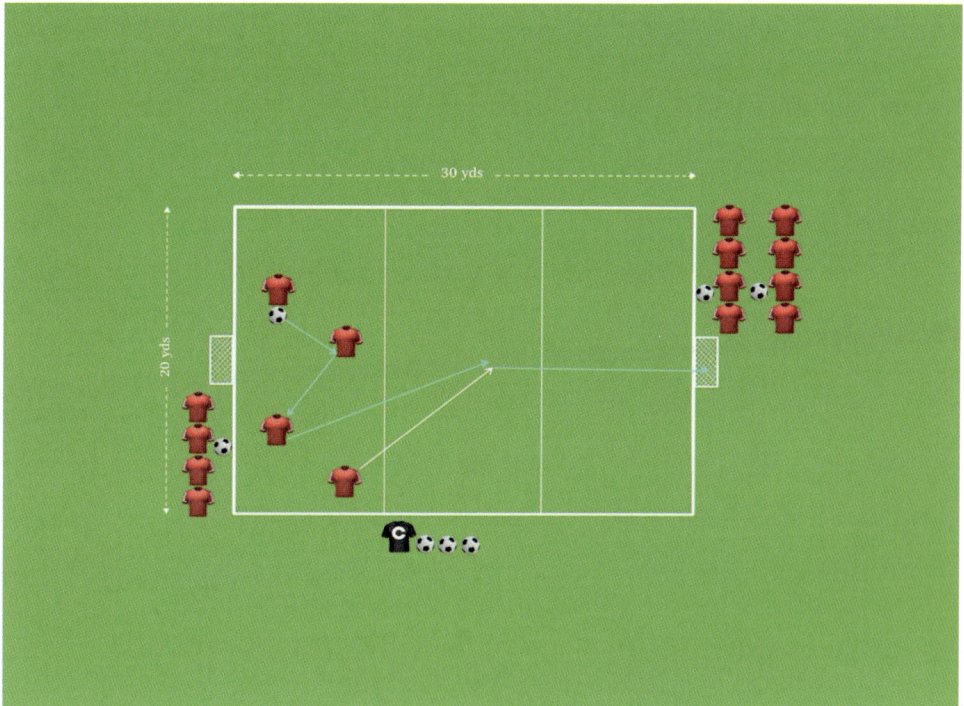

## Description

Divide players into four groups of four attackers. Divide the playing area into three equal-sized zones. Position a goal at both ends of the playing area. Position two groups of attackers at both ends of the playing area. Position each group of attackers side-by-side and a safe distance to either side of the goal. Position the groups of attackers at both ends in two rows (one behind the other). Each group requires one ball.

The activity starts when the first group of attackers at either end of the playing area attack the opposite goal. In the first zone, three of the attackers in the group must receive and pass the ball once. The final pass must be a through pass into the middle zone for the attacker that did not touch the ball to run onto. The attacker that receives the through pass is allowed one touch to receive the pass and one touch to shoot at goal.

As soon as the attacker has shot, all the attackers in the group run around the back of the opposite goal and to the back of the line. The activity continues immediately with an attack from the first group of attackers at the opposite end of the playing area.

## Key focus/Coaching points

**Primary focus:** Finishing

**Secondary focus:** Short passing

**Additional focus:** Speed

## Progressions/Adaptations

- Add a goalkeeper in both goals.
- Each attack starts with a roll out from the goalkeeper.
- Add a defender in both end zones.
- After the through pass into the middle zone, 2 attackers run into the middle zone. The defender in the zone that the attackers passed through follows the 2 attackers into the middle zone. The attackers are allowed a maximum of 3 passes in the middle zone before one of them must shoot. The defender tries to win possession or block the shot.

## ACTIVITY 142   ANGLED FINISHING

**Level:** Basic

**Type of activity:** Unopposed technical practice

**Number of participants:** 12 + 1 goalkeeper

**Equipment required:** Soccer balls, cones, 2 sets of bibs and 1 goal

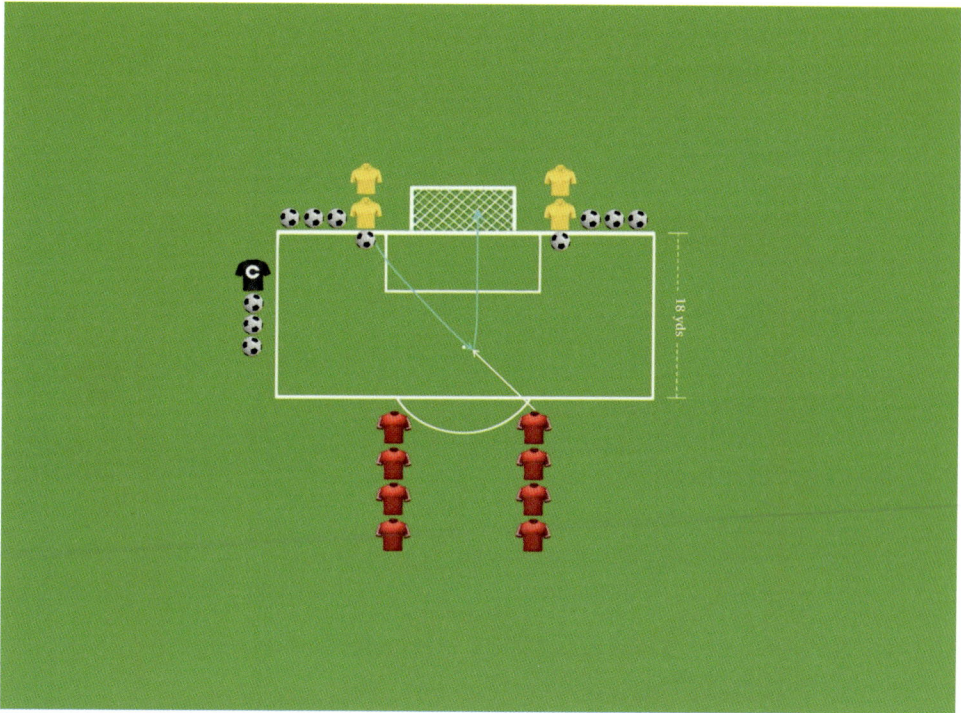

## Description

Divide players into two groups of four attackers and two groups of two ball feeders. Position a goal at one end of the playing area. Position one group of attackers in line with each goalpost. Position the groups of attackers in straight lines and approximately 20 yards from the goal. Position the ball feeders in straight lines and a safe distance to either side of the goal. Each group of ball feeders requires a supply of balls.

The activity starts when the first attacker in line from either group makes an attacking run towards the goal. The first ball feeder in the line diagonally opposite the attacker passes to the attacker as they make their run towards goal. The attacker approaches the ball and performs a first-time finish. Ideally, the attacker should be approximately 12 yards from goal as they perform the finish.

After the finish, the ball feeder and the attacker run to the back of the next line in a clockwise direction. The activity continues immediately with the first ball feeder in line from the other group of ball feeders and the first attacker in line from the other group of attackers. After each finish, the ball feeder and the attacker run to the back of the next line in a clockwise direction.

## Key focus/Coaching points

**Primary focus:** Finishing

**Secondary focus:** Movement

**Additional focus:** Receiving

## Progressions/Adaptations

- Encourage the attackers to make different types of runs before each finish, e.g., to the goal and away, away from the goal and toward it, and curved and straight.
- Vary the type of pass to the attacker, e.g., flat, lofted or 1-2 bounces.
- The ball feeder follows their pass towards the attacker and applies passive pressure to the finish.
- Add a goalkeeper.

# Finishing 341

## ACTIVITY 143 STRIKE FORCE

**Level:** Basic

**Type of activity:** Unopposed technical practice

**Number of participants:** 12 + 1 goalkeeper

**Equipment required:** Soccer balls, cones, 2 sets of bibs and 1 goal

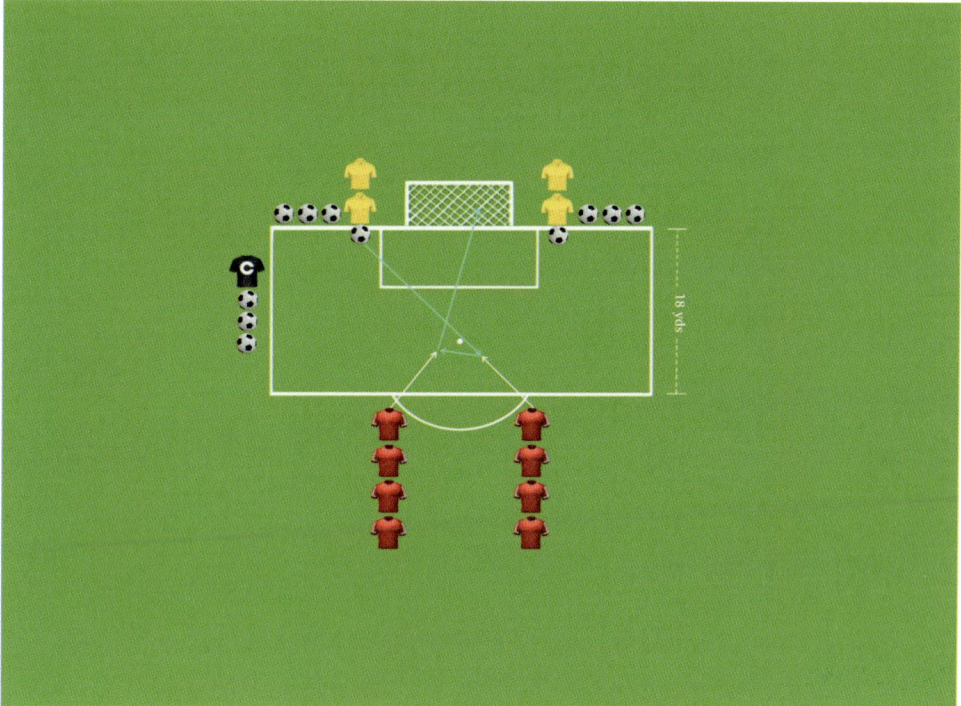

## Description

Divide players into two groups of four attackers and two groups of two ball feeders. Position a goal at one end of the playing area. Position one group of attackers in line with each goalpost. Position the groups of attackers in straight lines and approximately 20 yards from the goal. Position the ball feeders in straight lines and a safe distance to either side of the goal. Each group of ball feeders requires a supply of balls.

The activity starts when the first attacker in line from either group makes an attacking run towards the goal. The first ball feeder in the line diagonally opposite the attacker passes to the attacker as they make their run towards goal.

As the ball feeder passes the ball, the first attacker in line from the other group of attackers makes a supporting run towards the goal. The first attacker receives the pass and then passes to the supporting attacker. The supporting attacker performs a first-time finish. Ideally, the finish should be approximately 12 yards from goal.

After the finish, the ball feeder and the two attackers run to the back of the next line in a clockwise direction. The activity continues immediately with the first ball feeder in line from the other group of ball feeders and the first attacker in line from both groups of attackers. After each finish, the ball feeder and the two attackers run to the back of the next line in a clockwise direction.

## Key focus/Coaching points

**Primary focus:** Finishing

**Secondary focus:** Receiving

**Additional focus:** Movement

## Progressions/Adaptations

- Encourage the attackers to make different types of attacking runs, e.g., to the goal and away, away from the goal and toward it, curved and straight.
- Vary the type of passes to the first attacker, e.g., flat, lofted or 1-2 bounces.
- The ball feeder follows their pass towards the attacker and applies passive pressure to the finish.
- Add a goalkeeper.

# Finishing 343

## ACTIVITY 144  COCONUT SHY

**Level:** Basic

**Type of activity:** Unopposed technical practice

**Number of participants:** 10

**Equipment required:** Soccer balls, cones, domes, 2 sets of bibs and 1 goal

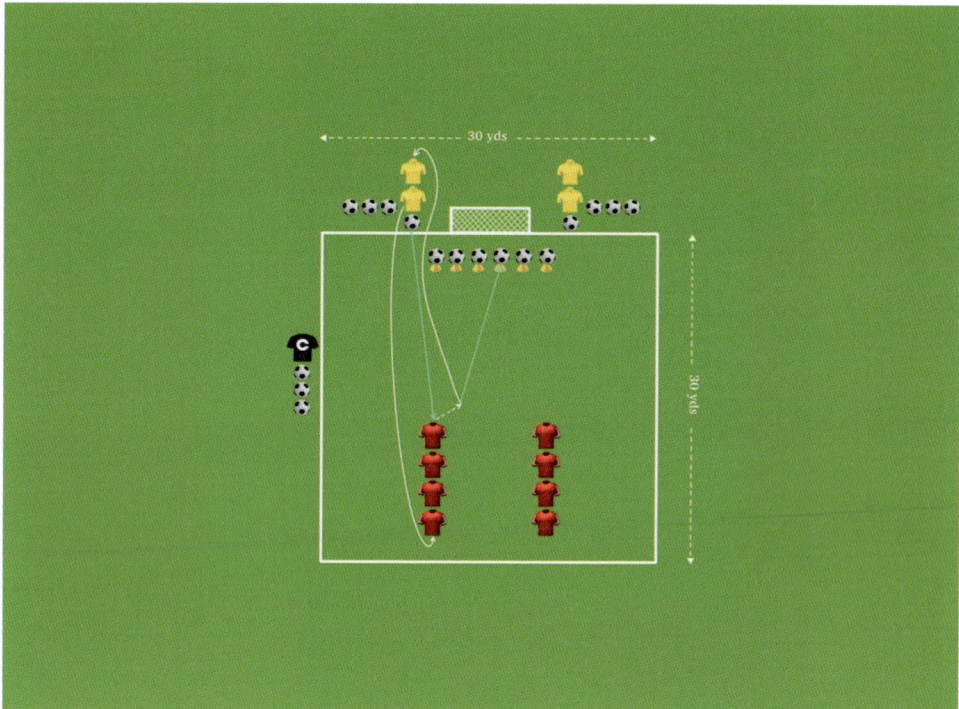

## Description

Divide players into two groups of three or four attackers and two groups of two ball feeders. Mark out a playing area with a goal positioned at one end. Position six balls on top of domes inside the goal. Position the domes side-by-side with 1-2 yards in between each dome.

Position the groups of attackers in straight lines approximately 15 yards from the goal. Position one group of attackers in line with each goalpost. Position one line of ball feeders a safe distance to the side of either goalpost. Each group of ball feeders requires a supply of balls.

The activity starts with a pass from the first player in line from either group of balls to the first attacker in the opposite line. The attacker has one touch to receive the pass and then one touch to try to knock any of the balls off the domes with a low finish.

After each finish, the ball feeder and the attacker run to the back of each other's line. The activity continues immediately from the first player in line in the other group of ball feeders. The activity continues until all the balls have been knocked off the domes.

## Key focus/Coaching points

**Primary focus:** Finishing

**Secondary focus:** Shooting

**Additional focus:** Ball manipulation

## Progressions/Adaptations

- Position a supply of balls with both groups of attackers. The first attacker in line from either group plays a 1-2 with the ball feeder in the opposite line. After receiving the pass back from the ball feeder, the attacker performs a first-time finish.
- After the 1-2, the ball feeder follows their pass and tries to block the finish.

# ACTIVITY 145  4V1 FINISHING

Level: Intermediate

Type of activity: Opposed technical practice

Number of participants: 19 + 2 goalkeepers

Equipment required: Soccer balls, cones, discs, 1 set of bibs and 2 goals

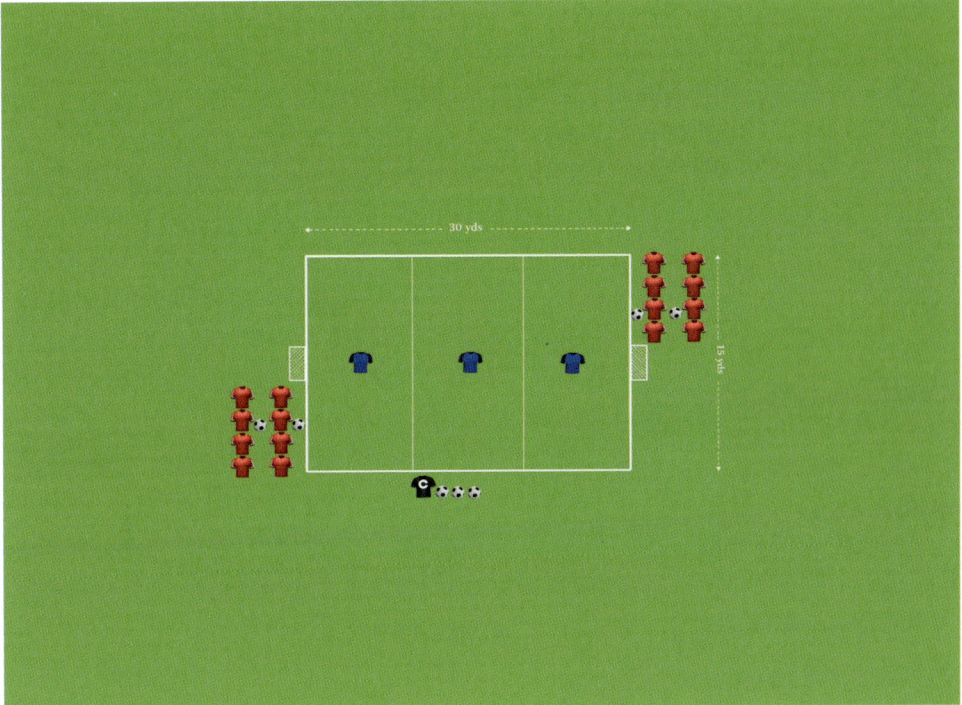

## Description

Divide players into four groups of four attackers and one group of three defenders. Divide the playing area into three equal-sized zones. Position a goal at one end of the playing area. Position one defender in each zone. Position two groups of attackers at both ends of the playing area. Position each group of players side-by-side and a safe distance to either side of the goal. Position the groups at both ends in two rows (one behind the other). Each group requires one ball.

The activity starts with the first group of attackers from either end of the playing area attacking the goal at the opposite end of the playing area. The attackers must keep possession and avoid the defender in each zone. If the attackers successfully reach the far end zone, they try to score.

If any of the defenders make a tackle, an interception or kick the ball out of the playing area, the attack is over. When the attack is over, all the attackers run around the back of the goal that they were attacking and join the back of the line. The activity continues immediately with the first group from the opposite end of the playing area.

## Key focus/Coaching points

**Primary focus:** Finishing

**Secondary focus:** Short passing

**Additional focus:** Creativity

## Progressions/Adaptations

- The attackers must complete 3 passes in each zone.
- Condition the type of finish, e.g., first time, left foot, right foot or volley.
- Allow the defender in the middle zone to retreat to the final zone to create a 4v2 attacking overload.
- Add a goalkeeper in both goals.

# ACTIVITY 146  THREE-SECOND FINISH

**Level:** Intermediate

**Type of activity:** Opposed technical practice

**Number of participants:** 7 + 1 goalkeeper

**Equipment required:** Soccer balls, cones, 4 set of bibs and 1 goal

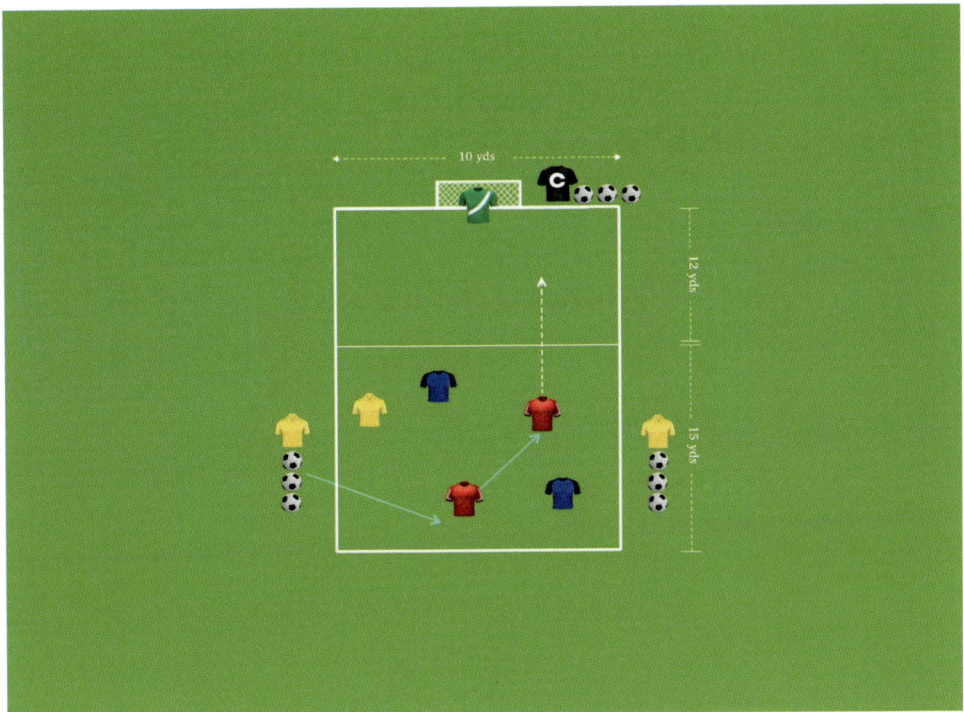

## Description

Divide players into two teams of two, one support player and two ball feeders. Mark out a main playing area and position a scoring zone at one end of the main playing area. Position a goal and goalkeeper at the end of the scoring zone. Position the two teams and the support player inside the main playing area. Position one ball feeder on the outside of either side of the main playing area. Both ball feeders require a supply of balls.

The activity starts when one of the ball feeders passes to either team. The two teams compete for possession and try to create an opportunity for one player to run into the scoring zone. The players can either dribble or receive a through pass into the scoring zone. The support player supports the team in possession but cannot dribble into the scoring zone. The support player can complete through passes into the scoring zone.

When a player has possession inside the scoring zone, they have 3 seconds to try to score. After each attempt at goal, the player retreats to the main playing area. The activity continues with a pass to either team from the other ball feeder. Rotate the ball feeders every 5 minutes.

## Key focus/Coaching points

**Primary focus:** Finishing

**Secondary focus:** Short passing

**Additional focus:** Speed

## Progressions/Adaptations

- When a player enters the scoring zone, 1 defender can enter the scoring zone to pressurise the attacker. If the defender wins the ball they can try to score.
- The support player can join the attacking player in the scoring zone to make a 2v1 attacking overload.
- Set teams a winning target, e.g., first team to 10 goals wins.

# ACTIVITY 147  SET TO SCORE

**Level:** Intermediate

**Type of activity:** Unopposed technical practice

**Number of participants:** 9 + 1 goalkeeper

**Equipment required:** Soccer balls, cones, 2 sets of bibs and 1 goal

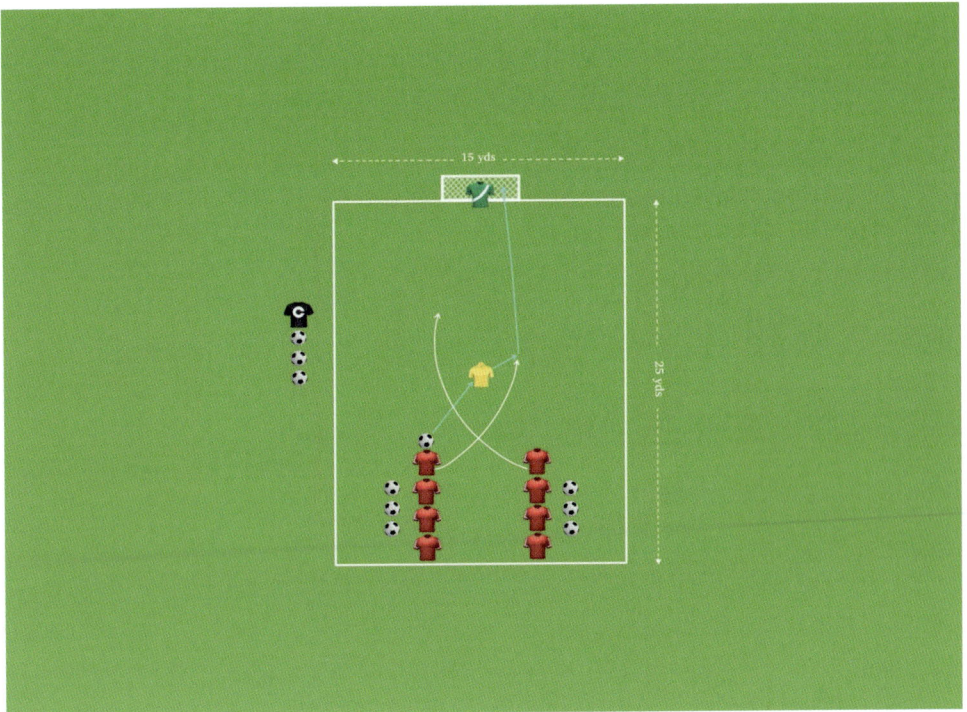

## Description

Divide players into two groups of four attackers and one target player. Mark out a playing area and position a goal and goalkeeper at one end of the playing area. Position the groups of attackers in straight lines, 25 yards from the goal. Position one group of attackers in line with each goalpost. Each group of attackers requires a supply of balls. Position the target player with their back to the centre of the goal and 5 yards in front of both groups of attackers.

The activity starts when the first attacker in either line passes to the target player. The attacker makes a diagonal run across the front of the target player towards goal. At the same time as the pass to the target player, the first attacker in the other line makes a supporting run across the front of the target player towards the goal.

The target player plays a return pass towards the goal and into the path of the first attacker's run. The first attacker follows the pass towards goal and tries to score with a first-time finish. If the first attacker scores, both attackers run to the back of the opposite line and the next attack starts from the other line of attackers.

If the goalkeeper makes a save or the finish rebounds back into play off the goalpost, the supporting attacker has one touch to finish the rebound.

## Key focus/Coaching points

**Primary focus:** Finishing

**Secondary focus:** Shooting

**Additional focus:** Speed

## Progressions/Adaptations

- Vary the type of return pass from the target player, e.g., flat, lofted or bobbly.

- The supporting attacker now acts as a defender. After the pass from the attacker, the defender makes a recovery run across the front of the target player and tries to catch the attacker. If the defender wins possession of the ball, they can try to score. The defender can only use 2 touches before trying to score.

# Finishing

## ACTIVITY 148  THINKING FINISHING

**Level:** Advanced

**Type of activity:** Opposed technical practice

**Number of participants:** 14 + 2 goalkeepers

**Equipment required:** Soccer balls, cones, discs, 2 sets of bibs and 2 goals

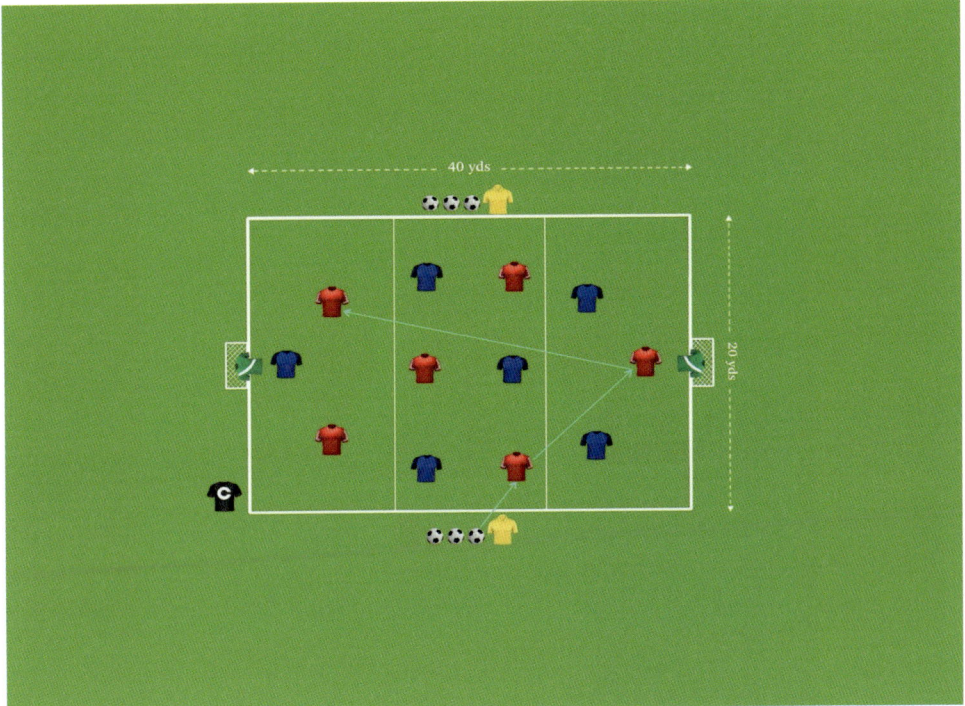

## Description

Divide players into two teams of seven (including goalkeepers) and two ball feeders. Divide the playing area into three zones with a goal and goalkeeper at both ends of the playing area. The teams attack opposite ends of the playing area.

Organise both teams of outfield players into a 1-3-2 formation. For both teams, position one defender in their defensive zone, three midfielders in the middle zone and two attackers in their attacking zone. Position one ball feeder on either side of the playing area with a supply of balls each.

At the start of the activity, all players must play within their zones. The activity starts when either ball feeder passes to any of the midfielders. The teams compete in a 7v7 conditioned match.

The defenders and midfielders in both teams are allowed as many passes as they need to keep possession and transfer the ball between zones. Once the ball is in either attacking zone, the attackers cannot pass the ball backwards into another zone. The attackers are allowed a maximum of three passes in the attacking zone before they must try to score.

If the goalkeeper makes a save and the attackers win possession of the ball after the rebound, they are allowed another three passes before they must try to score.

## Key focus/Coaching points

**Primary focus:** Finishing

**Secondary focus:** Movement

**Additional focus:** Support play

## Progressions/Adaptations

- When the ball is an attacking zone, 1 midfielder from the attacking team and 1 midfielder from the defending team run into the attacking zone to create a 3v2 attacking overload. When the attack is over, both midfielders return to the middle zone.

- The attackers are allowed a maximum of 2 passes in the attacking zone before trying to score.

# Finishing

## ACTIVITY 149   DREAM GOALS

**Level:** Advanced

**Type of activity:** Opposed technical practice

**Number of participants:** 9 + 1 goalkeeper

**Equipment required:** Soccer balls, cones, 3 sets of bibs and 1 goal

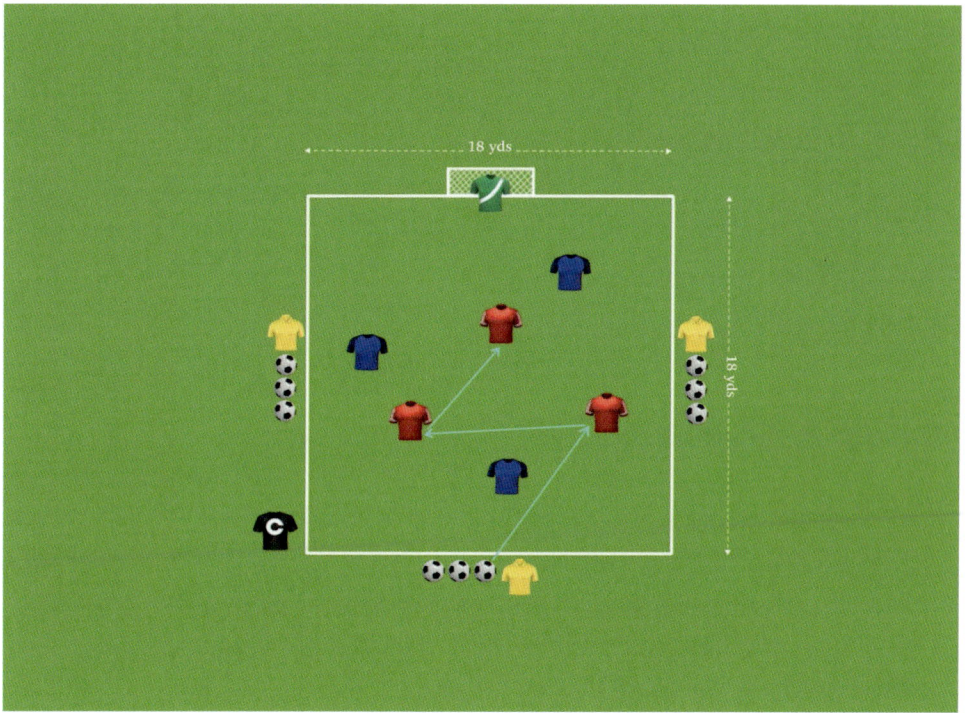

## Description

Divide players into one team of three attackers, one team of three defenders and one group of three ball feeders. Position a goal and goalkeeper at one end of the playing area. Position the group of attackers and the group of defenders inside the playing area. Position the group of ball feeders around the outside of the playing area. Each ball feeder requires a supply of balls.

The activity starts when one of the ball feeders passes into the playing area to one of the attackers. The attackers try to keep possession from the defenders and score. The defenders can apply passive pressure to the attackers by closing space and marking the attackers.

Encourage the attackers to keep the attacks realistic and to play at a high intensity. The attackers should perform each finish at least 10 yards from the goal. All finishes must be first-time finishes. As soon as each attack is over, another ball feeder passes into the playing area to one of the attackers. Once the ball feeders have used up all the soccer balls, rotate the players.

## Key focus/Coaching points

**Primary focus:** Finishing

**Secondary focus:** Receiving

**Additional focus:** Attacking and defending

## Progressions/Adaptations

- The defenders apply active pressure to the attackers. Encourage the defenders to make tackles, mark the attackers tightly and to force the attackers away from goal.
- If the defenders win possession of the ball, they can try to score. If the defending team score, they receive the next ball feed. When the defending team fails to score, the attacking team receives the next ball feed.

# ACTIVITY 150  HIGH-PRESSURE FINISHING

**Level:** Advanced

**Type of activity:** Opposed technical practice

**Number of participants:** 12 + 1 goalkeeper

**Equipment required:** Soccer balls, cones, 3 sets of bibs and 1 goal

## Description

Divide players into two teams of four and one group of four support players. Mark out an arc-shaped playing area. Position a goal and goalkeeper at the straight end of the playing area. Position the two teams inside the playing area and the group of support players around the outside of the playing area. The coach should be positioned outside the playing area with a supply of balls.

The activity starts when the coach passes a ball to either team inside the playing area. The two teams compete for possession and try to score in the goal. Both teams can pass to and receive passes back from the support players at any time during an attack. The support players are allowed a maximum of two touches to return the pass to the attacking team. Rotate the support players every 5 minutes.

## Key focus/Coaching points

**Primary focus:** Finishing

**Secondary focus:** Movement

**Additional focus:** Receiving

## Progressions/Adaptations

- Mark out a finishing zone 12 yards from goal. All goals must be scored inside the finishing zone.
- The players are allowed a maximum of 1 touch before each finish.

## ACTIVITY 151  FIND A FINISH

**Level:** Advanced

**Type of activity:** Implementation practice

**Number of participants:** 12 + 2 goalkeepers

**Equipment required:** Soccer balls, cones, discs, (preferable but not essential), 2 sets of bibs and 2 goals

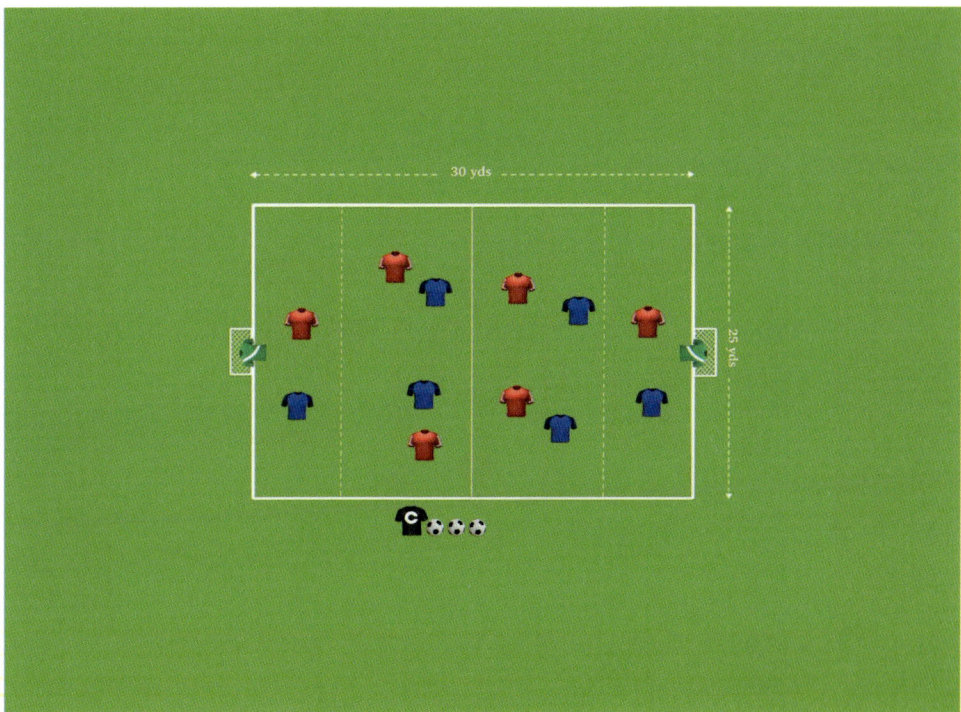

## Description

Divide players into two teams of seven (including goalkeepers). Position a goal and goalkeeper at both ends of the playing area. Position both teams inside the playing area. The playing area needs to be short in length so that most finishes are from close-/mid-range (no more than 15 yards from goal). Mark out a halfway line across the playing area and an offside line in both halves of the playing area (approximately 15 yards from the goal).

The teams compete in a 7v7 match and attack opposite ends of the playing area. The players follow normal match rules with the condition that players can only score in the opposition's half of the playing area.

## Key focus/Coaching points

**Primary focus:** Finishing

**Secondary focus:** Attacking and defending

**Additional focus:** Movement

## Progressions/Adaptations

- Mark out a scoring zone 12 yards from each goal. Goals can only be scored from inside this zone.

- Every finish inside the scoring zone must be a first-time finish.

# Volleys

## ACTIVITY 152   VOLLEY BASICS

**Level:** Basic

**Type of activity:** Unopposed technical practice

**Number of participants:** 16

**Equipment required:** Soccer balls, cones and 2 sets of bibs

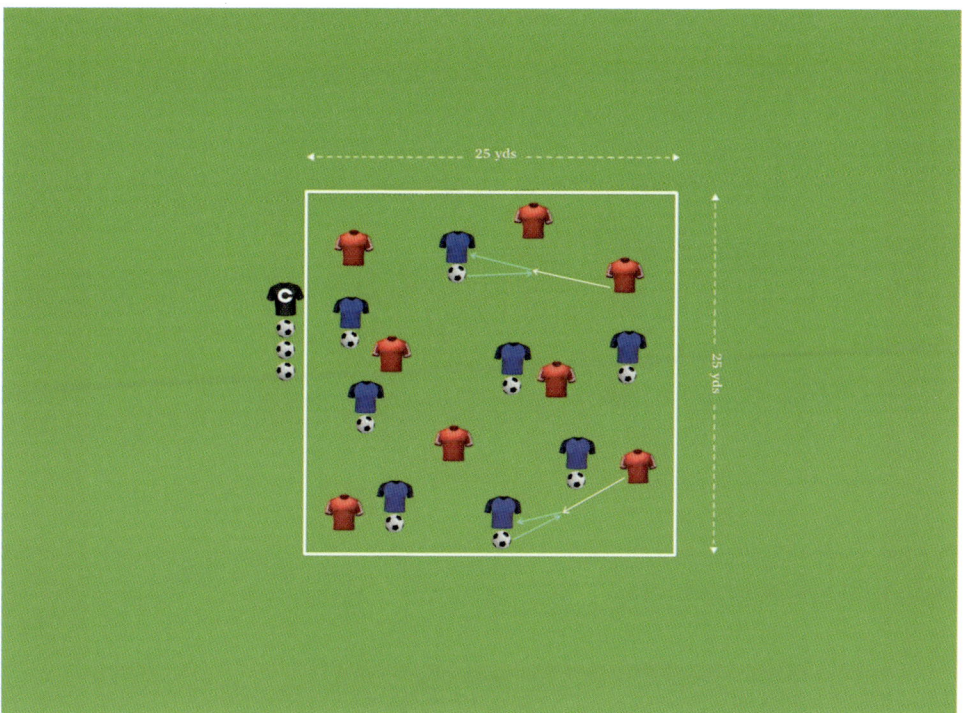

## Description

Divide players into one group of eight volley players and one group of eight ball feeders. Position the group of volley players and the group of ball feeders inside the playing area.

Each ball feeder requires one ball. The ball feeders must hold their soccer balls in both hands and stand still.

The group of eight volley players jog around the playing area. Each time that a volley player runs towards a ball feeder, they must call for the ball and stand opposite the ball feeder. The ball feeder gently throws the ball with both hands to the volley player.

The volley player returns the ball back into the hands of the ball feeder with a volley. For the first 2-3 minutes, allow the volley players to volley the ball using any part of their foot and decide the most appropriate type of volley for each feed.

Once the players are comfortable with the activity and have practiced different types of volleys, condition the activity so that they spend 60 seconds performing the following types of volleys: Side-foot volley, front-of-foot volley, thigh volley, thigh receive and side-foot volley, thigh receive and front-of-foot volley, front-of-foot receive and side-foot volley.

Encourage the ball feeders to give accurate feeds. The feeds need to be in a good position to comfortably perform each type of volley, e.g., a feed for a side-foot volley should be around knee height. Encourage the volley players to use both feet to perform the volleys. It is helpful if they tell the ball feeders which foot they want to use before each feed.

## Key focus/Coaching points

**Primary focus:** Volleys

**Secondary focus:** Headers

**Additional focus:** Receiving

## Progressions/Adaptations

- The ball feeders can move around the playing area.
- Increase the difficulty of the feeds by varying their speed, height and adding different types of spin.

## ACTIVITY 153  VOLLEY AND MOVE

**Level:** Basic

**Type of activity:** Unopposed technical practice

**Number of participants:** 16

**Equipment required:** Soccer balls and cones

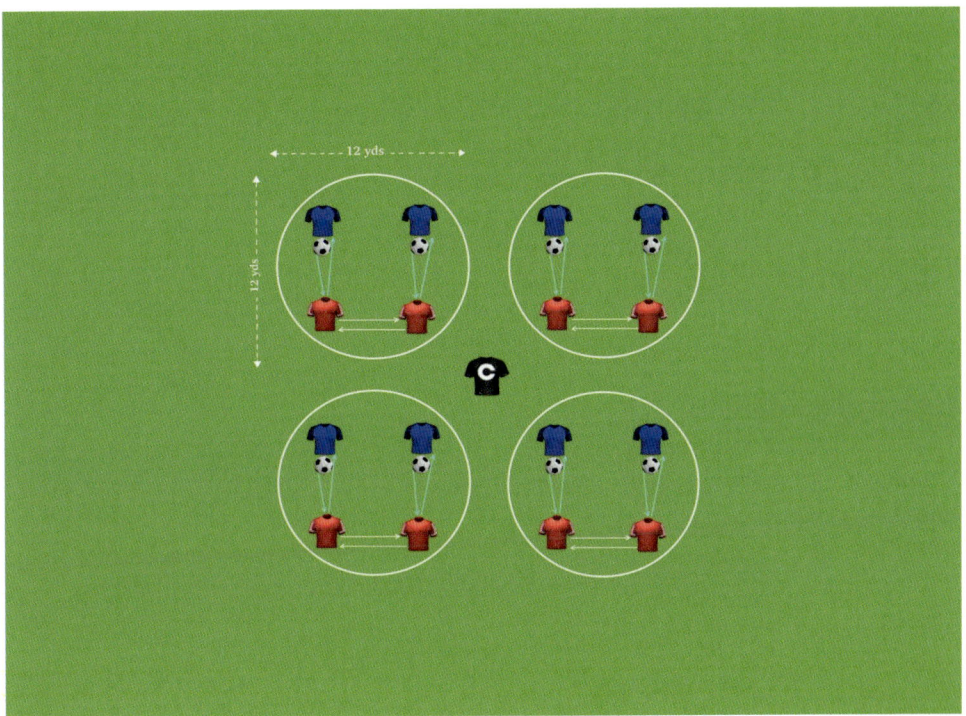

## Description

Divide players into four groups of four. Mark out four small circular playing areas. Position one group of players inside each playing area. Organise each group into two pairs. Nominate one player in each pair as the ball feeder and the other player as the volley player. Position the ball feeders in each group side-by-side and 6 yards apart. Position the volley players 10 yards opposite their partners. Each ball feeder requires a ball.

The activity starts when the ball feeders give a two-hands aerial feed to their partners. The volley players return the ball to their partner's hands with a volley. As soon as the volley players have completed their volley, they must sidestep across the playing area and switch ball feeders for the next volley.

The volley players continue the volleys and side steps for 60 seconds. After 60 seconds, rotate the ball feeders and volley players. Work through the following types of volleys: Side-foot volley, front-of-foot volley, thigh volley, thigh receive and side-foot volley, thigh receive and front-of-foot volley, front-of-foot receive and side-foot volley.

## Key focus/Coaching points

Primary focus: Volleys

Secondary focus: Physical/movement development

Additional focus: Receiving

## Progressions/Adaptations

- Before each volley, the volley player should quickly turn their back to and then turn around to face the ball feeder.
- Increase the difficulty of the feed by varying the speed, height and spin.

## ACTIVITY 154  WALL VOLLEYS

**Level:** Basic

**Type of activity:** Unopposed technical practice

**Number of participants:** 1-20

**Equipment required:** Soccer balls and wall or any other suitable upright surface

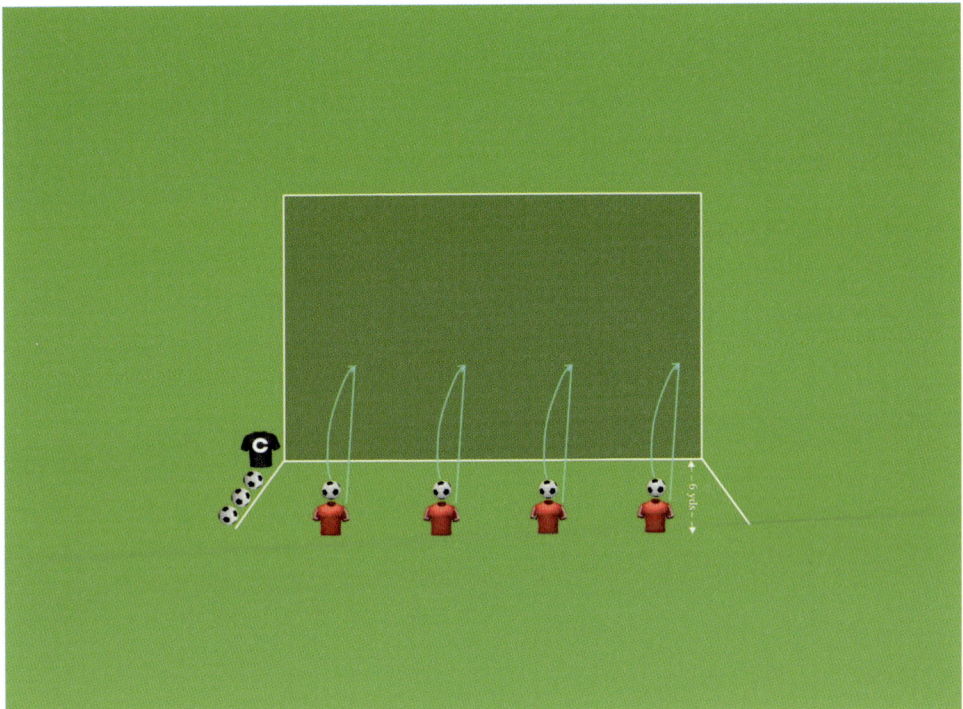

## Description

Players perform individually with a ball each. Position the players facing a wall approximately 6 yards away. Make sure that players have enough space to move a few steps left and right without interfering with other players. The players perform continuous volleys/half-volleys against the wall. Work through the following challenges:

Side-foot volleys, front-of-foot volleys, alternate-feet volleys, front-of-foot receive and front-of-foot volleys, front-of-foot receive and side-foot volleys, side-foot receive and side-foot volleys, side-foot receive and front-of-foot volleys, front-of-foot half-volleys, side-foot half-volleys, front-of-foot receive and front-of-foot half-volleys, front-of-foot receive and side-foot half-volleys, side-foot receive and side-foot half-volleys, side-foot receive and front-of-foot half-volleys.

## Key focus/Coaching points

Primary focus: Volleys

Secondary focus: Half-volleys

Additional focus: Receiving

## Progressions/Adaptations

- Use smaller balls and work towards using a tennis ball.
- Increase/decrease the power of each volley/half-volley.
- Increase/decrease the distance between the players and the wall.

# ACTIVITY 155 SOCCER TENNIS

**Level:** Intermediate

**Type of activity:** Opposed technical practice

**Number of participants:** 2-24

**Equipment required:** Soccer balls, cones, 2 sets of bibs and nets/benches

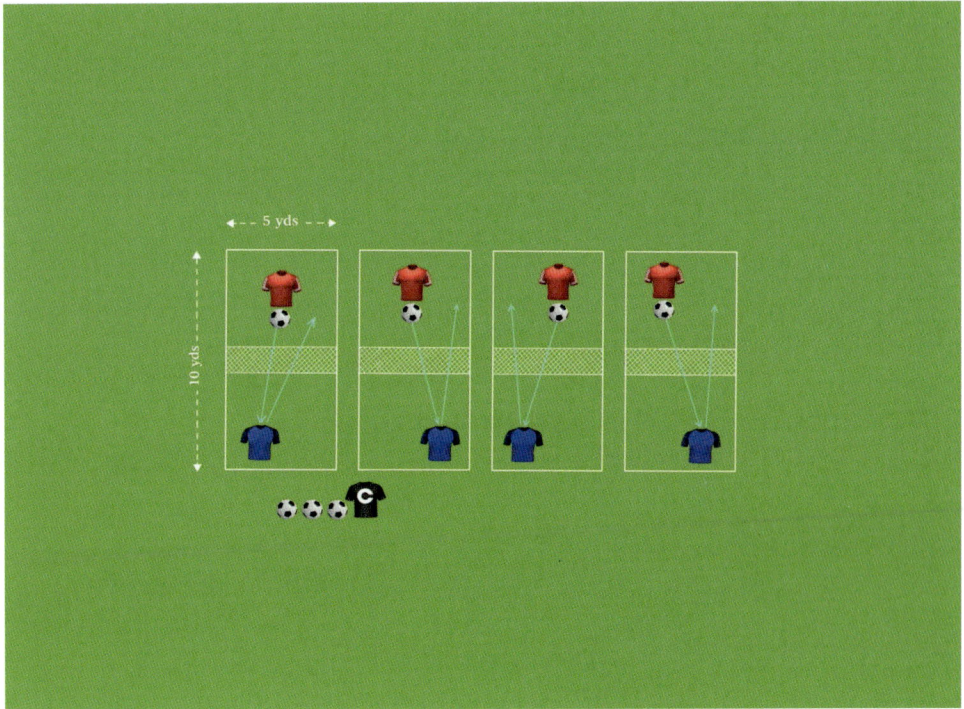

## Description

Divide players into pairs with one ball per pair. Mark out a small rectangular playing area for each pair of players. Position a net, bench or line of cones running across the middle of the playing area. Position one player on either side of the net. The players take part in a game of soccer tennis. The players must try to transfer the ball over the net with a volley or half-volley.

Each point starts with a volley or half-volley serve. The server moves to the back of their half of the playing area and serves the ball over the net. The server should hold the ball in two hands and let it drop towards the floor. The server can either volley it over the net or let it bounce once and half-volley it over the net. The players take turns to start each point.

If the server transfers the ball over the net and it lands inside their opponent's half of the playing area, the point starts. The player receiving the serve must return the ball back over the net with a half-volley. **The serve must not be returned with a volley.** If the player receiving the serve **volleys** the ball back over the net, fails to return the ball over the net or returns the ball back over the net but it lands outside the playing area, the server scores 1 point. If the server fails to get the ball over the net or the serve lands outside the playing area, their opponent scores 1 point.

After the serve and return of serve, the players can choose to either volley, half-volley with one bounce or half-volley with two bounces the ball over the net. When a player transfers the ball over the net, and their opponent fails to return it or returns the ball over the net, but it lands outside the playing area, the player that successfully transferred the ball over the net scores 1 point.

## Key focus/Coaching points

Primary focus: Volleys

Secondary focus: Headers

Additional focus: Half-volleys

## Progressions/Adaptations

- The players must volley/half-volley the ball with their weaker foot.
- Condition the type of volley/half-volley, e.g., side-foot or front-of-foot volley.
- Use a points system to challenge the players:
  - If a player wins a point with a volley, they score 3 points; if they win the point with a one-bounce half-volley they score 2 points; and if they win the point with a two-bounce half-volley they score 1 point.

# ACTIVITY 156  PRESSURE VOLLEYS

**Level:** Intermediate

**Type of activity:** Opposed technical practice

**Number of participants:** 18

**Equipment required:** Soccer ball, cones and 3 sets of bibs

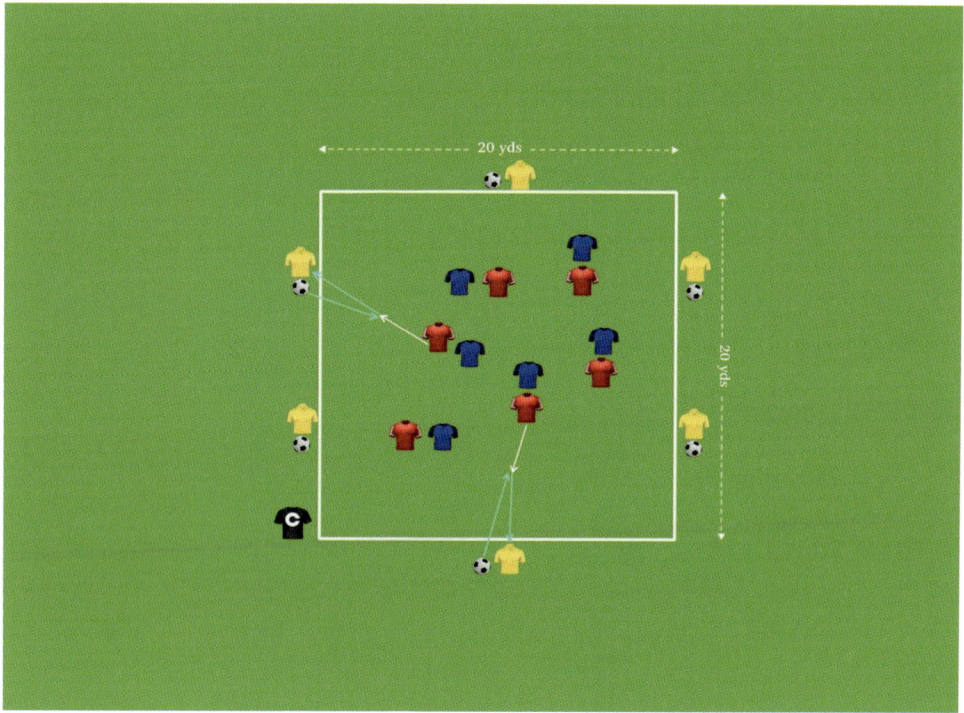

## Description

Divide players into one group of six volley players, one group of six passive defenders and one group of six ball feeders. Position the groups of volley players and the group of defenders inside the playing area. Organise the volley players and the defenders into pairs. Position the ball feeders around the outside of the playing area with a ball each.

The activity starts when the volley players run to an available ball feeder. The ball feeder gives a two-hand aerial feed to the volley player. The volley player returns the ball into the hands of the ball feeder with a volley. After each volley, the volley players move to a new ball feeder for another volley.

Throughout activity, the defenders should apply passive pressure to the volley players by marking them as closely as possible. After 60 seconds, rotate ball feeders, volley players and defenders. Once the players are comfortable with the organisation of the activity, work through the following types of volleys: Side-foot volley, front-of-foot volley, thigh volley, thigh receive and side-foot volley, thigh receive and front-of-foot volley, front-of-foot receive and side-foot volley.

## Key focus/Coaching points

**Primary focus:** Volleys

**Secondary focus:** Physical/movement development

**Additional focus:** Receiving

## Progressions/Adaptations

- The defenders apply active pressure and try to intercept each volley.
- Increase the difficulty of feed by varying the speed, flight and spin.

# ACTIVITY 157  VOLLEYS KEEP BALL

**Level:** Intermediate

**Type of activity:** Opposed technical practice

**Number of participants:** 11

**Equipment required:** Soccer balls, cones and 2 sets of bibs

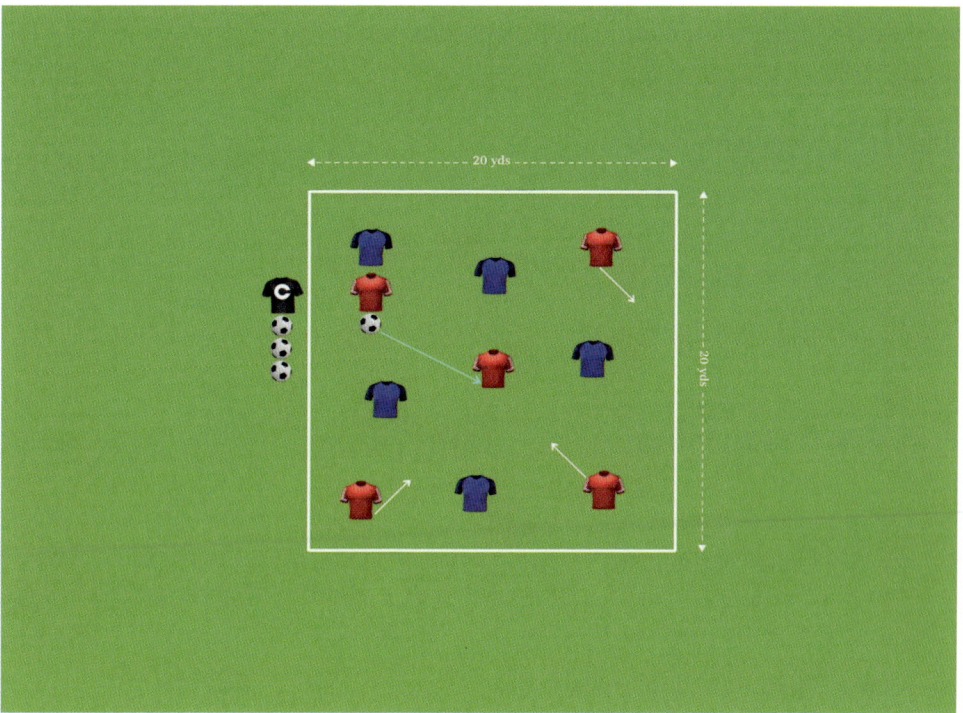

## Description

Divide players into two teams of five. Mark out a playing area and position both teams inside the playing area. The teams compete against each other for possession of the ball. The players keep possession by volleying it to a teammate to catch. The players serve themselves volleys by holding the ball in two hands and volleying it as they let the ball drop. When a team completes five consecutive passes, they score 1 point.

The player in possession of the ball must stand still and has a maximum of 3 seconds to perform a volley to a teammate. All players apart from the player in possession can move around the playing area. The players in the team in possession should try to create space and make angles to receive a volley.

The team out of possession tries to win possession by intercepting volleys. If the ball hits the floor, the first team to pick the ball up wins possession. Encourage the players to keep volleys at a comfortable catching height (e.g., waist height) and to use a sensible amount of power. **Advise players to stand a few steps back from the player in possession as they make a pass to avoid being hit by a misdirected volley.**

## Key focus/Coaching points

**Primary focus:** Volleys

**Secondary focus:** Support play

**Additional focus:** Movement

## Progressions/Adaptations

- Add a target player into the playing area who can catch the ball for both teams. The team in possession must complete a minimum of 3 volleys and then complete a volley to the target player to score 1 point. When a point is scored, the target player volleys the ball to the team previously out of possession and the activity continues.

- Allow players to perform half-volleys.

# ACTIVITY 158  SOCCER VOLLEYBALL

**Level:** Advanced

**Type of activity:** Opposed technical practice

**Number of participants:** 12

**Equipment required:** Soccer balls, cones, 2 sets of bibs and net/bench

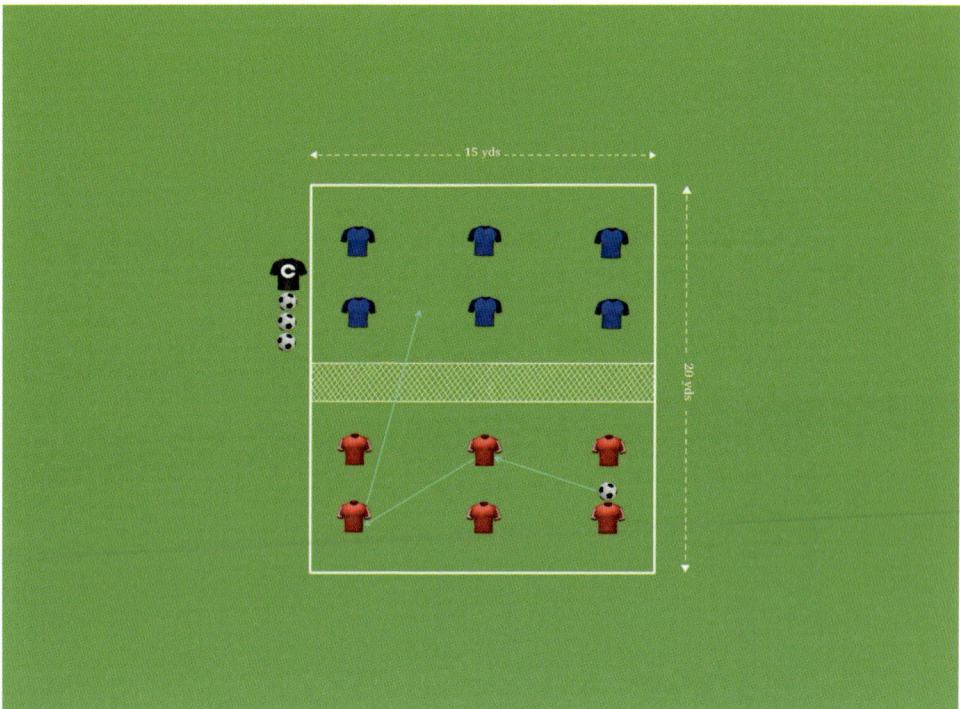

## Description

Divide players into two teams of six. Mark out a playing area with a net running across the width of the playing area. Position one team on either side of the net. The players in each team combine to volley the ball over the net. Points are scored when the ball is volleyed over the net and either lands inside the opponent's half of the playing area or the opposition team fails to return the ball back over the net.

The teams are allowed a maximum of three volleys in their own half of the playing area to volley the ball over the net. If a team wins the point, the number of volleys performed to win the point determines the value of the point, e.g., three volleys = 3 points, two volleys = 2 points and one volley = 1 point.

This method of scoring encourages players to pass to teammates and gives all players more opportunities to practice volleys. Players are not allowed consecutive touches of the ball. Each point starts with a self-feed volley from hands from the back line of the playing area. Teams take turns starting each point.

### Key focus/Coaching points

**Primary focus:** Volleys

**Secondary focus:** Headers

**Additional focus:** Support play

### Progressions/Adaptations

- Allow players to perform half-volleys.
- Allow players to use feet, thighs and heads to transfer the ball over the net.

# ACTIVITY 159  VOLLEY TO SCORE

**Level:** Advanced

**Type of activity:** Unopposed technical practice

**Number of participants:** 15 + 3 goalkeepers

**Equipment required:** Soccer balls, cones and 3 goals

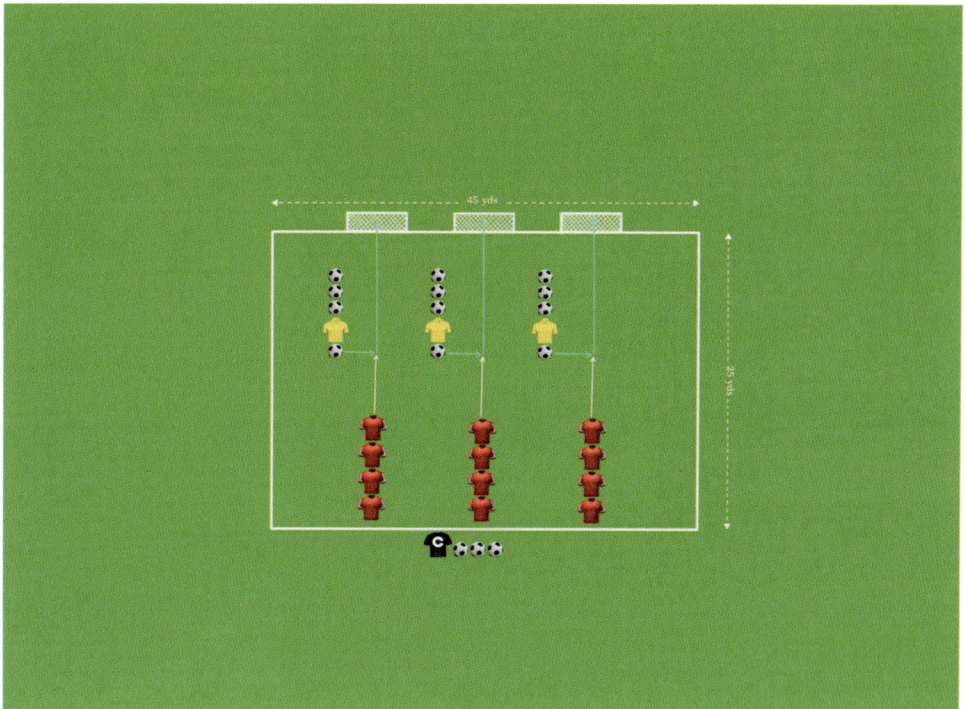

## Description

Divide players into three groups of four and one group of three ball feeders. Position three goals and goalkeepers at one end of the playing area. Position the goals 15-20 yards apart. Position each group of four players in straight lines opposite a goal. Position the groups approximately 20 yards from goal. Allocate one ball feeder to each group of players. Position the ball feeder 5 yards in front of, and 1-2 yards to the left of, the first player in line in their group.

The activity starts when the first player in line from each group runs towards goal. The ball feeders should give a two-hand aerial feed for the player to perform a right-foot volley at goal. After each volley, the player runs to the back of their line and the next player in line continues the activity. After 2-3 minutes rotate one player from each group with the ball feeder.

After each player has taken a turn as a ball feeder, re-start the activity with the ball feeders positioned in front of, and to the right of, their groups. As the players run towards goal, they receive a two-hand aerial feed and perform a left foot volley. Make sure that the ball feeder is out of the line of each volley and that the player performing the volley has a clear path to goal.

### Key focus/Coaching points

**Primary focus:** Volleys

**Secondary focus:** Half-volleys

**Additional focus:** Shooting

### Progressions/Adaptations

- The players perform half-volleys.
- The players must use 1 touch to receive the feed and then volley the ball at goal.
- Set a time limit of 3 minutes. The teams compete to score as many volleys/half-volleys as they can in 3 minutes.

# ACTIVITY 160  OPEN PLAY VOLLEYS

**Level:** Advanced

**Type of activity:** Opposed technical practice

**Number of participants:** 16

**Equipment required:** Soccer balls, cones and 3 sets of bibs

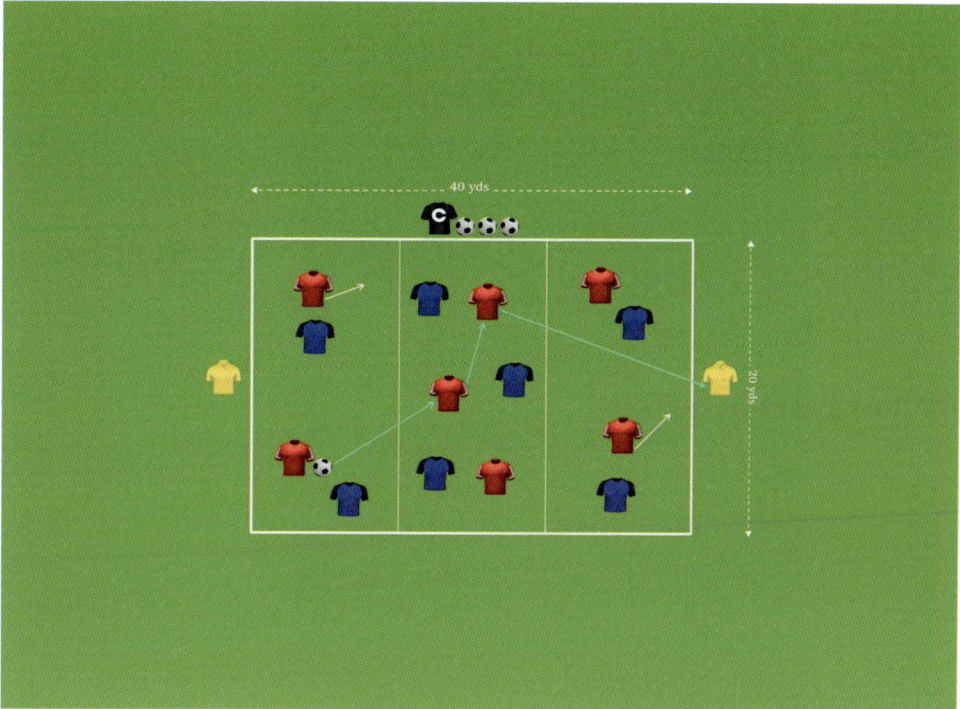

## Description

Divide players into two teams of eight (including one target player per team). Divide the playing area into three zones with the middle zone slightly larger than the end zones. The teams attack opposite ends of the playing area.

Organise both teams into a 2-3-2 formation. Position two defenders from both teams inside their defensive zone, three midfielders from both teams inside the middle zone and two attackers from both teams inside their attacking zone. The players must play within their zones. Position 1 target player from both teams at the end of their attacking zone.

The teams compete against each other for possession and try to score points by a self-feed volley from hands for their target player to catch. The scoring volley must be performed by an attacker inside their attacking zone. During each attack, the players keep possession and build the attack by performing self-feed volleys.

The volley passes must only be one zone forwards and backwards. The player in possession of the ball must stand still and has 3 seconds to perform a volley. All other players in the attacking team can move and make angles to receive a volley. The defending team try to win possession by either intercepting volleys or picking up the ball if it runs loose.

**Advise players to stand a few steps back from the player in possession as they make a pass to avoid being hit by a misdirected volley.** When a point is scored, the target player that caught the ball performs a self-feed volley to the team that just conceded the point to re-start the activity. Encourage the target players to move along the line to help create goal-scoring opportunities.

### Key focus/Coaching points

Primary focus: Volleys

Secondary focus: Movement

Additional focus: Support play

### Progressions/Adaptations

- Passes can be 2 zones forwards and backwards.
- The attacking team must complete 3 passes inside each zone before they can try to score.
- For advanced groups, change the possession sequence to: Aerial feed to a teammate, receiving player volleys the ball to another teammate to catch.

# ACTIVITY 161  VOLLEY RULES

**Level:** Advanced

**Type of activity:** Opposed technical practice

**Number of participants:** 14 + 2 goalkeepers

**Equipment required:** Soccer balls, cones, 2 sets of bibs and 2 goals

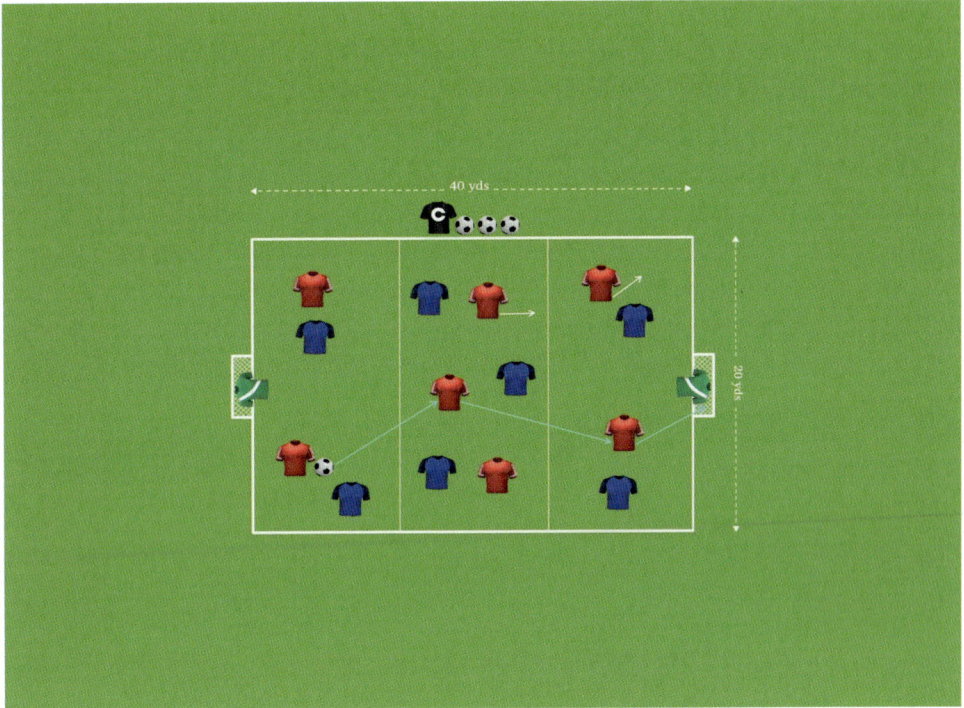

## Description

Divide players into two teams of eight (including goalkeepers). Divide the playing area into 3 zones with the middle zone slightly larger than the end zones. Position a goal and goalkeeper at both ends of the playing area. The teams attack opposite ends of the playing area.

Organise both teams of outfield players into a 2-3-2 formation. Position two defenders from both teams inside their defensive zone, three midfielders from both teams inside the middle zone and two attackers from both teams inside their attacking zone. The players must play within their zones.

The teams compete against each other for possession and try to score points by a self-feed volley or volley from hands past the goalkeeper and into the goal. The scoring volley must be performed by an attacker inside their attacking zone.

When an attacking player receives a volley in the attacking zone, all other players take five steps back and the player in possession has 2 seconds to perform an unopposed self-feed volley or half-volley at goal. Make sure that all players are out of the line of the volley. If an attacker catches the ball close to goal, they must take 10 steps back from where they received before they try to score in order to safeguard the goalkeeper.

During each attack, the players keep possession and build the attack by performing self-feed volleys and half-volleys. The volley passes must only be one zone forwards and backwards. The player in possession of the ball must stand still and has 3 seconds to perform a volley. All other players in the attacking team can move and make angles to receive a volley. The defending team tries to win possession by either intercepting volleys or picking up the ball if it runs loose. **Advise players to stand a few steps back from the player in possession as they make a pass to avoid being hit by a misdirected volley.**

## Key focus/Coaching points

Primary focus: Volleys

Secondary focus: Half-volleys

Additional focus: Attacking and defending

## Progressions/Adaptations

- Formations can be changed as the activity develops. Allow the teams to make sensible changes to the number of players in each zone.

- If the players are performing mainly hopeful, long-range volley passes, condition the activity so that the players must complete 3 passes in each zone before they can pass the ball into the next zone.

- When a player completes a volley to a teammate in another zone, allow them to follow the volley into the zone. The player must retreat to their original zone when their team loses possession.

# Heading 379

# HEADING

## ACTIVITY 162  HEADING BASICS

**Level:** Basic

**Type of activity:** Unopposed technical practice

**Number of participants:** 2-16

**Equipment required:** Soccer balls, cones and 2 sets of bibs

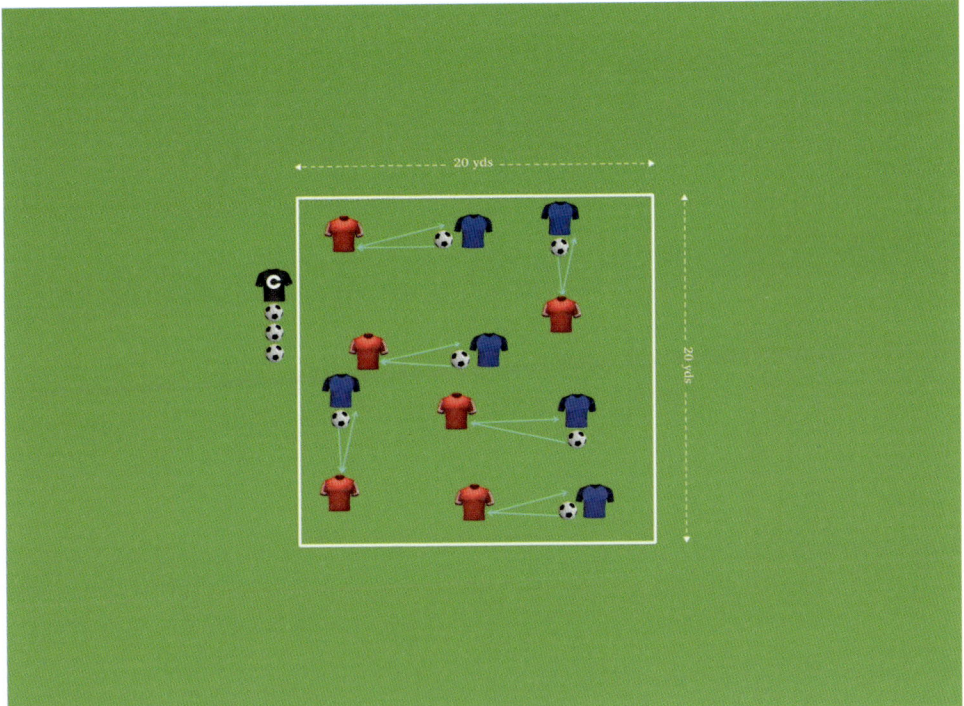

## Description

Divide players into pairs with one ball per pair. Position all players inside the playing area. Position the players in each pair 10 yards opposite each other. Nominate one player in each pair to start the activity as the ball feeder. The ball feeder feeds the ball with two hands for their partner to header back to them. The header should be aimed at chest height. After 8-10 headers, the players swap roles. Once the players are comfortable heading the ball, work through the following types of headers: Header to waist height, header to feet, header over partner's head.

## Key focus/Coaching points

**Primary focus:** Heading

**Secondary focus:** Ball manipulation

**Additional focus:** Receiving

## Progressions/Adaptations

- Vary the feed using different types of speed, spin, height and trajectory.
- The players try to keep the ball in the air by heading the ball backwards and forwards to each other.

# ACTIVITY 163: PIGGY IN THE MIDDLE

Level: Basic

Type of activity: Opposed technical practice

Number of participants: 3-21

Equipment required: Soccer balls, cones and 3 sets of bibs

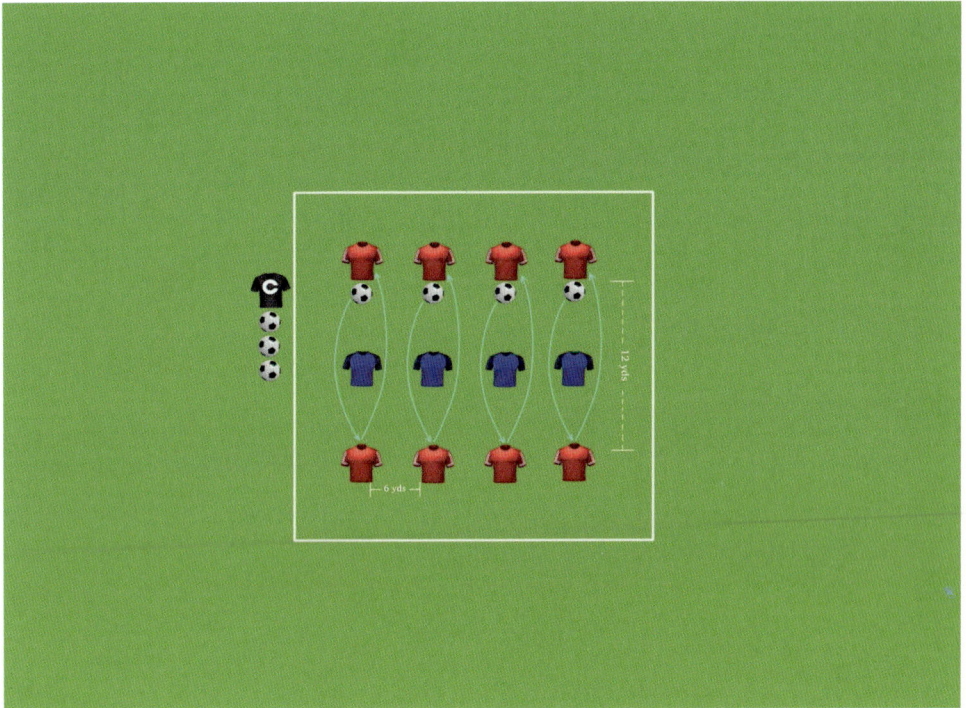

## Description

Divide players into groups of three with one ball per group. Position all groups inside the playing area. Nominate one player to start the activity as the ball feeder, one player to act as the "piggy" and one player as the header player. Position the ball feeder and the header player 12 yards apart with the piggy standing in between them.

The ball feeder performs a two-hand ball feed over the head of the piggy to the header player. The header player tries to head the ball back over the head of the piggy for the ball feeder to catch.

The piggy raises their hands above their head to try to catch the header. The piggy cannot move from where they are standing or jump to catch the ball. If the piggy catches the ball, they swap positions with the header player. Rotate the ball feeder every 2-3 minutes.

## Key focus/Coaching points

**Primary focus:** Heading

**Secondary focus:** Ball manipulation

**Additional focus:** Receiving

## Progressions/Adaptations

- Allow the piggy to jump to try to catch the ball.
- Allow the piggy to jump and move side-to-side to try to catch the ball.
- The ball feeder and the header player progress to the sequence of: Ball feed, header back to ball feeder, header to header player and catch.

## ACTIVITY 164  HEADING WORKOUT

**Level:** Basic

**Type of activity:** Unopposed technical practice

**Number of participants:** 12

**Equipment required:** Soccer balls, cones and 3 sets of bibs

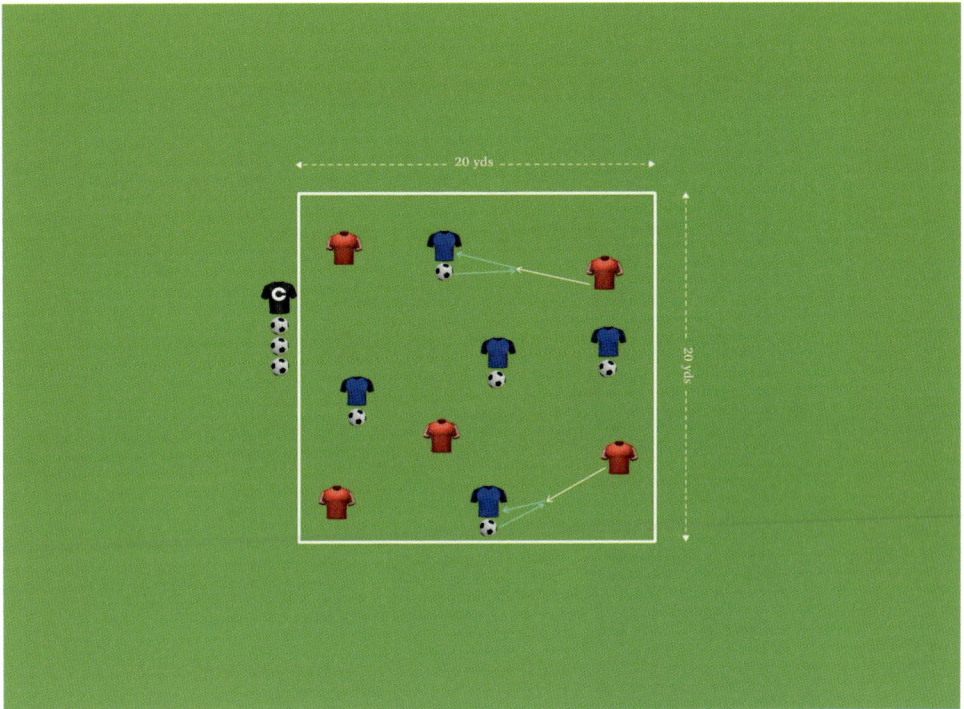

## Description

Divide players into one group of five header players and one group of five ball feeders. Position all players inside the playing area. Each ball feeder requires a ball. The group of header players move around inside the playing area. Each time a header player is 6-8 yards from an available ball feeder, they receive a two-hand feed and head the ball back to the ball feeder. Once the players are comfortable with the activity, work through the following techniques: Header to chest height, header to waist height, header to feet, receive the feed with a cushioned header and then header the ball back to the feeder.

## Key focus/Coaching points

**Primary focus:** Heading

**Secondary focus:** Movement

**Additional focus:** Receiving

## Progressions/Adaptations

- Allow the ball feeders to move around the area.
- Increase the difficulty of the header by varying the speed/spin/height/trajectory of each feed.
- Add 2 floating defenders to pressurise and block the headers.

# ACTIVITY 165  PAIRS HEADING

**Level:** Basic

**Type of activity:** Unopposed technical practice

**Number of participants:** 2-24

**Equipment required:** Soccer balls, cones and 2 sets of bibs

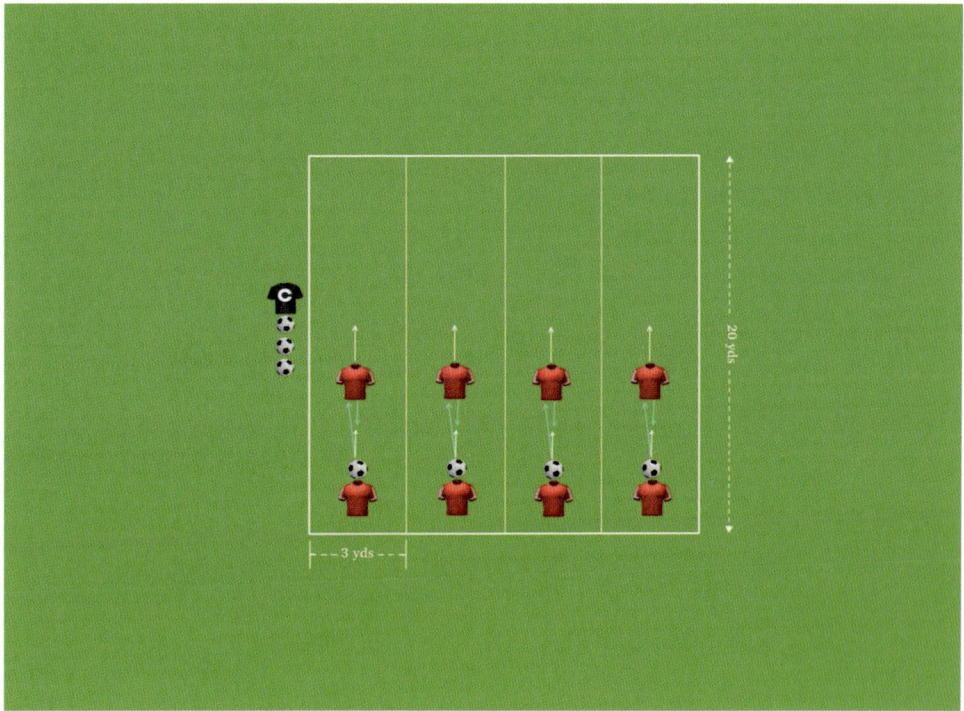

## Description

Divide players into pairs with one ball per pair. Divide the playing area into narrow lanes. Position one pair of players inside each lane. Nominate one player to start the activity as the ball feeder. Position the ball feeder at one end of the playing area facing forwards and their partner 2-3 yards opposite them.

The activity starts when the ball feeder jogs forwards and their partner jogs backwards towards the opposite end of the playing area. Every four to five steps, the ball feeder performs a two-hand feed for their partner to header. The header should be aimed at chest height for the ball feeder to catch. Once the pairs have reached the end of the playing area, the players swap roles and repeat the activity in the opposite direction.

## Key focus/Coaching points:

**Primary focus:** Heading

**Secondary focus:** Movement

**Additional focus:** Ball manipulation

## Progressions/Adaptations

- Encourage the players to work at a higher tempo.
- Add a passive defender in between the partners to pressurise the feed and header. The feed and the header can be over the top of, or to the side of, the defender.
- Increase the difficulty of the header by varying the speed/spin/height/trajectory of the feed.

# ACTIVITY 166  BULLET HEADERS

**Level:** Basic

**Type of activity:** Unopposed technical practice

**Number of participants:** 11 + 1 goalkeeper

**Equipment required:** Soccer balls, cones, 3 sets of bibs and 1 goal

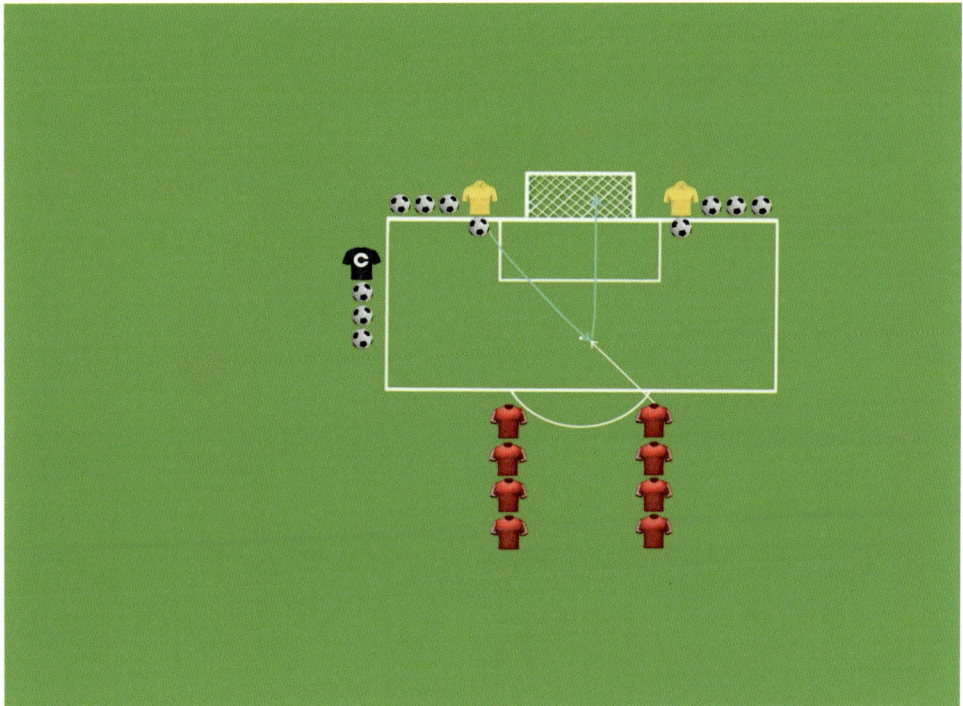

## Description

Divide players into two groups of four and one group of two ball feeders. Position a goal at one end of the playing area. Position the groups of players in straight lines opposite each goalpost. Position the groups 18 yards from the goal. Position one ball feeder a safe distance to the side of each goalpost. Each ball feeder requires a supply of balls.

The activity starts when the first player in line from either group runs diagonally towards the centre of the goal. The ball feeder diagonally opposite the player performs a two-hand aerial feed. The player approaches, receives the feed and performs a header at goal. The header should be performed approximately 10 yards from goal. After the header, the player runs to the back of the line in the other group of four players.

The activity continues with the first player in line from the other group who runs diagonally towards the centre of the goal. The ball feeder diagonally opposite the player performs a two-hand aerial feed. The activity continues for 2-3 minutes alternating between each group and ball feeder. Rotate the ball feeders after 2-3 minutes.

## Key focus/Coaching points

**Primary focus:** Heading

**Secondary focus:** Finishing

**Additional focus:** Movement

## Progressions/Adaptations

- The players make different types of runs (e.g., straight, diagonal, zigzag or curved). The players can now decide which feeder they receive the ball from.
- Add a goalkeeper.
- Add a defender to apply passive pressure to each header.

# ACTIVITY 167  SPEED HEADING

**Level:** Intermediate

**Type of activity:** Unopposed technical practice

**Number of participants:** 10 + 2 goalkeepers

**Equipment required:** Soccer balls, cones, 2 sets of bibs and 2 goals

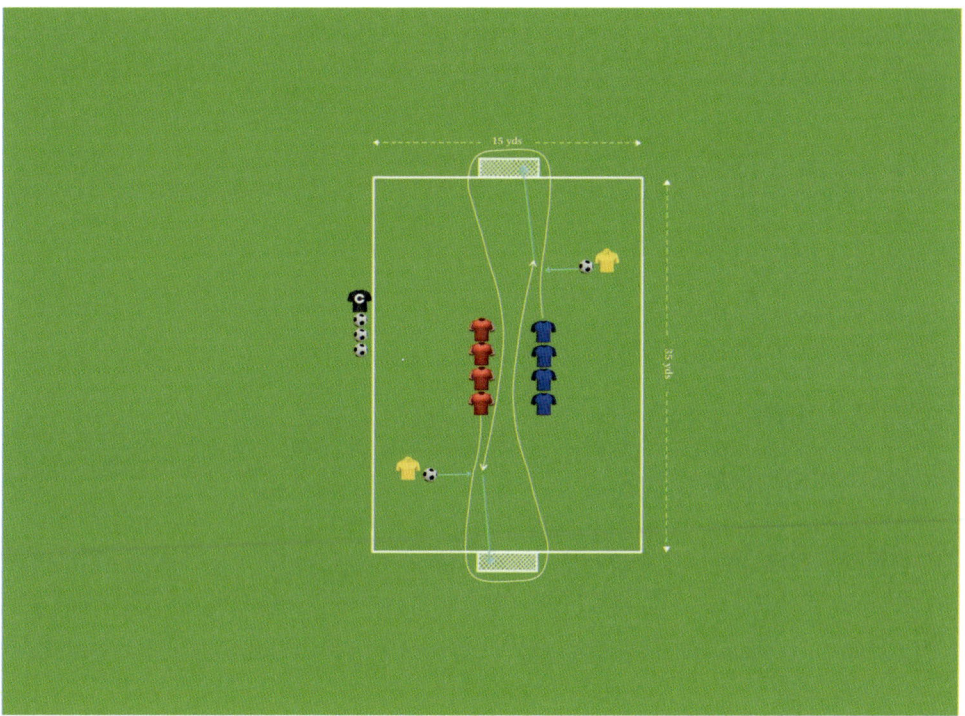

## Description

Divide players into two teams of four and two ball feeders. Position a goal at both ends of the playing area. Position the groups in straight lines in the middle of the playing area facing opposite goals. Position 1 ball feeder 8-10 yards in front of each team. Each ball feeder requires a supply of balls.

The activity starts when the first player in line from both teams sprints around the back of the goal they are facing and then towards the goal at the opposite end of the playing area. Both players run past the front end of the other team's line. As the players pass the front of the opposite line, the ball feeders perform a two-hand aerial feed for the players to header at goal.

As soon as the first player in each line has performed their header, they run to the back of their line. The next player in line for both teams immediately repeats the activity. Organise the activity as a relay race; award 10 points for the fastest team to complete all their headers and 3 points for every header they score. The team with most the points is the winning team. Rotate the ball feeders after each race.

## Key focus/Coaching points

**Primary focus:** Heading

**Secondary focus:** Movement

**Additional focus:** Finishing

## Progressions/Adaptations

- Add a goalkeeper in both goals. Award 5 points if a player scores a header and 3 points if the header is on target but the goalkeeper saves it.
- Increase the difficulty of the headers by varying the spin, height, speed and trajectory of each feed.

# ACTIVITY 168  HEADING MEDLEY

**Level:** Intermediate

**Type of activity:** Unopposed technical practice

**Number of participants:** 12 + 1 goalkeeper

**Equipment required:** Soccer balls, cones, 1 mannequin, 4 agility poles and 1 set of bibs

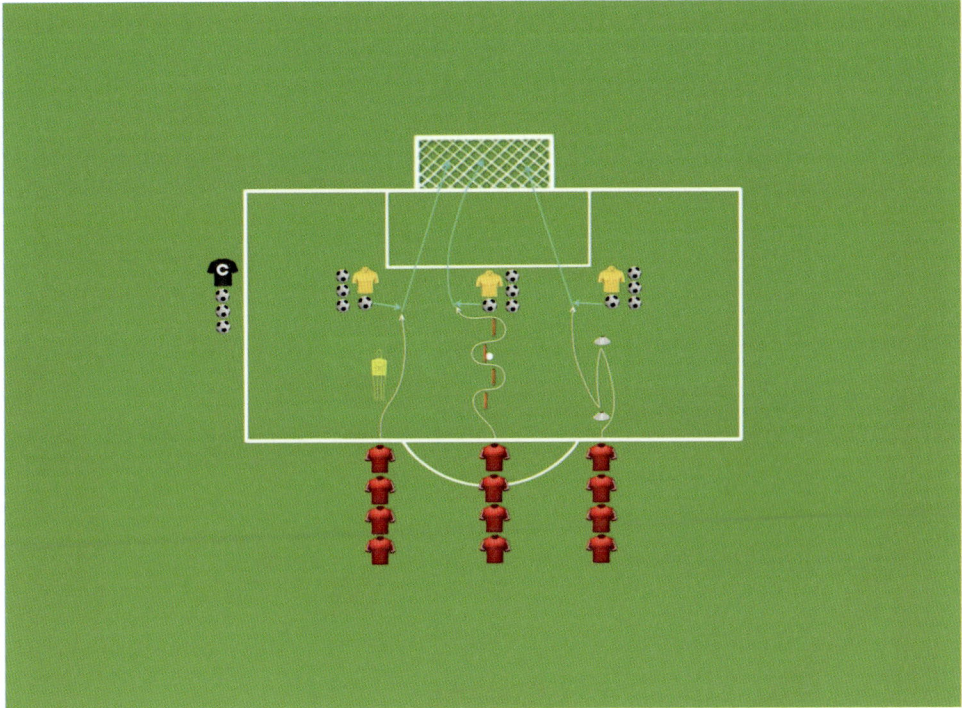

## Description

Divide players into three groups of four header players and one group of three ball feeders. Position a goal at one end of the playing area. Position each group of header players in straight lines and 20 yards from the goal. Position one group of header players in line with the left goalpost, one group of header players in line with the centre of the goal and one group of header players in line with the right goalpost.

Mark out an activity station in front of each group of header players (see below). Position one ball feeder 2-3 yards beyond each activity station with a supply of balls. The distance between the first player in line in each group of header players and the end of the activity station should be approximately 8 yards.

The activity starts when the first header player in line from each group runs through their activity station towards their ball feeder. When the header players reach the end of their activity stations, the ball feeders feed them a ball at head height. The header players move towards their ball feed and try to score with a header into the goal.

After a header player has performed a header, they run to the back of their line. The next header player in line repeats the activity. The groups perform the task at their activity station for 5 minutes continuously. Every 5 minutes, rotate the ball feeders and rotate the groups of header players to a new activity station. Each group must complete all three activity stations.

- **Station 1** – Run to the mannequin, dodge to the left/right and header the ball feed into the goal.
- **Station 2** – Slalom run between 4 agility poles and header the ball feed into the goal.
- **Station 3** – Run to the cone ahead, run backwards to the starting cone, run towards the ball feeder and header the feed into the goal.

## Key focus/Coaching points

Primary focus: Heading

Secondary focus: Movement

Additional focus: Finishing

## Progressions/Adaptations

- Add a goalkeeper.
- Increase the difficulty of each header by varying the speed, spin, height and trajectory of each feed.

# ACTIVITY 169  4V1 HEADING

**Level:** Intermediate

**Type of activity:** Opposed technical practice

**Number of participants:** 5-20

**Equipment required:** Soccer balls, cones and 2 sets of bibs

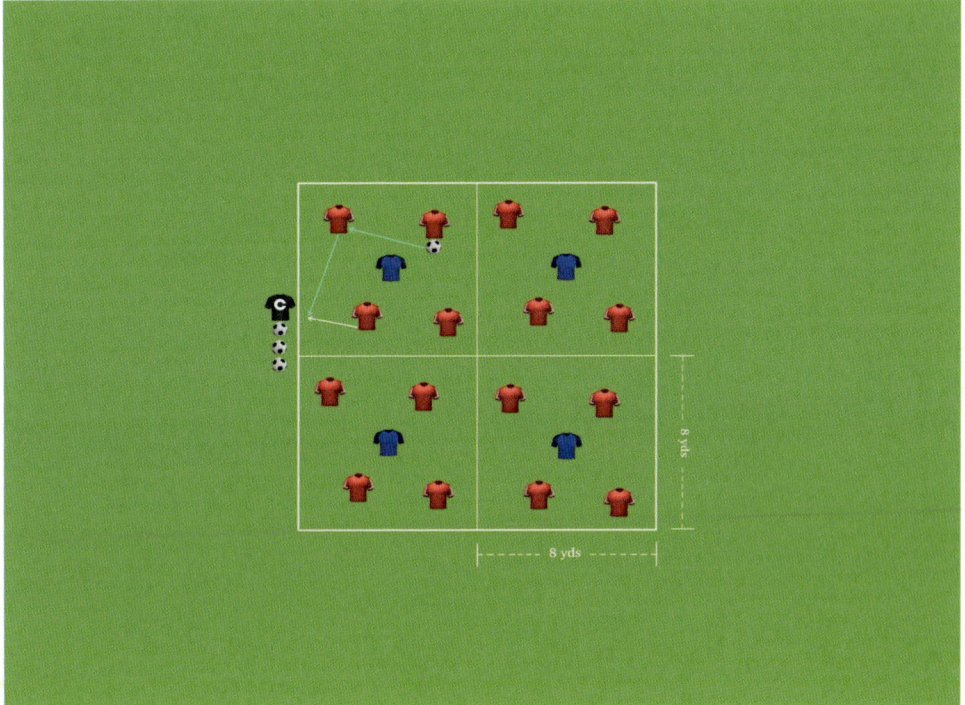

## Description

Divide players into four groups of five. Mark out a playing area divided into four squares. Position one group of players inside each square. Organise the players in each group into four attackers and one defender. Each group requires one ball.

The attackers move around their square and try to keep possession of the ball using the sequence of throw, header and catch. The defender tries to catch the ball to break the sequence.

The throw must be a two-hand feed to a teammate and the header must be caught by a third teammate. Perform the activity for 60 seconds or until the defender wins possession. Rotate the attackers and the defender every 60 seconds.

## Key focus/Coaching points

**Primary focus:** Heading

**Secondary focus:** Movement

**Additional focus:** Decision making

## Progressions/Adaptations

- Change the possession sequence to:
  - Throw to a teammate, header to a third teammate, header to a fourth teammate (this can be a player previously involved in the possession sequence) and catch.
- Progress to 3 attackers v 2 defenders inside each square.

# Heading 395

## ACTIVITY 170  HEADING FINESSE

**Level:** Intermediate

**Type of activity:** Opposed technical practice

**Number of participants:** 6

**Equipment required:** Soccer balls, cones and 3 sets of bibs

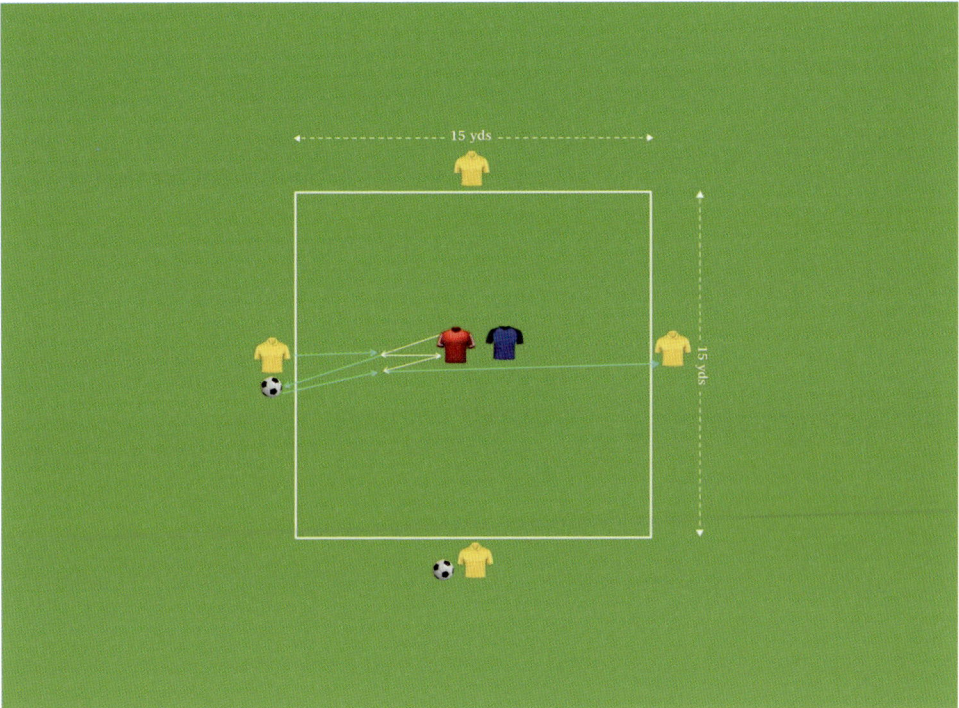

## Description

Divide players into one group of two players and one group of four ball feeders. Mark out a small playing area. Position the two players inside the playing area and the four ball feeders outside the playing area. Position one ball feeder outside each line of the playing area. Position one ball with two of the ball feeders. Any two ball feeders can have a ball; however, they must not be positioned on opposite sides of the playing area.

Before the activity starts, nominate one player inside the playing area as the heading player and the other player as a passive defender. The passive defender must follow and mark the heading player. The activity starts when the heading player runs towards one of the ball feeders. The ball feeder performs a two-hand aerial feed and heading player headers the ball back to them to catch. After the header, the heading player runs backwards to the middle of the playing area and then runs back to the initial ball feeder. The ball feeder performs another two-hand ball feed, and the heading player performs a backwards flick header for the ball feeder at the opposite end of the playing area to catch.

Once the heading player has performed both headers, the heading player and the passive defender immediately switch roles. The new heading player performs the same heading activity but uses the ball feeders that were not used by the previous heading player. After 2 minutes rotate two ball feeders with the heading player and the passive defender.

## Key focus/Coaching points

**Primary focus:** Heading

**Secondary focus:** Movement

**Additional focus:** Physical/movement development

## Progressions/Adaptations

- The heading player receives a feed and performs a header to the ball feeder on their right or left (this is determined by which ball feeder is without a ball and available to catch the header). The heading player then runs backwards to the middle of the playing area and towards the ball feeder they have just performed a header to. The heading player receives a feed from the ball feeder and performs a sideways header back to the original ball feeder.

- The defenders apply active pressure and try to intercept the headers before they reach the intended ball feeder.

- Increase the difficulty of the headers by varying the speed, spin, height and trajectory of each ball feed.

## ACTIVITY 171    IN THE ONION BAG

**Level:** Intermediate

**Type of activity:** Opposed technical practice

**Number of participants:** 11 + 1 goalkeeper

**Equipment required:** Soccer balls, cones, 2 set of bibs and 1 goal

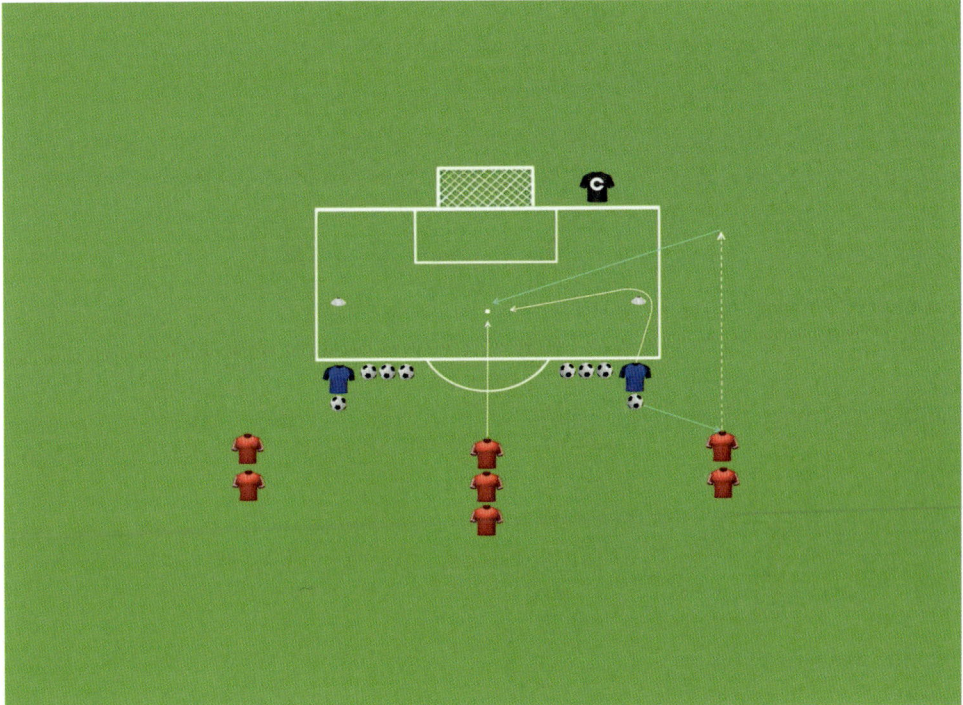

## Description

Divide players into one group of three central attackers, one group of two right wingers, one group of two left wingers, one right-sided defender and one left-sided defender. Mark out a playing area with a goal positioned at one end of the playing area.

Position the group of central attackers in a straight line and 35 yards opposite the centre of the goal. Position the group of right wingers in a straight line and 35 yards from the goal on the right side of the playing area. Position the group of left wingers in a straight line and 35 yards from the goal on the left side of the playing area. Position the right-sided defender 10 yards ahead of the group of left wingers and slightly in field towards the goal. Position the left-sided defender 10 yards ahead of the group of right wingers and slightly in field towards the goal. Position a cone 10 yards behind each defender.

The activity starts when either defender passes to the first winger in line on their side of the playing area. The defender makes a recovery run around the cone positioned behind them and then towards the centre of the goal. As the pass is played, the first central attacker in line makes an attacking run towards the goal.

The winger receives the pass and is allowed two more touches to dribble the ball towards the end of the playing area. After the second touch, the winger crosses the ball in the air for the central attacker to header at goal.

After the attack is finished, the central attacker runs to the back of their line, the winger replaces the defender, and the defender runs to the back of the line of wingers on their side of the playing area. The activity continues immediately from the other side of the playing area and continues from alternate sides of the playing area.

The quality of the cross is crucial to the success of this activity. The players need coaching and advice on how to cross ball in the air to create opportunities for headers at goal. If the crosses are consistently wayward then allow the wingers to either volley the ball from hands or the throw ball towards the goal.

## Key focus/Coaching points

**Primary focus:** Heading

**Secondary focus:** Crossing

**Additional focus:** Finishing

## Progressions/Adaptations

- Position 1 defender at a safe distance to the side of both goalposts. When the defender facing the winger passes the ball, the defender beside the goalpost on that side of the playing area runs towards the centre of the goal to help defend the cross. A second central attacker makes an attacking run towards goal to create a 2v2 attack v defence for the cross.

- Add a goalkeeper.

# ACTIVITY 172  THROW, HEAD AND CATCH

**Level:** Advanced

**Type of activity:** Opposed technical practice

**Number of participants:** 16

**Equipment required:** Soccer balls, cones and 2 sets of bibs

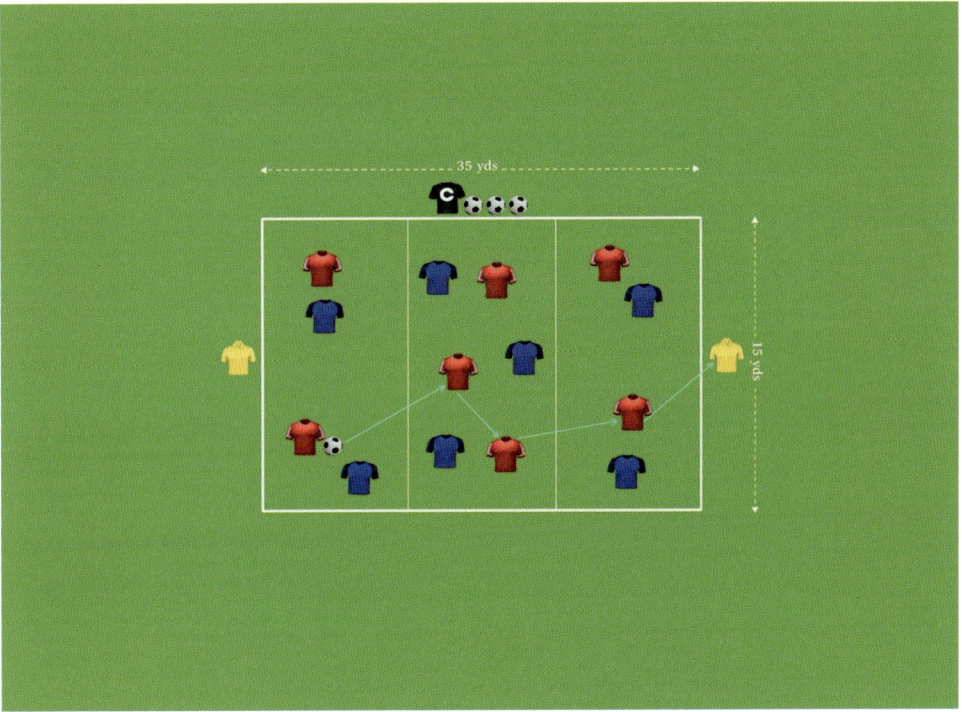

## Description

Divide players into two teams of eight (including one target player per team). Mark out a playing area divided into three zones. Organise both teams of players into a 2-3-2 formation (excluding target players). Position two defenders from both teams inside their defensive zone, three midfield players from both teams inside the middle zone and two attackers from both teams inside their attacking zone. Position one target player at opposite ends of the playing area. The teams attack opposite ends of the playing area. The players must play within their zones of the playing area.

The teams compete for possession and try score with a header to their target player for them to catch. The sequence of possession for both teams to follow is throw, head and catch. The player in possession of the ball throws it with two hands to a teammate who then tries to header it to a third teammate to catch. The player that throws the ball must stand still and has a maximum of 3 seconds to release the ball. All the player's teammates can move to create angles to receive the throw.

The team out of possession tries to win possession with a header or a catch, depending on the stage of the possession sequence of the team in possession. If the ball touches the floor during the activity, the first team to pick it up gain possession. The ball can travel any number of zones forwards and backwards. When a team scores with a header to their target player, the target player re-starts the activity with a throw to an opposition player.

## Key focus/Coaching points

**Primary focus:** Heading

**Secondary focus:** Movement

**Additional focus:** Support play

## Progressions/Adaptations

- If the activity is too difficult for the players, allow the ball to bounce once after each header before it is caught.

- For advanced players, change the possession sequence to: throw, header to a third teammate, header to a fourth teammate (any player previously in the possession sequence can be used) and catch.

- Allow 1 player from the team in possession to move from their defending zone into the middle zone when the ball travels from their defensive zone into the middle zone.

- Allow 1 player from the team in possession to move from the middle zone into their attacking zone when the ball travels from their middle zone into their attacking zone.

# ACTIVITY 173  HEAD SCRAMBLE

**Level:** Advanced

**Type of activity:** Opposed technical practice

**Number of participants:** 6 + 1 goalkeeper

**Equipment required:** Soccer balls, cones, 3 sets of bibs and 2 goals

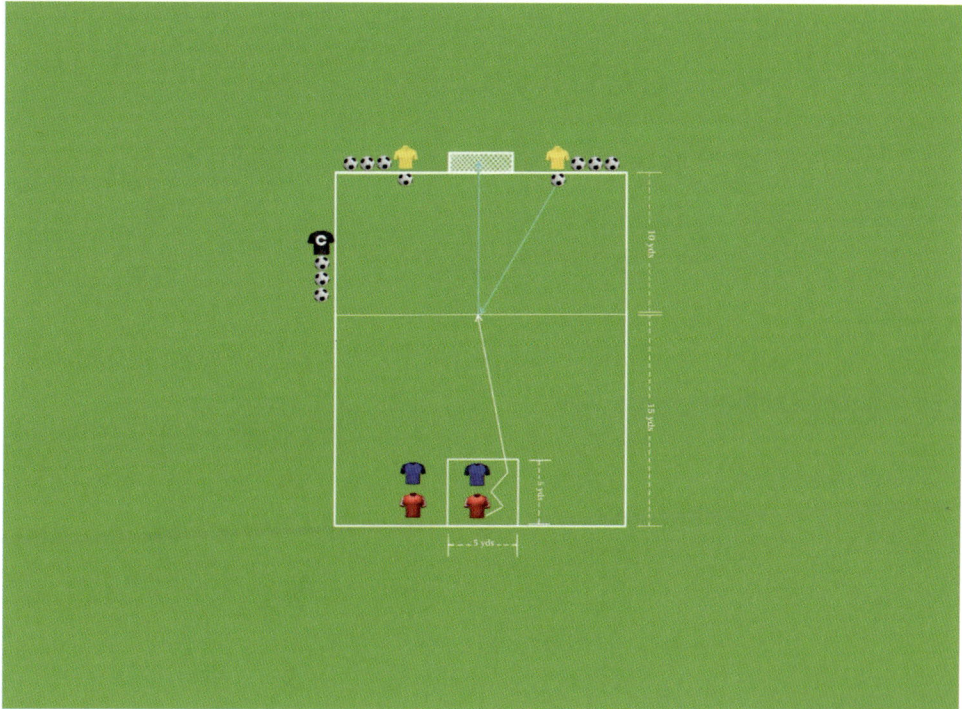

## Description

Divide players into one group of two attackers, one group of two defenders and one group of two ball feeders. Mark out a playing area with a small square at one end of the playing area and a goal at the opposite end of the playing area. Mark out a no-scoring zone across the width of the playing area 8-10 yards from the goal.

Position one attacker and one defender inside the square. Position the other attacker and defender outside the playing area. Position one ball feeder a safe distance to the side of each goalpost. Each ball feeder requires a supply of balls.

The activity starts when the attacker inside the square tries to create space away from the defender. The defender must apply active pressure to the attacker and mark the attacker as tightly as possible. When the attacker has created some space, they run out of the square towards either ball feeder. The defender must remain inside the square.

As the attacker approaches the ball feeder, they perform a two-hand feed for the attacker. The attacker tries to head the ball into the goal before they enter the no-scoring zone. Encourage the ball feeders to feed the ball with sufficient power so that the attacker receives the feed before the no-scoring zone. After the header, the attacker returns to the square and the attacker and defender swap roles for the next ball feed.

After both players have performed as an attacker and a defender, they rotate with the attacker and the defender waiting outside the square. Rotate the ball feeders after 5 minutes.

## Key focus/Coaching points

**Primary focus:** Heading

**Secondary focus:** Finishing

**Additional focus:** Movement

## Progressions/Adaptations

- The attacker performs the activity twice before switching roles with the defender.
- Position 2 attackers and 2 defenders inside the square. Either attacker can run out of the square to receive a feed and header at goal, depending on who creates space first.
- Allow 1 defender to follow the attacker out of the square to pressurise the header.
- Add a goalkeeper.

# ACTIVITY 174  KING OF HEADERS

**Level:** Advanced

**Type of activity:** Opposed technical practice

**Number of participants:** 14 +1 goalkeeper

**Equipment required:** Soccer balls, cones, 2 sets of bibs and 1 goal

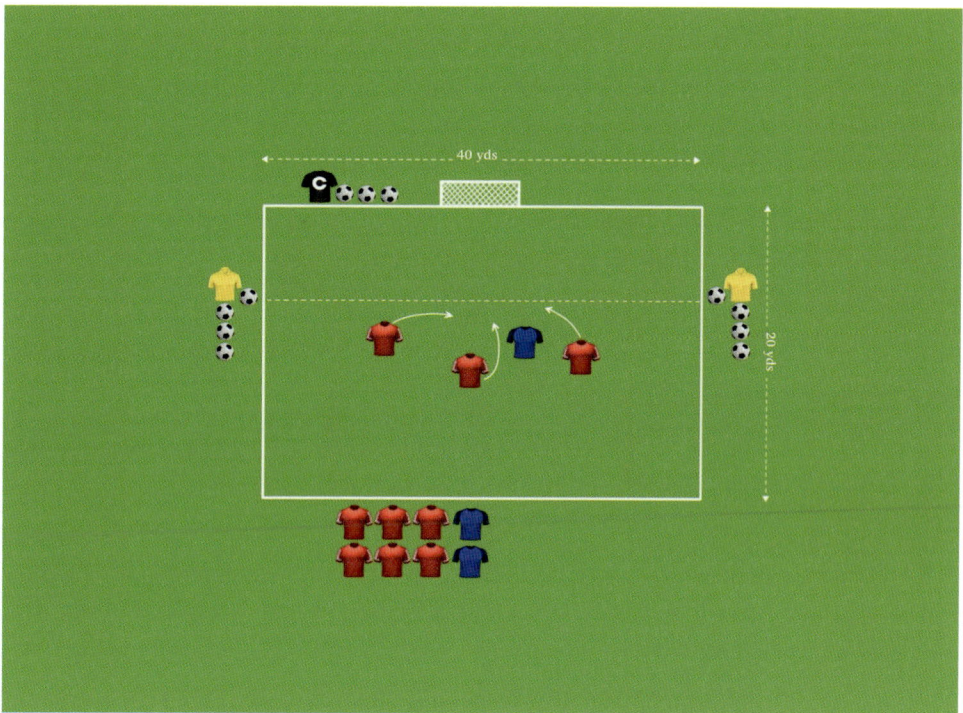

## Description

Divide players into three groups of four and one group of two wingers. Mark out a playing area and position a goal at one end of the playing area. Mark out an offside line across the width of the playing area. Position the offside line 10 yards from the goal. Initially, the offside line is not an active part of the activity.

Organise each group of four players into three attackers and one defender. Position the first group of three attackers 12-15 yards from the goal. The attackers can select their own starting positions between the width of the goalposts. Position the defender with their back to goal 12-15 yards from the goal. The defender can select their own starting position between the width of the goalposts.

Position one winger on each side of the playing area in line with the offside line. Each winger requires a supply of balls. Position the other groups of four players at the other end of the playing area.

The activity starts when the first group of three attackers make attacking runs towards the goal. The winger on the right side of the playing area crosses the ball in the air for the attackers to attack. The defender applies active pressure to the attackers and tries to block attempts at goal/header the ball away from the goal.

Any of the attackers can header the cross and try to score. After the first cross, the attackers and defenders re-set their starting positions. The activity continues from the left side of the playing area when the left winger crosses the ball.

After the attackers have received a cross from both sides, the group of 4 players leaves the playing area and the next group repeat the activity. Rotate the groups after each completion of the activity. Rotate the wingers after 5 minutes.

After 10-15 minutes, introduce the following point system to make the activity more competitive:

- **Attackers: 1 point** for a header off target, **2 points** for a header on target, **2 points** for a 1-touch finish (feet can be used) after a blocked header or any kind of rebound, **3 points** for a headed goal.

- **Defenders: 1 point** for header won by the defender(s), **2 points** for a header out of playing area, **3 points** for header out of playing area with no bounce.

## Key focus/Coaching points

**Primary focus:** Heading

**Secondary focus:** Attacking and defending

**Additional focus:** Physical/movement development

## Progressions/Adaptations

- Add a goalkeeper. Encourage the goalkeeper to punch or catch inaccurate crosses.
- The attackers decide which player crosses the ball by movement towards and communication with the crossing player.
- The defender can play offside against any of the attackers using the offside line.

# 406 THE SOCCER COACH'S TOOLKIT

## ACTIVITY 175   TAKE YOUR CHANCES

**Level:** Advanced

**Type of activity:** Opposed technical practice

**Number of participants:** 10

**Equipment required:** Soccer balls, cones, 3 sets of bibs and 4 mini goals

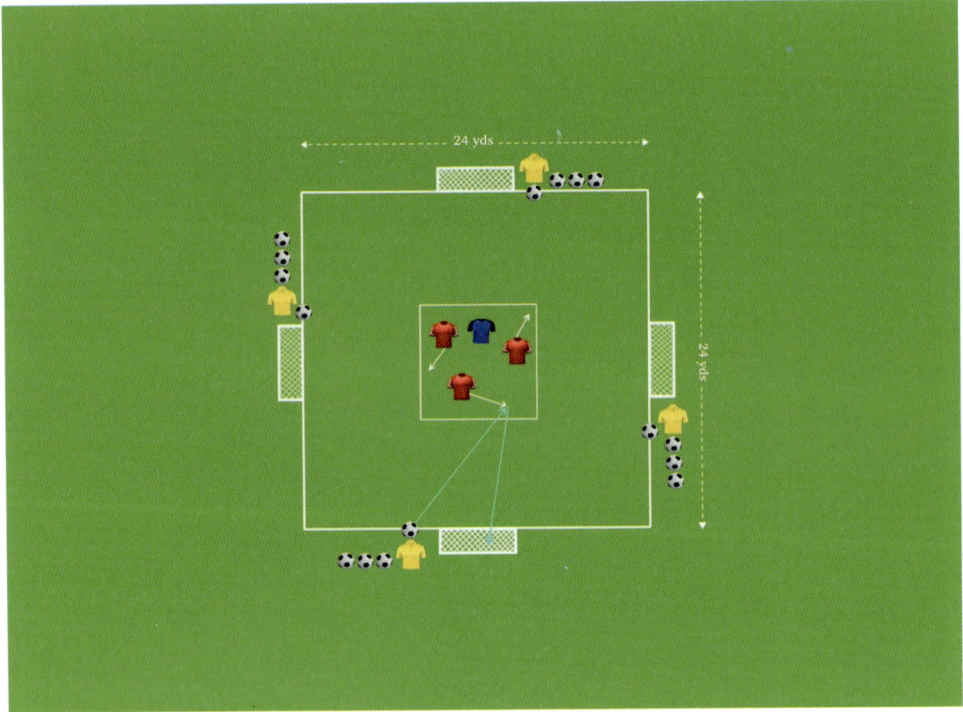

## Description

Divide players into one group of four and one group of four ball feeders. Mark out a small playing area with a square in the centre of the playing area. Position a mini goal on each side of the playing area. Position the group of four inside the playing area. Organise the group into three attackers and one defender. Position one ball feeder a safe distance to the side of each goal. Each ball feeder requires a supply of balls.

The attackers try to create space inside the square away from the defender. Any of the attackers can call for and receive a feed from any of the ball feeders. The ball feeder performs a two-hand feed to the attacking player. The attacker that receives the feed must try to header the ball into any of the mini-goals or start a sequence of headers among the attackers before one of the attackers tries to header the ball into any of the mini-goals.

The defender applies active pressure to the attackers and tries to block headers and header the ball out of the square. Use the following scoring system for each feed:

**Attackers:**

- 3 points for a headed goal.
- 4 points for 1 headed pass and then a headed goal.
- 5 points for 2 headed passes and then a headed goal.

**Defenders:**

- 3 points if the defender wins the first header.
- 2 points if the defender interrupts an attacking sequence of headers with a header out of the square.

Rotate the players after 5 minutes.

## Key focus/Coaching points

Primary focus: Heading

Secondary focus: Support play

Additional focus: Finishing

## Progressions/Adaptations

- Position the ball feeders 5-10 yards in front of the goals. When an attacker attempts a header at goal, the ball feeder in front of that goal tries to prevent the attacker from scoring by heading the ball away.
- Progress to 4 attackers v 2 defenders inside the square.

# GOALKEEPING

## ACTIVITY 176   GOALKEEPING BASICS

**Level:** Basic

**Type of activity:** Unopposed technical practice

**Number of participants:** 2-20 goalkeepers

**Equipment required:** Soccer balls and cones

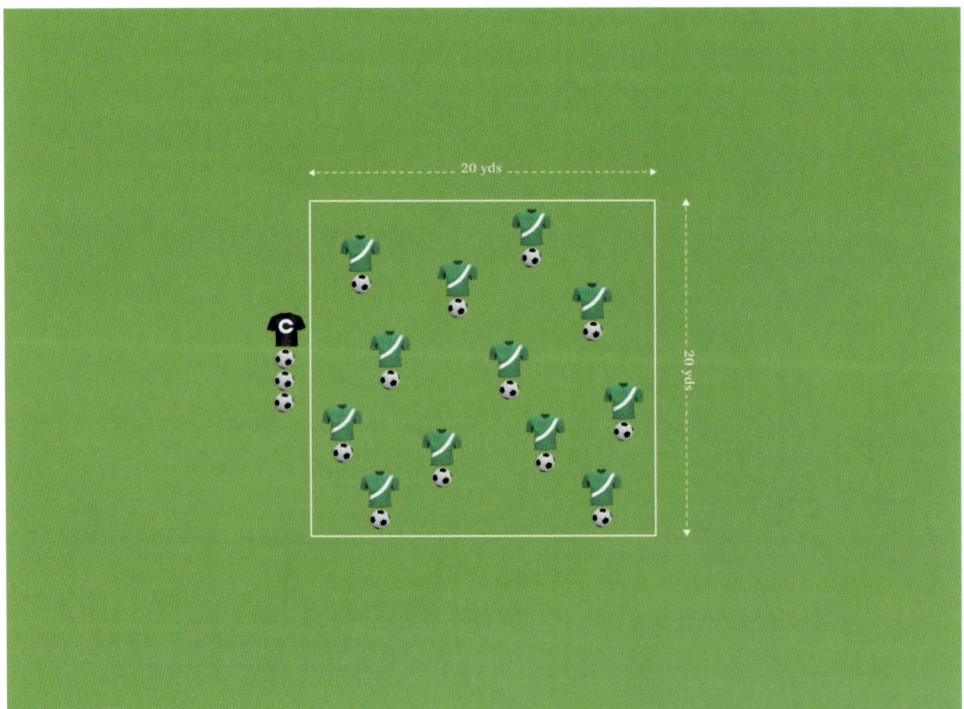

### Description

Players perform individually with a ball each. Position all players inside the playing area. The players perform the following techniques 10-12 times:

- Bounce the ball and catch.
- Throw the ball upwards and catch.
- Throw the ball upwards, jump and catch.
- Bounce the ball, throw the ball upwards, clap hands twice and catch.
- Throw the ball upwards, claps hands as many times as possible and catch.

Divide the players into pairs. Each player requires a ball. Position each pair of players inside the playing area. Position each pair of players 8-10 yards apart. The pairs of players perform the following techniques:

- The players simultaneously throw their ball to each other. The players try to catch each other's ball.
- One player throws their ball towards their partner. The other player deflects the ball back to them using their own ball.
- One player throws their ball towards their partner. The other player catches the ball on top of their own ball.
- Self-feed and swap balls with a volley/thigh/header.

## Key focus/Coaching points

**Primary focus:** Catching

**Secondary focus:** Reaction time

**Additional focus:** Agility

## Progressions/Adaptations

- Higher ability players should work at a faster tempo and perform repetitions quickly.
- Vary the speed, spin, bounce and trajectory of each bounce, feed and throw.

## ACTIVITY 177  GOALKEEPER BALL SKILLS

**Level:** Basic

**Type of activity:** Unopposed technical practice

**Number of participants:** 2-20 goalkeepers

**Equipment required:** Soccer balls and cones

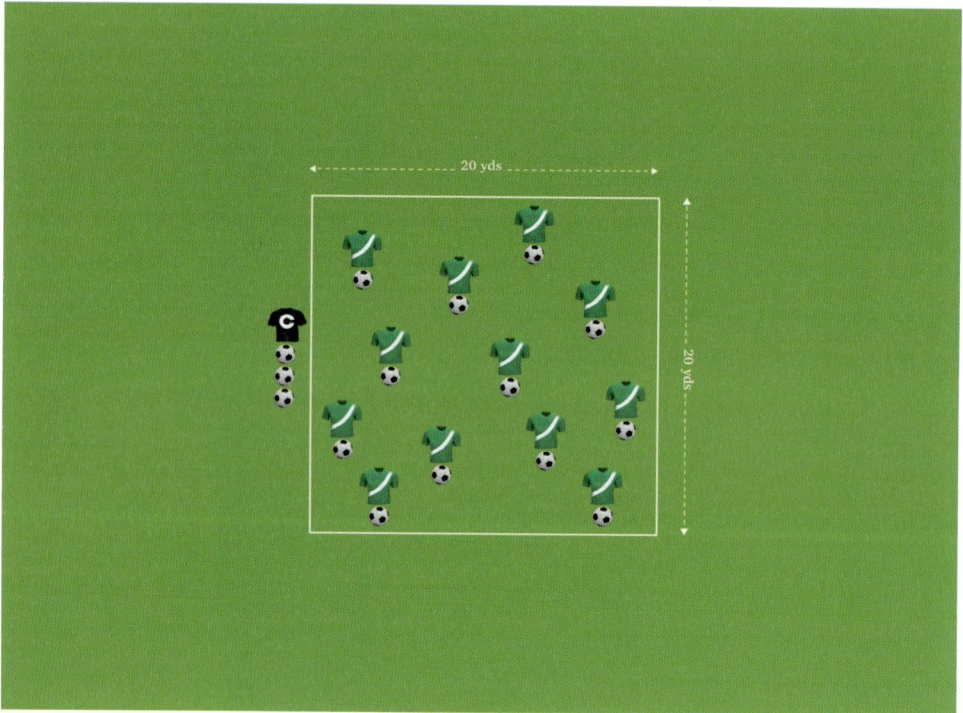

## Description

Players perform individually with a ball each. Position all players inside the playing area. Players work through the following techniques:

- Lean forward, bend knees, catch the ball in front of and behind legs.
- Move the ball around waist (circular motion and use hands).
- Figure-eights around and through legs (use hands).

- Basketball bounces between legs.
- Keep the ball in the air using fist.
- Perform a volleyball-style 2-arm shot (inside of the forearms) to keep the ball in the air.
- Bounce the ball hard into the floor. Let the ball rise and catch it at the top of the bounce.

## Key focus/Coaching points

**Primary focus:** Coordination

**Secondary focus:** Catching

**Additional focus:** Agility

## Progressions/Adaptations

- Higher ability players should work at a faster tempo and be encouraged to complete a high number of repetitions in 60 seconds.
- Vary the speed, spin, bounce and trajectory of each bounce, feed and throw.

## ACTIVITY 178  GOALKEEPER DUOS

**Level:** Basic

**Type of activity:** Unopposed technical practice

**Number of participants:** 2-20 goalkeepers

**Equipment required:** Soccer balls and cones

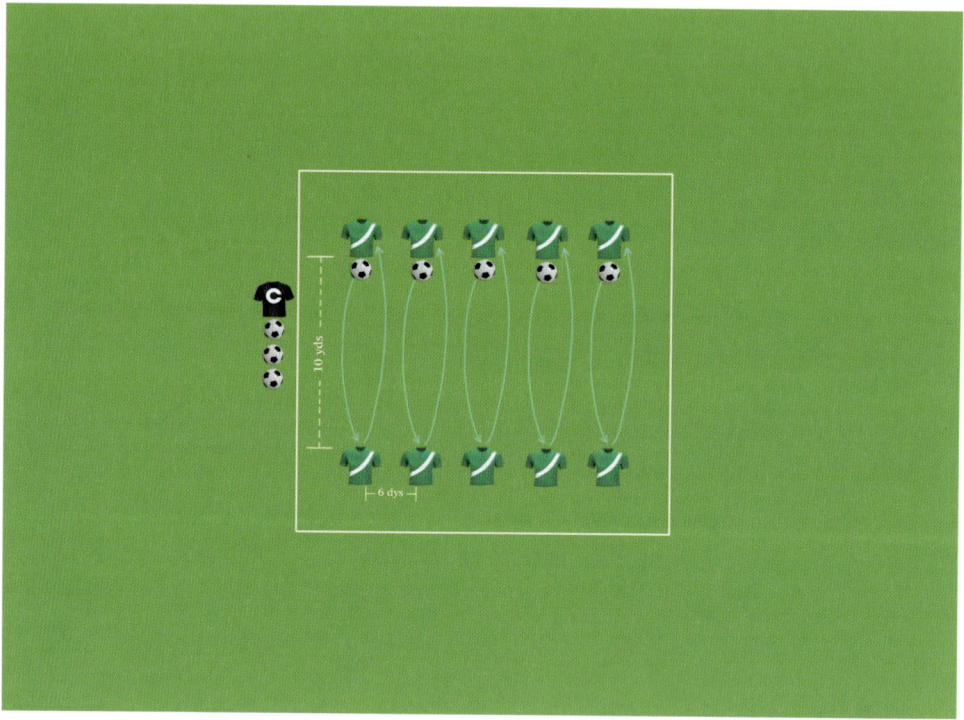

## Description

Divide players into pairs with one ball per pair. Position each pair of players inside the playing area. Position the players in each pair 8-10 yards apart. The pairs perform the following techniques:

- Underarm roll and pick up.
- Underarm throw and catch (waist height).

- Two-hand overarm throw and catch (chest height).
- Two-hand overarm throw with one bounce and catch (chest height).
- Volley from hands and catch (chest height).
- Half-volley from hands and catch (chest height).
- Two-hand underarm high throw and catch (jump to catch).
- Shot along the ground and diving save.
- Volley from hands and diving save.
- Shots from close range, partner on knees and rebound save back to the shooter.

## Key focus/Coaching points

Primary focus: Catching

Secondary focus: Coordination

Additional focus: Agility

## Progressions/Adaptations

- Vary the speed, spin, bounce and trajectory of each bounce, feed, throw and shot.
- Higher ability players should work at a faster tempo and be encouraged to complete a high number of repetitions in 60 seconds.

# 414 THE SOCCER COACH'S TOOLKIT

## ACTIVITY 179   LONG KICK OUTS

**Level:** Basic

**Type of activity:** Unopposed technical practice

**Number of participants:** 4 goalkeepers + 2 players

**Equipment required:** Soccer balls and cones

## Description

Divide players into one group of four. Mark out a playing area 40-50 yards long. Divide the group of four players into two pairs. Position each pair of players at opposite ends of the playing area. Position the players at the same end of the playing area 18-20 yards apart. Each pair of players requires a supply of balls.

# Goalkeeping

The pairs practice taking goal kicks end-to-end, using their partner as the target for each kick. Encourage the players to be as accurate as possible with each goal kick. Encourage the players to kick the ball through the air.

## Key focus/Coaching points

Primary focus: Long passing

Secondary focus: Distribution

Additional focus: Decision making

## Progressions/Adaptations

- Decrease/increase the distance between the pairs.
- After the receiving player catches the goal kick, they roll the ball forwards a few yards and kick the rolling ball to their partner.
- Position a defender in between both goalkeepers. The defender can intercept inaccurate goal kicks.
- The players practice kicking the ball from hands to their partner.

# 416 THE SOCCER COACH'S TOOLKIT

## ACTIVITY 180   DIAMOND ROLL

**Level:** Basic

**Type of activity:** Unopposed technical practice

**Number of participants:** 8 goalkeepers

**Equipment required:** Soccer balls, 8 mannequins or agility poles

## Description

Divide players into a group of eight. Mark out a diamond-shaped playing area using four mannequins. Position the mannequins 15 yards apart. Position two players (one behind the other) at each point of the diamond. Make sure that there are 4-5 yards between the players. Position a ball with both players at opposite points of the diamond. All other players start the activity without a ball.

The activity starts when each player with a ball rolls it to the first player in line at the next mannequin. The direction of the rolls should be clockwise. After each roll, the players follow their roll to the back of the line at the next mannequin. The activity continues clockwise around the diamond. Use the following throwing and rolling techniques sequentially: Left-hand underarm roll, right-hand underarm roll, one-hand overarm throw, two-hand overarm throw and two-hand throw from chest.

## Key focus/Coaching points

Primary focus: Throwing

Secondary focus: Rolling

Additional focus: Distribution

## Progressions/Adaptations

- Add a mannequin or agility pole in between each point of the diamond as an obstacle. Encourage the players to make space to the side before rolling/throwing the ball to avoid the obstacle.

- Increase/decrease the distance between the points of the diamond.

- Condition each throw so that it must bounce 1-2 times before it reaches the receiving player.

## ACTIVITY 181  FIVE IN A THROW

**Level:** Intermediate

**Type of activity:** Opposed technical practice

**Number of participants:** 8 goalkeepers

**Equipment required:** Soccer balls, cones, discs and 2 sets of bibs

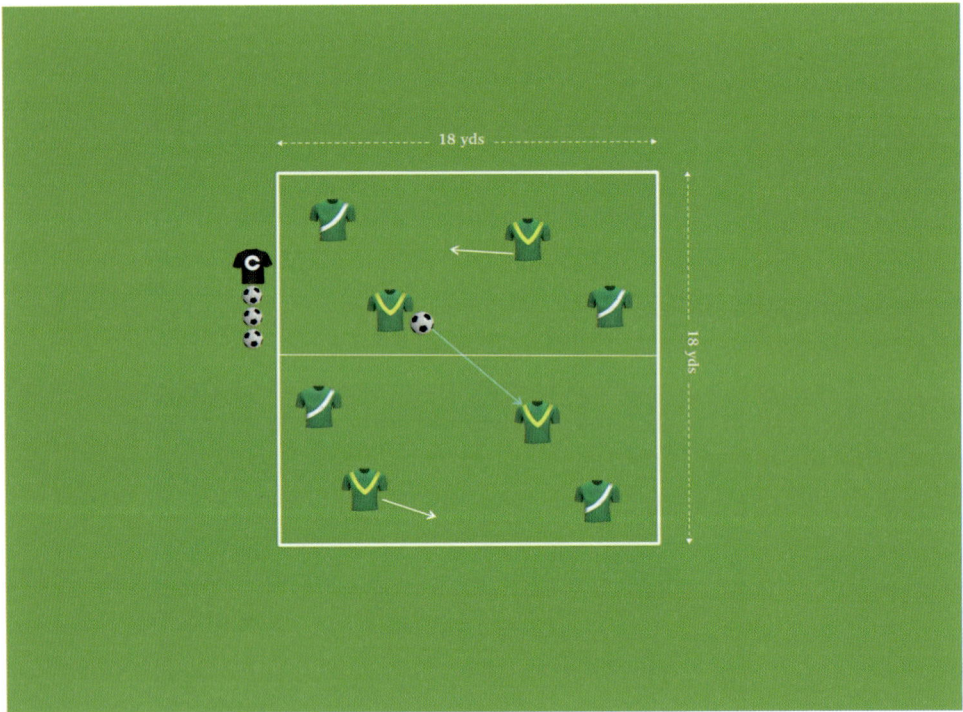

### Description

Divide players into two teams of four. Mark out a playing area with a halfway line across the middle. Players keep possession by throwing or rolling the ball to teammates. The player in possession must stand still and has 3 seconds to release the ball. All other players from the team in possession should move to create angles to receive the ball. All players from the team out of possession should move to try to intercept the ball. When either team completes five throws/rolls in the opposition half they score 1 point.

## Key focus/Coaching points

**Primary focus:** Throwing

**Secondary focus:** Catching

**Additional focus:** Receiving

## Progressions/Adaptations

- Condition the type of throw/rolls, e.g., 1/2-hand overhead throw, 1/2-hand underarm throw and 1/2-hand underarm roll.

- Condition the activity so that each team must complete different types of rolls or throws in each attack.

- The teams must complete 3 throws/rolls in each half of the playing area to score 1 point.

# 420 THE SOCCER COACH'S TOOLKIT

## ACTIVITY 182   GET DOWN

**Level:** Intermediate

**Type of activity:** Unopposed technical practice

**Number of participants:** 3 goalkeepers + 1 ball feeder

**Equipment required:** Soccer balls, cones and 1 goal

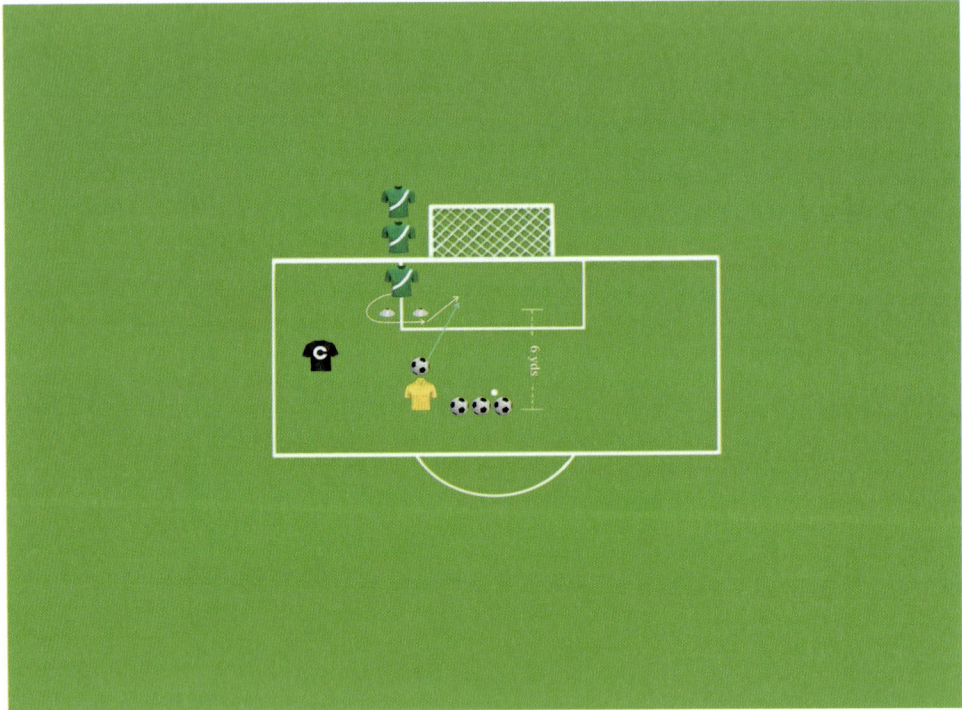

## Description

Divide players into one group of three goalkeepers and one ball feeder. Position a goal at one end of the playing area. Position two cones 6 yards apart, slightly to the left side of and 3 yards in front of the goal. Position one goalkeeper in between the two cones. Position the other two goalkeepers 4-5 yards behind the cones in a straight line. Position the ball feeder 6 yards opposite the cones. The ball feeder requires a supply of balls.

The goalkeepers perform each activity (see below) for 5-10 minutes. After each save, the goalkeeper that performed the save runs to the back of the line. The first goalkeeper in line immediately runs into position between the cones for the next save. The goalkeepers must move quickly in and out of the cones to maintain a high intensity.

- **Activity 1** – The goalkeeper side steps to the cone farthest from the goal and then to the cone nearest to the goal. As the goalkeeper reaches the cone closest to the goal, the ball feeder strikes a low side-foot shot towards the goal for the goalkeeper to make a diving save.

- **Activity 2** – The goalkeeper side steps around the cone nearest to the goal, across to and around the cone farthest from the goal and then back to a position in between the cones. As the goalkeeper reaches the middle of the cones, the ball feeder strikes a low side-foot shot towards the goal for the goalkeeper to make a diving save.

- **Activity 3** – Position two cones one behind the other facing the ball feeder. The cones should be approximately 6 yards apart. Position the cones slightly to the left side of and 3 yards forward from the goal. Position the goalkeeper next to the cone closest to the ball feeder. The goalkeeper backsteps to the cone behind them and as they reach this cone, the feeder strikes a low side-foot shot towards the goal for the goalkeeper to make a diving save.

Position the cones on the other side of the goal and repeat the three activities.

## Key focus/Coaching points

Primary focus: Agility

Secondary focus: Shot preparation

Additional focus: Reaction time

## Progressions/Adaptations

- Vary the type of shot at goal, e.g., volley and half-volley.
- Increase the power of each shot.

## ACTIVITY 183   GOALKEEPER 1V1S

Level: Intermediate

Type of activity: Opposed technical practice

Number of participants: 2 goalkeepers + 4 attackers

Equipment required: Soccer balls, cones, 2 sets of bibs and 1 goal

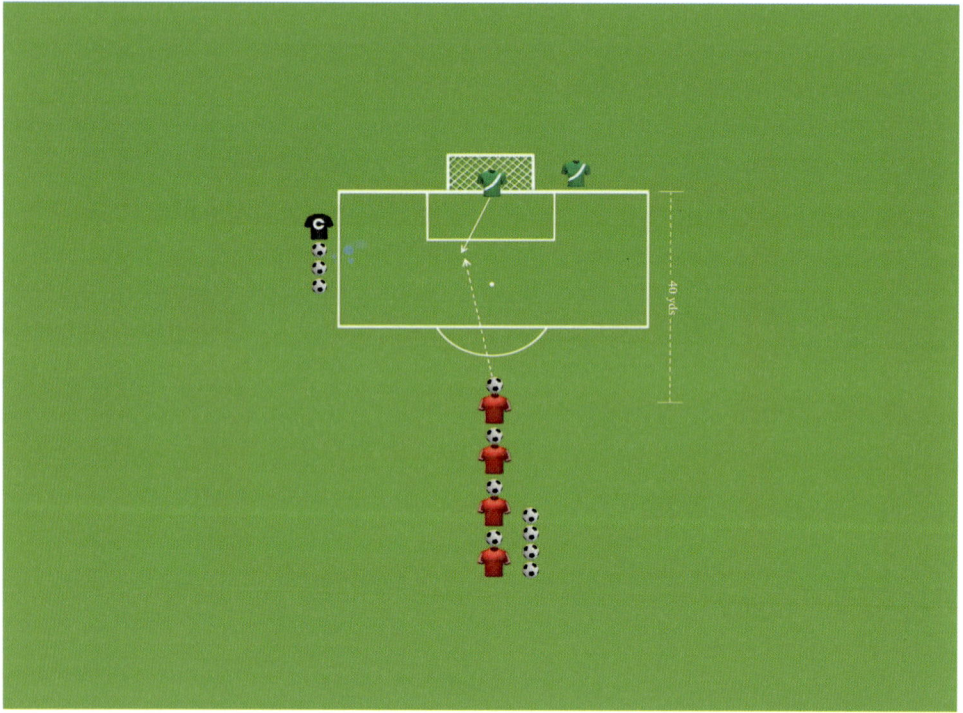

### Description

Divide players into one group of two goalkeepers and one group of four attackers. Position a goal at one end of the playing area. Position one goalkeeper in goal and the other goalkeeper a safe distance to the side of either goalpost. Position the attackers in a straight line 40 yards from goal. The group of attackers requires a supply of balls.

The activity starts when the first attacker in line runs with the ball towards the goal. As the attacker approaches the goal, the goalkeeper comes out of the goal. The goalkeeper either tries to dispossess the attacker by diving at their feet to grab the ball or force the attacker away from the goal. The attacker has 10 seconds from when they start their attack to try to dribble around the goalkeeper and score.

After each attack, the goalkeepers swap positions, the attacker runs to the back of their line and the next attacker in line starts an attack.

## Key focus/Coaching points

Primary focus: Decision making

Secondary focus: Agility

Additional focus: Positioning

## Progressions/Adaptations

- Allow the attacker to either dribble around the goalkeeper or shoot. Mark out a shooting line 18 yards from goal. The attacker must shoot before they cross the line.
- Allow the attackers to attack in pairs. As soon as the pair of attackers start their attack, the next player in line acts as a defender and chases the attackers. The defender works as a pair with the goalkeeper to try to dispossess the attackers.

# 424  THE SOCCER COACH'S TOOLKIT

## ACTIVITY 184   CLAIM AND DISTRIBUTE

**Level:** Intermediate

**Type of activity:** Opposed technical practice

**Number of participants:** 3 goalkeepers + 11 players

**Equipment required:** Soccer balls, cones, 2 sets of bibs and 1 goal

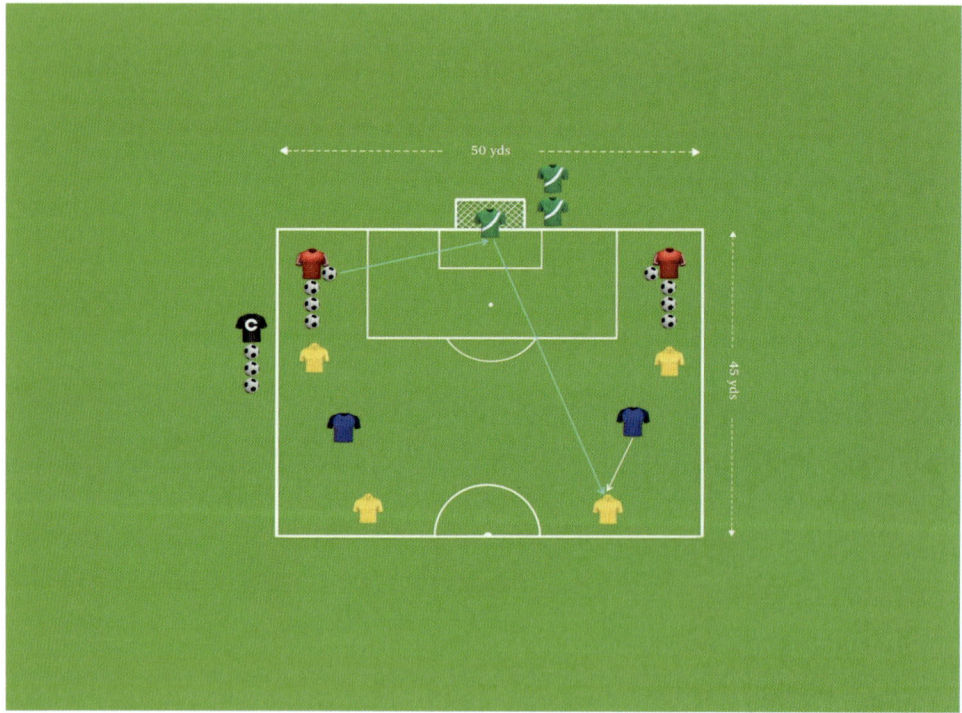

## Description

Divide players into one group of three goalkeepers, one group of four target players, one group of two defenders, one right winger and one left winger. Position a goal and goalkeeper at one end of the playing area. Position the other two goalkeepers one behind the other, next to the goal.

Position the right winger on the right side of the playing area and the left winger on the left side of the playing area. Position the wingers 6 yards from the end of the playing area. Each winger requires a supply of balls.

Position one target player 20 yards diagonally left and one target player 20 yards diagonally right from the centre of the goal. Position one target player 40 yards diagonally left and one target player 40 yards diagonally right from the centre of the goal. Position the target players farthest from the goal at a slightly straighter angle than the target players closest to the goal. Position one defender in between each target player.

The activity starts when either winger crosses a ball for the goalkeeper to jump and catch. After the catch, the goalkeeper can either throw the ball to the farthest target player or roll the ball to the closest target player on the opposite side of the playing area. For example, if the cross was from the right side of the playing area, the goalkeeper must distribute the ball to the left side of the playing area. As the goalkeeper distributes the ball to either target player, the defender closest to the target player runs towards them to pressure the accuracy of the distribution.

When the target player has received the ball, the goalkeeper returns to the centre of the goal and receives the next cross from the other winger. The goalkeeper repeats the catch and distribution to either target player on the opposite side of the pitch.

After the goalkeeper has received two crosses and distributed the ball, they run to the back of the line of goalkeepers next to the goal. The first goalkeeper in line enters the playing area to repeat the activity.

## Key focus/Coaching points

**Primary focus:** Catching

**Secondary focus:** Decision making

**Additional focus:** Distribution

## Progressions/Adaptations

- The defenders try to intercept the goalkeepers' throws and rolls.
- Add a defender to apply passive pressure to the goalkeepers as they catch the crosses.

# 426 THE SOCCER COACH'S TOOLKIT

## ACTIVITY 185  ON YOUR TOES

**Level:** Intermediate

**Type of activity:** Opposed technical practice

**Number of participants:** 2 goalkeepers + 6 players

**Equipment required:** Soccer balls, cones, discs, 2 sets of bibs and 2 goals

## Description

Divide players into two teams of four (including goalkeepers). Position a goal and goalkeeper at both ends of the playing area with a supply of balls beside both goals. Mark out a halfway line across the playing area. The teams attack opposite ends of the playing area. Position the teams in their defensive half of the playing area.

The activity starts when either goalkeeper rolls a ball out to teammate. The attacking team must keep possession of the ball in their own half of the playing area. The attacking team pass the ball and try to create an opportunity to shoot at the opposition goal from their defensive half of the playing area.

The defending team must stay in their own half of the playing area. The defending team tries to prevent the attacking team from shooting by closing space and blocking their route to goal. When the attacking team shoots, the defending team tries to block the shot.

If the attacking team scores from their shot, they score 1 point. If the shot is saved by the goalkeeper, blocked by the defenders, or misses the target, the attack is over. Once a shot has been attempted, the goalkeeper at the opposite end of the playing area rolls a ball out to a teammate to start an attack at the opposite end.

## Key focus/Coaching points

**Primary focus:** Shot stopping

**Secondary focus:** Positioning

**Additional focus:** Movement

## Progressions/Adaptations

- The attacking team can move into the opposition half to shoot. After the shot, they immediately retreat to their own half.
- If the ball stays in play after a shot and the defending team wins possession of the ball, they can attack the other end. Play continues until either a goal is scored, or the ball goes out of the playing area. The activity re-starts with a roll out from the goalkeeper of the team that had the last attempt at goal.

## ACTIVITY 186  STOP ALL SIX

**Level:** Intermediate

**Type of activity:** Unopposed technical practice

**Number of participants:** 2 goalkeepers + 7 attackers

**Equipment required:** Soccer balls, cones and 1 goal

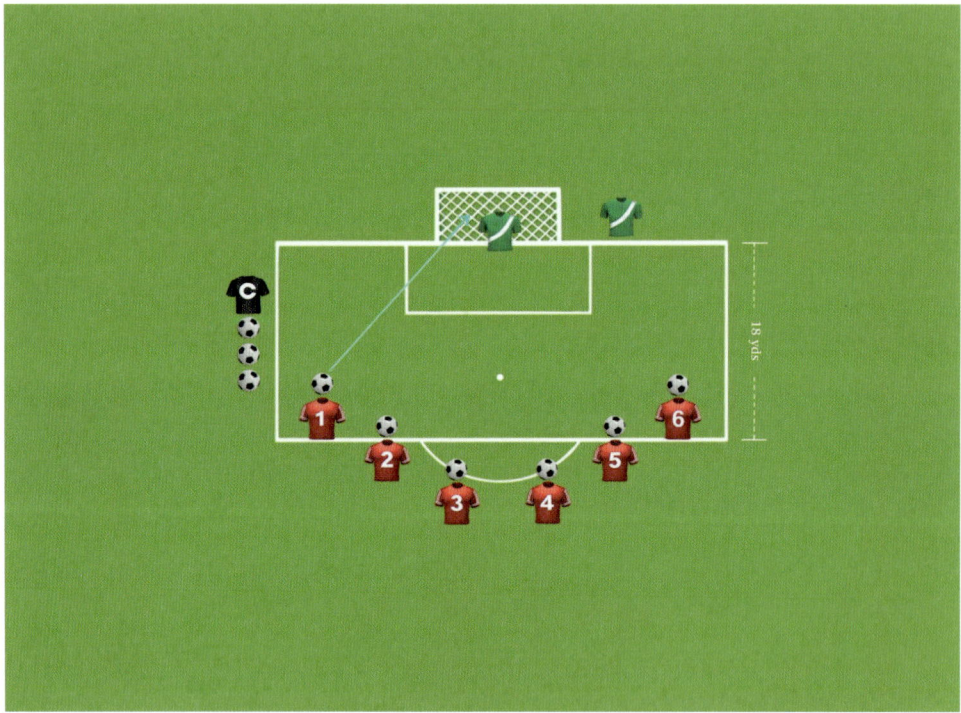

## Description

Divide players into one group of two goalkeepers and one group of six attackers. Position a goal and one goalkeeper at one end of the playing area. Position the other goalkeeper a safe distance to the side of the goal. Position the group of six attackers in an arc shape facing the goal. Position each player approximately 20 yards from the goal. Position the attackers 6-8 yards apart from each other. Number the attackers 1-6 from left to right. Each attacker requires a ball.

The activity starts when attacker number 1 shoots at goal and the goalkeeper tries to save the shot. As soon as the goalkeeper is back up on their feet, attacker number 2 shoots. Continue the activity with the attackers shooting in ascending numerical order. After the sixth shot, the goalkeeper moves to the side of the goal and the goalkeeper standing to the side of the goal moves into the goal for the next six shots.

## Key focus/Coaching points

Primary focus: Shot stopping

Secondary focus: Positioning

Additional focus: Catching

## Progressions/Adaptations

- Position an extra attacker near the centre of the goal to follow up shots that the goalkeeper pushes back into the playing area. Make sure that the attacker stands a safe distance outside the line of each shot.

- The extra attacker calls out the number of the player to shoot. This will encourage the goalkeeper to concentrate and react quickly to shots from different positions.

# 430 THE SOCCER COACH'S TOOLKIT

## ACTIVITY 187  CLOSE-RANGE SAVES

**Level:** Intermediate

**Type of activity:** Unopposed technical practice

**Number of participants:** 1 goalkeeper + 4 attackers

**Equipment required:** Soccer balls, cones and 1 goal

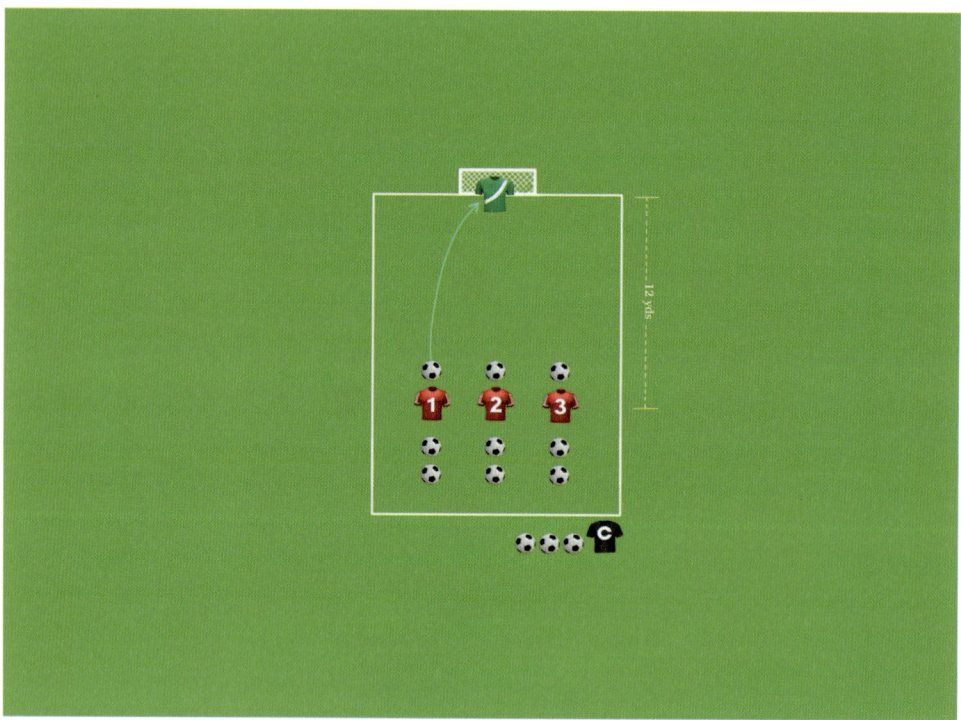

## Description

Divide players into one group of three attackers and one goalkeeper. Position a goal and the goalkeeper at one end of the playing area. Position each of the attackers 12 yards from the goal. Position one attacker in line with the left goalpost, one attacker in line with the centre of the goal and one attacker in line with the right goalpost. Number the attackers 1-3 from left to right. Each attacker requires a supply of balls.

The activity starts when attacker number 1 performs a shot/feed for the goalkeeper to catch or save. The activity continues with the attackers performing feeds/shots in ascending numerical order. After each shot/feed, allow the goalkeeper 2-3 seconds to prepare for the next shot/feed. After attacker number 3 has performed their shot/feed, player number 1 continues the activity. The attackers perform the shots/feeds continuously until all the balls have been used. The attackers perform the following techniques:

- **Attacker 1** – Volley from hands for a catch or parry away from the goal.
- **Attacker 2** – Low shot for a diving save.
- **Attacker 3** – High underarm throw. The goalkeeper must jump to the catch the ball at its highest point.

## Key focus/Coaching points

Primary focus: Agility

Secondary focus: Movement

Additional focus: Reaction time

## Progressions/Adaptations

- Position a fourth attacker close to the centre of the goal to finish any rebounds. Make sure that the attacker stands outside of the line of each shot/feed.
- The fourth attacker calls out the number of the player to shoot. This will encourage the goalkeeper to concentrate and react quickly to shots/feeds from different positions.

## ACTIVITY 188  LEAPING KEEPERS

**Level:** Advanced

**Type of activity:** Unopposed technical practice

**Number of participants:** 2 goalkeepers + 2 attackers

**Equipment required:** Soccer balls, cones and 1 goal

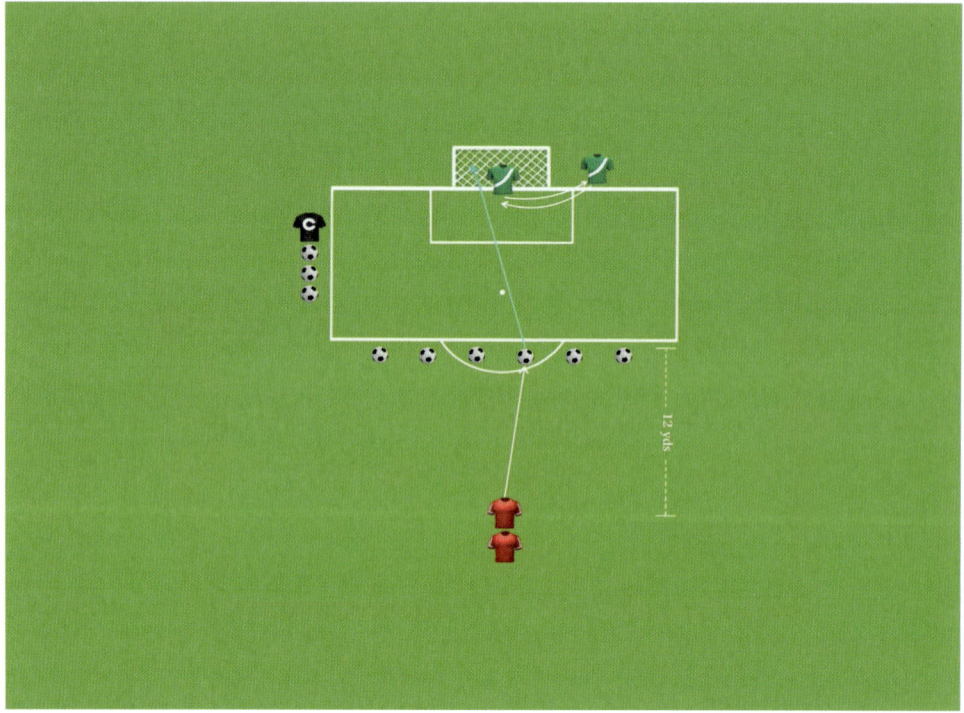

## Description

Divide players into one group of two goalkeepers and one group of two attackers. Position a goal and one goalkeeper at one end of the playing area. Position the other goalkeeper a safe distance to the side of the goal. Position the two attackers in a straight line 30 yards from goal. Position a line of six balls 10 yards in front of the attackers. Position the balls side-by-side and 4-5 yards apart.

# Goalkeeping

The activity starts when the first attacker in line runs to one of the balls and shoots at goal. The goalkeeper tries to save the shot. After the shot, the attacker runs to the other attacker and tags them. The goalkeeper stands up and side steps to the side of the goal as fast as they can. The goalkeeper next to the goal side steps into the goal as fast as they can. The next attacker runs to one of the balls and shoots at goal. The attackers take alternate shots at goal until all the balls have been used.

The time interval between each shot will allow the goalkeepers enough time to swap over and be ready for the next shot; however, they will need to move quickly for this to happen.

## Key focus/Coaching points

**Primary focus:** Shot stopping

**Secondary focus:** Agility

**Additional focus:** Catching

## Progressions/Adaptations

- Add a third attacker near to the centre of the goal to convert rebounds. Make sure that the attacker stands outside the line of each shot.
- The goalkeeper turns their back to the ball before each shot. As the attacker prepares to shoot, the coach shouts "Turn". The goalkeeper turns quickly to face the shot. Increase the distance between the players and the balls by 5 yards to give the goalkeepers time to turn their back and then face each shot.

# 434 THE SOCCER COACH'S TOOLKIT

## ACTIVITY 189  50 SAVES

**Level:** Advanced

**Type of activity:** Unopposed technical practice

**Number of participants:** 6 goalkeepers + 6 attackers

**Equipment required:** Soccer balls, cones and 6 mini-goals

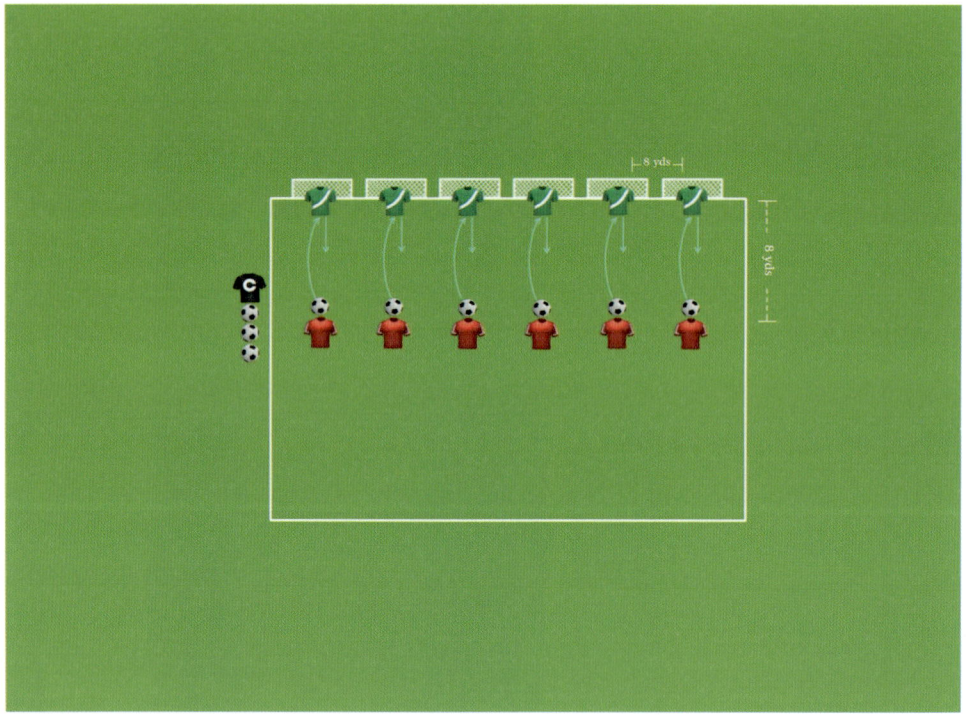

## Description

Divide players into six pairs. Position six mini goals 8-10 yards apart at one end of the playing area. Organise each pair into one goalkeeper and one attacker. Position each goalkeeper in a mini goal. Position each attacker 8 yards opposite their goalkeeper partner.

The attackers take 50 consecutive shots at goal. The goalkeepers try to save the shots and rebound them back to the attacker for the next shot. The attacker should not necessarily try to score with each shot but should try to force the goalkeeper to make a diving save.

After each save, the attacker immediately runs to the ball and shoots again. The attacker must move quickly and minimise the goalkeeper's recovery and preparation time between shots. Encourage the attackers to shoot first time. If necessary, the attackers can have one touch before each shot.

The attackers play an important role in making the saves challenging but realistic. The shots should not be too powerful, as this would be potentially dangerous for the goalkeeper and too difficult to save in relation to distance from the goal and the goalkeeper's level of fatigue. The attacker should try to vary the height, spin and trajectory of each shot.

Goalkeepers are generally coached to divert the ball away from goal or catch the ball when making saves. In this activity, the emphasis is on developing movement, fitness, agility and quick reactions. In order to develop these things, the shots must be continuous and so the goalkeeper must rebound the ball back to the attacker.

## Key focus/Coaching points

**Primary focus:** Physical/movement development

**Secondary focus:** Agility

**Additional focus:** Reaction time

## Progressions/Adaptations

- The goalkeepers must try to catch each shot. After each catch, the goalkeeper rolls the ball back to the attacker.

- Encourage the attackers to disguise each shot. The attackers can feint to shoot or perform a trick before each shot.

# 436 THE SOCCER COACH'S TOOLKIT

## ACTIVITY 190   PLAY IT SAFE

**Level:** Advanced

**Type of activity:** Implementation practice

**Number of participants:** 1 goalkeeper + 9 players

**Equipment required:** Soccer balls, cones, 2 sets of bibs and 1 goal

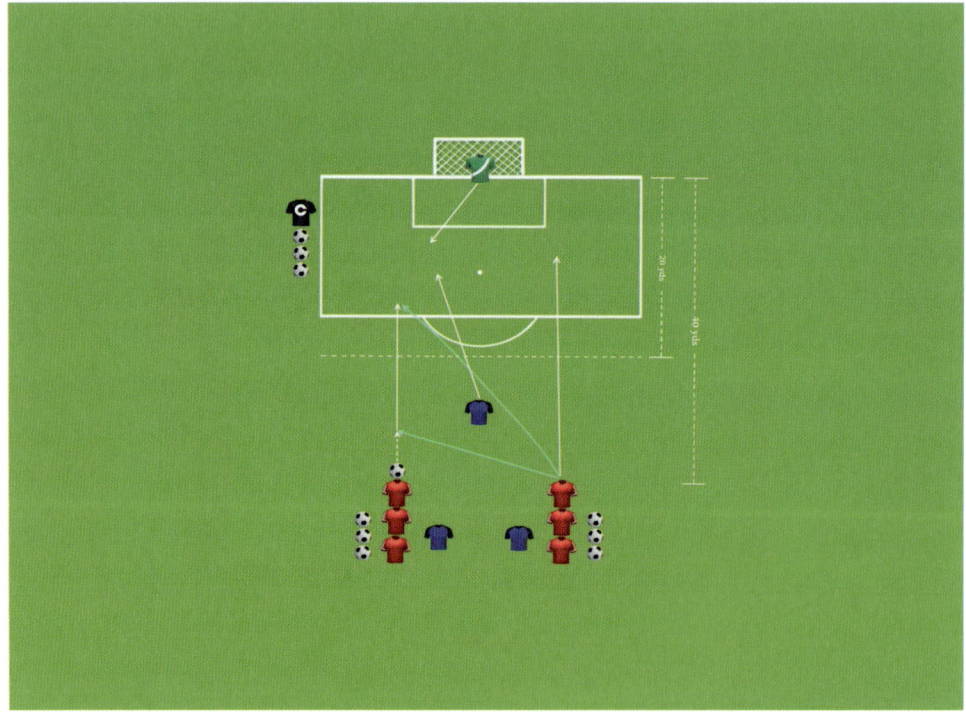

## Description

Divide players into a group of 10. Organise the players into three pairs of attackers, three defenders and one goalkeeper. Position a goal and the goalkeeper at one end of the playing area. Mark out an offside line 20 yards from goal. Position the pairs of attackers side-by-side in a straight line, 40 yards from goal. The attackers require a supply of balls. Position one defender 10 yards opposite the line of attackers. Position the remaining two defenders beside the attackers' line and out of the way of each attack.

The activity starts when the first pair of attackers in line attack the goal. The attackers try to keep possession and score as quickly as possible. The attackers combine using dribbles, passes and crosses to create a goal-scoring opportunity. The defender retreats towards the goal and works with the goalkeeper to try to stop the attackers from scoring. The defender tries to make a tackle, interception or force the attack out of play before the attackers create an opportunity to score.

If the defender fails to stop the attack, the goalkeeper tries to save the attempt at goal or force the attack out of play. After each attack, the attackers run to the back of the attackers' line and the defenders run to the group of defenders. The next pair of attackers and the next defender position themselves inside the playing area for the next attack.

## Key focus/Coaching points

**Primary focus:** Positioning

**Secondary focus:** Attacking and defending

**Additional focus:** Agility

## Progressions/Adaptations

- Introduce a points system for the goalkeeper:
    - 1 point for saving an attempt at goal.
    - 3 points for preventing an attempt at goal.
- Progress to 3 attackers v 2 defenders in each attack.

## ACTIVITY 191  1, 2, THROW

**Level:** Advanced

**Type of activity:** Opposed technical practice

**Number of participants:** 1 goalkeeper + 16 players

**Equipment required:** Soccer balls, cones, discs, 2 sets of bibs, 1 goal and 2 mini-goals

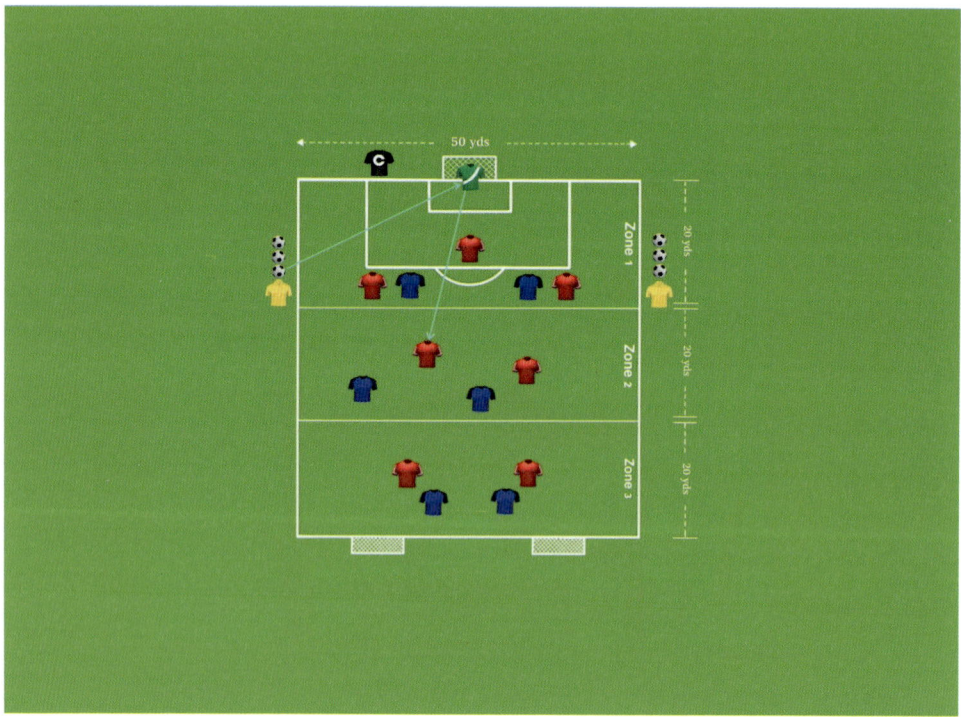

### Description

Divide players into one team of eight, one team of six and two ball feeders. Mark out a playing area with a goal positioned at one end and one mini-goal in each corner at the opposite end of the playing area. Divide the playing area into three zones.

Organise the team of eight into one goalkeeper, three defenders, two midfielders and two attackers. Organise the team of six into two defenders, two midfielders and two attackers. The team of eight attack the two mini-goals and the team of six attack the goal at the opposite end of the playing area. Position one ball feeder on either side of the playing area 20 yards from goal with a supply of balls each. Organise the team of eight with three defenders inside their defensive zone, two midfielders in the middle zone and two attackers in their attacking zone. Organise the team of six with two players in each zone. The players must play within their zones. Number the team of eight's defensive zone "Zone 1", their middle zone "Zone 2" and their attacking zone "Zone 3".

The activity starts when the coach calls out "1", "2" or "3". Nominate either ball feeder to deliver an aerial cross for the goalkeeper to catch. Once the goalkeeper has caught the cross, they have 4 seconds to distribute the ball to a teammate in the corresponding zone. The goalkeeper decides whether to throw, roll or kick the ball.

Once the goalkeeper has distributed the ball, the two teams compete for possession and try to score. The team of eight tries to score with a pass into either of the mini goals. The team of six tries to score past the goalkeeper at the opposite end of the playing area. When a goal is scored or the ball goes out of play, the activity re-starts with a cross to the goalkeeper from the ball feeder on the other side of the playing area.

## Key focus/Coaching points

Primary focus: Distribution

Secondary focus: Catching

Additional focus: Decision making

## Progressions/Adaptations

- The goalkeeper decides which zone and player to distribute the ball to.
- Allow 1 player in each zone from the team of 8 to move 1 zone in any direction before the goalkeeper distributes the ball. The players can move between this zone and their original zone during their team's attack. When the team of 8 loses possession, the players must retreat to their original zone.

# 440  THE SOCCER COACH'S TOOLKIT

## ACTIVITY 192   ONE FOR THE CAMERAS

**Level:** Advanced

**Type of activity:** Unopposed technical practice

**Number of participants:** 2 goalkeepers + 5 players

**Equipment required:** Soccer balls, cones and 1 goal

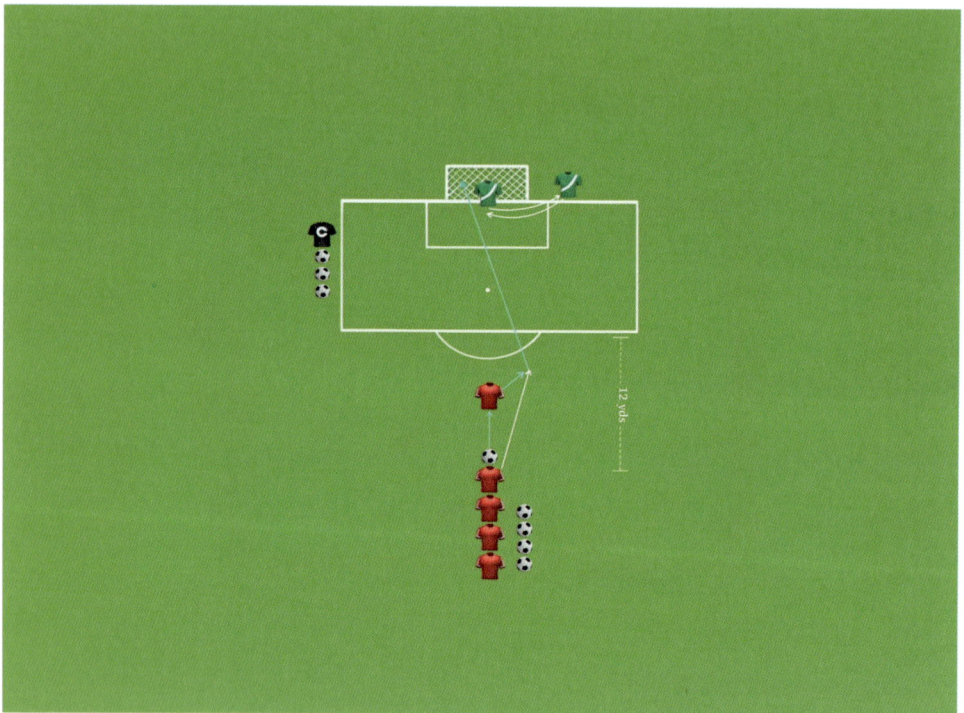

## Description

Divide players into one group of two goalkeepers, one group of four attackers and one ball receiver. Position a goal and one goalkeeper at one end of the playing area. Position the other goalkeeper a safe distance to the side of the goal. Position the attackers in a straight line, 30 yards from goal. The attackers require a supply of balls. Position the ball receiver with their back to goal 5 yards opposite the line of attackers.

The activity starts when the first attacker in the line passes the ball to the ball receiver. The ball receiver returns the pass to the left or right and towards the goal. The attacker follows the pass and shoots first time at goal. The goalkeeper tries to save the shot.

After the shot, the goalkeeper stands up (if they made a diving save) and side steps to the side of the goal. The other goalkeeper side steps into the goal for the next shot. The attacker runs to the back of the attackers' line. As soon as the new goalkeeper is in goal and the attacker is clear of the goal, the next attacker in line continues the activity.

## Key focus/Coaching points

**Primary focus:** Shot stopping

**Secondary focus:** Agility

**Additional focus:** Reaction time

## Progressions/Adaptations

- Before each shot, the goalkeeper runs to a cone positioned 6 yards from the goal line and then backwards to the goal. The goalkeeper must move quickly to be ready for the shot.

- Before each shot, the goalkeeper turns their back to the attacker. As the attacker passes to the ball receiver, the goalkeeper to the side of the goal calls out "Turn". The goalkeeper must turn quickly to face the shot.

## ACTIVITY 193   KEEPER IS THE KEY

**Level:** Advanced

**Type of activity:** Implementation practice

**Number of participants:** 2 goalkeepers + 14 players

**Equipment required:** Soccer balls, cones, 2 sets of bibs and 2 goals

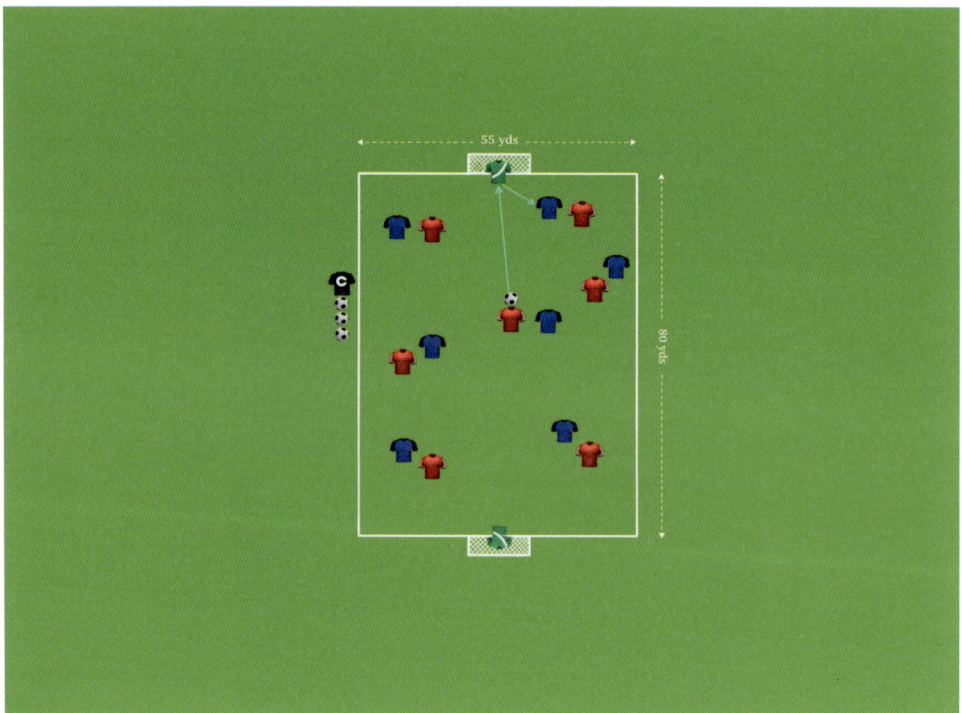

### Description

Divide players into two teams of eight (including goalkeepers). Position a goal and goalkeeper at both ends of the playing area. Organise both teams into a 2-3-2 formation for an 8v8 match.

The activity starts with an unopposed shot at the opposition goal from 25 yards by either team. The goalkeeper tries to catch or parry and retrieve the shot so that they are ready to distribute the ball. During the match, every time that either team concedes a corner or a throw-in in their own half of the playing area, the opposition re-starts the activity with an unopposed shot at their goal from 25 yards.

This method of re-starting the activity ensures that the goalkeepers face regular shots and are regularly involved in the activity. The re-start also allows the goalkeeper to practice ball distribution after making a save.

## Key focus/Coaching points

**Primary focus:** Positioning

**Secondary focus:** Shot stopping

**Additional focus:** Distribution

## Progressions/Adaptations

- Condition the maximum number of passes that the team in possession is allowed to make in the opposition half before shooting at goal. The fewer the number of passes allowed, the more shots at goal will be attempted.
- Before each re-start, the goalkeeper must turn their back to play. As the player shoots at goal, the coach calls out "Turn". The goalkeeper turns quickly to face the shot.

# 444 THE SOCCER COACH'S TOOLKIT

## ACTIVITY 194  KEEPER RE-STARTS

**Level:** Advanced

**Type of activity:** Implementation practice

**Number of participants:** 2 goalkeepers + 20 players

**Equipment required:** Soccer balls, discs, cones, 2 sets of bibs and 2 goals

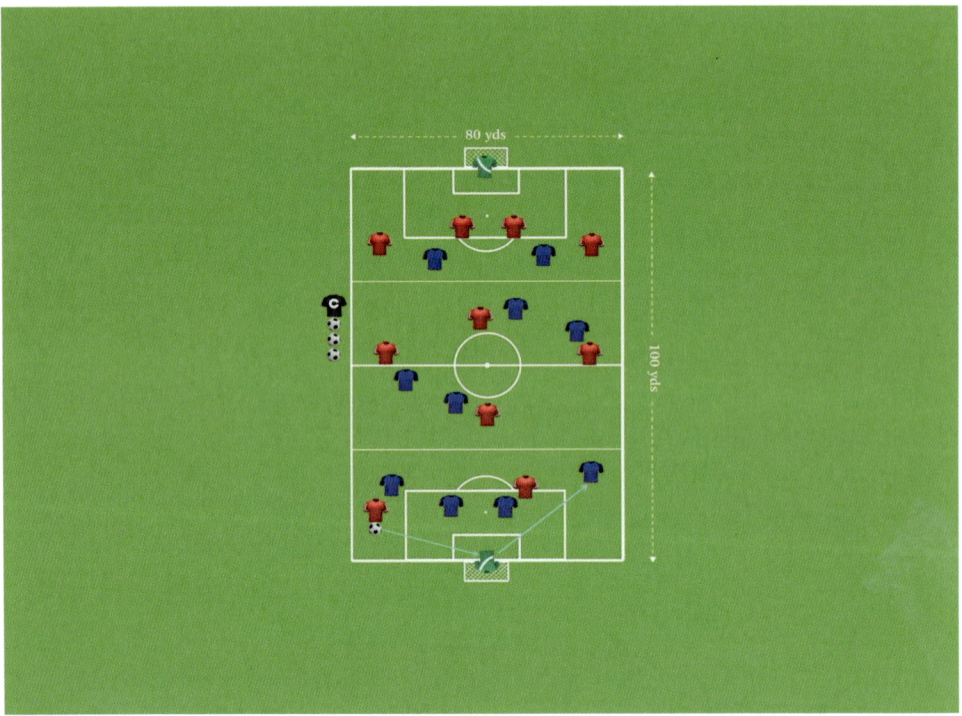

## Description

Divide players into two teams of 11 (including goalkeepers) for an 11v11 match. Position a goal and goalkeeper at both ends of the playing area. Divide the playing area into three zones. Organise both teams into a 4-4-2 formation. Position four defenders from both teams in their defensive zone, four midfielders from both teams in the middle zone and two attackers from the attacking team in their attacking zone. Initially, the players must play within their zone.

# Goalkeeping

The activity starts with an aerial cross from either team on either side of the playing area for the opposition goalkeeper to catch. The goalkeeper's catch should be unopposed. Once the goalkeeper has caught the ball, they can distribute the ball with a roll, throw or kick to a teammate.

During the match, when either team concedes a throw-in in their own half of the playing area, the opposition team re-starts the activity with an unopposed cross to the goalkeeper from either side of the playing area. This method of re-starting the activity allows the coach to work on the goalkeepers' distribution and their ability to deal with crosses.

## Key focus/Coaching points

**Primary focus:** Distribution

**Secondary focus:** Catching

**Additional focus:** Tactical/team shape

## Progressions/Adaptations

- The crosses to re-start must be opposed, i.e., the attackers can challenge the goalkeeper for the ball.
- The attackers are allowed a maximum of 4 passes in the attacking zone before they must try to score.
- Allow the players to move freely in and out of zones, but ensure they keep a sensible 4-4-2 shape. Each time a cross re-starts the activity allow no more than 3 attackers in their attacking zone to challenge the goalkeeper.

# 446 THE SOCCER COACH'S TOOLKIT

# ATTACKING AND DEFENDING

## ACTIVITY 195  STICK OR TWIST

**Level:** Basic

**Type of activity:** Opposed technical practice

**Number of participants:** 16 + 3 goalkeepers

**Equipment required:** Soccer balls, cones, 3 sets of bibs and 2 goals

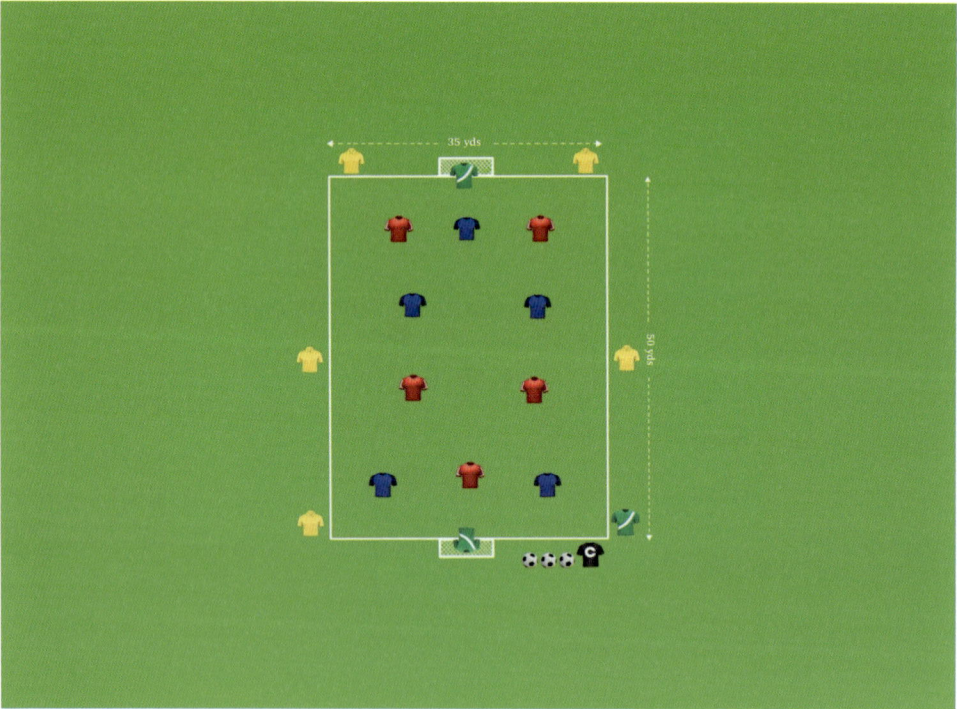

## Description

Divide players into three teams of six (including goalkeepers). Position a goal and goalkeeper at both ends of the playing area. Position two teams inside the playing area for a 6v6 match and the remaining team around the outside of the playing area to act as ball retrievers.

The first team to score two goals wins the match. At the end of the match, the coach asks the winning team if they want to "stick or twist". If the winning team chooses to "stick", they win 3 points, but they must leave the playing area and do not play in the next match. The losing team stays inside the playing area for the next match. The team of ball retrievers enters the playing area to play the next match against the losing team.

If the winning team chose to "twist", they gamble the 3 points won in the previous match and stay inside the playing area for the next match. The losing team leaves the playing area with 0 points. The team of ball retrievers enters the playing area to play the next match against the winning team.

If the winning team wins the next match, they must again decide whether to "stick" and keep all the points that they have won or "twist" again and play another match. If the winning team decides to "twist" and loses the next match, they lose all the points accumulated in that sequence of matches.

If a match is level after 5 minutes of play, award 1 point to both teams. The team that has played the longest sequence of matches get the choice to "stick or twist" for the next match. Set a point total of 15. The first team to win 15 points is the winner.

## Key focus/Coaching points

Primary focus: Attacking and defending

Secondary focus: Decision making

Additional focus: Tactical/team shape

## Progressions/Adaptations

- Add a support player who plays for the team in possession to create attacking overloads.
- The players can only score with a first-time finish.

# 448 THE SOCCER COACH'S TOOLKIT

## ACTIVITY 196  NUMBERS

**Level:** Basic

**Type of activity:** Opposed technical practice

**Number of participants:** 8 + 2 goalkeepers

**Equipment required:** Soccer balls, cones, 2 sets of bibs, and 2 goals

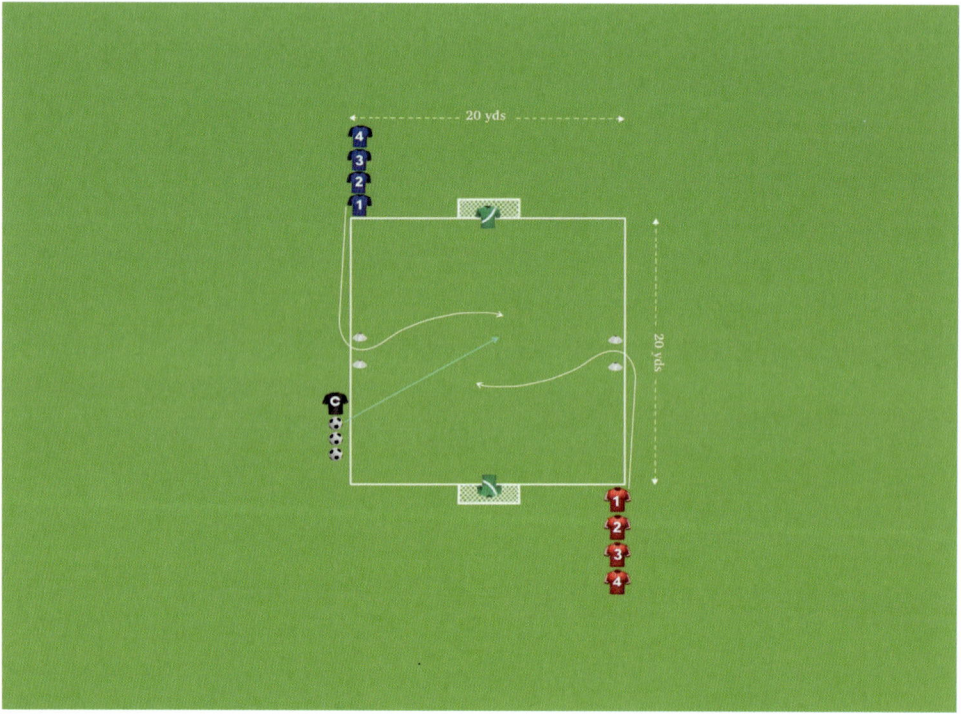

## Description

Divide players into two teams of four. Mark out a playing area and position a goal and goalkeeper at both ends of the playing area. Position a gate in the middle of both sides of the playing area. Position each team in a corner at the same end of the playing area. Position the teams in straight lines. Number each player in both teams 1-4. The teams attack opposite ends of the playing area. Make sure that the teams know which end they are attacking before the activity starts.

# Attacking and Defending

The activity starts when the coach calls out a number between 1-4. The coach feeds a ball into the middle of the playing area. The players with the corresponding number from both teams run towards and through the gate opposite them and into the playing area.

The two players compete in a 1v1 match. The match continues until a goal is scored or the ball goes out of the playing area. The first player to score wins 3 points for their team. If after 20 seconds neither player has scored, both players must leave the pitch. Award 1 point to both teams.

Once each 1v1 match is over, the players return to their team. The coach calls out another number and feeds a ball into the playing area.

## Key focus/Coaching points

**Primary focus:** Attacking and defending

**Secondary focus:** Physical/movement development

**Additional focus:** Ball manipulation

## Progressions/Adaptations

- The coach calls out 2 numbers. Progress to 2v2 matches.
- The team in possession must complete 3 passes before trying to score.

# 450 THE SOCCER COACH'S TOOLKIT

## ACTIVITY 197  CROSS THE LINE

**Level:** Basic

**Type of activity:** Opposed technical practice

**Number of participants:** 2-12

**Equipment required:** Soccer balls, cones, 2 sets of bibs and 2 goals

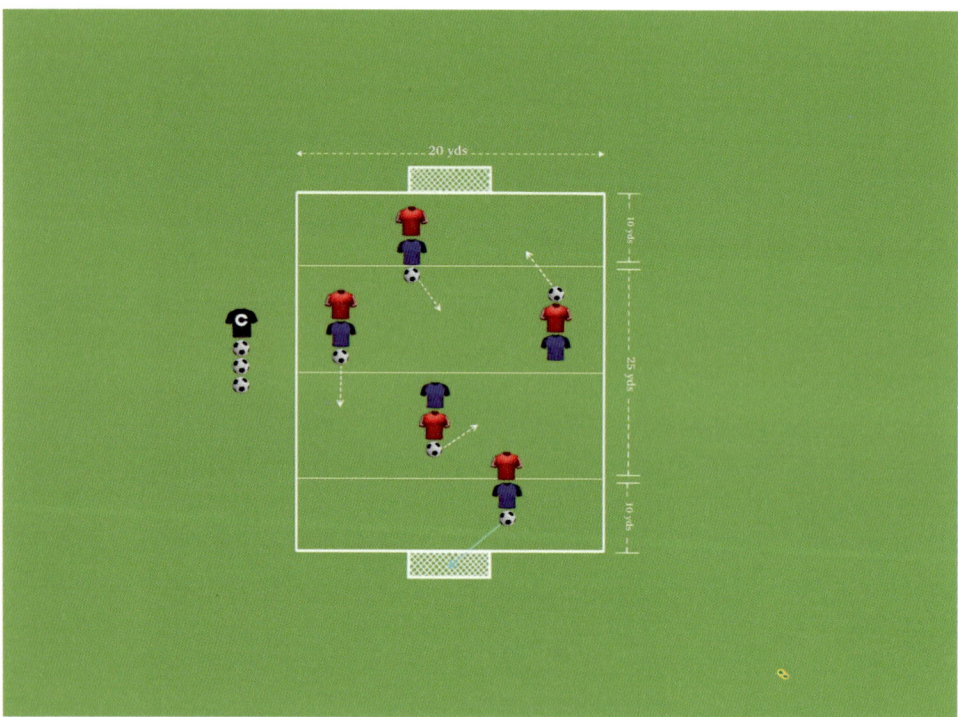

## Description

Divide players into pairs. Mark out a playing area with a goal at both ends. Mark out a halfway line across the middle of the playing area. Mark out a 10-yard scoring zone across both ends of the playing area.

Each pair of players competes in a 1v1 match, attacking opposite ends of the playing area. Players must dribble into the scoring zone at the end they are attacking and pass the ball into their opponent's goal to score. Whenever a player scores a goal, they must retreat to the halfway line. Once the player is on the halfway line, their opponent starts an attack.

There will be multiple 1v1 matches going on at the same time, so encourage the players to play with their heads up and to look around as much as possible. The activity works well if all players attacking the same end of the playing area wear the same colour bibs.

## Key focus/Coaching points

**Primary focus:** Attacking and defending

**Secondary focus:** Dribbling

**Additional focus:** Physical/movement development

## Progressions/Adaptations

- Progress to 2v2 matches.
- Progress to 3v3 matches.

# 452 THE SOCCER COACH'S TOOLKIT

## ACTIVITY 198   1V1 CONTINUOUS DRILL

**Level:** Basic

**Type of activity:** Opposed technical practice

**Number of participants:** 8 + 2 goalkeepers

**Equipment required:** Soccer balls, cones, 2 sets of bibs and 2 goals

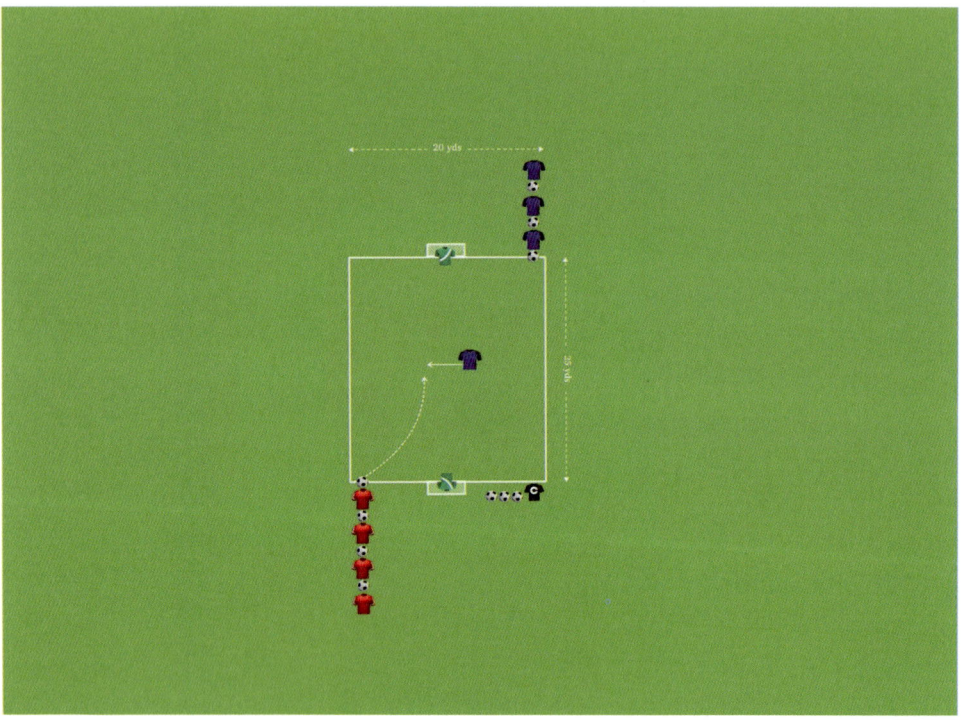

## Description

Divide players into two teams of four. Position a goal and goalkeeper at both ends of the playing area. Position the groups in straight lines, at opposite diagonal ends of the playing area and a safe distance to the side of the goals. Each player requires a ball.

Organise the player at the front of one line to start the activity as an attacker and the player at the front of the other line to start the activity as a defender. Position the attacker at the front of their line outside the playing area and the defender inside the playing area 12 yards from the centre of their goal. Apart from the defender, each player requires a ball. The activity starts when the attacker tries to dribble past the defender and score past the goalkeeper in the opposite goal. The defender tries to tackle or force the attacker out of the playing area.

Once the attack is finished, the defender runs to the back of their line and the attacker stays inside the playing area and switches to playing as a defender for the next attack. The first player in line at the opposite end of the playing area tries to dribble past the defender and score past the goalkeeper in the opposite goal. Once this attack is over, the defender runs to the back of their line and the attacker stays inside the playing area and switches to playing as a defender against the first player in line at the opposite end of the playing area.

The activity should be performed continuously at alternate ends of the playing area. Encourage the players to play at a high intensity and to rotate positions as quickly as possible after each attack.

## Key focus/Coaching points

Primary focus: Attacking and defending

Secondary focus: Dribbling

Additional focus: Turning

## Progressions/Adaptations

- Progress to 2v2 attack v defence. Each pair of players attacks and defends once.
- If the defenders win possession, they can attack the opposite goal. Play until a goal is scored or the ball goes out of the playing area.

## ACTIVITY 199   BOTH SIDES OF THE FENCE

**Level:** Basic

**Type of activity:** Opposed technical practice

**Number of participants:** 8 + 2 goalkeepers

**Equipment required:** Soccer balls, cones, 2 sets of bibs and 2 goals

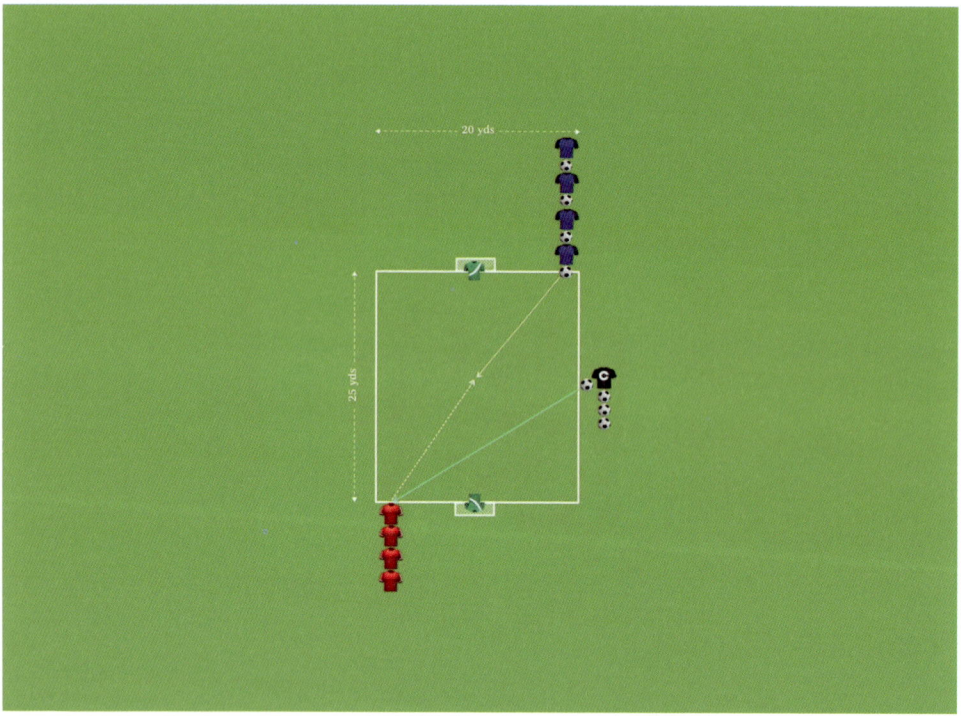

## Description

Divide players into groups of four. Position a goal and goalkeeper at both ends of the playing area. Position the groups in straight lines at opposite diagonal ends of the playing area and a safe distance to the side of the goals. The coach should be positioned in the middle of either sideline with a supply of balls.

The activity starts when the coach passes to the first player in line at either end of the playing area. The player that receives the ball becomes the attacker and attacks the goal at the opposite end of the playing area. The first player in the opposite line enters the playing area and plays as a defender. The attacker tries to dribble past the defender and score in the opposite goal. The attack is over when the attacker scores, the defender wins possession of the ball, or the ball travels outside the playing area. When the attack is over, the attacker runs to the back of the opposite line. The defender runs back to the front of their line and becomes the attacker for the next attack.

The coach passes a ball to the attacker who immediately attacks the goal at the opposite end of the playing area. The first player in line at the other end of the playing area enters the playing area and plays as a defender.

## Key focus/Coaching points

Primary focus: Attacking and defending

Secondary focus: Dribbling

Additional focus: Finishing

## Progressions/Adaptations

- Progress to 2v2 attack v defence. Each pair of players attacks and defends once.
- The attackers must complete 2 passes before attempting to score.
- 1 attacker must dribble past a defender before the attackers can attempt to score.

## ACTIVITY 200   HOLD FIRM

**Level:** Basic

**Type of activity:** Opposed technical practice

**Number of participants:** 8 + 1 goalkeeper

**Equipment required:** Soccer balls, cones, 2 sets of bibs, 2 mini-goals and 1 goal

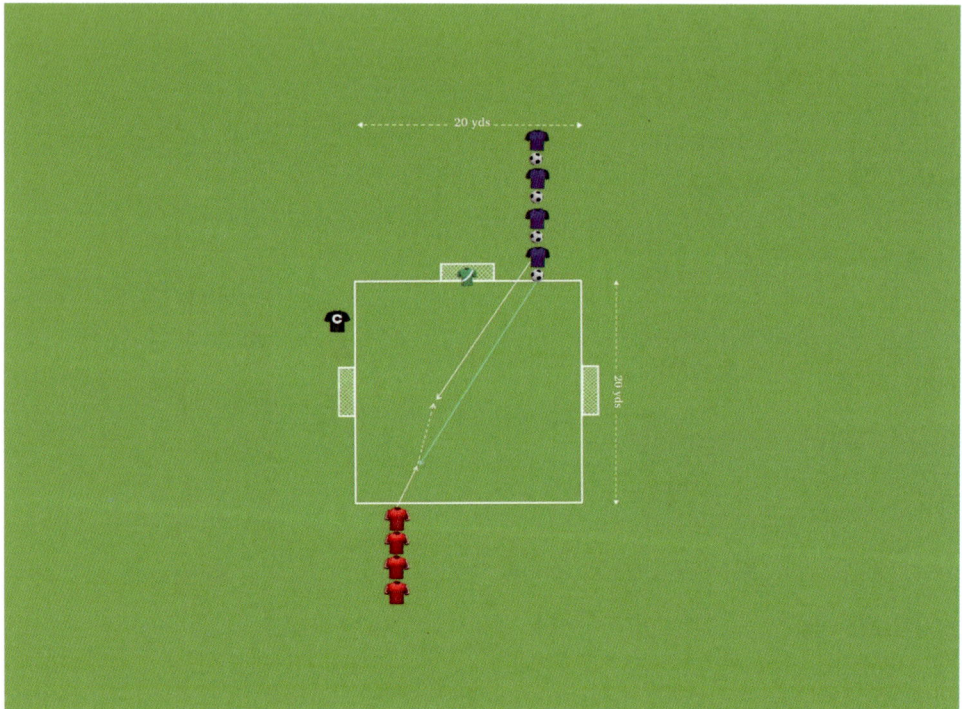

## Description

Divide players into one group of four attackers and one group of four defenders. Position a goal and goalkeeper at one end of the playing area. Position one mini-goal in the centre of both sidelines. Position the group of defenders in a straight line, a safe distance to the side of one goal. Position the group of attackers in a straight line, a safe distance to the side of the opposite goal and diagonally opposite the group of defenders. The group of defenders requires a supply of balls.

The activity starts when the first defender in line passes to the first attacker in line. The defender follows their pass and closes the space in front of the attacker. The attacker receives the ball and then tries to dribble past the defender and score past the goalkeeper in the opposite goal.

If the defender wins possession of the ball, they try to score a goal by dribbling the ball into either of the mini goals. The attacker can try to re-gain possession from the defender and start another attack. The activity continues until a goal is scored or the ball goes out of play. When the 1v1 is over, the defender and the attacker run to the back of the opposite line. The activity continues when the next defender in line passes to the next attacker in line.

## Key focus/Coaching points

Primary focus: Attacking and defending

Secondary focus: Dribbling

Additional focus: Shielding

## Progressions/Adaptations

- Progress to 2 attackers v 1 defender.
- Progress to 2 attackers v 2 defenders.

## ACTIVITY 201  1V1 FINISHING

Level: Basic

Type of activity: Opposed technical practice

Number of participants: 11 + 1 goalkeeper

Equipment required: Soccer balls, cones and 2 sets of bibs

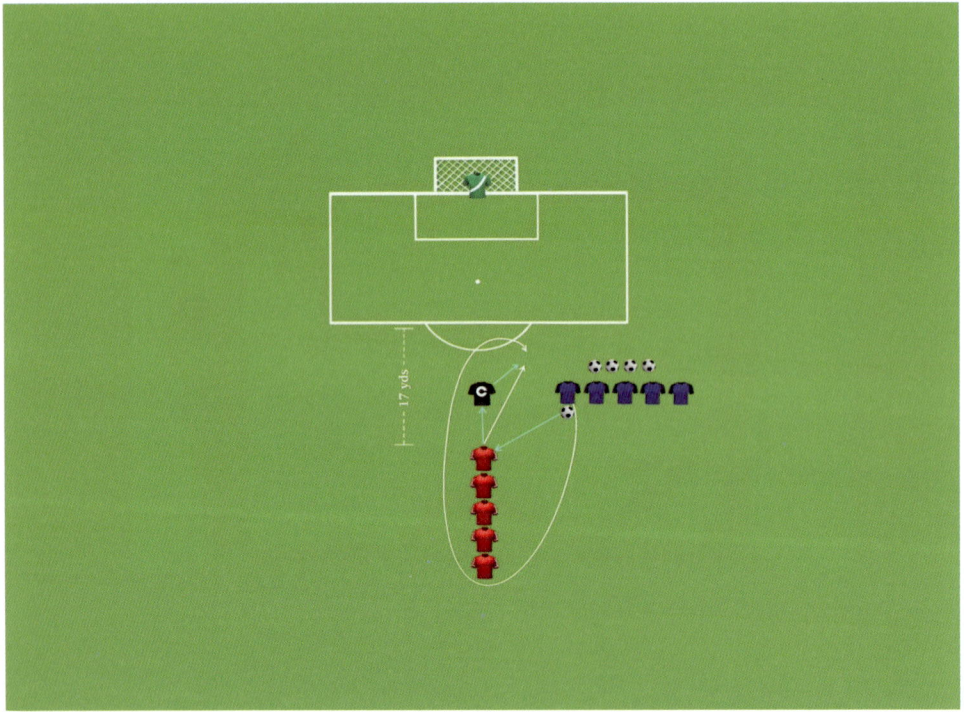

## Description

Divide players into one group of five attackers and one group of five defenders. Position a goal and goalkeeper at one end of the playing area. The coach should stand 25 yards from and with their back to the goal. Position the group of defenders in a straight line, 5-6 yards to either side of and facing the coach. Position the group of attackers in a straight line 10 yards opposite the coach. The defenders require a supply of balls.

The activity starts when the first defender in line passes the ball to the first attacker in line. The defender runs around the back of the attackers' line and then towards the goal as quickly as possible. The attacker receives the pass and then plays a 1-2 pass with the coach. The coach passes the ball towards the goal to the side that the defender ran from.

The defender and attacker race to win possession of the pass. The player that wins possession of the ball attacks the goal and tries to score past the goalkeeper. Often, the attacker will get to the ball first, which means the defender must try to get goal-side of the ball and into position to face the attacker.

If the defender wins possession from the pass, the attacker must quickly establish a good defending position and try to win possession. After 5 minutes rotate the attackers and defenders.

## Key focus/Coaching points

**Primary focus:** Attacking and defending

**Secondary focus:** Physical/movement development

**Additional focus:** Speed

## Progressions/Adaptations

- Progress to 2 attackers v 2 defenders.

- Position 1 support player 25 yards from the goal. The support player supports the team in possession to create 3v2 attacking overloads. The support player is not allowed to score.

# 460 THE SOCCER COACH'S TOOLKIT

## ACTIVITY 202   1V1 SPEED PLAY

**Level:** Basic

**Type of activity:** Opposed technical practice

**Number of participants:** 8 + 1 goalkeeper

**Equipment required:** Soccer balls, cones, 2 sets of bibs and 1 goal

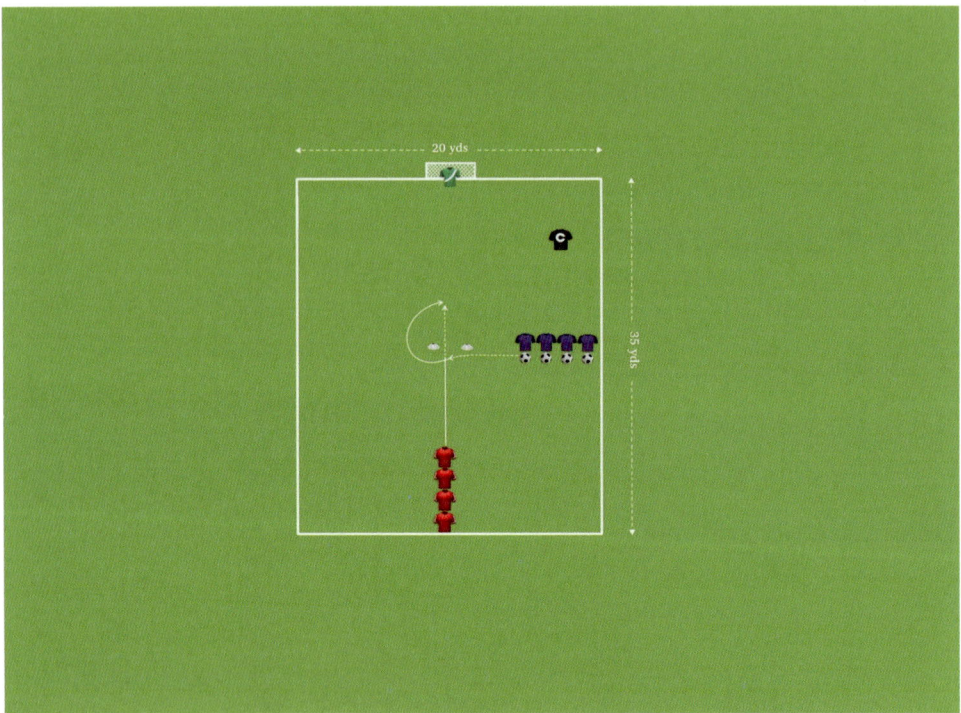

## Description

Divide players into one group of four attackers and one group of four defenders. Position a goal and goalkeeper at one end of the playing area. Position the group of attackers in a straight line at the opposite end of the playing area. Mark out a gate using two cones 10 yards opposite the group of attackers. Each attacker requires a ball. Position the group of defenders in a straight line on either side of the playing area and facing the gate.

# Attacking and Defending

The activity starts when first defender in line dribbles their ball into the playing area across the front of the gate and leaves the ball in the centre of the gate. The defender then runs around the far cone of the gate and towards the goal. As soon as the defender leaves the ball between the gate, the first attacker in line sprints to the ball. The attacker takes possession of the ball and dribbles towards the goal.

The defender must try to get goal-side of the ball as quickly as possible. The attacker tries to dribble past the defender to score past the goalkeeper. The defender tries to stop the attack by making a tackle or forcing the ball out of play.

Award 1 point to the defending team if the attack fails to produce a goal and 3 points for the attacking team if a goal is scored. After each attack, the players run to the back of their lines and the next attack starts. Rotate the attackers and the defenders after 5 minutes.

## Key focus/Coaching points

**Primary focus:** Attacking and defending

**Secondary focus:** Physical/movement development

**Additional focus:** Speed

## Progressions/Adaptations

- If the defender wins the ball, they become the attacker and try to score. The original attacker can try to regain possession and try to score again. Play until a goal is scored or the ball goes out of play.

- Progress to 2 attackers v 2 defenders. One of the defenders dribbles the ball between the gates and the other defender follows them without a ball.

## ACTIVITY 203  PICK YOUR PATH

**Level:** Basic

**Type of activity:** Opposed technical practice

**Number of participants:** 8

**Equipment required:** Soccer balls, cones, 2 sets of bibs and 2 mini-goals

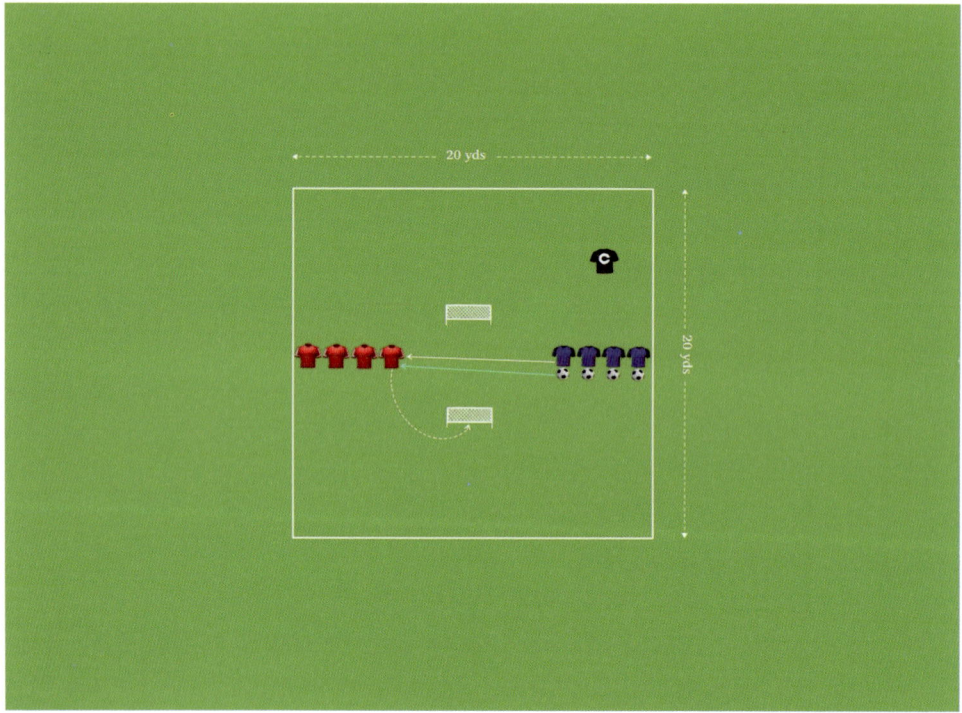

## Description

Divide players into one group of four attackers and one group of four defenders. Position two mini-goals back-to-back in the middle of the playing area with a channel 6 yards wide running between the mini-goals. Position the groups in straight lines opposite each other at either end of the channel. Leave 8-10 yards of space between the front of both lines and the start of the channel.

The activity starts when the first defender in line passes the ball through the channel to the first attacker in line. The defender sprints through the channel and follows their pass. The attacker receives the pass and dribbles towards the front of either goal. If the defender blocks the goal that the attacker is dribbling towards, the attacker can change direction and dribble to the other goal.

The attacker is allowed to score in either mini goal during the 1v1 but must not dribble through the channel. The defender tries to win possession of the ball and prevent the attacker from scoring.

Award 3 points to the attacking team if the attacker scores and 1 point to the defending if the defender wins possession of the ball. After each attack, the players run to the back of their line and the next attack starts with the first defender in line and the first attacker in line. Rotate the attackers and defenders after 5 minutes.

## Key focus/Coaching points

Primary focus: Attacking and defending

Secondary focus: Turning

Additional focus: Shielding

## Progressions/Adaptations

- If the defender wins possession of the ball, they become the attacker and try to score. The original attacker can try to regain possession and try to score again. Play until a goal is scored or the ball goes out of play.
- Progress to 2 attackers v 2 defenders.

## ACTIVITY 204  ATTACKING ANGLES

**Level:** Basic

**Type of activity:** Opposed technical practice

**Number of participants:** 3-18

**Equipment required:** Soccer balls and cones

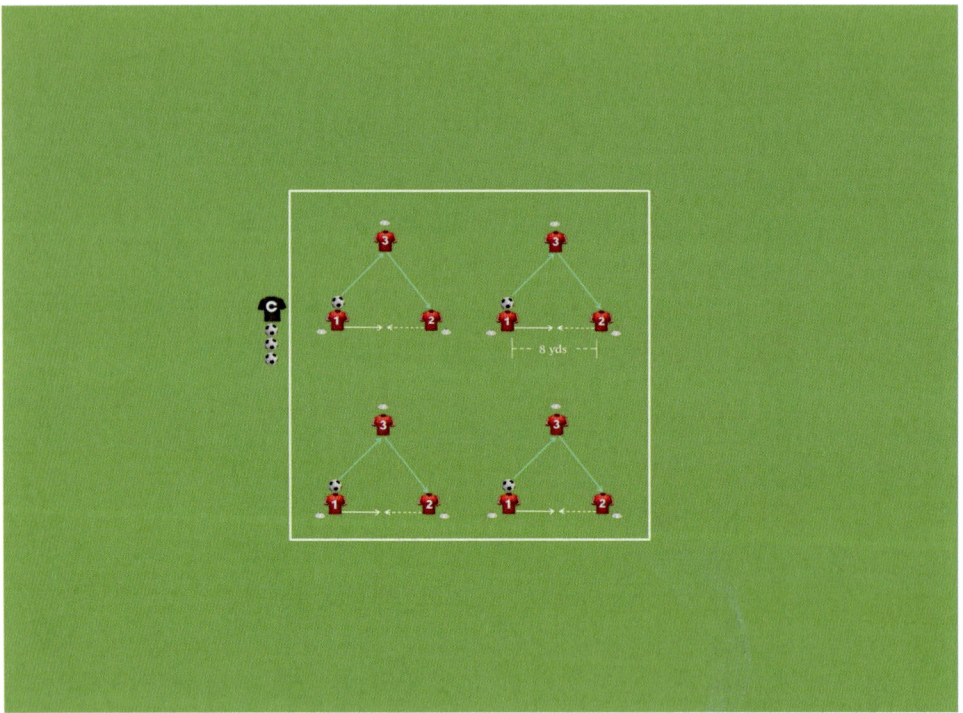

### Description

Divide players into groups of three. Position each group of players inside the playing area. Organise each group into a triangular shape. Position a cone 1-2 yards behind each player. Position the players at each point of the triangle 8-10 yards apart. Each group requires a ball. Number the players at the base of the triangle 1 and 2 and the player at the point of the triangle number 3.

The activity starts when player 1 passes the ball to player 3. Player 3 receives the pass and then passes to player 2. Player 2 dribbles towards and tries to go past player 1 and stop the ball on the cone behind player 1.

Player 1 runs towards and tries to tackle player 2. If player 1 wins possession of the ball, they try to dribble past player 2 and stop the ball on the cone behind player 2. The players rotate 1 position clockwise after each attack. Position the ball at the same point of the triangle for each attack.

## Key focus/Coaching points

Primary focus: Attacking and defending

Secondary focus: Dribbling

Additional focus: Turning

## Progressions/Adaptations

- Player 1 plays a 1-2 with player 2 and then passes to player 3. Player 3 tries to dribble past and stop the ball on the cone behind player number 1.
- Player 3 can pass to and receive passes from player during each attack.

## ACTIVITY 205   3V3 ATTACKING AND DEFENDING

**Level:** Intermediate

**Type of activity:** Opposed technical practice

**Number of participants:** 12 + 2 goalkeepers

**Equipment required:** Soccer balls, cones, discs, 2 sets of bibs and 2 goals

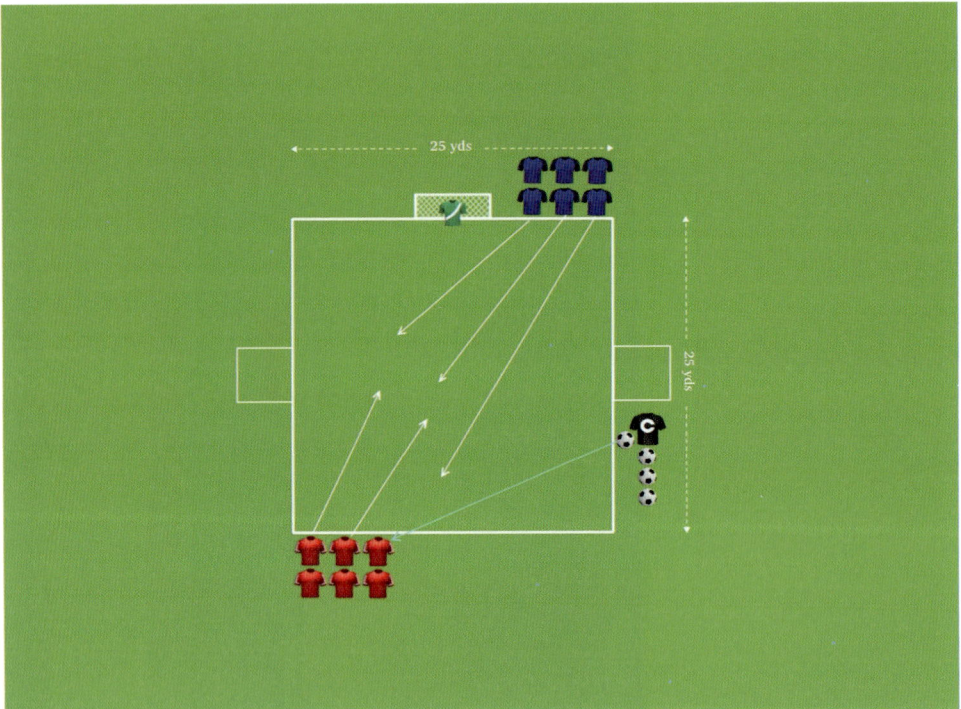

## Description

Divide players into two groups of three attackers and two groups of three defenders. Mark out a playing area with a square in the centre of each sideline. Position a goal and goalkeeper at one end of the playing area. Position both groups of attackers side-by-side in a corner, at the end of the playing area opposite the goal. Position both groups of defenders side-by-side in the corner diagonally opposite the groups of attackers. The coach should be positioned next to the square closest to the groups of attackers with a supply of balls.

# Attacking and Defending

The activity starts when the coach passes to the first attacking group in line. The attacking group enters the playing area and tries to score in the goal at the opposite end of the playing area. The first defending group in line enters the playing area, closes the space in front of the attackers and tries to prevent the attacking team from scoring.

If the defending group wins possession of the ball, they try to score by dribbling into either square. The attack is over when either team has scored, or the ball goes out of play. Both groups run to the back of their line. The activity re-starts when the coach passes to the first attacking group in line.

## Key focus/Coaching points

Primary focus: Attacking and defending

Secondary focus: Movement

Additional focus: Short passing

## Progressions/Adaptations

- The defending team passes the ball to the attacking team to start each attack. The defending team should vary the speed, flight and spin of the passes.
- Place a goal and goalkeeper at both ends of the playing area. If the defending team wins possession of the ball they try to score in the opposite goal.

## ACTIVITY 206  21

**Level:** Intermediate

**Type of activity:** Opposed technical practice

**Number of participants:** 10 + 2 goalkeepers

**Equipment required:** Soccer balls, cones, 2 sets of bibs and 2 goals

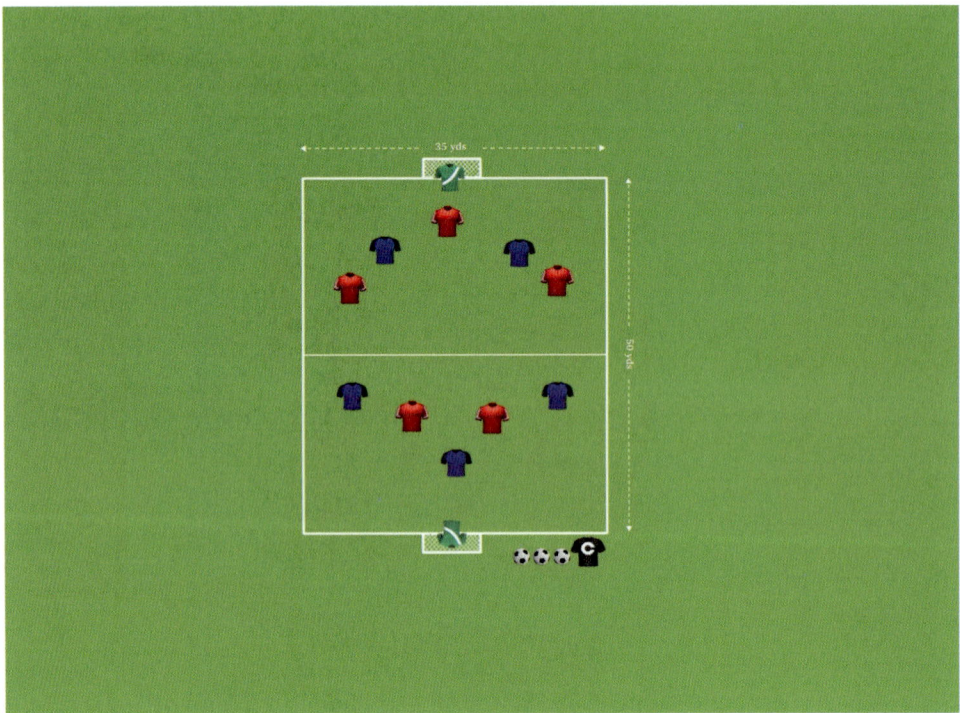

## Description

Divide players into two teams of six (including goalkeepers). Mark out a playing area with a halfway line running across the middle of the playing area. Position a goal and goalkeeper at both ends of the playing area. The teams compete in a 6v6 match with the playing condition that the number of completed passes before each goal dictates the value of the goal, e.g., 3 passes = 3 goals. The first team to score 21 points is the winning team.

Ensure that the playing area is quite small so that it is difficult for teams to keep possession for long periods of time. This means that teams must strike a balance between trying to build periods of possession with taking early opportunities to try to score.

## Key focus/Coaching points

**Primary focus:** Attacking and defending

**Secondary focus:** Decision making

**Additional focus:** Tactical/team shape

## Progressions/Adaptations

- The teams must complete at least 2 passes in both halves of the playing area before they can try to score.

- The teams must complete 1 first-time pass in both halves of the playing area.

# 470 THE SOCCER COACH'S TOOLKIT

## ACTIVITY 207   CLOSE TO HOME

**Level:** Intermediate

**Type of activity:** Opposed technical practice

**Number of participants:** 12

**Equipment required:** Soccer balls, cones, discs, 2 sets of bibs and 2 goals

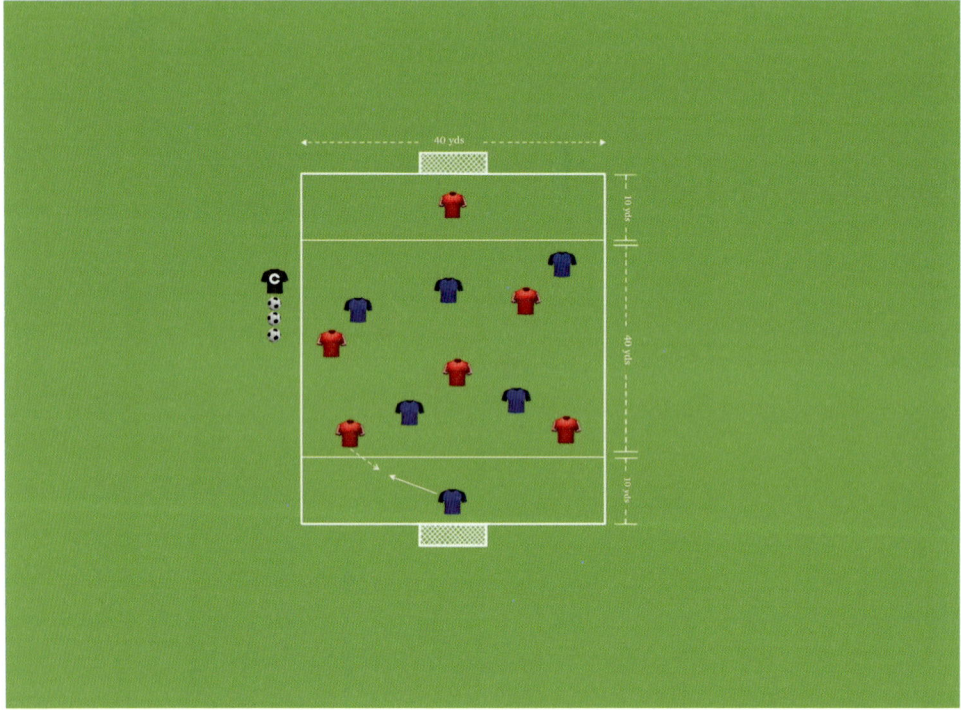

## Description

Divide players into two teams of six. Position a goal at both ends of the playing area. The teams compete in a 6v6 match and attack opposite ends of the playing area. Mark out an end zone at both ends of the playing area in which any player on the defending team can temporarily assume the role of goalkeeper if they are the defender nearest to their goal.

# Attacking and Defending

Neither team has a nominated goalkeeper. The player acting as the goalkeeper can use any part of their body to save attempts at goal. Encourage all the players to take part in outfield play as much as possible and to only act as a goalkeeper when trying to deny a goal-scoring opportunity.

## Key focus/Coaching points

Primary focus: Attacking and defending

Secondary focus: Tactical/team shape

Additional focus: Goalkeeping

## Progressions/Adaptations

- Condition the activity so that only 2 attackers and 2 defenders are allowed inside both end zones.

- The attacking team can only score with a first-time finish inside their attacking end zone.

- Acting goalkeepers are no longer allowed to save shots with their hands. This will encourage defenders to think creatively about how to block their goal when acting as the last line of defence.

## ACTIVITY 208  FOUR GOALS CLOSE TO HOME

**Level:** Intermediate

**Type of activity:** Opposed technical practice

**Number of participants:** 12

**Equipment required:** Soccer balls, cones, 4 sets of bibs and 4 goals

## Description

Divide players into two teams of six. Mark out a playing area and position one goal in the centre of each line of the playing area. Mark out a goalkeeper's zone in front of each goal. The teams play a 6v6 match with four goals. Nominate one team to attack two of the goals. The nominated goals must be at opposite ends of the playing area. Nominate the other team to attack the other two goals.

Any player can temporarily assume the role of goalkeeper when defending either of their goals if they are in the goalkeeper's zone and are the defender nearest to their goal. The player acting as the goalkeeper can use any part of their body to save attempts at goal.

Encourage all the players to take part in outfield play as much as possible and to only act as a goalkeeper when trying to deny a goal-scoring opportunity.

## Key focus/Coaching points

Primary focus: Attacking and defending

Secondary focus: Tactical/team shape

Additional focus: Shooting

## Progressions/Adaptations

- Divide players into 4 teams of 3. Each team defends 1 goal. Each team of 3 is competing to score the most goals. Give each team a partner team so that the teams work together in pairs. Each team can use their partner team to pass to and to build attacks. The partner teams must not score against each other. Each team needs to wear different colour bibs and be aware of who their partner team is before the activity starts.

- Follow the above organisation but now each team of 3 starts with 5 lives. Every time a team concedes a goal, they lose 1 life. When a team reaches zero lives they are eliminated from the activity. The winning team is the last team with lives intact. Once only 2 teams remain, partnerships no longer remain and both teams can score against each other.

# 474 THE SOCCER COACH'S TOOLKIT

## ACTIVITY 209  NO EASY OPTION

**Level:** Intermediate

**Type of activity:** Opposed technical practice

**Number of participants:** 8 + 2 goalkeepers

**Equipment required:** Soccer balls, cones, 2 sets of bibs and 2 goals

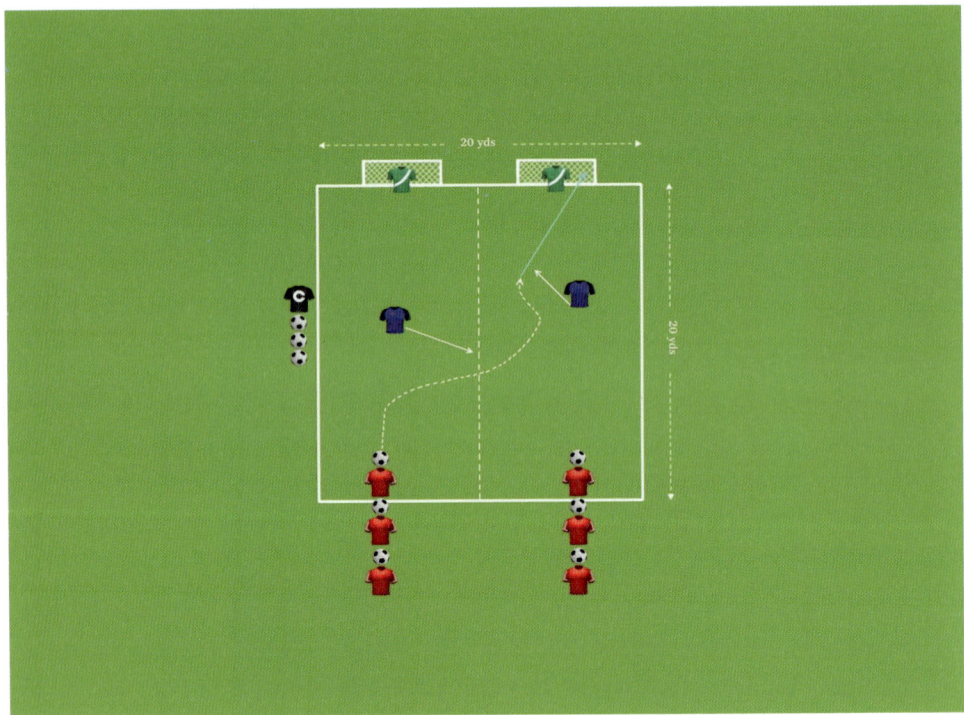

## Description

Divide players into two groups of five (including goalkeepers). Mark out a playing area divided into two zones. Position a goal and goalkeeper in both zones. The goals must be at the same end of the playing area. Organise the remaining players in each group into three attackers and one defender. Position one group of players inside each zone.

Position the defenders 12-15 yards from and with their back to their goal. Position the attackers in a straight line 20 yards opposite their goal. Each group of attackers requires a supply of balls. The activity starts when the first attacker in line from either group dribbles into either zone of the playing area. The attacker can dribble between the zones as often as required. The attacker tries to dribble past the defender in either zone. If the attacker dribbles past a defender, they try to score past the goalkeeper in the same zone. During each attack, the defenders must stay inside their zones. The attacker has 10 seconds to try to score.

The attack is over when a goal is scored, or when a defender wins possession of the ball or forces the ball out of play. If after 10 seconds the attacker has possession of the ball but has failed to score, the attack is over. After each attack, the attacker runs to the back of their line and the first attacker in the opposite line continues the activity.

Encourage the defenders to work together and position themselves in relation to one another as they would if there were no dividing line. Encourage the defenders to operate as a defensive pair. After 5 minutes, rotate the attackers and defenders.

## Key focus/Coaching points

**Primary focus:** Attacking and defending

**Secondary focus:** Decision making

**Additional focus:** Movement

## Progressions/Adaptations

- The first attackers in line in each group simultaneously only attack the goal in their zone. The attackers and defenders must play within their zones.
- The first attackers in line in each group combine against both defenders in a 2v2 attack v defence. The attackers can move between zones and score in either goal. The defenders can move between zones and try to defend both goals.

# 476 THE SOCCER COACH'S TOOLKIT

## ACTIVITY 210  LEADING FROM THE FRONT

**Level:** Intermediate

**Type of activity:** Opposed technical practice

**Number of participants:** 16 + 2 goalkeepers

**Equipment required:** Soccer balls, cones, 3 sets of bibs and 2 goals

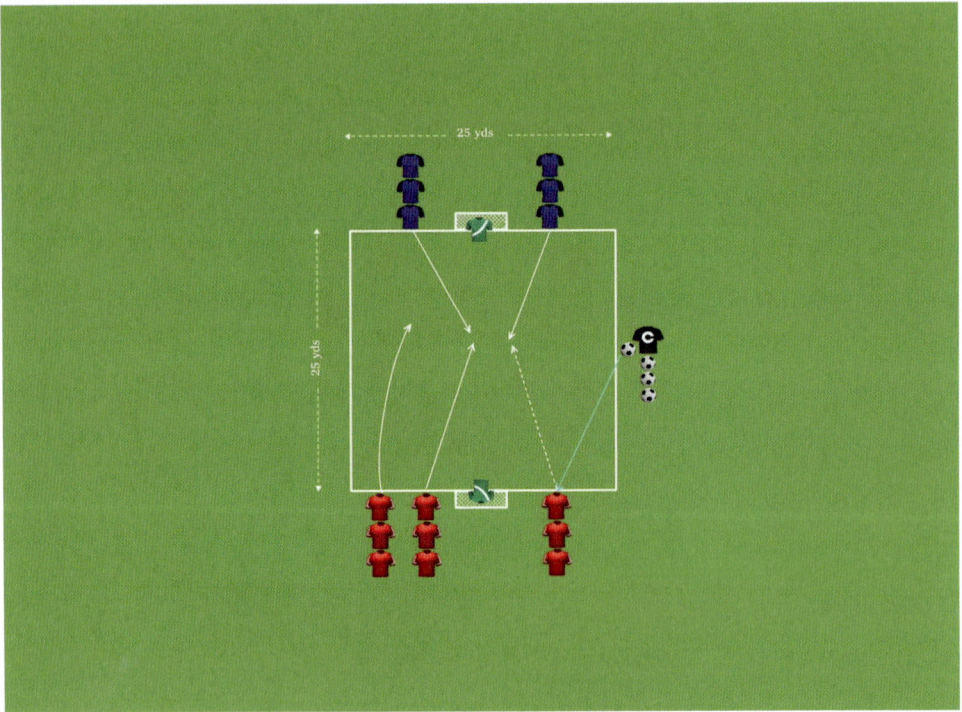

## Description

Divide players into three groups of three attackers and two groups of three defenders. Position a goal and goalkeeper at both ends of the playing area. Position the groups of attackers in rows at one end of the playing area. Organise each row of attackers so that there are two attackers a safe distance to one side of the goal and the third attacker a safe distance to the side of the goal.

Position the groups of defenders in rows of two at the opposite end of the playing area. Organise each row of defenders so that there is one defender a safe distance to either side of the goal. The coach should be positioned on either side of the playing area halfway between the groups. The coach requires a supply of balls.

The activity starts when the coach passes to any attacker in the first group of attackers. The attacker that receives the pass dribbles into the playing area and the other two attackers run into the playing area. The first two defenders run into the playing area and close the space in front of the attackers. The attackers combine to try to score past the goalkeeper. The defenders combine to try to prevent the attackers from scoring.

If the defenders win possession of the ball, they attack the goal at the opposite end. Play until a goal is scored, the ball goes out of play, or 30 seconds have elapsed. After each attack, the players run to the back of their line and the coach re-starts the activity with a pass to the next group of attackers. Rotate the attackers and defenders after 5 minutes.

## Key focus/Coaching points

Primary focus: Attacking and defending

Secondary focus: Movement

Additional focus: Finishing

## Progressions/Adaptations

- Add a support player to support the group in possession. The support player helps both teams to keep possession but is not allowed to score.

- If the attackers score, they score 2 points for the attacking groups. If the defenders win possession and score, they win 3 points for the defending groups. The attacking groups combine scores, and the defending groups combine scores. Rotate the groups after 5 minutes and see which group has scored the most points.

- If the attackers score, add an extra defender to the next group of defenders. If the defenders score, add an extra attacker to the next group of attackers. If neither team scores, revert to 3v2 attack v defence.

# 478 THE SOCCER COACH'S TOOLKIT

## ACTIVITY 211   BUILD UP TO SCORE

**Level:** Intermediate

**Type of activity:** Opposed technical practice

**Number of participants:** 8 + 1 goalkeeper

**Equipment required:** Soccer balls, cones, 2 sets of bibs and 1 goal

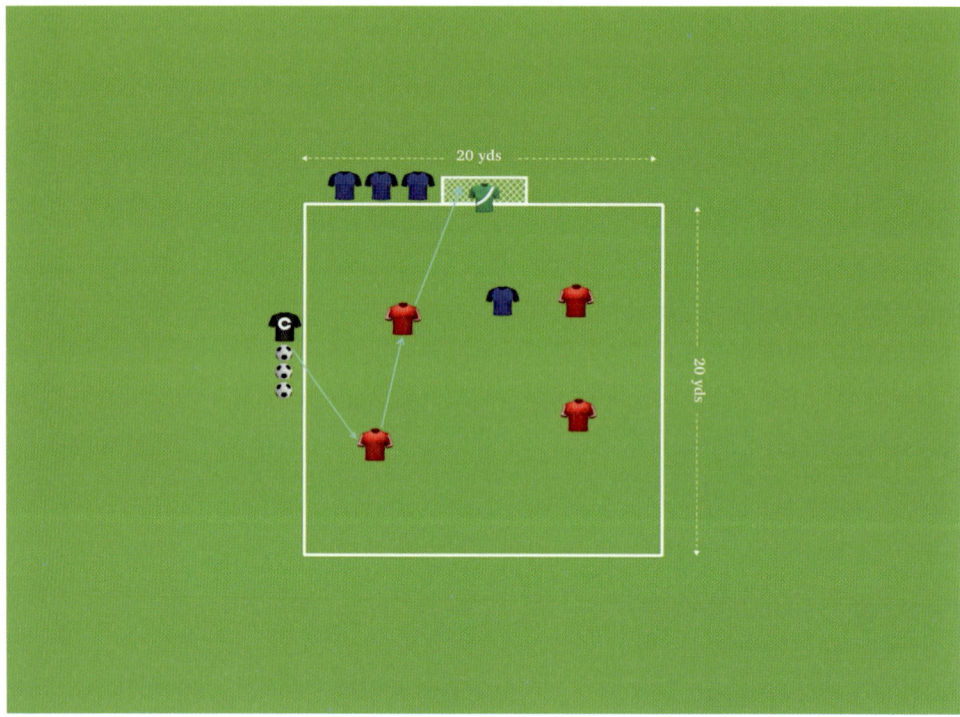

## Description

Divide the players into one team of four attackers and one team of four defenders. Position a goal and goalkeeper at one end of the playing area. Position the attacking team inside the playing area. Position one defender inside the playing area and three defenders a safe distance to the side of the goal. The coach should be positioned on the side of the playing area with a supply of balls.

The activity starts when the coach feeds a ball to the attacking team. The attacking team tries to score, and the defender tries to prevent the attackers from scoring. If the attacking team scores, they score 1 point, and a second defender enters the playing area for the next attack. The coach feeds another ball into the playing area and the attacking team tries to score against two defenders. If the attacking team scores, they score 2 points.

The attacking team continues playing until they have scored against three defenders (3 points) and then four defenders (4 points). Each time that the defending team prevents the attacking team from scoring either by winning possession of the ball or by forcing ball out of play, they score 1 point.

After the attacking team has scored against four defenders, the teams switch roles. Once both teams have scored against 4 defenders, add up all their points and see which team has scored more.

## Key focus/Coaching points

Primary focus: Attacking and defending

Secondary focus: Movement

Additional focus: Creativity

## Progressions/Adaptations

- When there is 1 defender inside the playing area, the attacking team is allowed a maximum of 3 passes before they try to score. For each extra defender allow 1 more pass.
- The attacking team must score with a first-time finish.
- If the defending team wins possession of the ball, they can score a bonus point by completing 2 passes for 2 defenders, 3 passes for 3 defenders and 4 passes for 4 defenders.

## ACTIVITY 212  POWERBALL

**Level:** Intermediate

**Type of activity:** Opposed technical practice

**Number of participants:** 8

**Equipment required:** Soccer balls, cones, discs, 2 sets of bibs and 4 mini-goals

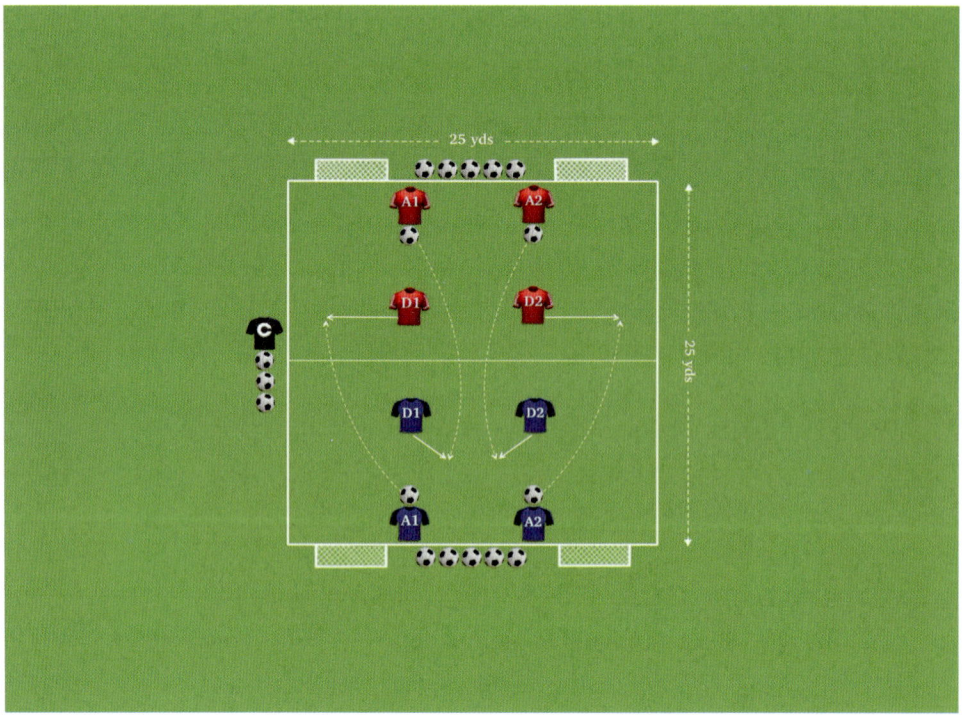

## Description

Divide players into two teams of four. Mark out a playing area divided into two zones. Position a mini goal in each corner of the playing area. Position one team inside each zone of the playing area. Divide each team into two attackers and two defenders. Pair up one attacker from each team with one defender from the other team so that there are four sets of 1v1 contests. Position the attackers in each team at opposite ends of the playing area. Position the defenders in each team 10 yards back from the dividing line in opposite zones of the playing area. Position a supply of balls at both ends of the playing area.

The activity starts when each attacker dribbles into the opposite zone and tries dribbling past their nominated defender. If the attacker dribbles past their nominated defender, they try to score by dribbling through either of the mini goals. Each defender tries to stop their nominated attacker from scoring by either tackling the attacker or forcing the ball out of play.

If the attacker scores, the defender takes up their starting position in the opposite zone and the attacker starts a new attack. The attacker collects a ball and tries to score at the opposite end of the playing area. Each time that an attacker scores, they attack the opposite end of the playing area.

If an attacker fails to score, they run back to the end line they started their attack from, collect a new ball and start a new attack. The attackers score 1 point each time they score. Rotate the attackers and defenders after 3-5 minutes. Once all the players in both teams have performed as attackers and defenders, add up the points scored by each team. The team with the most points is the winner.

## Key focus/Coaching points

**Primary focus:** Attacking and defending

**Secondary focus:** Dribbling

**Additional focus:** Running with the ball

## Progressions/Adaptations

- The defenders can try to stop either attacker scoring. The attackers must try to dribble past both defenders (if necessary) and score.
- The attackers work as a pair using 1 ball and try to score. The defenders work as a pair and try to prevent the attackers from scoring.

# 482 THE SOCCER COACH'S TOOLKIT

## ACTIVITY 213   COVER ALL BASES

**Level:** Intermediate

**Type of activity:** Opposed technical practice

**Number of participants:** 10

**Equipment required:** Soccer balls, cones, domes, 2 sets of bibs and 3 mini-goals

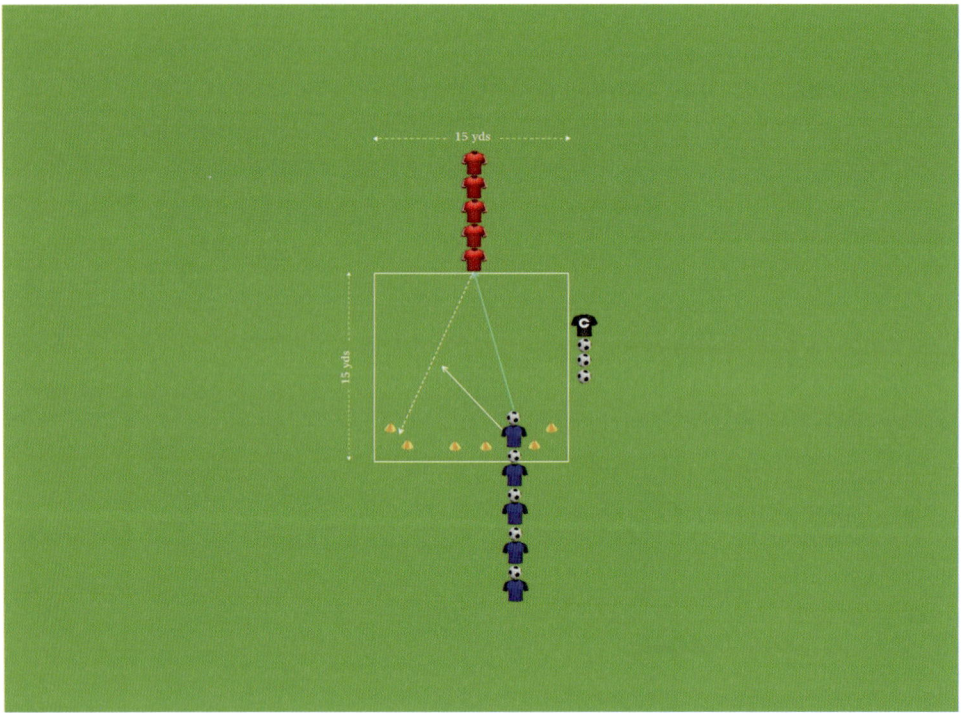

## Description

Divide players into one team of five attackers and one team of five defenders. Mark out a playing area with three mini goals positioned at one end of the playing area. Position one mini-goal in each corner and one mini-goal in the middle of the end line. Position the team of defenders in a straight line a safe distance to the side of the middle mini goal. Position the team of attackers in a straight line at the opposite end of the playing area. The team of defenders requires a supply of balls.

The activity starts with a pass from the first defender in line to the first attacker in line. The defender follows their pass and closes the space in front of the attacker. The attacker tries to dribble past the defender and score by dribbling through any of the mini goals. The defender tries to prevent the attacker from scoring by winning possession of the ball or forcing the ball out of play.

If the attacker dribbles through the middle mini-goal, they score 3 points. If the attacker dribbles through either of the corner mini goals they score 1 point. After each attack, the players run to the back of the opposite line and the activity continues when the first defender in line passes to the first attacker in line.

## Key focus/Coaching points

**Primary focus:** Attacking and defending

**Secondary focus:** Dribbling

**Additional focus:** Turning

## Progressions/Adaptations

- Progress to 2v2 attack v defence.
- Position 1 mini-goal at the attackers' end of the playing area. If the defenders win the ball, they can try to score by dribbling through the mini goal. If the defender(s) score, they score 5 points.

## ACTIVITY 214   BREAK THROUGH OR BREAK FREE

**Level:** Intermediate

**Type of activity:** Opposed technical practice

**Number of participants:** 6 + 1 goalkeeper

**Equipment required:** Soccer balls, cones, 3 sets of bibs, and 1 goal

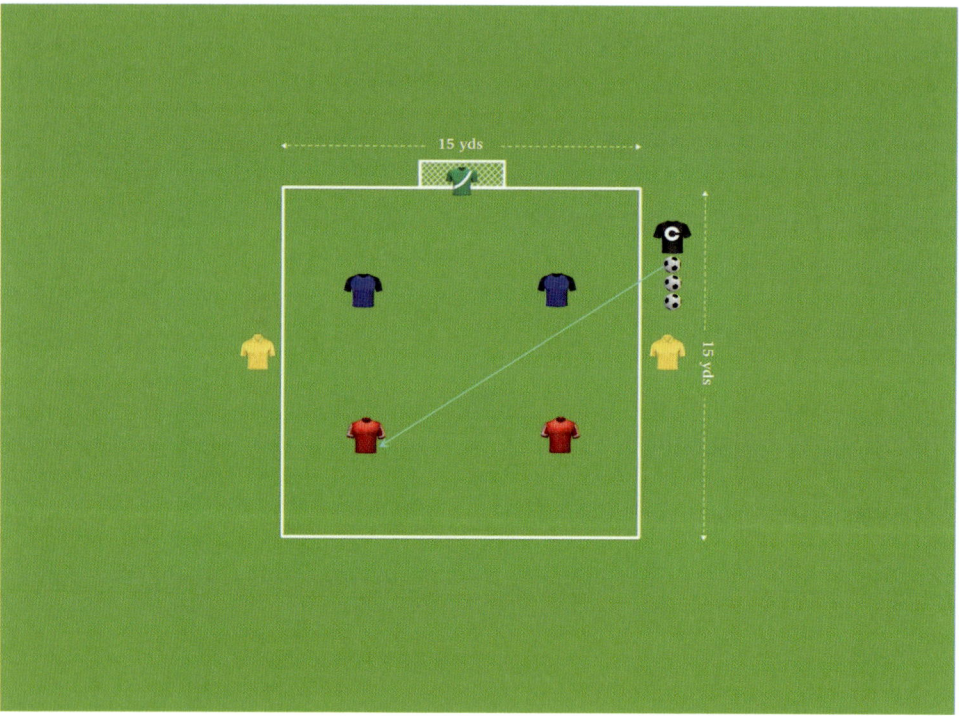

## Description

Divide players into one team of two attackers, one team of two defenders and one team of two support players. Mark out a small playing area. Position a goal and goalkeeper at one end of the playing area. Position the team of attackers and the team of defenders inside the playing area. Position one support player on the outside of each sideline. The coach should be positioned outside the playing area with a supply of balls.

The activity starts when the coach passes to the attacking team. The attacking team tries to keep possession of the ball and score past the goalkeeper within 30 seconds. The attackers can pass to and receive passes from the support players as often as required. If the attackers score, they score 1 point.

The defending team tries to prevent the attackers from scoring. If the defenders win possession of the ball, they must try to dribble out of the playing area. If the defenders manage to dribble out of the playing area, they score 1 point.

If the ball goes out of play before the 30 seconds elapse, the coach passes another ball to the attacking team, who have the remainder of the 30 seconds to try to score. If the attacking team scores, they remain as the attacking team for the next episode of play and the defending team swaps roles with the support players. If the defenders score or prevent the attacking team from scoring, they remain inside the playing area and become the attacking team for the next episode of play. The previous attacking team becomes the support players and the support players become the defenders for the next episode of play.

## Key focus/Coaching points

**Primary focus:** Attacking and defending

**Secondary focus:** Finishing

**Additional focus:** Short passing

## Progressions/Adaptations

- Award the attacking team a bonus point if they complete 3 passes before scoring.
- Award the defending team a bonus point if they complete 3 passes before dribbling the ball out of the playing area.

# 486 THE SOCCER COACH'S TOOLKIT

## ACTIVITY 215   FIVE GOALS FIVE WAYS

**Level:** Advanced

**Type of activity:** Opposed technical practice

**Number of participants:** 11 + 2 goalkeepers

**Equipment required:** Soccer balls, cones, 3 sets of bibs and 2 goals

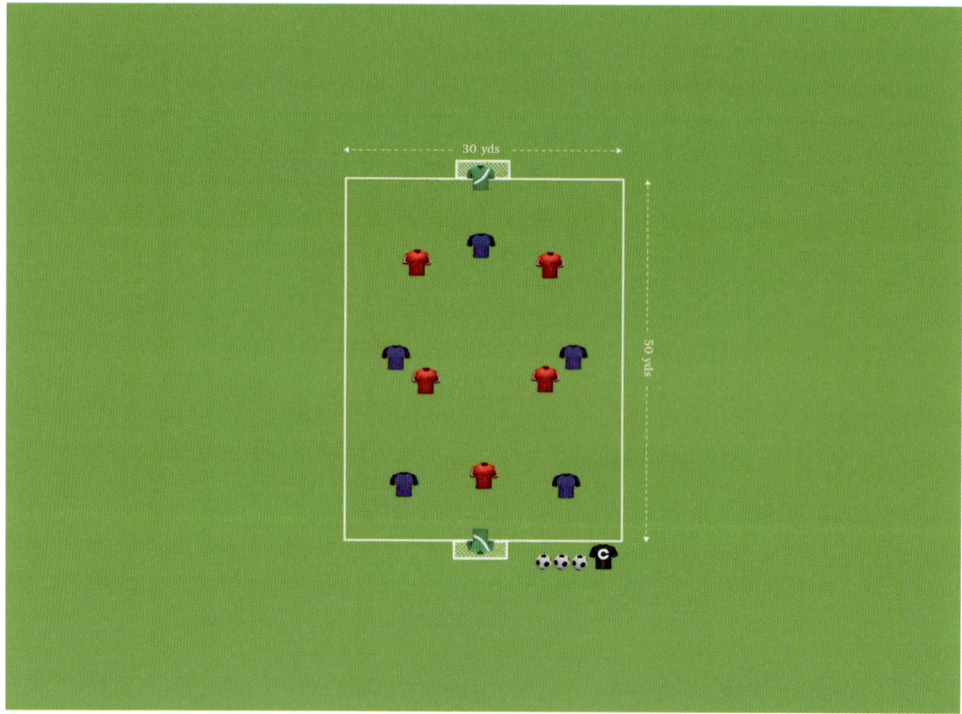

## Description

Divide players into two teams of six (including goalkeepers). Position a goal and goalkeeper at both ends of the playing area. The teams compete in a 6v6 match and attack opposite ends of the playing area. Before the activity starts, decide on five different ways of scoring (see below for ideas). The first team to score using all five ways wins the match.

## Suggested methods for scoring:

Left foot/right foot first-time finish, back-heel, header, volley, half-volley, long-range shot (20 yards minimum), chip, solo goal (the attacker must dribble past two players before scoring).

## Key focus/Coaching points

Primary focus: Attacking and defending

Secondary focus: Finishing

Additional focus: Decision making

## Progressions/Adaptations

- Add a floating support player to support the team in possession. The floating support player can score for both teams.
- Each outfield player within a team must score using a different method.

## ACTIVITY 216   NARROW PITCH SSG

**Level:** Advanced

**Type of activity:** Implementation practice

**Number of participants:** 12 + 2 goalkeepers

**Equipment required:** Soccer balls, cones, 2 sets of bibs and 2 goals

## Description

Divide players into two teams of seven (including goalkeepers). Mark out a narrow playing area. Position a goal and goalkeeper at both ends of the playing area. The teams compete in a 7v7 match and attack opposite ends of the playing area. The narrowness of the playing area emphasises the development of attacking and defending techniques and tactics in central areas of the pitch.

## Key focus/Coaching points

**Primary focus:** Attacking and defending

**Secondary focus:** Tactical/team shape

**Additional focus:** Decision making


## Progressions/Adaptations

- Mark out a channel on both sides of the playing area:
    - Allow 1 player from the attacking team to move into either channel during an attack. When the attacking team loses possession, the player returns to the playing area.
    - Position 1 player from both teams inside each channel. When an attacker passes to their teammate inside the channel, they can follow their pass into the channel. If the attacker follows the pass into the channel, 1 defender follows them into the channel to create a 2v2 attack v defence inside the channel. When the attacking team loses possession of the ball, the attacker that passed the ball and the defender that followed the pass must return to the playing area.
    - Divide the playing area into 3 zones. Position 2 defenders from both teams in their defensive zone, 2 midfielders from both teams in the middle zone and 2 attackers from both teams in their attacking zone. During play, both teams are allowed a maximum of 2 players to leave their playing zone and enter either channel. When a player moves into a channel, they are not allowed to move beyond the ends of their zone. Players can move in and out of the channels if there are no more than 2 players from either team inside the channels.

# 490 THE SOCCER COACH'S TOOLKIT

## ACTIVITY 217  WIDE PITCH SSG

**Level:** Advanced

**Type of activity:** Implementation practice

**Number of participants:** 14 + 2 goalkeepers

**Equipment required:** Soccer balls, cones, 2 sets of bibs and goals

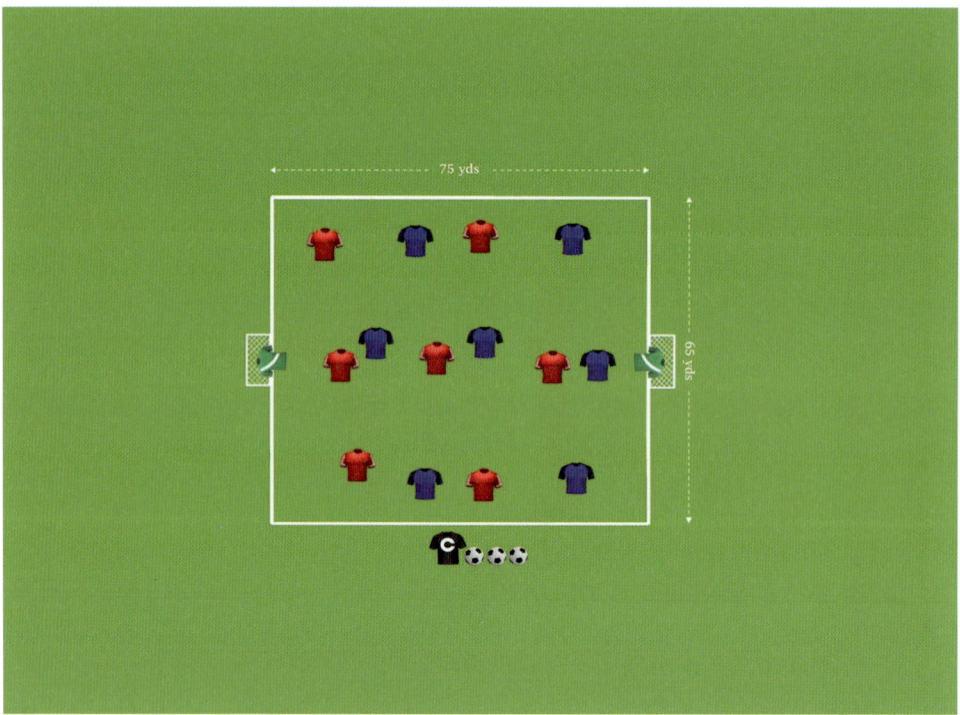

## Description

Divide players into two teams of eight (including goalkeepers). Mark out a wide playing area. Position a goal and goalkeeper at both ends of the playing area. The teams compete in an 8v8 match and attack opposite ends of the playing area. The width of the playing area emphasises the development of effective of attacking and defending techniques and tactics in wide areas of the pitch.

## Key focus/coaching points

**Primary focus:** Attacking and defending

**Secondary focus:** Tactical/team shape

**Additional focus:** Decision making

## Progressions/Adaptations

- Divide the playing area into 3 zones. Both teams position 2 defenders in their defensive zone, 3 midfielders in the middle zone and 2 attackers in their attacking zone.

- Mark out a channel 20-25 yards wide down the length of one side of the playing area. A maximum of 3 players from both teams (six in total) can be inside the channel at the same time.

- The players can move in and out of the channel and there is no limit on the number of players allowed inside the channel.

## ACTIVITY 218   VOLLEYS SSG

**Level:** Advanced

**Type of activity:** Opposed technical practice

**Number of participants:** 14

**Equipment required:** Soccer balls, cones, 2 sets of bibs and 6 mini-goals

## Description

Divide players into two teams of seven. Mark out a playing area and position three mini-goals at both ends of the playing area. Position one mini goal in each corner and one mini goal in the centre of both end lines.

The teams attack opposite ends of the playing area. The teams compete for possession and try to score with a volley from hands into a mini goal. The players keep possession with a volley-pass from hands to a teammate. The player in possession of the ball can either stand still or travel in any direction using one basketball-style bounce before stopping. Once the player in possession is standing still, they have 3 seconds to volley-pass the ball to a teammate. All other players are allowed to move freely.

If the player in possession fails to volley-pass after 3 seconds, possession is awarded to the other team. The attacking team tries to create space to receive a volley-pass and the defending team tries to intercept the pass. The defender nearest to the player in possession must stand approximately five steps back as they attempt a pass to minimise the risk of being hit by the ball.

If the ball runs loose, the first team player to pick up the ball wins possession for their team. When the ball goes outside the playing area, the player that re-starts play must do so with a volley pass from hands.

## Key focus/Coaching points

**Primary focus:** Attacking and defending

**Secondary focus:** Volleys

**Additional focus:** Tactical/team shape

## Progressions/Adaptations

- The player in possession is no longer allowed to travel with the ball.

- Before a goal can be scored, 2 players from the attacking team must have completed a 1-2 volley-pass, i.e., the player receiving the first volley-pass must volley-pass back to the player that volley-passed to them without catching the ball.

- The player in possession is allowed only 2 seconds before volley-passing.

- The players must score with a first-time volley i.e., they do not catch the ball before they volley it towards the goal.

# 494  THE SOCCER COACH'S TOOLKIT

## ACTIVITY 219   ONE BIG, TWO SMALL

**Level:** Advanced

**Type of activity:** Small-sided game

**Number of participants:** 15 + 1 goalkeeper

**Equipment required:** Soccer balls, cones, 3 sets of bibs, 2 mini-goals and 1 goal

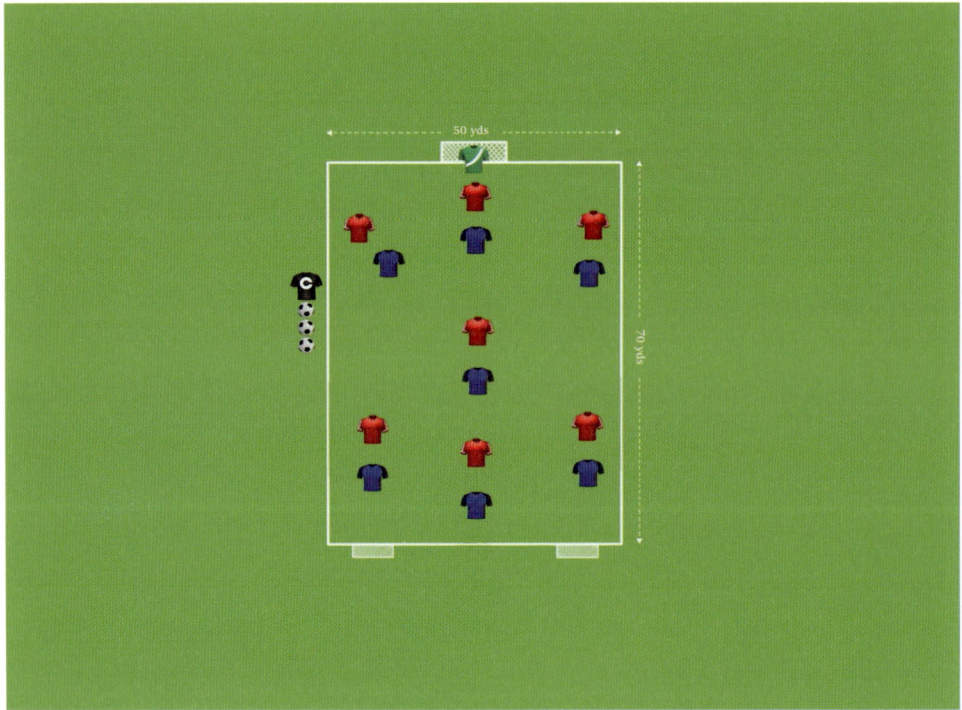

## Description

Divide players into one team of eight (including goalkeeper) and one team of seven (no goalkeeper). Mark out a playing area and position a goal at one end of the playing area. Position one mini-goal in each corner at the opposite end of the playing area.

The teams compete in an 8v7 match. The team of eight attacks the two mini-goals and tries to score by dribbling the ball through either of the mini-goals. The team of seven attacks the goal at the opposite end of the playing area and tries to score past the goalkeeper.

The positioning and size of the goals will encourage the teams to play in different ways. Both teams will have to experiment with different techniques and tactical approaches to attacking and defending. Rotate the teams after 20 minutes. The goalkeeper must stay in the same goal so that the original team of seven now has the numerical advantage.

## Key focus/Coaching points

Primary focus: Attacking and defending

Secondary focus: Decision making

Additional focus: Tactical/team shape

## Progressions/Adaptations

- Add a floating support player to support the team in possession.
- Players are allowed a maximum of 3 touches in possession.

## ACTIVITY 220  MYSTERY BOX

**Level:** Advanced

**Type of activity:** Small-sided game

**Number of participants:** 12 + 2 goalkeepers

**Equipment required:** Soccer balls, cones, 2 sets of bibs, a pen, a piece of paper and 2 goals

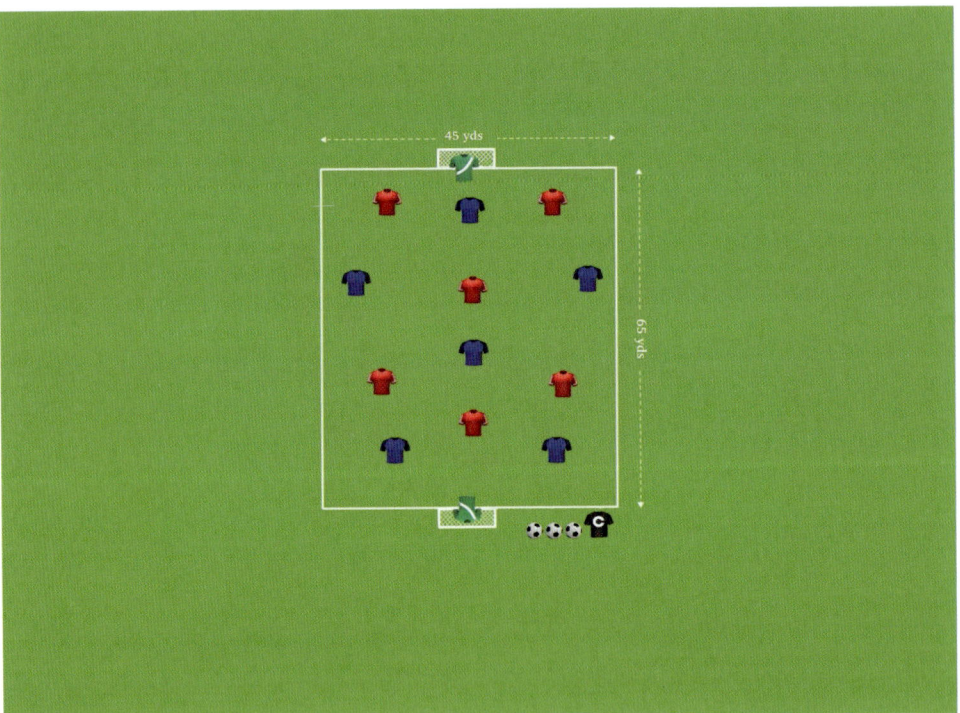

### Description

Divide players into two teams of seven (including goalkeepers). Position a goal and goalkeeper at both ends of the playing area. The teams compete in a 7v7 match and attack opposite ends of the playing area.

Before the activity starts, the coach and players create a list of significant scenarios that can happen during a soccer match. The coach writes down each scenario on a small piece of paper and puts each piece of paper in their pocket.

The activity starts with no scenarios in place until the first goal is scored. Once the first goal has been scored, a player from the team that conceded the goal runs to the coach. The coach takes 1 piece of paper from their pocket and reads out the scenario. The activity re-starts with the scenario in effect.

Each scenario stays in effect until the next goal is scored. When the next goal is scored, the coach takes another piece of paper from their pocket and reads out the scenario.

Here is a list of suggested scenarios, which can be added to or adapted by the coach and the players:

- Re-start with a penalty to the team that just scored/conceded the goal.
- Re-start with a corner/direct free kick 20 yards from goal to the team that just scored/conceded the goal.
- The referee sends 1 player from each team to the sin bin for 3 minutes. The teams number each player 1-7. The coach selects a number, and the corresponding players go to the sin bin.
- The goalkeepers are allowed to use their hands outside the penalty area for 3 minutes.
- The team that just scored/conceded the goal cannot score for the next 3 minutes.
- The next goal is worth double.
- The team that just scored/conceded the goal must play in silence for the next 5 minutes. Award a direct free kick to the opposition each time the rule is broken.
- The next goal scored must a header or a volley.

## Key focus/Coaching points

**Primary focus:** Attacking and defending

**Secondary focus:** Decision making

**Additional focus:** Tactical/team shape

## Progressions/Adaptations

- The player in possession is allowed a maximum of 3 touches.
- 1 player from each team is allowed only 1 touch in possession.

## ACTIVITY 221 TRIPLE TARGET

**Level:** Advanced

**Type of activity:** Opposed technical practice

**Number of participants:** 8

**Equipment required:** Soccer balls, cones, discs and 2 sets of bibs

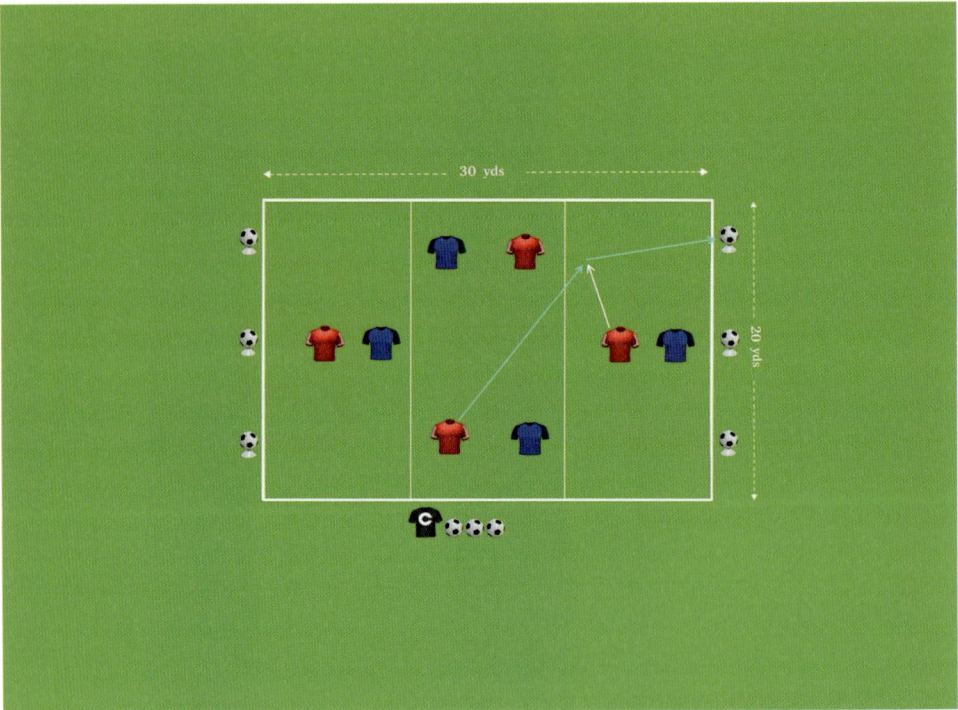

### Description

Divide players into two teams of four. Divide the playing area into three zones. Position three balls balanced on top of cones 3-4 yards apart at both ends of the playing area. Organise both teams into a 1-2-1 formation. The teams attack opposite ends of the playing area. Position one defender from each team inside their defensive zone, two midfielders from each team inside the middle zone and one attacker from both teams inside their attacking zone. Initially, the players must play within their zones.

The activity starts when the coach feeds a ball to either team. The teams compete for possession and try to score by passing or shooting the ball to knock the other balls off the cones at the end that they are attacking. Only the attackers are allowed to score, so the team in possession tries to create opportunities to pass to their teammate in their attacking zone.

All players can move freely within their allocated playing zones and pass forwards and backwards between the zones. The first team to knock all the balls off the cones at the end that they are attacking is the winning team.

## Key focus/Coaching points

Primary focus: Attacking and defending

Secondary focus: Short passing

Additional focus: Long passing

## Progressions/Adaptations

- 1 midfielder from the attacking team can dribble into their attacking zone, or pass to the attacker inside their attacking zone, to create a 2v1 attacking overload. Both players in their attacking zone can score. As soon as the attacking team loses possession, the midfielder must retreat to the middle zone.

- All players can move forward 1 zone after making a successful pass or dribble into the next zone. As soon as their team loses possession, they must retreat to their original zone. Any attacking player inside their attacking zone can score.

- All players can move freely between zones. Try to encourage teams to maintain a 1-2-1 formation to maintain realistic play. Any attacking player inside their attacking zone can score.

# 500  THE SOCCER COACH'S TOOLKIT

## ACTIVITY 222  PLAYER POWER

**Level:** Advanced

**Type of activity:** Opposed technical practice

**Number of participants:** 10 + 2 goalkeepers

**Equipment required:** Soccer balls, cones, 2 sets of bibs, and 2 goals

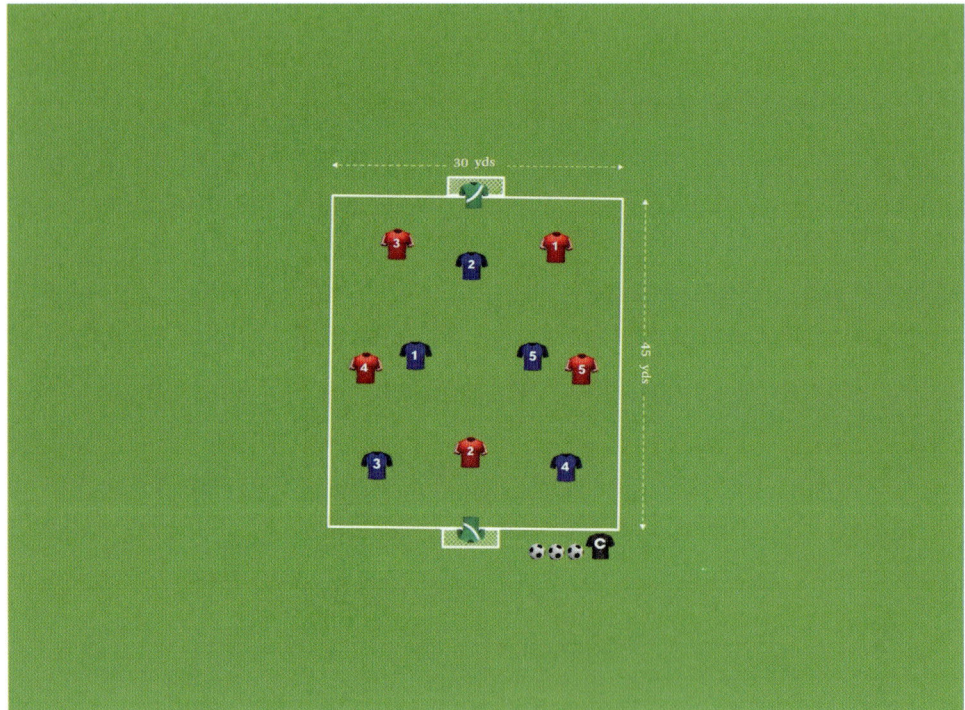

## Description

Divide players into two teams of six (including goalkeepers). Position a goal and goalkeeper at both ends of the playing area. The teams compete in a 6v6 match and attack opposite ends of the playing area. Before the activity starts, number the outfield players 1-5.

When a goal is scored, the value of the goal is equal to that of the number allocated to the scorer. For example, if player 3 scores, the value of the goal is three goals. The numbering system is helpful when the group is of mixed ability. In mixed-ability groups, the stronger players often dominate possession, which can limit the weaker players' development and engagement. To help avoid this problem, the coach can subtly number the players so that the weaker players are allocated higher numbers and the stronger players are allocated lower numbers. This will encourage the stronger players to involve the weaker players more in the activity.

When the groups of players are of a similar ability, the numbering system can be used to encourage players to play in new and different positions. The coach can allocate lower numbers to the players that prefer attacking roles and higher numbers to players that prefer defensive roles.

The more defensive players will be encouraged to play in attacking positions, as any goals that they score will be of high value to the team. More attacking-minded players will be encouraged to play a more defensive role because any goals that they score will be of less value to the team.

## Key focus/Coaching points

**Primary focus:** Attacking and defending

**Secondary focus:** Decision making

**Additional focus:** Movement

## Progressions/Adaptations

- Set the teams a goals target, e.g., the first to 20 goals wins. As well as reaching the winning target, all players on the winning team must score at least 1 goal.
- Award a bonus goal if a team completes 5 passes before scoring.

# 502 THE SOCCER COACH'S TOOLKIT

## ACTIVITY 223  DOUBLE TROUBLE

**Level:** Advanced

**Type of activity:** Opposed technical practice

**Number of participants:** 12

**Equipment required:** Soccer balls, cones, 2 sets of bibs and 4 mini-goals

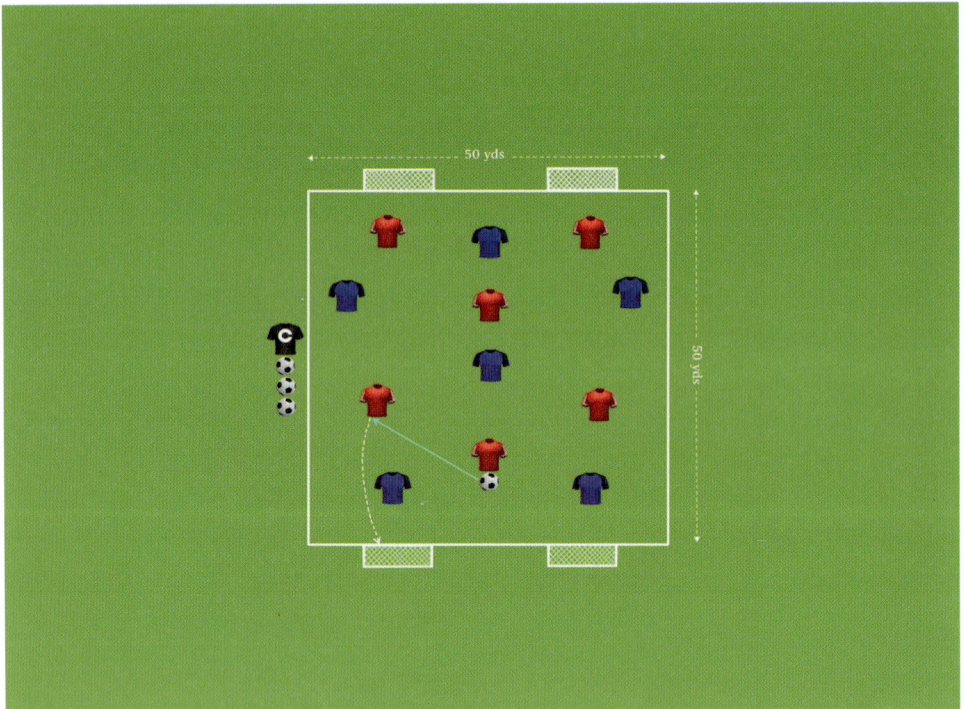

## Description

Divide players into two teams of six. Mark out a playing area and position one mini-goal in each corner of the playing area. The teams compete in a 6v6 match and attack opposite ends of the playing area. The players can score by either dribbling the ball through or passing the ball first time through a mini goal.

## Key focus/Coaching points

**Primary focus:** Attacking and defending

**Secondary focus:** Short passing

**Additional focus:** Running with the ball

## Progressions/Adaptations

- Increase/decrease the size of the mini goals.
- Add a second ball so that there are 2 balls in play at the same time.

# 504   THE SOCCER COACH'S TOOLKIT

## ACTIVITY 224   EMPTY THE NET

**Level:** Advanced

**Type of activity:** Small-sided game

**Number of participants:** 14 + 2 goalkeepers

**Equipment required:** Soccer balls, cones, 2 sets of bibs and 2 goals

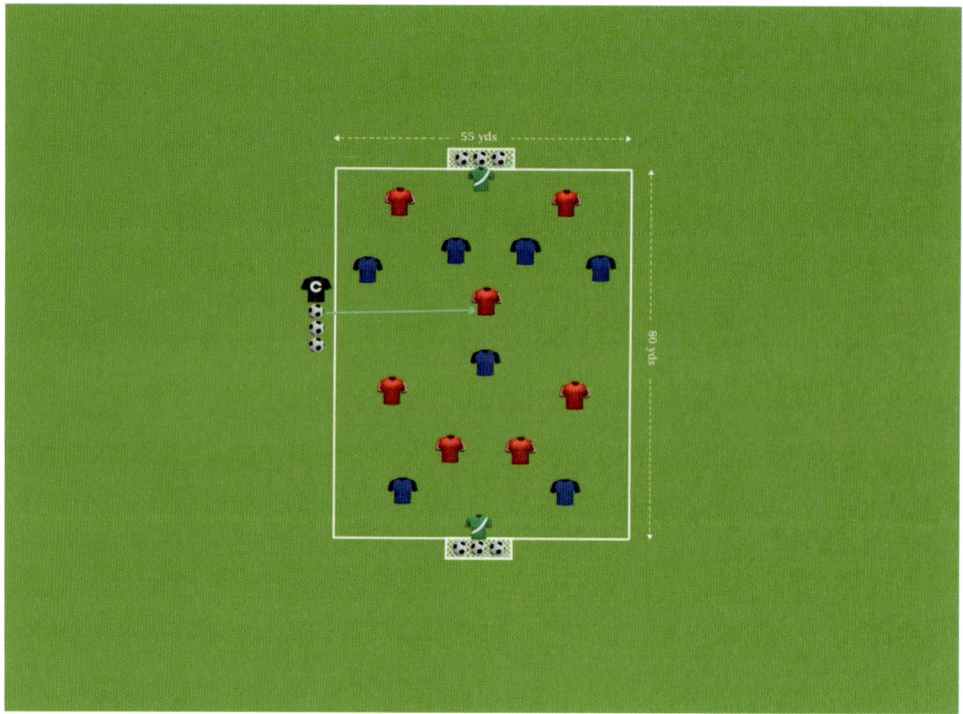

## Description

Divide players into two teams of eight (including goalkeepers). Position a goal and goalkeeper at both ends of the playing area. Position 3 balls in each team's goal. The teams compete in an 8v8 match and attack opposite ends of the playing area.

The activity starts when the coach feeds a ball into the playing area. The teams compete for possession and try to score. The first team to score with the ball in play immediately re-starts the activity from their goalkeeper. The goalkeeper takes one ball out of their team's goal and distributes it to a teammate. The teams now play with this ball until a goal is scored.

Each time a team scores, the goalkeeper removes one ball from their goal and distributes it to a teammate. The teams play with this ball until a goal is scored. The activity continues until one of the teams has removed all the balls from their own goal and scored with each ball in the other team's goal.

## Key focus/Coaching points

**Primary focus:** Attacking and defending

**Secondary focus:** Speed

**Additional focus:** Finishing

## Progressions/Adaptations

- Mark out a channel on both sides of the playing area. Position 1 player from each team in both channels. The players inside the channel and the players inside the playing area must play within their allocated areas.

- Remove the channel and divide the playing area into 3 zones. Organise both teams of outfield players into a 2-3-2 formation. Position 2 defenders from both teams inside their defensive zone, 2 midfielders from both teams inside the middle zone and 2 attackers from both teams inside their attacking zone.

# 506 THE SOCCER COACH'S TOOLKIT

# TACTICAL DEVELOPMENT/TEAM SHAPE

## ACTIVITY 225   CROSSING AND FINISHING

**Level:** Basic

**Type of activity:** Opposed technical practice

**Number of participants:** 14 + 1 goalkeeper

**Equipment required:** Soccer balls, cones, 2 sets of bibs and 1 goal

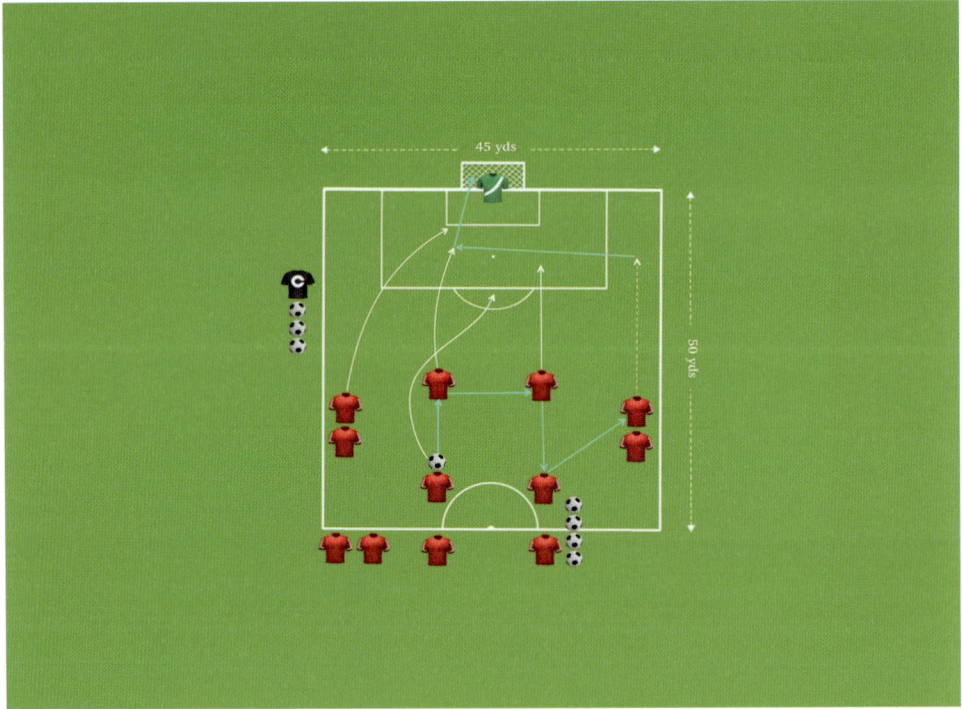

## Description

Divide players into one group of 12. Position a goal and goalkeeper at one end of the playing area. Organise the group into four central midfielders, two right wingers, two left wingers and four central attackers. The central midfielders require a supply of balls. Position the central midfielders in two rows, side-by-side at one end of the playing area facing the goal. Position the groups of wingers in straight lines on opposite sides of the playing area. Position the wingers close to the sideline on their side of the playing area and 10 yards ahead of the central midfielders. Position 1 group of central attackers side-by-side with their backs to the goal, 15 yards opposite the central midfielders. Position the other group of central attackers next to the group of central midfielders.

The activity starts when either of the first two central midfielders in line passes the ball to either of the central attackers. The central attacker that receives the pass then passes to the other central attacker. The central attacker now in possession passes the ball to the central midfielder that did not play the initial pass.

The central midfielder now in possession passes the ball wide to the first winger in line in either group. The winger that receives the pass dribbles the ball until they are 8-10 yards from the goal line.

Both central attackers make attacking runs towards the goal. The central midfielder that played the first pass makes a supporting run towards the goal and stops 18-20 yards from the goal. The winger on the opposite side of the playing area makes an attacking run towards the back post. The winger crosses the ball to either of the central attackers or the supporting winger. The player that receives the cross is allowed one touch to receive and one touch to finish. If the cross is misdirected or the ball deflects off an attacker towards the supporting central midfielder, the central midfielder is allowed one touch to receive the ball and one touch to shoot.

After each attack, the players run to the back of their line. The activity re-starts with the next player(s) in each group. Rotate the players after 5-10 minutes.

## Key focus/Coaching points

**Primary focus:** Tactical/team shape

**Secondary focus:** Crossing

**Additional focus:** Finishing

## Progressions/Adaptations

- Add 1 then 2 defenders to mark the central attackers. Start with passive defending then the allow defenders to block, intercept and tackle.
- Before receiving the first pass, the central attackers make runs to create space away from the defenders.

# Tactical Development/Team Shape

## ACTIVITY 226  BULL'S-EYE

**Level:** Basic

**Type of activity:** Implementation practice

**Number of participants:** 14 + 2 goalkeepers

**Equipment required:** Soccer balls, cones, discs, 2 sets of bibs and 2 goals

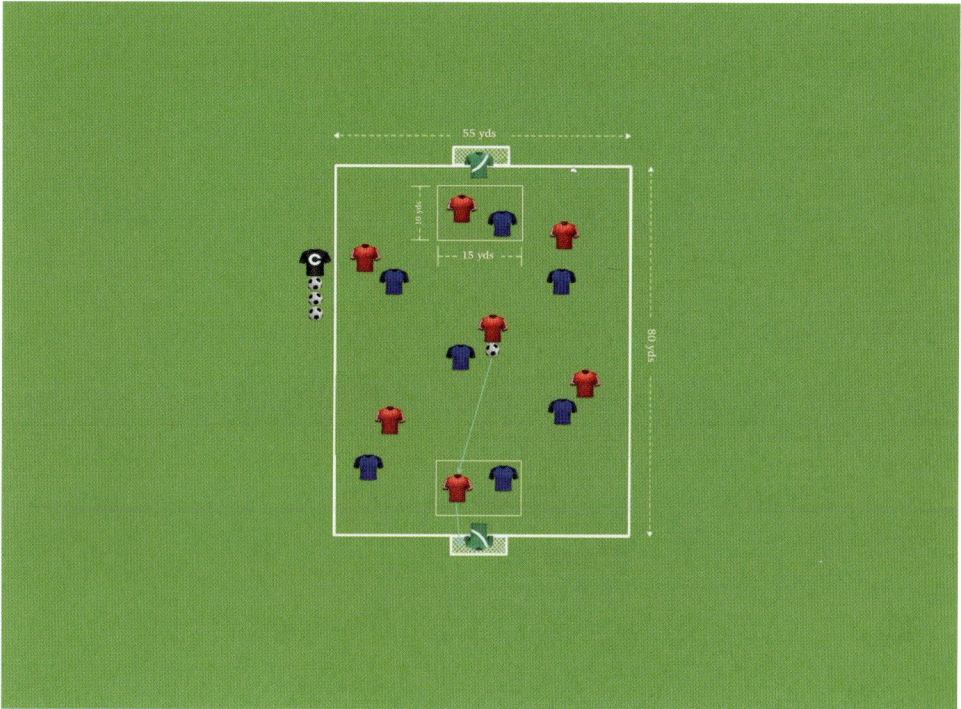

## Description

Divide players into two groups of eight (including goalkeepers). Position a goal and goalkeeper at both ends of the playing area. Mark out a 10x15-yard rectangle at both ends of the playing area 6 yards out from the goal. The teams attack opposite ends of the playing area. The players can only score goals from inside the rectangle closest to the goal that they are attacking.

All players can move freely in and out of the rectangles during the activity and there is no limit on the number of players allowed inside the rectangles at any one time. The attacking team faces the challenge of trying to keep the rectangle as open as possible to create space for when an attacker receives the ball inside the rectangle.

The activity encourages players to create opportunities to score from an area of play that statistically produces a high percentage of goals.

## Key focus/Coaching points

**Primary focus:** Tactical development/team shape

**Secondary focus:** Decision making

**Additional focus:** Movement

## Progressions/Adaptations

- If the attacking teams find it difficult to score from inside the squares, allow only 1 defender inside the square at any one time.
- Goals can be scored from any area of the pitch. Award 3 goals for each goal scored from inside the square.
- Goals scored from inside the square must be a first-time finish.

## ACTIVITY 227   DEFENDING DEEP

**Level:** Basic

**Type of activity:** Implementation practice

**Number of participants:** 7 + 1 goalkeeper

**Equipment required:** Soccer balls, cones, domes, discs, 2 sets of bibs and 1 goal

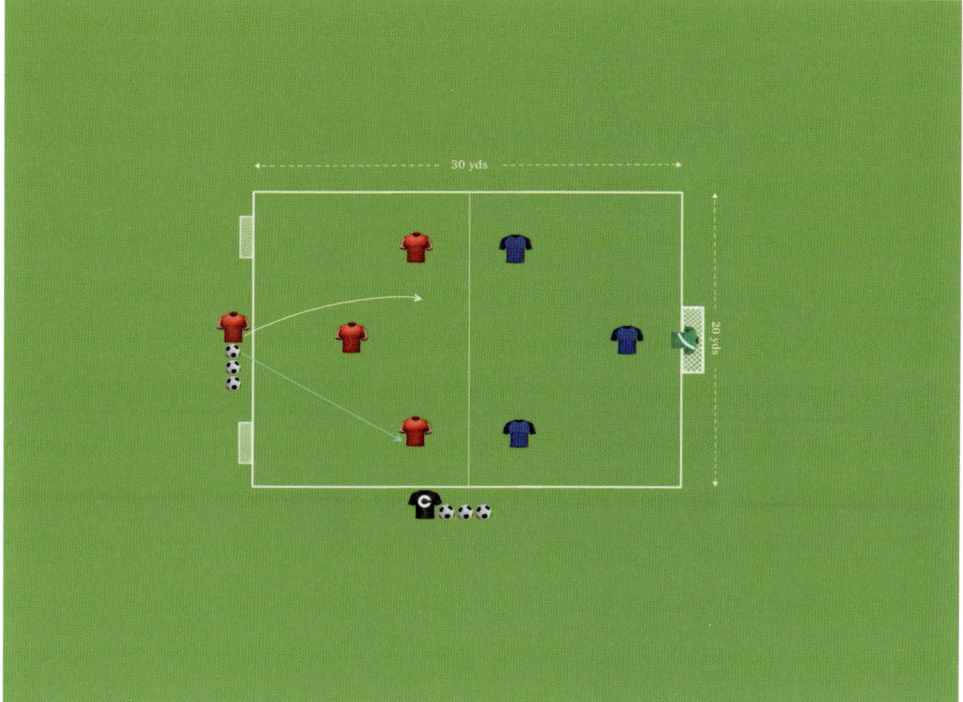

## Description

Divide players into one team of four attackers, one team of three defenders and a goalkeeper. Mark out a playing area divided into two zones. Position a goal and the goalkeeper at one end of the playing area and one mini-goal in both corners at the opposite end of the playing area. Position three of the attackers inside the zone farthest from the goal. Position the remaining attacker on the endline between the mini goals with a supply of balls. Position the group of defenders inside the zone closest to the goal.

The activity starts when the attacker between the mini goals passes to an attacker inside the playing area. The attacker that passed the ball follows their pass to create four attackers inside the zone farthest from the goal. The attackers try to keep possession and score. The attackers can move freely and dribble/pass between zones as they build their attack. The attackers can only score from inside the zone closest to the goal.

The defenders must stay inside their zone when they are defending. If the defenders win the ball from the attackers, they can move out of their zone and try to score by either dribbling through a mini-goal or with a first-time pass through a mini-goal from the zone closest to the mini-goals. The defenders can move freely and dribble/pass between the zones as they build their attack.

If the attackers win possession back, the defenders immediately retreat to the zone closest to the goal and continue defending. The attack continues until the ball goes out of play or a goal is scored. Rotate the attackers and defenders after 10 minutes.

## Key focus/Coaching points

**Primary focus:** Tactical development/team shape

**Secondary focus:** Defending against an overload

**Additional focus:** Defensive support

## Progressions/Adaptations

- Allow the defenders to break out of their zone and pressure the attackers as soon as the attack starts. The attackers are still only allowed to score from inside the zone nearest to the goal.
- The attacking team is allowed a maximum of 5 passes before attempting to score.

## ACTIVITY 228  GO CREATE

**Level:** Basic

**Type of activity:** Opposed technical practice

**Number of participants:** 10 + 1 goalkeeper

**Equipment required:** Soccer balls, cones, discs, domes, 2 sets of bibs, 2 mini-goals and 1 goal

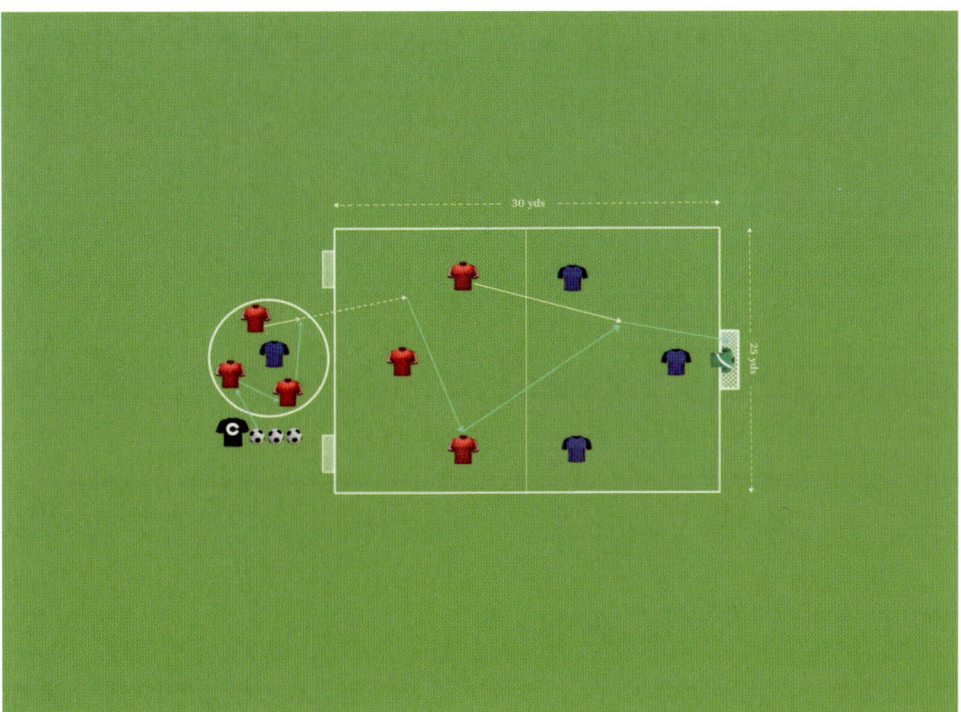

## Description

Divide players into a group of six attackers and four defenders. Mark out a main playing area divided into two zones. Position a goal and goalkeeper at one end of the playing area. Mark out a circle 2-3 yards beyond the opposite end of the playing area. Position one mini-goal in each corner of the zone nearest to the circle. Position three attackers and one defender inside the circle. Position three attackers inside the zone nearest to the circle. Position three defenders inside the zone nearest to the goal.

The activity starts when the coach feeds a ball to an attacker inside the circle. The attackers try to keep possession and complete two passes without interception or the ball going out of the circle. The attacker that receives the second pass must dribble out of the circle and into the nearest zone. The attackers try to score in the goal at the opposite end of the playing area. The attackers can move freely and dribble/pass between both zones as they build their attack but can only score when the ball is in the zone nearest to the goal.

The defending team must stay inside their zone when they are defending until they win possession of the ball. If they win possession, they can move out of their zone and try to score by dribbling the ball through either of the mini goals. The defenders can move freely and dribble/pass between the zones as they build their attack.

Once a goal is scored or ball goes out of play, all players immediately return to their starting positions and the coach feeds a new ball into the circle. Rotate attackers and defenders after 5-10 minutes.

## Key focus/Coaching points

**Primary focus:** Tactical development/team shape

**Secondary focus:** Attacking with an overload

**Additional focus:** Creativity

## Progressions/Adaptations

- Increase the number of passes that must be completed inside the circle before an attacker can move into the nearest zone.

- A second attacker and the defender move out of the circle when an attacker moves into the nearest zone. This creates a 5v4 attacking overload inside the playing area.

- Condition each attack to include a creative attacking movement before a goal can be scored. For example, the attack must include an overlap run, a 1-2 pass or a first-time finish.

## ACTIVITY 229 ATTACKING OVERLOADS

**Level:** Basic

**Type of activity:** Opposed technical practice

**Number of participants:** 8 + 2 goalkeepers

**Equipment required:** Soccer balls, cones, 2 sets of bibs and goals

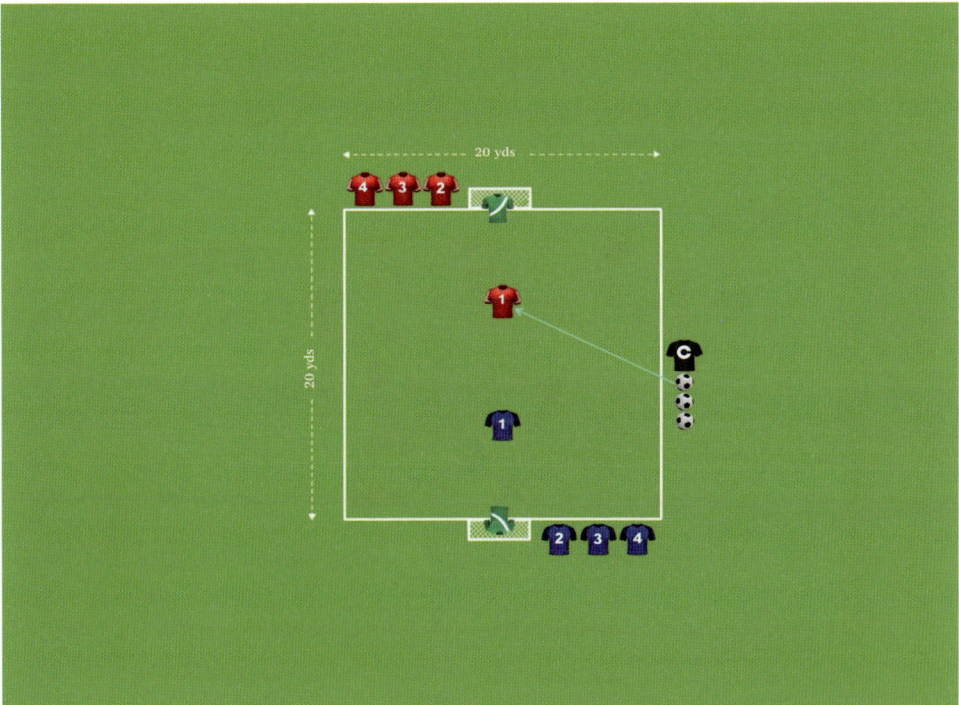

## Description

Divide players into two teams of five (including goalkeepers). Position a goal and goalkeepers at both ends of the playing area. Mark out a playing area that is an appropriate size for 2v2 (including goalkeepers) and up to 5v5 play (including goalkeepers).

Number the outfield players on both teams 1-4. Position player 1 from both teams inside the playing area and all other players a safe distance to the side of the playing area. The coach should be positioned outside the playing area with a supply of balls.

The activity starts when the coach passes to either player inside the playing area. The players compete against each other to score. The first player to concede a goal is joined by player 2 from their team to create a 2v1 attacking overload for their team in the next episode of play. When player number 2 is inside the playing area, the coach passes a new ball to the team with the attacking overload. The team of two compete against the team of one for possession and try to score.

The activity continues in this way with the team that concedes the goal bringing their next player (in ascending numerical order) into the playing area until all outfield players are in play. The activity allows the players to have more space during the early stages and less space as the activity progresses. This activity will also allow players to experience competitive play when team numbers are balanced and imbalanced.

### Key focus/Coaching points

**Primary focus:** Tactical development/team shape

**Secondary focus:** Dribbling

**Additional focus:** Ball manipulation

### Progressions/Adaptations

- Once either team has all 4 outfield players inside the playing area, they then remove a player (in ascending numerical order) each time they score until all their outfield players are outside the playing area. The first team to remove all their outfield players from the playing area this is the winning team.
- Introduce an alternative method of scoring, e.g., 4-6 passes = 1 goal.

# Tactical Development/Team Shape

## ACTIVITY 230  ATTACKING TEAM PLAY

**Level:** Basic

**Type of activity:** Implementation practice

**Number of participants:** 8 + 1 goalkeeper

**Equipment required:** Soccer balls, cones, discs, 2 sets of bibs and 1 goal

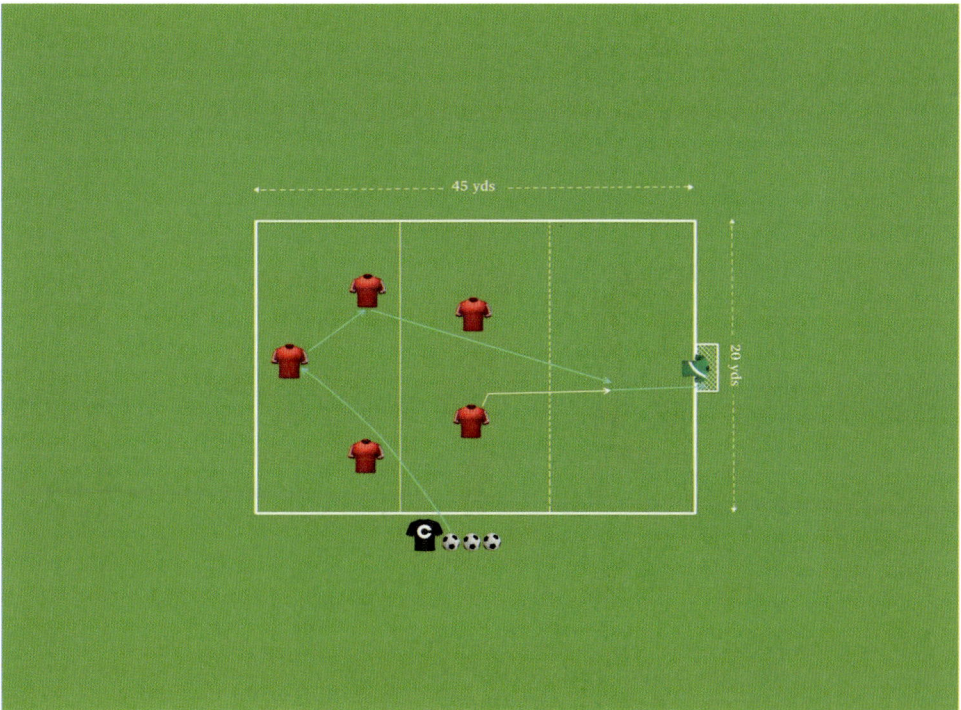

## Description

Divide players into a group of five. Mark out a playing area divided into three zones. Position a goal and goalkeeper at one end of the playing area. Organise the group into three midfielders and two attackers.

Position three midfielders inside the zone farthest from the goal. Position two attackers inside the middle zone. Use line nearest to the goal in the middle zone as an offside line. The coach should be positioned outside the playing area with a supply of balls.

The activity starts when the coach passes to one of midfielders. The midfielders keep possession inside their zone. The attackers support possession and make attacking runs, e.g., curved, cross-over and diagonal to receive a pass either inside the middle zone or inside the zone nearest to the goal.

Any of the midfielders can pass to an attacker. The pass can be to the feet of an attacker inside the middle zone or a through pass into the zone nearest the goal. Encourage the players in possession to keep the ball for a realistic amount of time i.e., no longer than 5-10 seconds.

If the pass to an attacker is received inside the middle zone, the attacker that receives the pass must dribble into the zone nearest to the goal. Once the attacker is inside the zone nearest to the goal, they are allowed one touch of the ball before they try to score. If the pass to an attacker is a through pass into the zone nearest the goal, the attacker is allowed two touches of the ball before they try to score. Use the offside line to help develop the timing of the pass and the timing of the attacking runs. If an attacker is offsides, re-start the activity with a pass to the midfielders.

## Key focus/Coaching points

**Primary focus:** Tactical development/team shape

**Secondary focus:** Movement

**Additional focus:** Finishing

## Progressions/Adaptations

- Add 1 defender inside the zone farthest from the goal and 1 defender inside the middle zone. The defenders try to make tackles and intercept passes.

- Add 1 defender inside the zone nearest to the goal. Allow both attackers to move into this zone to create a 2v1 attacking overload. The attackers are allowed a maximum of 3 passes inside the zone nearest to the goal before an attacker must try to score.

- Condition the number of passes allowed inside each zone to develop quick play. The midfielders are allowed a maximum of 3 passes inside the zone farthest from the goal zone, and the attackers are allowed a maximum of 2 passes inside the middle zone and 1 pass inside the zone nearest to the goal.

# ACTIVITY 231  HOG THE BALL

**Level:** Basic

**Type of activity:** Opposed technical practice

**Number of participants:** 11

**Equipment required:** Soccer balls, cones, discs and 3 sets of bibs

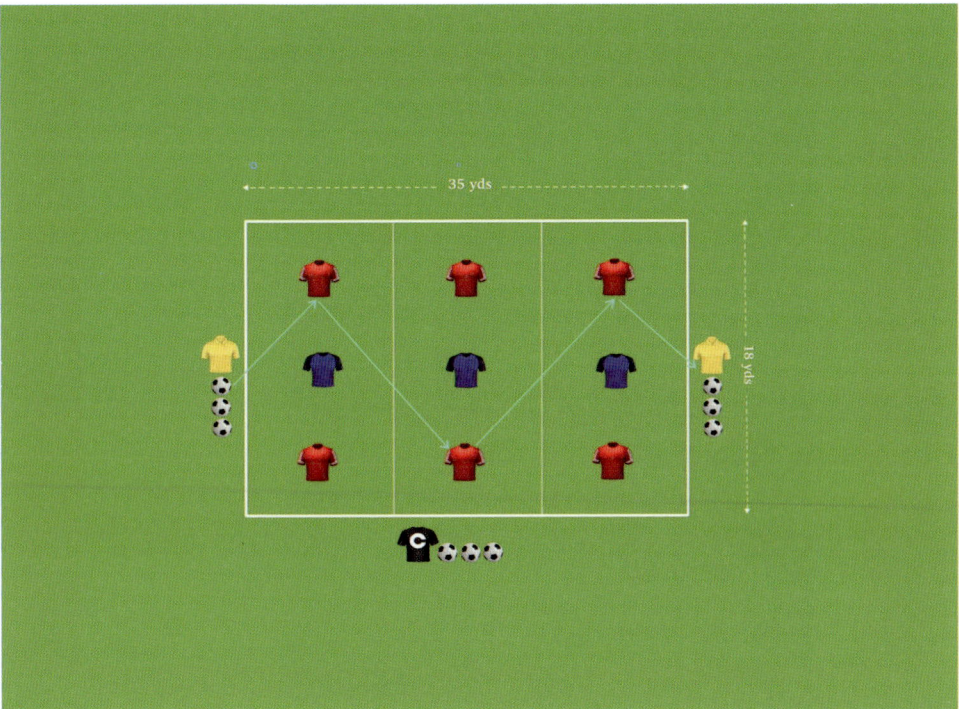

## Description

Divide players into one team of six attackers, one team of three defenders and two target players. Divide the playing area into three zones. Position two attackers and one defender inside each zone. Position one target player at both ends of the playing area with a supply of balls. Initially, all players must play within their allocated zones.

The activity starts when either of the target players passes to an attacker inside the zone nearest to them. The attackers try to keep possession through each zone and score with a pass to the target player at the opposite end of the playing area.

If the attacking team manages to pass the ball to the target player, the target player immediately passes to an attacker in the zone nearest to them. The attacking team now attacks the opposite end of the playing area.

If the defenders win possession or the ball goes out of play, the activity re-starts immediately with a pass from the target player at the other end of the playing area to an attacker inside the zone nearest to them. Rotate the players after 10 minutes.

## Key focus/Coaching points

**Primary focus:** Tactical development/team shape

**Secondary focus:** Movement

**Additional focus:** Speed

## Progressions/Adaptations

- Allow the attackers to move freely between the zones; however, they must always have 2 players inside each zone.
- Allow no more than 3 passes in each zone.

# ACTIVITY 232  PRESSING MATTERS

**Level:** Basic

**Type of activity:** Opposed technical practice

**Number of participants:** 10

**Equipment required:** Soccer balls, cones, discs, and 2 sets of bibs

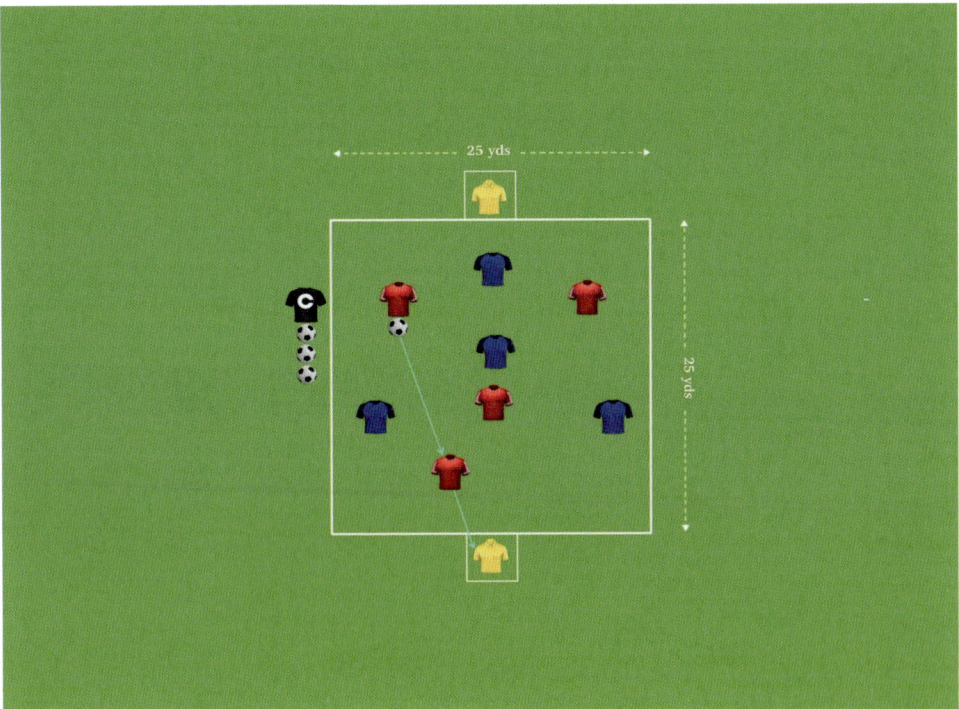

## Description

Divide players into two teams of four and two target players. Mark out a playing area and position a square at opposite ends of the playing area. Position one target player inside each square. The teams attack opposite ends of the playing area.

The teams compete for possession and try to score by passing the ball to the target player inside the square that they are attacking. When either team passes to their target player, the target player immediately passes the ball to the opposition team who then attacks the opposite end of the playing area. Each pass to a target player scores 1 point. Rotate the target players after 10 minutes.

## Key focus/Coaching points

**Primary focus:** Tactical development/team shape

**Secondary focus:** Pressing

**Additional focus:** Attacking and defending

## Progressions/Adaptations

- When a team passes to the target player at the end that they are attacking, the player that passed the ball and the target player switch possessions.

- Mark out a halfway line across the width of the playing area. When a team has possession in their defensive half of the playing area, only 1 player from the opposition team can remain inside their defensive half of the playing area. When a team has possession in their attacking half of the playing area, all players in the defending team must retreat to their defensive half of the playing area.

## ACTIVITY 233  COUNTERATTACKS

**Level:** Basic

**Type of activity:** Implementation practice

**Number of participants:** 10 + 2 goalkeepers

**Equipment required:** Soccer balls, cones, discs, 2 sets of bibs and 2 goals

## Description

Divide players into one team of six attackers and one team of four defenders. Mark out a playing area divided into two zones. Number the zones 1 and 2. Position a goal and goalkeeper at both ends of the playing area with a supply of balls each. Position four of the attackers inside zone 1 and two attackers inside zone 2. Position two defenders inside both zones.

The activity starts when the goalkeeper inside zone 1 rolls a ball out to any of the four attackers inside zone 1. The attackers try to keep possession from the defenders inside zone 1 and pass to an attacker inside zone 2. When a pass is received by an attacker inside zone 2, any two attackers from zone 1 can follow the pass into zone 2 to create a 4v2 attacking overload inside zone 2. The four attackers inside zone 2 try to keep possession from the two defenders and score past the goalkeeper inside zone 2.

When a goal is scored, the defenders win possession, or the ball goes out of play, the activity re-starts with a roll out from the goalkeeper inside the same zone as the four attackers. Rotate the players after 10-15 minutes.

## Key focus/Coaching points

**Primary focus:** Tactical development/team shape

**Secondary focus:** Counterattacking

**Additional focus:** Creativity

## Progressions/Adaptations

- If a defender wins possession, they can pass to a teammate in the opposite zone. Once a passed has been received by a defender in the opposite zone, the 2 defenders try to score past the goalkeeper at that end of the playing area. Two attackers from the zone where the pass was played from follow the pass to maintain a 4v2 numerical advantage for the attackers.

## ACTIVITY 234   4V4 PLAYING OUT OF DEFENCE

**Level:** Intermediate

**Type of activity:** Implementation practice

**Number of participants:** 8 + 1 goalkeeper

**Equipment required:** Soccer balls, cones, 2 sets of bibs, 3 mini-goals and 1 goal

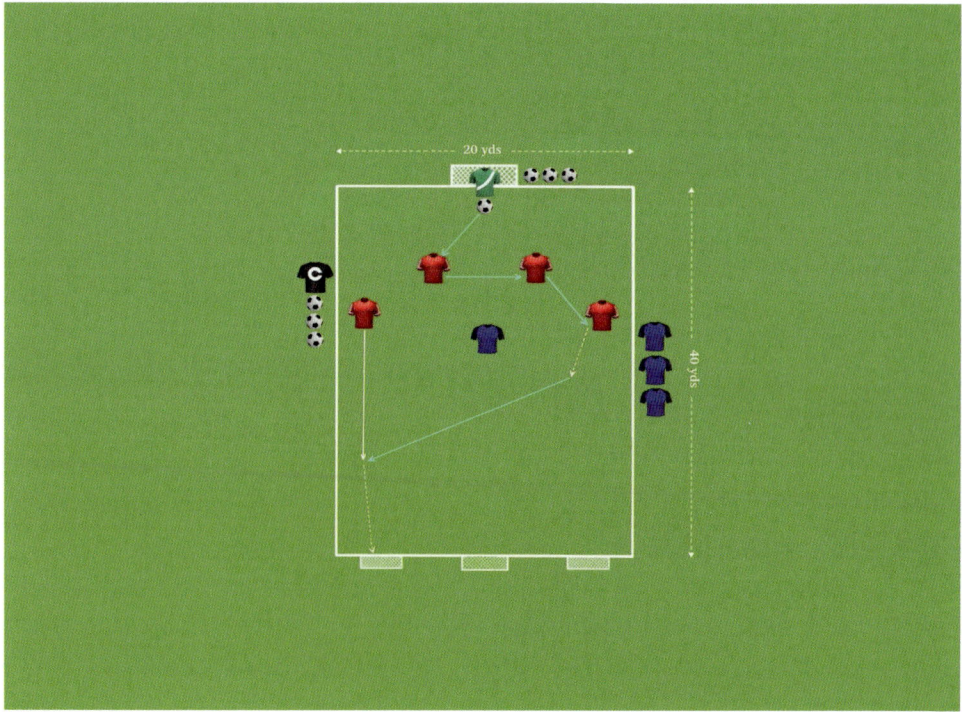

## Description

Divide players into one attacking team of four players and one defending team of four players. Position a goal and goalkeeper at one end of the playing area. The goalkeeper requires a supply of balls. Position three mini-goals across the opposite end of the playing area. The attacking team attack the three mini-goals and the defending team attack the goal at the opposite end of the playing area.

Organise the attacking team into a defensive formation of two centre-backs, one right-back and one left-back. Position all players from the attacking team inside the playing area. Position one player from the defending team inside the playing area and the remaining players from the defending team outside the playing area.

The activity starts when the goalkeeper rolls a ball out to a player in the attacking team. The attacking team tries to keep possession and score by dribbling through one of the mini goals. If the attacking team scores, they score 1 point. The player from the defending team tries to prevent the attackers from scoring. If the player from the team defending team wins possession of the ball, they score 1 point. If the defender wins possession of the ball, they can try to score past the goalkeeper to score 2 points.

When the attacking team scores, a second player from the defending team enters the playing area to defend the next attack. If the attacking team fails to score, the existing player from the defending team remains inside the playing area to defend the next attack. Each time the attacking team scores, another player from the defending team enters the playing area until all four players from the defending team are inside the playing area.

After each attack, the players in the attacking team return to their starting positions and the goalkeeper re-starts the activity with a roll out to a player in the attacking team. After 10 attacks rotate the attacking and defending teams. The team that scores the most points is the winning team.

## Key focus/Coaching points

**Primary focus:** Tactical development/team shape

**Secondary focus:** Receiving

**Additional focus:** Movement

## Progressions/Adaptations

- Each player in the attacking team must touch the ball before the attacking team can try to score.
- Introduce a maximum number of passes allowed in each attack, e.g., 4 passes v 1 defender, 5 passes v 2 defenders, 6 passes v 3 defenders and 7 passes v 4 defenders.

## ACTIVITY 235   SCENARIOS

**Level:** Intermediate

**Type of activity:** Small-sided game

**Number of participants:** 16 + 2 goalkeepers

**Equipment required:** Soccer balls, cones, 2 sets of bibs and 2 goals

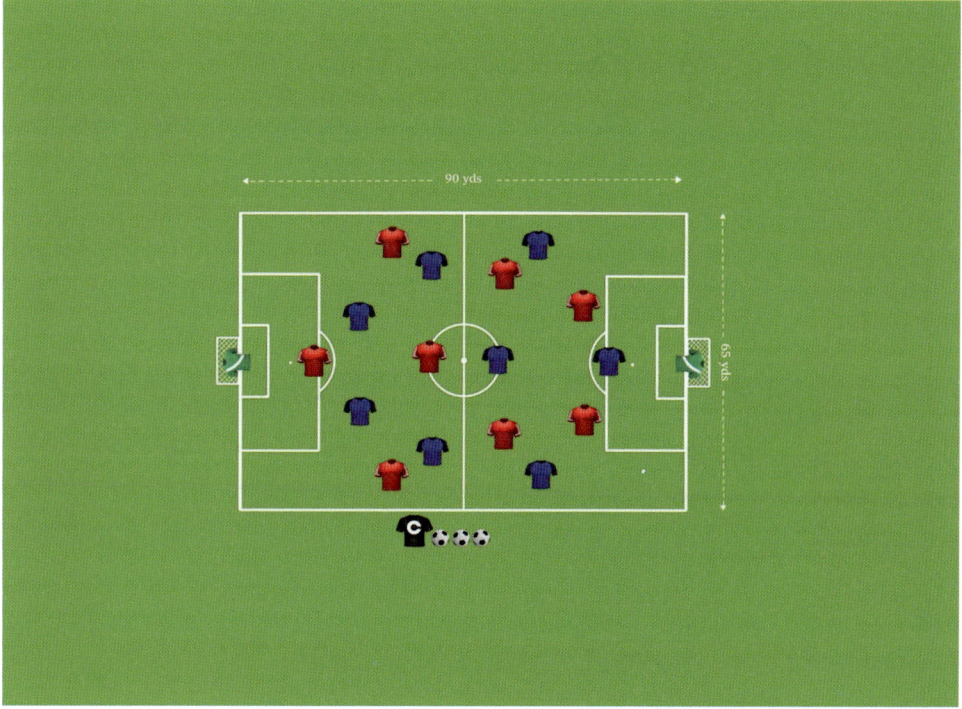

## Description

Divide players into two teams of nine (including goalkeepers). Position a goal and goalkeepers at both ends of the playing area. The teams compete in a 9v9 match and attack opposite ends of the playing area. Before the activity starts, the coach nominates one of the teams to counter a match-based scenario (see below for some examples). The coach should create a scenario that allows the team to focus on specific areas of team play and improve specific areas of technical and tactical weakness.

If, for example, a group of players needs to improve their defending, the scenario they encounter during the match should allow them to focus on defending techniques and tactics.

Before the activity starts, give the team 5 minutes without coach intervention to discuss their game plan, tactics and most suitable team shape to counter the scenario. After 5 minutes, the coach should discuss the players' ideas and add their own input before finalizing team game plan, tactics and team shape. Once the activity starts, the coach should take appropriate opportunities to make tactical changes, coach individual players and team units.

**Examples of scenarios:**

- 2-0 down with 10 minutes to play (focus on attacking and creating chances to score).
- 2-0 up with 20 minutes to play but with a 1 player numerical dis-advantage (focus on eliminating space for the opposition to attack and defending compactly).
- Play against a team with direct style of play. Condition the opposition to play in a direct style, i.e., pass forward as quickly as possible (focus on preventing forward passes and minimising space in front of and behind the opposition forwards).
- Playing against a team that defends narrowly and tries to block the centre of the pitch (focus on getting the ball wide quickly when attacking).

## Key focus/Coaching points

**Primary focus:** Tactical development/team shape

**Secondary focus:** Attacking and defending

**Additional focus:** Decision making

## Progressions/Adaptations

- Each scenario presents a new challenge and set of problems to counter. **Try to coach only 1 team during this activity and condition the other team to play as you require them to**.
- Further general progressions and adaptations can be added to make the scenario more challenging, e.g., a maximum of 3 touches in possession, only first-time attempts at goal, or dividing the playing area into zones and conditioning play in the zones (e.g., 2 players must perform a 1-2 in each zone).

# Tactical Development/Team Shape

## ACTIVITY 236  CHECKPOINT SOCCER

**Level:** Intermediate

**Type of activity:** Opposed technical practice

**Number of participants:** 10 + 2 goalkeepers

**Equipment required:** Soccer balls, cones, domes, 2 sets of bibs, 4 mini-goals and 1 goal

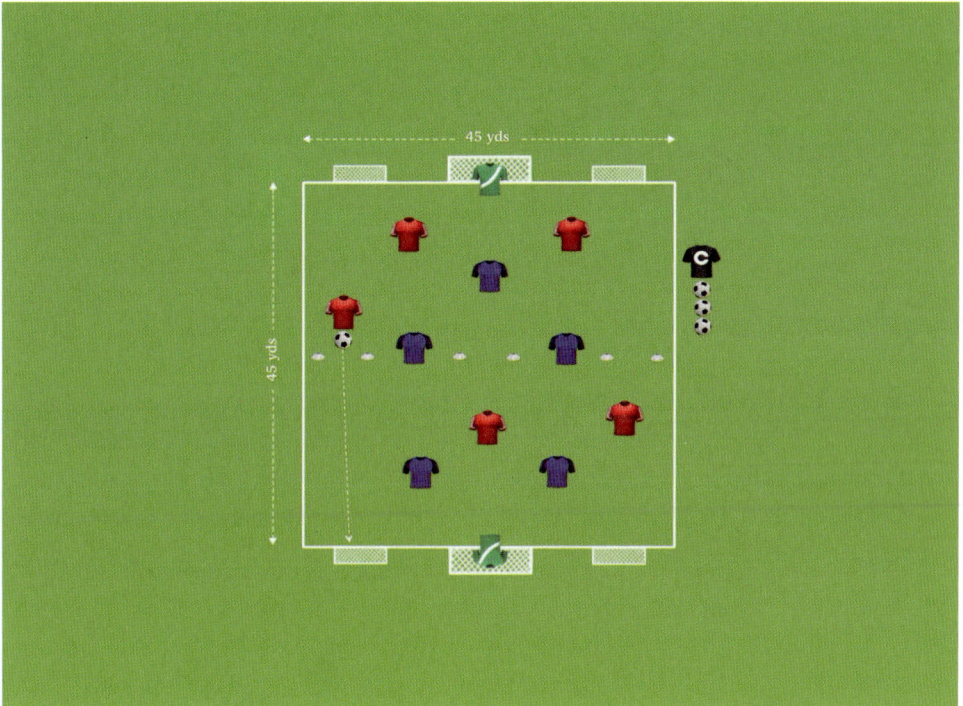

## Description

Divide players into two teams of six (including goalkeepers). Position a goal and goalkeeper centrally at both ends of the playing area and 1 mini-goal in each corner of the playing area. Mark out three gates across the middle of the playing area – one in line with the goal and one in line with each mini-goal. The teams attack opposite ends of the playing area.

The teams try to score by either dribbling the ball through a mini-goal or by passing to the goalkeeper at the opposite end of the playing area. Before either team can try to score, they must either dribble through – or pass to a teammate through – the gate in line with the goal they are attacking.

If a goal is scored with a pass to the goalkeeper, the activity re-starts immediately with a roll out from the goalkeeper to the team that conceded the goal.

## Key focus/Coaching points

**Primary focus:** Tactical development/team shape

**Secondary focus:** Decision making

**Additional focus:** Movement

## Progressions/Adaptations

- Move/add/take away the gates to emphasise different styles of play. For example, removing the middle gate will encourage the players to build attacks in wide positions and removing the wide gates will encourage the players to build attacks in central areas.

- Introduce a minimum/maximum number of passes to be completed in attack to encourage different styles of attacking play.

# Tactical Development/Team Shape 531

## ACTIVITY 237  DEFENDING IN WIDE AREAS

**Level:** Intermediate

**Type of activity:** Implementation practice

**Number of participants:** 16 + 1 goalkeeper

**Equipment required:** Soccer balls, cones, discs, 2 sets of bibs and 1 goal

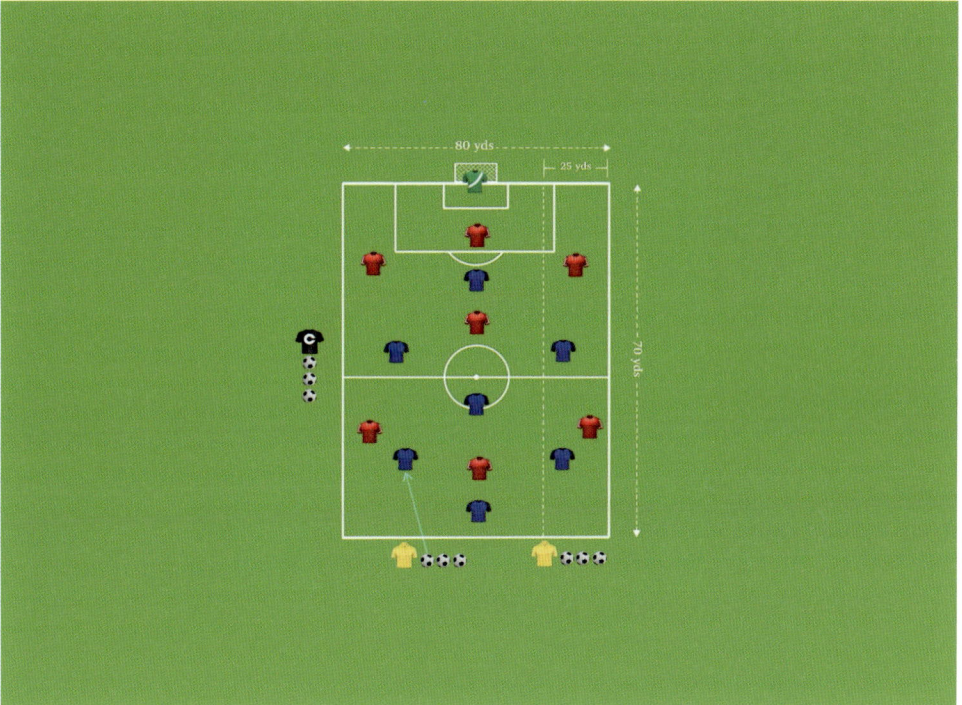

## Description

Divide players into one team of eight (including goalkeeper), one team of seven and two target players. Mark out a playing area approximately two thirds the length of a full-size pitch. Mark out a channel running the length of one side of the playing area. Position the channel 10 yards wide of either goalpost up to the nearest sideline. Position a goal and goalkeeper at one end of the playing area. Position the two target players at the opposite end of the playing area.

Organise both sets of outfield players into a 3-3-1 formation. The team of seven players attacks the goal and try to score past the goalkeeper. The team of eight attacks the opposite end and tries to score with a pass to either of the target players. The coach should focus on the team of eight and try to improve their individual, team-unit and whole-team defending in wide areas.

If the team of seven players scores, the activity re-starts with a goal kick from the goalkeeper. If the team of eight scores, the activity re-starts with a pass from the target player to the opposition team. Rotate the teams after 15-20 minutes.

For the first 10 minutes of the activity, players can move in and out of and play without restrictions inside the channel. Once the players are comfortable with the organisation of the activity, introduce the progressions/adaptations.

## Key focus/Coaching points

**Primary focus:** Tactical development/team shape

**Secondary focus:** Defending in wide areas

**Additional focus:** Movement

## Progressions/Adaptations

- Mark out a halfway line across the width of the playing area. Allow 1 player from the attacking team to play inside their attacking half of the channel when their team has possession in their attacking half of the playing area. Allow 1 defender to move into the channel to defend against the attacking player. When the attacking team loses possession, the attacker and the defender must return to the main playing area.

- Allow 2 players from the attacking team to play anywhere inside the channel when their team has possession in their defensive half of the playing area. Allow 2 defenders to move into the channel to defend against the attacking players. When the attacking team loses possession, the attackers and the defenders must return to the inside of the playing area.

# ACTIVITY 238 ATTACKING IN WIDE AREAS

**Level:** Intermediate

**Type of activity:** Implementation practice

**Number of participants:** 16 + 2 goalkeepers

**Equipment required:** Soccer balls, cones, discs, 3 sets of bibs and 2 goals

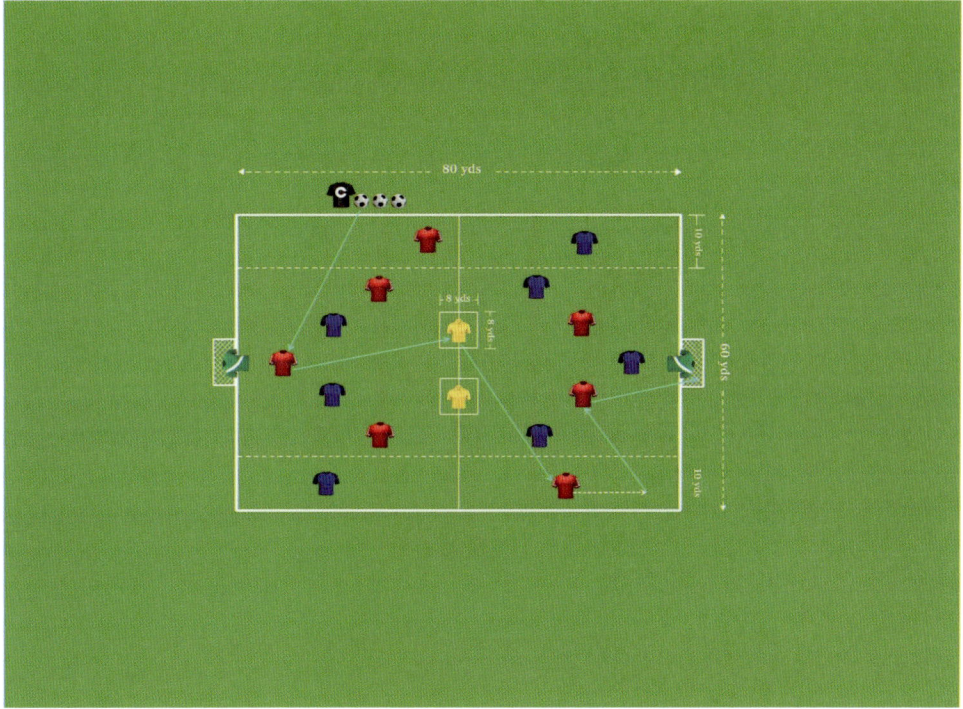

## Description

Divide players into two teams of eight (including goalkeepers) and two target players. Mark out a playing area with a halfway line across the width of the playing area. Position a channel 8-10 yards wide running the length of both sides of the playing area. Mark out two squares side-by-side (approximately 6 yards apart) on the halfway line. Position a goal and goalkeeper at both ends of the playing area. The coach should be positioned on the outside of the playing area with a supply of balls.

Organise each team of outfield players into three defenders, two attackers and two wingers. Position three defenders in their defensive half of the playing area, two attackers in their attacking half of the playing area and one winger inside each channel. Position one target player inside each square.

The teams attack opposite ends of the playing area. All players must play within their designated playing areas. The target players perform unopposed inside their squares. The wingers in each channel compete against each other for possession.

The activity starts when the coach feeds a ball to a defender on either team. The defenders try to keep possession in their own half and pass to either of the target players. When either of the target players receives possession, they try to pass to either winger from the team in possession. When the winger receives possession, they try to cross the ball to either attacker in their attacking half of the playing area. If the attackers receive possession from the cross, they can try to score directly from the cross or keep possession and build an attack inside their attacking half of the playing area.

If the defending team wins possession of the ball (including in the channels), they must play the ball back to a teammate in their defensive half (unless possession is won in the defensive half). The defenders start an attack from their defensive half of the playing area by passing to either target player. When a goal is scored or the ball goes out of play, the coach re-starts the activity with a pass to a defender from the team that defended the previous attack.

## Key focus/Coaching points

**Primary focus:** Tactical development/team shape

**Secondary focus:** Attacking in wide areas

**Additional focus:** Creativity

## Progressions/Adaptations

- Advanced players will be comfortable with contested play, but with less advanced players it may be necessary to allow teams to take alternate attacks with only passive pressure from the defending team.
- The wingers must play a 1-2 pass with a teammate or target player before delivering a cross.

# Tactical Development/Team Shape

## ACTIVITY 239  ATTACKING IN CENTRAL AREAS

**Level:** Intermediate

**Type of activity:** Implementation practice

**Number of participants:** 12 + 2 goalkeepers

**Equipment required:** Soccer balls, cones, discs, 2 sets of bibs and 2 goals

## Description

Divide players into two teams of seven (including goalkeepers). Mark out a narrow and long playing area (approximately the width of a penalty area and the full length of a full-size pitch). Mark out a channel 12 yards wide across the middle of the playing area. Position a goal and goalkeeper at both ends of the playing area. Each goalkeeper requires a supply of balls.

Position three defenders from both teams in their defensive half of the playing area, one midfielder from both teams inside the channel and two attackers from both teams in their attacking half of the playing area. All outfield players apart from the players in the channel must play within their designated areas. The teams attack opposite ends of the playing area.

The activity starts when either goalkeeper rolls a ball out to a defender in their team. The defenders try to keep possession and then pass the ball to their midfield teammate inside the channel.

If the defenders complete a pass to their midfield teammate, the midfielder must dribble (unopposed) into their attacking half of the playing area to create a 3v3 attack. The attacking team tries to keep possession and score. The attacking team attacks until either they score, lose possession or the ball goes out of the play. Once the attack is over, the goalkeeper from the defending team re-starts the activity with a roll out to a teammate in the defensive half of the playing area. If the defenders lose possession of the ball in their defensive half of the playing area or the ball goes out of play, the opposition goalkeeper re-starts the activity with a roll out to a defender in their team.

## Key focus/Coaching points

**Primary focus:** Tactical development/team shape

**Secondary focus:** Attacking in central areas

**Additional focus:** Creativity

## Progressions/Adaptations

- Remove the middle channel but maintain a 3-1-2 formation for both teams. When either midfielder receives a pass from a defender, they can either dribble forwards or pass to an attacker to create a 3v3 attack. The defender that passed to the midfielder moves forward and covers the vacant midfield area. When the attacking team loses possession, the defender and the midfielder retreat to their starting positions.

- Change both teams' formation to 3-2-1 and play normal match rules, i.e., not alternate attacks. Encourage the attacking players to move forward and to support attacking moves and then retreat to a 3-2-1 formation when they lose possession.

## ACTIVITY 240  CREATING SPACE

**Level:** Intermediate

**Type of activity:** Opposed technical practice

**Number of participants:** 16

**Equipment required:** Soccer balls, cones, discs* and 3 sets of bibs

*Discs rather than cones are essential to mark out the squares to ensure that the ball travels smoothly between the squares.

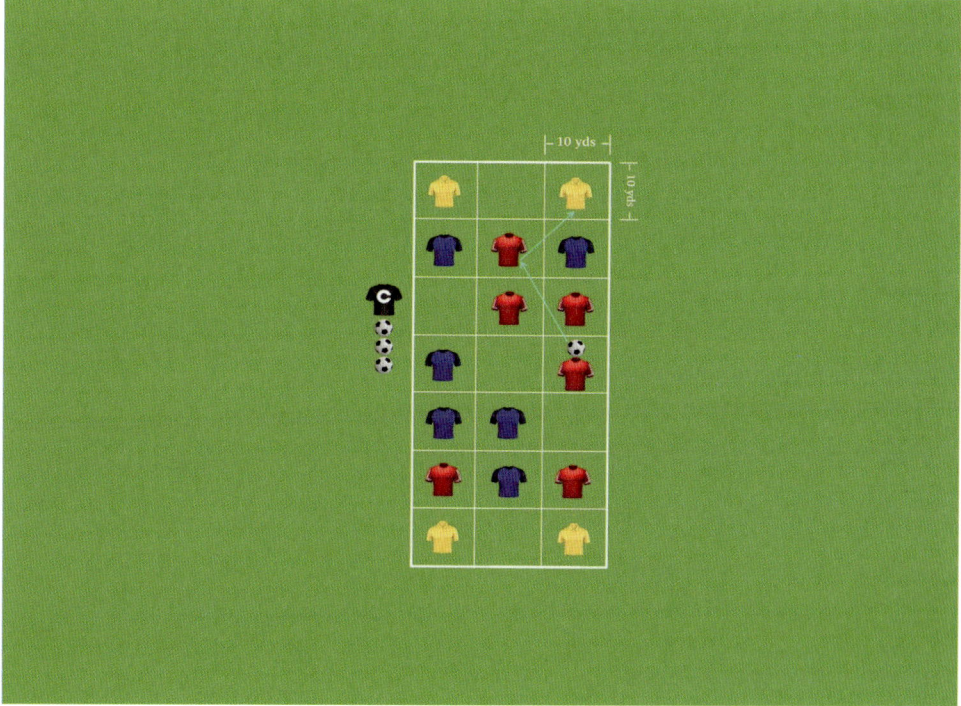

## Description

Divide players into two teams of six and four target players. Divide the playing area into 21 10x10 yard squares. Position one target player inside each of the corner squares and the remaining 12 players inside any other square (1 player per square). The teams compete against each other to keep possession and score points by passing to any of the target players. All players apart from the target players can move freely around the playing area but only one player is allowed inside a square at any one time. When a player receives possession, they must stay inside their square until they have passed the ball.

When a pass is completed to a target player, the target player performs an unopposed pass to the other target player at the same end of the playing area. When the second target player receives the ball, they must pass to any player from the team that has just scored. If the team that has just scored receives the pass from the target player, they must attack the opposite end of the playing area and try to pass to one of the target players at the opposite end of the playing area.

If the opposition intercepts the pass from the second target player, they must also attack the opposite end of the playing area and try to pass to one of the target players at that end. Whenever possession changes hands during normal play, the team that wins possession can attack either end of the playing area.

If, during the activity, there is more than one player inside a square at the same time as the ball, the player that receives the ball is only allowed one touch to play out of the square. If the player takes more than one touch, a free kick should be awarded to the opposition.

## Key focus/Coaching points

**Primary focus:** Tactical development/team shape

**Secondary focus:** Movement

**Additional focus:** Support play

## Progressions/Adaptations

- Every player in the attacking team must touch the ball before they can pass to a target player.
- When a player receives possession, they are allowed to move into a new square (1 square in any direction) if it is unoccupied before they pass the ball.

# Tactical Development/Team Shape

## ACTIVITY 241  PRINCIPLES OF DEFENDING

**Level:** Intermediate

**Type of activity:** Implementation practice

**Number of participants:** 14 + 1 goalkeeper

**Equipment required:** Soccer balls, cones, discs, 2 sets of bibs and 1 goal

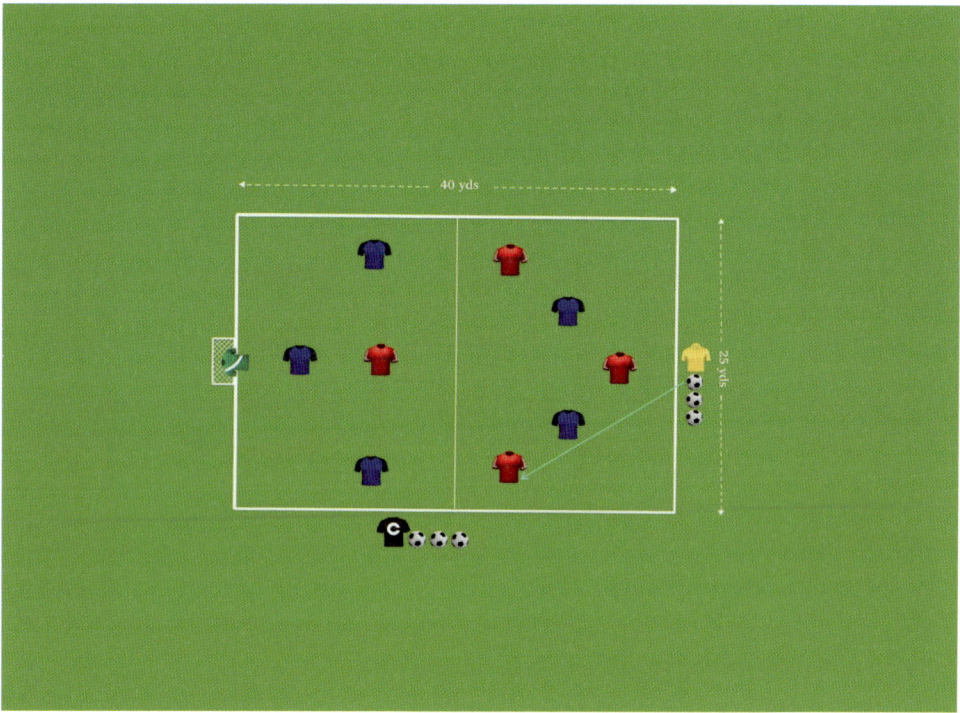

## Description

Divide players into one team of five defenders, one team of four attackers, one goalkeeper, and one target player. Divide the playing area into two zones. Position a goal and the goalkeeper at one end of the playing area. Position the target player at the opposite end of the playing area with a supply of balls. Encourage the target player to move along the end line to support play.

The attackers try to score past the goalkeeper, and the defenders try to score with a pass to the target player. Position three defenders inside their defensive zone and two defenders inside their attacking zone. Position three attackers inside their defensive zone and one attacker inside their attacking zone. Initially, the players must play within their designated zones. The teams must have possession inside their attacking zone before they can score.

The activity starts with a pass from the target player to one of the three attackers inside their defensive zone. The attackers try to keep possession and pass forward to one of the attackers inside their attacking zone. The defenders try to prevent the forward pass into the attacking zone. If the defenders win possession, they must pass back to a teammate in their defensive zone. When the defenders have possession inside their defensive zone, they attack the opposite end of the playing area.

If the attackers successfully pass forward to an attacker inside their attacking zone, the player that passed the ball runs into their attacking zone. The two attackers combine and try to score past the goalkeeper. The three defenders try to prevent the attackers from scoring and try to win possession of the ball. If the defenders win possession of the ball, they must pass forwards to the two defenders inside their attacking zone.

After each attack, the target player re-starts the activity with a pass to one of the three attackers inside their defensive zone. The coach should focus on coaching the defending team. Rotate the players after 10-15 minutes.

## Key focus/Coaching points

**Primary focus:** Tactical development/team shape

**Secondary focus:** Defensive support

**Additional focus:** Movement

## Progressions/Adaptations

- Allow 1 of the attackers from their defensive half to either dribble or follow their pass into the attacking half to create a 3v3 attack v defence.
- Add 2 players to the attackers and 2 players to the defenders. Position 1 attacker in each zone and 1 defender in each zone.

## Tactical Development/Team Shape 541

## ACTIVITY 242   DEFENDING AGAINST OVERLOADS

**Level:** Intermediate

**Type of activity:** Implementation practice

**Number of participants:** 15 + 2 goalkeepers

**Equipment required:** Soccer balls, cones, discs, 2 sets of bibs and 2 goals

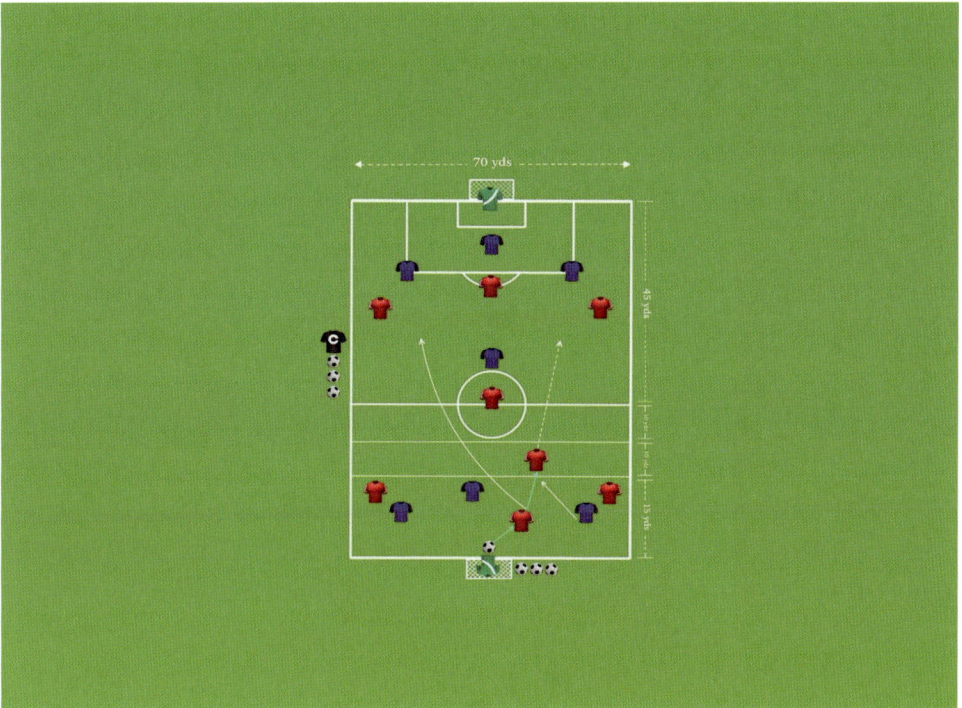

## Description

Divide players into one team of nine attackers and one team of eight defenders (including goalkeepers). Mark out a playing area divided into two zones with one zone 10-15 yards longer than the other. Mark out a channel 10 yards wide, 10 yards inside the shorter zone and running across the width of the zone.

Position a goal and goalkeeper at both ends of the playing area. The team of attackers attacks the goal positioned at the end of the longer zone. The team of defenders attacks the goal positioned at the end of the shorter zone. Position four attackers and four defenders from both teams inside the longer zone. Position three attackers and three defenders from both teams inside the shorter zone. Position one player from the attacking team inside the channel. The attackers' goalkeeper requires a supply of balls.

The activity starts when the attackers' goalkeeper rolls a ball out to an attacker inside the shorter zone. The attackers try to keep possession of the ball and pass to the midfielder in the channel. The defenders try to prevent the attackers from passing to the midfielder. If the defenders win possession inside the shorter zone, the activity re-starts with a roll out from the goalkeeper to an attacker inside the shorter zone.

If an attacker successfully passes to the midfielder, the player that passed the ball and the midfielder travel into the longer zone to create a 6v4 attacking overload. The six attackers try to score past the goalkeeper. If the attackers score, the activity re-starts with a roll out from the attackers' goalkeeper to an attacker inside the shorter zone.

If the defending team win possession in the longer zone, they must quickly pass to a defender in their shorter zone to create a 3v2 attacking overload. The three defenders try to score past the goalkeeper.

As soon as the defenders pass the ball into the shorter zone, the attacker that passed the ball into the channel must quickly retreat to the shorter zone to re-establish a 3v3 balance. The midfielder must also retreat to the channel.

If the attacking team wins possession back in the longer zone or the ball goes out of play, the attacking team's goalkeeper re-starts the activity with a roll out to an attacker in the shorter zone. The coach should focus on coaching the defenders in this activity. Rotate the teams after 10-15 minutes.

## Key focus/Coaching points

Primary focus: Tactical development/team shape

Secondary focus: Defending against an overload

Additional focus: Defensive support

## Progressions/Adaptations

- When the attackers have possession inside the longer zone, 1 defender from the shorter zone runs into the longer zone to create a 6v5 attacking overload.

- When the attackers have possession inside the longer zone, allow them the option of sending 1 or 2 attackers from the shorter zone plus the midfielder into the longer zone to create either a 6 or 7v5 attacking overload.

## ACTIVITY 243  PRINCIPLES OF ATTACK

**Level:** Advanced

**Type of activity:** Small-sided game

**Number of participants:** 14 + 2 goalkeepers

**Equipment required:** Soccer balls, cones, 2 sets of bibs and 2 goals

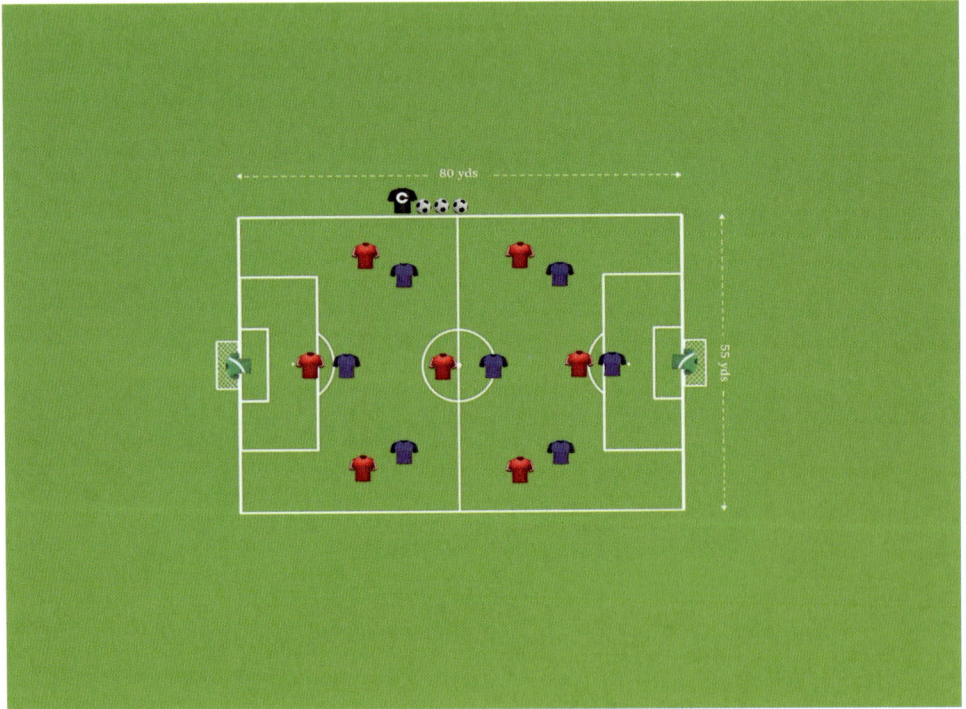

## Description

Divide players into two teams of eight (including goalkeepers). Position a goal and goalkeeper at both ends of the playing area. Organise both sets of outfield players into a 3-3-1 formation. The teams compete in an 8v8 match and follow normal match rules. The coach should focus on coaching one team and focus on improving their attacking shape, movement and productivity. Encourage the team to attack using a variety of techniques and tactics. The coach can condition the other team to play in a certain style, e.g., pressing high or defending in a low block.

## Key focus/Coaching points

**Primary focus:** Tactical development/team shape

**Secondary focus:** Creativity

**Additional focus:** Movement

## Progressions/Adaptations

- Change the formation of one/both teams, e.g., 2-3-2 or 3-2-2.
- Divide the playing area into three zones and/or two wide channels. Limit the number of players allowed inside each zone or channel at any one time. The use of channels and zones presents the players with different attacking challenges to overcome and introduces them to different technical/tactical attacking approaches e.g., attacking in wide/central areas or maintaining possession and penetrating the opposition.

# 546 THE SOCCER COACH'S TOOLKIT

## ACTIVITY 244   MOVEMENT AND FINISHING IN CENTRAL AREAS

**Level:** Advanced

**Type of activity:** Small-sided game

**Number of participants:** 16 + 2 goalkeepers

**Equipment required:** Soccer balls, cones, 2 sets of bibs and 2 goals

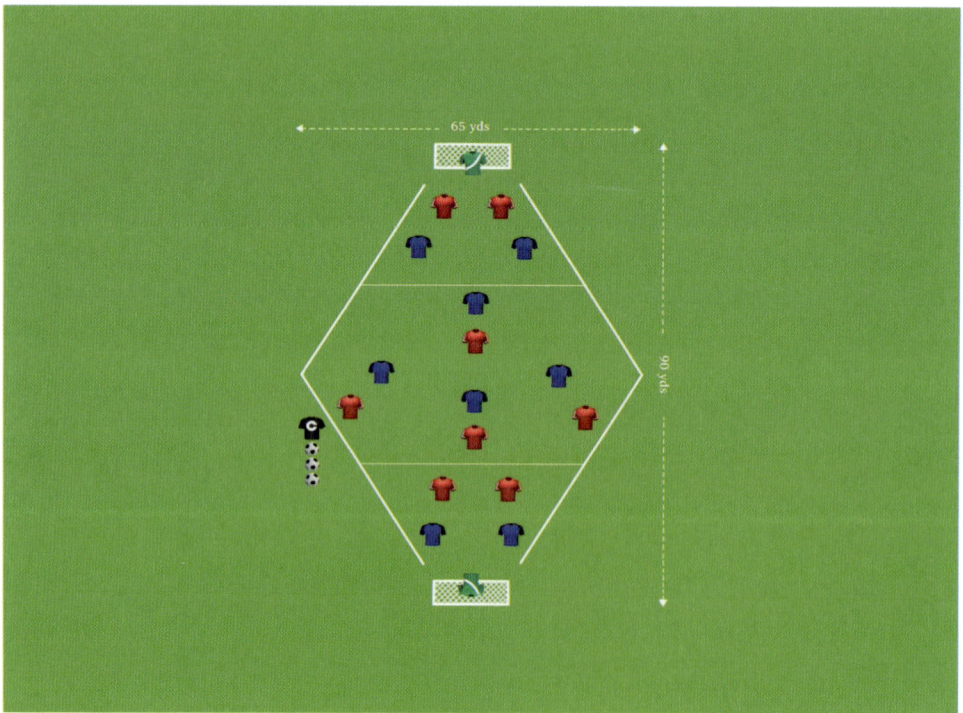

## Description

Divide players into two teams of nine (including goalkeepers). Mark out a diamond-shaped playing area. Divide the playing area into three zones. Position a goal and goalkeeper at both ends of the playing area. The teams compete in a 9v9 match and attack opposite ends of the playing area.

# Tactical Development/Team Shape

Position two players from both teams inside their defensive zone, four midfielders from both teams inside the middle zone and two attackers from both teams inside their attacking zone. Initially, all players must play within their designated zones.

When the ball goes out of play on either side of the playing area, play re-starts with a throw-in as normal. When the ball goes out of play beyond the goal line for a goal kick, play re-starts with a goal kick as normal. When the ball goes beyond the goal line for a corner, the team whose corner it is re-starts play with a roll out from their goalkeeper to a teammate in either their defensive zone or the middle zone.

The shape of the playing area directs attacks towards the centre of the playing area. The coach should focus on coaching one team and on improving their attacking shape, movement and productivity in central areas. Rotate the teams after 20 minutes.

## Key focus/Coaching points

**Primary focus:** Tactical development/team shape

**Secondary focus:** Creativity

**Additional focus:** Finishing

## Progressions/Adaptations

- The attacking team can only pass forward 1 zone at a time.

- Allow attacking players to either dribble into the next zone or pass and follow their pass forward into it. When the attacking team loses possession, the player must immediately retreat to their original zone.

- All players can move freely between the zones but must maintain a balance of 2 players in their defensive zone, 4 players in their midfield zone and 2 players in their attacking zone.

# 548 THE SOCCER COACH'S TOOLKIT

## ACTIVITY 245   GOAL SCORING ON THE TURN AND RUNNING ONTO PASSES

**Level:** Advanced

**Type of activity:** Simulated match activity

**Number of participants:** 19 + 1 goalkeeper

**Equipment required:** Soccer balls, cones, 2 sets of bibs and 1 goal

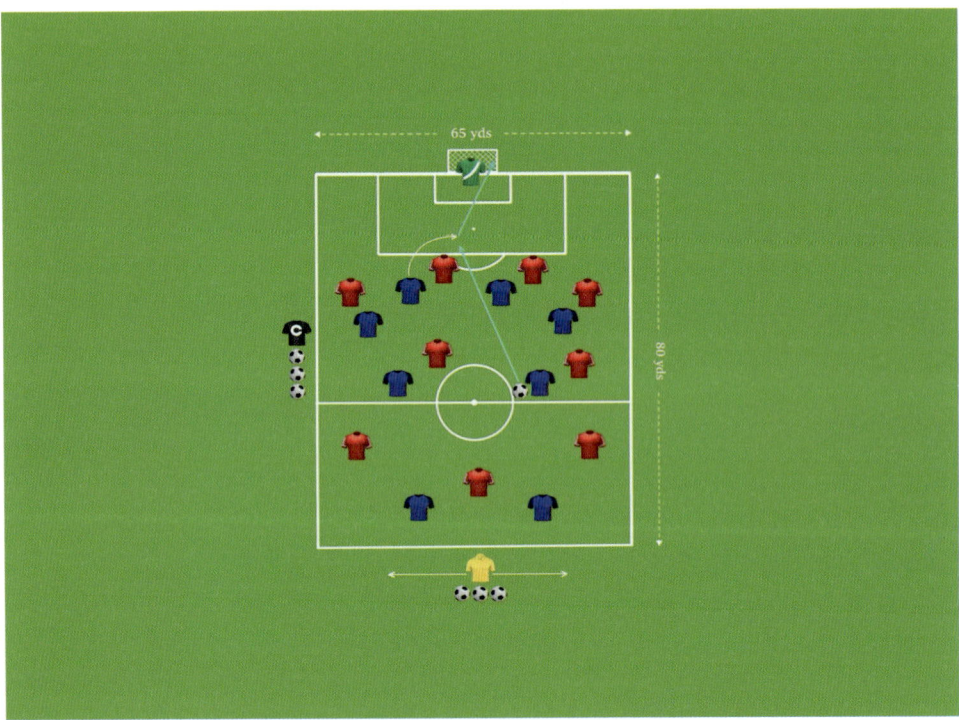

## Description

Divide players into one team of 10 (including goalkeeper), one team of eight and one target player. Mark out a playing area approximately 65 yards wide, and two-thirds the length of, a full-size pitch. Position a goal and the goalkeeper at one end of playing area and the target player at the opposite end of the playing area. Encourage the target to move along the end line and support play. The target player requires a supply of balls.

Organise the out-field players in the team of 10 into a 4-4-1 formation and the team of eight into a 2-4-2 formation.

The team of 10 tries to score by passing to the target player and the team of eight tries to score past the goalkeeper. When the team of eight scores a goal where either of the two strikers turn past a defender and score or run onto a through pass and score, it is worth two goals. After each goal, play re-starts when the target player passes to a player in the team of eight. Rotate the teams after 20-30 minutes.

## Key focus/Coaching points

Primary focus: Tactical development/team shape

Secondary focus: Movement

Additional focus: Finishing.

## Progressions/Adaptations

- Award 3 points to the team of 8 if their strikers combine to score or if either of the strikers scores with a first-time finish.
- Add a player to the team of 8 who plays between the midfield and the strikers. This player should focus on trying to create goal-scoring opportunities for the 2 strikers.

# 550 THE SOCCER COACH'S TOOLKIT

## ACTIVITY 246   PRESSING AS A TEAM

**Level:** Advanced

**Type of activity:** Small-sided game

**Number of participants:** 14 + 2 goalkeepers

**Equipment required:** Soccer balls, cones, 2 sets of bibs and 2 goals

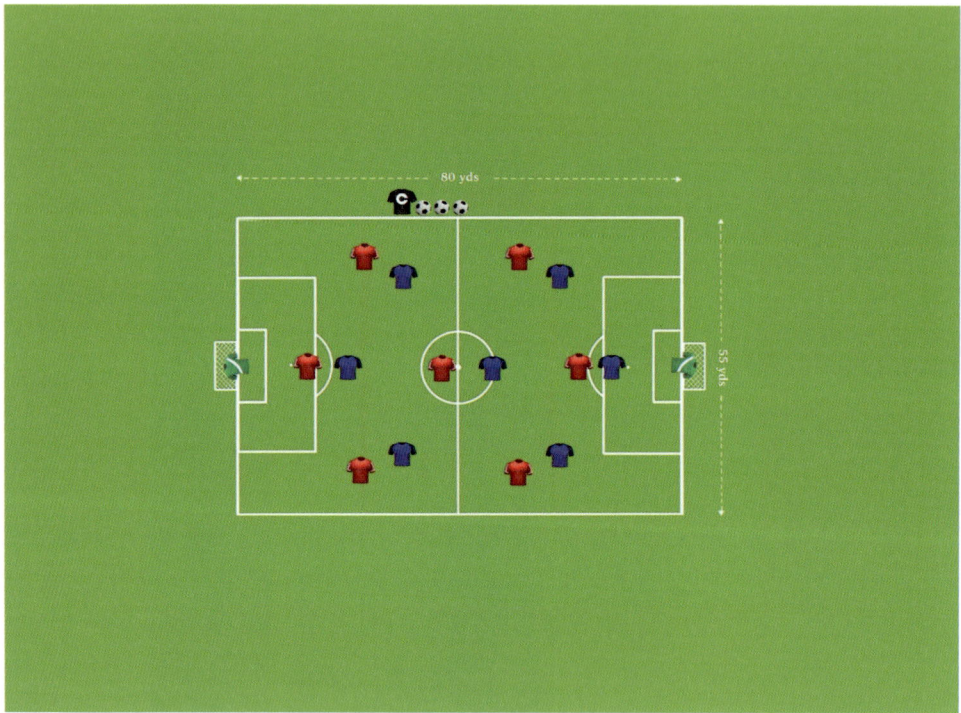

## Description

Divide players into two teams of eight (including goalkeepers). Mark out a playing area with a goal and goalkeeper at both ends of the playing area. Organise both teams into a 3-3-1 formation. The teams compete in an 8v8 match and follow normal match rules. The coach should focus on coaching one team at a time to improve the players' individual, team-unit and whole-team pressing.

## Key focus/Coaching points

**Primary focus:** Tactical development/team shape

**Secondary focus:** Pressing

**Additional focus:** Movement

## Progressions/Adaptations

- Divide the playing area into 3 zones. Position 3 defenders from both teams inside their defensive zone, 3 midfielders from both teams inside their middle zone and 1 attacker from both teams inside their attacking zone. All players must play within their designated zone.

- Allow 1 defender to move forward into the middle zone to press the attacking team when the ball is in the middle zone. Allow 1 defender to move into the middle zone and 1 midfielder to move into their attacking zone to press the attacking team when the ball is in their defensive zone. The defender and midfielder must immediately retreat to their designated zones if their team wins possession.

## ACTIVITY 247   IMPROVE GOALKEEPING

**Level:** Advanced

**Type of activity:** Small-sided game

**Number of participants:** 14 +2 goalkeepers

**Equipment required:** Soccer balls, cones, 2 sets of bibs, and 2 goals

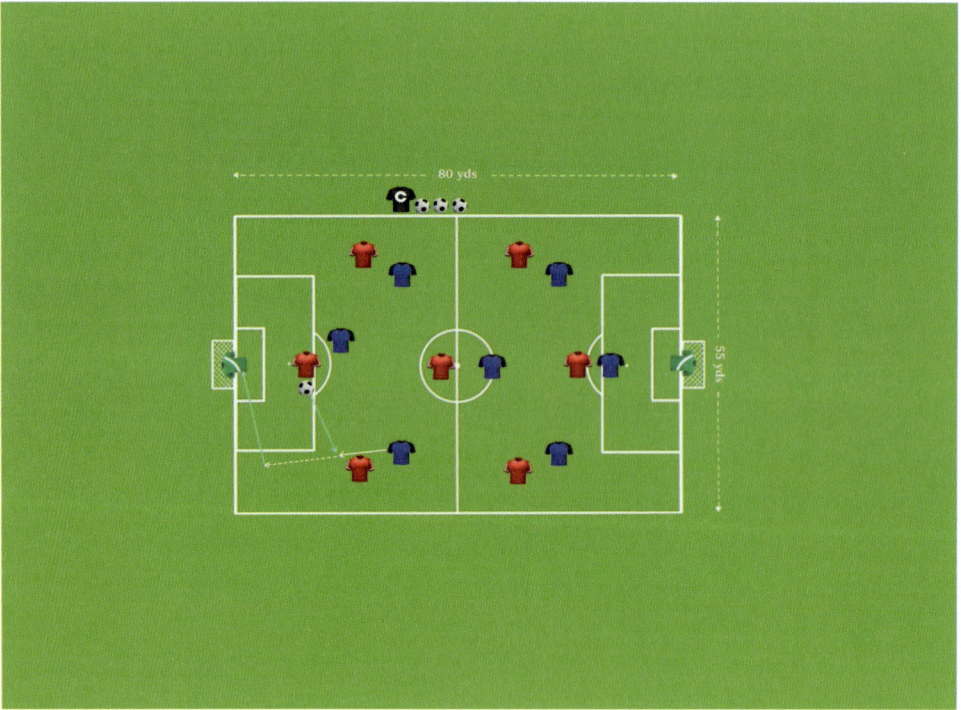

## Description

Divide players into two teams of eight (including goalkeepers). Mark out a playing area with a goal and goalkeeper at both ends of the playing area. Organise both teams of outfield players into a 3-3-1 formation. The teams compete in an 8v8 match. The coach should focus on coaching one goalkeeper at a time to improve their individual performance and function within the team of the goalkeeper.

The activity has a specific starting position, and the coach can bring play back to this starting position at any time during the activity. The opposing team's left-sided midfielder intercepts a pass from the central defender to the right-sided defender. The opposing team's left midfielder dribbles towards the goal line their team is attacking and crosses for the goalkeeper to catch. The goalkeeper now has possession and must distribute the ball to a teammate.

## Key focus/Coaching points

**Primary focus:** Tactical development/team shape

**Secondary focus:** Goalkeeping

**Additional focus:** Attacking and defending

## Progressions/Adaptations

- Allow 1 opposition striker to apply passive pressure to the goalkeeper during each re-start.

- Divide the playing area into 3 zones. Position 3 defenders from both teams inside their defensive zone, position 2 midfielders from both teams inside their middle zone and position 1 attacker from both teams inside their attacking zone. All players must play within their designated zones. Focus on the goalkeeper's relationship with each team unit.

## ACTIVITY 248   MOVEMENT TO CREATE SPACE

**Level:** Advanced

**Type of activity:** Simulated match activity

**Number of participants:** 19 +1 goalkeeper

**Equipment required:** Soccer balls, cones, discs, 2 sets of bibs and 1 goal

## Description

Divide players into an attacking team of 10 (including goalkeeper), a defending team of nine and one ball feeder. Mark out a playing area approximately 70 yards wide and two-thirds the length of a full-size pitch. Mark out a halfway line across the playing area and an offside line.

Position the offside line halfway between the halfway line and the defending team's end of the playing area. At the start of the activity, do not play offsides. Use the offside line as a progression/adaption to the activity (see progressions/adaptations section). Position a goal and the goalkeeper at one end of the playing area. The defending team tries to score past the goalkeeper. The attacking team tries to score by either dribbling past or receiving a through pass beyond the end line at the opposite end of the playing area.

Organise the outfield players in the attacking team into a 3-4-2 formation and the defending team into a 4-4-1 formation. Position the ball feeder on the defending team's end line with a supply of balls. When either team scores or the ball goes out of play, the ball feeder re-starts the activity with a pass to the defending team.

The activity has a specific starting position, and the coach can bring play back to this starting position at any time during the activity: One of the defending team's central midfielders over-hits a pass to the central attacker. The attacking team's central defender intercepts the pass. The central defender now has possession and can start an attack.

The coach should focus on coaching the attacking team. The coach should focus on the players' individual, team-unit and whole-team movement and ability to create space. Rotate the teams after 20-30 minutes.

## Key focus/Coaching points

Primary focus: Tactical development/team shape

Secondary focus: Movement

Additional focus: Support play

## Progressions/Adaptations

- The players in the attacking team are only allowed 3 touches in possession.
- The attacking team are allowed a maximum of 7 passes before attempting to score.
- Play offsides against the attacking team beyond the offside line.

## ACTIVITY 249  CREATE SPACE TO MAKE GOAL-SCORING OPPORTUNITIES

**Level:** Advanced

**Type of activity:** Simulated match activity

**Number of participants:** 17 + 1 goalkeeper

**Equipment required:** Soccer balls, cones, discs, 2 sets of bibs and 1 goal

### Description

Divide players into an attacking team of nine (including goalkeeper), a defending team of eight and one target player. Mark out a playing area approximately 65 yards wide and two-thirds the length of a full-size pitch. Mark out a halfway line across the playing area and an offside line.

Position the offside line halfway between the halfway line and the defending team's end of the playing area. At the start of the activity, do not play offsides. Use the offside line as a progression/adaption to the activity (see progressions/adaptations section). Position a goal and the goalkeeper at one end of the playing area. Position the target player at the opposite end of the playing area. Encourage the target player to move along the end line and support play. Organise the outfield players in the attacking team into a 2-4-2 formation and the defending team into a 3-4-1 formation.

The attacking team tries to score by passing to the target player. If the attacking team successfully passes to the target player, the target player immediately passes to the defending team to start their own attack. The defending team tries to score past the goalkeeper. When either team scores or the ball goes out of play, the target player re-starts the activity with a pass to the defending team.

The activity has a specific starting position and coaches can bring play back to this starting position at any time during the activity: The defending team's right midfielder over-hits a pass to the central attacker. One of the attacking team's central defenders intercepts the pass. The central defender now has possession and can start an attack.

The coach should focus on coaching the attacking team. The coach should focus on the players' individual, team-unit and whole-team movement and ability to make space to create goal-scoring opportunities. Rotate the teams after 20-30 minutes.

## Key focus/Coaching points

**Primary focus:** Tactical development/team shape

**Secondary focus:** Movement

**Additional focus:** Support play

## Progressions/Adaptations

- Players in the attacking team are only allowed 3 touches in possession.
- Divide the playing area into 3 zones. Position the players from both teams inside their designated zone, i.e., position the defenders from both teams inside their team's defensive zone, position the midfielders from both teams inside the middle zone and position the attackers from both teams inside their team's attacking zone. All players must play within their designated zones. Focus on the movement of the attacking team's players within their zones.
- Play offsides against the attacking team beyond the offside line.

# 558 THE SOCCER COACH'S TOOLKIT

## ACTIVITY 250  COMBINATION PLAYS BETWEEN TEAM UNITS

**Level:** Advanced

**Type of activity:** Simulated match activity

**Number of participants:** 18 +1 goalkeeper

**Equipment required:** Soccer balls, cones, discs, 3 sets of bibs and 1 goal

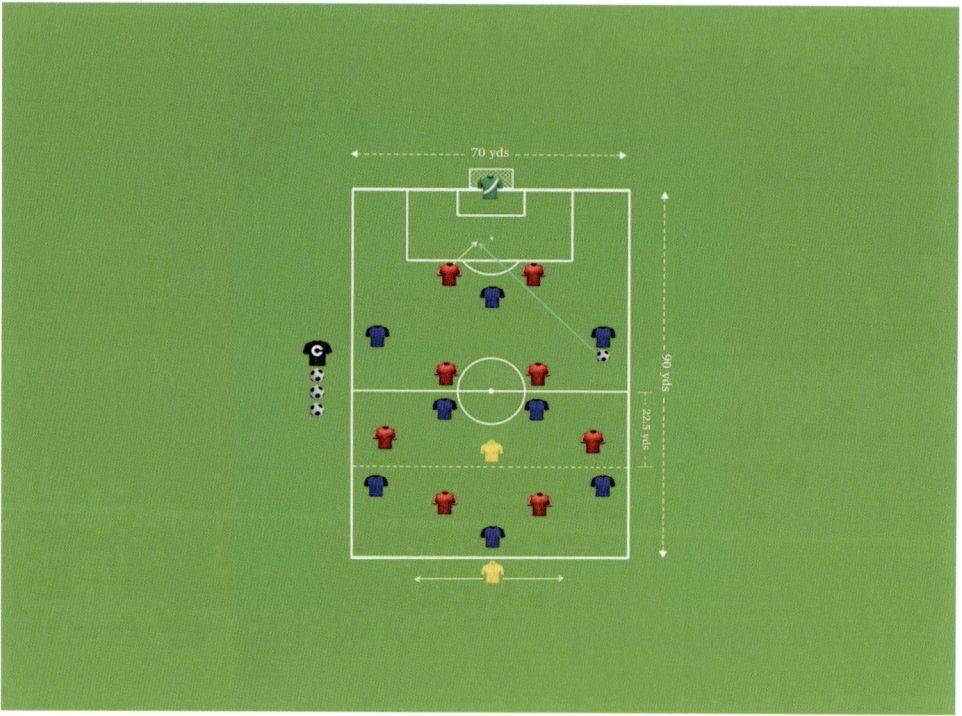

## Description

Divide players into an attacking team of nine (including goalkeeper), a defending team of eight, a floating support player and a target player. Mark out a playing area approximately 70 yards wide and two-thirds the length of a full-size pitch. Mark out a halfway line across the playing area and an offside line.

Position the offside line halfway between the halfway line and the defending team's end of the playing area. At the start of the activity, do not play offsides. Use the offside line as a progression/adaption to the activity (see progressions/adaptations section). Position a goal and the goalkeeper at one end of the playing area. Position the target player at the opposite end of the playing area. Encourage the target player to move along the end line and support play. Organise the outfield players in the attacking team into a 2-4-2 formation and the defending team into a 3-4-1 formation.

The attacking team tries to score by passing to the target player. The defending team tries to score past the goalkeeper at the opposite end of the playing area. When either team scores or the ball goes out of play, the target player re-starts the activity with a pass to the defending team. Both teams can pass to, and receive passes from, the floating support player. Encourage the floating support player to create space to receive passes and support the team in possession. The floating support player is not allowed to score.

The activity has a specific starting position and coaches can bring play back to this starting position at any time during the activity: The defending team's right midfielder over-hits a pass to the central attacker. One of the attacking team's central defenders intercepts the pass. The central defender now has possession and can start an attack.

## Key focus/Coaching points

**Primary focus:** Tactical development/team shape

**Secondary focus:** Movement

**Additional focus:** Speed

## Progressions/Adaptations

- Players in the attacking team are only allowed 3 touches in possession.
- One of the attacking team's midfielders can only play first-time passes.
- Divide the playing area into 3 zones. Position the players from both teams inside their designated zone, i.e., position the defenders from both teams inside their team's defensive zone, position the midfielders from both teams inside the middle zone, and position the attackers from both teams inside their team's attacking zone. All players must play within their designated zones. Focus on the movement of the attacking team's players within their zones.
- Play offsides against the attacking team beyond the offside line.

# 560 THE SOCCER COACH'S TOOLKIT

## ACTIVITY 251   SUPPORT PLAY

**Level:** Advanced

**Type of activity:** Small-sided game

**Number of participants:** 16 +2 goalkeepers

**Equipment required:** Soccer balls, cones, discs, 2 sets of bibs and 2 goals

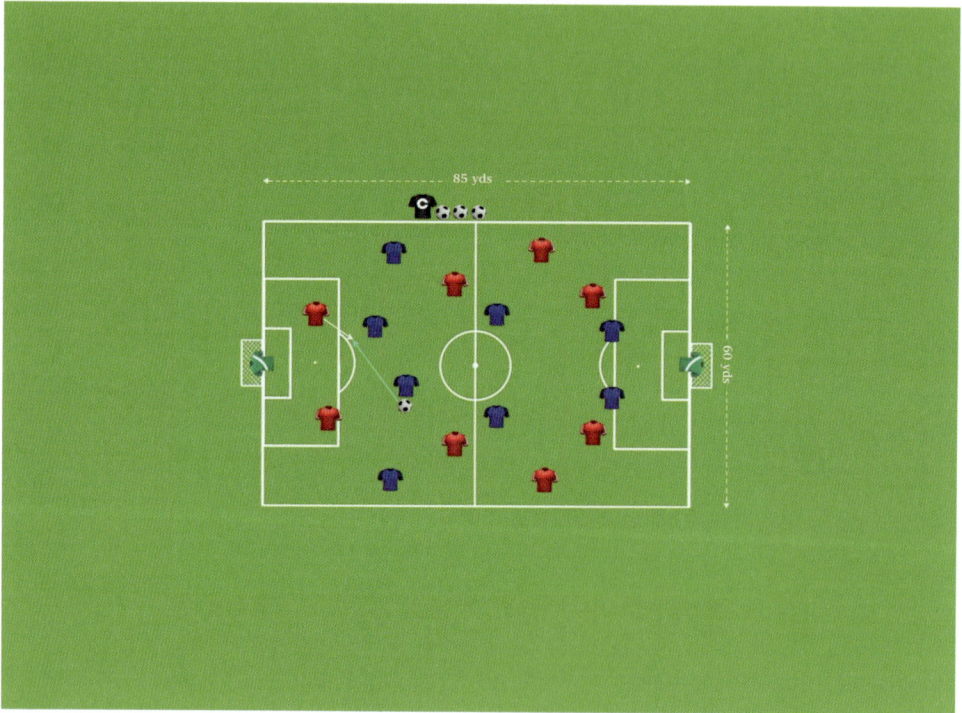

## Description

Divide players into two teams of nine (including goalkeepers). Position a goal and goalkeeper at both ends of the playing area. Organise both teams of out-field players into a 2-4-2 formation. The teams compete in an 9v9 match. The coach should focus on the players' individual, team-unit and whole-team support play.

The activity has a specific starting position, and the coach can bring play back to this starting position at any time during the activity: One of the opposition team's central attackers misplaces a sideways pass to the other central attacker. One of the central defenders intercepts the pass. The central defender now has possession and can start an attack.

## Key focus/Coaching points

**Primary focus:** Tactical development/team shape

**Secondary focus:** Movement

**Additional focus:** Support play

## Progressions/Adaptations

- Add 1 extra defender/midfielder/attacker to the team being coached to help create more support options.

- Divide the playing area into 3 zones. Position the players from both teams inside their designated zone, i.e., position the defenders from both teams inside their team's defensive zone, position the midfielders from both teams inside the middle zone and position the attackers from both teams inside their team's attacking zone. All players must play within their designated zones. Focus on support play within the defending, midfield and attacking zones.

# 562 THE SOCCER COACH'S TOOLKIT

## ACTIVITY 252  CREATIVE AND PENETRATIVE ATTACKING

**Level:** Advanced

**Type of activity:** Simulated match activity

**Number of participants:** 18 + 1 goalkeeper

**Equipment required:** Soccer balls, cones, discs, 2 sets of bibs and 1 goal

## Description

Divide players into an attacking team of 10 (including goalkeeper), a defending team of eight and one ball feeder. Mark out a playing area approximately 65 yards wide and two-thirds the length of a full-size pitch. Mark out a scoring zone approximately 12 yards wide running across the defending team's end of the playing area. Position a goal and the goalkeeper at the opposite end of the playing area. Position the ball feeder on the defending team's end line with a supply of balls.

Organise the outfield players from the attacking team into a 3-4-2 formation and the defending team into a 2-4-2 formation. The attacking team scores by either a dribble into, or by running onto and receiving a through pass inside the scoring zone. The defending team tries to score past the goalkeeper at the opposite end of the playing area. If either team scores, the ball feeder immediately passes a ball to the defending team to start an attack.

The activity has a specific starting position, and the coach can bring play back to this starting position at any time during the activity: The defending team's right midfielder over-hits a pass to their centre forward. The attacking team's central defender intercepts the pass. The central defender now has possession and can start an attack.

## Key focus/Coaching points

**Primary focus:** Tactical development/team shape

**Secondary focus:** Creativity

**Additional focus:** Movement

## Progressions/Adaptations

- Divide the playing area into 3 zones. Position the players from both teams inside their designated zone, i.e., position the defenders from both teams inside their team's defensive zone, position the midfielders from both teams inside the middle zone, and position the attackers from both teams inside their team's attacking zone. **Use the following conditions:**
    - The attacking team is allowed a maximum of 3 passes inside their defensive zone and 2 in the middle zone before the ball must travel forwards into the next zone.
    - When a defender or a midfielder from the attacking team dribbles or passes forwards into the next zone, they must remain inside that zone until the attacking team loses possession. When the attacking team loses possession of the ball, the attacking player(s) must return to their original zone.
    - Award 2 points to the attacking team if two players from the attacking team complete a 1-2 pass into the scoring zone, an attacking player performs a first-time pass to a teammate inside the scoring zone or an attacker successfully dribbles past a defender in their attacking zone before dribbling into the scoring zone.

**Credits**

**Cover and interior design:** Anja Elsen

**Layout:** DiTech Publishing Services, www.ditechpubs.com

**Cover photo:** © AdobeStock

**Interior diagrams:** Courtesy of Rob Ellis

**Illustrator:** Zara Derik

**Managing editor:** Elizabeth Evans

**Copyeditor:** Stephanie Kramer